MW00339746

THE OXFORD HANDBOOK OF

PUBLIC
ACCOUNTABILITY

THE OXFORD HANDBOOK OF

PUBLIC

ACCOUNTABILITY

Edited by

MARK BOVENS, ROBERT E. GOODIN

and

THOMAS SCHILLEMANS

OXFORD

UNIVERSITY PRESS

OXFORD

UNIVERSITY PRESS

Great Clarendon Street, Oxford, OX2 6DP,
United Kingdom

Oxford University Press is a department of the University of Oxford.
It furthers the University's objective of excellence in research, scholarship,
and education by publishing worldwide. Oxford is a registered trade mark of
Oxford University Press in the UK and in certain other countries

© The several contributors 2014

The moral rights of the authors have been asserted

First Edition published in 2014

Impression: 1

All rights reserved. No part of this publication may be reproduced, stored in
a retrieval system, or transmitted, in any form or by any means, without the
prior permission in writing of Oxford University Press, or as expressly permitted
by law, by licence or under terms agreed with the appropriate reprographics
rights organization. Enquiries concerning reproduction outside the scope of the
above should be sent to the Rights Department, Oxford University Press, at the
address above

You must not circulate this work in any other form
and you must impose this same condition on any acquirer

Published in the United States of America by Oxford University Press
198 Madison Avenue, New York, NY 10016, United States of America

British Library Cataloguing in Publication Data
Data available

Library of Congress Control Number: 2014936658

ISBN 978-0-19-964125-3

Printed and bound by
CPI Group (UK) Ltd, Croydon, CR0 4YY

Links to third party websites are provided by Oxford in good faith and
for information only. Oxford disclaims any responsibility for the materials
contained in any third party website referenced in this work.

Contents

PART I   ANALYTICAL PERSPECTIVES

PART II   STUDYING ACCOUNTABILITY

PART V ACCOUNTABILITY MECHANISMS

PART VI DEBATING ACCOUNTABILITY

PART VII REFLECTIONS ON THE FUTURE OF ACCOUNTABILITY STUDIES

List of Figures

List of Tables

LIST OF CONTRIBUTORS

Robert D. Behn, John F. Kennedy School of Government, Harvard University, Cambridge, Massachusetts, United States.

Mark Bovens, Utrecht School of Governance, Utrecht University, The Netherlands.

Gijs Jan Brandsma, Utrecht School of Governance, Utrecht University, The Netherlands.

Floor Cornelissen, Maasstad Hospital, Rotterdam, The Netherlands.

Bodil Damgaard, Centre for Democratic Network Governance, University of Roskilde, Denmark.

Jane Davison, School of Management, Royal Holloway, University of London, United Kingdom.

Melvin J. Dubnick, Department of Political Science, University of New Hampshire, Durham, New Hampshire, United States.

Matthew Flinders, Department of Politics, University of Sheffield, United Kingdom & Murdoch University, Perth, Western Australia, Australia.

Mark N. Franklin, Department of Political and Social Science, European University Institute, San Domenico di Fiesole, Italy.

Sean Gailmard, Political Science Department, University of California, Berkeley, California, United States.

Michael Goodhart, Department of Political Science, University of Pittsburgh, Pennsylvania, United States.

Robert E. Goodin, Department of Government, University of Essex, United Kingdom & School of Philosophy, Australian National University, Canberra, Australia.

Dorothea Greiling, Institute of Management Accounting, Johannes Kepler University, Linz, Austria.

Arie Halachmi, Department of Public Administration, Tennessee State University, Nashville, Tennessee, United States.

Carol Harlow, Department of Law, London School of Economics, United Kingdom.

Christie Hayne, Queen's School of Business, Queen's University, Kingston, Ontario, Canada.

Christopher Hood, All Souls College, University of Oxford, United Kingdom.

Mark D. Jarvis, School of Public Administration, University of Victoria, Victoria, Canada.

Erik Hans Klijn, Department of Public Administration, Erasmus University Rotterdam, The Netherlands.

Christopher Koch, Gutenberg School of Management and Economics, Johannes Gutenberg University Mainz, Germany.

Jonathan G. S. Koppell, College of Public Programs, Arizona State University, Phoenix, Arizona, United States.

Joop F. M. Koppenjan, Department of Public Administration, Erasmus University Rotterdam, The Netherlands.

Sanneke Kuipers, Utrecht School of Governance, Utrecht University, The Netherlands.

Per Lægreid, Department of Administration and Organization Theory, University of Bergen, Norway.

Sheldon Leader, School of Law and Essex Business and Human Rights Project, University of Essex, United Kingdom.

Jenny M. Lewis, School of Social and Political Sciences, University of Melbourne, Australia.

Jane Mansbridge, John F. Kennedy School of Government, Harvard University, Cambridge, Massachusetts, United States.

Jerry L. Mashaw, Yale Law School, Yale University, New Haven, Connecticut, United States.

Albert Meijer, Utrecht School of Governance, Utrecht University, The Netherlands.

Mark H. Moore, John F. Kennedy School of Government, Harvard University, Cambridge, Massachusetts, United States.

Richard Mulgan, Crawford School of Public Policy, Australian National University, Canberra, Australia.

Pippa Norris, John F. Kennedy School of Government, Harvard University, Cambridge, Massachusetts, United States & Department of Government and International Relations, University of Sydney, Australia.

Johan P. Olsen, Arena Centre for European Studies, University of Oslo, Norway.

Yannis Papadopoulos, LAGAPE (Laboratoire d'analyse de la gouvernance et de l'action publique en Europe), University of Lausanne, Switzerland.

Shefali V. Patil, Management Department, Wharton University of Pennsylvania, Philadelphia, Pennsylvania, United States.

B. Guy Peters, Department of Political Science, University of Pittsburgh, Pennsylvania, United States.

Paul L. Posner, Public and International Affairs, George Mason University, Washington DC, United States.

Barbara S. Romzek, School of Public Affairs, American University, Washington DC, United States.

Steven E. Salterio, Queen's School of Business, Queen's University, Kingston, Ontario, Canada.

Thomas Schillemans, Utrecht School of Governance, Utrecht University, The Netherlands.

Colin Scott, UCD Sutherland School of Law, University College Dublin, Ireland.

Asif Shahan, Development Studies, University of Dhaka, Bangladesh.

Steven Rathgeb Smith, Maxwell School, Syracuse University, New York, United States.

Stuart Soroka, Department of Political Science, McGill University, Montreal, Canada & Department of Communication Studies and the Center for Political Studies at the Institute for Social Research, University of Michigan, Ann Arbor, Michigan, United States.

Paul 't Hart, Utrecht School of Governance, Utrecht University, The Netherlands & Netherlands School of Public Administration, The Hague, The Netherlands.

Philip E. Tetlock, Management Department, Wharton University of Pennsylvania, Philadelphia, Pennsylvania, United States.

John Uhr, School of Politics & International Relations, Australian National University, Canberra, Australia.

Steven van de Walle, Department of Public Administration, Erasmus University Rotterdam, the Netherlands.

Frank Vibert, Department of Government, London School of Economics, United Kingdom.

Ferdinand Vieider, Risk and Development Research Unit, Social Science Research Center Berlin (WZB), Berlin, Germany.

Mark E. Warren, Department of Political Science, University of British Columbia, Vancouver, Canada.

Christopher Wlezien, Department of Government, University of Texas, Austin, Texas, United States.

Jens Wüstemann, Business School, University of Mannheim, Germany.

Kaifeng Yang, Askew School of Public Administration and Policy, Florida State University, Tallahassee, Florida, United States.

CHAPTER 1

....

PUBLIC ACCOUNTABILITY

....

MARK BOVENS, THOMAS SCHILLEMANS, AND ROBERT E. GOODIN

PROLIFERATION AND FRAGMENTATION

ACCOUNTABILITY is the buzzword of modern governance. In legislation introduced between 2001 and 2006 into the US Congress, the word "accountability" occurred in the title of between 50 and 70 proposed bills in each two-year cycle (Dubnick 2007, 8). More recently, when US President Obama launched his Recovery Act in response to the global financial crisis, it had three main goals: creating new jobs, spurring economic activity, and to "foster unprecedented levels of *accountability* and transparency in government spending."[1] The quest for accountability also manifests itself in many other national jurisdictions, as well as in supranational policy actors such as the European Union (EU), the World Bank, or the Intergovernmental Panel on Climate Change. Indeed, "public accountability" has been a key theme in public management reforms around the globe (Christensen and Lægreid 2011, 12). In the first part of this handbook, Melvin J. Dubnick provides empirical evidence of the growing frequency of the term's use, based on a million scanned volumes drawn from works published in English between 1800 and 2005. While the term first appears in the plotted sample during the early 1800s, it remains a culturally innocuous term until the 1960s and 1970s, when we see a very sharp and increasing upturn in its usage, which continues well into the twenty-first century. In the final part of this volume, Matthew Flinders claims that because of the industrious accountability work by so many scholars, accountability is emerging as the *Über-concept* of the twenty-first century.

The rising prominence of "accountability" in public discourse has given rise in turn to a burgeoning of attention to "accountability" in recent academic scholarship. It has been an object of scholarly debate and analysis in, for example, political science, public administration, international relations (IR), social psychology, constitutional law, and business administration. However, in each of the sub-disciplines, scholars analyze concepts of accountability and practices of account-giving unaware of, and still less building on, each other's achievements. As a result, academic scholarship on accountability, although booming, is highly fragmented and non-cumulative. Virtually every different author sets out to produce his or her own definition of accountability. Virtually every new author or editor uses his or her own concepts, conceptualizations, and frames for studying accountability—often with different conceptualizations being employed across chapters within the same edited volume. Some writers use the concept very loosely, others define it much more narrowly and tightly. But few of these definitions are fully compatible. Cumulative and commensurable research is difficult if not impossible in such circumstances.

Against this background of proliferation and fragmentation, this handbook aims to unify. This volume provides, for the first time, a comprehensive overview of the current scholarship on the topic—one which systematically takes stock of this burgeoning field organized around the conceptual framework developed in this chapter. It provides a state of the art overview of the recent scholarship on public accountability, collecting, consolidating, and integrating inquiries currently scattered across a broad range of disciplines and sub disciplines. Its comprehensive character, incorporating a wide range of topics and disciplines, will make it a touchstone not only for practitioners and established students of good governance in the public and the private sectors, but also for students and other newcomers to the field.

As background to the endeavor, this introductory chapter will provide a basic, conceptual framework for the analysis of accountability. In the course of doing that, it will also provide an overview of recent work in accountability across various fields, illustrating some of the important commonalities and differences. Finally, this introduction also provides a roadmap situating the different parts of this handbook in the landscape of current accountability studies.

HISTORICAL ROOTS

Accountability is a concept that has taken on ever-new shades of meaning, with its increased usage over the course of the past decades (Mulgan 2000; Flinders 2011). Accountability has been described as an "icon," a "hurrah-word," and a "chameleon"; it is an elusive and much (perhaps essentially) contested concept. Clearly, accountability means many different things to different authors and readers. Still and all, accountability—if not the concept then at least the underlying practices—has ancient and fairly unequivocal roots.

The idea of accountability is historically rooted in the practice of book-keeping and in the discipline of accounting (see Bovens 2005; Hayne and Salterio in this volume). Accounting always has a dual meaning: it is about listing and counting important "things"—possessions, debts, agreements, promises—and about providing an account concerning this count. Thus it implies telling a story, based on some obligation and with some consequence in view.

Accountability is anchored in the mundane yet important practice of record-keeping and gives rise to story-telling in a context of social (power) relations within which enforcement of standards and the fulfillment of obligations is a reasonable expectation.

This connection between counting, accounting, story-telling, and social power relations has ancient roots. In his tale of the development of written languages, Jared Diamond (1999)—without actually making too much of it—describes how the few independently developed written languages have evolved from record-keeping activities. Consider the Sumerians in Mesopotamia, who before 3000 BC developed the first written language. They used clay tokens for accounting purposes, "recording numbers of sheep and amounts of grain" (1999, 218). A system of writing gradually developed, which increasingly allowed Sumerians to convey more complex, and arguably more interesting, messages than stock-keeping records. Similarly, the written Cherokee language was developed by an Indian called Sequoyah around 1820, in a conscious effort to copy the white man's apparently beneficial use of "scribbling on paper." Sequoyah's code was also, initially, a book-keeper's tool. Diamond (1999, 228) recounts: "Sequoyah was illiterate and could neither speak nor read English. Because he was a blacksmith, Sequoyah began by devising an accounting system to help him keep track of his customers' debts." His approach soon became more sophisticated—he started borrowing signs from English and attributed totally new meanings to them. Within a short span of time, the Cherokee community became 100 percent literate and "they began printing books and newspapers." Here, again, clever and pretty straightforward book-keeping soon led to an ability to convey more complex stories in public settings.

The etymological roots of the English concept of "accountability" stem from the Middle Ages when, as Dubnick (2007) points out, it was first used in its current connotation in the Domesday books by William I in 1085, as a translation for the French expression "comptes a rendre." The Domesday books held very accurate accounts of all the possessions of the king, which is to say, everything in his realm. In roughly the same vein, the 13th century French Archbishop of Rouen, Eudes de Rigaud, visited all the religious houses in his jurisdiction and made detailed notes of his findings (Dunbabin 2007; Vincent 2007). In both medieval examples, accountability refers to the counting of possessions and classifying information on the basis of implicit or explicit norms and conventions. In both instances, also, agents were *obliged* to provide answers to the questions posed to them by the accountants on behalf of their master, be it William I or Eudes de Rigaud. Accountability thus has a relational core to it; it refers to the obligation to provide an account *to*, usually, a superior or at least someone with a legitimate stake.

ACCOUNTABILITY RESEARCH: A MINIMAL CONCEPTUAL CONSENSUS

The historical legacy of accountability contains a number of constants that can serve as a basis for a minimal conceptual consensus. It would be a gross overstatement to claim that all contemporary scholars of public accountability adhere to this minimal definitional consensus of accountability. For one thing, quite a few authors often provide *no* formal definitions at all. Many others develop their own typologies of accountability; in the process they elaborate a bewildering and ever growing variety of overlapping and competing conceptions of accountability. Nevertheless, beneath all this confusion, many authors base their analyses, either explicitly or more often implicitly, on this minimal conceptual consensus as will become evident from an overview of accountability research in various relevant disciplines.[2]

The *relational* and *communicative* core of accountability is clearly seen in the *social psychological* literature on accountability. Here, most authors define accountability as the expectation that one may be asked, often by an authority or one's superior, to justify one's thoughts, beliefs, or actions. Not all social psychology authors explicate this formal definition. Yet in their customary (quasi-)experimental approaches, this relational and communicative approach is inevitably manifest. Tetlock describes the social psychological approach as follows:

> Accountability is a critical rule and an enforcement mechanism—the social psychological link between individual decision-makers on the one hand and social systems on the other. Expectations of accountability are an implicit or explicit constraint on virtually everything people do, "If I do this, how will others react?" Failure to act in ways for which one can construct acceptable accounts leads to varying degrees of censure, depending on the gravity of the offense and the norms of the society.
> (Tetlock 1992, 337; see also his Chapter 5 with Patil and Vieider in this volume)

The *accounting* literature is, at root, surprisingly concomitant with the social psychological approach just described. In accountancy, the agent's obligation to provide an account of his behavior to an external party is the thread connecting the myriad of definitions and research approaches deployed in the academic literature (see also Hayne and Salterio in this volume). Accountability, here, is about the "exchange of reasons for conduct" and aims to "verbally bridge the gap between action and expectation" (Messner 2009). But where the social psychological research primarily focuses on the communicative interaction between an agent and an audience and its effects on his (or her) choices and behavior, the accountancy literature logically connects with reporting and book-keeping on the one side and with procedures and practices of audit and review on the other. The similarity between those disciplines lies in their use of the same base definitions of accountability that give rise to hugely disparate research interests and professional practices.

The above research traditions generally focus on individual persons, managers, firms, organizations or book-keepers as accountable actors. The *public administration* literature, in contrast, often shifts attention to the overarching perspective of governments, public bodies, policy fields, or entire sectors. Where accounting and social psychology scholars will often look at non-public and informal forms of accountability, public administration adamantly focuses on the *public* character of *formal* accountability. Its focus is on systemic, structural forms of accountability for public service provision or governments. In this branch of the literature, most authors adopt relational definitions of accountability, often leaning on the work by Romzek and Dubnick (1998), but also on Mulgan (2003), Strøm (2000), and Day and Klein (1987). It is striking to see here, how almost all authors start their definition with some variation on the theme that "accountability is about providing answers for your behavior" and then proceed to thicken this definition, which leads different authors in different directions. This superficial disparity masks the underlying consensus on first principles among such scholars regarding the conceptual fundamentals of accountability.

Public administration studies of public accountability tend to focus on forms of accountability in public service provision and regulation and on systemic, structural forms of accountability. The remaining three disciplines depart from this notion and display a more outspoken interest in *political* forms of accountability. These disciplines display a healthy appetite for the irregular, incidental case of accountability regarding incidents, misconduct, or criminal behavior, and, following from that, an appetite for the analysis of specific cases.

Political scientists often approach the issue from the perspective of power. Here, accountability generally denotes a relationship between elected politicians and their voters, sometimes mediated by parties, government representatives, or bureaucrats. Political scientists adopting this focus often define accountability along these lines: "accountability usually means that voters know, or can make good inferences about, what parties have done in office and reward or punish them conditional on these actions" (Stokes 2005, 316). As the opportunity for communication between actor and forum—captured in face-to-face accountability in social psychology—is virtually absent in large scale democracies, the hygienic role of sanctions and the opportunity to throw or vote the rascals out is more important. "Accountability = punishment" predominates in this branch of the literature (see Mansbridge, Chapter 4 in this volume).

International relations research often focuses on specific cases of internationalization and its implications for accountability. Even when such authors refrain from providing formal definitions, they often implicitly assume that accountability essentially involves the idea that politicians, government representatives, and NGOs may be called upon to explain and justify their behavior to a variety of stakeholders—be they national, local, or transnational. As Mulgan (2003) has suggested, accountability can be rendered towards two types of accountability forums on the basis of different principles: one is the principle of ownership, which is central to most of the research in the political science literature. Citizens may demand answers from their representatives on the basis of ownership, as do the representatives themselves from the bureaucrats serving them. The other general basis for accountability is the principle of affected rights and interests, which is more often applicable to IR research (see Goodhart, Chapter 18 in this volume) and is also highly relevant in legal research. Third parties may demand accountability when some agent—be it a politician, government, agency, or firm—harms some right or interest, for instance when s/he pollutes the environment or violates human rights.

Where political science focuses on the behavior of powerful political agents, *constitutional law* scholars often focus on the norms that do or ought to govern political accountability, the institutions embodying and guarding those norms, and the commensurability of existing norms with new developments in governance, such as, for example, the emergence of multi-level governance. A review of some of the key journals in this field suggests that a lot of the accountability-related papers aim to come to terms with new forms of governance and the internationalization in some policy fields, which challenge existing constitutional and legal norms and values. This interest in the changing circumstances and practices of governance permeates the various disciplinary approaches of accountability, as we will return to near the end of this introduction. In its core definition, most constitutional law scholars (see Harlow in this volume) also stick to the relational core definition of public accountability. As Auel (2007, 495), building on Schedler (1999), puts it: "Accountability in its fundamental sense means being answerable for one's actions to some authority and having to suffer sanctions for those actions: 'A is accountable to B when A is obliged to inform B about A's (past or future) actions and decisions, to justify them, and to suffer punishment in the case of eventual misconduct.'"

To sum up: there is a bewildering array of approaches across the multitude of academic fields that concern themselves with accountability. At root, however, most researchers use fairly similar notions of what constitutes the core of accountability. Furthermore, these notions are reasonably comparable across the various disciplines.

The upshot of this brief survey of different disciplinary approaches is simply this. There may be more similarity in our thinking about accountability than we generally acknowledge. Approximately 40 percent of the recent papers on accountability use formal definitions of accountability that are compatible with this minimal conceptual consensus (see Schillemans 2013).[3] This is a hopeful sign for those who wish to deepen and expand our knowledge of accountability in a cumulative way, with advances in each discipline and sub-discipline providing a springboard for advances in others.

The minimal conceptual consensus entails, first of all, that accountability is about providing answers; is about answerability towards others with a legitimate claim to demand an account. Accountability is then a relational concept, linking those who owe an account and those to whom it is owed. Accountability is a relational concept in another sense as well, linking agents and others for whom they perform tasks or who are affected by the tasks they perform. This relation is most commonly described in the current literature in terms of agents and principals, although some also speak about accountors and accountees, actors and forums, or agents and audiences. Accountability is furthermore a retrospective—ex post—activity. Finally, accountability is a consequential activity as anyone who is being held accountable may testify—as Behn (2001) says, only a little hyperbolically, "accountability means punishment."

"PUBLIC" ACCOUNTABILITY

In our daily lives we are often accountable to others. Our partners, parents, bosses, and neighbors may, from time to time, demand an account from us for something or another, and we may feel a genuine obligation to provide answers that we hope they will find satisfactory. But luckily, these forms of accountability are rarely public. This handbook does not concern all of those private forms of accountability. Instead, it is about *public* accountability.

"Public" in public accountability may take to a number of different referents. In the context of this handbook, "public" refers to "openness" or "transparency." That is to say the account is not rendered discreetly, behind closed doors. Rather, it is in principle open to the general public. The information provided about the actor's conduct is generally accessible, hearings and debates are open to the public, and the forum promulgates its judgment to the public at large. Secondly, "public" can refer to the *object* of the account-giving. Public accountability mainly regards matters of public concern, such as the spending of public funds, the exercise of public powers, or the conduct of public institutions. It is not necessarily limited to public organizations, but can extend to private bodies that exercise public privileges or receive public funding (Scott 2000, 41). Thirdly, "public" can refer to the accounting perspective and standards. Public accountability implies the rendering of account for matters of public interest, i.e. an accounting that is performed with a view to the public interest or to public responsibilities.

In general, one could say this: Public accountability is accountability in, and about, the public domain.

ACCOUNTABILITY AS A VIRTUE AND AS A MECHANISM

In both the scholarly literature and in the political and policy discourse, two different usages of "accountability" can be observed. Those are reflected in the way this handbook is organized. We can reduce some of the conceptual confusion by distinguishing between "accountability as a virtue" and "accountability as a mechanism." Both usages are useful. They nonetheless address different kinds of issues, imply different standards and evoke different analytical dimensions (Bovens 2010).

Accountability as a Virtue

In the first usage, accountability is seen as a virtue, as a desirable quality of states, government organizations, firms, or officials. This is reflected in the emotive use of "accountability" in the many titles of legislative acts of Congress, mentioned at the outset of this chapter. For example, the purpose of the Syria Accountability Act, adopted in 2003, was not to provide a series of mechanisms for rendering an account regarding dealings with Syria, but to end what the United States saw as Syrian support for terrorism, to end Syria's presence in Lebanon, to stop Syria's alleged development of weapons of mass destruction, and to cease Syria's illegal importation of Iraqi oil. In a similar vein, the United Nations Voting Accountability Act prohibits United States assistance to foreign countries that oppose the position of the United States in the United Nations. In this usage, accountability is not primarily about instituting mechanisms, but about defining and preventing undesirable behavior.

Likewise, accountability studies that use accountability in this rather active sense of virtue focus on the actual performance of governments, officials, and agencies. Implicitly or explicitly, they formulate a set of substantive standards for good governance and assess whether officials or organizations comply with these standards (Wang 2002; Considine 2002; O'Connell 2005; Koppell 2005). Accountability in this very broad sense comes close to "responsiveness," "a sense of responsibility," or a willingness to act in a transparent, fair, compliant, and equitable way. The main items on this research agenda are the evaluation of the *conduct of actors* and an analysis of the factors that induce accountable behavior. In this line of research, accountability is the *dependent* variable, the outcome of a series of interactions between various factors, actors, and variables. In these types of studies, accountability deficits manifest themselves as inappropriate behavior, or "bad" governance—unresponsive, opaque, irresponsible, and ineffective. Of course, there is no general consensus about the standards for accountable behavior, and these standards differ depending on role, institutional context, era, and political perspective. So accountability in this sense is inevitably essentially contested, and domain-specific.

Part 3 of the handbook explores the norms and practices of accountable behavior in some of the most important domains of public governance. This part focuses on accountability in constitutional law (Harlow, Chapter 12), public administration (Peters, Chapter 13), civil servants (Uhr, Chapter 14), networks (Klijn and Koppenjan, Chapter 15), citizen participation (Damgaard and Lewis, Chapter 16), multi-level governance (Papadopoulos, Chapter 17), and international relations (Goodhart, Chapter 18). Each of these chapters explores just how accountability as a virtue is seen in different domains. Together these chapters display an overview of the state of affairs in our thinking of accountable, proper behavior in some of the most important and challenging contemporary contexts of governance.

Accountability as a Mechanism

The dominant usage of accountability, in accord with the minimal conceptual consensus we provided earlier, is as a social, political, or administrative mechanism. In this usage, accountability is conceptualized as an institutional relation or arrangement in which an agent can be held to account by another agent or institution (Day and Klein 1987; Scott 2000; Mulgan 2003; Goodin 2003; Aucoin and Jarvis 2005; Bovens 2007; Philp 2009). In this line of research, the primary object of accountability studies is not so much the behavior of public agents as it is the way in which these institutional arrangements govern the behavior of public agents. And the focus of accountability studies in this mode is not whether the agents have acted in an accountable way, but rather whether and how they are or can be held to account ex post facto by accountability forums. For example, the study of Busuioc (2013) describes and analyzes how a web of formal and informal accountability mechanisms, such as management boards, internal audits, and parliamentary hearings, has been spun around EU agencies and how these mechanisms operate in practice.

When discussing accountability as a social or political mechanism, some further analytical distinctions may be helpful. Account-giving usually consists of at least three elements or stages. First of all, for a relationship to qualify as account-giving, it is crucial that the actor is obliged to inform the forum about his or her conduct, by providing various sorts of information about the performance of tasks, about outcomes, or about procedures. Often (particularly with failures), this also involves the provision of explanations and justifications. Secondly, there needs to be a possibility for the forum to interrogate the actor and to *question* the adequacy of the explanation or the legitimacy of the conduct—hence, the close semantic connection between "accountability" and "answerability." Thirdly, the forum may *pass judgment* on the conduct of the actor. It may approve an annual account, denounce a policy, or publicly condemn the behavior of an official or an agency. In passing a negative judgment, the forum frequently imposes sanctions of some kind on the actor. In case of a positive judgment, the forum may commend or even reward the actor.

Studies conceiving of accountability as a mechanism focus on the relationship between agents and forums. Some such studies are basically descriptive; they chart the intricate webs of accountability arrangements surrounding modern public actors (Scott 2000). Others assess how these arrangements operate and with what effects (Day and Klein 1987; Schillemans 2011). Legal scholars, for example, are interested in the propriety of a particular accountability mechanism or of a specific, concrete accountability process: is the forum sufficiently independent from the actor? Does it have serious inquisitorial and sanctioning powers? Is the forum impartial, and does it provide due process? Political scientists and public management scholars are more interested in the effects these arrangements have on the way public actors operate. Do they enhance democratic control of the executive? Do they provide for checks and balances? Do they induce public organizations to improve their performance? The main items on the political science research agenda are the evaluation of *mechanisms* and the positive or negative effects of these mechanisms. These are basically studies about political or social control. In these studies accountability is the *independent* variable, a factor that may or may not have an effect on the behavior of actors. Accountability deficits, within this line of research, are defined in terms of gaps in the web of control mechanisms.

In this handbook, Part 5 discusses many of the most important mechanisms of accountability in contemporary democratic systems of governance. The part starts with elections (Franklin, Soroka, and Wlezien) as the most important mechanism of democratic accountability and then proceeds to discuss important additional mechanisms such as hierarchy (Jarvis), accounting and auditing (Hayne and Salterio), performance reporting (Van de Walle and Cornelissen), PerformanceStat (Behn), independent regulators (Scott), audit institutions (Posner and Shahan), transparency (Meijer), and watchdog journalism (Norris). Together, these mechanisms provide extensive regimes of accountability in modern states, fueling concerns regarding the rise of an audit society (Power 1997), pressing accountability overloads (see Halachmi, Chapter 34 in this handbook) and, ultimately, multiple accountabilities disorder (Koppell 2005).

Typologies of Public Accountability

Public accountability comes in many guises. Public institutions and actors are required to account for their conduct to various forums and in a variety of ways. These dimensions revolve around essential questions to be asked about accountability: **who** is accountable to **whom**, for **what**, by **which** standards, and **why**?

The Accountable Actor

Who should render an account? Who is the *actor* that is required to answer to the forum? In ordinary social relationships amongst citizens, it is usually clear who should account for what. As a child we are accountable to our parents, as a pupil to our teachers, and as an employee to our superiors. This is far more complicated however when it comes to public organizations and institutions. Here one can distinguish, for example, between *corporate* accountability in which the organization as a legal entity is to give account; *hierarchical* accountability, in which only the apex of the organization (the CEO or the minister) needs to render an account externally; *collective* accountability, in which every member of the organization can be called upon to give account, irrespective of his or her contribution; or *individual* accountability, in which individual officials are held accountable in so far as they have contributed to or are responsible for the acts of the organization.

These differences are reflected in the varying focuses in the relevant academic disciplines on different accountable actors. In international relations, law, public administration, and accounting, the focus is often on organizations and institutions as actors (government agencies, legal bodies, or transnational organizations). Other important incorporated actors discussed in other corners of the public accountability literature are political parties (in political science), NGOs (IR and accountancy), public contractors (law), semi-independent public bodies (public administration and accountancy), and even private enterprises (accountancy). Politicians, such as heads of state or cabinet ministers, are "popular" accountable actors in international relations studies, constitutional law, political science, and public administration.

The Accountability Forum

To *whom* is an account to be rendered? Addressing this question yields a classification based on the type of *forum* to which the actor is required to render account. Public organizations and officials operating in a constitutional democracy find themselves confronting different types of forums and hence different kinds of accountability. These forums generally demand different sorts of information and apply different criteria in assessing what constitutes responsible conduct. They are therefore likely to render different judgments on the conduct of the public organization or the public official. The literature distinguishes a variety of accountability relationships, based on a variety of forums (Day and Klein 1987; Romzek 1996; Sinclair 1995; Romzek and Dubnick 1998; Behn 2001, 59; Pollitt 2003, 93; Mulgan 2003).

When we focus on *political* accountability, for instance, the account is given in political forums, to voters, members of Parliament and other political representatives, ministers, or political parties. The next type that may be distinguished is bureaucratic or *managerial* accountability, in which the forum is part of the chain of command within a bureaucratic organization. This is sometimes also called hierarchical accountability. Here the forums involve organizational superiors, all the way up to the management board, the CEO, or the minister. Then there is *administrative* accountability, where the forums are administrative bodies and regulators, involving courts of audit, ombudsmen, inspectorates, and regulatory agencies. This form of accountability may sometimes overlap with *legal* accountability, where the forums are legal bodies, such as courts, prosecutors, judges, and other magistrates. In the case of *professional* accountability, the account-giving is vis-à-vis peers and professional bodies of oversight. Another subset of forums involve clients, interest groups, affected third parties, and other societal stakeholders, which are often classified under the heading of *social*, or horizontal, accountability.

The Nature of the Conduct

The third question is: *about what* is an account to be rendered? This question concerns the nature of the conduct about which information is to be provided. Is it about the way money is being spent? Is it about the content of policy decisions? Is it about compliance with legal requirements? Accountability relationships may thus center on various types of "content," financial, procedural, communicative, and so forth (cf. Day and Klein 1987, 26; Sinclair 1995; and Behn 2001, 6–10).

The various disciplines focus on different dimensions of an actor's conduct and performance for which an account may be demanded. Financial accountability is the official focus among accounting researchers, although their research focus is much broader. Accountability for due process and appropriate conduct would generally fall in the realms of constitutional and administrative law, although many political scientists, public administration and IR scholars also take to this procedural perspective. Social psychologists focus on the process and quality of decision-making, which precedes the other dimensions. Accountability for products, outputs, or outcomes permeates all disciplines.

The Accountability Standards

The fourth question regards the *standards* by which the conduct of the actor is to be judged by the forum. Which substantive standards apply when assessing whether the actor has acted in an acceptable manner? As we have already seen, a large variety of standards is available, depending on role, context, and the nature of the forum. Often multiple standards apply. One of the most commonly used typologies of accountability is Romzek and Dubnick's. They analyze accountability as: "The means by which public agencies and their workers manage the diverse expectations generated within and outside the organization" (Romzek and Dubnick 1987, 228). They distinguished four types of accountability, which are not mutually exclusive. In *bureaucratic* accountability, for example, the expectations faced by organizations or officials in public administration are shaped by bureaucratic hierarchies, emphasizing adherence to rules and procedures and deference to political or organizational superiors. The expectations could also be based on legal norms and rules, such as due process (*legal* accountability), professional norms and standards (*professional* accountability), or political demands (*political* accountability). The number of standards is potentially quite large, as roles, contexts, and perspectives may all differ from one case to another. One could also distinguish various outcome-oriented standards, such as democratic controllability, good governance, and effectiveness and efficiency.

The Nature of the Obligation

The fifth question is *why* the actor feels (or indeed *is*) compelled to render an account. This relates largely to the nature of the relationship between the actor and the forum. *Mandatory* accountability arises where the forum formally wields power over the actor, perhaps due to a hierarchical relationship between actor and forum. A case in point is that of an administrative body that is accountable to the minister or through the minister to Parliament. Most political accountability arrangements, which are based on the delegation from principal to agent, are forms of *vertical*, mandatory accountability. In most cases of legal accountability too, the forum has the formal authority to compel the actor to give account, although based in that case not on a principal–agent (PA) relationship but rather on laws and regulations. At the opposite end of the spectrum one finds social accountability (see Moore in this volume). Here, there is generally no hierarchical relationship between actor and forum and no formal obligation to render account. Instead, giving account to various stakeholders in society occurs basically on a voluntary basis. Such accountability could hence be termed *voluntary accountability*.

Between these two extremes there are many intermediate forms. Sometimes agents are compelled by governments to arrange for sectorial or professional systems of self-regulation and account-giving. Other times agents pre-empt looming public regulation with self-imposed tightened norms for and practices of accountability. In a formal sense these types of accountability should be understood as voluntary forms of accountability, yet in practice the actors have no real choice. These types of accountability can be seen as *quasi-voluntary forms of accountability*.

The distinctions provided in this section will run through many of the chapters in this handbook. Specifically, these distinctions are central to Part 4, where the accountabilities of some of the most important actors are discussed. The chapters focus on the accountability of public services (Romzek), public management (Lægreid), the third sector (Rathgeb Smith), the corporate sector (Leader), and global governance organizations (Koppell).

STUDYING PUBLIC ACCOUNTABILITY

Against the background of all these various classifications and types of accountability, it should come as no surprise that the practice of studying public accountability is immensely diverse. There is an enormous variety in approaches both across and within academic disciplines. The purpose of this handbook is to provide an overview of existing work, not for its own sake, but as a stimulus and a guide to future research on public accountability. Accordingly, this section will provide a short overview of existing research in various disciplines, pointing to some encouraging commonalities, particularly at the theoretical level.

Theories

Across the various disciplines, two central theoretical models stand out in accountability research. In accountancy, international relations, political science, and public administration, the rational *principal–agent* theory has become the most common—and most criticized—dynamic theory for analyzing accountability. The *social contingency model* has evolved primarily in social psychology, but with echoes in more sociological approaches of public accountability. Both theoretical models are based on a relational core, and support substantive expectations about the likely behavior of parties in an accountability setting—although both models are highly flexible and eschew any easy attempt at ratification or falsification (see Gailmard in this volume).

The assumption of the rational actor is most visible in the majority of theoretical studies that use agency. Strøm's (2000) and Müller's (2000) work on accountability and delegation is exemplary of this strand in the literature. Strøm consciously models accountability in the "democratic chain of delegation." He stipulates that a modern representative democracy can be described as a concatenation of principal–agent (PA) relationships (Strøm 2000). The citizens, who are the primary principals in a democracy, have delegated their power to popular representatives, who, in turn, have delegated to the government the power of drafting and enforcement of laws and policy. Ministers subsequently entrust policy implementation to their ministries, who proceed to delegate parts of these tasks to more or less independent bodies and institutions or, indeed, to street-level bureaucrats. Each principal in the chain of delegation seeks to monitor the execution of the delegated public tasks by calling the agent to account. At the end of the accountability chain are the citizens, who pass judgment on the conduct of the government and who indicate their (dis)pleasure at the ballot box. Public accountability is an essential precondition for the democratic process to work, since it provides citizens and their representatives with the information needed for judging the conduct of government (see also Przeworski et al. 1999; Dowdle 2006).

Application of the agency model derives great advantage from assigning ideal types of accountability relations. Strøm for instance stipulates that accountability will work best in presidential systems, in which the number of delegations is the lowest and relations of delegation and accountability are unidirectional. The agency model also provides practical tips for principals aiming to fashion their relations with their agents, derived from the behavioral assumptions of the model. The lucidity of this model has inspired more authors to ground their work—albeit often loosely or partially—in it (Auel 2007; Romzek and Johnston 2000; Bardach and Lesser 1996; Bovens, 't Hart, and Schillemans 2008; Mörth 2007; Whitaker et al. 2004). And while some find success with it, others report that PA-based expectations fail to hold. Breaux et al. (2002) for instance report that in one case of welfare reform, the PA theory-based decision to privatize, in the words of one respondent, "undermin[ed] what we are trying to achieve." A similar finding was reported by Lehn (2008). He used the PA model to assess organizational performance of contracted not-for-profit organizations. He found that the model was only partially applicable to relationships between governments and contracted not-for-profits, since these organizations also have relational goals with their constituencies which are difficult to accommodate within the strongly performance-oriented model of agency theory. In these and other studies (see Brandsma and Schillemans 2013), PA theory could only partially explain the actual behavior of agents and principals. Principals are often found to be less interested in specific results than PA theory would assume and agents are often much less opportunistic. Moreover, where PA theory focuses on dyadic relationships between some agent and some principal, the more general public character and social settings in which they operate can be easily ignored. It is here that the social contingency model of accountability has added value.

The social contingency model of accountability, developed in social psychology and incorporating insights from sociology and behavioral economics, is the second major strand of theorizing on accountability. Social psychologists essentially see accountability as a bridging element between an individual and an external constituency, be it friends, strangers, or superiors (Lupson 2007). The behavior of individuals is then assumed to be strongly influenced by intra-personal cognitive processes (Chaiken and Trope 1999; Patil et al. and Koch and Wüsteman, in this volume; see also Olsen and Mansbridge, in this volume).

The social contingency model assumes that actors are rational, as does agency theory. The difference, however, is that the social contingency model does not focus on goal-directed behavior and relationships of "ownership," but instead focuses on the impact of an agent's social environment on his or her behavior. The theory generally assumes that the expectation that one is to justify one's judgments, actions, and decisions to others—that one is accountable—has a marked influence on those judgments, actions, and decisions. As people seek approval, as choices are often based on the logic of appropriateness (see Olsen in this volume), they will adjust their actions and decisions to societal norms and expectations of appropriate conduct. Tetlock (1992) has pointed out that the model is inherently *functionalistic*. Behaviors are explained from their "functionality" in relation to social goals and personal standings; decisions by decision-makers are often more influenced by their need for approval and support from important social constituencies than their desire to bring about specific results (what March and Olsen termed the "logic of consequences").

On the basis of this rather elementary framework, where accountability refers to situations where decision-makers are (potentially) obliged to account for their behavior to others, an expansive stream of research has emerged. In a series of often experimental research designs, the effects of differently institutionalized forms of accountability on actions or decisions have been investigated (see Lerner and Tetlock 1999 for an overview). This research sheds light on questions that are of acute relevance to political and public accountability as a number of relevant institutional factors have been addressed, for instance: What types of accountability foster precision in judgments and what types of accountability enhance critical reflection? What happens to the agent when the accountability audience focuses on processes rather than on results? How do factors such as timing, reputation, and political leanings affect accountability processes and their outcomes?

Part 1 of this handbook will look more closely at the different theoretical approaches to accountability. It begins with Dubnick's assessment of the historical roots and pedigree of accountability and Warren's situating of accountability within democratic theory. After that, the theoretical battlefield comes into view. Patil, Vieider, and Tetlock build on the psychological social contingency model to elucidate the differences between process and outcome accountability. Mansbridge draws the contours of a social contingency model of accountability. Gailmard argues for agency theory as the appropriate approach to accountability while Olsen focuses on institutions and accountability, and, in the process, contests many of the assumptions of rationality that agency theory relies upon.

Methods

Part 2 will subsequently discuss the most commonly used methods in studying public accountability. It features chapters on experimental analysis (Koch and Wüstemann), quantitative analysis (Brandsma), qualitative analysis (Yang), and visual analysis (Davison). The discussion aims to help researchers starting their inquiries to adopt appropriate research tools. Currently, scholars tend to adopt the specific type of methodological approach that is current in their field. Legal scholars prefer theoretical approaches, a preference shared with political scientists who, together with international relations scholars, also seek quantitative evidence. Social psychologists rely on experiments and are the most rigorous mono-methodologists. In contrast, accountancy scholars display the most varied approaches to studying accountability.

Themes

Why have so many authors "suddenly" begun working on public accountability in the recent past? What happened in the real world to boost such a vigorous academic cottage industry?

The growing complexity of government—both in terms of organization, societal relations, types of tasks, and formal regulation—is a recurring theme in the public accountability literature. This concern mirrors the large scale reorganizations of contemporary systems of governance. According to conventional accounts, the process began at the end of the nineteen sixties, at exactly the same time that accountability studies started to gain some traction, and it escalated in the course of the nineteen eighties and nineties. This idea is that ever increasing complexity of governance is a main driver of the research on accountability. More complex, multi-level systems of governance make accountability more difficult. When public policies are the product of difficult collaborations between many agents, private as well as public, it is more difficult to deliver; more difficult to call to account; more difficult even to understand who we should hold accountable.

The importance of the notion of governmental complexity for the ascent of accountability studies can be easily adduced from an analysis of the subjects driving public accountability research. For instance, in the large field of public administration studies, almost a third of the papers focus on situations where services are not delivered by bureaucracies or via established bureaucratic routines, but rather are provided by more-or-less independent, more-or-less public organizations faced with incentives from a (quasi-)market environment. Nearly another third of the public administration papers focus on the consequences of policy networks, notably the rise of public–private partnerships. What ties both types of papers together is that the specific forms of service delivery (through marketization, privatization, disaggregation, or the use of networks) blurs the strict lines of command and accountability that Strøm envisioned for the public service and that are said to have existed in the past.

In international relations, political science, constitutional law, and even accounting, the same types of issues resurface. Moreover, in many policy fields, policies increasingly are made on supra or international levels, including the EU, where traditional, national mechanisms of accountability are lacking or insufficient.

Part 6 in the handbook visits some of the key issues arising in public accountability research. The rise to prominence of accountability studies is first commented on from the perspective of accountability *deficits* by Richard Mulgan and then from the reverse angle of accountability *overloads* by Arie Halachmi. A further set of chapters then relate accountability to time (Mashaw), crises (Kuipers and 't Hart), blame (Hood), and to trust

(Greiling). Moore closes this part with a chapter on accountability, legitimacy, and the court of public opinion.

A HANDBOOK OF PUBLIC ACCOUNTABILITY

This handbook, as other OUP handbooks, is designed to be the one-stop-shop on the subject for those already working in the field—not only for academic scholars who study accountability, but also for practitioners in both the public and private sector who are designing, adjusting, or just struggling with, accountable governance and accountability mechanisms. Its comprehensiveness shows itself in a variety of ways. It showcases both conceptual and normative as well as empirical approaches in public accountability studies. It does not only give an overview of the scholarly research in a variety of disciplines, but it also takes stock of a wide range of accountability mechanisms and practices. In doing so, it is intended to be valuable to both accountability scholars and accountability practitioners. The handbook also covers accountability in the public, the private, and the non-profit sector, drawing on scholars from around the world and encouraging cross-national comparative perspectives. Most of all, this handbook aims to bring together insights from different fields as a stepping stone for future studies on public accountability that learn to benefit from existing studies. There is a dormant minimal conceptual consensus on what constitutes accountability across the different academic disciplines, as we have discussed at length in this chapter, which allows future research projects on accountability to benefit from existing theoretical analyses and methodological approaches from different fields. This, we hope, can contribute to more cumulative and integrative work on the subject in the future of accountability studies.

The handbook ends with Part 7, shorter reflective notes by some seasoned accountability scholars on valuable future areas for accountability research, as part of a new agenda for accountability studies. Mel Dubnick argues for a relational approach to accountability, and proposes to loosen the ties with neo-institutional and positive theory; by giving priority to ethnography over design, a better understanding of the role of accountability in governance can be achieved. Frank Vibert's chapter makes a claim for a more institutional research approach to accountability. As most analyses of accountability tend to carry rationalist assumptions of human behavior, are static in nature, and focus on isolated mechanisms or organizations, future studies of accountability would benefit from richer assumptions of human nature and more institutional and dynamic approaches. Our own proposal is a shift in focus in accountability studies from *deficit* to *overload* studies and, ultimately, to questions of meaningful accountability. Our proposal aligns with Matthew Flinders' earlier warning against the self-evident truth that we seem to need more accountability and more reforms in the age of complex governance. Flinders states: "academics are not passive or neutral analysts but are themselves one important strand of the social fabric that produces, supports or questions dominant assumptions about the expected standard of public accountability." He cautions authors to be more self-reflective about the *outcomes* and *assumptions* guiding their accountability research. We hope this handbook will achieve just that.

ACKNOWLEDGMENTS

During the spring semester of 2012, Mark Bovens was Van Doorn Fellow at the Netherlands Institute for Advanced Study in the Humanities and Social Sciences (NIAS) in Wassenaar. This fellowship and the hospitality of the NIAS towards the other editors has greatly enhanced the quality of the editorial process.

We would also like to thank our research assistant Armin Djogic for his excellent work and careful attention to detail as copy editor of this handbook.

NOTES

1. Quoted from the website recovery.gov, dedicated to this task. The Bill does not specify this goal, although it pays a lot of attention to accountability. See <http://www.recovery.gov>.
2. This overview is based on a review of 212 academic papers that focused on accountability. These were collected from 40 journals in the field of Public Administration, Political Science, Constitutional Law, International Relations, Accounting and Business Administration, and Social Psychology. See Schillemans (2013).
3. Actually, almost half of the papers analyzed in Schillemans (2013) abstain from a formal definition of accountability. When we limit our comparison of accountability definitions to only those papers that provide explicit definitions, more than two thirds of the definitions are broadly similar to the minimal conceptual consensus.

REFERENCES

Aucoin, P. and Jarvis, M. D. 2005. *Modernizing Government: A Framework for Reform.* Ottawa: Canada School of Public Service.

Auel, K. 2007. "Democratic Accountability and National Parliaments: Redefining the Impact of Parliamentary Scrutiny in EU Affairs." *European Law Journal*, 13: 487–504.

Bardach, E. and Lesser, C. 1996. "Accountability in Human Services Collaboratives—For What? and To Whom?" *Journal of Public Administration Research & Theory*, 6: 197–224.

Behn, R. D. 2001. *Rethinking Democratic Accountability*. Washington, DC: Brookings Institution Press.

Bovens, M. 2005. From Financial Accounting to Public Accountability, pp. 183–94 in *Bestandsaufnahme und Perspektiven des Haushalts- und Finanzmanagements*, ed. H. Hill. Baden Baden: Nomos Verlag.

Bovens, M. 2007. "Analysing and Assessing Accountability: A Conceptual Framework." *European Law Journal*, 13: 447–68.

Bovens, M. 2010. "Two Concepts of Accountability: Accountability as a Virtue and as a Mechanism." *West European Politics*, 33: 946–67.

Bovens, M., 't Hart, P., and Schillemans, T. 2008. "Does Accountability Work? An Assessment Tool." *Public Administration*, 86: 225–42.

Brandsma, G. J. and Schillemans, T. 2013. "The Accountability Cube: Measuring Accountability." *Journal of Public Administration Research & Theory*, 23 (4): 953-975.

Breaux, D. A., Duncan, C. M., Keller, C. D., and Morris, J. C. 2002. "Welfare Reform, Mississippi Style: Temporary Assistance for Needy Families and the Search for Accountability." *Public Administration Review*, 62: 92–103.

Busuioc, M. 2013. *European Agencies: Law and Practices of Accountability*. Oxford: Oxford University Press.

Christensen, T. and Lægreid, P., eds. 2011. *The Ashgate Research Companion to New Public Management*. Burlington: Ashgate.

Considine, M. 2002. "The End of the Line? Accountable Governance in the Age of Networks, Partnerships, and Joined-up Services." *Governance*, 15: 21–40.

Day, P. and Klein, R. 1987. *Accountabilities: Five Public Services*. London: Tavistock.

Diamond, J. 1999. *Gun, Germs and Steel: The Fates of Human Societies*. New York: W.W. Norton.

Dowdle, M. W. 2006. Public Accountability: Conceptual, Historical, and Epistemic Mapping, pp. 1–26 in *Public Accountability: Designs, Dilemmas and Experiences*, ed. M. W. Dowdle. Cambridge: Cambridge University Press.

Dubnick, M. J. 2007. *Situating Accountability: Seeking Salvation for the Core Concept of Modern Governance*. Unpublished paper. <mjdubnick.dubnick.net/papers/2002/salv2002.pdf>

Dunbabin, J. 2007. "Review: The Holy Bureaucrat: Eudes Rigaud and Religious Reform in Thirteenth-Century Normandy." *English Historical Review*, 122: 1385–87.

Flinders, M. 2011. "Daring to be a Daniel: The Pathology of Politicized Accountability in a Monitory Democracy." *Administration & Society*, 43: 595–619.

Goodin, R. E. 2003. "Democratic Accountability: The Distinctiveness of the Third Sector." *Archives Européennes de Sociologie*, XLIV: 359–96.

Koppell, J. G. S. 2005. "Pathologies of Accountability: ICANN and the Challenge of 'Multiple Accountabilities Disorder.'" *Public Administration Review*, 65: 94–107.

Lehn, B. 2008. "Bearing More Risk for Results: Performance Accountability and Nonprofit Relational Work." *Administration & Society*, 39: 959–83.

Lerner, J. and Tetlock, P. E. 1999. "Accounting for the Effects of Accountability." *Psychological Bulletin*, 125: 255–75.

Lupson, J. 2007. *A Phenomenographic Study of British Civil Servants' Conceptions of Accountability*. PhD Thesis. Cranfield University.

Messner, M. 2009. "The Limits of Accountability." *Accounting, Organizations and Society*, 34: 918–38.

Mörth, U. 2007. "Public and Private Partnerships as Dilemmas Between Efficiency and Democratic Accountability: The Case of Galileo." *Journal of European Integration*, 29: 601–17.

Müller, W. C. 2000. "Political Parties in Parliamentary Democracies: Making Delegation and Accountability Work." *European Journal of Political Research*, 37: 309–33.

Mulgan, R. 2000. "'Accountability': An Ever-Expanding Concept?" *Public Administration*, 78: 555–73.

Mulgan, R. 2003. *Holding Power to Account: Accountability in Modern Democracies*. London: Palgrave Macmillan.

O'Connell, L. 2005. "Program Accountability as an Emergent Property: The Role of Stakeholders in a Program's Field." *Public Administration Review*, 65: 85–93.

Philp, M. 2009. "Delimiting Democratic Accountability." *Political Studies*, 57: 28–53.

Pollitt, C. 2003. *The Essential Public Manager*. London: Open University Press/McGraw-Hill.

Power, M. 1997. *The Audit Society: Rituals of Verification*. Oxford: Oxford University Press.

Przeworski, A., Stokes, S. C., and Manin, B., eds. 1999. *Democracy, Accountability, and Representation*. Cambridge: Cambridge University Press.

Romzek, B. S. 1996. Enhancing Accountability, pp. 94–114 in *Handbook of Public Administration* (second edition), ed. J. L. Perry. San Francisco: Jossey Bass.

Romzek, B. S. and Dubnick, M. J. 1987. "Accountability in the Public Sector: Lessons from the Challenger Tragedy." *Public Administration Review*, 47: 227–38.

Romzek, B. S. and Dubnick, M. J. 1998. Accountability: Volume 1, pp. 6–11 in *International Encyclopedia of Public Policy and Administration*, ed. J. M. Shafritz. Boulder, CO: Westview Press.

Romzek, B. S. and Johnston, J. M. 2000. "State Social Services Contracting: Exploring the Determinants of Effective Contract Accountability." *Public Administration Review*, 4: 436–49.

Schedler, A. 1999. Conceptualizing Accountability, pp. 13–28 in *The Self-Restraining State: Power and Accountability in New Democracies*, eds. A. Schedler, L. Diamond, and M. F. Plattner. Boulder: Lynne Rienner.

Schillemans, T. 2011. "Does Horizontal Accountability Work? Evaluating Potential Remedies for the Accountability Deficit of Agencies." *Administration & Society*, 43: 387–416.

Schillemans, T. 2013. *The Public Accountability Review: A Meta-Analysis of Public Accountability Research in Six Academic Disciplines*. Working Paper. Utrecht University School of Governance. <http://igitur-archive.library.uu.nl/USBO/2013-0517-200614/UUindex.html>.

Scott, C. 2000. "Accountability in the Regulatory State." *Journal of Law and Society*, 27: 38–60.

Sinclair, A. 1995. "The Chameleon of Accountability: Forms and Discourses." *Accounting, Organizations and Society*, 20: 219–37.

Stokes, S. C. 2005. "Perverse Accountability: A Formal Model of Machine Politics with Evidence from Argentina." *American Political Science Review*, 99: 315–25.

Strøm, K. 2000. "Delegation and Accountability in Parliamentary Democracies." *European Journal of Political Research*, 37: 261–89.

Tetlock, P. E. 1992. The Impact of Accountability on Judgment and Choice: Toward a Social Contingency Model, pp. 331–76 in *Advances in Experimental Social Psychology: Vol. 25*, ed. M. P. Zanna. San Diego: Academic Press.

Vincent, N. 2007. "Review: The Holy Bureaucrat: Eudes Rigaud and Religious Reform in Thirteenth-Century Normandy." *Biography*, 30: 389–92.

Wang, X. 2002. "Assessing Administrative Accountability: Results from a National Survey." *American Review of Public Administration*, 32: 350–70.

Whitaker, G. P., Altman-Sauer, L., and Henderson, M. 2004. "Mutual Accountability Between Governments and Nonprofits: Moving Beyond 'Surveillance' to 'Service.'" *American Review of Public Administration*, 34: 115–33.

PART I

ANALYTICAL PERSPECTIVES

CHAPTER **2**

ACCOUNTABILITY AS A CULTURAL KEYWORD

MELVIN J. DUBNICK

WORDS MATTER

WORDS matter, and at any specified time and place some words matter more than others.[1] Raymond Williams, often cited as the founder of cultural studies, regarded certain words as "keys" to understanding cultures and changes in the society. In his study of industrialization from 1780 to 1950, Williams highlighted five such *keywords* as pivotal: industry, democracy, class, art, and culture. "The changes in their use" during that period

> bear witness to a general change in our characteristic ways of thinking about our common life: about our social, political and economic institutions; about the purposes which these institutions are designed to embody; and about the relations to these institutions and purposes of our activities in learning, education and the arts. (Williams 1958, xiii)

In 1976 Williams extended his list of culturally significant keywords to 110 terms and published his examination of each in a volume under the title *Keywords*; an additional 21 terms were included in a 1983 revised edition, and one can assume there would have been more additions and changes had he published further revisions (Williams died in 1988).[2]

This chapter focuses on a particular word—*accountability*—that, despite its absence from Williams's original lists, would likely have taken a prominent place among contemporary cultural keywords. As support for that contention, Figure 2.1 provides evidence of the growing frequency of the term's use in a sampling of books based on a million

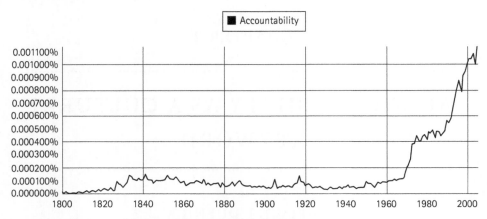

FIGURE 2.1 Frequency of accountability in English language texts, 1800–2005

scanned volumes drawn from works published in English (in the US and UK) between 1800 and 2005.[3] While accountability first appears in the plotted sample during the early 1800s, it remains a culturally innocuous term until the 1960s and 1970s, when we start to see a sharp and significant upturn in its usage.

Accountability's claim to cultural keyword status can also be based on *how* the term has been used in this period, for it has gone from a relatively narrow range of applications reflecting a simple sense of its meaning (typically indicating a condition where one party is answerable to another for some X) to an expansive, ambiguous, and often enigmatic term with considerable cultural gravitas cutting across many cultural domains (Mulgan 2000).

Evidence of this development is literally everywhere. There is hardly any aspect of our lives that has not been touched by the growing obsession with accountability. Teachers are held accountable for the performance of their students, and presidents are assumed accountable for the state of the economy; we hold parents accountable for the behavior of their children, and police accountable for higher crime rates; we demand accountability for bankers who we believe caused a financial crisis, and call for greater accountability when the potholes in our local roads go unrepaired. We react to all crimes and scandals (and even natural disasters!) by calling for someone to be held to account, and we expect there to be accountability systems in place to prevent the recurrence of just about any untoward behavior. Pervasive is one way to characterize our collective obsession with accountability. Pollitt and Hupe (2011) note it as one of the "magic words" shared widely by students and practitioners of governance.[4]

The elevation of accountability to cultural keyword status is as puzzling as it is important for our comprehension of changes that are taking place in the domains of politics and governance. Here is a term that has been part of the modern governance paradigm for nearly a millennium (Dubnick 1998), but has only of late become the iconic manifestation of "good governance." While the term has been treated positively for decades as a desirable characteristic of modern states (Fukuyama 2011), there have been no new major theoretical breakthroughs in the study of politics or government pushing accountability to the foreground as the defining feature of modern governance.[5] Nor has its recent rise to global salience been the result of any coherent social movement or reformist ideology; in fact, the push for greater accountability seems to be a point of agreement in even the most partisan and divided political contexts. In that regard, accountability has truly become a "golden concept" (Bovens, Schillemans, and 't Hart 2008).

Whatever the cause of accountability's emergence as a keyword, there is little doubt that its newly gained importance as a cultural icon has transformed its form and function in governance and politics. Accountability is no longer merely a term of the governance arts—a useful instrument to be pulled from the policy or management toolbox to deal with some specific problem. The aura of legitimacy is now associated with its use, even in instances where it is obviously an irrelevant or inappropriate instrument for the job (Mashaw 2006). In addition, over the past several decades a strong belief has developed in the capacity of accountability to achieve some of our most highly-valued objectives. Expressed as the "promises of accountability" (Dubnick and Frederickson 2011), these include unquestioned—and often unsubstantiated—assumptions that various forms of accountability will result in a more democratically responsive government, improvements in the efficient and effective performance of government agencies, a more ethical public sector workforce, and the enhanced capacity of government to generate just and equitable policy outcomes.

In short, given its emergence as a cultural keyword, we can no longer rely on our knowledge of accountability in its older, simpler, and more precise forms. What we are dealing with is not merely a set of institutional arrangements or managerial mechanisms, but a cultural phenomenon that is dominating, altering, and consuming our traditional notions of governance. Our objective here is to enhance our understanding of this emergent form of accountability as it relates to the domains of governance and politics.

This exploration of accountability as a cultural phenomenon is limited to the lexical and conceptual manifestations of our subject, and in that sense it touches on just two among a wider range of culturally significant forms taken by account-giving norms and actions in socio-cultural relationships. Accountability is also a social psychological phenomenon (Lerner and Tetlock 1999), and even the utterance of the term within various contexts can be treated as a linguistic speech act with social impact and cultural significance (Lupia 2011). In that sense, this chapter is only an indication of what is yet to be explored in the study of accountability as a cultural phenomenon.

AND THEN THERE WAS "THE WORD"

We start with the most obvious manifestation of accountability-as-cultural-phenomenon—the word itself. There are three options open to those of us who would analyze the pedigree and development of any particular word. First, we can focus on the definitions offered in authoritative dictionaries or carefully collected from other sources. Second, we can explore the etymological origins of the word. Finally, we can seek insight through studies of the usage of a term.

The definition: Seeking a definition for this "notoriously ambiguous" (Brooks 1995) term can prove very frustrating, and often results in the adoption of a version deemed best suited to the narrowly delineated topic at hand. Unfortunately, this tactic generates problems of conceptual omission or commission (cf. Keohane 2003).

We begin our search for meaning in the usual place, with the authoritative *Oxford English Dictionary* (OED):

> The quality of being accountable; liability to account for and answer for one's conduct, performance of duties, etc. (in modern use often with regard to parliamentary, corporate, or financial liability to the public, shareholders, etc.); responsibility. Freq. with modifying word.

Three notable features of that definition include: (1) it is an abstract noun designating an immaterial "quality" or characteristic; (2) its definition is strongly tied to synonyms, such as liability, answerability, responsibility; and (3) it is often accompanied by a "modifying word" that effectively renders it meaningful only in context. These points, individually and together, make the task of defining accountability at best problematic.

The first problem is that upon close scrutiny one realizes that the definition begs the question of what constitutes "accountableness" rather than providing any substantive basis for a definition. What is the nature of that quality or characteristic? The state of "being accountable" would suffice if there was some way of characterizing that condition, but what we are provided with is circular:[6] accountability is what it means to be accountable, and being accountable is what it means to possess accountability. This is a definition going nowhere, requiring reliance on the second feature of the definition—synonyms.

As we see below when addressing accountability as a concept, the reliance of the OED definition on synonyms makes sense in the attempt to generate a meaningful understanding of the term but is a weak basis for a definition that truly differentiates the word within the linguistic community. This is most evident when we try to deal with the word in translation or out of specific contexts.

Although English speakers take the term accountability for granted, few languages have an equivalent word. Until recently, romance languages translated accountability as "responsibility," and languages like Japanese and modern Hebrew relied on awkward transliterations when necessary (Dubnick 1998). To be responsible—to possess the quality of responsibility—does not communicate what it means to be accountable, answerable, liable, obliged, etc. Synonyms are often more similar than they are equivalent, and that gap (the dissimilarity) can prove troublesome, not only across language boundaries but also across contexts.

Which brings us to the third feature of the OED definition—its noting that the word accountability is frequently accompanied by a modifying term, e.g., *political* accountability, *financial* accountability, *corporate* accountability, *legal* accountability, etc. Here the word's definition is surrendered to its contextualized meanings, and thus to the various synonyms associated with those settings. In law, accountability is liability; in politics it is answerability and responsiveness; in finance and corporate governance, it is fiduciary relationships and fidelity; etc. Whatever substantive meaning might be in the word accountability is overwhelmed and subordinated to the demands of the specific task environment.

The problems with the definition highlighted here help explain the relative ease with which accountability was elevated to cultural keyword status. The lack of any inherent definable characteristic that could act as an anchor for the notion of accountability rendered it vulnerable to assuming a broadened meaning tied to the modifying contexts and/or the synonyms with which the word is often associated.

Origins: Additional insight can often be gained by turning to a word's etymology— a search for meaning in its origins and roots. But here, too, we confront an ambiguity fostered by the very structure (or morphology) of the word. Among students of etymology, a word such as accountability is regarded as a complex noun of two parts (e.g., in the OED, the adjective *accountable* + the suffix *-bility*) and the etymological task seems simple enough—find and combine the meaningful roots of each word. The next step, however, proves somewhat more challenging, for the word's roots tend to justify a much narrower sense of what accountability means than common contemporary usage implies.

For the adjective *accountable*, the roots are deep (Old French) and deeper (Latin). The deep roots are in the Old French, and are commonly cited as still another complex term, the verb *aconter* (*a-* + *conter*), to count, to reckon. This, in turn, is linked to the Latin verb *computare*, to compute or calculate. Taken literally, an accountable person is "able" (has the capacity) to offer an account or reckoning of some sort, and accountability can be seen in that rather limited light as characterizing someone having the ability to provide a response to those calling for a count or calculation.[7]

In basic terms, an accountable person is an "accountant" in the strictest, most literal, and legalistic sense of that word. The label was once formally applied to those individuals called to testify before the court because they maintained the books for an enterprise that was part of some legal dispute.[8] If there is a sense of qualities usually attributed to the appellation "accountable person" (someone with accountability)—responsibility, obligation, liability, etc.—they are not inherent in the meanings derived from etymological roots. If there is any sense of designating someone with responsibility, it is the implication that the accountant will fulfill the role of offering the expected "count" on demand.

In this seemingly trivial exercise in etymology, an important point stands out: nothing in the word's origins supports its contemporary use as a higher standard by which to operate or judge individuals, groups, or nations. The characteristic of accountability was narrowly associated with the actions of an individual engaged as a book-keeper in the nascent profession of accounting.

Usage: If neither dictionary definitions nor etymological analysis can help us with the meaning of accountability, we need to turn to pragmatics—the examination of meaning

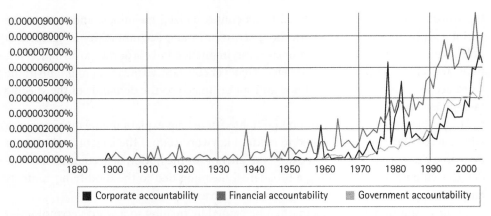

FIGURE 2.2 Frequency of mediated forms of accountability in English language texts, 1890–2005

derived from usage. There are several analytic approaches to the study of word usage,[9] but under the heading of pragmatics are those that emphasize the role of context in shaping meaning.

The Google scanned books data in Figure 2.1 can be used to indicate meanings derived from word usage at a more contextualized level. As noted in the comments about the definition of accountability, the term often derives its meaning from the adjectives with which it is associated. In line with that logic, Figure 2.2 tracks the phrases "corporate accountability," "accountable government,"[10] and "financial accountability" from 1890 to 2005 using the English language corpus developed by the Google project team. The plotted patterns follow the more general trends in Figure 2.1 related to the unqualified term itself, but the findings also reflect some interesting variations related to the question of meaning. It is not surprising to see financial accountability emerge first and most prominently over this extended period, and we can speculate that there is some relationship between its first occurrence during a time characterized by our first major nationwide economic and banking crises. The phrase "corporate accountability" seems to have its initial boost during the 1950s when the power of corporations became a major issue, and given shifting political views during the 1960s, it is not surprising that government accountability starts to draw increasing reference during the 1970s. While these conjectures should be treated with caution given the nature of the dataset, each of these trend lines indicates just how sensitive the word accountability has been to political and economic conditions.[11]

Of course, noting increased frequency of usage is not the same as analyzing the meanings of words derived from such usage. The most common pragmatics approaches have been associated with the concept of "language games," a perspective developed by the philosopher Ludwig Wittgenstein in his later works (1968) that has had a profound effect on the study of what words "mean." As with other pragmatics approaches, the emphasis is on the role that context plays in determining the meaning of words and their related discourses (Stalnaker 1970).

There are many kinds of language games that use (and shape the meaning of) accountability, and those relevant to the present effort occur within the context of discourses and narratives about governance. While we use the terms in our daily lives, the concepts of "discourse" and "narrative" are analytic tools in the hands of linguists and philosophers[12] interested in human communication. Analytically, discourses are the most general form of language-based verbal communication produced as a means to generate a response from the receiving population, and narratives are a particular form of discourse based on the use of "stories" (broadly defined; Rudrum 2005). Within the context of such stories of governance, we can see how the meaning of accountability has been altered from the core OED definition ("quality of being accountable")—a definition that all but disappears as the word is transformed through a variety of narrative means.

In Figure 2.3 we see that in some discourses, the word is *institutionalized* by its association with constitutional and electoral arrangements designed to constrain and control the power of political authorities, rendering them more answerable and responsive. More than just mechanisms (see below), these arrangements provide a framework within which accountability is to be achieved and sustained, even if any or all the players involved lack (or never achieve) the "quality of being accountable." This is the discourse of democratic accountability, and the language game that takes place within it raises accountability to the level of the legitimizing standard (i.e., ends) for modern governance. It is supported by a narrative in which there is an implied promise that such arrangements will result in greater degrees of democratic governance (e.g., Fukuyama 2011).

Discourse focused on	Narrative	Accountability as	Examples
Institutionalization	Promise of democracy	Arrangements (usually constitutional) intended to constrain power and foster answerability and responsiveness of officials.	Constitution making; Self-restraining State; Accountability forums; Horizontal accountability
Mechanization	Promise of control	Means used to oversee and direct operations and behavior within organized context.	Administrative control; Bureaucratization; Rules; Reporting; Auditing
Juridicization	Promise of justice	Formalization (usually legal in nature) of rules and procedures designed to deal with undesirable and unacceptable behavior.	Formalization; Legal rulemaking; Criminalization; Enforcement; Truth & Reconciliation
Incentivization	Promise of performance	Standards and metrics designed to influence behavior.	TQM; Performance measurement; Performance management; Standards

FIGURE 2.3 Discourses and narrative of accountability

In other discourses, accountability has been *mechanized*—that is, reconfigured as a means for facilitating control. While the institutional form is designed to achieve answerability, responsiveness, etc., here organizational arrangements (e.g., hierarchies, bureaucracies, audits, reporting) are designed to solicit obedience and greater efficiency. In this language game, to be accountable is to be subject to active control, but from the perspective of those charged with managing organizations, it fosters a positive narrative of control.

In a third type of discourse, accountability has been *juridicized* and incorporated into the language games of both criminal and civil legal systems as well as the formalized sanctioning process within organizations. Here the underlying narrative is that accountability produces justice for those victimized by malicious or damaging behavior.

In still another discourse, accountability has been *incentivized*—turned into a set of benchmarks or metrics against which performance is measured. Here, the meaning of accountability becomes the basis for assessment in an effort to promote (or force) adjustments in performance in order to demonstrate that one has become more accountable. The narrative is based on a view of human nature that assumes individuals will respond in a positive way to information about their performance.

What is interesting about these discourses is that they are frequently about more than descriptions of governance (public, private, and third sector); they are also generating narratives of reform. Whether focused on attaining higher ends (democracy and justice) or basic means (facilitating control or enhanced performance), discursive forms of accountability are closely tied to efforts to bring about change and reflect views that accountability (however it is defined) is either lacking or insufficient under current circumstances. In this regard, within these language games, accountability carries the burden of being either the cause or the cure for what ails the governance system.

We obviously learn a good deal more about the meaning of accountability by relying on pragmatics, most significantly that the word draws its meaningfulness not from its defined content, but from its context and functionality, or dysfunctionality, within the realm of modern forms of governance. Again, we can see that this tendency to be contextualized and fitted into different discursive formats helps explain why accountability was suitable for cultural keyword status. The question as to why it attained that status when it did remains unanswered.

Conceptualizing Accountability

As a cultural phenomenon, accountability is more than merely a distinct and "definable" term. It is also at the center of a powerful conceptual construct that plays a major role in how we perceive the operations of modern government. In this section we examine the nature of that conceptual construct to see if it can add to our understanding of the cultural primacy of accountability among that class of terms that shape our understanding of politics and governance.

We begin by highlighting a central fact about the definition of the word accountability; it is a term characterized by an exceptionally high degree of synonymity. Whether focusing on typical definitions or efforts to translate this very English word, we find frequent reliance on several common synonyms—words that users or translators accept as sufficiently similar in "meaning" to substitute for accountability. What this synonymic condition implies is that our efforts to develop a meaningful understanding of accountability as a cultural keyword may require that we abandon our focus on the word per se and reset it on the more general **concept** of accountability that has emerged in recent years.

In its purest form, a synonym of one word is another that can be used interchangeably with the first regardless of context. The word and its synonym are in the strictest sense identical in meaning. A "bachelor" is an "unmarried man," a "mother" is a "female parent," a "car" is an "automobile," etc. Is accountability *identical* in this way to responsibility, liability, answerability, etc.? Not quite, especially in light of the contextual (i.e., pragmatic) variation in usage of each of those terms. In our complex and interconnected world, I can be responsible for some event, for example the marriage of two people who met because I did not take the empty seat between them on the bus, without being held to account for it (nor for whatever happiness or miseries that befall the couple in the years that follow). Nevertheless, there is some degree of overlap in meaning among these terms as they are put to use in everyday language games. They may not be synonyms in the "purist" sense, but they share a level or degree of synonymity.

Implied in the high degree of synonymity characterizing accountability and related terms is the suggestion of a more general idea—a concept—that ties them together despite their autonomous existence in various language games and discourses. Shifting our focus from word to concept can prove significant in comprehending the keyword status of accountability. Lexicographers define a concept as some basic unit of thought reflecting an idea, "an abstraction from a number of ideas about individual referents" that share something in common (Svensén 2009, 213). To grasp the nature and importance of accountability in this conceptual sense, we need to explore just how the associated terms relate to each other in a cultural sense.

To uncover concept-defining ideas, some analysts look for some core term around which conceptualizations cluster (Motter et al. 2002; Wille 2005). Others find concepts emerging from a variety of common metaphorical tropes (Morgan 1980; 1983). For example, as already noted, the synonymic character of accountability is frequently treated metonymically, as if it is one among several interchangeable terms that roughly conveys the same meaning. We hear this conceptual device at work when reporters frequently use the word accountability in lieu of more obtuse (at least for the layperson) terms such as legal liability or to communicate the meaning of fiduciary relationships. The problem with this approach, as well as the cluster analysis method, is that neither provides leads as to why it is accountability, rather than other terms in the synonymic class, that has become so central to the ideas being represented.

Another relevant metaphorical trope (synecdoche) involves viewing accountability as part of a family of synonymic terms sharing a close relationship to some referent concept. We see this in the common association of accountability with the concept of democracy. Discourses on democracies reflect an assumption that some form of accountability to the public is among the defining features of political systems that warrant that label. An accountable government is more often than not understood to be democratic, and vice versa. In such discourses, certain of the standard synonyms for accountability (e.g., answerability, responsiveness) tend to be applied freely, generating a sense of what it means for a system of governance to be (democratically) accountable.

Nevertheless, the discursive relationship between democracy and accountability is hardly direct or precise, primarily due to the impreciseness of meanings associated with both terms. Tilly (2007, 7-11) has highlighted at least four types of definitions for democracy: constitutional (based on the legal form of the regime), substantive (focused on quality of life under a regime), procedural (tied to the use of a range of "democratic" practices, e.g. contested elections, universal suffrage, etc.), and process-oriented (highlighting the existence of certain conditions, e.g., rule of law, voting equality, effective participation, transparency, etc.). The tethered relationship assumed to exist between democracy and accountability is reflected in the role that various forms of accountability play in each of these approaches, from constitutional provisions related to suffrage, to holding regular elections and public hearings, to guaranteeing a number of political rights and civil liberties.

In searching for a meaningful sense of the concept of accountability, however, such an approach poses a major challenge. Here the concept melds into its referent concept, democracy—and in the process falls back into the chameleon-like state that has rendered it a widely applied cultural phenomenon. What is lost, however, is the idea of accountability as a distinct form of behavior and social relationships that are as much a part of authoritarian hierarchies as they are a characteristic of democratic regimes. The fact that democracy is itself a keyword (Williams 1976) makes the task even more challenging. The same holds true for attempts to derive a meaningful sense of accountability by tethering it to the management of private firms or corporate governance (Sinclair 1995)—in each instance, the concept of accountability is transformed and reconstructed, often to the point of obscuring its essential characteristics as a social relationship.

There remains the question of why, among this cluster of accountability-related concepts, it is accountability that currently holds such a prominent place. Certainly, there are other members of this synonymic class of words (e.g., responsibility: Bovens 1998) that are not as parochial in their origin and are far more translatable across many languages. In addition, there are words in that synonymic class far more meaningful within specific domains as "terms of art" (e.g., liability in law). Nevertheless, at least within the past half century, it is accountability that has emerged as the salient concept—the keyword—among this collection of concepts.

One possible reason why accountability has become so prominent among its synonymic class may be its discursive association with what are perceived to be higher public values. As the concept of accountability became narratively intertwined with the promises of democracy, justice, efficiency (control), and greater administrative performance, its status as a public virtue (Bovens 2010) also rose, to the point that it has come

	Legal Setting	Organizational Setting	Professional Setting	Political Setting
Moral pulls	Liability	Answerability	Responsibility	Responsiveness
Moral pushes	Obligation	Obedience	Fidelity	Amenability

Source: Dubnick (1998).

FIGURE **2.4** Species of the genus accountability

to dominate its class of related concepts.[13] Whatever the relationship among the concepts in the past, the centrality of accountability is now well established.

As Bovens (2010) has noted, however, accountability is more than a virtue; it is also a mechanism and instrument of administrative and political power that can be applied to bring about policy compliance as well as to force changes in governance. Nevertheless, these two aspects of accountability are related. As a highly regarded (virtuous) public value, accountability has emerged as a moral force which can be—and often is—used to promote and foster the application of compliance mechanisms and instruments of change. This moral force can be brought to bear through both external pressure stressing the desirability of accountable governance—what Nozick (1981) called "moral pull"—and managerial efforts to instill and internalize an ethical commitment to accountability within public agencies (i.e., "moral push").

It would be a mistake, therefore, to see the relationships among these related concepts as merely hierarchical or simplistically metaphorical. A more appropriate means for framing the current (keyword-based) relationship is through the substantive metaphor of genus and species, with accountability situated as the concept-encompassing genus to which each species (sub-concept) relates. Such a scheme requires that we establish rules that define the relationship between accountability and its sub-concepts as well as articulate characteristics that distinguish among the different species. As illustrated in Figure 2.4, the different species can be sorted not only by the relevant settings within which they are likely to appear, but also by whether they are related to accountability through the process of moral push or moral pull.

This conceptual framing of accountability provides a broader sense of meaning than the earlier focus on definitions and etymology. It also addresses the enhanced (cultural) reach of the idea of accountability in recent decades and its elevated status within its family of synonyms. By viewing it within this genus–species framework, we are adopting the view that today the concept of accountability encompasses (rather than replaces) many of the synonymic terms and ideas with which it has been associated. In common usage today as a cultural keyword, to be accountable is to be responsible, and amenable, and answerable, and obliged, etc. As importantly, this framing also provides a contextual basis for understanding the variations in what the concept of accountability means in various settings.

Conclusion

There is a growing consensus among students of contemporary governance that we are in the midst of major changes requiring a basic reformulation of how we view the institutions through which we govern our social, economic, and political relationships (OECD 2001). Some see these changes as foundational, involving the disassembling and reassembling of nation-state focused governance patterns (Sassen 2008; Valaskakis 2001), while others have noted the capacity of modern governments to adapt to changing conditions without altering the fundamental arrangements of state-based governance (Weiss 1998).

The increased attention to accountability and its development as a cultural keyword can be regarded as an indicator and measure of the unsettled nature of governance in this tumultuous and transitional time. Implied as well is the strong likelihood that, if and when the debates over the nature of governance are somewhat settled, accountability will likely assume a central role in the dominant discourse that emerges. It is reasonable to ask what form that central role will take.

The answer perhaps lies in the historical precedent of two other governance-related keywords: efficiency and planning. In his classic study of ideas that underpinned the rise of the American administrative state, Waldo (1948) took note of how efficiency—"a term generally regarded as descriptive, 'mechanical' "—had become "invested with moral significance" during the Progressive era, developing into a "key concept" in the political theory of the administrative state.[14]

Similarly, the concept of planning has a history extending back to efforts to build defensive fortifications around ancient and medieval cities (Mumford 1961), and yet by the mid-20th century it had gained keyword status reflecting the widespread acceptance of corporate, social, and national economic planning (Galbraith 1971; Scott 1998; Miller and Rose 2008). Despite analytic critiques (Dahl and Lindblom 1953; Wildavsky 1973), powerful ideological challenges (e.g., Hayek 1944), and its association with the failed economies of the Soviet bloc, planning has remained (albeit in more subtle forms) a basic part of the logic of modern governance thinking—part of what Foucault (1991) terms our collective "governmentality."

Accountability seems to be following the same historical arc as both efficiency and planning—terms initially associated with certain mechanisms of governing transformed into culturally salient concepts that became the very definition of "good governance" at the height of their popularity. Accountability has already been transfigured from an instrument of governing to what MacIntyre (1984) characterized as a "virtuous practice"—an endeavor in which the act of holding to account (or being held to account) is now regarded as an end in itself within the context of governing. But as a cultural keyword, accountability is also becoming something much more—a lens through which we perceive, understand, and shape all aspects of our social lives.

For those engaged in the study of accountability, the implications of this "culturation" of the concept are significant. It not only challenges the myopic perspectives that currently inform accountability research (cf. Ebrahim 2005), but also begs for a radical rethinking of the ontological foundations upon which current thinking is based (Dubnick 2011). Moreover, it establishes the need for a theory of accountable governance rooted in a greater appreciation of how the words we use both reflect and determine the lives we lead.

Notes

1. On the power of words in different contexts, see Bourdieu (1991), Tambiah (1968), and Edelman (1977; 1985).
2. An updated revision incorporating Williams's terms was attempted in Bennett et al. (2005). For a more historical approach to keyword analysis, see Frantzen (2012).
3. This analysis is based on books scanned by Google as part of its effort to digitize the holdings of major libraries; see <http://www.google.com/googlebooks/library.html>. A major sub-project aimed at facilitating the use of data generated by the Google Books Library Project is reflected in the "N-Gram" initiative explained at <http://books.google.com/ngrams/info>. See Michel et al. (2011) for further elaboration.
4. To some critics, the term "perverse" might be a more fitting characterization; see O'Neill (2002); Stein (2002, Ch. 2); Flinders (2011).
5. Ferejohn (1999, 133) initiated an effort to develop an accountability-based theory of democracy by laying the groundwork for what he termed a "fuller theory of endogenous accountability," but there has been little effort to follow through on that project.
6. See Burgess (2008) for the case for circularity in definitions.
7. The relationship of accountability to its Old French roots is clearer in Samuel Johnson's 1755 *A Dictionary of the English Language* in which he defines the word "comptible" as "ready to give an account." He notes the reference source as Shakespeare.
8. Originally (c. 15th century), in British law the term "accountant" designated any "defendant in an action of account" (i.e., anyone capable of being held to account in matters of trust, such as in financial relationships). By the 16th century, it was used to designate anyone (defendant or witness) who made a living through the keeping of accounts; eventually the designation was applied to those legally certified as accountants (in contrast to bookkeepers). See Garner (2011, 117).
9. The Google book scan project cited earlier (see Figure 2.1) has opened up the possibility of a more empirically based examination of word usage that goes beyond mere frequency counts; see Michel et al. (2011). At this juncture, however, that capacity is limited and the significance of the analysis should be approached with caution.
10. The phrase entered into the viewer was "government accountability", but that was integrated by the program with the more commonly used "accountable government."
11. Seeking another indicator of usage patterns, we attempted to find out if the word "accountability"—not in any translated form or transliterated—appeared in foreign language books that are part of the Google Books database. With all due consideration for the limitations of this measure, it was clear that the word had crossed language barriers and become part of the discourse in at least three European languages: French, German, and Spanish.

During the post-World War Two period, but especially since the early 1970s, the word itself has become globalized—the result, perhaps, of Anglo-American dominance of the legal aspects of globalization as well as its influence in other aspects (cultural, social, and political) of the constantly expanding international arena.

12. For a general overview of the logic and structure of discourse and narrative analyses, see Brockmier and Harre (1997).

13. There is historical precedent for this situation in parliamentary systems in which the concept of "ministerial responsibility" became the standard measure of what we would today term "good governance"; see Barberis (1998); also Flinders (2002a; 2002b).

14. "The high point in the popularity of 'efficiency' came in the years immediately preceding the First Great War. It was a rallying cry of Progressivism. Indeed, it was recognized as a 'movement' within the larger movement, and became in certain circles a veritable fetish" (Waldo 1948, 190).

References

Barberis, P. 1998. "The New Public Management and a New Accountability." *Public Administration*, 76: 451–70.

Bennett, T., Grossberg, L., Morris, M., and Williams, R. 2005. *New Keywords: A Revised Vocabulary of Culture and Society*. Malden, MA: Blackwell Publishers.

Bourdieu, P. 1991. *Language and Symbolic Power*. Cambridge, MA: Harvard University Press.

Bovens, M., Schillemans, T., and 't Hart, P. 2008. "Does Public Accountability Work? An Assessment Tool." *Public Administration*, 86: 225–42.

Bovens, M. 1998. *The Quest for Responsibility: Accountability and Citizenship in Complex Organisations*. Cambridge, UK: Cambridge University Press.

Bovens, M. 2010. "Two Concepts of Accountability: Accountability as a Virtue and as a Mechanism." *West European Politics*, 33: 946–67.

Brockmier, J. and Harre, R. 1997. "Narrative: Problems and Promises of an Alternative Paradigm." *Research on Language & Social Interaction*, 30: 263–83.

Brooks, T. 1995. *Accountability: It All Depends on What You Mean*. Clifton, NJ: Akkad Press.

Burgess, J. A. 2008. "When is Circularity in Definitions Benign?" *The Philosophical Quarterly*, 58: 214–33.

Dahl, R. A. and Lindblom, C. E. 1953. *Politics, Economics, and Welfare: Planning and Politico-economic Systems Resolved into Basic Social Processes*. New York: Harper Torchbooks.

Dubnick, M. J. 1998. Clarifying Accountability: An Ethical Theory Framework, pp. 68–81 in *Public Sector Ethics: Finding and Implementing Values*, eds. C. Sampford, N. Preston, and C. A. Bois. Leichhardt, NSW: The Federation Press/Routledge.

Dubnick, M. J. 2011. "Move Over Daniel: We Need Some 'Accountability Space.'" *Administration & Society*, 43: 704–16.

Dubnick, M. J. and Frederickson, H. G. 2011. Introduction, pp. xi–xxx in *Accountable Governance: Problems and Promises*, eds. M. J. Dubnick and H. G. Frederickson. Armonk, NY: M.E. Sharpe.

Ebrahim, A. 2005. "Accountability Myopia: Losing Sight of Organizational Learning." *Nonprofit and Voluntary Sector Quarterly*, 34: 56–87.

Edelman, M. J. 1977. *Political Language: Words That Succeed and Policies That Fail*. New York: Academic Press.

Edelman, M. 1985. "Political Language and Political Reality." *PS*, 18: 10–19.

Ferejohn, J. 1999. Accountability and Authority: Toward a Theory of Political Accountability, pp. 131–53 in *Democracy, Accountability, and Representation*, eds. A. Przeworski, S. C. Stokes, and B. Manin. New York: Cambridge University Press.

Flinders, M. 2002a. "Shifting the Balance? Parliament, the Executive and the British Constitution." *Political Studies*, 50: 23–42.

Flinders, M. 2002b. "Governance in Whitehall." *Public Administration*, 80: 51–75.

Flinders, M. 2011. "Daring to be a Daniel." *Administration & Society*, 43: 595–619.

Foucault, M. 1991. Governmentality, pp. 87–104 in *The Foucault Effect: Studies in Governmentality*, eds. G. Burchell, C. Gordon, and P. Miller. Chicago: University of Chicago.

Frantzen, A. J. 2012. *Anglo-Saxon Keywords*. Malden, MA: Wiley-Blackwell.

Fukuyama, F. 2011. *The Origins of Political Order: From Prehuman Times to the French Revolution*. First edition. New York: Farrar, Straus and Giroux.

Galbraith, J. K. 1971. *The New Industrial State*. Second edition. New York: New American Library.

Garner, B. A. 2011. *A Dictionary of Modern Legal Usage*. New York: Oxford University Press.

Hayek, F. A. 1944. *The Road to Serfdom*. Chicago: University of Chicago Press.

Johnson, S. 1755. *A Dictionary of the English Language*. London: Printed by W. Strahan, for J. and P. Knapton [etc.].

Keohane, R. O. 2003. "The Concept of Accountability in World Politics and the Use of Force." *Michigan Journal of International Law*, 24: 1121–41.

Lerner, J. S. and Tetlock, P. E. 1999. "Accounting for the Effects of Accountability." *Psychological Bulletin*, 125: 255–75.

Lupia, A. 2011. Necessary Conditions for Increasing Accountability, pp. 85–93 in *Accountability Through Public Opinion: From Inertia to Public Action*, eds. S. Odugbemi and T. Lee. Washington: World Bank Publications.

MacIntyre, A. C. 1984. *After Virtue: A Study in Moral Theory*. Second edition. Notre Dame, Ind.: University of Notre Dame Press.

Mashaw, J. L. 2006. Accountability and Institutional Design: Some Thoughts on the Grammar of Governance, pp. 115–56 in *Public Accountability: Designs, Dilemmas and Experiences*, ed. M. D. Dowdle. Cambridge, UK: Cambridge University Press.

Michel, J. B., Shen, Y. K., Aiden, A. P., Veres, A., Gray, M. K., Google Books Team, Pickett, J. P., Hoiberg, D., Clancy, D., Norvig, P., Orwant, J., Pinker, S., Nowak, M. A., and Aiden, E. L. 2011. "Quantitative Analysis of Culture Using Millions of Digitized Books." *Science*, 331: 176–82.

Miller, P. and Rose, N. 2008. *Governing the Present: Administering Economic, Social and Personal Life*. Cambridge: Polity Press.

Morgan, G. 1980. "Paradigms, Metaphors, and Puzzle Solving in Organization Theory." *Administrative Science Quarterly*, 25: 605–22.

Morgan, G. 1983. "More on Metaphor: Why We Cannot Control Tropes in Administrative Science." *Administrative Science Quarterly*, 28: 601–07.

Motter, A. E., Moura, A. P. S. de, Lai, Y. C., and Dasgupta, P. 2002. "Topology of the Conceptual Network of Language." *Physical Review*, E 65: 065102.

Mulgan, R. 2000. "'Accountability': An Ever-expanding Concept?" *Public Administration*, 78: 555–73.

Mumford, L. 1961. *The City in History: Its Origins, Its Transformations, and Its Prospects*. First edition. New York: Harcourt, Brace & World.

Nozick, R. 1981. *Philosophical Explanations*. Cambridge, MA: Belknap/Harvard.

O'Neill, O. 2002. *A Question of Trust*. Cambridge: Cambridge University Press.

OECD. 2001. *Governance in the 21st Century*. Paris: Organisation for Economic Co-operation and Development.

OED. *Oxford English Dictionary Online*. Retrieved from <http://www.oed.com/>.

Pollitt, C. and Hupe, P. 2011. "Talking About Government." *Public Management Review*, 13: 641–58.

Rudrum, D. 2005. "From Narrative Representation to Narrative Use: Towards the Limits of Definition." *Narrative*, 13: 195–204.

Sassen, S. 2008. *Territory, Authority, Rights: From Medieval to Global Assemblages*. Princeton: Princeton University Press.

Scott, J. C. 1998. *Seeing Like a State: How Certain Schemes to Improve the Human Condition Have Failed*. New Haven: Yale University Press.

Sinclair, A. 1995. "The Chameleon of Accountability: Forms and Discourses." *Accounting, Organizations and Society*, 20: 219–37.

Stalnaker, R. C. 1970. "Pragmatics." *Synthese*, 22: 272–89.

Stein, J. G. 2002. *The Cult of Efficiency*. Toronto: House of Anansi Press.

Svensén, B. 2009. *A Handbook of Lexicography: The Theory and Practice of Dictionary-Making*. New York: Cambridge University Press.

Tambiah, S. J. 1968. "The Magical Power of Words." *Man*, 3: 175–208.

Tilly, C. 2007. *Democracy*. New York: Cambridge University Press.

Valaskakis, K. 2001. Long-Term Trends in Global Governance: From "Westphalia" to "Seattle", pp. 45–66 in *Governance in the 21st Century*. Paris: Organisation for Economic Co-operation and Development.

Waldo, D. 1948. *The Administrative State: A Study of the Political Theory of American Public Administration*. New York: Ronald Press Co.

Weiss, L. 1998. *The Myth of the Powerless State*. Ithaca, NY: Cornell University Press.

Wildavsky, A. 1973. "If Planning is Everything, Maybe it's Nothing." *Policy Sciences*, 4: 127–53.

Wille, R. 2005. Formal Concept Analysis as Mathematical Theory of Concepts and Concept Hierarchies, pp. 1–33 in *Formal Concept Analysis: Foundations and Applications*, eds. B. Ganter, G. Stumme, and R. Wille. New York: Springer.

Williams, R. 1958. *Culture and Society, 1780–1950*. New York: Columbia University Press.

Williams, R. 1976. *Keywords: A Vocabulary of Culture and Society*. New York: Oxford University Press.

Williams, R. 1983. *Keywords: A Vocabulary of Culture and Society*. London: Fontana Paperbacks.

Wittgenstein, L. 1968. *Philosophical Investigations*. New York: Macmillan.

CHAPTER 3

....

ACCOUNTABILITY AND DEMOCRACY

....

MARK E. WARREN

DEMOCRACY is the kind of political system in which the people rule. But because "the people" is not a single entity, nor are the purposes or loci of rule unified, any democracy is also a system of accountabilities: of representatives to the people they represent, of officials for the public trust they hold, and even of the people to themselves for past and future decisions. There are many forms of accountability that have nothing to do with democracy, but democracy could not be conceived, let alone practiced, without vast and complex webs of accountabilities between peoples and those who govern on their behalf and in their name. Indeed, accountability is so central to democracy that much of the literature on democracy could be recast in these terms.

I shall limit my discussion to six tasks. First, I identify the basic elements of democratic accountability. The condition of vulnerability to power creates the need for democratic accountability, which is comprised of justifications for the exercise of power that can be sanctioned by those affected by its use. Second, I argue that a key problem in the development of democratic politics has to do with forming principals and agents among whom relations of accountability might develop. Third, I discuss the considerable costs of enforcing accountability relationships—costs that any system of democratic accountabilities should anticipate. Fourth, I examine voting as a mechanism of democratic accountability. Because voting is a relatively weak form of democratic accountability I argue, fifth, that we should think about accountability in terms of *regimes*: systems of complementary mechanisms that combine with voting to ensure greater accountability. Finally, I discuss several challenges to democratic accountability under contemporary conditions of politics. I shall suggest that we have the conceptual and practical resources to address these challenges, so long as we think beyond democracy as simply voting and elections.

THE PROBLEM OF DEMOCRATIC ACCOUNTABILITY: VULNERABILITY, JUSTIFICATION, EMPOWERMENT

What kind of problem is accountability for democracy? Normatively, democracy is defined by individuals' entitlement to proportional influence over collective decisions that affect them—a norm often called the "all affected (or all affected interests) principle" (Goodin 2007; Habermas 1996; Young 2000). Accountability supports this democracy-defining norm by connecting those entitled to influence collective decisions by virtue of their real or potential affectedness to agents who make and organize these decisions on their behalf (Borowiak 2011, 11). Problems of *democratic* accountability arise from individuals' dependence upon these delegated powers in two senses: *negatively*, insofar they are vulnerable to the powers agents wield, and *positively*, insofar as their capacities to exert influence over collectivities depend upon agents' responsiveness and answerability (Mulgan 2003, 12). Thus, in these very generic terms, we can think about democratic accountability as enacting entitlements that are normatively justified by the all affected principle, and backed by powers that enable those (potentially) affected to demand and enforce answerability from those who hold and use delegated powers.

Following this formulation, we can elaborate three basic features of the problem of democratic accountability. The first, *vulnerability to delegated power*, is common to all relations of co-dependence that arise from social coordination and cooperation. These vulnerabilities increase as societies grow in size and scale, concentrating powers in the hands of elites who occupy key locations within social organizations and whose interests do not necessarily encapsulate the interests of those their powers affect. Potential interest divergence between power holders and those they affect is thus essential to identifying needs and demands for accountability. To the extent that the interests of co-dependents *converge*, relations of trust mitigate vulnerabilities. Under these circumstances there is no need for accountability; the risks of social cooperation are minimal because each actor holds the interests of those they affect in view, removing the need to monitor and "hold to account" (Baier 1986; Luhmann 1979; Warren 1999). So the need for accountability arises from the intersection of *social co-dependence* and *interest divergence*. Accountability relations are important when social co-ordination risks exploitation, oppression, or other harms to the interests of those affected. It follows that in a democracy the most basic problem to which accountability is the solution is that even though government is "owned" by the people, the powers of collective decision and action are held by elites, to which the people are vulnerable, both negatively (the possibilities for harms) and positively (the opportunities for collective action) (Mulgan 2003, 12).

The second generic element of democratic accountability is answerability, especially in the form of *justification*. All relations of accountability involve a discursive dimension: "To be 'accountable' for one's activities is both to explicate the reasons for them and to supply the normative grounds whereby they may be 'justified'" (Giddens 1984, 30). Accountability to someone for something involves "giving an account"—justifying decisions and actions in terms that are acceptable to those (potentially) affected (Borowiak 2011, Ch. 4). This element of justification corresponds to what the editors of this volume call "accountability as a virtue," encompassing the responsiveness and answerability of public agents. The *democratic* element of justification has to do with those to whom an account is owed, namely those affected or potentially affected by the powers in question. And it has to do with how members of a collectivity hold discursive entitlements; they must be able ask for, receive, and accept (or reject) reasons and justifications for the exercise of powers. Democracy does not, of course, require that each public agent provide continuous accounts of each and every decision they make. Rather it requires that each agent *could* provide an account—and understand this expectation—should it be called upon to do so (Warren 1996). The element of justification distinguishes accountability from *responsibility*: one can be responsible for something or someone without justifying this responsibility to them—as a parent is responsible for a child (Mulgan 2003, 15–18; Philp 2009, 30).

The third generic element of democratic accountability is *empowerment*. Those entitled to hold power-holders to account must be empowered to demand and sanction an account of a decision or potential decision (Bovens 2007; Goodin 2003). This element corresponds to what the editors of this volume term "accountability as a social mechanism"; the institutional arrangements that enable those (potentially) affected by decisions to require an account. A democratic system of accountabilities is therefore a system of distributed empowerments. It requires those entitled to accountability have the power to hold accountable those who make and execute collective decisions on their behalf. The ways and means of doing so are many, including voting, rights of speaking, pressure, petition, and association, standings to sue, and rights to information relevant to the power to question authorities. They also include agents whose duty it is to oversee decision-makers through checks and balances, such as legislative oversight committees, courts engaging in judicial review, and government auditors.

These three basic elements can be, and often are, conceptualized as intrinsic to *democratic representation*, which involves an initial authorization by a representative constituency—such as through an election—followed by some kind of accountability of the representative to the constituency—such as through a subsequent election (Mansbridge 2003; Pitkin 1967; Rehfeld 2005; Saward 2010; Urbinati and Warren 2008). Democratic accountability is thus inherent in the representation cycle: authorization constitutes and empowers representatives who are then held to account for their decisions.

THE FORMATION OF PRINCIPALS AND AGENTS IN ACCOUNTABILITY RELATIONSHIPS

These theoretical considerations indicate why accountability is intrinsic to democracy, both normatively and structurally. A second kind of conceptual problem has to do with the contingencies of accountability. For accountability to come into existence there must already exist social entities among whom accountability relationships can come into being. It is now common to specify these relationships with *principal–agent* language: an individual, group, or institution acts as an agent for a principal with respect to some need, good, or vulnerability, and is conceived as accountable to that principal. Principal–agent theory is covered thoroughly elsewhere in this volume (see Gailmard). The theory is much criticized within democratic theory for oversimplifying accountability relationships as well as overburdening them with disciplinary assumptions, especially from law and economics (Borowiak 2011; Philp 2009).

This said, much of the problem of enacting accountability relationships occurs "prior" to principals and agents. The achievements of democracy depend upon processes that constitute principals and agents—particularly "peoples" and "representatives"—such that they have an existence and an identity over time and space, and so that promises, commitments, and other elements of accountability can come into being. Contemporary uses of principal–agent theory rarely frame these existential questions, but they do throw them into relief. Principal–agent language originated to clarify fiduciary duties and responsibilities in law and was adapted subsequently to highlight ways and means by which principals might control agents more generally (Przeworski, Stokes, and Manin 1999). Strong systems of democratic accountability were built on states with capacities and identities sufficient that principals—emerging publics, social movements, and political organizations—could "demand" an account from agents capable of providing an account. On the one hand, the consolidation of power in the nation-state form, combined with the specification of power in written constitutions and statute law, produced the kinds of collective entities of which accountability could be demanded (Warren 2006). On the other hand, this same form created "peoples" by subjecting territorially discrete populations to jurisdiction.

Historically, accountability systems have been integral to state capacity building, and they have tended to precede democratic accountabilities (Philp 2009). This is why an important feature of modern state-building was the development of bureaucracies with written descriptions of offices, including not just the duties of an office but also the office's place within hierarchies of command and control, such that elites could hold subordinates accountable for their performances (Weber 1978, 969ff). Modern bureaucratic accountability systems—the Prussian system ideal-typed by Max Weber

(1978, Vol. 2, Ch. XI) being one of the most impressive—were driven by consolidations of power and expansions of empire rather than by considerations of democracy. The ability of monarchs to organize administrative systems to extract economic surpluses enabled not only more effective exploitation of national populations, but also rapacious colonialism, from the Spanish and later British genocides in the Americas to Belgium's unimaginably cruel plantations in the Belgian Congo. Similarly, consolidated state capacities were at work in both world wars, which resulted in deaths numbering in the hundreds of millions. The first task for democratic accountability was to make state power accountable to those subjected to state violence. In doing so, mechanisms of democratic accountability built on prior development of state capacities, just because these processes amounted to the formation of agents of which accountability demands could be made (Tilly 2007).

We can say something similar about the formation of principals who have interests affected by a collectivity such as the state. As suggested above, democracies empower individuals to demand accountability through distributions of rights and powers. But these empowerments are only effective to the extent that individuals are formed into "peoples"—formed into publics, groups, associations, or other kinds of organization that transform, say, an aggregation of voters, into a "principal" with the capacity to make demands—to ask for a justification and to hold to account. It is often the case that principals of this kind are formed as a result of distributed empowerments, such as votes. But it can also be that principals develop in resistance to collectivities with agent-like powers, as with union movements in Europe, opposition to British rule in India, or the civil rights movement in the US. The more functional democracies were built within relatively high-capacity states, in part because these states provided a locus for accountability demands as part of democratization struggles. As a result, the modern democratization process is one of progressive empowerments of peoples, initially defined by virtue of their subjection to state powers and related social powers. It has advanced primarily by expanding and empowering features of citizenship—forming principals—initially with respect to various state-based jurisdictions, which define actual or potential agents, as well as potential loci of redress in legislation and judicial judgments. "Democratic" accountability is one consequence of these kinds of empowerments.

COSTS OF ACCOUNTABILITY

A second heuristic advantage of principal–agent theory is that it highlights the costliness of accountability, which in turn underscores the challenges of designing workable accountabilities into political institutions in ways that are not overwhelmed by their costs. Because the theory assumes that agents will have interests that diverge from principals, accountability relationships are effective to the extent principals bear the costs of monitoring agents. These costs can be extensive (Mulgan 2003, Ch. 7). From the standpoint of principals, accountability requires information and attentiveness. One problem is that scale, distance, and complexity increase the opaqueness of organizations and citizens, increasing the costs of accountability to such an extent that it is hard to imagine that any citizen (or group of citizens) could marshal the information necessary for close and thorough monitoring.

Not only must costs of information be manageable, but so too must the costs of sanctioning agents who fail to act in the interests of principals. Agents often amass considerable power in the form of control over economic resources, police powers, regulatory bottlenecks, and so on. As a result, principals are typically at a power disadvantage, as evidenced by the high costs borne by whistleblowers, even in those jurisdictions in which whistleblowing is legally enabled and politically encouraged. Costs become manageable when citizens can overcome collective action problems that off-load risks onto individuals—as does, for example, institutionalized voting.

But there are also opportunity costs of accountability measured in lost performance by agents (Mulgan 2003, 236ff). Accountability that is systematized, as with most government and business finances, exacts collective costs simply owing to the burdens of compliance. In addition, accountability that is closely focused on specific behaviors and performances can undermine professional judgment, initiative, and creativity—precisely the reasons why principals might need and want agents to work on their behalf.

Finally, any society in which accountability relationships are both pervasive and always acted upon would not be a very good society from the standpoint of commitments, trust, freedom, and solidarity. Any system of accountability will have inflection points at which accountability degenerates into mutual suspicion and intrusive surveillance, undermining the very agent capacities that would be held to account. Trust—which is not only efficient but essential to most working social relationships—can be crowded out by accountability. Thus we should think of good accountability systems as backstopping rather replacing trust, so that accountability costs are assumed only when trust fails. In this way, the very availability of accountability mechanisms should cause them to be used less, both because principals and agents understand that they *could* be used, and also because of the high costs and undesirable consequences of their deployment. When accountability systems mitigate the vulnerabilities inherent in social co-dependence, trust relations are less risky and more likely to grow—evidence for which is found in the fact that societies with high degrees of democratic accountability also tend to be societies with high levels of generalized trust (Rothstein 2005; Uslaner 2002). The presence of democratic accountability also enables agents to learn, as they anticipate and receive feedback (Bovens 2007). So, in principle, the better the accountability systems, the less burdensome they are likely to become.

These considerations help to put problems of democratic accountability in perspective. Accountability is essential to a democracy, but it is organizationally and institutionally challenging to build, and comes with costs that must be weighed against the (often substantial) harms that it addresses. Principals and agents must be identifiable and tractable, and burdens on citizens must be manageable and achievable. Owing to their costs, accountability relationships should only be built into those areas where they are most likely to prevent harm. And, ideally, accountability should enable rather than replace trust relationships, primarily by hedging the risks of cooperation.

Voting as Democratic Accountability

Among the means available to instantiate these dimensions of democratic accountability, pride of place is traditionally given to electoral accountability. The reason is that voting in competitive elections addresses each of these dimensions: on average, principals and agents are identifiable and tractable, and the costs of voting, including the costs of information and monitoring, are relatively low. Nor (on average) does electoral selection and removal of representatives produce such invasive forms of monitoring that they cannot do their jobs. Voting-based empowerments can also be widely and equally distributed, while the kinds of knowledge that align voter interests and government policy are relatively easy to come by—though, of course, there are significant differences among electoral systems in both these respects

Yet despite its democracy-defining centrality, voting is not a very powerful accountability mechanism, even when differences among institutional arrangements are taken into account. With respect to their elected representatives, voters have two general kinds of accountability powers through which they can enforce principal–agent relations. The first is *selection* from among the available choices. Voters can choose agents they believe more likely to represent their interests, and then remove them if they are disappointed. The second is *monitoring* an agent's activities, with the aim of ensuring its actions align with voters' preferences (Mansbridge 2009; Przeworski, Stokes, and Manin 1999, Ch. 1; Strøm 2000).

But even though both activities would seem to have relatively low informational and cognitive requirements, many voters seem unable to meet even these. The extent to which voters can use their powers to identify and enforce principal–agent relations remains unclear (Achen and Bartels 2004; Anderson 2007). Voters probably make better choices than these factors would predict, owing to the prevalence of trustworthy information proxies (Lupia and McCubbins 1998). Yet it is hard to avoid the conclusion that when these factors combine with institutional barriers—especially systems that diffuse loci of accountability—voting appears to be a weak accountability device. As Przeworski (2010, Ch. 2) argues, electoral accountability provides little direct citizen control over government, at best serving to constrain the most egregious abuses of power, and functioning to align policies with the preferences of the median voter only over periods of several decades.

It is in part owing to these weaknesses that we have seen an upsurge in so-called "direct democracy"—that is, initiatives and referendums through which citizens might stem the "agency losses" that are endemic to electoral democracy by voting directly upon proposals or policies. Initiatives and referendums have an important place in contemporary democracies, especially as devices for generating democratic legitimacy for policy proposals that are politically hazardous for legislators. But these forms of voting suffer from low citizen capacities in the same ways electoral democracy suffers more generally. They also come at high cost to retrospective accountability. "The people" who votes a policy into law has no accountability for the constraints on executing the policy or for its consequences—leading, at the extreme, to the kinds of contradictory taxing and spending directives that have made California very difficult to govern over the last three decades. Democratic accountability requires agents that have coherent identities over time, such that they can be held accountable for subsequent consequences of decisions. A key challenge is to design initiative and referendum processes that strengthen rather than undermine democratic accountability. Recent experiments have involved constituting randomly-selected groups of citizens to propose or evaluate proposals with the goal of increasing voter knowledge or providing new kinds of trusted information proxies with strong democratic credentials (Lang and Warren 2012; Mackenzie and Warren 2012; Warren 2008). These proposals do not in themselves resolve temporal problems of accountability inherent in ballot measures. But these kinds of deliberative supplements may help voters to anticipate the consequences of their votes for future peoples, in this way introducing a temporally-focused accountability that is exercised at the moment of the vote.

DEMOCRATIC ACCOUNTABILITY REGIMES

If we are to adequately sketch the terrain upon which democratic accountability operates, we need to step back and see voting and elections as parts of broader systems of mechanisms that comprise and enable democratic accountability regimes. All developed democracies have institutionalized a broad variety of accountability mechanisms defined, on one side, by governmental jurisdictions, and on the other, by the power of citizens to hold to account. These mechanisms include not only elections, but also rights to petition and standings to sue; associations, organizations, and other kinds of publics with political freedoms protected by law; rules regarding transparency and access to information by journalists, advocates, and other civil society actors; modes of accountability between agencies and branches of government; and public offices that act to demand accountability as trustees of the people (such as public auditors) and function to make accountability more tractable to the people. Ideally, these mechanisms work together to instantiate the three basic elements of democratic accountability: limits to vulnerabilities, justification, and empowerment.

The extent to which these ideal effects occur in any given regime is, of course, a complex empirical question, one far beyond the scope of this chapter. What I can do, however, is underscore some of the more important mechanisms. The most basic are constitutions that subject the powers of the state to law—especially to laws that establish political institutions, including the ways and means of conducting political conflict, the rights that establish the limits to state power, the zones of freedom and forms of security citizens can enjoy and take for granted, as well as formally equal standing before the law. These basic accountabilities require executive agencies that have clear, ordered responsibilities, defined by jurisdictions, and organized through chains of command that enable legislatures to impose direction and policy on government on behalf of those they represent. On the standard model of a democratic accountability regime, bureaucratic accountability is, in the first instance, to the elected branches of government, with accountability relationships enforced by reporting requirements, oversight committees, and auditors responsible to the bodies and officials elected by the people.

These forms of accountability based in rule of law gain their democratic elements largely from the availability of sanctions that can be used by citizens. The most important of these follow from functional judicial institutions with some insulation from partisan conflict, and a good deal of credible commitment to the rule of law (Rosanvallon 2011, part 2). Their importance to democracy is that they establish the accountability of the state for publicly knowable laws, while empowering citizens to use law to hold agents of the state accountable. This is why the standing that citizens have to sue agents of the state for harm or failures to uphold laws is a key indicator of the extent and depth of democratic accountability.

It is, of course, one thing to hold state agents accountable for enacted laws—and indeed it is, one of the easier kinds of accountability to design into democratic regimes, since mechanisms can be specific, targeted, and actionable. It is another thing to hold agents accountable for the laws they enact—the defining feature of *political* accountability. Democracies do so through two kinds of constitutional arrangement, which differ primarily in the ways agents and principals are constituted (Strøm 2000). Parliamentary systems concentrate power, producing relatively clear agents who can be held accountable by voters and opposition parties; presidential systems separate powers, so that agents have motivations to hold one another accountable on behalf of differentiated constituencies.

In England, parliamentary powers originated as an accountability bargain with the Crown: in return for the right to tax, the Crown accepted accountability to Parliament for the use of public monies (Bates 1991). Parliament, we might say, was the principal that constituted the Crown as an accountable agent. As Parliament democratized with the spread of the franchise, and power shifted into the House of Commons, the locus of accountability came to rest with the Prime Minister, who today is accountable to the members of the Commons, and retains the power to govern so long as he or she, as head of the party of government, maintains their confidence. The majority party, the party that forms a government, is accountable for the platform proposed to voters, and voters are empowered to hold parties accountable at moments of election. In this way, parliamentary systems tend to concentrate power, and thus focus the location of agency in ways that provide citizens strong moments of retrospective accountability in the manner of a referendum on the performance of incumbent governments.

In contrast, constitutional systems based on checks and balances—"presidential" systems—typically combine a bicameral legislature with a separately elected executive. In the United States, the framers of the constitution modified Montesquieu's "mixed constitution" into a system of separated powers that would check and balance one another. They did so by defining areas of responsibility and power, and then providing for these powers to be shared among branches of government in such a way that each owes accountability to the other. Whereas parliamentary systems concentrate powers, presidential systems spread them in such a way that no agent can act alone, without the cooperation of other agents with separate constituencies and constitutional powers. In these systems the central accountability mechanisms are the justifications agents must provide to one another as the price of avoiding vetoes. Accountability is "democratic" insofar as agents demand accounts on behalf of multiple and overlapping constituencies (the principals). The strength of presidential systems is that they induce "horizontal" accountability within the state on behalf of constituencies. Their weakness is that they diffuse the locus of agency as well as fragmenting constituencies, making voting-based accountability more difficult because there are no clear moments in which agents and principals are simultaneously constituted.

Constitutional systems may also be unitary or federal, with the former concentrating powers and the latter dividing powers among levels of government. As with separated powers, federal systems produce more agents to oversee other agents on behalf of multiple and overlapping constituencies. And, as with separated power systems, federal governments also diffuse loci of agency, leading to systems with more horizontal checks, but at the cost of less transparency to citizens (Cutler 2004).

The various ways these features of constitutions mix with differing kinds of electoral systems also affect democratic accountability mechanisms. Single member plurality (SMP) systems (based on single member districts) tend to reward winning parties with a disproportionate number of seats in legislatures. There are many variants of proportional representation (PR) systems, but most are based on multi-member districts, and allocate seats to parties in proportion to their electoral success. From the perspective of accountability, the trade-offs are well theorized. PR systems tend to be more responsive and inclusive than SMP systems; voters can maintain closer relationships with smaller parties that have more specific platforms relative to parties in SMP systems. There is more *prospective* accountability in PR systems, owing to the more focused relationships between voters and parties, particularly in open-list systems. But because PR systems tend to result in coalition governments within multi-party legislatures, they also diffuse loci of accountability. In contrast, SMP systems tend to produce majorities that can form governments without needing to bargain with coalition partners, thus producing clear agents that can (retrospectively) be held accountable (Powell 2000).

Looking Forward: Resources for Democratic Accountability

Measured by basic norms of democracy—particularly the all affected interests principle—it is far from evident the democratic accountability regimes we have inherited are sufficient to meet present and future challenges to democracy. Among the most daunting are those introduced by complexity and scale, as well as those that follow from mismatches between organized political jurisdictions and those affected by collective decisions. The challenge for democratic theory is thus to conceive principals with the organization and capacities to enforce accountability relationships, and to conceive agents with the capacities to respond. In theory, we can imagine new kinds of principals that are issue-specific and form around affected publics. Imagining corresponding agents, however, is more challenging, primarily because outside of already organized political jurisdictions, there is often no "there" there: In many emerging issue areas, we lack tractable agents of the kind that could be the locus of accountability demands. That said, we are not without conceptual resources for these kinds of challenges, many of which can be generalized from existing institutions and practices. In what follows, I summarize six areas within which we might look for these resources.

Mediated accountability: Like virtually every other activity in complex societies, labors of accountability are divided and specialized. One consequence is that the most pervasive and often most effective forms of accountability are *mediated* (or *compounded*— see Mulgan 2003, 229–32) by agents that hold other agents accountable on behalf of the principals they represent. As suggested above, democracies embody *systems* or *regimes* that depend upon many forms of mediated accountability. Within parliamentary systems, such agents are part of the design of competitive legislatures; it is the responsibility of "Her Majesty's loyal opposition" to hold the party (or coalition) of government to account on behalf of those who lost the last election. Presidential systems like the American one add checks and balances. Institutionalized oversight of executive agencies by legislative committees, for example, was part of the system of political incentives designed into the US Constitution of 1789. Some forms of mediated accountability are more recent, such as auditing offices working on behalf of legislatures. The US General Accounting Office, established in 1921, is tasked with the mission of monitoring executive agencies on behalf of Congress. Still other forms of mediated accountability are features of protected publics and civil societies. At least since De Tocqueville published *Democracy in America*, a free press has been justified as a vigilant overseer of power, acting as agents of the people. More recently, civil society organizations such as the Conference Board of Canada, Human Rights Watch, and many others have taken on the roles of watchdog on behalf of issues or constituencies, issuing reports (and sometimes report cards) on governments and corporations. Over the last few decades, the accountability powers of both kinds of agents have been deepened by Freedom of Information acts and Sunshine laws in virtually all of the developed democracies (Cain, Fabrinni, and Egan 2003). Beyond these kinds of agents, contemporary politics has numerous interest and advocacy groups that claim to oversee elites on behalf of a huge variety of constituencies. Our challenge is to understand how these kinds of agents contribute to systems of democratic accountabilities (Montanaro 2012; Urbinati and Warren 2008).

Proximate and specific accountability: One key challenge to democratic accountability in contemporary polities has to do with the migration of policy-making into a multitude of government agencies and entities in ways that bypass, as it were, electoral accountability altogether—particularly in areas of urban planning, education, health care, medical and old age insurance, and environmental policy (Warren 2009). There are two complementary forces at work here. From the side of citizens—the demand side—even though broad electoral accountability mechanisms are blunt instruments, citizens want fair treatment and responsive government with respect to particular services. The demands for accountability are specific and proximate (Rosanvallon 2011, Part 4). From the side of government, agencies and the professionals who work in them have been accountable to the demands of their offices since the civil services began to professionalize in the late 1800s. But these actors also increasingly view themselves as accountable to those they serve: patients, students and parents, citizens requiring protection, commuters needing safe and effective transportation, consumers depending upon safe products, and so on. Within each of these policy areas, we are now likely to find organized citizens involved in policy development and service delivery. We are also sometimes seeing government entities encouraging citizen organization and oversight—often by providing enabling information, but sometimes more proactively, inviting organizations to assess new policies and proposals, or expanding standing for civil suits so citizens (or groups) can hold (say) businesses directly accountable for harm resulting from contravened regulatory regimes. Our challenge is to assess the ways in which these emerging proximate and specific forms of accountability supplement or detract from democratic accountability.

"Governance" accountability: In a closely related trend, in many areas of policy we are seeing "governance" replace "government"—that is, policies are often developed in cooperation with civil society organizations or with other kinds of non-governmental partners in the form of public–private partnerships. Many government services are devolved or "de-concentrated" to lower units of government, while others are contracted out. The overall picture is not necessarily bad for democracy, as these developments can lead to more responsiveness as well as new arenas of political participation (Rosanvallon 2011, Part 4; Sørenson and Torfing 2008; Warren 2009). It is probably the case that on average "governance" increases capacities for collective organization and action—as governance regimes can incorporate higher levels of political and technical complexity than the command and control bureaucracies they are replacing. But these developments also mean that loci of accountability increasingly lack the generality and simplicity necessary for agents to be tractable for citizens (Poggi 1990; Papadopoulos 2003, 2007). Few government officials, offices, or institutions can now claim, with Harry Truman, that "the buck stops here"—representing a challenge for democratic accountability under conditions of "governance."

Global accountability: A parallel challenge exists at the global level. To the extent we buy into the all affected principle, we must also notice that "chains of affectedness" are increasingly global in nature (Bohman 2007)—while, of course, also acknowledging that there is no global equivalent to the state (Keohane 2002). In part, the causes of globalization are the expansions of markets and market capitalism in the wake of post-World War II settlements and post-1989 openings that made the world, as it were, "safe for investment." States in the capitalist democracies have always served two masters: the people and markets. That said, with sufficient pressure, high capacity states can impose regulative regimes on markets, addressing (even if inadequately) their most burdensome externalities for labor, the environment, and consumers. The nature and democratic potentials of these accountabilities can be disputed. The 2008 banking crisis in the US, for example, demonstrated that Wall Street exerts disproportionate influence in Washington, primarily owing it its ability to hold the economy hostage. Yet at least in this case there were identifiable agents of accountability struggles, albeit agents with a good deal more complexity than suggested by the shorthand: "Washington" and "Wall Street." The global context is different: most issue areas lack state-like entities that could function as the agents of accountability demands. One of the lessons, perhaps, of the often erratic focus of anti-globalization movements of the last two decades is that there are few global agents from which to demand accountability, as is possible of states. "Global capital" may be responsible for a variety of problems, but it lacks the qualities of agency necessary for relationships of accountability with affected constituencies. This does not mean that there are no agents—there are multiple and overlapping international and regional organizations, many of which exist to deal with specific issues. But it does mean that the nature and kinds of accountability are at best complicated (Grant and Keohane 2005). One of our foremost challenges is to conceive and actualize agents and their corresponding principals that are global in scope but organized in ways that track chains of affectedness rather than territorial sovereignties.

Exit-based accountability: Under conditions of high complexity and scope, we should ask whether market-like accountability—the entrance and exit of buyers and sellers into contracts, or members into organizations, or voters into political parties in competitive party systems—might be put to democratic uses (Hirschman 1970; Warren 2011). The democratic benefits of exit-based accountability are considerable: entrance and exit are powers that can be exercised by individuals (and so not subject to collective action problems involved in constituting peoples as principals), often at relatively low cost depending on the levels of competition and an individual's relative powers of choice. Suitably empowered with demand—rights to education or healthcare services, for example—individuals can evoke specific and timely accountability from organizations—even public organizations—as long as there is competition among them. Any well-developed democratic accountability system will seek ways of benefitting from the advantages of exit-based accountability by using state-based power to construct and distribute demand as well as to address externalities of market transactions (Warren 2011).

Association-based accountability: As issues flow beyond jurisdictionally constituted principals and agents, norms of accountability should play a greater role in shoring up democratic deficits. Norms can and do generate principals as well as agents of mediated accountability through associations—organizations built around purposes that people share, and for which they voluntarily organize—purposes such as a common faith, a common activity like a sport, a common goal like developing a neighborhood, or a common set of valued distinctions, from ethnicity to lifestyle (Warren 2001). Accountability in such cases works primarily through normative commitments that generate associations. Because association-based accountability is normative in character, it works primarily though discursive means. Associations must, ultimately, make the case for their activities to their members or to the publics they claim to represent, or they fade into irrelevance. They have high capacities to motivate and legitimate collective actions, and high capacities for attentiveness to specific and often complex issues. Assuming they are protected (itself a state-based condition), associations can motivate across borders, since their form is not limited by territorial jurisdictions. Democracies should (and do) protect and enable association-based organization where possible but they should also find ways of introducing association-based accountability into state-based organization as well as international regimes. Association-based accountability is one of the potentials—yet to be fully appreciated—that comes with shifts from "government" to "governance."

Conclusion: Rethinking Democratic Accountability Regimes

Democracies have managed mostly to solve the most pressing accountability problems faced by any political system: those having to do with the use and deployment of state coercion. They have developed some generalized responsiveness through combinations of electoral mechanisms, checks and balances, and professionalized bureaucracies. This said, considerable challenges remain if democratic accountability is to advance, particularly as the conditions of politics change. Elections, although essential to democratic accountability, are crude mechanisms at best, and certainly insufficient for addressing a host of emerging challenges, from the decentralization of the nation-state as the primary locus of accountability, to citizen demands for high levels of specific performance and responsiveness from governments. But if we keep in mind that we have many resources beyond elections for democratic accountability, we should be able to reform and invent democratic accountability regimes that can bear the weight of the future.

Acknowledgments

I am grateful to Edana Beauvais and Sean Gray for their research assistance.

References

Achen, C. H. and Bartels, L. M. 2004. *Musical Chairs: Pocketbook Voting and the Limits of Democratic Accountability*. In APSA (American Political Science Association) 100th Annual Meeting. Chicago, 2–5 September 2004.

Anderson, C. J. 2007. "The End of Economic Voting? Contingency Dilemmas and the Limits of Democratic Accountability." *Annual Review of Political Science*, 10: 271–96.

Baier, A. 1986. "Trust and Anti-Trust." *Ethics*, 96: 231–60.

Bates, R. H. 1991. "The Economics of Transitions to Democracy." *PS: Political Science and Politics*, 24: 24–27.

Bohman, J. 2007. *Democracy Across Borders: From Dêmos to Dêmoi*. Cambridge: MIT Press.

Borowiak, C. T. 2011. *Accountability and Democracy. The Pitfalls and Promise of Popular Control*. New York: Oxford University Press.

Bovens, M. 2007. "Analysing and Assessing Accountability: A Conceptual Framework." *European Law Journal*, 13: 447–68.

Cain, B. E., Fabrinni, S. and Egan, P. 2003. Toward More Open Democracies: The Expansion of Freedom of Information Laws, pp. 115–39 in *Democracy Transformed? Expanding Political Opportunities in Advanced Industrial Democracies*, eds. B. E. Cain, R. J. Dalton, and S. E. Scarrow. New York: Oxford University Press.

Cutler, F. 2004. "Government Responsibility and Electoral Accountability in Federations." *Publius: The Journal of Federalism*, 34: 19–38.

De Tocqueville, A. 1968. *Democracy in America*. 2 Vols, ed. J. P. Mayer. New York: Harper and Row.

Giddens, A. 1984. *The Constitution of Society*. Berkeley: University of California Press.

Goodin, R. E. 2003. "Democratic Accountability: The Distinctiveness of the Third Sector." *European Journal of Sociology*, 56: 359–96.

Goodin, R. E. 2007. "Enfranchising All Affected Interests, and Its Alternatives." *Philosophy and Public Affairs*, 35: 40–68.

Grant, R. W. and Keohane, R. O. 2005. "Accountability and Abuses of Power in World Politics." *American Political Science Review*, 99: 29–43.

Habermas, J. 1996. *Between Facts and Norms*. Massachusetts: MIT Press.

Hirschman, A. O. 1970. *Exit, Voice, and Loyalty: Responses to Decline in Firms, Organizations, and States*. Cambridge, MA: Harvard University Press.

Keohane, R. O. 2002. *Global Governance and Democratic Accountability*. Paper presented as a Miliband Lecture. London: London School of Economics.

Lang, A. and Warren, M. E. 2012. Supplementary Democracy? Democratic Deficits and Citizens' Assemblies, pp. 291–314 in *Imperfect Democracies: The Democratic Deficit in Canada and the United States*, eds. P. T. Lenard and R. Simeon. Vancouver: University of British Columbia Press.

Luhmann, N. 1979. *Trust and Power*. Toronto: Wiley.

Lupia, A. and McCubbins, M. 1998. *The Democratic Dilemma: Can Citizens Learn What They Need to Know?* New York: Cambridge University Press.

Mackenzie, M. K. and Warren, M. E. 2012. Two Trust-Based Uses of Minipublics in Democratic Systems, pp. 95–124 in *Deliberative Systems*, eds. J. Mansbridge and J. Parkinson. Cambridge: Cambridge University Press.

Mansbridge, J. 2003. "Rethinking Representation." *American Political Science Review*, 97: 515–28.

Mansbridge, J. 2009. "A 'Selection Model' of Political Representation." *Journal of Political Philosophy*, 17: 369–98.

Montanaro, L. 2012. "The Democratic Legitimacy of Self-Appointed Representatives." *Journal of Politics*, 74: 1094–1107.

Mulgan, R. 2003. *Holding Power to Account: Accountability in Modern Democracies*. London: Palgrave.

Papadopoulos, Y. 2003. "Cooperative Forms of Governance: Problems of Democratic Accountability in Complex Environments." *European Journal of Political Research*, 42: 473–501.

Papadopoulos, Y. 2007. "Problems of Democratic Accountability in Network and Multilevel Governance." *European Law Journal*, 13: 469–86.

Philp, M. 2009. "Delimiting Democratic Accountability." *Political Studies*, 57: 28–53.

Pitkin, H. F. 1967. *The Concept of Representation*. Berkeley: University of California Press.

Poggi, G. 1990. *The State. Its Nature, Development, and Prospects*. Stanford: Stanford University Press.

Powell, G. B. 2000. *Elections as Instruments of Democracy: Majoritarian and Proportional Visions*. New Haven: Yale University Press.

Przeworski, A., Stokes, S. C., and Manin, B., eds. 1999. *Democracy, Accountability, and Representation*. New York: Cambridge University Press.

Przeworski, A. 2010. *Democracy and the Limits of Self-Government*. New York: Cambridge University Press.

Rehfeld, A. 2005. "Toward A General Theory of Representation." *Journal of Politics*, 68: 1–21.

Rosanvallon, P. 2011. *Democratic Legitimacy: Impartiality, Reflexivity, Proximity*. Princeton: Princeton University Press.

Rothstein, B. 2005. *Social Traps and the Problem of Trust*. New York: Cambridge University Press.

Saward, M. 2010. *The Representative Claim*. New York: Oxford University Press.

Sørenson, E. and Torfing, J. 2008. *Theories of Democratic Network Governance*. Basingstoke, UK: Palgrave Macmillan.

Strøm, K. 2000. *Delegation and Accountability in Parliamentary Democracies*. Presented at the Conference on "Re-Thinking Democracy at the New Millennium." University of Houston, 17–20 February 2000.

Tilly, C. 2007. *Democracy*. Cambridge: Cambridge University Press.

Urbinati, N. and Warren, M. E. 2008. "The Concept of Representation in Contemporary Democratic Theory." *Annual Review of Political Science*, 11: 387–412.

Uslaner, E. 2002. *The Moral Foundations of Trust*. New York: Cambridge University Press.

Warren, M. E. 1996. "Deliberative Democracy and Authority." *American Political Science Review*, 90: 46–60.

Warren, M. E. 1999. Democratic Theory and Trust, pp. 310–45 in *Democracy and Trust*, ed. M. E. Warren. Cambridge: Cambridge University Press.

Warren, M. E. 2001. *Democracy and Association*. Princeton: Princeton University Press.

Warren, M. E. 2006. Democracy and the State, pp. 382–99 in *The Oxford Handbook of Political Theory*, eds. J. Dryzek, B. Honig, and A. Phillips. Oxford: Oxford University Press.

Warren, M. E. 2008. Citizen Representatives, pp. 50–69 in *Designing Deliberative Democracy: The British Columbia Citizens' Assembly*, eds. M. Warren and H. Pearse. Cambridge: Cambridge University Press.

Warren, M. E. 2009. "Governance-Driven Democratization." *Critical Policy Analysis*, 3: 3–13.

Warren, M. E. 2011. "Voting with Your Feet: Exit-Based Empowerment in Democratic Theory." *American Political Science Review*, 105: 683–701.

Weber, M. 1978. *Economy and Society*. 2 Vols, eds. G. Roth and C. Wittich. Berkeley: University of California Press.

Young, I. M. 2000. *Inclusion and Democracy*. Oxford: Oxford University Press.

CHAPTER 4

A CONTINGENCY THEORY OF ACCOUNTABILITY

JANE MANSBRIDGE

ACCOUNTABILITY AND PUNISHMENT

ACCOUNTABILITY has become synonymous with punishment. When angry citizens and consumers demand accountability, they want someone's head on the block. When political scientists model accountability, they model incentives produced by the threat of sanctions. Accountability scholars should avoid this one-dimensional sanction-based definition by adding back in the traditional definition of accountability—as giving an account of, explaining, and justifying one's actions to those to whom one is responsible—and recognizing that two substantively different forms of accountability are associated with these two definitions, each being appropriate in a different context. *Sanction-based* accountability is most appropriate in contexts of justified distrust. Yet it also creates distrust, which then undermines the foundation of trust-based accountability. *Trust-based* accountability, which relies heavily on giving an account, is most appropriate in contexts of justified trust. A *contingency theory* of accountability underscores the importance of getting the mix right, because sanction-based accountability not only stems from distrust; it creates distrust.

SANCTION-BASED ACCOUNTABILITY

Toward the end of the 1960s, writers of books in English began to use the word "accountability" more frequently. The meaning of the word "accountability" also began to change. Traditional understandings of the concept stressed "giving an account," not only in English but in French (*rendre compte*) and in German (*Rechenschaft abgeben*). The *Oxford English Dictionary* (2nd ed.), for example, defines "accountability" substantively as "liability to give an account of, and answer for, discharge of duties or conduct."[1] This traditional concept had emphasized explaining and justifying one's actions. Yet in the last several decades, the term has slowly begun to connote primarily the application of sanctions after a process of monitoring. By 1999, an influential volume on accountability in politics could define accountability as follows:

> Governments are 'accountable' if citizens can discern representative from unrepresentative governments and can sanction them appropriately, retaining in office those incumbents who perform well and ousting from office those who do not. An 'accountability mechanism' is thus a map from the outcomes of actions (including messages that explain those actions) of public officials to sanctions by citizens. (Przeworski et al. 1999, 10)

Based on economic principal–agent theory, this new definition of accountability came to focus on punishment.

The change in definition accompanied a change in practice. In 1994, Power gave the label "the audit explosion" to a massive increase in Great Britain in the use of quantitative metrics to measure performance and establish accountability in the new sanction-based sense. For public servants in particular, punishment and reward began to depend more heavily on quantitatively measured performance. In some contexts, the sanctions that accompanied the new quantitative metrics undoubtedly acted as a stimulus to better performance. In other contexts, the sanctions seemed to crowd out the motivations that in the past had produced good performance. Yet most analyses did not distinguish, as a contingency theory should, between contexts in which sanctions-based accountability is most productive and those in which trust-based accountability would perform better.

The clash between proponents of the two systems goes back at least to the 1940s, when Friedrich (1940) argued that the best way to secure responsible and ethical conduct among public officials was first to select self-motivated persons who sincerely wanted to work for the public interest and then to reinforce those internal commitments. Finer (1941) argued instead for external sanctions and controls (see Carr (1999) for the "great debate" between these two). In management theory, by 1960 McGregor was pointing out that employees are more likely to exercise imagination, ingenuity, and creativity in their work when they intrinsically care about that work and about the organization's goals ("Theory Y") than when they work only because of external incentives ("Theory X"). In psychology, in the early 1970s Deci began a long line of experiments demonstrating that when individuals have intrinsic reasons for taking an action, giving them extrinsic material rewards crowds out the intrinsic motivation. Paying college students to do puzzles, for example, reduced their later likelihood of doing puzzles voluntarily, compared to a control group asked to do puzzles with no pay. Giving the students verbal rewards, by contrast, had a positive effect (Deci 1971).

Neither the early theorists nor Deci paid much attention to contextual differences, whether among individuals or situations. Only later did Deci and his collaborators discover that extrinsic rewards do not drive out intrinsic motivation when the extrinsic rewards can be framed not as controlling but as inherent to the task or as honoring the recipient (Deci, Koestner, and Ryan 1999; see also Deci and Ryan 1985).

In the field of political and social design, in 1980 Goodin noted more generally that "*material incentives destroy rather than supplement moral incentives*" and pointed out that this proposition "discredits one of the most popular approaches to social engineering" since Hume's "famous and influential advice . . . to 'design institutions for knaves'" (Goodin 1980, 140, emphasis in original). Frey, an economist, then provided empirical support for this proposition in an article entitled "A constitution for knaves crowds out civic virtues." In his survey, 51 percent of Swiss respondents agreed to accept siting a nuclear waste repository in their town when simply asked without any compensation, but when they were offered compensation, the acceptance rate dropped to 25 percent. Frey concluded that "care must be taken to design a system of laws fundamentally trusting citizens and politicians." Although he recognized in one sentence that viable systems must also have sufficient monitoring and sanctioning "to effectively deter exploitative behavior, not least because [such behavior] undermines civic virtue if it becomes widespread" (Frey 1997, 1052), he never asked the contextual question of when one ought to design laws for knaves and when for the public spirited.

By 2000, the "audit explosion" of sanction-based accountability in Great Britain was in full swing. O'Neil, a philosopher, took note and decried the way the new sanction-based systems were eroding morale in the traditional civil service: "Plants don't flourish when we pull them up too often to check how their roots are growing." Auditing and sanctioning, she decided, were damaging the "real work" of professionals, because although "trust often invites reciprocal trust" in a virtuous spiral, "when trust starts spiraling downwards . . . we may lose it altogether" (O'Neill 2002, 19). In Behn's (2001, 83) words, "institutionalized suspicion undermines trust". Philp focused specifically on probity and honor among the forms of intrinsic motivation, distinguishing between "integrity-based systems" of public office and rule (which I call more broadly "trust-based" and "selection-based" systems) and "compliance-based systems" (which I call "sanction-based" systems). An integrity-based system, he wrote, "requires that the agent has the appropriate dispositions and character and behaves appropriately because he or she has that degree of probity, rather than simply acting in a response to external incentives." Such a system "expects people to be guided by the desire to act in keeping with their responsibilities and fundamental commitments." A compliance-based or sanctions-based system, by contrast, is founded on distrust and is therefore inherently dishonoring. Thus Philp (2008, 37, 42) concluded that "Someone who regards his or her conduct . . . as a matter of honour should not be held to account in a way that is itself dishonouring". In practice, he added, sanction-based systems threaten to repel individuals with integrity or encourage them to adopt more self-interested motivations.

Most recently Tamir, also a philosopher, has taken up Campbell's (1979, 85) law on the corrupting effect of quantitative metrics for accountability: "The more any quantitative social indicator is used for social-decision making, the more subject it will be to corruption pressures and the more apt it will be to distort and corrupt the social processes it is intended to monitor." Accountability, she argues, can become "malignant" when distrust generates a desire for "continuous comparable monitoring, which in turn leads to numerical assessments that corrupt what they intend to measure, thus intensifying distrust." She suggests that groups with a free-market or conservative agenda may actively foster this distrust and the consequent downward-spiraling patterns of malignant accountability because disempowering the state allows the market to shape social life, fosters conditions of conservatism, and hinders the ability to bring about social change (Tamir 2012).

TRUST-BASED ACCOUNTABILITY

An alternative to sanction-based accountability is possible, but only when the world makes available a set of potential agents who, for one or another exogenous reason, already want to do much of what the principals want them to do.

When this fortuitous circumstance obtains, it pays the principal to put in considerable effort ex ante, to select the right agent, whose interests are aligned with the principal's own interests, and then afterward let that agent act more or less on her own initiative—rather than putting in all the effort ex post, to monitor and sanction the agent. If the agent's and the principal's interests are aligned well, the principal can afford to engage in less monitoring and sanctioning after the selection, because research before the selection—for example, looking at the agent's past reputation—has given the principal sufficient reason to believe that the principal's and agent's interests are aligned. This is the *selection model* of principal–agent relations (Mansbridge 2009; see also Fearon 1999; Besley 2006).

For some, the choosing of a childcare provider exemplifies the selection model. If you hire caregivers to take care of your children, you will look extensively to find people you think feel warm toward children intrinsically, so that when you are absent, they will act as much as possible the way you would like to have acted. You know you are not going to be able to monitor well what happens when you are gone and that many unexpected circumstances will arise in which you will want your caregivers to use their best judgment.

Similarly, if citizens appoint a judge, they will want to find someone who intrinsically cares about justice. For constitutional reasons they may want to make that judge's tenure relatively secure. So constitutionally they may limit sharply their own capacity to sanction. In this case they will want to invest relatively heavily beforehand in processes of both training and selection that will produce judges who, because of their own internal motivation, will act the way the citizens want them to act. The training and the creation of a profession do not eliminate all sanction; rather they displace much of the sanctioning, both formal and informal, to the profession. If the system works well, the judges themselves sanction those who depart from the norms of good judging. The organizational literature calls this *horizontal* or *network* accountability. It has the problem, which Goodin (2003) has noted, of needing to find ways to call the network itself to account. *Dynamic accountability*, treated later, may respond in part to this problem. In the judicial systems of most developed countries, training, self-selection (sorting) into the profession, and reputation make it relatively easy to find potential agents who have internalized the norms of justice and who then, for their own internal reasons, want to judge justly. Because of this fact—external to anything the citizens as principals have done—citizens can now select such individuals for a position in which constitutionally the citizens have deprived themselves of much capacity to sanction.

Academic tenure provides another example. In order to promote knowledge, universities often want their senior academics to be relatively insulated from political pressures and their superiors' whims. But bestowing tenure also limits sharply the university's future capacity to sanction. In that case, a university will want to invest relatively heavily in an *ex ante* process of selection that will choose scholars whose own internal motivation will lead them to continue to study and write with the same intensity, dedication, and intelligence as they had before tenure.

A system of accountability based on selection and justified trust, when achievable, has significant advantages over one based on sanctions. The agent's autonomy in such a system tends to produce in that agent greater psychological wellbeing, greater involvement in the task, and greater persistence on the task in the face of obstacles (Ryan and Deci 2006). Public service motivation, a significant form of intrinsic motivation, seems to be linked with better performance through greater job satisfaction and organizational commitment (Vandenabeele 2009, based on informants' self-reports). The quality of communication between principal and agent is also likely to be better, with the agent more likely to volunteer accurate information. The normative relationship of principal and agent, founded on trust, is likely to be more satisfying.

Human nature is so constituted, however, that we can rarely do away entirely with sanction. Both individuals and systems often need a little threat of sanction in the mix in order to provide an ecological niche in which intrinsic motivation, particularly public-interested motivation, can flourish. Almost any accountability system will therefore require what I have called a *selection core* and a *sanction periphery*, with some balance between trust- and sanction-based accountability (Mansbridge 2009). The question is in each set of different circumstances: How big can we make the selection core and how light and delicate the sanction periphery? The goal is to create a system of accountability subtle enough so that the sanction periphery does a gentle job of disciplining, but remains as thin as possible and as congruent with honoring as possible, so as not to interfere with the internal motivations that drive the selection core.

Whether or not organizations and polities can depend primarily on trust-based accountability depends on several factors.

First, and most importantly, the creation of trust-based, accountability in a selection model of principal–agent relations depends on whether in any given situation there are or could be enough potential agents with internally motivated interests that are aligned with the interests of potential principals. Take, for example, mowing a lawn. Relatively few people want to mow a lawn without any external inducement. The accountability relationship between me and the person I hire to mow some grass will therefore be based to a large degree on sanctions (the reward of pay and the threat of not being hired again) and to a relatively small degree on selection for intrinsic motivation. On the other hand, this relationship will probably have *some* selection component. There may be some people in my world who, perhaps for reasons of internal pride, want to work hard and do a job that meets the standards of the craft. When this is the case, I will try to discover and select one of those people. I will ask my friends whether they know anyone who is honest, works hard, and cares about the quality of the work. I will look for someone who has a reputation for this kind of internal motivation.

Another homely example comes from a university administrator whose position required her to hire undergraduates to work over the summer on the university's grounds. Having found that students on the university's athletic teams generally wanted to keep in good physical shape, she hired them because they had the internal motivation to work hard at the manual labor she asked of them (Pratt and Zeckhauser 1985, 15).

Even with lawn-mowing and landscaping, in short, the world may produce some differences among individuals in the degree to which they are internally motivated to do that work. When this is the case, if a principal can invest sufficient time and effort ex ante to find such agents and select them, that principal can save time and effort ex post on monitoring and sanctioning.

A second factor is how easy it is in a particular job to monitor the work closely. With a caregiver, for example, I could install video cameras in all the rooms in my house to tape everything that happened while I was away at work. I could spend my evenings watching the tapes to uncover deviations from duty. Most of us do not want to do that. We therefore have to trust the caregiver most of the time. Because we cannot monitor easily, we will invest fairly heavily ex ante in trying to find and select people who want, for their own reasons, to do well by our child.

A third factor is the effects of monitoring and sanctioning on the worker. A care-giver who knew that he or she was being taped constantly might not like it. The lack of trust that such a procedure signaled might even poison the caregiver's relationship with the parent and perhaps the child. The act of monitoring could also undermine whatever internal motivation the agent might have. So might working under the threat of sanction.

Finally, the more a principal wants an agent to use initiative and act flexibly in future unforeseeable circumstances, the more a selection model is efficient. By contrast, systems based on monitoring and sanctioning tend to induce the agent to focus primarily on the acts that can be monitored and sanctioned, that is, on the measurable means and not the real goal.

In sum, of the four important conditions that determine when one should choose a selection model, only the first is a necessary condition. A selection model is viable only when aligned agents exist and are in reasonable supply. The other conditions are contingent, making a selection model, with its trust-based form of accountability, cost-effective to the degree that monitoring is hard, monitoring and sanctioning have high costs or bad effects, and flexibility in unpredictable circumstances is an important part of the job.

The selection model depicted here does not feature the kind of accountability that many mean these days when they say, "We need more accountability." They mean: "We want to be able to make our agents do what we want them to do." That is, "We want to exercise power over them. We want to be able to watch them carefully and punish them when they do not do what we want them to do." This is sanction-based accountability. The more traditional understanding of accountability, giving an account, is more compatible with the selection model. It can take either a one-way *narrative* form, as in the opinions of the justices of the U.S. Supreme Court, or a more two-way *deliberative* form, in which the principal not only listens to the agent's narrative but asks questions and perhaps volunteers information. Here the interaction can be mutually educative. It can also have positive normative properties, in that it can be an interaction among equals, or at least conduce to equality among the interlocutors.

These two models, the sanctions model and the selection model, apply in many realms. In the funding world, for example, donors in an earlier era would select as recipients organizations with a reputation for integrity, managed by individuals with a reputation for competence, honesty, and commitment to the same goals as the donors. They would then trust that their money was being used flexibly and with initiative in a relatively unpredictable future with unpredictable conditions. Now, by contrast, donors often want measurable outcomes, so that they can monitor the process and punish and reward accordingly. As a result, they sometimes get efforts aimed at creating only the highest marks on measurable outcomes, which may not be the deeper outcomes they actually want.

CONTINGENCY IN ACCOUNTABILITY SYSTEMS

Accountability studies can profitably ask when accountability systems should rely most heavily on sanctions and when they can mix in more elements of selection and justifiable trust.

In past debates and in past work on intrinsic motivation, the scholars who have rightly pointed out the benefits of trust-based accountability have not given great attention to the benefits of sanctions when the conditions supporting a selection model of principal–agent relations are absent or weak. Each of the theorists discussed above, for example, wrote as if one kind of system simply had predictable effects in one direction and another system had predictable effects in a different direction. But accountability theorists should recognize that individuals and contexts differ. One accountability regime will not fit all.

Brennan (1996) was one of the first accountability theorists to stress differences among individuals. In a work that generally argued for the efficacy of selection over sanction, he pointed out that the resulting accountability regime would work only for certain kinds of agents—those I have identified here as intrinsically motivated in ways that align with a principal's objectives. Rather than assuming "motivational homogeneity," he argued, in the realm of public action one should try to identify the more and less "knavish" individuals, then "locate the less knavish in those employments in which knavishness is most destructive." Because "such virtue as exists in society will be a positive resource for that society, and should be located in its highest valued use just like any other resource," and because in his view politics, bureaucracy, the judiciary, and other non-market offices were the highest uses, "the good functioning of society will depend on the extent to which the relatively virtuous are selected for non-market offices" (1996, 257–60). He further suggested that rewarding the intrinsically-motivated agents in a "currency" that has worth only to the intrinsically-motivated will encourage those individuals to self-select into the appropriate jobs.

Besley (2006), who, like Brennan, contrasted the sanctions and selection models of principal–agent relations, also stressed that individuals come in different "types." Although in standard economic theory, "agents are homogeneous," in practice, potential agents vary according to "the extent to which...they agree with the *mission* being pursued" by the entity for which they work. Being a "trustworthy" individual "is a type rather than a consequence of incentives" (2006, 100, 41, emphasis in original).

With their observation that individuals vary by type, Brennan and Besley began to create something like a contingency theory of accountability. Yet as pioneers in a field that, as Besley (2008, 37, 42) puts it, "is in its infancy" they failed to mention two considerations that should be central to any such theory. First, each individual is not one type but many. The social context activates the different features of one's identity on which one will draw. Second, social contexts differ greatly in the density of individuals with different kinds of intrinsic motivation. A contingency theory of accountability would focus both on the mix of motivations within each potential agent and the mix of intrinsically motivated actors in a particular context.

It is hard to design systems of accountability that maximize the efficiencies available through selection-based, trust-based forms of accountability and also deploy the sanction-based forms when necessary. Any such design requires deep attention to context. A currently deeply corrupt government or administration may need to introduce strong sanction-based accountability systems to disrupt the highly integrated equilibria based on self-interest or group interest that have evolved over the years (Rothstein 2011). Denmark did just this in the period from the last half of the seventeenth century to the mid-nineteenth (Mungiu-Pippidi 2011, 62–67). Even systems that have evolved to work largely on public-spirited internal motivation, selection, and justified trust need some sanction-based accountability at the edges of the system. Without any disciplinary sanctions at all, an accountability system based on selection and trust will tend to unravel like prisoners' dilemma games where cooperators gradually decide not to remain suckers as they see others benefit from defecting. On the other hand, when internal motivation is doing most of the work, sanction-based accountability must discipline only lightly and in the most important places in order not to disrupt the delicate balance of the selection-trust system.

Experimentation is usually the best way to evolve an accountability system, although social science is beginning to allow us to become more precise about which systemic features to embrace or avoid. We are beginning to learn more about the emotions, such as pride and disgust that are, relevant to different accountability systems (see e.g., Kelly (2011) on disgust). We are also learning that when injunctions to better behavior ("injunctive norms") are inadvertently set in a descriptive context indicating that many people in fact behave badly ("descriptive norms"), the injunctions may backfire. Gerber and Rogers (2009, 181), for example, have shown that when potential voters are contacted and urged to vote after hearing that "in the most recent election ... voter turnout was the lowest it had been in over 30 years," they were less likely to signal an intention to vote than after hearing that the last election turnout was the highest in decades along with an expressed hope that they would join the trend. People may quite reasonably take their signals on how to act from what the majority does. When this is the case, accountability systems that signal that most people are acting self-interestedly may inadvertently convey a descriptive norm that reinforces self-interest.[2]

The effects of pride, disgust, and descriptive norms are only a few of many features that anyone trying to improve a system of accountability should consider. The problem is compounded by the delicate nature of balancing trust-based and sanction-based accountability systems. Organizations, governments, and administrations are not likely to be able to apply from a book a set of rules establishing the best balance in their particular contexts. Instead, they will probably have to work incrementally and experimentally with existing and evolving traditions, cultures, people, and demands of the work.

DYNAMIC ACCOUNTABILITY

Sabel and Zeitlin give the name *dynamic accountability* to a process that may succeed in combining, in ways that are sensitive to context, the most important features of both sanction-based and trust- based accountability regimes. The key features of dynamic accountability are networks, recursivity, deliberation, innovation, inclusion, and publicity. In the many instances that Sabel and Zeitlin have observed in the European Union (EU), superordinate bodies (such as the Member States acting jointly or other EU institutions) set framework goals and measures for gauging the achievement of these goals. Then, as they put it, "Lower-level units (such as national ministries or regulatory authorities and the actors with whom they collaborate) are given the freedom to advance these ends as they see fit. But in return for this autonomy, they must report regularly on their performance and participate in a peer review in which their results are compared with the results of other groups using other means to achieve the same general ends. Finally, the framework goals, performance measures, and decision-making procedures themselves are periodically revised by the actors, including new participants whose views come to be seen as indispensable to full and fair deliberation" (Sabel and Zeitlin 2008, 271).

In this new "experimentalist architecture," mutual consultation, network accountability, and interaction between "principal" and "agent" work through what I have termed deliberative accountability. Sabel and Zeitlin argue persuasively that the very terms "principal" and "agent" become almost meaningless in this context of rapid evolution, experimentation, and recursivity. Peer networks do much of the job of accountability, as each member needs to explain and justify his or her actions to peers who know enough to understand and evaluate the situation. But the networks themselves are checked by the requirement of giving public reasons susceptible to scrutiny by governments, NGOs, and other stakeholders. Sabel and Zeitlin point out that in these systems of dynamic accountability, "a single function, such as monitoring and review of implementation experience, can be performed through a variety of institutional devices, operating singly and/or in combination with one another. Conversely, a single institutional mechanism, such as a formal peer review exercise, can perform a number of distinct governance functions, such as assessing the comparative effectiveness of different national and subnational implementation approaches, opening up opportunities for civil society actors to hold governments accountable at national and EU levels, identifying areas where new forms of national or transnational capacity building are required, and/or contributing to the redefinition of common policy objectives" (2008, 274). The process of dynamic accountability that Sabel and Zeitlin have observed "routinely results either in revisions of EU directives, regulations, and administrative decisions, or in the elaboration of revisable standards mandated by law and the enunciation of new principles which may eventually be given binding force" (2008, 276). In this process of continuous institutional revision, regulation "increasingly takes the novel form of contestable rules to be understood as rebuttable guides to action even when they are also taken as enforceable sovereign commands" (2008, 275). The entire process, they conclude, "is a machine for learning from diversity" (2008, 276).

Dynamic accountability is also especially likely to generate the "pre-emptive self-criticism" that Tetlock and his colleagues have shown produces more thoughts than other processes and reduces many forms of cognitive bias. Pre-emptive self-criticism is "the predecisional strategy of anticipating plausible objections of would-be critics, factoring those objections into one's mental representation of the problem, and reaching a complex synthesis that specifies how to deal with tradeoffs" (Tetlock 2002, 455). Such thinking is triggered by "forms of accountability that activate the metacognitive maxim 'anticipate plausible objections'" (2002, 456) and is particularly likely when "the views of the audience are unknown or known to conflict, the audience is knowledgeable and powerful, and the audience possesses a legitimate right to inquire into the reasons behind opinions or decisions" (2002, 455, citing Lerner and Tetlock 1999). These conditions are often met in the dynamic accountability processes in the EU because the individuals in these networks are accountable to other individuals within the network who have different and sometimes contradictory views, have relatively powerful sanctions against one another, and have the legitimate right to ask for the reasons behind any opinion or decision. At the same time the networks themselves are accountable to other authorities and stakeholders with the same characteristics. These conditions tend to produce the "internalized dialogue" with a "dialectical 'on the one hand' and 'on the other hand' rhythm" that Tetlock (2002, 456) has shown attenuates cognitive bias.

Processes of dynamic accountability seem plausibly applicable to far smaller contexts than the EU. When an academic department sets up a committee, the chair may appoint members from different disciplinary approaches to the committee (inclusion). As the members do their work, they may share information about the different needs of their subfields as well as, perhaps, new ideas on what is best for the department in this context (deliberation and innovation). They watch one another to see that the representation of needs within the committee is fair and that no member is acting underhandedly (internal network accountability). But that mutual watching is relatively integral to their colleagueship. It need not be perceived as the threat of sanction. The members may collectively try out one solution that works badly and then revisit the problem, or they may take the question to the whole department to discuss together (recursivity). When the committee makes its report to the department, it does not usually share all of the details of its discussions (that is, it does not provide *transparency in process*), but it justifies and explains, giving the reasons for its decision, thus providing a *transparency in rationale* that is open to scrutiny by the relevant public (Mansbridge 2009, 386). When other members of the department question the members of the committee and those members respond, they engage together in a process of deliberative accountability external to the network. When the process is also recursive, it meets all the criteria for dynamic accountability.

The same process might profitably be applied to the interaction of funding agencies with health clinics in poorer countries (Heimer and Gazley 2012), or to many other situations in which participants are now discovering problems with hierarchical and sanction-based accountability, with its strict separation of principal and agent. The network features of dynamic accountability also provide some response to the responsibility diffusion inherent in the "problem of many hands" (Thompson 1980).

Sabel and Zeitlin do not point out that within dynamic accountability in the EU the processes of selection into the peer networks and the *esprit de corps* and socialization that accompanies figuring out solutions and acting together probably create some intrinsic motivation and some bases for justifiable mutual trust.[3] Yet the process they describe of dynamic accountability seems likely to both create and support a selection model of principal–agent relations and a trust-based accountability regime. This combination, when achievable, is likely to be more efficient than a regime based primarily on sanctions.

FUTURE ACCOUNTABILITY STUDIES

The future of accountability studies depends in part on finding ways to combine sanction-based accountability with a selection model of principal–agent relations and trust-based accountability. It depends on developing context-sensitive forms of accountability that introduce adaptability, recursivity, inclusion, publicity—and sanctions when necessary—while trying to sustain or build upon existing sources of accurate selection and trust-based accountability. Contexts differ. Before instituting anything close to a pure selection and trust regime, one should ask: "Can the situation support a selection model? Would it be viable? Are there sufficient numbers of available agents with trustworthy internal motivations? Would it be hard to monitor the behavior I want? Do monitoring and sanctioning have relatively high costs? Do I want from my agent flexible behavior adapted to unforeseeable circumstances?" If the answer to these questions is "yes," an accountability model with a large selection core and a small sanction periphery will be better than one based primarily on sanctions. Bringing in more sanctions might well be counterproductive.

In most cases, a contingency theory of accountability sensitive to context is likely to be more effective than simply demanding "more accountability" in the sense of more monitoring and punishment.

Notes

1. Chambers (2003, 38) writes congruently that in deliberative democratic theory "account-ability is primarily understood in terms of 'giving an account' of something, that is, publicly articulating, explaining, and most importantly, justifying, public policy." See also Sabel and Zeitlin (2008, 305): "Accountability generically understood means presenting an account of one's choices that is owed to others…"
2. An experiment with signs urging hikers not to pick up fossils in Cialdini et al. (2006), most frequently cited for the unintended effect of creating a descriptive norm, achieves statistically significant results only by comparing non-comparables.
3. See Haas (1989) on epistemic communities and Sherif et al. (1988) on acting together for a superordinate goal.

References

Behn, R. D. 2001. *Rethinking Democratic Accountability*. Washington, DC: Brookings Institute.

Besley, T. 2006. *Principled Agents: The Political Economy of Good Government*. Oxford: Oxford University Press.

Brennan, G. 1996. Selection and the Currency of Reward, pp. 256–76 in *The Theory of Institutional Design*, ed. R. E. Goodin. Cambridge: Cambridge University Press.

Campbell, D. T. 1979. "Assessing the Impact of Planned Social Change." *Evaluation and Program Planning*, 2: 67–90.

Carr, F. 1999. "The Public Service Ethos: Decline and Renewal?" *Public Policy and Administration*, 14: 1–16.

Chambers, S. 2003. "Deliberative Democratic Theory." *Annual Review of Political Science*, 6: 307–26.

Cialdini, R. R., Demaine, L. J., Sagarin, B. J., Barrett, D. W., Rhoads, K., and Winters, P. L. 2006. "Activating and Aligning Social Norms for Persuasive Impact." *Social Influence*, 1: 3–15.

Deci, E. L. 1971. "Effects of Externally Mediated Rewards on Intrinsic Motivation." *Journal of Personality and Social Psychology*, 18: 105–15.

Deci, E. L., Koestner, R., and Ryan, R. M. 1999. "A Meta-Analytic Review of Experiments Examining the Effects of Extrinsic Rewards on Intrinsic Motivation." *Psychological Bulletin*, 125: 627–68.

Deci, E. L. and Ryan, R. M. 1985. *Intrinsic Motivation and Self-determination in Human Behavior*. New York: Plenum.

Fearon, J. 1999. Electoral Accountability and the Control of Politicians, pp. 55–97 in *Democracy, Accountability and Representation*, eds. A. Przeworski, S. C. Stokes and B. Manin. Cambridge: Cambridge University Press.

Finer, H. 1941. "Administrative Responsibility in Democratic Government." *Public Administration Review*, 1: 335–50.

Frey, B. S. 1997. "A Constitution for Knaves Crowds Out Civic Virtues." *The Economic Journal*, 107: 1043–53.

Friedrich, C. J. 1940. Public Policy and the Nature of Administrative Responsibility, pp. 3–24 in *Public Policy: A Yearbook of the Graduate School of Public Administration*, eds. C. J. Friedrich and E. S. Mason. Cambridge, Mass.: Harvard University Press.

Gerber, A. S. and Rogers, T. 2009. "Descriptive Social Norms and Motivation to Vote: Everybody's Voting and so Should You." *The Journal of Politics*, 71: 178–91.

Goodin, R. E. 1980. "Making Moral Incentives Pay." *Policy Sciences*, 12: 131–45.

Goodin, R. E. 2003. "Democratic Accountability: The Distinctiveness of the Third Sector." *European Journal of Sociology*, 44: 359–96.

Haas, P. M. 1989. "Do Regimes Matter? Epistemic Communities and Mediterranean Pollution Control." *International Organization*, 43: 377–403.

Heimer, C. A. and Gazley, J. L. 2012. "Performing Regulation: Transcending Regulatory Ritualism in HIV Clinics." *Law and Society Review*, 46: 853–87.

Kelly, D. 2011. *Yuck! The Nature and Moral Significance of Disgust*. Cambridge, MA: The MIT Press.

Lerner, J. S. and Tetlock, P. E. 1999. "Accounting for the Effects of Accountability." *Psychological Bulletin*, 125: 255–75.

Mansbridge, J. 2005. "The Fallacy of Tightening the Reins." *Österreichische Zeitschrift für Politikwissenschaft*, 34: 233–47.

Mansbridge, J. 2009. "A 'Selection Model' of Political Representation." *The Journal of Political Philosophy*, 17: 369–98.

Mansbridge, J. 2010. *Against Accountability*. EUI Max Weber Lecture. October 25. Florence: European University Institute.

McGregor, D. 1960. *The Human Side of Enterprise*. New York: McGraw-Hill.

Mungiu-Pippidi, A. 2011. Becoming Denmark: Understanding Good Governance Historical Achievers, pp. 36–47 in *Contextual Choices in Fighting Corruption*, eds. A. Mungiu-Pippidi, M. Loncaric, B. V. Mundo, A. C. S. Braga, M. Weinhardt, A. P. Solares, A. Skardziute, M. Martini, F. Agbele, M. F. Jensen, C. von Soest, and M. Gabedava. Oslo: Norwegian Agency for Development and Cooperation.

O'Neill, O. 2002. *A Question of Trust*. Cambridge: Cambridge University Press.

Philp, M. 2008. "Delimiting Democratic Accountability." *Political Studies*, 57: 28–53.

Power, M. 1994. *The Audit Explosion*. London: Demos.

Pratt, J. W. and Zeckhauser, R. J., eds. 1985. *Principals and Agents: The Structure of Business*. Boston: Harvard Business School Press.

Przeworski, A., Stokes, S. C., and Manin, B. 1999. *Democracy, Accountability and Representation*. Cambridge: Cambridge University Press.

Rothstein, B. 2011. *The Quality of Government: Corruption, Social Trust, and Inequality in International Perspective*. Chicago: University of Chicago Press.

Ryan, R. M. and Deci, E. L. 2006. "Self-Regulation and the Problem of Human Autonomy." *Journal of Personality*, 74: 1557–85.

Sabel, C. F. and Zeitlin, J. 2008. "Learning from Difference: The New Architecture of Experimentalist Governance in the EU." *European Law Journal*, 14: 271–327.

Sherif, M., Harvey, O. J., White, B. J., Hood, W. R., and Sherif, C. W. 1988. *Intergroup Conflict and Cooperation: The Robbers Cave Experiment*. Scranton, PA: Harper and Row; originally published 1954.

Tamir, Y. 2012. *Malignant Accountability*. Presented at the Seminar on *Moral Controversies and Public Policy*. Harvard Kennedy School, 10 October 2012.

Tetlock, P. E. 2002. "Social Functionalist Frameworks for Judgment and Choice: Intuitive Politicians, Theologians, and Prosecutors." *Psychological Review*, 109: 451–71.

Thompson, D. F. 1980. "Responsibility of Public Officials: The Problem of Many Hands." *American Political Science Review*, 74: 905–16.

Vandenabeele, W. 2009. "The Mediating Effect of Job Satisfaction and Organizational Commitment on Self-Reported Performance." *International Review of Administrative Sciences*, 75: 11–33.

CHAPTER 5

PROCESS VERSUS OUTCOME ACCOUNTABILITY

SHEFALI V. PATIL, FERDINAND VIEIDER, AND
PHILIP E. TETLOCK

INTRODUCTION

As this handbook attests, accountability is a multifaceted phenomenon that can be studied from a wide range of theoretical and methodological perspectives. This chapter grapples with a problem that has largely fallen between the disciplinary cracks: the choice that both private- and public-sector managers often face between oversight systems that focus on holding others accountable either for their efforts to achieve outcomes (with minimal regard for the accuracy or quality of those outcomes—pure process accountability) or for their effectiveness in actually delivering outcomes (with minimal regard for the processes utilized to arrive at these outcomes—pure outcome accountability) (Beach and Mitchell 1978; Curley, Yates, and Abrams 1986). Of course, the choice need not be dichotomous. Most accountability systems are evolving process-outcome hybrids that lean in one direction or another but that, depending on task and context, assign shifting weights to process-oriented versus outcome-oriented standards for judging performance (Eisenhardt 1985; 1989; Tetlock and Mellers 2011b).

Although one might suppose designing process or outcome accountability systems to be a dry, technocratic affair of "principals" crafting optimal incentives for "agents" who have varying degrees of risk aversion, debates between proponents of process-oriented vs. outcome-oriented systems have proven surprisingly spirited and even occasionally acrimonious, breaking out in diverse organizational domains, including intelligence analysis (Tetlock and Mellers 2011a), public schools (Chubb and Moe 1988), equal employment opportunity (EEO) enforcement (Tetlock, Vieider, Patil, and Grant 2013), auditing (Cohen, Krishnamoorthy, Peytcheva, and Wright 2011), investment strategies (Sutcliffe and McNamara 2001), sales-force management (Anderson and Oliver 1987; Cravens, Ingram, LaForge, and Young 1993), health care (Rubin, Pronovost, and Diette 2001), information systems development (Kirsch 1996), human resource systems (Arthur 1994), product manufacturing (Hammer and Stanton 1999), and business innovation (Coyne 1997; Simons 2005). Proponents of process accountability often argue that it is prudent to incentivize the adoption of best practices (processes) that employees can control—and, that it is both inefficient and unfair to hold subordinates responsible for outcomes beyond their control (a policy that merely rewards the lucky and punishes the unlucky (Bertrand and Mullainathan 2001)). By contrast, proponents of outcome accountability often counter that it is essential to pressure employees to find new ingenious ways of bringing "uncontrollable" outcomes under control (Simons 2005). In this view, process accountability can too easily degenerate into bureaucratic rituals in which employees adhere to widely-accepted processes within the organization and make excuses for poor outcomes by claiming that they did all they could within the bounds of organizational norms and "best practices" (Meyer and Rowan 1977; Tetlock and Mellers 2011b; Wilson 1989).

The remainder of this chapter is dedicated to exploring the actual and perceived consequences of process and outcome accountability—and is divided into three sections. First, we summarize the experimental literature on the actual pros and cons of process versus outcome accountability with respect to judgment and choice dependent variables—a literature that stresses the advantages of process accountability but that has serious methodological limitations. Second, we examine some real-world political debates that have arisen over the pros and cons of process versus outcome accountability—a body of work that highlights the perceived strengths and weaknesses of each type of accountability among observers of varying ideological persuasions but that sheds less light on actual strengths and weaknesses. Third, we propose a conceptual framework that generates novel hypotheses about the conditions under which process and outcome forms of accountability are likely to improve or degrade the quality of judgment and choice and that offers guidelines for practitioners about how to achieve the best of both accountability worlds.

THE LABORATORY LITERATURE ON PROCESS VERSUS OUTCOME ACCOUNTABILITY

Experimental research on process versus outcome accountability tends to emphasize the relative benefits of process accountability (Lerner and Tetlock 1999). For example, studies have shown that process accountability reduces escalating commitment to sunk costs (Simonson and Staw 1992), produces better-calibrated probability judgments (Siegel-Jacobs and Yates 1996), enhances performance on tasks requiring analytical processing (Langhe, Osselaer, and Wierenga 2011), enriches attentiveness and alertness in making judgments (Brtek and Motowidlo 2002), and motivates more thorough information search and analysis (Doney and Armstrong 1996).

Experimental psychologists have advanced a number of reasons why, relative to outcome accountability, process accountability often yields more empirically accurate and logically defensible judgments. For instance, they have proposed that outcome accountability pushes decision-makers' stress levels into a super-optimal zone that rigidifies cognition, whereas process accountability mitigates evaluation apprehension by reassuring decision-makers that they will be "socially safe" as long as they deploy defensible procedures (Siegel-Jacobs and Yates 1996). This reassurance is especially important for decision-makers who believe they live in a world of irreducible uncertainty (Hammond 1995).

Experimental psychologists have also suggested that process accountability, by encouraging more thorough evaluation of available information (Brtek and Motowidlo 2002; Dreu, Koole, and Steinel 2000; Ford and Weldon 1981; Tetlock 1983; Tetlock and Boettger 1989) focuses decision-makers' attention on "how" to make sound decisions (Siegel-Jacobs and Yates 1996). Outcome accountability, by contrast, merely conveys to the decision-maker that judgments need to be accurate without providing guidance on how to achieve this goal. This argument is also advanced in debates about how best to improve health care quality (a sector where outcomes are often beyond the provider's control). Process, as opposed to outcome, measures provide information that is actionable—i.e., they identify for clinicians which processes have the potential to affect patient outcomes—and thus can be used to provide feedback for quality improvement (Rubin et al. 2001).

Outcome accountability, however, is not without its advocates. For example, Langhe et al. (2011) demonstrate that the benefits of process accountability accrue only for tasks with certain characteristics. They found that although outcome accountability decreased performance on simple tasks that required analytical processing, it increased performance on configural tasks that required more holistic processing. Studies have also found that pressures to justify procedures can lead people under process accountability to shift decision-making weights rapidly, causing them to fall prey to the decoy effect and to adopt narrower decision-making strategies (Slaughter, Bagger, and Li 2006). Lastly, Arkes, Dawes, and Christensen (1986) found that when held accountable for the accuracy of their judgments, decision makers were less likely to base their judgments on linear additive rules that the experimenters explicitly conveyed to them to complete the probabilistic task, instead setting out to find more optimal outcomes beyond what decision process norms allowed. This suggests that outcome accountability can sometimes motivate decision makers to seek novel and ingenious strategies that compensate for inadequate established procedures, in order to optimize desired outcomes (Simons 2005; Tetlock and Mellers 2011b).

However, the experimental work reviewed here suffers from at least two major methodological limitations which call into question its applicability to actual organizations. The first concerns the mismatch between experimental manipulations of process accountability and real-world forms of process accountability. Institutional theorists have long noted that decision makers in social systems are typically constrained by normative guidelines when they select judgment and choice strategies (Edelman 1985; Feldman and March 1981; Meyer and Rowan 1977; Pfeffer 1981). To meet societal demands for rationality and fairness, organizations often adopt formal processes and rules for gathering, storing, communicating, and using information (Feldman and March 1981). These rules are deeply embedded within the institutions' symbolic systems, relational systems, routines, and artifacts (Scott 2008) and passed on to newcomers during organizational socialization (Maanen and Schein 1979).

However, the vast majority of laboratory experiments reviewed above have tended to create unusual (deliberately normatively ambiguous) forms of process accountability in which participants are unaware of what their evaluators deem to be "effective" or "quality" procedures for making judgments and decisions (Ashton 1992; Brtek and Motowidlo 2002; Dreu et al. 2000; Slaughter et al. 2006). By contrast, decision makers under outcome accountability are often told that their performance evaluations will be based on comparison of their responses to predictions derived from statistical models (Arkes et al. 1986; Langhe et al. 2011; Siegel-Jacobs and Yates 1996), or to the judgments of fictitious subject matter experts (Brtek and Motowidlo 2002; Slaughter et al. 2006), or to judgments of team members (Klimoski 1972), or based on the reactions of recipients of the decisions (Adelberg and Batson 1978; Fandt and Ferris 1990). In brief, the normative standards governing what constitutes a high quality decision were often known to the decision maker.

The benefits of process accountability in the lab then are not wholly surprising. Most research demonstrates that under normative ambiguity, people select the most broadly defensible decision strategies possible, which in turn, leads to more systematic, even-handed, and integratively complex thinking (Tetlock 1983; Tetlock, Skitka, and Boettger 1989). However, process accountability in organizations with well-defined norms about what constitutes "quality" procedures could potentially degrade quality of judgment and choice if it simply encourages decision makers to rely on the acceptability heuristic to convince influential constituencies that their processes are rational and that they are reasonably intelligent (Pfeffer 1981; Schlenker 1980; Tedeschi 1981)—after all, utilizing widely accepted beliefs of what is deemed "intelligent" often serves to assure managers that due care was taken to make rational decisions (Langley 1989). As such, conformity to inadequate or defective practices can be a potential consequence of heavy-handed types of process accountability.

The second limitation concerns the extent to which experimental manipulations of process and outcome accountability convey socio-relational signals to the decision maker. The imposition of accountability systems often places the decision maker in a de facto subordinate relationship by defining to whom he or she is accountable and the normative grounds under which evaluations will be made (Tetlock 1985). Situated-identity theory and related frameworks suggest that people in any interpersonal interaction are in a continuous process of negotiating identities vis-à-vis each other, often alternating rapidly between the roles of claiming identities for themselves (e.g., trustworthy, competent, likable) and granting, to varying degrees, the identity claims of others (Tetlock 1984). In principle, everything people do can be scaled for its identity implications—if I do x or y, what conclusions will others draw about my character? Given that this other party has acted in x or y fashion toward me, what message does that send about the types of situated identities that they are prepared to grant me in this situation?

These micro-signals can have major effects on the cognitive, emotional, or behavioral responses of agents to accountability demands. An ongoing meta-analysis of the accountability literature by Vieider and Tetlock (2011) sheds light on the various micro-signals that can be conveyed between principal and agent and the sensitivity of these signals to minimal changes in context or messaging. A shift in one or two words can reframe accountability from polite request to categorical demand (from "we ask that you explain how you reached your conclusions…" to "you will be required to explain how you reached your conclusions…") and from an inquisitorial-prosecutorial tone to a friendly expression-of-curiosity tone (from "justify/defend your views" to "help us to understand why you see things as you do"). A shift in one or two words can also change from whom people believe the request or demand has sprung; an audience more likely to be sympathetic (e.g., members of one's team or in-group) or intelligently skeptical (e.g., neutral experts) or hostile (e.g., members of a rival team or out-group); an audience comprised of lower-, same-, or higher-status persons (e.g., fellow students or doctoral fellows); an audience whose goal is simply judging you (e.g., someone "grading" your responses) versus one whose goal is getting to know you and treating you with respect as someone who has a capacity to contribute to the investigation (e.g., someone who is genuinely curious about your views).

Although the effects of various micro-signals on decision-making remain to be fully investigated, it is quite plausible that previous studies have conveyed more positive relational signals to those under process accountability than to those under outcome accountability. For example, in most process accountability manipulations, participants were informed that an interview would be conducted where they would be asked about the processes they utilized to make their decisions, potentially conveying a sense of acceptance of the subjects as important and valuable contributors to the experiment (Arkes, Christensen, Lai and Blumer 1987; Ashton 1992; Brtek and Motowidlo 2002; Dreu, Beersma, Stroebe, and Euwema 2006; Dreu et al. 2000; Langhe et al. 2011; Ford and Weldon 1981; Hagafors and Brehmer 1983; McAllister, Mitchell, and Beach 1979; Rozelle and Baxter 1981; Siegel-Jacobs and Yates 1996; Simonson and Nye 1992; Simonson and Staw 1992; Tetlock and Boettger 1989; Tetlock and Kim 1987). For the outcome accountability manipulations, the opportunity to justify one's outcomes face-to-face varied across studies, and quite likely signaled a lack of respect and regard for the competencies, abilities, and contributions of the subjects. The studies that did allow for an interview were only conducted so the participants could explain why they succeeded or failed in reaching optimal outcomes (Adelberg and Batson 1978; Brtek and Motowidlo 2002; Fandt and Ferris 1990; Klimoski 1972; Simonson and Staw 1992). In other cases, there was no face-to-face interaction with the interviewer, and decision makers only received monetary bonuses for reaching optimal outcomes (Arkes et al. 1986; Langhe et al. 2011; Siegel-Jacobs and Yates 1996; Slaughter et al. 2006). If this analysis of the relational signals in each accountability condition is accurate, it suggests another possible explanation for the cognitive benefits of process accountability.

There is no inherent reason, however, why process and outcome accountability must always be linked respectively to positive and negative relational signals. For instance, it is easy to imagine forms of process accountability that convey to participants a lack of respect for the competencies of the decision maker—e.g., they are being held accountable for processes because the evaluators lack the confidence in their ability to choose sound processes on their own and want to ensure that they are adopting agreed-upon strategies to achieve desired objectives (Jaworski 1988; Merchant 1988). Here we should expect the effects of process accountability to be less beneficial. Substantial bodies of work in social psychology and organizational behavior demonstrate that people react negatively to institutional control systems that depict them as lazy and incompetent (Enzle and Anderson 1993; Schoorman, Mayer, and Davis 2007; Sutton and Galunic 1996). For example, instituting close-knit monitoring systems that signal lack of trust has been shown to lead experimental agents to become less creative (Amabile 1979), less trustworthy (Malhotra and Murnighan 2002), and less willing to engage in organizational citizenship behavior crucial for the effective function of most collectivities (Organ 1988).

Because of the lack of consideration of normative structures and relational micro-signaling in laboratory research on process and outcome accountability, it is difficult to generalize these studies to supplement a broader understanding of these accountability systems as they operate in organizational life. As an alternative, we now turn our attention to real-world debates about these accountability systems in the realm of public policy.

REAL-WORLD DEBATES ABOUT THE PROS AND CONS OF PROCESS VERSUS OUTCOME ACCOUNTABILITY

Debates over the merits of process vs. outcome accountability have popped up in a variety of policy arenas. Here we focus on three spheres: disputes over the criteria for evaluating teacher performance in public schools, for evaluating the equal employment opportunity (EEO) performance of personnel managers, and for evaluating the accuracy of national intelligence estimates generated by intelligence analysts.

The same underlying question about normative ground rules recurs across domains. To what extent should people be responsible for *how* they do their jobs (trying hard to achieve organizational goals using best known practices) and secondarily for *what* they actually accomplish, versus responsible for *what* they accomplish and secondarily for *how* they manage to do it? Proponents of pure-process accountability favor the former—enforcing EEO norms on the basis of how carefully managers ensure that personnel decisions are grounded in job-relevant performance data, not on statistical quotas specifying the target representation of minorities across jobs; judging teachers on their teaching performance (e.g., lesson plans, clarity of delivery), not on student test scores; and judging intelligence analysts on how rigorously they assess available evidence, not on whether they get it right or wrong. By contrast, proponents of pure-outcome accountability favor the latter, shifting focus from evaluating inputs to evaluating outcomes—evaluating managerial efforts to create an EEO workplace by the actual minority numbers in the firm; evaluating teacher performance by student test scores; and evaluating intelligence analysts' efforts by actual predictive track records.

In a correlational field study, Tetlock et al. (2013) found a rather strong connection between support for outcome accountability and suspicions about agent trustworthiness, or perceptions of how likely these agents are to be "opportunistic" when no one is looking. Managers often tacitly assume that outcome accountability is harder to game than is process accountability—and therefore more appropriate for less conscientious or honest agents. Process accountability is seen as too vulnerable to the critique of "cosmetic compliance" in which skeptics worry that it is too easy to fake inputs: for personnel officers in corporations to pretend to be in compliance with equal-employment-opportunity rules even though they are not and minority advancement is languishing; or for public school administrators to pretend to implement best educational practices even though they are not and student achievement test scores are languishing; or for intelligence analysts to pretend to be in compliance with rigorous epistemic norms for processing evidence even though they are not and serious errors are creeping into national intelligence estimates. Political observers may offer kinder, gentler forms of process accountability only to those agents whom they classify as trustworthy.

Consistent with this reasoning, Tetlock et al. (2013) found a strong ideology-by-institutional-domain interaction. In early twenty-first-century America, liberal managers tended to be more skeptical of private-sector corporations and more tolerant of public-sector employees and their unions whereas conservatives tended to have the mirror-image orientation. As such, American liberals were more likely to prefer low-tolerance-for-excuses, outcome accountability for personnel decision-makers charged with implementing equal employment opportunity laws in private sector organizations, whereas American conservatives were more likely to prefer strict outcome accountability for public school teachers and their unions.

Tetlock et al. (2013) also examined the extent to which liberals and conservatives would alter their accountability-regime preferences in response to evidence. They found that ideologically motivated observers often find ingenious ways of preserving their preconceptions about agent trustworthiness. For example, participants were informed that teachers have responded to an outcome accountability system by finding sneaky ways of adjusting test scores. The dominant reaction of liberals was that, although this was deplorable, the outcome-accountability system drove teachers to this desperate measure (thereby protecting the perception of teachers as fundamentally trustworthy, albeit corruptible by a flawed system). Liberals thus preferred shifting from an outcome to a process accountability system. The dominant reaction of conservatives was that the cheating reinforced their view of the public school system—and of the need for more rigorous outcome accountability.

The flipside pattern arose when liberals and conservatives learned that corporate personnel managers had responded to an outcome accountability system mandating numerical goals for minority advancement by finding sneaky ways of playing the numbers. Now the dominant reaction of conservatives was that, although this was deplorable, the perverse outcome-accountability system drove managers to this extreme (again, thereby protecting the perceived trustworthiness of the agents who had been corrupted by a flawed accountability system). By contrast, liberals saw the pattern of cheating as reinforcing their view of continuing racial bias among managers—and their view of the need for even more rigorous outcome accountability.

These ideologically driven debates over accountability systems tell us quite a bit about the power of motivated reasoning in managerial judgments about how to design accountability systems. All too often, managers appear to be prisoners of their accountability preconceptions. Unfortunately, however, these debates tell us little about the actual effectiveness of process versus outcome accountability.

An Integrative Framework: Accountability and Empowerment

In this section, we attempt to correct for the limitations of both previous laboratory work on accountability and correlational field studies of debates over accountability design. We propose an integrative framework for exploring the impact of process and outcome accountability grounded in the classic tension between exploitation and exploration in organizational learning (Levitt and March 1988; March 1991): the tension between extracting maximum utility from established routines (by encouraging process compliance with best practices, often by reducing discretion by relying on statistical models) and the need to encourage agents to think outside the proverbial box (by identifying shortcomings in standard processes and innovating). We shall also argue that the effects of process and outcome accountability hinge less on the process–outcome distinction than they do on the social-identity signals that accountability sends to employees about how managers view them—and the resulting impact on psychological empowerment. Those forms of process and outcome accountability that "empower" employees are more likely to stimulate innovation whereas those that "disempower" employees are more likely to yield perfunctory compliance (if not passive or active resistance).

The Challenge of Balancing Control and Innovation

Organizations are often under pressure—from both regulators and competitors—to standardize decision practices to conform to best practice guidelines of one form or another (Sutcliffe and McNamara 2001). This trend is evident in many settings, including intelligence analysis, risk analysis of financial products, tax compliance, patient medical care, product manufacturing companies, and human resources (e.g., termination, layoff, and hiring processes). By formalizing decision processes, organizations can both communicate regulatory compliance and exploit existing knowledge routines for enhancing reliability (Dean and Sharfman 1993; Hackman and Wageman 1995). Research on organizational politics suggests that control over process is a key source of power (Crozier 1964; Pettigrew 1973), and given the information asymmetries about how things really work that often favor employees over management, implementing formal procedures is one means by which management can reduce its disadvantage and gain control over its agents (Eisenhardt 1985; Fama and Jensen 1986).

Of course, there is always the risk that best practices will ossify into bureaucratic ritualism and persist long after a changing world has made them obsolete. Such stagnation is often explained by a mix of organizational processes. For instance, organizational socialization, the process by which one learns "the ropes" of particular roles, fosters the internalization of standard practices among newcomers and shapes their perspectives for interpreting new information (Maanen and Schein 1979). These practices gradually become taken for granted as "the way things are done" (Berger and Luckmann 1966)—and eventually become automated and unfold unconsciously (DiMaggio and Powell 1983; Meyer and Rowan 1977). This automation can result in rigidities or organizational inertia (Mintzberg 1978; Starbuck 1983; Tushman and Romanelli 1985).

The net result is that managers confront trade-offs between control and innovation. They want to encourage process compliance but also to encourage creative workarounds for processes that have outlived their usefulness. This trade-off is a recurring refrain in management theory (Detert, Schroeder, and Mauriel 2000; Eisenhardt and Tabrizi 1995; Levinthal and March 1993; Shea and Howell 1998; Sitkin, Sutcliffe, and Schroeder 1994).

Linking Process and Outcome Accountability to Balancing Control and Innovation

Accountability can shape how decision makers perform this balancing act. Two theories in social psychology—construal level theory (Liberman and Trope 1998; 2003) and regulatory focus theory (Higgins 1997; 1998)—imply that process accountability is more conducive to achieving goals of control and outcome accountability is more conducive to innovation. Pure process accountability directs attention toward the "means" of the judgment task, rather than the "end" of accuracy, in order to meet evaluation demands. As a result, agents adopt low-level, concrete interpretations of their tasks and a prevention-focused emphasis on duties, obligations, and compliance (Liberman, Idson,

Camacho, and Higgins 1999). The resulting mindset enables detailed attention to control how one makes up one's mind whereas the resulting prevention-focused motivation enables compliance with standard decision practices of the organization.

By contrast, pure outcome accountability tends to direct attention toward ends rather than means—an end-state focus that facilitates high-level, abstract mental interpretations of tasks and motivates promotion-focused coping that includes proactive information-searching, risk-taking, and openness to change (Liberman, Molden, Idson, and Higgins 2001). This high-level processing also facilitates novel thinking because it renders common associations, which impede innovation, less accessible (Friedman, Fishbach, Förster, and Werth 2003; Friedman and Förster 2001). This, coupled with promotion-focused motivation, enables agents to think beyond standard practices and to experiment with new methods of achieving better outcomes (Arkes et al. 1986).

The relationship between process and outcome accountability and the actual achievement of control and innovation goals is however inevitably precarious, because both systems have the potential to backfire. We can deduce this precariousness from construal-level theory itself, which posits that activation of abstract (concrete) construal levels automatically deactivates concrete (abstract) construal levels (Trope and Liberman 2010). In this view, low-level or concrete construals induced by process accountability must subtract attention from the high-level or abstract attributes of the judgment task. This "getting lost in the trees" phenomenon can cause agents to stick with standard practices with little to no recognition of their shortcomings in achieving outcomes. The control that an organization tries to achieve through process accountability can thus spiral downward into blind conformity that sustains deficient decision practices.

Conversely, high-level construals induced by outcome accountability necessarily subtract attention from how judgments are made. Under outcome accountability, decision-making increasingly relies on "intuitive" means or what feels "right" in the race to achieve optimal judgments (Brtek and Motowidlo 2002). This can be detrimental for organizations as innovation not only requires discovering more effective practices but also cross-validation testing and codification of the new practices so they can be implemented elsewhere in the organization. Standard practices are supposed to prescribe effective strategies—and this is thwarted if these processes are never incorporated into collective memory (Eisenhardt and Tabrizi 1995; Weick, Sutcliffe, and Obstfeld 1999).

Organizational theories also lend support to this analysis of process and outcome accountability. As noted before, pressures to adopt "sound" processes under process accountability can cause people to seek out the most easily defensible procedures—as standard practices offer political cover that allows agents to claim competence, rationality, and legitimacy, with minimal risk of pushback (Langley 1989; Pfeffer 1981; Schlenker 1980; Tedeschi 1981). After all, these practices represent "how we do things here," offering political cover to agents seeking to assure evaluators that due diligence was exercised. Coping reduces to conformity in which people merely shift their views in accord with those of their evaluators (Tetlock 1983; Tetlock et al. 1989). Moreover, conformity confers political cover, regardless of whether the chosen processes yield negative or positive outcomes (Feldman and March 1981). When negative outcomes flow from deficient processes, the defense is that everything was done "by the book" ("my hands were tied") or that the use of procedures was a sign of one's commitment to the institution (Berger and Luckmann 1966; Scott 2008).

Agency theories in micro-economics also highlight the potential pitfalls of outcome accountability (Eisenhardt 1989). Outcome-based contracting transfers risk to the agent, which can be problematic when outcomes are only partly a function of the agents' behaviors and can be affected by exogenous factors—and the agent is rewarded or penalized for outcomes partly outside his or her control (Demski and Feltham 1978; Harris and Raviv 1979; Shavell 1979). Agents may then resort to various forms of corner-cutting and shirking (Baker, Gibbons, and Murphy 2002). Again, the conclusion is similar: outcome accountability can reduce attention to "how" questions, which means that, even if outcome accountability stimulates innovation, it will be hard to reproduce the success as long as the inattention to process prevents us from learning which processes should be replaced and which implemented to increase overall effectiveness (Douglas and Judge 2001).

The result is a design dilemma: implement process accountability to minimize variance in decision-making and increase reliability (ensuring some control over how decisions are made), but run the risk of prolonged reliance on deficient practices with little regard for outcomes, or implement outcome accountability to encourage attention to actual outcomes (ensuring some innovation and flexibility), but run the risk of encouraging gaming of poorly understood metrics.

The best path forward would appear to be some form of compromise—movement toward various hybrid systems that blend features of process and outcome accountability as appropriate to each new context. Indeed, many hybrids of process and outcome accountability do exist—such as RAROC (risk-adjusted return on capital) guidelines that place constraints on the risks that investment decision makers are allowed to make to mitigate excessive risk-taking, but also incentivize maximizing returns within those guidelines (Tetlock and Mellers 2011b).

Unfortunately, designing viable hybrid models is easier said than done. Hybrid models often go astray—bringing out the worst rather than the best consequences of process and outcome accountability. For example, consistent with work on social dilemmas (Komorita and Barth 1985) and on goal conflict (Locke, Smith, Erez, Chah, and Schaffer 1994), research on hybrid individual vs. collective rewards in teamwork shows that members cope with contradictory pressures to maximize personal vs. group interests by concentrating on one goal (at the expense of the other), thus undermining performance (Quigley, Tesluk, Locke, and Bortol 2007; Sniezek, May, and Sawyer 1990; Wageman 1995). Competing goals also have the potential to produce "analysis-paralysis" (Ethiraj and Levinthal 2009).

Some trade-offs are inevitable here but we suspect that the hypothesized adverse effects of both process and outcome accountability can often be contained by designing accountability systems that "empower" agents. Specifically, agents who feel empowered under process accountability are likely to resist conformity to deficient standard practices as well as attend to outcomes whereas those who feel empowered under outcome accountability are likely to attend to processes as well as outcomes, thereby facilitating organizational learning.

The key to "empowering" agents lies in the micro details of the symbolic interactions between principals and agents—and the meanings that participants assign to their relationships within the accountability system. Principals are concerned with establishing the legitimacy of their authority and agents with evaluating the legitimacy of that authority. Given that principals cannot always monitor agents, it is in their best interests to communicate to agents that they are legitimate and fair, in order to encourage norm internalization (Tyler 1997). And given that agents who enter authority relationships are vulnerable to both exploitation (with attendant loss of outcomes) and exclusion (with attendant loss of social identity) (Lind 2001), it is in their best interests to be sensitive to the micro-signals that authorities intentionally or unintentionally communicate about how they see the agents and why they feel the agents need to be held accountable in certain ways rather than others.

Factors that Empower Agents through Process and Outcome Accountability

Psychological empowerment is theoretically an additive function of four factors that reflect an individual's active (as opposed to passive) orientation to his or her work: meaning, competence, self-determination, and impact (Spreitzer 1995; 1996). According to Spreitzer, meaning involves the fit between the requirements of a person's work role and his or her beliefs and values (Hackman and Oldham 1980), competence refers to confidence in one's capability to perform work activities (Wood and Bandura 1989), self-determination involves a sense of personal control and autonomy in initiating and directing one's actions (Deci, Connell, and Ryan 1989), and impact is the degree to which a person can influence key organizational outcomes and beneficiaries (Ashforth 1989). These four factors of empowerment have been shown to increase innovation and initiative (Spreitzer 1995).

This analysis meshes with our concern for balancing control and innovation through process and outcome accountability. To reiterate, our goal is to explain how relational factors can compensate for the deficiencies in each accountability system—that is, prevent continued conformity to inadequate decision practices under process accountability and prevent codification of processes under outcome accountability. In explicit conditions of process accountability, empowerment is hypothesized to induce an implicit sense of outcome accountability; conversely, in explicit conditions of outcome accountability, empowerment is hypothesized to induce an implicit sense of process accountability.

Meaning and Impact

To empower agents via process accountability, agents need to see the system as providing meaningful opportunities to improve the welfare of others by adopting sound practices that yield better decisions (Hackman and Oldham 1976). Agents then feel their own actions will make a difference for others, increasing the sense of having a prosocial impact (Grant 2007; Grant et al. 2007). A loss in meaning and sense of impact can cause an agent simply to conform to inadequate processes as the only end in sight. This may be especially likely when a decision maker perceives that he or she is being held accountable for processes only as a means for an organization to meet external regulatory demands or as a way to keep order.

Principals can increase the meaning of the accountability system and the agent's perceived impact by communicating cues that induce a psychological connection between the decision processes he or she must justify and end-state goals involving the well-being of identifiable beneficiaries—for example, standard medical procedures are linked to benefitting patients, decision criteria for making intelligence forecasts are linked to benefitting national security, procedures for air traffic control are linked to passenger safety. Research demonstrates that perceptions of task significance can be enhanced by frequently communicating how jobs can make a difference to the lives of others (Grant 2008), suggesting that continuous messaging about how decision processes enhance the welfare of beneficiaries can imbue otherwise arbitrary rules with significance.

By contrast, outcome accountability already focuses agents on end-state outcomes so the challenge is instilling a sense of meaning and impact around the importance of "process" for long-term organizational effectiveness. Inattention to decision processes under outcome accountability is exacerbated when decision makers find little or no meaning in the decision processes themselves. However such inattention can be curbed when agents see the processes as benefitting the organization, in essence, creating a mental link between process and outcome.

Self-Determination and Competence

Accountability and self-determination may seem inherently at odds, but theories of organizational justice suggest otherwise. When principals act in a procedurally fair manner towards agents, agents may experience substantial autonomy even though embedded in a complex accountability system of normative constraints.

Process accountability can enhance procedural justice when principals adopt more egalitarian-adversarial (as opposed to hierarchical-inquisitorial) approaches to resolving disputes over who should be responsible for what. Adversarial models stress the importance of "voice," of convincing all parties that they have equal opportunities to present their perspectives. People tend to believe that after an authority has provided opportunities for "voice" by soliciting their opinions, those opinions will be taken into consideration when determining the distribution of outcomes (Avery and Quiñones 2002; Greenberg 2000; Tyler 1987). Given this well-established empirical result, the opportunity for "voice" inherent in more adversarial models of justice should provide agents with a sense of autonomy in determining which procedures to adopt in decision-making, as they will have the chance to defend their actions to a receptive audience. This sense of self-determination can give decision makers the confidence necessary to abandon inadequate decision practices in favor of more effective ones because they believe their accounts will be given a fair hearing.

Self-determination and autonomy can also be enhanced under outcome accountability when principals adopt more egalitarian-adversarial approaches to managing agents. The opportunity for "voice" may provide agents with a sense of freedom to deviate from optimizing outcomes when doing so would require processes that violate other organizational norms and values. This greater sense of freedom is rooted in the sense that they will have an opportunity to explain the reasons behind their deviations—and their accounts will be taken seriously.

Principals can also instill a sense of competence in agents by conveying respect when implementing process and outcome accountability systems. Giving respect signals that agents are valued, high status members in the organization (Tyler and Smith 1997; 1998; Tyler, Degoey, and Smith 1996), increasing the self-efficacy they feel in conducting their tasks and coping with accountability demands. Respect can be signaled through process accountability by emphasizing that the organization sees employee potential in providing feedback for quality improvement initiatives, and that the organization encourages employees to monitor which processes do or do not lead to desired outcomes (thereby signaling employee competence in making meaningful contributions). Respect can be signaled through outcome accountability by emphasizing that the organization is confident in the skills and ingenuity of employees to obtain outcomes and that it is decreasing the monitoring of processes so as to allow for autonomy and flexibility.

Perceptions of competence enhanced through respect have the potential to encourage agents to abandon deficient standard practices. Some scholars have argued that respect makes the individual characteristics of the receiver salient (Blader and Tyler 2009; Smith and Tyler 1997), suggesting that respected people are more likely to "stand up" by engaging in riskier behavior such as dissent (Grant and Patil 2012; Packer 2008). Possible explanations include: (a) higher status increases perceptions that dissent will lead to rewards (Hirschman 1970; Sherif and Sherif 1967); (b) higher status decreases the threat of penalties for dissent (Hollander 1958; Kelley and Shapiro 1954; Phillips and Zuckerman 2001).

Respect, by increasing feelings of competence, can also encourage attention to "how one thinks" and decrease reliance on intuition (incommunicable private knowledge) under outcome accountability. Respect from organizational authorities has been linked to increased social identification (Simon and Stürmer 2003; Spears, Ellemers, Doosje, and Branscombe 2006), in which employees feel part of the group (Tajfel and Turner 1986) and work toward achieving organizational goals (Tyler and Blader 2000). These findings suggest that employees who feel respected and competent under outcome accountability are more likely to attend to decision processes if they believe doing so will promote organizational goals of control.

CONCLUDING REMARKS

Accountability is often defined as the answer to the question "who must answer to whom, for what, under whose ground rules?" (Tetlock 1985). Our analysis adds the "why?" question: "why do people believe they are accountable?" It matters whether people think the answer is "because we lack confidence in your integrity or competence" or "because we want to help you achieve objectives we all share." Exploring the social-identity signals conveyed by different types of accountability can help us achieve a deeper understanding of the complicated patchwork quilt of laboratory results on accountability and the often acrimonious debates that arise in the real world over how best to design accountability systems. And understanding the messages that their accountability systems send to employees can help managers cope more effectively with the classic trade-off between control and innovation. Although the trade-off will never disappear, managers should be able to push out the Pareto frontier for trade-offs between control and innovation and get more of the best of both worlds, to the degree they design accountability systems that send "empowering" messages to employees, messages of the form: the work we do together is meaningful; we value your contributions to the collective effort; we take your point of view seriously; and we plan to continue working together to achieve shared goals in a mutually respectful fashion.

REFERENCES

Adelberg, S. and Batson, C. D. 1978. "Accountability and Helping: When Needs Exceed Resources." *Journal of Personality and Social Psychology*, 36: 343–50.

Amabile, T. 1979. "Effects of External Evaluation on Artistic Creativity." *Journal of Personality and Social Psychology*, 37: 221–33.

Anderson, E. and Oliver, R. L. 1987. "Perspectives on Behavior-Based Verus Outcome-Based Salesforce Control Systems." *Journal of Marketing*, 51: 76–88.

Arkes, H. R., Christensen, C., Lai, C., and Blumer, C. 1987. "Two Methods of Reducing Overconfidence." *Organizational Behavior and Human Decision Processes*, 39: 133–44.

Arkes, H. R., Dawes, R. M., and Christensen, C. 1986. "Factors Influencing the Use of a Decision Rule in a Probabilistic Task." *Organizational Behavior and Human Decision Processes*, 37: 93–110.

Arthur, J. B. 1994. "Effects of Human Resource Systems on Manufacturing Performance and Turnover." *Academy of Management Journal*, 37: 670–87.

Ashforth, B. E. 1989. "The Experience of Powerlessness in Organizations." *Organizational Behavior and Human Decision Processes*, 43: 207–42.

Ashton, R. H. 1992. "Effects of Justification and a Mechanical Aid On Judgment Performance." *Organizational Behavior and Human Decision Processes*, 52: 292–306.

Avery, D. R. and Quiñones, M. A. 2002. "Disentangling the Effects of Voice: The Incremental Roles of Opportunity, Behavior, and Instrumentality in Predicting Procedural Fairness." *Journal of Applied Psychology*, 87: 81–6.

Baker, G., Gibbons, R., and Murphy, K. J. 2002. "Relational Contracts and the Theory of the Firm." *Quarterly Journal of Economics*, 117: 39–84.

Beach, L. R. and Mitchell, T. R. 1978. "A Contingency Model for the Selection of Decision Strategies." *Academy of Management Review*, 3: 439–49.

Berger, P. and Luckmann, T. 1966. *The Social Construction of Reality: A Treatise in the Sociology of Knowledge*. Garden City, NY: Anchor Books.

Bertrand, M. and Mullainathan, S. 2001. "Do People Mean What They Say? Implications for Subjective Survey Data." *The American Economic Review*, 91: 67–72.

Blader, S. L. and Tyler, T. R. 2009. "Testing and Extending the Group Engagement Model: Linkages Between Social Identity, Procedural Justice, Economic Outcomes, and Extrarole Behavior." *Journal of Applied Psychology*, 94: 445–64.

Brtek, M. D. and Motowidlo, S. J. 2002. "Effects of Procedure and Outcome Accountability on Interview Validity." *Journal of Applied Psychology*, 87: 185–91.

Chubb, J. E. and Moe, T. M. 1988. "Politics, Markets, and the Organization of Schools." *The American Political Science Review*, 82: 1066–87.

Cohen, J. R., Krishnamoorthy, G., Peytcheva, M., and Wright, A. 2011. Will Regulatory Enforcement and Principles-Based Accounting Influence Auditors' Ethical Judgments to Constrain Aggressive Reporting? Working paper, available at SSRN: <http://ssrn.com/abstract=1817684>.

Coyne, W. 1997. *Innovation: Breakthrough Thinking at 3M, Du Pont, GE, Pfizer, and Rubbermaid*, eds. R. Kanter, J. Kao and F. Wiersema. New York: Harper Business.

Cravens, D. W., Ingram, T. N., LaForge, R. W., and Young, C. E. 1993. "Behavior-Based and Outcome-Based Salesforce Control Systems." *Journal of Marketing*, 57: 47–59.

Crozier, M. 1964. *The Bureaucratic Phenomenon*. Chicago: University of Chicago Press.

Curley, S., Yates, J. and Abrams, R. 1986. "Psychological Sources of Ambiguity Avoidance." *Organizational Behavior and Human Decision Processes*, 38: 230–56.

Dean, J. W. and Sharfman, M. P. 1993. "Procedural Rationality in the Strategic Decision-Making Process." *Journal of Management Studies*, 30: 587–610.

Deci, E. L., Connell, J. P. and Ryan, R. M. 1989. "Self-Determination in a Work Organization." *Journal of Applied Psychology*, 74: 580–90.

Demski, J. S. and Feltham, G. A. 1978. "Economic Incentives in Budgetary Control Systems." *Accounting Review*, 53: 336–59.

Detert, J. R., Schroeder, R. G., and Mauriel, J. J. 2000. "A Framework for Linking Culture and Improvement Initiatives in Organizations." *Academy of Management Review*, 25: 850–63.

DiMaggio, P. and Powell, W. 1983. "The Iron Cage Revisited. Institutional Isomorphism and Collective Rationality in Organizational Fields." *American Sociological Review*, 48: 147–60.

Doney, P. M. and Armstrong, G. M. 1996. "Effects of Accountability on Symbolic Information Search and Information Analysis by Organizational Buyers." *Journal of the Academy of Marketing Science*, 24: 57–65.

Douglas, T. J. and Judge, W. Q. 2001. "Total Quality Management Implementation and Competitive Advantage: The Role of Structural Control and Exploration." *Academy of Management Journal*, 44: 158–69.

Dreu, C. K. W. de, Beersma, B., Stroebe, K., and Euwema, M. C. 2006. "Motivated Information Processing, Strategic Choice, and the Quality of Negotiated Agreement." *Journal of Personality and Social Psychology*, 90: 927–43.

Dreu, C. K. W. de, Koole, S. L., and Steinel, W. 2000. "Unfixing the Fixed Pie: A Motivated Information-Processing Approach to Integrative Negotiation." *Journal of Personality and Social Psychology*, 79: 975–87.

Edelman, M. J. 1985. *The Symbolic Uses of Politics*. Urbana: University of Illinois Press.

Eisenhardt, K. M. 1985. "Control: Organizational and Economic Approaches." *Management Science*, 31: 134–49.

Eisenhardt, K. M. 1989. "Agency Theory: An Assessment and Review." *Academy of Management Review*, 14: 57–74.

Eisenhardt, K. M. and Tabrizi, B. N. 1995. "Accelerating Adaptive Processes. Product Innovation in the Global Computer Industry." *Administrative Science Quarterly*, 40: 84–110.

Enzle, M. E. and Anderson, S. C. 1993. "Surveillant Intentions and Intrinsic Motivation." *Journal of Personality and Social Psychology*, 64: 257–66.

Ethiraj, S. K. and Levinthal, D. 2009. "Hoping for A to Z While Rewarding Only A. Complex Organizations and Multiple Goals." *Organization Science*, 20: 4–21.

Fama, E. F. and Jensen, M. C. 1986. Separation of Ownership and Control, pp. 276–98 in *Organizational economics*, eds. J. Barney and W. Ouchi. San Francisco: Jossey-Bass.

Fandt, P. M. and Ferris, G. R. 1990. "The Management of Information and Impressions: When Employees Behave Opportunistically." *Organizational Behavior and Human Decision Processes*, 45: 140–58.

Feldman, M. S. and March, J. G. 1981. "Information in Organizations as Signal and Symbol." *Administrative Science Quarterly*, 26: 171–86.

Ford, J. K. and Weldon, E. 1981. "Forewarning and Accountability." *Personality and Social Psychology Bulletin*, 7: 264–68.

Friedman, R. S., Fishbach, A., Förster, J., and Werth, L. 2003. "Attentional Priming Effects on Creativity." *Creativity Research Journal*, 15: 277–86.

Friedman, R. S. and Förster, J. 2001. "The Effects of Promotion and Prevention Cues on Creativity." *Journal of Personality and Social Psychology*, 81: 1001–13.

Grant, A. M. 2007. "Relational Job Design and the Motivation to Make a Prosocial Difference." *Academy of Management Review*, 32: 393–417.

Grant, A. M. 2008. "The Significance of Task Significance: Job Performance Effects, Relational Mechanisms, and Boundary Conditions." *Journal of Applied Psychology*, 93: 108–24.

Grant, A. M., Campbell, E., Chen, G., Cottone, K., Lapedis, D., and Lee, K. 2007. "Impact and the Art of Motivation Maintenance: The Effects of Contact with Beneficiaries on Persistence Behavior." *Organizational Behavior and Human Decision Processes*, 103: 53–67.

Grant, A. M. and Patil, S. V. 2012. "Challenging the Norm of Self-Interest: Minority Influence and Transitions to Helping Norms in Work Units." *Academy of Management Review*, 37: 547–68.

Greenberg, J. 2000. Promote Procedural Justice to Enhance Acceptance of Work Outcomes. *Handbook of Principles of Organizational Behavior*, ed. E. Locke. Malden, MA: Blackwell Publishing.

Hackman, J. R. and Oldham, G. R. 1976. "Motivation Through the Design of Work: Test of a Theory." *Organizational Behavior and Human Performance*, 16: 250–79.

Hackman, J. R. and Oldham, G. R. 1980. *Work Redesign*. Reading, MA: Addison-Wesley.

Hackman, J. R. and Wageman, R. 1995. "Total Quality Management: Empirical, Conceptual, and Practical Issues." *Administrative Science Quarterly*, 40: 309–42.

Hagafors, R. and Brehmer, B. 1983." Does Having to Justify One's Judgments Change the Nature of the Judgment Process?" *Organizational Behavior and Human Process*, 31: 223–32.

Hammer, M. and Stanton, S. 1999. "How Process Enterprises Really Work." *Harvard Business Review*, 77: 108–18.

Hammond, K. 1995. *Human Judgment and Social Policy: Irreducible Uncertainty, Inevitable Error, Unavoidable Injustice*. New York: Oxford University Press.

Harris, M. and Raviv, A. 1979. "Optimal Incentive Contracts with Imperfect Information." *Journal of Economic Theory*, 20: 231–59.

Higgins, E. T. 1997. "Beyond Pleasure and Pain." *American Psychologist*, 52: 1280–1300.

Higgins, E. T. 1998. "Promotion and Prevention: Regulatory Focus as a Motivational Principle." *Advances in Experimental Social Psychology*, 30: 1–46.

Hirschman, A. O. 1970. *Exit, Voice, and Loyalty: Responses to Decline in Firms, Organizations, and States*. Cambridge, MA: Harvard University Press.

Hollander, E. 1958. "Conformity, Status, and Idiosyncracy Credit." *Psychological Review*, 65: 117–27.

Jaworski, B. 1988. "Toward a Theory of Marketing Control: Environmental Context, Control Types, and Consequences." *Journal of Marketing*, 52: 23–39.

Kelley, H. H. and Shapiro, M. M. 1954. "An Experiment on Conformity to Group Norms Where Conformity is Detrimental to Group Achievement." *American Sociological Review*, 19: 667–77.

Kirsch, L. 1996. "The Management of Complex Tasks in Organizations: Controlling the Systems Development Process." *Organization Science*, 7: 1–21.

Klimoski, R. J. 1972. "The Effects of Intragroup Forces on Intergroup Conflict Resolution." *Organizational Behavior and Human Performance*, 8: 363–83.

Komorita, S. S. and Barth, J. M. 1985. "Components of Reward in Social Dilemmas." *Journal of Personality and Social Psychology*, 48: 364–73.

Langhe, B. de, Osselaer, S. M. J. van, and Wierenga, B. 2011. "The Effects of Process and Outcome Accountability on Judgment Process and Performance." *Organizational Behavior and Human Decision Processes*, 115: 238–52.

Langley, A. 1989. "In Search of Rationality: The Purposes Behind the Use of Formal Analysis in Organizations." *Administrative Science Quarterly*, 34: 598–631.

Lerner, J. S. and Tetlock, P. E. 1999. "Accounting for the Effects of Accountability." *Psychological Bulletin*, 125: 255–75.

Levinthal, D. A. and March, J. G. 1993. "The Myopia of Learning." *Strategic Management Journal*, 14: 95–112.

Levitt, B. and March, J. G. 1988. "Organizational Learning." *Annual Review of Sociology*, 14: 319–40.

Liberman, N., Idson, L. C., Camacho, C. J., and Higgins, E. T. 1999. "Promotion and Prevention Choices Between Stability and Change." *Journal of Personality and Social Psychology*, 77: 1135–45.

Liberman, N., Molden, D. C., Idson, L. C., and Higgins, E. T. 2001. "Promotion and Prevention Focus on Alternative Hypotheses: Implications for Attributional Functions." *Journal of Personality and Social Psychology*, 80: 5–18.

Liberman, N. and Trope, Y. 1998. "The Role of Feasibility and Desirability Considerations in Near and Distant Future Decisions: A Test of Temporal Construal Theory." *Journal of Personality and Social Psychology*, 75: 5–18.

Lind, E. A. 2001. "Fairness Heuristic Theory: Justice Judgments as Pivotal Cognitions in Organizational Relations." *Advances in Organizational Justice*, 56–88.

Locke, E. A., Smith, K., Erez, M., Chah, D., and Schaffer, A. 1994. "The Effects of Intra-Individual Goal Conflict on Performance." *Journal of Management*, 20: 67–91.

Maanen, S. van and Schein, E. 1979. Toward a Theory of Organizational Socialization, pp. 209–64 in *Research in Organizational Behavior*, eds. A. Brief and B. Staw. Stamford: JAI Press.

Malhotra, D. and Murnighan, J. K. 2002. "The Effects of Contracts on Interpersonal Trust." *Administrative Science Quarterly*, 47: 534–59.

March, J. G. 1991. "Exploration and Exploitation in Organizational Learning." *Organization Science*, 2: 71–87.

McAllister, D. W., Mitchell, T. R., and Beach, L. R. 1979. "The Contingency Model for the Selection of Decision Strategies: An Empirical Test of the Effects of Significance, Accountability, and Reversibility." *Organizational Behavior and Human Performance*, 24: 228–44.

Merchant, K. A. 1988. "Progressing Toward a Theory of Marketing Control: A Comment." *Journal of Marketing*, 52: 40–4.

Meyer, J. W. and Rowan, B. 1977. "Institutionalized Organizations: Formal Structure as Myth and Ceremony." *American Journal of Sociology*, 83: 340–63.

Mintzberg, H. 1978. "Patterns in Strategy Formation." *Management Science*, 24: 934–48.

Organ, D. W. 1988. *Organizational Citizenship Behavior: The Good Soldier Syndrome*. Lexington, MA: Lexington.

Packer, D. J. 2008. "On Being Both With Us and Against Us: A Normative Conflict Model of Dissent in Social Groups." *Personality and Social Psychology Review*, 12: 50–72.

Pettigrew, A. 1973. *The Politics of Organizational Decision Making*. London: Tavistock.

Pfeffer, J. 1981. Management as Symbolic Action: The Creation and Maintenance of Organizational Paradigms, pp. 1–52 in *Research in Organizational Behavior*, eds. L. Cummings and B. Shaw. Greenwich, CT: JAI Press.

Phillips, D. and Zuckerman, E. 2001. "Middle-Status Conformity: Theoretical Restatement and Empirical Demonstration in Two Markets." *American Journal of Sociology*, 107: 379–429.

Quigley, N., Tesluk, P., Locke, E. A., and Bortol, K. 2007. "A Multilevel Investigation of the Motivational Mechanisms Underlying Knowledge Sharing and Performance." *Organization Science*, 18: 71–88.

Rozelle, R. M. and Baxter, J. C. 1981. "Influence of Role Pressures on the Perceiver: Judgments of Videotaped Interviews Varying Judge Accountability and Responsibility." *Journal of Applied Psychology*, 66: 437–41.

Rubin, H. R., Pronovost, P., and Diette, G. B. 2001. "The Advantages and Disadvantages of Process Based Measures of Health Care Quality." *International Journal for Quality in Health Care*, 13: 489–96.

Schlenker, B. R. 1980. *Impression Management: The Self-Concept, Social Identity, and Interpersonal Relations*. Monterey, CA: Brooks/Cole Publishing Company.

Schoorman, F. D., Mayer, R. C., and Davis, J. H. 2007. "An Integrative Model of Organizational Trust: Past, Present, and Future." *Academy of Management Review*, 32: 344–54.

Scott, W. 2008. *Institutions and Organizations: Ideas and Interests*. Third edition. Los Angeles: Sage Publications.

Shavell, S. 1979. "Risk Sharing and Incentives in the Principal and Agent Relationship." *The Bell Journal of Economics*, 10: 55–73.

Shea, C. M. and Howell, J. M. 1998. "Organizational Antecedents to the Successful Implementation of Total Quality Management: A Social Cognitive Perspective." *Journal of Quality Management*, 3: 3–24.

Sherif, M. and Sherif, C. 1967. Conformity-Deviation, Norms, and Group Relations, pp. 164–89 in *Social Interaction*, ed. M. Sherif. Chicago: Aldine.

Siegel-Jacobs, K. and Yates, J. F. 1996. "Effects of Procedural and Outcome Accountability on Judgment Quality." *Organizational Behavior and Human Decision Processes*, 65: 1–17.

Simon, B. and Stürmer, S. 2003. "Respect for Group Members: Intragroup Determinants of Collective Identification and Group-Serving Behavior." *Personality and Social Psychology Bulletin*, 29: 183–93.

Simons, R. 2005. *Levers of Organization Design: How Managers Use Accountability Systems for Greater Performance and Commitment*. Boston, MA: Harvard Business School Press.

Simonson, I. and Nye, P. 1992. "The Effect of Accountability on Susceptibility to Decision Errors." *Organizational Behavior and Human Decision Processes*, 51: 416–46.

Simonson, I. and Staw, B. M. 1992. "Deescalation Strategies: A Comparison of Techniques for Reducing Commitment to Losing Courses of Action." *Journal of Applied Psychology*, 77: 419–26.

Sitkin, S. B., Sutcliffe, K. M., and Schroeder, R. G. 1994. "Distinguishing Control from Learning in Total Quality Management: A Contingency Perspective." *Academy of Management Review*, 19: 537–64.

Slaughter, J. E., Bagger, J., and Li, A. 2006. "Context Effects on Group-Based Employee Selection Decisions." *Organizational Behavior and Human Decision Processes*, 100: 47–59.

Smith, H. and Tyler, T. 1997. "Choosing the Right Pond: The Impact of Group Membership on Self-Esteem and Group-Oriented Behavior." *Journal of Experimental Social Psychology*, 33: 146–70.

Sniezek, J., May, D., and Sawyer, J. 1990. "Social Uncertainty and Interdependence: A Study of Resource-Allocation Decisions in Groups." *Organizational Behavior and Human Decision Processes*, 46: 155–80.

Spears, R., Ellemers, N., Doosje, B., and Branscombe, N. 2006. The Individual Within the Group: Respect!, pp. 175–95 in *Individuality and the Group: Advances in Social Identity*, eds. T. Postmes and J. Jetten. Thousand Oaks, CA: Sage Publications.

Spreitzer, G. M. 1995. "Psychological Empowerment in the Workplace: Dimensions, Measurement, and Validation." *Academy of Management Journal*, 38: 1442–65.

Spreitzer, G. M. 1996. "Social Structural Characteristics of Psychological Empowerment." *Academy of Management Journal*, 39: 483–504.

Starbuck, W. 1983. "Organizations as Action Generators." *American Sociological Review*, 48: 91–102.

Sutcliffe, K. M. and McNamara, G. 2001. "Controlling Decision-Making Practice in Organizations." *Organization Science*, 12: 484–501.

Sutton, R. and Galunic, D. 1996. Consequences of Public Scrutiny for Leaders and Their Organizations, pp. 201–50 in *Research in Organizational Behavior*, eds. B. Staw and L. Cummings. Greenwich, CT: JAI Press.

Tajfel, H. and Turner, J. C. 1986. The Social Identity Theory of Intergroup Behavior, pp. 7–24 in *Psychology of Intergroup Relations*, eds. S. Worchel and W. G. Austin. Chicago: Nelson Hall.

Tedeschi, J. T. 1981. *Impression Management Theory and Social Psychological Research*. New York: Academic Press.

Tetlock, P. E. 1983. "Accountability and Complexity of Thought." *Journal of Personality and Social Psychology*, 45: 74–83.

Tetlock, P. E. 1984. "Cognitive Style and Political Belief Systems in the British House of Commons." *Journal of Personality and Social Psychology*, 46: 365–75.

Tetlock, P. E. 1985. Accountability: The Neglected Social Context of Judgment and Choice, pp. 297–332 in *Research in Organizational Behavior*, eds. A. Brief and B. Staw. Stamford: JAI Press.

Tetlock, P. E. and Boettger, R. 1989. "Accountability: A Social Magnifier of the Dilution Effect." *Journal of Personality and Social Psychology*, 57: 388–98.

Tetlock, P. E. and Kim, J. I. 1987. "Accountability and Judgment Processes in a Personality Prediction Task." *Journal of Personality and Social Psychology*, 52: 700–9.

Tetlock, P. E. and Mellers, B. A. 2011a. "Intelligent Management of Intelligence Agencies: Beyond Accountability Ping-Pong." *American Psychologist*, 66: 542–52.

Tetlock, P. E. and Mellers, B. A. 2011b. Structuring Accountability Systems in Organizations: Key Trade-Offs and Critical Unknowns, pp. 249–70 in *Intelligence Analysis: Behavioral and Social Scientific Foundations*, eds. B. Fischhoff and C. Chauvin. Washington, DC: National Academies Press.

Tetlock, P. E., Skitka, L. and Boettger, R. 1989. "Social and Cognitive Strategies for Coping With Accountability. Conformity, Complexity, and Bolstering." *Journal of Personality and Social Psychology*, 57: 632–40.

Tetlock, P. E., Vieider, F., Patil, S. V., and Grant, A. M. 2013. "Ideology, Agency, and Accountability: Explaining Shifting Managerial Preferences for Alternative Accountability Regimes.". *Organizational Behavior and Human Decision Processes*, 122: 22-35.

Trope, Y. and Liberman, N. 2003. "Temporal Construal." *Psychological Review*, 110: 403–21.

Trope, Y. and Liberman, N. 2010. "Construal-Level Theory of Psychological Distance." *Psychological Review*, 117: 440–63.

Tushman, M. L. and Romanelli, E. 1985. "Organizational Evolution. A Metamorphosis Model of Convergence and Reorientation." *Research in Organizational Behavior*, 7: 171–222.

Tyler, T. 1997. "The Psychology of Legitimacy: A Relational Perspective on Voluntary Deference to Authorities." *Personality and Social Psychology Review*, 1: 323–45.

Tyler, T., Degoey, P., and Smith, H. 1996. "Understanding Why the Justice of Group Procedures Matters: A Test of the Psychological Dynamics of the Group-Value Model." *Journal of Personality and Social Psychology*, 70: 913–30.

Tyler, T. R. 1987. "Conditions Leading to Value-Expressive Effects in Judgments of Procedural Justice: A Test of Four Models." *Journal of Personality and Social Psychology*, 52: 333–44.

Tyler, T. R. and Blader, S. L. 2000. *Cooperation in Groups. Procedural Justice, Social Identity, and Behavioral Engagement*. Philadelphia: Psychology Press.

Tyler, T. R. and Smith, H. J. 1998. Social Justice and Social Movements, pp. 595–629 in *Handbook of Social Psychology*, eds. D. Gillbert, S. Fiske and G. Lindzey. New York: McGraw-Hill.

Vieider, F. and Tetlock, P. E. 2011. Accountability: A Meta-Analysis of Effect Sizes and Situated-Identity Analysis of Research Settings. Working paper.

Wageman, R. 1995. "Interdependence and Group Effectiveness." *Administrative Science Quarterly*, 40: 145–80.

Weick, K., Sutcliffe, K., and Obstfeld, D. 1999. Organizing for High Reliability. Processes of Collective Mindfulness, pp. 81–123 in *Research in Organizational Behavior*, eds. B. Staw and R. Sutton. Greenwich, CT: JAI.

Wilson, J. 1989. *Bureaucracy: What Government Agencies Do and Why*. New York: Basic Books.

Wood, R. and Bandura, A. 1989. "Social Cognitive Theory of Organizational Management." *Academy of Management Review*, 14: 361–84.

CHAPTER 6

ACCOUNTABILITY AND PRINCIPAL–AGENT THEORY

SEAN GAILMARD

CONCEPTUAL FLAVOR OF PRINCIPAL–AGENT THEORY

PUBLIC accountability is a function of the capabilities of principals to judge the performance of their agents (Achen and Bartels 2002; Healy and Malhotra 2010; Lenz 2012; Lupia and McCubbins 1998). But it is also in part a function of institutions themselves. To make sense of the relationship between accountability and institutional structure it is useful to make use of a theoretical framework that can express widely varying institutional details and express their consequences for accountability in commensurate terms. Principal–agent theory has become a widely used paradigm for analyzing public accountability. This is because it provides a flexible framework for modeling innumerable variations in institutional arrangements, and comparing their potential for inducing desirable behavior by agents.

Applications of principal–agent theory in the study of public accountability have become sufficiently common and widespread that it is hopeless to attempt a comprehensive review of the literature in so short a space, and this chapter will not attempt such a review. Instead it attempts to give a sense of the conceptual flavor of principal–agent analysis,[1] as well as insights gleaned from two of the original and still more common substantive areas of its application in political science—control of politicians through electoral institutions; and control of bureaucracies by legislative, executive, and/or judicial actors. Thus this chapter is organized as follows. We will first briefly review the basic structure and central tenets shared by principal–agent models. We will then proceed to discuss applications of principal-agent models to electoral politics, discuss insights gleaned from applications to bureaucratic accountability and end with a conclusion.

Principal–Agent Theory: An Overview

Analysis and evaluation of public accountability requires a specification of who is (or is supposed to be) accountable to whom. This is a core ingredient of principal–agent theory. In principal–agent models, some actor (or group of actors) called an agent undertakes an action on behalf of another actor (or group of actors) called a principal. The principal, for its part, can make decisions that affect the incentives of the agent to take any of its various possible actions.

This process of structuring incentives for the agent is the central focus of principal–agent theory. The decisions made by the principal that structure the agent's incentives to take various actions constitute a *contract*, in the language of principal–agent theory, and principal–agent theory is often taken as a specific area of contract theory more generally (Bolton and Dewatripont 2004).

Perhaps the most elemental point about principal–agent theory is that it is not in fact a single overarching theory with a specific set of assumptions or conclusions. Principal-agent theory is more accurately described as a family of formal models addressing related concerns with similar styles of analysis. It is not much of a stretch to suppose that for any given actors labeled "principal" and "agent," and any pattern of interaction between the two, a principal–agent model can be written down with that pattern as an equilibrium outcome—and modelers might consider it a parlor game of sorts to do it. Given that, one must be wary of claims to "test" principal–agent theory empirically in any broad sense. By the same token it is always possible to defend any status quo interaction between a "principal" and an "agent" as reflecting the greatest degree of accountability to which the agent can be held by the principal, given various informational asymmetries and commitment problems.

Specifying a member of the principal–agent family of models requires specifying (1) what the agent(s) can do and how this affects the principal(s), (2) what the principal(s) can do and how this affect the agent(s), and (3) who the principal(s) and the agent(s) are. In other words, principal–agent models specify a set of actors; possible actions they can take; and how they evaluate consequences of those actions. In this respect a principal–agent model is necessarily a game in the formal sense, and correspondingly, principal–agent models in contemporary literature are almost exclusively analyzed with the tools of noncooperative game theory.

While this chapter stresses the flexibility of principal–agent theory, this background suggests some of its limitations. First, it inherits the limitations of game theory as a tool for explaining behavior. Principal–agent analysis is also inappropriate for analyzing accountability of some actor to another, when the second is unaware of its dependence on the first and/or can do literally nothing to affect the behavior of the first. Finally, its very flexibility is also a sort of limitation. Within its domain of application there does not seem to be any pattern of behavior that a principal–agent model cannot explain. While any particular model in this family may have empirical content, it is not clear what content the family as a whole has.

A fundamental distinction in types of principal–agent models is between those dealing with moral hazard or hidden actions, and those dealing with adverse selection or hidden information. In moral hazard problems, the agent takes one of several possible actions that affect the principal's utility, the principal and agent have different preferences over the possible actions the agent can take, and the principal cannot directly control the agent's action. However, to make the problem interesting the principal observes some information affected by or correlated with the agent's action, and administers a reward or punishment (e.g., a bonus payment, re-election) based on that information.[2]

In adverse selection problems, the agent is privy to some information that the principal needs to make a decision in her own interest, but the agent prefers that the information be used differently. In pure adverse selection models, the principal may be able to specify costs the agent must incur to take various decisions, or even prohibit outright certain decisions by the agent or require a particular one. All of these types of direct control over the agent's action are unavailable in pure moral hazard models. In adverse selection, the problem for the principal is that it does not know how to use this control; it does not know which action to direct the agent to take.

Key to the analysis of both moral hazard and adverse selection problems is incentive compatibility. If the principal is unrestricted in the types of contracts it can offer the agent—e.g., in moral hazard, bonus pay for results that are correlated with the principal's preferred action—it is often possible for the principal to induce the agent to take the principal's own most preferred action. Incentive compatibility simply means that the principal must make it worth the agent's while to behave in this way. In general, incentive compatibility imposes constraints on the principal: the principal must trade-off the benefits of an improved decision from its own point of view, against the costs of inducing the agent to take that particular decision. If the agent also has an option to exit the relationship with the principal (an individual rationality or participation constraint), or if the agent's liability for poor performance is limited in some way, then in general incentive compatibility constraints imply that the principal will generally not induce the agent to pursue the principal's own most preferred course of action, even if the principal is able to do so in theory. The difference in the action the principal prefers to induce, given incentive compatibility (and participation) constraints, and the action the principal would take itself if it could (and had the information and capabilities of the agent) gives rise to agency loss. Principals must trade off agency loss against the cost of satisfying incentive compatibility. When these two costs to the principal are in direct conflict, as they typically are in principal-agent models, the principal generally does not wish to eliminate one cost at the expense of the other. Agency loss is what occurs when the agent gets a bit of extra slack from the principal to pursue its own interests rather than the principal's.

In general, then, principal–agent models suggest that agents need not in fact be perfect agents of their principals. Agency loss is not necessarily inevitable, in the sense that principals may (in some models) be able to eliminate it if they somehow prefer to do so. But even in these models, principals typically would find it prohibitively costly to eliminate agency loss completely, so they choose to tolerate some. Therefore, the mere existence of agency loss does not imply that accountability of the agent is suboptimal or defective from the principal's standpoint.

Electoral Agency

The plenary power of the state raises serious threats to the welfare of citizens. What is to prevent the political officials who hold the reins of state power from behaving opportunistically in policy making, elevating their own interests over those of voters? The promise of electoral democracy is that voters can hold political officials accountable for their policy choices, and thereby ensure a close connection between public will and public policy. Setting aside imperfections in voters themselves (their attentiveness, their rationality, etc.), are electoral institutions themselves up to this task? Even in a world of perfect voter attention and rationality, do electoral institutions themselves limit the accountability of policy to voters' interests?

This issue is exactly the one explored in principal–agent analyses of elections. Voters are the principal(s) and politicians are the agents.[3] One of the classics of the genre is due to Ferejohn (1986), who developed a pure moral hazard model of electoral accountability that taps into key concerns about elections as instruments of control.[4] The concern of political opportunism and mitigating agency loss with elections is inherently dynamic, so Ferejohn's model involves multiple periods—an infinite horizon to be exact. In Ferejohn's model an incumbent politician can exert effort on behalf of (homogenous, in the baseline case) citizens, who prefer more effort to less. But the value of effort changes randomly from one period to the next. This value is observed by the incumbent politician but not by the voters, who only observe their overall utility in each period. For politicians effort is costly but holding office has some value irrespective of how much effort the politician supplies. In equilibrium, voters use a simple retrospective voting rule: they reelect the incumbent for another period if their period t utility exceeds a specific threshold. But voters incur significant agency loss to politicians. If the value of effort is too small to voters, the incumbent shirks completely, knowing even very high effort will not be enough to put voters' utility over its retrospective threshold. If the value of effort to voters is large enough, politicians exert some effort but only the minimal amount necessary to be re-elected. This effort gets smaller when the value of effort gets larger, because the incumbent can work less hard and still satisfy the voters' retrospective threshold.

Of course, the magnitude of agency loss in any environment can only be judged relative to an alternative institutional arrangement. In an important paper, Persson, Roland,

and Tabellini (1997) show that separation of powers institutions combined with checks and balances, can mitigate the agency loss identified by Ferejohn. In essence, these authors argue, separation of powers when political actors have inherent preference conflicts (as between a legislature and executive) can lead to better information for voters about the possible value of policy making, and therefore allows voters to better tailor their voting threshold to the situation at hand. Persson, Roland, and Tabellini also show that these beneficial effects of separation of powers depend on checks and balances—in their case, political actors must come together for the purpose of determining policy.[5]

Until the last decade or so, principal–agent analyses of the electoral connection focused on the moral hazard dimension. The focus of this literature was on elections as instruments of control over politicians' behavior, given their preferences and capabilities. Banks and Sundaram (1993; 1998) initiated the formal analysis of elections with both moral hazard and adverse selection. In an influential essay, Fearon (1999) noted that elections not only provide an instrument with which to sanction wayward politicians, but also an instrument for selecting politicians with desirable traits or preferences in the first place.

At first blush, the possibility that elections can serve two purposes, sanctioning and selection, may suggest that, based on moral hazard models alone, they are more effective at mitigating agency problems than previously thought. However, this turns out not to be the case. Note that in the classic Ferejohn moral hazard model the voter has no trouble implementing the evaluation standard that most tightly constrains the politician. This is because the politician and her possible replacement are identical from the voter's standpoint—neither is better at generating favorable results than the other. If the voter were to learn that one of the pool of politicians had a more desirable "type" on the dimension of hidden information, and expected that "type" to generate better results in the future, then the voter would have no rational course of action but to select that type—regardless of their past performance. This is the case, for instance, in Canes-Wrone, Herron, and Shotts (2001). Though voters face both adverse selection (selecting competent politicians) and moral hazard problems (inducing the politician's choice of the voter's preferred policy), the adverse selection dimension trumps the moral hazard one in equilibrium. The key point of their model is that rational behavior by voters, combined with their information asymmetry and limited instruments of control over politicians, can lead to "pandering"—or the decision by politicians to neglect their own private information about socially desirable policies and pursue a course of action that the less-informed electorate considers beneficial.[6]

This is illustrative of a common theme in the electoral agency literature: demonstrating that perfectly rational behavior under the right (or wrong) constellation of information asymmetries and limitations on precommitment power can lead to specific kinds of agency loss. The focus of this sort of analysis is on electoral institutions themselves. Principal–agent models make the point that public accountability in electoral democracies is inherently limited, regardless of any imperfections voters may exhibit in their decision-making process.[7] This also illustrates a useful feature of the rationality postulate in principal–agent models, quite apart from its verisimilitude or lack thereof. It is useful to know the outer limits of public accountability that can be induced by elections, because this reveals that the limitations of voters can only be blamed so much for accountability pathologies in democracies.

BUREAUCRATIC AGENCY

One of the earliest, and still most robust, principal–agent literatures in political science takes bureaucrats as agents of some constellation of political principals—most often Congress, the president or executive actors, and/or courts. The 1970s saw profound scholarly disillusionment in Political Science, Law, and Economics with the bureaucratic policymaking apparatus created mostly since the Great Depression. In Political Science, scholars such as Theodore Lowi (1979) and Hugh Heclo (1977) argued that the bureaucratic institutions created by ostensibly well-meaning Congresses had become ungovernable, and that Congress had reached a point of abdicating its responsibilities to govern by creating one new bureaucracy after another while constraining them with little more than an directive to "Go forth and do good." Given this abdication, bureaucrats may or may not "do good" but they do so at best according to their own ideals and conception of what that means—not according to any vision that is guided by, or accountable to, Congress. Whatever doubts one may express about the democratic pedigree or legitimacy of the US Congress, it certainly occupies a seat closer to the governed than most bureaucratic policymakers do, and so this interpretation of bureaucratic architecture throws into doubt the public accountability of much of modern social and economic policy.

William Niskanen (1971) articulated similar concerns. Niskanen advanced several interrelated postulates in an economic model of bureaucratic service delivery: that bureaucrats seek to maximize their budgets; that bureaucrats know the value that legislators attach to the services they provide; that bureaucrats know more than those legislators about the cost of services they provide; and that bureaucrats essentially make "take it or leave it" budget offers to the legislature. The implication of this set of assumptions, Niskanen showed, is that bureaucrats extract rents from the legislature. Bureaucrats are willing to do so owing to the assumption about the bureaucrat's objective; they are able to do so because of the asymmetric information and proposal rights they enjoy (or are assumed to enjoy) over the legislature. Niskanen's model gave rise to a school of thought explaining the growth in government spending as well as the ostensible inefficiency of bureaucratic service provision. The implications for public accountability are obvious and serious: service delivery by specific bureaucracies, and government budgets as a whole, are not meaningfully held in check by Congress, and the actual government at the ground level is not accountable in any serious way to others than those making the decisions and spending the money.

The first wave of self-aware applications of principal–agent theory in the analysis of bureaucratic policy-making took issue with the inter-related concerns raised by

Lowi (1979), Heclo (1977), Niskanen (1971), and others. The common theme these scholars articulated is that the US Congress does not seem to be doing well by bureaucrats. The simple observation of Morris Fiorina (1979) was that it is difficult to square the assumption that Congress is good at minding its own interests (Mayhew 1974) with the argument that bureaucrats systematically undermine those interests. The reason is that, whatever the institutional arrangements by which bureaucrats interact with Congress, Congress designed them. It would be bizarre for Congress to actively design institutions that lead to the undermining of Congress's own interests, and yet that is what the disillusioned scholarship on bureaucracy through the 1970s seemed to suggest.

The germ of insight in Fiorina's argument stems directly from a principal–agent perspective on the situation. One should understand Congress as a principal and various bureaucrats as its agents. Therefore one should interpret bureaucratic institutions and legislative–bureaucratic interaction, inasmuch as these institutions and interactions are designed or affected by legislative principals, as promoting the interests of the principal to the greatest extent possible. This is the central premise of thought on bureaucratic institutions based on principal-agent theory. Left for debate are the precise meanings of the terms in that central premise—most conspicuously, what exactly Congress can do to design or affect bureaucratic institutions, and what exactly is the meaning of "to the greatest extent possible."

A simple but also stark illustration of this reasoning comes from a reinterpretation of a long-observed regularity in legislative–bureaucratic interaction in the US: that when agencies submit budget requests to the Office of Management and Budget in the Executive Office of the President, and the President in turn submits a budget proposal to Congress, Congress for its part often makes trivial modifications (or none at all) to the line items for particular agencies. Before the stream of principal-agent thought on the topic took hold in the literature this pattern could be interpreted as providing grounds for Niskanen's assumption that bureaucrats have nearly monopoly proposal power over budgets. After all, Congress often leaves the proposed amounts intact, and that is exactly what one would expect when an agenda setter has monopoly proposal rights and certain knowledge of the preferences of Congress (Romer and Rosenthal 1978). But it is also exactly what one would expect if bureaucrats are completely under the control of Congress and know that they cannot get away with budgeting one cent more than Congress wants them to spend—with full knowledge of the costs and benefits of their expenditures (Kiewiet and McCubbins 1991). Never mind that Congress often, in fact, does modify executive budget proposals; even the supposed stylized fact that it does not is entirely consistent with a principal-agent perspective on bureaucratic accountability.

The school of thought on bureaucratic accountability known as "Congressional dominance" takes principal–agent-inspired thought to its outermost possible reaches. This specific perspective is most closely associated with McCubbins, Noll, and Weingast (1987; 1989) (see also Weingast and Moran 1983), who elaborated an entire theory of administrative structure and procedure as a set of devices for Congress to mitigate its information asymmetries with respect to agencies and achieve the best possible outcomes in the bureaucratic policy process from its own point of view.[8] McCubbins, Noll, and Weingast offered a particularly insightful interpretation of the range of instruments available to Congress to influence choices made by bureaucratic agencies. For example, they pointed out that Congress can influence rights of standing with respect to the decisions of bureaucratic agencies (the right to sue agencies in court due to harms inflicted by their actions), as well as the jurisdiction of federal courts that review agency actions when they are sued (as they always are in important policy matters). In this way Congress can make it easier for favored interest groups to keep a close eye on and potentially help to rein in wayward agencies. In other words, Congress designs these administrative procedures not primarily out of concern with due process and such-like legal niceties, but rather out of a desire to mitigate agency loss due to moral hazard problems in the bureaucracy.

An important point about principal–agent perspectives on bureaucratic accountability, and one sometimes lost in translation from formal principal-agent models to the substantive issue of bureaucratic policymaking (cf. Moe 1987), is that nothing in these models implies that Congress "gets its way" in interactions with bureaucrats. Indeed, the ubiquity of agency loss in formal principal–agent models, as noted above, should be sufficient to indicate that this is not the case. In other words, principal–agent scholars of bureaucratic accountability must concede that in general some accountability of policy and administrative decisions to the interests of principals is lost in delegation. The formal concept of agency loss and the substantive concern of sacrificed accountability are inextricably linked.

The best case that can be made for delegation on principal–agent grounds is not that there is no compromise in accountability; it is that this compromise is better for the principal than the alternatives. This is perhaps best clarified in a canonical formal model of delegation due to Holmström (1984), and subsequently elaborated by Epstein and O'Halloran (1994; 1999), Gailmard (2002), Huber and Shipan (2002), Volden (2002), and Bendor and Meirowitz (2004). The agent is presumed to have some expertise the principal does not have, represented as information the principal needs to know to choose the best decision. And the principal and agent have different "ideologies," specifically different conceptions of the optimal result of the policy decision. The principal's instrument to influence the agent is to specify a set of policy decisions the agent is permitted to make, and allow the agent to pick freely from them. In the most basic variant of this model, once the agent so chooses, the game is over. When this model is represented formally as a game, its equilibrium involves the agent picking its own most preferred policy (the one that, given the agent's expert information, leads to its own most desired end result) whenever it is in the set of policies delegated by the principal. Since the principal and the agent, by assumption, have different ideal outcomes, this necessarily implies that the principal does not (ever, in equilibrium) obtain its most preferred outcome—but for at least some possible states of its information, the agent does.

Given this assumed information asymmetry and this device (controlling policy discretion) available to the principal to mitigate agency loss from that asymmetry, it is not possible for the principal to hold the agent accountable to the principal's goals better than the equilibrium specifies. If it were, then by assumption since the principal is assumed to be the best possible steward of its own interests, the "equilibrium" would not in fact be an equilibrium. Now the principal in this model certainly has the power to specify once and for all the decision the agent must make—it can restrict the agent to choose one particular policy. In this way the principal can attain complete control over the decision made by the agent. The principal does not (generally) behave this way in the equilibrium of the model, because it is counterproductive from the principal's own interests. Control per se over the agent is not the point; the point is for the principal to get as close as it can to its most preferred outcome, and by extension, to induce the agent to deploy its expertise as much as possible in the principal's interest. The principal sacrifices control because doing so gives the agent greater incentive to use its information—because by doing so the agent is allowed to pursue its own interest. The degree of accountability attained by the principal in equilibrium may not be the maximal degree of control possible in any circumstance, and if effort or information is sought from the agent, is always constrained by the agent's incentive compatibility conditions.

Policy discretion in the Holmström model is only one way for a principal to address its hidden information problem with respect to its agent. Another possible approach is for the principal simply to ask the agent for a direct report of its information, which the principal could then use itself in crafting policy. For instance, rather than delegating policy authority to a regulatory agency that is putatively an expert on the policy area in question, Congress might hold hearings in which it elicits this expertise, and writes statutes around it that are better tailored to Congress's own interests and ideological stance than are the regulations promulgated by agencies pursuant to their delegated policy discretion. Obviously, this would quickly become an unwieldy and impracticable approach: for Congress to ask the Environmental Protection Agency to report in a hearing everything it knows about mitigating the impact of water pollutants in rivers, and reflect that digested knowledge in a statute, would likely not be a fruitful exercise. Setting aside this eminently sensible point for a moment reveals an interesting aspect of the character of principal–agent models.

These two approaches to eliciting an agent's information, delegating policy discretion versus obtaining a direct report, can be directly and formally compared in terms of "how much" of the agent's information gets applied in policymaking, and the linkage between policy decisions and the principal's goals (the key point in analysis of accountability). This is the subject of an insightful paper by Dessein (2002) and elaborations and applications by Gailmard (2009) and Gailmard and Patty (2013). In particular, the principal is better off by simply delegating authority to the agent and completely relinquishing control over the decision (within the agent's range of discretion), than by requesting information from the agent and making a decision based on the report. The reason is that in the latter arrangement, the principal knows that she cannot fully trust the agent to be truthful for if she did, the agent would mislead her about the true state of the information so that the principal would act in the interests of the agent rather than the principal herself. But when the agent receives delegated authority from the principal, the agent can use all available information in pursuit of his own interests. So under the delegation arrangement more information gets applied to the improvement of the principal's (and the agent's) utility.

What's more, the exact same logic reveals that when delegation is used by a principal to elicit an agent's information, the principal may actually be better off if it cannot oversee or review the agent's decision in any way. For if the agent believes that the principal can revise its decision after the fact, the agent will not consider its decision to be an act of policy–making with any finality, but at best an advisory opinion that the principal may set aside. The principal may of course be interested in the agent's initial choice to the extent that it conveys information that the agent knows better than the principal. But then a game of delegation with revision by the principal devolves into nothing more than a game in which the agent sends a report of its information to the principal and the principal decides the actual policy accordingly. And we have already sketched the logic demonstrating that this arrangement is inferior from the principal's point of view than a (firm, irrevocable) delegation of policy authority to the agent.[9]

This toy example illustrates an important point about principal–agent models. Depending on the nature of the contracting environment, information asymmetries, and incentive problems facing the principal with respect to the agent, the optimal behavior of the principal may not comport with commonsense notions of exerting control. In the above example, oversight and review by the principal is counterproductive. This does not explain how an actual political principal would go about tying its hands to keep them off the decisions of a bureaucratic agent, but it does hint that in some situations it might want to tie its hands if it can. Therefore, to observe a principal limiting its own ability ostensibly to control an agent does not in itself suggest a challenge to principal-agent theory. A principal–agent model need only show that the putatively puzzling behavior of the principal is an equilibrium of some game to show that the principal is doing the best it can to guard its interests vis-à-vis the agent in the problem postulated in that model.

Situations in which agents must not only be induced to apply their information faithfully in the interests of the principal, but to acquire that information in the first place, are particularly ripe for this sort of twist. The reason is that if information is costly for agents to obtain, they must obtain some rents from information in order to be willing to invest in it. Apparently strange behavior by principals, such as conceding seemingly irrational degrees of autonomy over policy decisions that agents care about, can sometimes be interpreted as a de facto method for principals to guarantee that agents will obtain the necessary rents, and therefore make it worth the agent's while to invest in information (Gailmard and Patty 2007; 2013).

As is apparent by now, principal–agent theory is an extremely flexible theoretical framework (rather than a theory in and of itself) that is more about how one interprets observed interactions, than about predictions of specific patterns of interaction that may or may not occur. Recent work in political science has shown that principal–agent theory is even consistent with substantially less control of bureaucrats by political principals, and substantially less accountability of bureaucrats to those principals, than has previously been considered in this stream of thought. Two substantively quite different contributions (Carpenter 2001; Moe 2006) share an interesting theoretical similarity on this point. Carpenter's book is not explicitly steeped in the language or concepts of principal–agent theory (though see Gailmard and Patty (2007) for a formal principal-agent model that is similar in several ways), while Moe's paper is. But both scholars explore the implications for bureaucratic accountability of the fact that bureaucrats may assemble electoral coalitions to influence the identity and ideology of who their legislative principals are in the first place. That is, scholars must consider that interaction between legislative principals and bureaucratic agents is embedded in a larger political system in which legislators are themselves agents. If bureaucrats occupy a dedicated enough share of the electorate to whom legislators answer, they can induce titular legislative principals to treat favorably the policy concerns and favored agencies of those bureaucrats. If the dedicated bureaucrats-in-electorate willing to work for their cause are in fact an intense minority, then this arrangement can skew the ultimate accountability of policy choices to the will of voters in general. Carpenter (2001) contends and adduces historical evidence that bureaucrats can act as opinion leaders in constellations of interest groups allied around related concerns—and thereby induce those groups to lobby Congress in support of the very bureaucrats that Congress is nominally directing. In this way, Carpenter argues, bureaucrats can carve out some autonomy—not mere discretion—from political principals to pursue policy initiatives of their own choosing on their own terms. Whether the ends pursued by such bureaucrats in particular cases are salutary from the standpoint of public welfare or not, the point remains that this inversion of the canonical legislative principal–bureaucratic agent relationship reflects a failure of political institutions to engender accountability of bureaucrats to the will of Congress.

Some degree of confusion has arisen from the subsidiary observation that bureaucrats in fact have multiple principals. For one thing, Congress is a "they," not an "it," and furthermore bureaucrats have *other* principals besides the multiple principals in Congress itself. These points are valid and should be considered in principal–agent thought on the topic (and have been many times over; Moe 1985; Bendor, Taylor, and Van Gaalen 1987; Calvert, McCubbins, and Weingast 1989; McCarty 2002; Whitford 2006; Gailmard 2009). However, the multiple principals (or "common agency," as it is known in the principal–agent literature; cf. Bernheim and Whinston 1986; Laffont and Tirole 1993; Laffont and Martimort 2001) point does not negate the principal–agent-based reaction to concerns over bureaucratic accountability. Instead, it simply means that one should interpret the system on the assumption that each principal is doing its best, with whatever tools it has, to induce a favorable reaction from bureaucratic agents, taking as given that each other principal is trying to do so as well. This may lead to a more complicated model than single-principal variants, but does not resuscitate interpretations based on bureaucratic dominance. It is of course possible to postulate a model in which the attempts at influence by multiple principals cancel each other out completely, leaving the bureaucrat in a position of complete autonomy with respect to its principals; accounts of bureaucratic drift due to stalemate among multiple principals (McCubbins, Nolland, and Weingast 1987) have some of this flavor on a small scale. But this would appear to be a relatively specialized model rather than one encompassing some general thrust of the implications of common agency for bureaucratic accountability.

In summary, the principal–agent perspective has fundamentally reshaped how political scientists view bureaucratic arrangements (see Gailmard and Patty (2012) for a more detailed review). But this cannot be said to arise from incontrovertible evidence that principal–agent models in which political principals tightly control agents, and only those models, are consistent with observed events. Rather, it is in some part because of an assumption that political principals pursue desirable outcomes from their agents, and principals understand that these outcomes must be achieved in the most effective way possible given the problems and constraints that they face. The flexibility of principal–agent theory has made it possible to reconcile this interpretation with a great variety of seemingly puzzling or pathological bureaucratic institutions (Miller 1993; Prendergast 2003; 2007; Gailmard and Patty 2007; Ting 2009). But that flexibility is not so great that the core idea of political principals exercising direction over policy as best they can is fundamentally compromised.

CONCLUSION

Principal–agent theory has proven to be a flexible and useful approach for interpreting the effects of institutional arrangements on accountability of public decision-makers and public policy. Continuing development of this approach is the subject of a rich and ongoing literature. Particularly active areas at present include intrinsic motivation of agents (Prendergast 2007; Besley 2007; Gailmard and Patty 2007); the power of legal precedent in multi-tiered court systems (Carrubba and Clark 2012); and delegation in parliamentary systems (Huber and Shipan 2002; Dewan and Myatt 2010).

The "theory" is better understood as a family of models with a related perspective than as a single encompassing theory with a specific set of assumptions and conclusions. It is hard to imagine how the theory as a whole, rather than a specific model, could be falsified. Principal–agent theorists in political science have been reasonably adept at postulating configurations of information asymmetries, incentive problems, and contracting limitations to rationalize, as the best that a principal can expect to attain under the circumstances, a wide variety of seemingly puzzling and pathological institutions and behaviors. By the same token, when used in this particular way, principal–agent theory does not help us to be more demanding of our public officials. Instead this approach to principal–agent analyses of institutions asks how it could be that these pathologies might nevertheless result from principals doing the best job they can at holding their agents accountable. In this way it reveals the fundamental limitations on accountability imposed by political institutions, apart from the capabilities of the principals that operate within them.

Notes

1. For reasons of space this essay therefore does not consider the large empirical literatures on public accountability inspired by principal–agent theory. I am not aware of any published review of this empirical literature as a whole, but Besley and Case (2003) review significant portions, particularly those related to elections and selection of policy makers. Miller (2005) presents an insightful review of both theory and empirical research, focused particularly on the bureaucracy.

2. It is perfectly possible for a moral hazard problem to lack this feature, but then the agent simply takes its own preferred action irrespective of the interests of the principal.

3. Dixit, Grossman, and Helpman (1997) present an interesting twist on this, in which politicians are agents but (multiple, competing) interest groups are the principals. This illustrates the positive use of principal agent analysis without any normative connection to public accountability.

4. See also Barro (1973) for a complete information, finite horizon moral hazard model tapping into a similar concern as Ferejohn's.

5. Austen-Smith and Banks (1998) offer another extension dealing with incumbency advantage.

6. Majumdar and Mukand (2004) offer a related analysis of the incentives of politicians to invest in socially desirable experimentation with new policies.

7. See Fox and Shotts (2009), who present a model in which voters sometimes re-elect politicians known not to share the voters' preferences; or Ashworth and Bueno de Mesquita (2009), who present a model of elections in an adverse selection problem in which incumbency advantage arises in equilibrium.

8. Also see Horn and Shepsle (1989), Horn (1995), and DeFigueiredo, Spiller, and Urbiztando (1999). Banks and Weingast (1992) present a formal model in which agency budget requests serve as signals of agency costs. While signaling games are not necessarily applications of a principal–agent perspective, Banks and Weingast's model was explicitly inspired by Niskanen's assumptions.

9. Bueno de Mesquita and Stephenson (2007) present an explicit model making a similar but deeper point about the value of limiting review of agency actions. However, their model turns on hidden actions by bureaucrats, rather than hidden information. Their model shows that when some agency effort is observable and some is not, ex post review may induce the agent to substitute observable for unobservable effort, to the detriment of the principal in some cases. See also the multitask moral hazard model of Holmström and Milgrom (1987) for a similar point in economic contracting.

References

Achen, C. and Bartels, L. M. 2002. *Blind Retrospection: Electoral Responses to Droughts, Flu, and Shark Attacks.* In APSA (The American Political Science Association) Annual Meeting. Boston, MA September 2002.

Ashworth, S. and Bueno de Mesquita, E. 2009. "Electoral Selection, Strategic Challenger Entry, and the Incumbency Advantage." *Journal of Politics,* 70: 1006–25.

Austen-Smith, D. and Banks, J. 1998. Electoral Accountability and Incumbency, pp. 121–48 in *Models of Strategic Choice in Politics*, ed. P. Ordeshook. Ann Arbor, MI: University of Michigan Press.

Banks, J. and Weingast, B. 1992. "The Political Control of Bureaucracies Under Asymmetric Information." *American Journal of Political Science*, 36: 509–24.

Banks, J. and Sundaram, R. 1993. Adverse Selection and Moral Hazard in a Repeated Elections Model, pp. 295–312 in *Political Economy: Institutions, Information Competition, and Representation*, eds.W. A. Barnett, N. J. Schofield, and M. J. Hinich. New York: Cambridge University Press.

Banks, J. and Sundaram, R. 1998. "Optimal Retention in Agency Problems." *Journal of Economic Theory*, 82: 293–323.

Barro, R. 1973. "The Control of Politicians: An Economic Model." *Public Choice*, 14: 19–42.

Bendor, J. and Meirowitz, A. 2004. "Spatial Models of Delegation." *American Political Science Review*, 98: 293–310.

Bendor, J., Taylor, S., and Van Gaalen, R. 1987. "Politicians, Bureaucrats, and Asymmetric Information." *American Journal of Political Science*, 31: 796–828.

Bernheim, D. and Whinston, M. 1986. "Common Agency." *Econometrica*, 54: 923–42.

Besley, T. 2007. *Principled Agents? The Political Economy of Good Government*. New York: Oxford University Press.

Besley, T. and Case, A. 2003. "Political Institutions and Policy Choices: Evidence from the United States." *Journal of Economic Literature*, 41: 7–73.

Bolton, P. and Dewatripont, M. 2004. *Contract Theory*. Cambridge, MA: MIT Press.

Bueno de Mesquita, E. and Stephenson, M. 2007. "Regulatory Quality with Imperfect Oversight." *American Political Science Review*, 101: 605–20.

Calvert, R., McCubbins, M., and Weingast, B. 1989. "A Theory of Political Control and Agency Discretion." *American Journal of Political Science*, 33: 588–611.

Canes-Wrone, B., Herron, M., and Shotts, K. 2001. "Leadership and Pandering: A Theory of Executive Policymaking." *American Journal of Political Science*, 45: 532–50.

Carpenter, D. 2001. *The Forging of Bureaucratic Autonomy*. Princeton, NJ: Princeton University Press.

Carrubba, C. and Clark, T. 2012. "Rule Creation in a Political Hierarchy." *American Political Science Review*, 106: 622–43.

DeFigueiredo, R. J. P., Spiller, P., and Urbiztando, S. 1999. "An Informational Perspective on Administrative Procedures." *Journal of Law, Economics, and Organization*, 15: 283–305.

Dessein, W. 2002. "Authority and Communication in Organizations." *Review of Economic Studies*, 69: 811–38.

Dewan, T. and Myatt, D. 2010. "The Declining Talent Pool of Government." *American Journal of Political Science*, 54: 267–86.

Dixit, A., Grossman, G., and Helpman, E. 1997. "Common Agency and Coordination: General Theory and Application to Government Policy Making." *Journal of Political Economy*, 105: 752–69.

Epstein, D. and O'Halloran, S. 1994. "Administrative Procedures, Information, and Agency Discretion. Slack vs. Flexibility." *American Journal of Political Science*, 38: 697–722.

Epstein, D. and O'Halloran, S. 1999. *Delegating Powers*. New York: Cambridge University Press.

Fearon, J. 1999. Electoral Accountability and the Control of Politicians: Selecting Good Types versus Sanctioning Poor Performance, pp. 55–97 in *Democracy, Accountability, and Representation*, eds. A. Przeworski, B. Manin, and S. Stokes. New York: Cambridge University Press.

Ferejohn, J. 1986. "Incumbent Performance and Electoral Control." *Public Choice*, 50: 5–25.

Fiorina, M. 1979. Control of the Bureaucracy: A Mismatch of Incentives and Capabilities, pp. 124–42 in *The Presidency and the Congress: A Shifting Balance of Powers?* eds. W. Livingston, L. Dodd, and R. Schott. Austin, Texas: Lyndon B. Johnson School of Public Affairs, Lyndon Baines Johnson Library.

Fox, J. and Shotts, K. 2009. "Delegates or Trustees? A Theory of Political Accountability." *Journal of Politics*, 71: 1225–37.

Gailmard, S. 2002. "Expertise, Subversion, and Bureaucratic Discretion." *Journal of Law, Economics, and Organization*, 18: 536–55.

Gailmard, S. 2009. "Multiple Principals and Oversight of Bureaucratic Policy Making." *Journal of Theoretical Politics*, 21: 161–86.

Gailmard, S. and Patty, J. 2007. "Slackers and Zealots: Civil Service, Bureaucratic Discretion, and Policy Expertise." *American Journal of Political Science*, 51: 873–89.

Gailmard, S. and Patty, J. 2012. "Formal Models of Bureaucracy." *Annual Review of Political Science*, 15: 353–77.

Gailmard, S. and Patty, J. 2013. *Learning While Governing: Expertise and Accountability in the Executive Branch*. Chicago: University of Chicago Press.

Healy, A. and Malhotra, N. 2010. "Random Events, Economic Losses, and Retrospective Voting: Implications for Democratic Competence." *Quarterly Journal of Political Science*, 5: 193–208.

Heclo, H. 1977. *A Government of Strangers: Executive Politics in Washington*. Washington, DC: Brookings Institution Press.

Holmström, B. 1984. On the Theory of Delegation, pp. 115–41 in *Bayesian Models in Economic Theory*, eds. M. Boyer and R. Kihlstrom. New York: North-Holland.

Holmström, B. and Milgrom, P. 1991. "Multitask Principal Agent Analyses." *Journal of Law, Economics, and Organization*, 7: 24–52.

Horn, M. 1995. *The Political Economy of Public Administration*. New York: Cambridge University Press.

Horn, M. and Shepsle, K. 1989. "Administrative Process and Organizational Form as Legislative Responses to Agency Costs." *Virginia Law Review*, 75: 499–508.

Huber, J. and Shipan, C. 2002. *Deliberate Discretion? The Institutional Foundations of Bureaucratic Autonomy*. New York: Cambridge University Press.

Kiewiet, D. R. and McCubbins, M. 1991. *The Logic of Delegation*. Chicago: University of Chicago Press.

Laffont, J. J. and Martimort, D. 2001. *The Theory of Incentives: The Principal-Agent Model*. Princeton, NJ: Princeton University Press.

Laffont, J.J. and Tirole, J. 1993. *A Theory of Incentives in Procurement and Regulation*. Cambridge, MA: MIT Press.

Lenz, G. 2012. *Follow the Leader: How Voters Respond to Politicians' Performance and Policies*. Chicago: University of Chicago Press.

Lowi, T. 1979. *The End of Liberalism*. Second edition. New York: Norton.

Lupia, A. and McCubbins, M. 1998. *The Democratic Dilemma: Can Citizens Learn What They Need to Know?* New York: Cambridge University Press.

Majumdar, S. and Mukand, S. 2004. "Policy Gambles." *American Economic Review*, 94: 1207–22.

Mayhew, D. 1974. *Congress: The Electoral Connection*. New Haven: Yale University Press.

McCarty, N. 2002. "The Appointments Dilemma." *American Journal of Political Science*, 48: 413–28.

McCubbins, M., Noll, R., and Weingast, B. 1987. "Administrative Procedures as Instruments of Political Control." *Journal of Law, Economics, and Organization*, 3: 243–77.

McCubbins, M., Noll, R., and Weingast, B. 1989. "Structure and Process, Politics and Policy: Administrative Arrangements and the Political Control of Agencies." *Virginia Law Review*, 75: 431–89.

Miller, G. 1993. *Managerial Dilemmas: The Political Economy of Hierarchy.* New York: Cambridge University Press.

Miller, G. 2005. "The Political Evolution of Principal-Agent Models." *Annual Review of Political Science*, 8: 203–25.

Moe, T. 1985. "Control and Feedback in Economic Regulation: The Case of the NLRB." *American Political Science Review*, 79: 1094–1116.

Moe, T. 1987. "An Assessment of the Positive Theory of 'Congressional Dominance'." *Legislative Studies Quarterly*, 12: 475–520.

Moe, T. 2006. "Political Control and the Power of the Agent." *Journal of Law, Economics, and Organization*, 22: 1–29.

Niskanen, W. 1971. *Bureaucracy and Representative Government.* Chicago: Aldine.

Persson, T., Roland, G., and Tabellini, G. 1997. "Separation of Powers and Political Accountability." *Quarterly Journal of Economics*, 112: 1163–202.

Prendergast, C. 2003. "The Limits of Bureaucratic Efficiency." *Journal of Political Economy*, 111: 929–58.

Prendergast, C. 2007. "The Motivation and Bias of Bureaucrats." *American Economic Review*, 97: 180–96.

Romer, T. and Rosenthal, H. 1978. "Political Resource Allocation, Controlled Agendas, and the Status Quo." *Public Choice*, 33: 27–43.

Ting, M. 2009. "Whistleblowing." *American Political Science Review*, 102: 249–67.

Volden, C. 2002. "A Formal Model of the Politics of Delegation in a Separation of Powers System." *American Journal of Political Science*, 46: 111–33.

Weingast, B. and Moran, M. 1983. "Bureaucratic Discretion and Political Control." *Journal of Political Economy*, 91: 765–800.

Whitford, A. 2006. "The Pursuit of Political Control by Multiple Principals." *Journal of Politics*, 67: 28–49.

CHAPTER 7

....

ACCOUNTABILITY AND AMBIGUITY

....

JOHAN P. OLSEN

BEYOND COMPLIANCE AND CONTROL

THE argument of this chapter is that mainstream accountability theory reduces its own area of application by not taking ambiguity seriously enough. Theorizing accountability requires going beyond the dominant concern in the literature organized around compliance and control: to detect and measure deviance from authoritative orders, rules, standards and contracts; to discipline unruly agents and make them comply, thereby solving the problems of principals.[1]

The compliance-control perspective is too static, treating too many aspects of accountability as exogenous to politics and accountability processes. For example, principal–agent approaches usually assume pre-determined principals and agents. Authority and success criteria are embedded in normative theories and formal-legal institutions prescribing chains of delegation/authorization and representation/accountability. A priori assumptions are made about information asymmetry and conflict and the mechanisms through which accountability works. These assumptions about political institutions and agency are likely to apply to some political orders, settings, and situations, and not to others. They are in particular unlikely to capture accountability in polities in transformation, and the aim of the chapter is to supplement mainstream theory by offering an institutional perspective.

Compliance-control is only one aspect of accountability relations and processes. It may, therefore, be fruitful to relax assumptions regarding what accountability means and implies; what is involved in demanding, rendering, assessing, and responding to accounts; what factors foster effective accountability; and how accountability regimes emerge and change. It may be useful to examine a priori assumptions regarding purposes formulated by pre-determined principals, mediated through competitive elections, laws, hierarchical arrangements, and dyadic relationships between the people, a representative assembly, government, and non-elected agents.

"Accountability" refers to being answerable to somebody else, to be obligated to explain and justify action and inaction—how mandates, authority, and resources have been applied, with what results, and whether outcomes meet relevant standards and principles. However, the precise content of and assumed best way to ensure accountability vary across polities, policy areas, groups, and time (Stone 1995; Bovens 2007; Bovens, Curtin, and t'Hart 2010). In European democracies committed to the idea that rulers should be accountable to the ruled, there are huge variations in what accountability means and implies and when the demand for compliance is met (Verhey, Broeksteeg, and Driessche 2008).

"Ambiguity" implies a state of having more than one meaning and accountability under ambiguity refers to calling for, rendering, assessing, and sanctioning accounts in situations where objectives, technology, and experience are unclear, participation is fluid, and the legitimacy of different resources is contested. It is commonplace to assert that accountability thrives on clear and consistent authority, mandates, responsibility, rules, standards, goals, and expectations. Ambiguity is the enemy of effective accountability and should be eliminated. In contrast, the chapter explores implications of seeing ambiguity as intrinsic to democratic politics and human existence.

AMBIGUITY AS THE ENEMY OF ACCOUNTABILITY

In democracies accountability is linked to a belief in human agency, purposeful choice and history determined by human will, causal understanding, and control. Actors are accountable for the exercise of their powers, differentiating between authorized and unauthorized use of discretion. "Accountability abhors ambiguity" and requires that "clarity of accountability and contribution must be one of the attributes of every single role that makes up the system" (Porter-O'Grady, Hawkins, and Parker 1997, 54). The aim of accountability regimes is to reveal incompetence, fraud, malpractice, and abuse of power.

The idea that ambiguity is the enemy of accountability has roots in democratic theory and organization theory. A democratic article of faith is that "the public is ultimately the sole source of sovereign authority, and it is the public to whom all public officials ought ultimately to be accountable" (Goodin 2008, 164). Public accounts are vehicles for popular sovereignty (March and Olsen 1995) and effective accountability requires constitutional and formal-legal clarity regarding who is obligated to render an account, and who can call whom to account for what under different circumstances and sanction malpractice.

The idea is also central to conceptions of formal organizations as instruments for problem-solving and conflict resolution. Organizations are tools of rationality, effectiveness, and efficiency characterized by clear and consistent goals and formalized division of work, information, power, and responsibilities. Organizations are deliberately structured and restructured and there is a constant need to provide mechanisms of control to check on fulfillment of orders and adherence to rules. Supervision is built into the hierarchy of authority. The role of "higher-in-rank" includes the obligation to check on the performance of the "lower-in-rank" (Etzioni 1964, 25).

AMBIGUITY AS INTRINSIC TO LIFE

Ambiguity is not necessarily transitory or pathological. Ambiguity is intrinsic to human existence according to existential philosophy (Beauvoir 1972) and a core aspect of political and organizational life (Cohen, March, and Olsen 1972, 2012; March and Olsen 1976; March and Weissinger-Baylon 1986). When theorizing accountability it is necessary to take into account the ambiguous character of the foundational standards and principles of democracies (Connolly 1987). Demands for clarity and consistency are hard to meet because western culture is incoherent. There are unresolved conflicts between rival traditions regarding how concepts such as rationality and justice should be interpreted (MacIntyre 1988) and a cacophony of interpretations of what democracy means and implies (Hanson 1987, 69). Normative theories and formal-legal institutions give limited behavioral guidance. Democracies legitimize competing opinions and there is disagreement regarding what institutions make accountability effective (March and Olsen 1995, 59,162).

Since modern politics unfolds within and between organizations and institutions, it is worthwhile to observe that organizations are sometimes "organized anarchies" characterized by ambiguous preferences, unclear causal understanding, contested authority, and fluid participation (Cohen, March, and Olsen 1972, 2012). Accountability processes are then less integrated by institutions, and politics is event-driven, involving improvisation and elements of chance. Ambiguity is also embraced because detailed rules may be counterproductive in terms of outcomes and adaptability (Goodin 1982, 59–72).

The relevance of ambiguity is illustrated by processes of political transformation such as those currently taking place in Europe. For centuries the sovereign state has been the basic unit of political organization and identification and conceptions of accountability have developed in the context of the emerging state. The institutional foundations of the Westphalian state have, however, been challenged. Challenges embrace Europeanization, internationalization, a new *Zeitgeist*, and an international wave of public sector reforms. The role and significance of the territorial state, representative democracy, elected representatives, experts, and citizens have changed in ways that require reconsideration of conceptions of accountability. "Monitoring democracy" is presented as a new historical type of democracy involving continuous public scrutiny and control over power-holders across territorial boundaries and institutional settings (Keane 2009). The development calls attention to how institutions affect ambiguity and accountability.

INSTITUTIONS, AMBIGUITY, AND ACCOUNTABILITY

Institutions draw the borders of, but do not eliminate, ambiguity. The ordering effect is strongest in settled polities with well-entrenched institutions staffed by experienced, well-socialized people performing socially standardized activities. It is less strong in unsettled polities with weak or competing institutions staffed by inexperienced personnel doing novel things (March and Olsen 1976, 50).

Institutionalization refers to processes through which something diffuse, unstable, and unfixed turns into something that is settled and integrated (Selznick 1992). Institutionalization implies increasing clarity and agreement about accountability practices. Standardization and formalization reduce ambiguity, uncertainty, and conflict concerning who is accountable for what, to whom, when, and how. Some ways of acting are perceived as natural and legitimate. Thus there is less need for using incentives or coercion to make people follow prescribed accountability rules, the need to explain and justify practices is reduced, and there is less need to struggle for resources (Olsen 2008, 196). Attribution of accountability is guided by socially validated, relatively well-known, clear, and stable roles, rules, routines, procedures, doctrines, expectations, and resources. However, institutions exist because people believe they exist. They require continued public recognition and acceptance (Searle 1995, 1, 45) and sometimes institutions face erosion, decay, and revolt. De-institutionalization generates ambiguity, uncertainty, disorientation, and conflict.

As a supplement to formal-legal interpretations of accountability institutions, an institutional approach offers ideas regarding how "living" institutions affect conceptions and practices of accountability and how accounts are influenced by and influence a political order. A living institution prescribes rules of appropriate behavior for different actors in different situations. Organizing ideas provide norms of assessment and conceptions of reality that explain and justify rules and practices, and institutionalized endowments make it (more or less) possible to act in accordance with prescriptions. Institutions constitute and influence actors, identities, and affective ties. They have some autonomy and dynamics of their own and robustness regarding deliberate reform efforts and environmental change, generating "historical inefficiency," rather than simple equilibria (March and Olsen 1989).

The organization of accountability in contemporary democracies is characterized by varying degrees of institutionalization, specialization, and coordination. Over the years a multitude of institutions, organizations, networks, and communities of account formation, authorization, legitimation, dissemination, and assessment have emerged. Some have specialized in providing normative standards and certifying institutions, or monitoring, analyzing, and assessing performance without authority or resources to sanction misconduct. Others sanction abuse of power, but depend on information and analysis from outside. Besides legislative and judicial scrutiny, there are independent auditors, ombudsmen and other complaint mechanisms, epistemic communities, think-tanks, credit-rating and standard-settings agencies, tribunals, and committees of inquiry operating at an arm's length of popular control. New accountability relationships have been added to old ones, creating complex layers and combinations of co-existing, dynamic accountability structures and processes.

Multiplication of scrutiny and account-giving may foster redundancy that generates waste and inefficiencies. Yet redundancy may also make accountability arrangements more reliable and facilitate adaptation to shifting circumstances (Landau 1969). Theorizing accountability, therefore, requires attention to the complexity and dynamics of accountability relations and processes, rather than assuming hierarchical, dyadic, and predetermined principal–agent relations. Theorizing implies exploring how accountability regimes work and change in more or less institutionalized settings and well-structured, recurring, and consensual situations, involving different degrees of ambiguity.

INSTITUTIONAL SOURCES OF AMBIGUITY

To legitimately call someone to account requires that an actor has some autonomy and discretion that can be used or misused judged by some normative standard. Principals and agents are less likely to deviate from what they are supposed to do when (Olsen 2013):

- Compliance is secured through external controls of opportunity and incentive structures and the expected utility of complying is always greater than not complying.
- Reciprocal control is established through vertical or horizontal separation of power and expertise, checks and balances.
- Congruence in norms, common understandings, and role expectations are achieved through recruitment. Reliable and competent behavior is guaranteed by selecting and removing actors with certain characteristics (e.g. members of a specific party or profession) to/from office.
- Agreement is reached through communicative action and reciprocal discovery of normative validity and the best argument through deliberation among initially conflicting parties.
- Self-control is achieved through socialization, internalization, habituation, and character formation, rendering the appropriate norms and codes of conduct understandable and respected.
- Available resources make it possible to follow behavioral prescriptions and proscriptions.

In settled polities there is widespread agreement regarding who is accountable to whom, for what, under what circumstances, according to which criteria, and therefore who should be blamed if things go wrong. Normative concerns and causal beliefs are embedded in traditions, morals, and institutional spheres with some autonomy and resources of their own. There are repertoires of socially constructed and validated accounts and responses to accounts, influenced by what is intelligible and appropriate in specific political-cultural contexts. Favored stories are embedded in ideologies and traditions and there are continuous attempts to fit events to those stories. Routinized accounts focus on deviances from shared rules and expectations and provide reassurance that events are controllable or have the appearance of control (March and Olsen 1995, 149,161). Those authorized to call someone to account do so with reference to shared norms, commitments, purposes, and expectations. Those who have an obligation to render accounts to some legitimate authority do what they are supposed to do. Activities are recorded in routinized reports, but there is little perceived need to explain and justify what is done. Whereas there is interpretation, deliberation, and bargaining regarding what accountability means and implies in individual cases and situations, the politics of accountability takes place within institutional constraints and with modest controversy.

Under such conditions it is not unreasonable to treat authority, power, mandates, standards, goals, and conflicts as exogenous and pre-determined. The task is to identify the technically most efficient means for reaching pre-determined ends within existing constraints and sanction violation of rules and contracts. For students of politics, however, accountability is more interesting when such factors are seen as endogenous to politics and accountability processes. Accountability is related to fundamental issues in political life and accountability processes provide occasions for debates and struggles over authority, power, norms, worldviews, and responsibility, crucial for the legitimacy of a political order. A complication is that the meaning of "accountability" becomes more complex, a fact with special relevance for unsettled polities characterized by weak or competing institutions with a modest ordering effect.

In unsettled polities there are competing claims of representation and role-conceptions, procedural and result-oriented assessments. Normative standards and rules are rarely exhaustive or self-interpreting. Understanding causal systems and assigning accountability is difficult. It is not clear what has happened, why it happened, and whether what happened was good, making it difficult to establish how well different institutions or actors have performed. Under conditions of complex and dynamic interdependencies, where the performance of one actor is dependent on the performance of others, chance events, and long and uncertain causal chains with significant effects surfacing years later, the assumption that actors can be made accountable by disentangling their contribution to fiascos and successes is problematic (March and Olsen 1995, 157–58). The assignment of accountability may be capricious, mistaken, controversial, and politicized.

THE POLITICS OF ACCOUNTABILITY

Institutions affect but do not determine ambiguity and accountability. If institutions were perfect, there would be no discretion and no reason for studying accountability.

Or, accountability would be limited to detecting misunderstandings, incompetence, and criminal acts. However, claims about accountability deficits and disillusion with traditional forms of representative democracy suggest that practice is less than perfect, and when causality is too obscure to be established validly in terms of correctly assigning responsibility politics acquires a more important role in accountability processes. Possibilities arise for exercising political visions, claiming virtue and victory, blaming, shaming and identifying scapegoats. Polities in transformation, therefore, provide "windows" to understanding aspects of accountability largely ignored by compliance-control approaches.

Democratic politics involves more than making, implementing, and enforcing policies. Democracies are also collections of interlocking communities of explanation, justification, and criticism. Making the world intelligible in normative and causal terms is central to political life (March and Olsen 1976) and the search for identity, belonging, purpose, direction, and meaning can be as important an aspect of accountability processes as compliance and control. Accountability processes may promote a culture of cooperation, compromise, and integration, or suspicion, confrontation, and disintegration. Under some conditions accountability processes have an integrative effect and are conducive to intellectual and moral self-*development* as well as self-*government*. They ameliorate the moral qualities of individuals and society through the internalization of a democratic and civic ethos; improve communication, learning, and epistemic quality; contribute to power-equalization and political equality; and help actors find meaning in life through reflection and reasoning together. Under other conditions accountability processes provide a rhetorical arena for political struggle, splitting the population.

Rendering and responding to accounts may create controversies and denial, or become accepted as legitimate. An event may be interpreted as the result of purposeful acts or a necessity, accident, or misunderstanding. Responsibility may be disclaimed and shifted to someone else, or poor results said to be caused by inadequate resources. Behavior may be excused, forgiven, and justified, or disapproved of and punished. The style of presentation of an account, for example, humbly submitting to criticism, expressing regret; or excusing, justifying, defending, or reframing interpretations may be more important for responses than the act to be accounted for (Dubnick 2005). Sometimes account-giving may become a ritual providing illusions (Gustavsson, Karlsson, and Persson 2009).

Ambiguity may be seen as a political necessity. In order to reach agreement, compromises are made sufficiently ambiguous to allow competing interpretations, and change may be easier when it involves modifying the relations between co-existing, ambiguous principles rather than one clear principle replacing another. Under some conditions ambiguity, concealing one's preferences rather than taking a clear stand, may be an electoral strategy (Shepsle 1972; Page 1976; Alesina and Cukierman 1990). Superiors wanting to avoid association with torture may prefer ambiguity regarding how to handle prisoners. By not defining precisely what it means to "apply pressure" they shift accountability onto the lowest ranking and least powerful (Manning 2004).

Who to praise or blame does not necessarily depend on hard evidence and correct causal understanding. Interpretations of experience compete for acceptance on the basis of evidence or power (March 2010) and the ability to gain acceptance for a specific frame, type of discourse, language, interpretative community, or a particular interpretation, is a source and indicator of power (March and Olsen 1995, 180). The politics of accountability involve both the pursuit of accountability within an accountability regime and efforts to change established regimes. There is no clear-cut separation between the two, yet they are discussed separately in the next sections.

THE PURSUIT OF ACCOUNTABILITY

Through what mechanisms is effective accountability obtained? Democratic theories emphasize providing information and imposing sanctions as requirements for effective accountability. Because in democracies accounts are likely to be contested, they are often constructed in encounters among contending accounts. The influence of citizens is seen to depend on competing accounts and sources of information, and mechanisms for exploring, testing, gathering support for, and authorizing accounts are assumed to be supported by institutions securing freedom of expression, legitimate opposition, independent auditors, an active civil society, and a free press (March and Olsen 1995, 163).

The standard story of representative democracy gives priority to accountability through electoral mechanisms, and compliance-control approaches mainly deal with accountability in settled polities embracing ideas such as the sovereign people, sovereign parliament, and responsible minister. Popular rule is assumed to be expressed, implemented, and enforced through elections (Przeworski, Stokes, and Manin 1999). An example is parliamentarianism portrayed as a chain of dyadic relations. The authentic will of the people is expressed and control is exercised through competitive elections. The legislature makes laws and delegates authority to a hierarchy of non-elected public officials and holds them accountable (Strøm, Müller, and Bergman 2003). Self-interested principals control self-interested agents through incentives.

The problems of the standard story are well known. Problems do not necessarily originate with agents. Accountability deficit is caused by institutions and actors who are assumed to call others to account, but lack the motivation, time and energy, knowledge, or capabilities for reliably monitoring, assessing, and sanctioning agents' behavior and performance (Busuioc 2010, 220–23). For example, democratic accountability assumes an informed citizenry that knows what powerful agents are doing and the evidence and reasons behind their behavior. This ideal is difficult to realize and the European Union (EU) illustrates that theorizing accountability must include situations where there is no unitary and stable "people" to be served. There are competing claims regarding what citizens want and what their interests and needs are. What normative criteria and causal understandings shall have priority, and what jurisdictions and responsibilities different levels of government, institutions, and actors shall have are contested. Many criteria and audiences are mobilized in partly uncoordinated ways and it is not clear who can legitimately call whom to account for what, or who controls relevant incentives and information.

Concerns regarding citizens' inability to make rulers accountable need to be supplemented by citizens' responsibilities toward the community at large as the foundation of democracy and ultimate source of power. Rather than assuming a sovereign people accountable to no one, it is important to study how citizen exemption from accountability masks the contribution of ordinary citizens to democratic successes and failures (March and Olsen 1995, 153). An institutional approach takes into account processes of internalization and identification through which citizens come to accept codes of appropriate behavior as legitimate, and at stake is whether citizenship is primarily seen as carrying rights and consuming public services or implies adherence to socially validated behavioral rules. It is a question of whether citizens see themselves as responsible members of a political community, accountable to each other not only for following laws but for participating in political and civic life, keeping informed, not making unattainable demands, and accepting duties towards the welfare of other citizens. The issue is not only whether representative democracies are able to live up to the expectations of citizens, but also whether citizens' expectations make democracy possible and where expectations and aspirations come from.

Principals may provide agents with contradictory or unrealistic criteria, expectations, and aspirations. A culture of compromise with ambiguous lines between incumbents and opposition makes responsibility and accountability unclear. Political rhetoric fit for mobilizing support is not always fit for making programs work well. Reforms driven by political ideology rather than evidence and analysis produce perverse effects. Trust and deference are weakened through intense monitoring. Tripartite accountability relations among logics of politics, administration, and markets have turned out to be difficult to reconcile. Administrators have to decipher political decisions, legal documents, and a variety of pressures, and develop practical, viable solutions, and it has been argued that the current wave of delegation requires a reinvention of accountability (Gilmour and Jensen 1998; Klinger, Nalbandian, and Romzek 2001, 134–7).

For example, in the European Union, actors are required to provide accounts to a multitude of forums and satisfy multiple, contested, and ambiguous accountability claims. They are expected to do so in a variety of ways and through different channels, requiring different types of information, explanations, and justifications in terms of competing normative standards (Bovens, Curtin, and t'Hart 2010, 40). At different points in time, different accountability relationships are activated by and in relation to elected representatives, individual citizens, specific constituencies, mass media, democratic and civil standards, laws, financial auditing institutions, epistemic communities, professional codes of good practice, and the ethos of office. Calling to account and rendering, assessing, and sanctioning accounts often require pooling resources from several institutions and actors (Magnette 2000; Busuioc 2010).

Conceptions of accountability have come to rely on non-majoritarian, guardian institutions populated by officials neither directly elected nor managed by elected officials and loosely coupled to public opinion (Thatcher and Stone Sweet 2002). Judges, central bankers, and experts are assumed to act in a principled way, with competence, integrity, and impartiality, in accordance with laws, professional codes, the mandates of their office, and the common good. However, self-control and checks and balances among guardians have been assessed as democratically inadequate and simultaneously there are perceived to be accountability deficits and overloads. For instance, the Commission has become more accountable horizontally to other EU institutions, but less so to citizens. As a result, the Commission perceives itself as overloaded with accountability claims. In the eyes of the public it is unaccountable and deserves closer public scrutiny (Wille 2010, 83–85).

Living with Ambiguity and Conflict

When democracies face inconsistent claims, standards, and understandings, the task is usually seen as "striking a balance." Claims are weighted. Trade-offs are made. Conflict is resolved and equilibrium reached. An alternative to assuming authoritative conflict resolution is to consider how democracies live with ambiguity and unresolved conflict. Democracies search for "satisficing" or acceptable solutions and accountability processes may be institution-specific or involve the interaction of a variety of institutions.

In settled polities and routine situations accountability processes are likely to take place in parallel, relatively autonomous, institutional spheres. They are incremental, institution-specific, and influenced by the history, organization, and dynamics of the institution, yet in the shadow of a common understanding of political order. Existing beliefs, status, and power relationships bias interpretation towards familiar templates. Inspired by Cyert and March (1963) it is hypothesized that in settled polities and well-understood situations repeatedly confronted, there are co-existing dyadic accountability relations, routines, standard operating procedures, self-restraint, and de-politicization. There is local rationality, where different institutions define accountability and hold different types of actors accountable for different things and in accordance with different normative standards. There is also sequential attention to claims, and demands for coordination are buffered by limited attention and slack resources. Rather than being collapsed into a coherent preference order through trade-offs, competing accountability claims are treated as independent constraints, together defining a satisfying solution. Reduced slack or austerity may generate demands for coordination. The search for new alternatives is driven by performance crises and change follows from shifts in attention and aspiration levels.

In unsettled polities and unchartered waters institutions and actors have to learn their place in the larger political order through experience with what is seen as acceptable and politically possible. There are likely to be demands for coordinated behavior, and accountability relationships and processes develop in a dynamic interplay between levels of governance and institutional spheres. The pursuit of accountability and the dynamics of accountability become indistinguishable.

THE DYNAMICS OF ACCOUNTABILITY REGIMES

Accountability processes are part of the emergence and transformation of accountability regimes. They provide opportunities for exploring how accountability may be enhanced, inhibited, and legitimized by alternative regimes for challenging old accountability relations and processes and developing new ones. There are debates and struggles over whether and why the principles organizing and governing common affairs deserve the allegiance of citizens. Questions are raised about why specific institutions and office-holders should have the right and capacity to call to account, render and assess accounts, and sanction unacceptable behavior. These are issues closely linked to competing visions of political order. In the European Union, for example, proposals for making institutions and actors accountable have been based upon different conceptions of the nature, purpose, and desired future of the EU. Visions have varied among those seeing the Union as an intergovernmental, or supranational, or regulatory entity (Bovens 2007; Harlow and Rawlings 2007; Bovens, Curtin, and t'Hart 2010, 180, 189).

THE BELIEF IN DESIGN AND LEARNING

Core democratic beliefs are that citizens should decide through what institutional arrangements they are to be governed and that democracies have a unique ability to learn from experience. Correctly assigning causal credit or blame is assumed to increase the frequency of success and reduce the frequency of failure (March and Olsen 1995). Issues are resolved over time, with agreed-upon results encoded into trustworthy institutions (Warren 2011, 523,526). Contemporary democracies are also involved in reconsideration of accountability relations and processes and reformers believe in auditing and account-giving as instruments for collective intelligence and improved performance (Pollitt and Summa 1997, 331). Principal–agent approaches likewise assume that "agency loss" is mitigated and citizens and legislators cope with conflicting preferences and information asymmetry through a variety of institutional devices, providing information about what agents are doing and why, as well as capacities for holding them to account. Control is embedded in the shifting design of electoral, legislative, and bureaucratic institutions, in processes of selecting agents, monitoring structures, reports from agents and from third parties, penalties for lying and misrepresenting facts, overturning and reversing agents' decisions (Waterman and Meier 1998; Lupia and McCubbins 2000).

Deliberate design and reform is, however, only one among several change processes and it is problematic to assume that accountability regimes emerge and develop through institutional engineering and choice or competitive selection. Accountability arrangements may evolve slowly in relation to repeated encounters with well-structured, recurring problems in standardized situations. Yet, what are exceptions at one point in time become more common and gradually replace historically evolved routines, standards, and causal understandings. Key institutions, for example the Parliament, have developed through historical processes rather than deliberate design. In Westminster democracies the principle of ministerial responsibility has been adapted to shifting circumstances (Stone 1995), and the European Parliament (EP) has only recently succeeded in its appeal to "parliamentary democracy," moving its relationship to the Commission closer to a traditional Parliament–Executive relationship with the Commission accountable to the EP.

Democracies *do* learn from experience on the basis of accounts, but experience is an unreliable teacher. It is difficult to give precise and valid accounts of what has happened and what could have happened, and to conclude precisely what lessons to extract. Lessons are often ambiguous and contested and they are sometimes lost. Learning may be spurious and contribute to mistakes rather than intelligence (March 2010). New routines for information collection are not automatically followed by routines of analysis, debate, and sanctioning. Information is gathered but not attended to or acted upon (Feldman and March 1981). Accounts may be perverted by incompetence, fraud, deceptions, disinformation, and indoctrination, raising questions regarding how citizens and office-holders actually interpret the relevance, validity, and implications of accounts, and how different accountability institutions support intelligence and learning (March and Olsen 1995).

In brief, institutional design and experiential learning do not guarantee efficient adaptation to human purposes or environmental change, and neither does competitive selection, bargaining, deliberation, imitation, diffusion, or other adaptive processes. An empirical lesson is that practice is likely to come before theory in complex, contested, and dynamic polities with multiple accountability claims. The meaning and implications of "accountability" are defined and changed when principles meet practical situations and generate specific implications, cleavages, and relationships.

PRACTICE PRECEDES THEORY

The European Union, as an unsettled polity with no shared vision of how accountability is to be organized and legitimized, provides several examples of evolving practice being theorized, explained, and justified post hoc. The Union *has* been concerned with how codes of conduct may nurture accountability, responsibility, and integrity. There has been criticism of the weak links between the European Parliament and citizens, the modest position of the EP and member state parliaments, and the lack of transparency and accountability of the Council. Bargaining in networks has created an accountability problem by making it difficult to identify who has been influential and should be held accountable. "Guardian" institutions such as the Commission, the Court of Justice, and the Central Bank have been shielded from popular control, making it difficult to hold them accountable.

Consistent with continental traditions the EU has great confidence in formal-legal institutions and decisions. Nevertheless, after institutions have been formally established, living institutions and their practices have evolved gradually through a more or less coordinated struggle for attention, resources, and support, and ahead of political visions and academic theories (Olsen 2007; 2010; 2012). Processes of delegation and accountability have developed in parallel and partly informally and independent of each other during "normal times." Performance crises have generated demands for coordination and improved accountability.

Consider legal accountability and the birth of a new legal order in Europe. The origins of what has been called a juridical *coup d'état*, because courts in fundamental ways have transformed the normative foundations of the legal order through constitutional law-making (Stone Sweet 2007, 915), have a history. The ambiguities of the Treaties and different legal styles of interpretation allowed turf wars and struggle over competence and accountability. There have been gradual changes in judicial institutions, networks, and culture, based upon interaction between the European Court of Justice (ECJ), national courts, and the law profession. Through several partly autonomous events and decisions, and with significant elements of coincidence and chance, legal actors provided a "sufficient legal basis for the ECJ to revolutionize European law" and create an autonomous European legal order (Rasmussen 2008, 86, 98). A result was competing legal orders and ambiguous accountability relations.

Similar processes have taken place regarding administrative and financial accountability. European agencies (Busuioc 2010) and ombudsmen have struggled to establish an institutional identity, winning acceptance for the office, and building a Europe-wide professional network (Curtin 2007; Harlow and Rawlings 2007; Bovens, Curtin, and t'Hart 2010). The European Court of Auditors had difficulties developing an institutional identity as the guardian of sound financial management and gaining the attention of the EU's executive powers. Contest and resistance arose before action capacity was built and the Court was able to assert its role as a central node in a matrix of financial accountability. The Court gradually gained confidence and was accepted, helped by the growing power of the Union, bigger budgets, more net contributors to the budget, broad media coverage of fraud and scandals, and support from the European Parliament (Laffan 2003).

The EU cohesion policy saw an audit explosion triggered by financial management scandals and loss of legitimacy. However, whereas the aim was to achieve better policy performance, attention became focused on compliance and traditional financial accounting practice related to legality, regularity, and detecting errors, fraud, and corruption more than on learning and discovering how performance could be improved. There were complaints regarding the scale, intensity, redundancy, inefficiency, and overlapping of audits, diverting attention from results, strangling risk-taking and innovation, and generating disappointment and distrust. Resources and power were redistributed in favor of the "watchdogs" rather than those implementing cohesion policies and new auditing practices and regimes were layered on top of old ones (Mendez and Bachtler 2011).

Ambiguity and Accountability

Understanding how contemporary representative democracies live with ambiguity and multiple, contested, and dynamic conceptions of accountability that are not subject to enduring resolution requires going beyond mainstream compliance-control approaches. Accountability cannot be captured assuming a single, formal-legal chain of dyadic relationships or a checks-and-balances system in equilibrium. Theorizing what accountability is all about, through what mechanisms accountability is pursued, assigned, assessed, and sanctioned, and how regimes change, makes it necessary to go beyond a historical and non-contextual conception of accountability, making normative standards, epistemic quality, and the distribution of authority and power endogenous to politics and accountability processes. However, approaches based on different foundational assumptions are likely to be complementary rather than excluding each other. Theory-builders need to explore competing ideas, their areas of application, strengths and weaknesses, and the circumstances under which different processes are likely to foster or hinder effective accountability and regime change.

An institutional approach based on an expanded conception of accountability has been offered as a starting point for understanding how accountability regimes are organized, work, and change in representative democracies characterized by ambiguity, uncertainty, and tensions. Whereas there is a long way to go before a proper theory of accountability is within reach, some elements of a research agenda can be offered. Understanding accountability assumes reconstructing how decisions are made and whether things could and should have been done differently.

Political and organizational decision-making is often messy. The fluidity, inconsistencies, and conflicts of political life—incompletely reconciled desires and understandings that evolve in the context of pursuing them, variable participation, and shifting legitimacy of resources—make it difficult to correctly assign causal responsibility, credit, and blame. Democratic politics, nevertheless, emphasizing human will, understanding, and control and responsive and accountable government, foster demands for calling someone to account, and institutions are social conventions that create elements of temporary and imperfect order and predictability. Rules and practices define appropriate behavior and specify what is natural, normal, reasonable, right, good, and true; what must be expected, can be relied on and makes sense in a community; and institutionalized resources affect the degree to which actors are capable of complying with what rules prescribe and proscribe. Beliefs in a legitimate accountability regime simplify political life and reduce the degree of ambiguity by ensuring that many things are taken as given.

The institutional approach offered has gone beyond the stylized categories of compliance-control approaches privileging the electoral channel, legislation, hierarchies, and dyadic relations. It has invited comparisons between accountability regimes and argued that standard assumptions are most applicable in settled polities and routine situations characterized by low degrees of ambiguity. The assumptions are likely to be fruitful in polities with a sovereign center of normative and coercive authority or a single dominant set of normative and organizational principles, and in polities where formal-legal authority and external control dominate other concerns. Compliance-control approaches are less applicable in capturing accountability in unsettled polities and unfamiliar situations, especially in multi-level and multi-centered polities embedded in heterogeneous, pluralistic, and dynamic societies, such as the European Union. Under such conditions ambiguity plays a significant role because there are a variety of accountability regimes stretching over levels of government and institutional spheres. There is no unified, sovereign people, legitimate way of formulating unambiguous mandates, or authoritative political center. There are competing sources of information and conflicting role demands and internalized identities. Several actors hold roles as both "principals" and "agents," differently mobilized in different settings, and resources and capabilities are not necessarily adequate for prescribed roles. Possible next steps are to address in detail the actual operation and interaction of contested, co-existing accountability institutions, networks, and regimes, to develop typologies of accountability arrangements, and relate them to competing conceptions of what accountability is all about and what regimes foster effective accountability.

The institutional approach has gone beyond the assumptions that discovering and sanctioning deviance from pre-determined rules is the dominant aspect of accountability relations and processes, and that efficient accountability is best achieved through incentives and external control motivating a self-interested agent to behave as a self-interested principal desires. The approach has called attention to how accountability processes, especially in unsettled polities, provide occasions for searching for and testing collective purpose, intelligence, and meaning and political equality, and how internalization of different logics of appropriate behavior works as a mechanism through which institutions have an impact on calls for, rendering of, and responses to accounts. An institutional research agenda calls attention to the conditions under which accountability processes attract few or a variety of issues and participants; how training, socialization, and internalization may be stronger or weaker and more or less consistent across institutions; and how incentives and internalized rules interact in forming behavior. An underdeveloped issue is how accountability regimes affect how resources, rights, and capabilities are developed, distributed, regulated, and mobilized; how they make it more or less possible to act in accordance with key identities, roles, mandates, and responsibilities in representative democracies and, possibly, empower the powerless.

Finally, the institutional approach goes beyond the assumption that accountability regimes emerge, are maintained, and change as a result of the deliberate choices of pre-determined principals. It interprets the dynamics of accountability regimes as parts of complex institutionalization and de-institutionalization processes, and holds that compliance-control approaches are more likely to apply in a short-term perspective than in capturing long-term developments. The institutional agenda calls attention to how accountability processes provide opportunities for debates and struggles over what is a legitimate political order; how government is and should be organized; and where responsibility and accountability over different issues reside and should reside. Possible next steps are to examine what are stabilizing and de-stabilizing factors and frictions in change processes such as deliberate design, bargaining, deliberation, experiential learning, diffusion, and evolving historical processes. An institutional agenda in particular has to examine the internal dynamics of accountability regimes. In contemporary democracies accountability institutions are structured according to different principles and rules, providing competing analyses and prescriptions. Each institution is, furthermore, a collection of more or less tightly-coupled action programs determining possible actions over a range of circumstances that satisfies complex sets of standards, goals, rules, requirements, and constraints. There is therefore a need to explore how change follows because tensions and disputes are endemic in institutions and accountability regimes are never fully integrated or accepted by everyone.

NOTE

1. Thanks to Mark Bovens, Robert E. Goodin, and Thomas Schillemans for challenging comments and to James G. March for constructive suggestions and more than 40 years of discussions of ambiguity.

REFERENCES

Alesina, A. and Cukierman, A. 1990. "The Politics of Ambiguity." *Quarterly Journal of Economics*, 105: 829–50.

Beauvoir, S. de. 1972. *The Ethics of Ambiguity*. Secaucus, NJ: Citadel Press; originally published 1947.

Bovens, M. 2007. "Analysing and Assessing Accountability: A Conceptual Framework." *European Law Journal*, 13: 447–68.

Bovens, M., Curtin, D., and 't Hart, P. 2010. *The Real World of EU Accountability: What Deficit?* Oxford: Oxford University Press.

Busuioc, M. 2010. *The Accountability of European Agencies: Legal Provisions and Ongoing Practices*. Delft: Eburon.

Cohen, M. D., March, J. G., and Olsen, J. P. 1972. "A Garbage Can Model of Organizational Choice." *Administrative Science Quarterly*, 17: 1–25.

Cohen, M. D., March, J. G., and Olsen, J. P. 2012, "A garbage can model" at forty: A solution that still attracts problems, pp. 19–30 in *The Grabage Can Model of Organizational Choice: Looking Forward at Forty*, eds. A. Lomi and J. R. Harrison. Bingley, UK: Emerald Books.

Connolly, W. E. 1987. *Politics and Ambiguity*. Madison: University of Wisconsin Press.

Curtin, D. 2007. "Holding (Quasi-) Autonomous EU Administrative Actors to Public Account." *European Law Journal*, 13: 523–41.

Cyert, R. M. and March, J. G. 1963. *A Behavioral Theory of the Firm*. Englewood Cliffs, NJ: Prentice Hall.

Dubnick, M. J. 2005. "Accountability and the Promise of Performance: In Search of Mechanisms." *Public Performance & Management Review*, 28: 376–417.

Etzioni, A. 1964. *Modern Organizations*. Englewood Cliffs, NJ: Prentice-Hall.

Feldman, M. S. and March, J. G. 1981. "Information in Organizations as Signal and Symbol." *Administrative Science Quarterly*, 26: 171–86.

Gilmour, R. S. and Jensen, L. J. 1998. "Reinventing Government Accountability: Public Functions, Privatization, and the Meaning of 'State Action.'" *Public Administration Review*, 58: 247–58.

Goodin, R. E. 1982. *Political Theory and Public Policy*. Chicago: University of Chicago Press.

Goodin, R. E. 2008. *Innovating Democracy: Democratic Theory and Practice After the Deliberative Turn*. Oxford: Oxford University Press.

Gustavsson, S., Karlsson, C., and Persson, T. 2009. *The Illusion of Accountability in the European Union*. London: Routledge.

Hanson, R. L. 1987. Democracy, pp. 68–69 in *Political Innovation and Conceptual Change*, eds. T. Ball, J. Farr and R.L. Hanson. Cambridge: Cambridge University Press.

Harlow, C. and Rawlings, R. 2007. "Promoting Accountability in Multilevel Governance: A Network Approach." *European Law Journal*, 13: 542–62.

Keane, J. 2009. *The Life and Death of Democracy*. London: Simon & Schuster.

Klinger, D. E., Nalbandian, J., and Romzek, B. S. 2001. "Politics, Administration, and Markets: Conflicting Expectations and Accountability." *American Review of Public Administration*, 32: 117–44.

Laffan, B. 2003. "Auditing and Accountability in the European Union." *Journal of European Public Policy*, 10: 762–77.

Landau, M. 1969. "Redundancy, Rationality, and the Problem of Duplication and Overlap." *Public Administration Review*, 29: 346–58.

Lupia, A. and McCubbins, M. D. 2000. "Representation or Abdication? How Citizens Use Institutions to Help Delegation Succeed." *European Journal of Political Research*, 37: 291–307.

MacIntyre, A. 1988. *Whose Justice? Which Rationality?* Notre Dame: University of Notre Dame Press.

Magnette, P. 2000. "Towards 'Accountable Independence'? Parliamentary Controls of the European Central Bank and the Rise of a New Democratic Model." *European Law Journal*, 6: 326–40.

Manning, M. 2004. *Torture and the Politics of Ambiguity: Project Syndicate*. Retrieved from <www.project-syndicate.org/commentary/torture-and-the-politics-of-ambiguity>.

March, J. G. 2010. *The Ambiguities of Experience*. Ithaca: Cornell University Press.

March, J.G. and Olsen, J. P. 1976. *Ambiguity and Choice in Organizations*. Bergen: Universitetsforlaget.

March, J. G. and Olsen, J. P. 1989. *Rediscovering Institutions: The Organizational Basis of Politics*. New York: Free Press.

March, J. G. and Olsen, J. P. 1995. *Democratic Governance*. New York: Free Press.

March, J. G. and Weissinger-Baylon, R. 1986. *Ambiguity and Command: Organizational Perspectives on Military Decision Making*. Marshfield: Pitman.

Mendez, C. and Bachtler, J. 2011. "Administrative Reform and Unintended Consequences: An Assessment of the EU Cohesion Policy 'Audit Explosion.' " *Journal of European Public Policy*, 18: 746–65.

Olsen, J. P. 2007. *Europe in Search of Political Order*. Oxford: Oxford University Press.

Olsen, J. P. 2008. Explorations in Institutions and Logics of Appropriateness: An Introductory Essay, pp. 191–202 in *Explorations in Organizations*, ed. J.G. March. Stanford: Stanford Business Books.

Olsen, J. P. 2010. *Governing Through Institution Building: Institutional Theory and Recent European Experiments in Democratic Organization*. Oxford: Oxford University Press.

Olsen, J. P. 2013. "The Institutional Basis of Democratic Accountability." *West European Politics*, 36 (3): 447–73.

Page, B. I. 1976. "The Theory of Political Ambiguity." *The American Political Science Review*, 70: 742–52.

Pollitt, C. and Summa, H. 1997. "Reflexive Watchdogs? How Supreme Audit Institutions Account for Themselves." *Public Administration*, 75: 313–36.

Porter-O'Grady, T., Hawkins, M. A., and Parker, M. L. 1997. *Whole-Systems Shared Governance: Architecture for Integration*. Gaithersburg, MD: Aspen Publishers.

Przeworski, A., Stokes, S. C., and Manin, B. 1999. *Democracy, Accountability, and Representation*. Cambridge: Cambridge University Press.

Rasmussen, M. 2008. "The Origins of a Legal Revolution: The Early History of the European Court of Justice." *Journal of European Integration History*, 14: 77–98.

Searle, J. R. 1995. *The Construction of Social Reality*. London: Penguin.

Selznick, P. 1992. *The Moral Commonwealth: Social Theory and the Compromise of Community*. Berkeley: University of California Press.

Shepsle, K. A. 1972. "The Strategy of Ambiguity: Uncertainty and Electoral Competition." *The American Political Science Review*, 66: 555–68.

Stone Sweet, A. 2007. "The Juridical Coup d'État and the Problem of Authority." *German Law Journal*, 8: 915–28.

Stone, B. 1995. "Administrative Accountability in the 'Westminster' Democracies: Towards a New Conceptual Framework." *Governance*, 8: 505–26.

Strøm, K., Müller, W. C., and Bergman, T. 2003. *Delegation and Accountability in Parliamentary Democracies*. Oxford: Oxford University Press.

Thatcher, M. and Stone Sweet, A. 2002. "Theory and Practice of Delegation to Non-Majoritarian Institutions." *West European Politics*, 25: 1–22.

Verhey, L., Broeksteeg, H., and Driessche, I. van den 2008. *Political Accountability in Europe: Which Way Forward: A Traditional Concept of Parliamentary Democracy in a EU Context*. Groningen: Europa Law Publishing.

Warren, M. E. 2011. Democracy, pp. 517–29 in *The Oxford Handbook of the History of Political Philosophy*, ed. G. Klosko. Oxford: Oxford University Press.

Waterman, R. W. and Meier, K. J. 1998. "Principal-Agent Models: An Expansion?" *Journal of Public Administration Research and Theory*, 8: 173–202.

Wille, A. 2010. The European Commission's Accountability Paradox, pp. 63–86 in *The Real World of EU Accountability: What Deficit?* eds. M. Bovens, D. Curtin and P. 't Hart. Oxford: Oxford University Press.

PART II

STUDYING
ACCOUNTABILITY

CHAPTER 8

....

EXPERIMENTAL ANALYSIS

....

CHRISTOPHER KOCH AND JENS WÜSTEMANN

INTRODUCTION

....

EXPERIMENTAL research is about observing the effects of a deliberate intervention within a controlled setting. It offers the opportunity to establish causality through the powerful tool of random assignment. In a randomized experiment, participants are randomly allocated into a treatment group that receives the intervention and a control group that does not receive the intervention. Random assignment has the desired consequence that the participants in both groups can, on average, be expected to share similar characteristics and beliefs. In addition, the experimenter can control the setting. That means he or she can ensure that both groups face the same setting except for the intervention and that the intervention precedes the observed outcome. These elements of a controlled randomized experiment leave the intervention as the only plausible cause for the observed effect. In that case, the experiment is said to have high internal validity (e.g., Shadish et al. 2002, Ch. 2).

Experimental research can address issues on public accountability given that the experimental findings can be transferred to real world phenomena. This transfer is justified even if the experimental setting is a simpler version of reality as long as the experimental setting incorporates the real world features that are most important from a theoretical perspective. Other differences, for example, the characteristics of the intervention, the setting, the task, or the participants, do not hinder generalizing the experimental findings to the real world provided that these differences are unlikely to change the nature of the observed effect. An experiment with results that can be generalized to the real world setting is said to have high external validity (e.g., Shadish et al. 2002, Ch. 3).

This discussion shows that the external validity of experimental research rests on the strength of its theoretical foundations. The social contingency model provides such a theoretical fundament (Tetlock 1992). According to the model, an important aspect of accountability relationships is the expectation that one may be called on to justify one's judgment and decision-making to others. Being accountable to someone else is predicted to influence judgment and decision-making because people seek the social approval of others and will unconsciously apply strategies to ensure this approval. The social contingency model has facilitated the application of experimental accountability research to other fields, including politics (e.g., Gerber et al. 2008), auditing (e.g., Kennedy 1993), marketing (Zhang and Mittal 2005), negotiations (e.g., De Dreu et al. 2006), and many others. Experimental economics has only recently acquired interest in the construct of accountability and has investigated its impact on ambiguity aversion and loss aversion (e.g., Trautmann et al. 2008; Vieider 2011).

Experimental analysis can contribute to public accountability research in several ways. First, it is possible to integrate important elements of existing public accountability mechanisms into the experimental setting and to observe their causal effects on information processing, judgment, and decision-making. Second, experiments offer an opportunity to also consider alternative accountability mechanisms not implemented yet and their effects. Finally, experiments can be useful for identifying preferences for specific accountability mechanisms which may help to explain their existence in the real world.

Tetlock (1983): Towards the Development of the Social Contingency Theory

At the time of Tetlock's study (1983), the research on accountability was fragmented, with mixed results. It used a variety of different constructs for accountability including the level of social responsibility (Cvetkovich 1978), the degree of involvement (Chaiken 1980), and the need to inform a forum (Adelberg and Batson 1978). These studies found that while accountability often enhances effort, it can also influence people to exert little effort and simply adopt the position taken by the forum.

Tetlock emphasized the importance of considering the view of the forum when making predictions about the effects of accountability. If the actor knows the view of the forum, the simplest strategy for the actor is to shift their own view towards the view of the forum. The situation is different if the actor does not know the view of the forum. In that case, the actor might fear criticism for taking on a view without thinking the issue through. In response, he or she will exert high effort to build a defensible position.

To test these predictions Tetlock designed an experiment in which he asked the participants to record their thoughts and feelings on various controversial social issues (e.g., capital punishment), and then to express overtly their attitude on these issues. The study assigned the participants randomly to the experimental conditions. In a control condition of non-accountability, actors were assured that all of their responses would be completely confidential and anonymous. In the treatment conditions, participants expected to meet another subject to whom they had to justify their responses. The political views of the other subject were either not described at all ("unknown view treatment") or described as liberal or conservative ("known view treatments"). To strengthen the treatment effect, participants were informed that the upcoming meeting would be audiotaped. The study's finding supported that only accountability to a forum with unknown views enhances efforts measured by the level of integrative complexity, whereas accountability towards a forum with known views leads to a shift in attitude towards the views of the forum.

Tetlock's experimental design served as the model for many later studies. Together with a series of follow-up studies (Tetlock and Kim 1987; Tetlock and Boettger 1989; Tetlock et al. 1989), it led to the development of the social contingency theory (Tetlock 1985; Tetlock 1992).

RESEARCH QUESTIONS AND ISSUES

Accountability to Whom? The Forum

Public accountability relationships can be distinguished based on the variety of the forum. Examples of potentially relevant forums are political, regulatory, legal, or professional bodies. These forums are likely to differ in their informational demands and criteria of good behavior (Bovens 2007, 455–7).

Experimental research offers the opportunity to investigate how the actor's behavior is influenced by the anticipation of evaluation by a forum. That is, experimental research can test which characteristics of the forum have a causal impact on the judgment and decision-making of actors. An experimental study on this research question would systematically vary the characteristics of the forum across experimental conditions and observe the effects on the behavior of the participants. It can also capture the process of judgment and decision-making, which allows a greater understanding of how the effect emerges.

One key finding is that accountability does not have a uniform effect on judgment and decision-making; rather, its impact greatly depends on whether the preferences of the forum are known or unknown to the actor. If the preferences of the forum are known, actors tend to be biased towards these preferences in both the way they process information and their final judgment and decision (Tetlock 1983; Pennington and Schlenker 1999). Participants being accountable to a supervisor with a known view are more likely to selectively present defensive information that covers their mistakes (Fandt and Ferris 1990). The social contingency theory explains this finding through two main human motives, to minimize effort and to seek the social approval of others (Tetlock 1985; Tetlock 1992).

Experimental research observes a more balanced and diligent processing of information that leads to more balanced judgments and accurate decisions when the views of the forum are unknown to the actor (e.g., Tetlock 1983; Tetlock et al. 1989). Social contingency theory explains this behavior as the actors' attempt to ensure the social approval of a forum with unknown preferences by appearing well informed. To achieve this goal, actors tend to engage in pre-emptive self-criticism and integrative complexity. They attempt to anticipate potential criticism and develop well-grounded responses to it. This strategy also seems useful for coping with accountability pressure from two forums with opposing preferences (Green et al. 2000).

Who is Accountable? The Actor

Public accountability research is concerned with the question of who should render account. Should it be the organization as a legal entity or the members of the organization (Bovens 2007, 457–9)?

Experimental analysis focuses on the decision-making of persons. Therefore, experiments cannot directly investigate corporate accountability in which the legal entity must give account. However, it is possible to investigate this scenario indirectly by determining what corporate accountability means in practice. Does it mean that the head of the organization, the board, or a particular employee must be accountable? When corporate accountability is reduced to the individual level, it is possible to investigate it in experimental studies.

Experimental research on sole versus group accountability addresses the effects of collective versus individual accountability. One finding is that the diffusion of responsibility within a group reduces the impact of being held accountable for the outcome. The consequence is that sole decision-makers often perform better than groups when held accountable (O'Connor 1997). On the other hand, accountability can motivate groups to share increasingly relevant information which can enhance decision quality (Scholten et al. 2007).

One interesting issue is whether individuals differ in their ability to cope with accountability. However, experimental research is not best suited for the investigation of personality traits because the experimenter cannot directly manipulate these factors. Experimenters can only measure personality traits that reduce the ability to detect causal effects. This issue may partially explain why most studies observe rather weak interactive effects between accountability and personality traits or personal values (e.g., Tetlock et al. 1989; Brief and Dukerich 1991). As an exception, there is some evidence that participants with a low level of social anxiety and a high need for cognition are better able to cope with accountability (Tetlock et al. 1989; Green et al. 2000).

Experimental research has developed methods for manipulating factors that are related to personality traits. For example, Lerner et al. (1998) used video clips to prime their participants emotionally and found that accountability mitigates anger-related punitive attributions. Quinn and Schlenker (2002) employed short stories to motivate participants to either get along with others or make accurate decisions and found that those motivated to make accurate decisions can withstand the pressure to conform with the known views of a forum.

Accountability About What? The Content

Public accountability relationships can be constructed around various types of content; for example, they can concern the way financial resources are spent or whether specific rules of conduct have been followed (e.g., Adelberg and Batson 1978; Arkes et al. 1986). Important structural elements of the content include whether the accountability relationship is about the procedure followed or the outcome quality achieved and whether it is established before or after the processing of information (Bovens 2007, 459–60).

The social contingency model suggests that the timing of the formation of the accountability relationship is an important factor. In most cases, experimental studies hold the actor accountable from the start of the experiment. These studies often find that actors experience a strategic attitude switch for forums of known preferences and that they engage in pre-emptive self-criticism for forums whose preferences are unknown. Alternatively, experimental studies can inform participants of the accountability relationship only after they have made their judgment or decision. In this scenario, the social contingency theory predicts a strategy of defensive bolstering where participants focus on justifying their past decision rather than identifying a better solution to the problem (Tetlock et al. 1989).

Accountability mechanisms can hold the participant accountable for the procedure used in the decision process or the quality of the outcome achieved. These different types of accountability may trigger different behavioral responses. Simonson and Staw (1992) found that procedural accountability is helpful in reducing the escalation of commitment bias, but outcome accountability is not helpful. Siegel-Jacobs and Yates (1996) argued that procedural accountability is more likely to enhance performance than outcome accountability because the focus on the procedure implicitly suggests ways to improve. They further argued that procedural accountability is less stressful than outcome accountability as participants can protect against being blamed for failure by following the suggested procedures. Further studies have supported the finding that procedural accountability is superior to outcome accountability. Procedural accountability leads regularly to more conscientious behavior (Brtek and Motowidlo 2002) and makes tasks appear more solvable (Zhang and Mittal 2005). Procedural accountability can turn out to be problematic, however, if the optimal decision rule is more difficult to justify, because it is less intuitive (e.g., Slaughter et al. 2006) or more complex (De Langhe et al. 2011).

Accountability effects sometimes offer explanations for the existence of biases. For example, it can be rational for actors asked about the the ex ante likelihood of an event to consider ex post and therefore irrelevant information about outcomes given that they anticipate that the forum is prone to the hindsight bias. Similarly, the presence of accountability relationships can provide an explanation for ambiguity aversion as selecting an unambiguous choice is often easier to justify than selecting an ambiguous choice (Curley et al. 1986; Trautmann et al. 2008).

Kennedy (1993): Applying Accountability Research in Experimental Studies with Professionals

Kennedy (1993) applied the social contingency model to an experimental study with professional auditors and extended it by outlining a framework that explains in which circumstances accountability reduces biases in judgment and decision-making. Auditors are an interesting group of professionals to study because they exercise their professional judgment in a context of high accountability pressure from a variety of sources, e.g., internal quality reviewers, clients, and regulators (Gibbins and Newton 1994).

Kennedy developed a framework for the de-biasing effects of accountability based on prior literature. She argued that the effort-enhancing effects of accountability to a forum with unknown preferences indicate that accountability diminishes biases related to low effort, but does not have an effect on biases related to the non-optimal processing of information.

Kennedy tested her de-biasing framework in experimental studies that compared the judgment and decision-making of students and auditors. Accountability towards a forum with unknown views was varied across experimental conditions in which the participants were unaccountable, pre-accountable, and post-accountable. In the pre- and post-accountability conditions, the materials stated that some of the participants would be interviewed about their decisions by a forum and that a small number of these interviews were conducted. Pre-accountable indicates that participants were accountable from the start of the study, whereas post-accountable, indicates that they were only informed about their accountability after they had made their preliminary judgments, but before they made their final decision.

In line with her expectations, she found that pre-accountability diminished the effort-related recency bias for students. Expert auditors were not prone to the effort-related bias in both the accountable and non-accountable condition (Kennedy 1993). Further, she demonstrated that accountability had no effects on the data-related hindsight bias in which both students and auditors continue to make biased judgments even when held accountable (Kennedy 1995).

TESTING THE EFFECTS OF ACCOUNTABILITY

Formulating the Research Question Based on Theory

Theory plays an important role in experimental research. The first step in a research project is the formulation of the research question and the identification of relevant theory for developing the hypotheses. For accountability research, Tetlock's (1992) social contingency model provides a valuable framework.

Experimental studies gain their external validity from the underlying theory. Experiments that test a theory can claim that their findings are not only relevant within the specific experimental setting but also in other settings to which the theory applies. One can assume, therefore, that experimental settings that incorporate all of the important elements of the theory have high external validity. External validity is only endangered if elements of the real world differ from the experimental implementation in ways that are theoretically important (Bardsley et al. 2010, 56–71). The following sections discuss the implementation of important elements of accountability theory into experimental designs.

Selecting Participants in Consideration of their Background

Social contingency theory considers the motive of seeking the approval of others as an important driver for the effects of accountability (Baumeister and Leary 1995). Further, it assumes that this motive is a universal phenomenon that applies equally to young and old, men and women, laymen and professionals (Semin and Manstead 1983). The general applicability of the social contingency theory suggests that the findings of an experimental study should be generalizable to people with various backgrounds. As students are easy to recruit into studies, they are commonly chosen as participants. Theoretical arguments for students as participants are their low opportunity wage, steep learning curve, and open-mindedness towards the experimental setting (Friedman and Sunder 1994, 39).

But if the experiment will inform a certain domain, the experimenter must consider whether the participants in the experiment differ systematically from the population of the domain on theoretically important characteristics. Prior research has identified some characteristics of actors that interact with the effects of accountability. One might challenge, for example, whether the findings of experimental studies with students as subjects generalize to professionals, on the grounds of differences in social anxiety or need for cognition.

The beliefs of the participants about the view and preferences of the forum are an important aspect in the design and interpretation of experimental research. In the construction of experimental conditions in which the actors are informed about the views of the forum, the experimenter should ensure that the participants hold the intended beliefs about the views of the forum by explicitly describing these views (Brief and Dukerich 1991). If, however, the participants associate strong real world experiences with the setting, their own experiences might have a greater influence on their beliefs than the experimental description. For example, Russo et al. (2000) found that auditors react less strongly to accountability pressure from a forum with known views than do sales people. One explanation for this finding is that auditors carried the high accountability pressure of their daily work life into the experiment such that they acted as if they were accountable to a forum regardless of the actual experimental scenario.

In the experimental condition of unknown views, the experimenters typically expect that the participants believe that the forum may hold various views. However, they must be aware that participants might use any cue available to infer the forum's view. For example, actors could infer that the forum values optimal decision-making if told the members of the forum are researchers (Simonson and Nye 1992). Another possibility is that participants project their own views onto the audience. For example, Weigold and Schlenker (1991) observed that accountability had a magnifying effect, making participants who assessed themselves as risk-averse even more risk-averse. This finding suggests that participants expected the forum to share their own views. Similarly, Gelfand and Realo (1999) observed that individualists and collectivists behaved as if the forum shared their respective values.

Constructing a Relevant Task Environment

Social contingency theory can be applied to various tasks. Prior studies have accordingly investigated a diversity of experimental tasks that included statements of political attitude (e.g., Tetlock 1983), predictions of personality attributes (e.g., Tetlock and Kim 1987), evaluations of performance (e.g., Klimoski and Inks 1990), conduct of negotiations (e.g, Ben-Yoav and Pruitt 1984), and choices between risky options (e.g., Weigold and Schlenker 1991). The experimental task typically demands that the participants make hypothetical judgments and decisions. Some studies have provided the participants with the option to avoid making judgments and decisions, namely by choosing to pass the buck, procrastinate, or escape the decision (e.g., Green et al. 2000).

Experimenters strive to construct the task and its environment in a way that ensures experimental realism. Experimental realism is achieved if the participants behave in the experiment in a manner that is meaningful with respect to the research hypothesis. The task should motivate the participants to take the experiment seriously and to exert as much effort as they would in reality. One way to achieve experimental realism is to construct an experimental task that is similar to real world tasks important to the participants. Some studies have even acted as though the experimental task had real world consequences. For example, Pennington and Schlenker (1999) asked participants to make a recommendation on an ostensibly highly consequential real cheating case. Lord (1992) informed the participants that their judgment in the experiment would influence their performance evaluation in the real world. The degree of the similarity of the experimental task with the real world task is called mundane realism. Mundane realism is not an end in itself, but it can be a means to achieve experimental realism.

Economists often employ abstract tasks that are largely context-free. To achieve experimental realism, they utilize financial incentives (Hertwig and Ortmann 2001). However, providing financial incentives can be problematic in accountability research. Accountability constitutes a social incentive that motivates participants to exert additional effort if they are accountable to a forum with unknown preferences. The apparent similarity between social and financial incentives renders it likely that both factors interact, and recent studies have supported this intuition (Vieider 2011). The potential interaction effect represents a research opportunity, but it can also present a challenge for studies that attempt to focus on the main effects of accountability.

COMPARING DIFFERENT TYPES OF ACCOUNTABILITY MECHANISMS

Accountability is the expectation that one may be called on to justify one's judgment and decisions to others (Tetlock 1992). Experimental research investigates this phenomenon by comparing the behavior under accountability to a control condition of non-accountability. In the control condition of non-accountability, participants are assured of the anonymity and confidentiality of their responses. In contrast, in the treatment condition, participants are informed that they will meet a forum to which they must justify their decisions. Depending on the research question, the preferences of the forum are either explicitly described (known preferences) or not described (unknown preferences). The effectiveness of the manipulation is checked in post-experimental questions.

Accountability primarily includes the expectation that a meeting with a forum will take place, so from a theoretical perspective, it is not necessary to actually stage the meeting. Accordingly, upon the completion of the task, earlier studies have regularly informed the participants that the meeting had been cancelled and that they should continue with the post-experimental questionnaire. A debriefing session following the study informed the participant about the use of deception.

The use of deception is controversial. Deception can help to create effective and engaging treatment conditions, but it can also shatter participants' trust in the truthfulness of experimental settings and procedures. The loss of trust is problematic for future research because participants' distrust in the experimental setting reduces experimental realism and control. For this reason, deception in the form of providing false information to the participants is taboo in experimental economics (Davis and Holt 1993, 24). In psychology, deception is allowed, but only if it is justified by the study's significant scientific value and if effective non-deceptive alternatives are not feasible (American Psychologist Association 2002, Section 6.15). One way to achieve an efficient non-deceptive design in accountability research is to inform the participants that a specific fraction of all participants will be called on to justify their decision (e.g., Kennedy 1993; Vieider 2011). The downside of this method is that it might reduce the strength of the treatment because actors perceive it less likely that they will be called on to justify their judgments.

It is challenging to implement accountability mechanisms in experimental studies with professionals. Studies with professionals aim to investigate how the participants behave in the real world. The studies attempt to achieve this goal by integrating the real world context into the experimental setting. The challenge is to identify ways to incorporate a forum into the experimental design in a realistic manner. For example, how should an experimental design introduce a member of an executive board to whom a professional must justify his or her judgments in a realistic way? Alternative methods include the use of deception and informing the participants that their responses will be forwarded to the client (Buchman et al. 1996), informing them that they will have a simulated meeting with a person acting as the client (Koch et al. 2012), or asking them to imagine a forthcoming meeting with key constituents (Brown 1999).

IDENTIFYING ANTECEDENTS OF ACCOUNTABILITY

Accountability is a complex construct. It involves the multi-pronged question of who is accountable to whom about what and why. The complexity of the construct provides a challenge for experimental research because it makes it difficult to design various experimental conditions that differ only on some specified aspects but are comparable on all other features. For example, introducing a forum into an experimental condition incorporates a whole set of new aspects such as the concreteness and the characteristics of the forum, the identifiability of the actor, the perceived importance of the task, the presence of communication, and the immediacy of expected feedback. If the experimental conditions differ from each other in several aspects, experimental control is lost, and it becomes difficult to determine which aspect is driving the observed effect. The experimenter must conduct further studies to tease out the effects of the individual elements of accountability. For example, Sedikides et al. (2002) conducted a series of follow-up experiments to identify the incremental effects of the identifiability of the actor, the concreteness of the forum, and the status of the forum.

From a different perspective, the multi-dimensionality of the accountability construct can also represent a research opportunity. Experimental studies can be used to investigate whether the complex construct of accountability can be reduced to a more parsimonious construct that still captures all of the relevant features. An example of a construct that is more parsimonious than accountability is cognitive tuning. Cognitive tuning involves the expectation to communicate one's view to another individual, but it does not include a justification requirement (Zajonc 1960). However, Tetlock (1985) showed that accountability cannot be reduced to cognitive tuning because these constructs induce different behaviors. While accountability to a forum with unknown preferences triggers more complex information processing, a communication requirement triggers a suppression of complexity to produce a clear message. Further studies have demonstrated that it is impossible to reduce the accountability construct to decision importance or personal involvement (Tetlock 1992).

INVESTIGATING HOW ACCOUNTABILITY INFLUENCES INFORMATION PROCESSING

Experimental research offers the opportunity to investigate the manner of information processing that is triggered by accountability demands. Researchers can directly test whether actors engage in more thoughtful and balanced information processing when the preferences of the forum are unknown. Further, they can investigate whether a forum with known preferences not only influences what actors say but also how they think.

Information processing can be captured in multiple ways. One method is to ask the participants to list their thoughts and explain their reasoning. Studies that have used this approach have found that accountability to a forum with unknown preferences increases the number of arguments provided. Further, the arguments are expressed at higher levels of integrative complexity and are more balanced (e.g., Tetlock 1983). Other possibilities to analyze the impact of accountability on information processing are to measure the time required for the participants to complete the task or physiological measures such as blood pressure or heart rate (Brandts and Garofalo 2012). In a group setting, information processing can be captured by observing the intra-group interaction. For example, Scholten et al. (2007) found that accountability enhances the sharing of relevant information. An alternative approach is to structure the task and to elicit the participant's judgment on intermediary tasks (e.g., Koch et al. 2012).

Experimental techniques that actively interfere with information processing or manipulate the timing of accountability are most suitable for detecting causal relationships. Experimenters can interfere with the information processing of participants by placing them under cognitive load. For example, they can test whether time pressure reduces the presumably effort-related effects of accountability (Kruglanski and Freund 1983).

Experimental studies can also manipulate the timing of the accountability relationship. The effects of accountability should be weaker when the participants are placed under accountability pressure only after having processed most of the information. In line with this reasoning, Kennedy (1993) found that the mitigating effects of accountability for the effort-related recency bias are weaker for participants who are held accountable only after they have evaluated several pieces of evidence compared to participants who are informed about the accountability relationship from the beginning. Researchers can also test whether eliminating accountability by cancelling the meeting diminishes the effects of accountability. A persistence of the effects of accountability even if the meeting is cancelled would provide evidence that accountability influences not only what people say, but also how they process information (Pennington and Schlenker 1999).

Hoffman et al. (1996): The Role of Accountability In Experimental Economics

Experimental economics research often regards the social context as a nuisance. It regularly attempts to avoid the social context to ensure experimental control. For example, textbooks on experimental economics recommend paying participants privately. The intention of this rule is to avoid the social context in which the other participants observe how well each individual performed to ensure that the social incentives do not dominate the financial incentives (Friedman and Sunder 1994, 81).

Hoffman et al. (1996) is an important study that tested whether the social context introduced by making the decisions of the participants known to other participants or to the experimenter influences the level of altruistic behavior. The experimental design constructed a treatment group that ensured a complete absence of any social context by making sure that it was impossible for the other participants and for the experimenter to infer the decisions of the participant. The experimental task was the dictator game, in which a subject must determine how to divide $10 between herself and an anonymous counterpart. Several mechanisms were implemented to ensure complete privacy. First, the participant acting as the dictator received the money in cash and was able to replace the money taken out with fake money. The responses were then collected in sealed envelopes that made it impossible to tell whether it contained fake money or real money. In addition, some participants were randomly given no choice at all to ensure that the experimenter cannot infer the individual behavior of the participants even in a setting where all participants give the same response. The "no choice" scenario was implemented by having some envelopes that contained only fake money. After all envelopes were collected, they were shuffled and given out to the randomly assigned counterparts. The study finds that isolating participants from any social consequences increases the proportion of participants acting selfishly. The authors conclude that giving money in a dictator game that does not ensure complete privacy might be driven by reciprocity concerns instead of true altruism.

Experimental economics research that considers accountability as an interesting phenomenon and not as a potentially confounding factor has only recently begun. The first findings of this newly emerging research field are that accountability effects play an important role even in settings where counteracting financial incentives are provided (Vieider 2011) and that accountability demands reduce loss aversion (Pahlke et al. 2012), but magnify ambiguity aversion (Trautmann et al. 2008).

CONCLUSIONS

Experimental analysis is a useful research method for investigating how accountability to a forum influences the behavior of actors. Experimental research helps to identify which strategies actors use to cope with accountability and which factors trigger or moderate the use of these strategies. It also enables the investigation of the information processing that underlies the various strategies. These capabilities of experimental research explain why it is the main method for developing and testing the social contingency theory.

Another advantage of experimental accountability research is that it provides an avenue for bridging individual, interpersonal, and institutional approaches to judgment and decision-making (Lerner and Tetlock 2003). This bridging can be achieved by integrating the institutional elements of public accountability mechanisms into the experimental study and by investigating their causal effects on information processing as well as final judgment and decision-making. Thereby, experimental research on accountability connects cognitive psychology with social psychology.

The experimental method is less suitable for documenting which accountability mechanisms are in place in the real world and for identifying the ways in which accountability mechanisms differ from each other. Experimenters must be aware of these aspects, however, when designing experimental studies that are relevant for the real world. Therefore, they must rely on other research approaches to uncover this information.

Future research should consider the effects of accountability mechanisms in a broader context. For example, there has been little research on the topic with regard to which accountability mechanisms people prefer. One study by Tetlock (2000) found that political ideology influences whether people prefer accountability mechanisms that focus on the process or the outcome. Based on this finding, an interesting question is the effects of accountability on behavior when people can voluntarily choose whether they want to be held accountable and in which ways. Another possible extension relates to the way the preferences and beliefs of the forum are introduced. Rather than simply providing this information to the participants, future studies could investigate how and under what circumstances actors actively search for details concerning the forum's views. Finally, prior studies have often asked the participants only about their judgment and decisions. Social contingency theory predicts alternative strategies for coping with accountability that involve buck-passing or procrastination, but their attractiveness has rarely been tested (Green et al. 2000).

Experimental research on accountability that employs the paradigm of experimental economics has only recently begun. The method of experimental economics provides the opportunity to address new research questions that would be more difficult to investigate under a psychology-based framework. One important research question addresses the relationship between accountability and financial incentives. One study suggested that both constructs have different and sometimes interactive effects on behavior (Vieider 2011). Another interesting approach could be to integrate the accountability relationship between the forum and the actor within a game theoretical framework. This approach would allow the investigation of whether the predictions of game theory hold under accountability (e.g., Camerer 2003) and whether the effects of accountability can be observed in settings with repeated interactions that allow for learning (e.g., Camerer et al. 2003).

One final promising venue for future research is field experiments. Laboratory experiments cannot provide a definite answer on how relevant their findings are for the real world. Intervening in the real world by implementing an accountability mechanism on a random basis offers the potential to inform us which laboratory findings hold in reality and might provide us with new insights (e.g., DellaVigna 2009). An example of a field study is Gerber et al. (2008) that puts a group of voters under social pressure by promising them that their turnout will be publicized to their neighbors. Future studies could investigate the impact of specific features of accountability mechanisms within a work context through field experiments with real organizations and real employees.

References

Adelberg, S. and Batson, C. D. 1978. "Accountability and Helping: When Needs Exceed Resources." *Journal of Personality and Social Psychology*, 36: 343–50.

American Psychologist Association. 2002. *Ethical Principles of Psychologists and Code of Conduct*. Retrieved from <http://www.apa.org/ethics/code/>.

Arkes, H. R., Dawes, R. M., and Christensen, C. 1986. "Factors Influencing the Use of a Decision Rule in a Probabilistic Task." *Organizational Behavior and Human Decision Processes*, 37: 93–110.

Bardsley, N., Cubitt, R., Loomes, G., Moffatt, P., Starmer, C., and Sugden, R. 2010. *Experimental Economics*. Princeton and Oxford: Princeton University Press.

Baumeister, R. F. and Leary, M. R. 1995. "The Need to Belong: Desire for Interpersonal Attachments as a Fundamental Human Motivation." *Psychological Bulletin*, 117: 497–529.

Ben-Yoav, O. and Pruitt, D. G. 1984. "Accountability to Constituents: A Two-Edged Sword." *Organizational Behavior and Human Performance*, 34: 283–95.

Bovens, M. 2007. "Analysing and Assessing Accountability: A Conceptual Framework." *European Law Journal*, 13: 447–68.

Brandts, J. and Garofalo, O. 2012. "Gender Pairings and Accountability Effects." *Journal of Economic Behavior and Organization*, 83: 31–41.

Brief, A. P. and Dukerich, J. M. 1991. "Resolving Ethical Dilemmas in Management: Experimental Investigations of Values, Accountability, and Choice." *Journal of Applied Social Psychology*, 21: 380–96.

Brown, C. 1999. "Do the Right Thing: Diverging Effects of Accountability in a Managerial Context." *Marketing Science*, 18: 230–46.

Brtek, M. D. and Motowidlo, S. J. 2002. "Effects of Procedure and Outcome Accountability on Interview Validity." *Journal of Applied Psychology*, 87: 185–91.

Buchman, T. A., Tetlock, P. E., and Reed, R. O. 1996. "Accountability and Auditors' Judgments About Contingent Events." *Journal of Business Finance and Accounting*, 23: 379–98.

Camerer, C., Ho, T., and Chong, K. 2003. "Models of Thinking, Learning, and Teaching in Games." *American Economic Review*, 93: 192–5.

Camerer, C. F. 2003. *Behavioral Game Theory: Experiments in Strategic Interaction*. Princeton, NJ: Princeton University Press.

Chaiken, S. 1980. "Heuristic Versus Systematic Information Processing and the Use of Source Versus Message Cues in Persuasion." *Journal of Personality and Social Psychology*, 39: 752–66.

Curley, S. P., Yates, J. F., and Abrams, R. A. 1986. "Psychological Sources of Ambiguity Avoidance." *Organizational Behavior and Human Decision Processes*, 38: 230–56.

Cvetkovich, G. 1978. "Cognitive Accomodation, Language and Social Responsibility." *Social Psychology*, 41: 149–55.

Davis, D. D. and Holt, C. A. 1993. *Experimental Economics*. Princeton, NJ: Princeton University Press.

De Dreu, C. K. W., Beersma, B., Stroebe, K., and Euwema, M. C. 2006. "Motivated Information Processing, Strategic Choice, and the Quality of Megotiated Agreement." *Journal of Personality and Social Psychology*, 90: 927–43.

De Langhe, B., van Osselaer, S. M. J., and Wierenga, B. 2011. "The Effects of Process and Outcome Accountability on Judgment Process and Performance." *Organizational Behavior and Human Decision Processes*, 115: 238–52.

DellaVigna, S. 2009. "Psychology and Economics: Evidence from the Field." *Journal of Economic Literature*, 47: 315–72.

Fandt, P. M. and Ferris, G. R. 1990. "The Management of Information and Impressions. When Employees Behave Opportunistically." *Organizational Behavior and Human Decision Processes*, 45: 140–58.

Friedman, D. and Sunder, S. 1994. *Experimental Methods: A Primer for Economists*. New York City: Cambridge University Press.

Gelfand, M. J. and Realo, A. 1999. "Individualism-Collectivism and Accountability in Intergroup Negotiations." *Journal of Applied Psychology*, 84: 721–36.

Gerber, A. S., Green, D. P., and Larimer, C. W. 2008. "Social Pressure and Voter Turnout: Evidence from a Large-Scale Field Experiment." *American Political Science Review*, 102: 33–48.

Gibbins, M. and Newton, J. D. 1994. "An Empirical Exploration of Complex Accountability in Public Accounting." *Journal of Accounting Research*, 32: 165–86.

Green, M. C., Visser, P. S., and Tetlock, P. E. 2000. "Coping With Accountability Cross-Pressures: Low-Effort Evasive Tactics and High-Effort Quests for Complex Compromises." *Personality and Social Psychology Bulletin*, 26: 1380–91.

Hertwig, R. and Ortmann, A. 2001. "Experimental Practices in Economics: A Methodological Challenge for Psychologists." *Behavioral and Brain Sciences*, 24: 383–451.

Hoffman, E., McCabe, K. A., and Smith, V. L. 1996. "On Expectations and the Monetary Stakes in Ultimatum Games." *International Journal of Game Theory*, 25: 289–301.

Kennedy, J. 1993. "Debiasing Audit Judgment With Accountability: A Framework and Experimental Results." *Journal of Accounting Research*, 31: 231–45.

Kennedy, J. 1995. "Debiasing the Curse of Knowledge in Audit Judgment." *The Accounting Review*, 70: 249–73.

Klimoski, R. and Inks, L. 1990. "Accountability Forces in Performance Appraisal." *Organizational Behavior and Human Decision Processes*, 45: 194–208.

Koch, C., Weber, M., and Wüstemann, J. 2012. "Can Auditors be Independent? Experimental Evidence on the Effects of Auditors' Client Type." *European Accounting Review*, 21: 797–823.

Kruglanski, A. W. and Freund, T. 1983. "The Freezing and Unfreezing of Lay-Inferences: Effects on Impressional Primacy, Ethnic Stereotyping, and Numerical Anchoring." *Journal of Experimental Social Psychology*, 19: 448–68.

Lerner, J. S., Goldberg, J. H., and Tetlock, P. E. 1998. "Sober Second Thought: The Effects of Accountability, Anger, and Authoritarianism on Attributions of Responsibility." *Personality and Social Psychology Bulletin*, 24: 563–74.

Lerner, J. S. and Tetlock, P. E. 2003. Bridging Individual, Interpersonal, and Institutional Approaches to Judgment and Decision Making: The Impact of Accountability on Cognitive Bias, pp. 431–57 in *Emerging Perspectives on Judgment and Decision Research*, eds. S. Schneider and J. Shanteau. Cambridge, UK: Cambridge University Press.

Lord, A. T. 1992. "Pressure: A Methodological Consideration for Behavioral Research in Auditing." *Auditing*, 11: 89–108.

O'Connor, K. M. 1997. "Groups and Solos in Context: The Effects of Accountability on Team Negotiation." *Organizational Behavior and Human Decision Processes*, 72: 384–407.

Pahlke, J., Strasser, S., and Vieider, F. M. 2012. "Risk-Taking for Others under Accountability." *Economics Letters*, 114: 102–5.

Pennington, J. and Schlenker, B. R. 1999. "Accountability for Consequential Decisions: Justifying Ethical Judgments to Audiences." *Personality and Social Psychology Bulletin*, 25: 1067–81.

Quinn, A. and Schlenker, B. R. 2002. "Can Accountability Produce Independence? Goals as Determinants of the Impact of Accountability on Conformity." *Personality and Social Psychology Bulletin*, 28: 472–83.

Russo, J. E., Meloy, M. G., and Wilks, T. J. 2000. "Predecisional Distortion of Information by Auditors and Salespersons." *Management Science*, 46: 13–27.

Scholten, L., Knippenberg, D. van, Nijstad, B. A., and De Dreu, C. K. W. 2007. "Motivated Information Processing and Group Decision-Making: Effects of Process Accountability on Information Processing and Decision Quality." *Journal of Experimental Social Psychology*, 43: 539–52.

Sedikides, C., Herbst, K. C., Hardin, D. P., and Dardis, G. J. 2002. "Accountability as a Deterrent to Self-Enhancement: The Search for Mechanisms." *Journal of Personality and Social Psychology*, 83: 592–605.

Semin, G. R. and Manstead, A. S. R. 1983. *The Accountability of Conduct: A Social Psychological Analysis*. New York, NY: Academic Press.

Shadish, W. R., Cook, T. D., and Campbell, D. T. 2002. *Experimental and Quasi-Experimental Designs for Generalized Causal Inference*. Boston, MA: Houghton-Mifflin Company.

Siegel-Jacobs, K. and Yates, J. F. 1996. "Effects of Procedural and Outcome Accountability on Judgment Quality." *Organizational Behavior and Human Decision Processes*, 65: 1–17.

Simonson, I. and Nye, P. 1992. "The Effect of Accountability on Susceptibility to Decision Errors." *Organizational Behavior and Human Decision Processes*, 51: 416–46.

Simonson, I. and Staw, B. M. 1992. "Deescalation Strategies: A Comparison of Techniques for Reducing Commitment to Losing Courses of Action." *Journal of Applied Psychology*, 77: 419–26.

Slaughter, J. E., Bagger, J., and Li, A. 2006. "Context Effects on Group-Based Employee Selection Decisions." *Organizational Behavior and Human Decision Processes*, 100: 47–59.

Tetlock, P. E. 1983. "Accountability and Complexity of Thought." *Journal of Personality and Social Psychology*, 45: 74–83.

Tetlock, P. E. 1985. "Accountability: The Neglected Social Context of Judgment and Choice." *Research in Organizational Behavior*, 7: 297–332.

Tetlock, P. E. 1992. "The Impact of Accountability on Judgment and Choice: Toward a Social Contingency Model." *Advances in Experimental Social Psychology*, 25: 331–76.

Tetlock, P. E. 2000. "Cognitive Biases and Organizational Correctives: Do Both Disease and Cure Depend on the Politics of the Beholder?" *Administrative Science Quarterly*, 45: 293–326.

Tetlock, P. E. and Boettger, R. 1989. "Accountability: A Social Magnifier of the Dilution Effect." *Journal of Personality and Social Psychology*, 57: 388–98.

Tetlock, P. E. and Kim, J. I. 1987. "Accountability and Judgment Processes in a Personality Prediction Task." *Journal of Personality and Social Psychology*, 52: 700–9.

Tetlock, P. E., Skitka, L., and Boettger, R. 1989. "Social and Cognitive Strategies for Coping with Accountability: Conformity, Complexity, and Bolstering." *Journal of Personality and Social Psychology*, 57: 632–40.

Trautmann, S. T., Vieider, F. M., and Wakker, P. P. 2008. "Causes of Ambiguity Aversion. Known Versus Unknown Preferences." *Journal of Risk and Uncertainty*, 36: 225–43.

Vieider, F. M. 2011. "Separating Real Incentives and Accountability." *Experimental Economics*, 14: 507–18.

Weigold, M. F. and Schlenker, B. R. 1991. "Accountability and Risk Taking." *Personality and Social Psychology Bulletin*, 17: 25–9.

Zajonc, R. B. 1960. "The Process of Cognitive Tuning in Communication." *Journal of Abnormal and Social Psychology*, 61: 159–67.

Zhang, Y. and Mittal, V. 2005. "Decision Difficulty: Effects of Procedural and Outcome Accountability." *Journal of Consumer Research*, 32: 465–72.

CHAPTER 9

QUANTITATIVE ANALYSIS

GIJS JAN BRANDSMA

INTRODUCTION

QUANTITATIVE empirical studies into accountability are scarce. Much of the available literature provides definitions, typologies, theoretical models, or case studies, but research that compares findings on the basis of a fixed set of indicators is to a great degree still lacking. Comparability of findings is typically seen as the strength of quantitative methodology, but in the domain of accountability the necessary indicators have not become established enough in the field to allow for such systematic comparison. Operationalizations differ greatly, not only between studies using different definitions of accountability but even within sets of studies using similar definitions. Key methodological choices that directly follow from the respective research questions are often left implicit. The result is that empirical findings are mostly not cumulative, leaving the actual workings of accountability poorly understood beyond the domains of single cases.

This chapter maps out this largely uncharted terrain. It navigates through the many different indicators used in existing quantitative accountability research, and demonstrates which indicators are relevant for which particular classes of research questions. Singular, unbiased, and unambiguous indicators for accountability regrettably do not exist. For that, the scope of the concept simply is too big, and also it has multiple appearances depending on which aspects of accountability are researched in which context (cf. Tetlock 1985; Bovens 2007).

Finding the most appropriate indicators for accountability thus depends primarily on the main research question as well as the debate to which the according research aims to contribute. This chapter is structured along the lines of a number of questions, that together point towards particular sets of indicators. How is accountability understood?

Are formal accountability structures in scope, or rather practices? Do findings need to be comparable, and if so, between individuals or between organizations? Are changes over time part of the research question? And, is accountability in the end to be assessed or evaluated, or not? By answering these and more questions systematically, the relevance of certain previous studies becomes more easily apparent than when the concept "accountability" is used in a rather generic sense. This chapter organizes the approaches of existing quantitative studies into accountability by going through these guiding questions in turn.

Two Understandings of Accountability

Previous chapters in this volume have delved extensively into definitions of accountability and therefore I will not discuss these in detail (see Bovens, Schillemans, and Goodin in this handbook). What matters most at this point is that there are two distinct classes of definitions, those that define accountability *as a virtue* and those that define it *as a mechanism* (see Bovens (2010) for a more detailed discussion). These two classes of definitions give rise to different research questions and hence also different research designs and indicators.

Accountability *as a virtue* treats accountability as the derivate of the general desirability of an actor's behavior, for example in terms of effectiveness, efficiency, or, more broadly, good governance. Hence, the exact components of accountability as a virtue are not exhaustively identified. It is an umbrella concept used for a wide range of virtuous behaviors (cf. Considine 2002, 33). Thus the focus in the virtue approach of accountability is on the behavior of actors in terms of the outputs they deliver.

Accountability *as a mechanism* taps into the relationship between an actor and an accountability forum. Thus the focus is not on the (public) goods produced by the actor, but rather on accountability *for* the actor's behavior. Approaches of accountability as a mechanism can include identifying and mapping actor–forum relationships within a particular domain (e.g., Hanretty and Koop 2009; Schillemans 2008), as well as actors' expectations that they may eventually be held to account for their behavior (e.g. Tetlock 1983), as well as the actual practices of informing, discussing, judging, and imposing consequences (e.g., Brandsma 2010).

One word of caution is warranted about the level of aggregation. It needs to be properly specified whether the actors and forums are *individuals* or *organizations*, or that individual level data is required in order to say something about organizational behavior. These require different data resources and different research designs, since, for example, organizational structure varies between organizations and not between individuals within the same organization.[1]

When accountability is defined and actors and forums have been selected, it becomes possible to gauge accountability quantitatively. Even though the number of quantitative accountability studies is low, taken together they have made use of a plethora of different indicators and different methods that may serve as a basis for more cumulative research in this area. Because accountability as a virtue refers to a different object under study than accountability as a mechanism, the indicators fitting in each of these two strands of research will be discussed separately.

Measuring Accountability as a Virtue

Accountability as a virtue refers to a wide set of behaviors, and the set of indicators that has so far been used for this is accordingly large. For *political actors* for instance, a common indicator is pledge fulfillment by political parties (e.g., Ashworth 2000; Klingemann, Hoffebert, and Budge 1994). A disadvantage of using this indicator is that it does not capture pledge fulfillment by opposition parties since they do not govern, and furthermore it is incapable of assessing the behavior of politicians with respect to issues that only entered the political agenda after the election. Hence, alternative measures that compare the conflict dimensions in parliamentary debates to the conflict dimensions in electoral campaigns are more accurate (Louwerse 2011), and the more congruent these areas of competition are found to be, the better.

For accountability of *non-elected organizations*, operationalizations are used that either include popular approval ratings (e.g. Gelleny and Anderson 2000), or that closely tie in with notions of open government. A landmark research endeavor in the latter respect is the annual "Global Accountability Report" published by One World Trust (Lloyd, Warren, and Hammer 2008), a British non-governmental organization advocating accountability and transparency in global governance. The "Global Accountability Report," as published from 2005 onwards, analyzes accountability according to four dimensions: transparency, participation, complaints and response handling, and evaluation. In every report, a different sample of 30 globally active organizations is drawn, being international governmental organizations, non-governmental organizations, and corporations. The four dimensions of accountability are scored through an evaluation of the organization's internal procedures by means of a large number of indicators gauging, for example, whether there is stakeholder engagement, the timing of responses to requests from outside, the degree to which appeals mechanisms are impartial, and how the organization's procedures are communicated to its environment (Lloyd, Warren, and Hammer 2008). In the domain of global affairs, this research is the most extensive accountability study of its kind, but it may equally well be applicable within the national domain. The most recent coding scheme was published in 2011 (Hammer and Lloyd 2011; see also Box 1).

In managerial studies, accountability is also operationalized as performance, or rather high performance is seen as a proxy of accountable behavior. In this vein O'Connell (2005) operationalizes accountability as finance and client performance ratings. Weibel, Rost, and Osterloh (2010) reviewed previous studies on the effect of merit pay on performance by means of a meta-regression. They conclude that merit pay schemes have a slight positive effect.

Since accountability as a virtue can take up very broad meanings that overlap with notions of good governance, responsiveness, performance, and other desiderata, indicators of those concepts that are not literally labeled "accountability" may also be useful. It would go beyond the scope of this chapter to discuss these in detail. But since the number of quantitative studies into these issues is relatively large, students of accountability should have no problem finding appropriate indicators that arguably also tap into accountability as a virtue. Bouckaert and Van de Walle (2003), for instance, list and critically discuss operationalizations of trust and good governance. Thomas and Palfrey (1996) provide a generic evaluative framework, including among other concepts, effectiveness, efficiency, appropriateness, acceptability, and responsiveness, extended by Vigoda (2002) to include more specific indicators of public satisfaction with government services.

Box 9.1 Landmark study of accountability as a virtue

Hammer and Lloyd (2011) use 73 indicators for measuring accountability on four dimensions. All items are four-point scales. A selection:

Indicator	Extreme 1	Extreme 2
Transparency		
Transparency policy	Organization has no position, or makes vague commitments	There are formal, mandatory, and public policies
Rewards and incentives	No formal system of rewarding transparent behavior among staff	Transparency is part of job targets and is appraised against
Appeals process	No process exists for appeal against decision of non-disclosure	There is an independent appeal body, reporting to the board
Participation		
Process commitments	No commitments as to how to consult stakeholders	Commitment to balancing stakeholder voices, information before consultation, feedback
Staff capacity	No provision of support to staff in engaging with stakeholders	Training of staff, provision of overview of commitments, guidelines for implementing these
Quality management systems	No monitoring of engagement	Organization-wide monitoring, with stakeholders results periodically published internally and externally

Evaluation		
Independence of evaluation	No procedures or commitments for independence of evaluations	There is an independent body evaluating periodically
Level of evaluation	No commitment to evaluating	Requirements for evaluating specific issues operational, policy, and strategic activities
Stakeholder involvement	No consultation with stakeholders in developing approach to and external valuations	Wide consultations with internal stakeholders on approach to evaluations
Complaints and response		
Process	No procedures on handling complaints from external stakeholders	Multiple channels for making complaints, procedures clearly specified
Protection	No commitment to protecting stakeholders that make complaints	Ensuring confidentiality and non-retaliation; sanctioning those who do retaliate
Whistle-blower policy	No commitment to responding to internal complaints	Policy of responding to internal complaints, applicable to all categories of staff

MEASURING ACCOUNTABILITY AS A MECHANISM

Many observers have noted that governance structures get increasingly complex and that this results in a dispersion of accountability over an ever-growing number of forums and actors. In addition, there may well be a wide range of informal accountability forums to which actors *feel* obliged to render account (Doney and Armstrong 1996). Gauging all possible accountabilities for certain actors or forums therefore defies one's best efforts.

Researchers therefore usually investigate just one or only a few *types* of accountability relationship, depending on the nature of the most relevant actors or forums and the type of behavior for which account is rendered (Tetlock 1985). This chapter will not repeat the typology of accountabilities presented earlier, but it is evident that accountability towards the electorate requires a different research design as well as different indicators than when accountability within a bureaucracy is in scope, even though both may be conceptualized as hierarchical, principal–agent type relationships.

Accountability as a mechanism essentially consists of three elements: information provided by the actor to the forum, debate or discussion between actor and forum, and judgment (eventually including imposing consequences) passed by the forum. Not all the three elements have been investigated to the same degree.

Information has been investigated most extensively, and quite a large range of indicators is available for tapping into this element. Perhaps this is because information is seen as a prerequisite for the other elements of accountability (Bovens 2007: but see Brandsma and Schillemans 2013). In the context of multilateral negotiations (in which the negotiator is the agent of a domestic principal), Delreux (2011) plainly asks principals to report if they feel they receive the same information as their agent during feedback meetings, but he also taps into information asymmetries in favor of the principals by asking if they put all their cards on the table regarding fallback positions. For a small set of European parliamentary debates on European Council affairs, Van de Steeg (2009) simply codes whether or not the European Council has provided the European Parliament with information. In coding agency statutory requirements, Koop (2011) scores if agencies are obliged to provide to ministers information on request, annual plans, annual budgets, annual activity reports, and annual financial reports. Brandsma (2010) uses multiple indicators for different types of information on committee meetings as presented to the hierarchical superiors of its participants, including items on issues on the agenda, the input of the participants, the results of any votes, and the proceedings of the discussions in committee. Wang (2002) surveyed American municipal chief administrators and asked them to what degree their cities inform residents, elected officials, and the business community. This item is repeated for a large number of municipal activities (such as projects), organizational performance indicators (such as goal attainment), professional tools (such as audit reports), and disclosure strategies (such as media or hearings).

The debate on information as part of accountability to some degree overlaps with the debate on transparency. The conceptual difference is that transparency is about the availability of information which is often not targeted at a specific recipient (usually at the public at large), whereas accountability is about the actual transfer of information to a specific recipient (the accountability forum). For transparency to contribute to accountability, the recipient thus actually needs to read and process the available information (Hueller 2007; Naurin 2007). Nevertheless, indicators of transparency may well be useful for gauging the information element of accountability, especially where accountability towards the general public is concerned.

Welch and Wong (2001), for instance, study transparency for one medium of information only, namely government websites. The websites are scored quite crudely (i.e. only 0 or 1 scores) on a very large number of indicators including for example the provision of contact details, an organization chart, easily readable reports and documents, and clickable e-mail links towards subdivisions of the organization. Pina, Torres, and Royo (2007) perform a similar analysis for European local and regional governments, but score observed frequencies as opposed to dichotomized scores. Brandsma, Curtin, and Meijer (2008) discuss the capability of NGOs and the general public to act as fire alarms to the European Parliament by counting the number of times that the lists of participants, agendas, minutes, vote results, and draft decisions of executive decision-making committees are made available through the internet. The completeness of the committees' internet registry is assessed by comparing its contents to the European Commission's annual report on committee workings, which lists the number of meetings and decisions per committee. These transparency indicators arguably are useful for tapping into the information dimension of accountability as a mechanism.

As many indicators as there are available for gauging information, so few exist for tapping into *discussions* or *debates*. But this is also the dimension that is hardest to quantify. Whereas information and sanctions relate to observable acts, to formal capacities or to documents, indicators on discussion tap into a less observable aspect. Still, some have used indicators to gauge it. Brandsma (2010) used indicators to gauge frequency as well as intensity of discussion between a superior and a hierarchic subordinate. For non-profit organizations, Carman (2009) recorded, amongst other items, if those organizations hire external evaluators to do site visits. In their study on government websites that was mentioned earlier, Welch and Wong (2001) measure interactivity between local governments and residents through the availability of clickable e-mail links towards subdivisions of the organization, thereby gauging opportunities for discussions rather than actual practices. Brehm and Gates (1997) gauge the frequency of receiving feedback that helps street level bureaucrats to improve performance. Van de Steeg (2009) coded the recordings of complete parliamentary debates for a relatively small number of issues. Indicators include efficient use of speaking time, clarity of the questions asked, listening to questions asked, and actual answering of the questions. On a more abstract note, McGraw (1991) provides a typology of justifications and excuses, and tested in a laboratory setting how evaluations of past behavior differ between types of justification and excuses provided.

The number of indicators for the *judgment and consequences* phase of accountability is somewhat higher. In the context of electoral accountability, Strøm (1997) investigates electoral volatility and the timing before the election at which voters make their final vote choice, which he uses as a proxy to describe the strength of retrospective voting as a form of sanctioning political leaders. For political accountability, Van de Steeg (2009) codes whether the European Parliament is able to adopt a resolution following debates with European Council presidents. With respect to agencies, Hanretty and Koop (2009) and Koop (2011) study structural features of regulatory agencies, and among other items score the possibilities for forums to overturn agency decisions, dismiss agency heads, ignore appointment nominees, and renew terms for board members. Lamothe and Lamothe (2009) have looked at the consequences of non-compliance in a dataset consisting of no less than 6,061 contracts between governments and external service providers. Their main indicators were if the service provider was able to maintain any contracts in the following periods, and if the relative number of contracts decreased over time, both of which serving as proxies for sanctions. Brehm and Gates (1997) mainly tap into the effectiveness of rewards and sanctions, using indicators such as preferences for promotions, bonuses, paid leave, and applying disciplinary actions. Brandsma (2010) gauges the availability of certain sanctioning and rewarding instruments to heads of unit in bureaucracies, including the actual application of these instruments.

One striking aspect of the existing quantitative researches of accountability as a mechanism is that, except for Van de Steeg (2009), Brandsma (2010), and Brandsma and Schillemans (2013), studies always focus on one or two elements of accountability mechanisms as opposed to the full set. This may well relate to a general lack of conceptual clarity as to how accountability is to be defined. But if we take the threefold distinction between information, discussion, and judgment/consequences as a starting point, the clustering of research into all elements but discussion is striking (Brandsma and Schillemans 2013).

In sum there are a fair number of indicators available for both approaches to accountability, but the different indicators used do not completely correspond to each other. In fact, there are even some researchers who alternate researching accountability as a virtue and accountability as a mechanism between separate studies (e.g. the quality of government institute, cf. Dahlberg 2011; Teorell et al. 2011), or even within the same research (e.g. Transparency International 2000).

Box 9.2 Examples of indicators of accountability as a mechanism

Indicator	Author	Method
Information		
Availability of information on a webpage (different types, yes/no)	Welch and Wong 2001	Content analysis
Same (different types, counted)	Pina et al. 2007	Content analysis
Completeness of information on a webpage (percentage)	Brandsma et al. 2008	Content analysis
Information obligations from agencies to ministers: various categories (yes/no)	Koop 2011	Content analysis
How often are you informed [by the actor] on [list]	Brandsma 2010	Survey
Do principals feel they receive the same information as their agents?	Delreux 2011	Survey
Discussion		
[The actor's behavior] is often discussed with him afterwards	Brandsma 2010	Survey
Evaluation discussions are on matters of principle	Brandsma 2010	Survey
Clarity of questions asked and answers given	Van de Steeg 2009	Content analysis
Site visits by external evaluators	Carman 2009	Survey
Different types of justifications	McGraw 1991	Experiment
Clickable e-mail links (proxy for opportunities for interactive engagement) (yes/no)	Welch and Wong 2001	Content analysis
Consequences		
To what extent would you prefer to receive each of the following as a reward for good performance? (cash, recognition, etc.)	Brehm and Gates 1997	Survey

Failure to treat customers fairly results in reprimands	Brehm and Gates 1997	Survey
Are you able to use each of the following options to let your staff know that you are very satisfied/dissatisfied with their work? (firing staff, bonuses, reallocation of tasks, etc.)	Brandsma 2010	Survey
Can ministers overturn agency decisions?	Koop 2011	Content analysis
Relative amount of government contracts maintained	Lamothe and Lamothe 2009	Govt data

Unless otherwise noted the indicators are scales ranging from never to always, very much to very little, or agree to disagree as appropriate.

COMPARING ACCOUNTABILITY SCORES
BETWEEN SUBJECTS

The fact that accountability can be scored quantitatively implies that scores can be compared. Besides honing in on the question of how much accountability there is, it is also possible to investigate the obvious but salient follow-up question of whether certain accountability regimes are stronger or weaker than others. This follow-up question is particularly salient due to the commonly observed shift from government to governance, in which authority increasingly moves away from the national political realm towards non-majoritarian institutions, public–private partnerships, networks of national and supranational actors, and to international or global institutions and networks. This does not only implicate shifts in types of accountabilities, but moreover policy-makers are subject to a larger number of accountabilities at the same time. Assessing the strength of each of these accountabilities essentially is a matter of comparison, and especially here lies the strength of quantitative methodology: different situations are made comparable by means of using standardized indicators.

Essentially, three types of comparisons can be made. First, comparisons can be made across actors towards the same forum. Which actors are most accountable? This is, for example, the type of comparison made by One World Trust. Their annual "Global Accountability Report," which has been described before, explicitly aims to provide comparative scores of 30 organizations per year and to rank them. Top ranked organizations include UNICEF, the European Bank for Reconstruction and Development, and the International Federation of Organic Agriculture Movements (IFOAM), whereas Halliburton, the International Atomic Energy Agency, and the International Olympic Committee are found at the bottom of their rankings (Lloyd, Warren, and Hammer 2008). Moving beyond mapping variation only, Koop (2011) identifies four factors that affect the number of accountability requirements in the statutes of independent agencies: political salience of the issues the agency deals with, political salience of accountability as such at the time the agency was founded, the legal basis of the organization, and the number of veto players.

The second type of comparison is across forums by the same actor. To which forums is the strongest accountability rendered? This requires a fixed set of indicators to be repeated across a number of forums. This is what Dunn and Legge (2001) did, for example, for top local civil servants in finding out which forums were most relevant to them. They found they give most attention to local elected officials, to the preferences of stakeholders and citizens, and only to a lesser extent to local media and court cases, which suggests that traditional accountability relationships are still dominant.

The third type of comparison is across actor–forum relationships within a given domain. Which actor–forum relationships are stronger than others? Brandsma's (2010) study of hierarchic accountability in a complex administrative setting includes items on all three constitutive elements of accountability as a mechanism, and also displays their scores on the according three dimensions simultaneously in a three-dimensional graph (see also Brandsma 2010, 174, 187; Brandsma and Schillemans 2013). This allows for identifying which relationships between which individual actors and forums have higher or lower scores on information provision, discussion, imposition of consequences, or any combination of these. Scores on each dimension have been grouped in relatively high and low scores. It would have been possible to provide more precise information on the scores of specific cases within the dataset when using a three-dimensional scatterplot, but regrettably that type of plot is not intelligible in print.

In similar vein, but using fewer cases and without using a graphical display, Van de Steeg (2009) identified which particular post-summit debates between members of the European Parliament and European Council presidents provided for most accountability. Although developments over time were not explicitly part of the research design, it appeared from her results that accountability—even in the absence of any formal obligation—steadily strengthened over time. Whereas in the early 1990s a European Council president left the floor immediately after his opening statement, debates in the years after provided for an ever increasing degree of accountability.

DETECTING CHANGES OVER TIME

There is also a fourth type of comparison that can be made which needs to be singled out from the discussion: comparisons of accountability before and after regime transformation. This is of particular relevance, again, to evaluating the effects of shifts in governance. However, most research is limited to mapping and scoring accountability *after* the reorganization of public services. For assessing the changes to accountability as induced by shifts in governance, a longitudinal research design is necessary. The same is true for the assessment of changes in accountability over time that may be due to socio-cultural changes rather than to reorganization of the public sector.

It is for this salient type of question that most gaps in research still exist. As the references in this chapter already indicate, quantitative research into accountability or into aspects thereof has for the most part only developed recently. This implies that historical information, which is vital for making longitudinal assessments, is lacking. Another logical explanation is that the issue of shifts in governance only becomes relevant from the moment shifts start taking place, which makes it hard to create sound measurements of the pre-shift situation that go beyond mappings of formal accountability structures.

Nevertheless, there are some studies that include a longitudinal component, or at least that include data collected over several years, so that a longitudinal measurement would have been possible. Brehm and Gates (1997) seek to establish the degree to which the image of the leisure-seeking bureaucrat is correct and by what means accountability forums constrain the agent's behavior in practice. Their research shows on the basis of formal modeling, computer simulations, and survey data analysis that rather than hierarchic superiors, peers and clients are the most important forums for bureaucrats. The authors identify several existing large-scale data resources, including a large number of indicators that measure, for instance, rewards preferred by bureaucrats, variables explaining actual shirking, reprimands, feedback, job evaluation by supervisors, and organizational checks. To some degree this includes the same or similar indicators measured in different years. However, because their research question does not include a longitudinal component, no systematic identification has been made of developments over time.

Most of the few longitudinal studies relate to electoral accountability. A key question in this domain is to what degree voters actually punish previously elected officials for past performance. Longitudinal studies into retrospective voting show a mixed picture. Some indicate that voters do punish incumbents for, for example, general economic or policy-specific underperformance, while other studies question these findings (e.g. Kramer 1971; Fiorina 1978; Holbrook and Garand 1996; Kiewit and Udell 1998; Berry and Howell 2007). Another key question, more relating to accountability as a virtue, is to evaluate to what degree political parties behave in parliament as they promised at election time. Louwerse (2011) compared conflict dimensions in British and Dutch parliamentary debates to those in electoral campaigns, and found that contrary to widespread popular belief these arenas of competition become more congruent over time.

FEEDING EMPIRICAL FINDINGS INTO NORMATIVE EVALUATIONS

Many studies into accountability mean to identify to what degree an existing accountability regime is sufficient or appropriate, either by virtue of the main research question or, more commonly, reflections in the concluding paragraph. In this sense, many speak of accountability "deficits," "overloads," or even a "crisis of accountability." Quantitative research into regimes and practices of accountability can contribute greatly to this research aim. Even though quantitative research is not capable of defining assessment criteria as such, it does provide valuable information against which pre-defined norms or benchmarks can be tested. In this way, evaluative statements on shortages or over-loads of accountability can be underpinned empirically.

The accountability cube proposed by Brandsma (2010) and Brandsma and Schillemans (2013), for instance, can be used for detecting potentially problematic cases within one type of accountability relationship. In this sense the cube can be used to identify the magnitude of an accountability deficit empirically, given a certain norma-tive benchmark. This benchmark may, for instance, relate to popular control, checks and balances, or to learning by actors (cf. Bovens 2007). Using multiple benchmarks based on popular control, Brandsma (2010, 188–90) concludes that 40.9 percent of hierarchi-cal accountability relationships within the Dutch and Danish national civil services, with respect to input given in European technical meetings, score relatively low accord-ing to multiple benchmarks simultaneously, and hence display a risk of a deficit.

Besides this, as the discussion of accountability as a virtue has already revealed, posi-tive or negative outcomes of accountability can also serve as normative benchmarks. Does accountability bring about social desiderata such as trust, efficiency, and effective-ness? This is the type of approach that is dominant in psychological research, and many studies find effects that can only to some degree be seen as positive. Several experimen-tal studies demonstrate that the existence of an accountability mechanism, or at least the actor's perception that he will be held to account for his behavior, leads to more accurate decision-making and to more diligent information processing, but also to the symbolic manufacturing of superfluous information in order to demonstrate the actor's good intentions (Doney and Armstrong 1996; Mero and Motowidlo 1995; Tetlock 1983). Similarly, Ossege (2012) investigated the effect of accountability processes on the perfor-mance of public managers, and concluded that accountability to some degree leads to pro-social behavior, but also to a stronger degree to pleasing behavior. These effects lead him to conclude that under certain conditions 'we are better off without accountability' (Ossege 2012, 601).

Research Agenda

Quantitative studies are relatively new and few in the domain of accountability. Aside from a small number of older studies, nearly all research dates back to the mid-1990s and, mostly, later. But already the number of different indicators used in the literature is vast. Also researchers have used a plurality of methods, ranging from surveys and document codings to coded and quantified interviews. Experiments have been used as well, but only in more psychological accountability research. In a nutshell, this shows that accountability is an issue that can be researched quantitatively just like any other politico-administrative concept.

Substantively, nearly all existing studies have in common that they limit themselves to describing, in a quantitative sense that is, the state of accountability within a particular domain. Admittedly this is already complicated enough in an uncharted terrain like accountability. But there are three types of questions for which quantitative methodology is a great asset, but which are hardly addressed in empirical accountability studies.

One deals with the causes of accountability, be it formal accountability rules or practices. Quantitative methodology is particularly helpful for tracing correlations so that theories can be statistically tested, but there is still hardly anything we know about factors that influence emergent degrees of accountability, and yet plenty of theories have been introduced and are well-developed enough to be put to the test in real-life settings. These include, for instance, rational choice-inspired theories that fit the principal–agent framework (see Gailmard in this volume), or the more sociologically-inspired stewardship theory (see Mansbridge or Olsen in this volume). This is not to say that those theories have never been put to the test at all, but in the context of explaining accountability they have not been subject to empirical scrutiny to a large degree (but see Brandsma 2010; Koop 2011).

The same is true with respect to the consequences of accountability, but here the harvest is not as meager as with its causes. Social-psychological research traces accountability effects on a variety of individual properties, such as posturing, pro-social or egocentric behavior (Doney and Armstrong 1996; Frink and Ferris 1998; Ossege 2012), efficient allocation of resources (Adelberg and Batson 1978), or the actor's satisfaction with his own achievements (Markman and Tetlock 2000). Most studies, however, do not focus particularly on governmental settings.

A final underexplored territory relates to systematic comparison of accountability settings and accountability practices between policy domains, governmental settings, and countries. Nearly all comparative studies (of which only a few exist) compare within policy domains only. But with all normative concerns that relate to shifts from government towards governance, many intriguing questions have yet been left aside. For example—are independent agencies less accountable than government departments, and if so, to what degree? Do public sector reforms lead to different accountability practices between countries? Quantitative methodology is particularly suitable for comparative questions like these as it allows for more systematic comparison.

Empirical research, be it quantitative or qualitative, is a laborious exercise, especially when it concerns (internationally) comparative research. For closing the salient gaps mentioned in accountability research, it would be particularly helpful if there would be agreement on definitions and operationalizations. As this chapter has demonstrated, indicators are very different not only because they are context specific but also because authors tend to invent their own definitions and operationalizations of accountability. This chapter hopes to have made a contribution to spurring more cumulative research in which particular relevant indicators of existing research are used again in a different context, or in which even a full quantitative research is replicated elsewhere. In the end, only cumulation will lead to more complete insights into the actual workings of accountability and also to more empirically informed normative conclusions.

NOTE

1. For a more elaborate discussion of various types and sub-types of accountability, see Bovens (2007), Tetlock (1985), Doney and Armstrong (1996).

REFERENCES

Adelberg, S. and Batson, C. D. 1978. "Accountability and Helping: When Needs Exceed Resources." *Personality and Social Psychology*, 36: 343–50.

Ashworth, R. E. 2000. "Party Manifestos and Local Accountability: A Content Analysis of Local Election Pledges in Wales." *Local Government Studies*, 26: 11–30.

Berry, C. R. and Howell, W. G. 2007. "Accountability and Local Elections: Rethinking Retrospective Voting." *Journal of Politics*, 69: 844–58.

Bouckaert, G. and Van de Walle, S. 2003. "Comparing Measures of Citizen Trust and User Satisfaction as Indicators of 'Good Governance': Difficulties in Linking Trust and Satisfaction Indicators." *International Review of Administrative Sciences*, 69: 329–43.

Bovens, M. A. P. 2007. "Analysing and Assessing Accountability: A Conceptual Framework." *European Law Journal*, 13: 447–68.

Bovens, M. A. P. 2010. "Two Concepts of Accountability: Accountability as a Virtue and as a Mechanism." *West European Politics*, 33: 946–67.

Brandsma, G. J. 2010. *Backstage Europe: Comitology, Accountability and Democracy in the European Union*. Dissertation. Utrecht: Utrecht University.

Brandsma, G. J. and Schillemans, T. 2013. "The Accountability Cube: Measuring Accountability." *Journal of Public Administration Research and Theory*, 23 (4): 953–75.

Brandsma, G. J., Curtin, D. M., and Meijer, A. J. 2008. "How Transparent are EU "Comitology" Committees in Practice?" *European Law Journal*, 14: 819–38.

Brehm, J. and Gates, S. 1997. *Working, Shirking and Sabotage: Bureaucratic Response to a Democratic Public*. Ann Arbor: The University of Michigan Press.

Carman, J. 2009. "Nonprofits, Funders, and Evaluation: Accountability in Action." *The American Review of Public Administration*, 39: 374–90.

Considine, M. 2002. "The End of the Line? Accountable Governance in the Age of Networks, Partnerships, and Joined-Up Services." *Governance*, 15: 21–40.

Dahlberg, S. 2011. *Codebook for the QoG Web-Survey Study 2008/2009 and 2010*. Gothenburg: University of Gothenburg. The Quality of Government Institute.

Delreux, T. 2011. *The EU as International Environmental Negotiator*. Farnham: Ashgate.

Doney, P. M. and Armstrong, G. M. 1996. "Effects of Accountability on Symbolic Information Search and Information Analysis by Organizational Buyers." *Journal of the Academy of Marketing Science*, 24: 57–65.

Dunn, D. D. and Legge, J. S. 2001. "U.S. Local Government Managers and the Complexity of Responsibility and Accountability in Democratic Governance." *Journal of Public Administration Research and Theory*, 11: 73–88.

Fiorina, M. P. 1978. "Economic Retrospective Voting in American National Elections: A Micro-Analysis." *American Journal of Political Science*, 22: 426–43.

Frink, D. D. and Ferris, G. R. 1998. "Accountability, Impression Management, and Goal Setting in the Performance Evaluation Process." *Human Relations*, 51: 1259–83.

Gelleny, R. D. and Anderson, C. J. 2000. "The Economy, Accountability, and Public Support for the President of the European Commission." *European Union Politics*, 1: 173–200.

Hammer, M. and Lloyd, R. 2011. *Pathways to Accountability II: The 2011 Revised Global Accountability Framework: Report on the Stakeholder Consultation and the New Indicator Framework*. London: One World Trust.

Hanretty, C. and Koop, C. 2009. *Comparing Regulatory Agencies: Report on the Results of a Worldwide Survey*. EUI Working Papers, No. 2009/63. RSCAS.

Holbrook, T. and Garand, J. C. 1996. "Homo Economus? Economic Information and Economic Voting." *Political Research Quarterly*, 49: 351–75.

Hueller, T. 2007. "Assessing EU Strategies for Publicity." *Journal of European Public Policy*, 14: 563–81.

Kiewit, D. R. and Udell, M. 1998. "Twenty-Five Years After Kramer: An Assessment of Economic Retrospective Voting Based Upon Improved Estimates of Income and Unemployment." *Economics & Politics*, 10: 219–48.

Klingemann, H. D., Hofferbert, R. I., and Budge, I. 1994. *Parties, Policy and Democracy*. Boulder, CO: Westview.

Koop, C. 2011. "Explaining the Accountability of Independent Agencies: The Importance of Political Salience." *Journal of Public Policy*, 31: 209–34.

Kramer, G. 1971. "Short-Term Fluctuations in U.S. Voting Behavior, 1896–1964." *American Political Science Review*, 64: 131–43.

Lamothe, M. and Lamothe, S. 2009. "Beyond the Search for Competition in Social Service Contracting: Procurement, Consolidation, and Accountability." *American Review of Public Administration*, 39: 164–88.

Lloyd, R., Warren, S., and Hammer, M. 2008. *2008 Global Accountability Report*. London: One World Trust.

Louwerse, T. P. 2011. *Political Parties and the Democratic Mandate: Comparing Collective Mandate Fulfilment in the United Kingdom and the Netherlands*. Leiden: Leiden University.

Markman, K. D. and Tetlock, P. E. 2000. "Accountability and Close-Call Counterfactuals: The Loser Who Nearly Won and the Winner Who Nearly Lost." *Personality and Social Psychology Bulletin*, 26: 1213–24.

McGraw, K. M. 1991. "Managing Blame: An Experimental Test of the Effects of Political Accounts." *The American Political Science Review*, 85: 1133–57.

Mero, N. P. and Motowidlo, S. J. 1995. "Effects of Rater Accountability on the Accuracy and the Favorability of Performance Ratings." *Journal of Applied Psychology*, 80: 514–24.

Naurin, D. 2007. *Deliberation Behind Closed Doors: Transparency and Lobbying in the European Union*. Colchester: ECPR Press.

O'Connell, L. 2005. "Program Accountability as an Emergent Property: The Role of Stakeholders in a Program's Field." *Public Administration Review*, 65: 85–93.

Ossege, C. 2012. "Accountability—Are We Better Off Without It? An Empirical Study into the Effects of Accountability on Public Managers' Work Behaviour." *Public Management Review*, 14: 585–607.

Pina, V., Torres, L., and Royo, S. 2007. "Are ICTs Improving Transparency and Accountability in the EU Regional and Local Governments? An Empirical Study." *Public Administration*, 85: 449–72.

Schillemans, T. 2008. "Accountability in the Shadow of Hierarchy: The Horizontal Accountability of Agencies." *Public Organization Review*, 8: 175–94.

Strøm, K. 1997. "Democracy, Accountability and Coalition Bargaining." *European Journal of Political Research*, 31: 47–62.

Teorell, J., Samanni, M., Holmberg, S., and Rothstein, B. 2011. *The Quality of Government Dataset Codebook*. Version 6 April 2011. Gothenburg: University of Gothenburg. The Quality of Government Institute.

Tetlock, P. E. 1983. "Accountability and the Perseverance of First Impressions." *Social Psychology Quarterly*, 46: 285–92.

Tetlock, P. E. 1985. "Accountability: The Neglected Social Context of Judgment and Choice." *Research in Organizational Behavior*, 7: 297–332.

Thomas, P. and Palfrey, C. 1996. "Evaluation: Stakeholder-Focused Criteria." *Social Policy & Administration*, 30: 125–42.

Transparency International. 2000. *The TI Source Book 2000*. Berlin and London: Transparency International.

Van de Steeg, M. W. 2009. *Public Accountability in the European Union: Is the European Parliament Able to Hold the European Council Accountable?* European Integration Online Papers, No. 13.

Vigoda, E. 2002. "Are You Being Served? The Responsiveness of Public Administration to Citizens' Demands: An Empirical Examination in Israel." *Public Administration*, 78: 165–91.

Wang, X. 2002. "Assessing Administrative Accountability: Results from a National Survey." *The American Review of Public Administration*, 32: 350–70.

Weibel, A., Rost, K., and Osterloh, M. 2010. "Pay for Performance in the Public Sector: Benefits and (Hidden) Costs." *Journal for Public Administration Research and Theory*, 20: 387–412.

Welch, E. W. and Wong, W. 2001. "Global Information Technology Pressure and Government Accountability: The Mediating Effect of Domestic Context on Website Openness." *Journal for Public Administration Research and Theory*, 11: 509–38.

CHAPTER 10

....

QUALITATIVE ANALYSIS

....

KAIFENG YANG

THE DOMINANT APPROACH

....

PUBLIC accountability research refers to an embryonic field of study that seriously engages in theorizing or conceptualizing accountability as the central subject in the public governance context (Dubnick and Frederickson 2011), leaving aside the publications that use accountability conveniently or casually as a variable. Most empirical studies in this literature so far have used qualitative designs, and the well-designed ones have greatly advanced our understanding of accountability. Generally the nature of research questions dictates the choice of research methods. Specifically, why have qualitative designs been dominant in accountability research? How are they used? What issues should researchers attend to in the future? This chapter provides some preliminary discussions.

QUALITATIVE RESEARCH

....

Defining qualitative research is difficult because it means different things. Some scholars emphasize qualitative epistemologies that are non-positivistic, some refer to qualitative research strategies that facilitate interpreting or revealing meanings, and others point to qualitative techniques that are not operationalized with numbers and statistics. The qualitative camp includes paradigms that assume different ontology, epistemology, methodology, nature of knowledge, inquiry style, and quality criteria (Gabrielian, Yang, and Spice 2008).

This chapter uses qualitative research as an overarching category that includes a diverse array of approaches and methods. Two definitions are helpful, although not without critics and problems. Denzin and Lincoln (2000, 3) refer to qualitative research as an interpretive, naturalistic approach to understanding the world: "study things in their natural settings, attempting to make sense of, or to interpret, phenomena in terms of the meanings people bring to them." This definition captures the core unique characteristics of qualitative research. Strauss and Corbin (1998, 11) define it as "any type of research that produces findings not arrived at by statistical procedures or other means of quantification." This definition emphasizes that qualitative research is relative to quantitative research.

At the risk of offending sophisticated readers, I focus on a number of commonly agreed-upon elements that seem to be important or salient for qualitative research (Snape and Spencer 2003, 3-5; Brower, Abolafia, and Carr 2000):

- An in-depth and interpreted understanding of the social world by learning participants' circumstances, experiences, perspectives, and histories
- Samples are small in size and purposively selected
- Data collection usually involves close contact between the researcher and the participants in an interactive, developmental, and emergent process
- Data are detailed and rich
- A heavy inductive component or orientation in the analytic process
- Analysis is open to emergent concepts and ideas, which may produce detailed description and classification, identify patterns, or develop typologies and explanations
- Outputs tend to focus on the interpretation of social world through mapping meanings, processes, and contexts
- Particularly useful for hypothesis generating instead of testing

Why Qualitative Research in Studying Accountability

Qualitative research is suited for certain types of questions, such as those that are in need of understanding or explanation of social phenomena and their context, complex, involving processes that occur over time, ill-defined, deeply rooted, sensitive, or entailing information that can only be collected from special individuals (Brower et al. 2000; Ritchie 2003; Snape and Spencer 2003). Accountability researchers have to address these issues.

First, accountability is ill-defined and not well understood. Before a researcher measures and explains/predicts the level of accountability, s/he needs to know what accountability means. But accountability has been a confusing, ever-expanding, chameleon-like construct. This is partly due to the fact that while accountability relates to almost everything important in public administration, explicitly studying it does not have a long history. When phenomena are ambiguous, qualitative research helps clarify them. This is why a stream of accountability research examines how accountability is understood or interpreted by practitioners. For example, recognizing the lack of consensus regarding the meaning of governance and accountability, Goddard (2005) sought the participants' viewpoints and adopted the grounded theory procedure.

Understanding the meaning and functions of accountability is particularly important when researchers start to examine new environments or settings. Partnerships and networks are an example. Network governance has become increasingly important, but our traditional understanding of accountability is based on single, autonomous, and hierarchical organizations. We cannot reasonably infer network accountability from organizational accountability, so studying network accountability requires a discovery process that relies heavily on inductive and qualitative methods. This is why Acar, Guo, and Yang (2008) conducted interviews to find out how partnership participants thought about accountability, believing that stories managers tell are "as valid as science" (Hummel 1991, 31). This is also why, when Romzek and colleagues (2012) examined informal accountability in networks, they collected case and interview data from network actors and then used grounded analysis to identify shared elements and patterns.

Second, accountability is an emergent property (Yang 2012). Individuals both create and are constrained by accountability structures; accountability is constantly changing and shifting as actors act and interact. The changing dynamics of accountability cannot be captured by cross-sectional surveys, which collect data at a given time, nor can it be effectively examined in experimental designs, which usually control confounders such as time. Doing longitudinal analysis would be difficult as the meaning of accountability shifts over time. In contrast, qualitative research is appropriate for tracking and mapping the changes and dynamics across time. One example is O'Connell's (2005) study of a statewide reform of the social service delivery system. By tracking the accountability relationships before and after the reform, O'Connell was able to show that accountability emerged from the relationships among actors in the program's field.

Sometimes the changing accountability relationship reflects a cat and mouse game between principals and agents. When the principal designs an accountability system, the agent does not simply comply but learns how to game it. Observing the agent's gaming, the principal will revise the system, leading to further gaming. Thus, understanding an accountability system requires one to track the mutual adaptation process. In understanding how the US government holds federally-funded local training centers accountable for job creation, Courty and Marschke (2007) showed that one has to go back over thirty years. Originally the government held the centers accountable for "employment and wage rates at the termination of training," but the centers gamed by placing on file participants who could not find employment even if they had not been trained for 2 or 3 years. The government responded by adding that participants who had not received any training for 90 days must be terminated, only to find that the centers gamed the 90-day window by gaming between years. The government then changed to hold the centers accountable for "employment and earnings three months after the termination," but the centers reacted by selecting enrollees who are most able to obtain employment and pressing employers to retain the clients until the third month.

Third, accountability is deeply rooted and is often delicate and intangible. While accountability is sometimes understood as a virtue or an institutional arrangement, its manifestation or implementation cannot be separated from actors' values, perceptions, interpretations, and strategic responses. As a result, fully studying accountability requires accessing actors' inner knowledge that either has been suppressed or is largely unconscious. A phenomenon like this is appropriate for qualitative inquiry. Goddard (2005) recognized the importance of explaining how individual and social perceptions interact with structures and practices. Borrowing Bourdieu's concept of habitus, Goddard referred to his approach as studying accountability habitus—"the set of dispositions within the organization to develop practices in certain ways in accordance with the shared perceptions of accountability in existence" (2005, 192). This explains why he chose interviewing. Similarly, Ezzamel, Robson, Stapleton, and McLean (2007) emphasized that there is not only accountability based on formal institutional requirements, but also accountability based on the way actors legitimate themselves in everyday activities—"folk" accountability. The latter is not only deeply rooted but also largely untouched in the previous literature. No existing or apparent categories or theories existed to allow quantitative research, so document analysis and interviews were used.

The fact that accountability relates to actors' perceptions and mental models suggests that an interpretive approach is often useful in uncovering the social construction of accountability. There are different and sometimes contradictory interpretations of accountability, which lead people to have varied beliefs and behaviors. Researchers must keep an open mind in exploring the beliefs and meanings through which people construct their world. This is why Poulsen (2009) used qualitative methods to unveil multiple accountability perceptions rooted in competing governance traditions.

Fourth, accountability information is often sensitive and can only be collected from individuals or groups that have a special role in society such as public figures and leading professionals who are directly involved in accountability relationships. In particular, if researchers are interested in exposing the motives and strategies of those who design the accountability system or discovering how certain individuals perceive and react to the system, they need research designs that enable them to obtain honest responses. This suggests the use of theoretical sampling and establishing rapport and trust before obtaining the information. Quantitative research in this case is much less appropriate.

In some cases, the study subjects or potential informants are so few that in-depth qualitative research is a natural option. For example, Boin and colleagues (2010) aimed to understand how top political leaders' leadership style affected their responses to blame in the aftermath of crises. They chose George W. Bush and Hurricane Katrina, arguing that "this is a particularly interesting case because it features George W. Bush, a previously successful crisis leader in the immediate aftermath of the 9/11 attacks" (2010, 707). In other cases, the potential subjects may not be too few, but qualitative methods are required to obtain their truthful opinion. For example, Farrell and Law (1999) attempted to find out whether the promotion of market accountability by legislation had reduced the powers of local education authorities (LEAs) in Wales and thus changed the LEA accountability in practice. Relevant information could only be obtained from those who were involved in the matter, including the Education Director and the Education Committee Chair in each Welsh County. In order to discover their honest reaction to the market-oriented mechanisms, the authors conducted semi-structured interviews.

Fifth, insights about accountability are often gained from accountability crises, which are special and naturally occurring events that usually cannot be replicated. "Typically, accountability problems or dilemmas become observable when dramatic events occur and change the configuration of accountability systems or pressures" (Yang 2012, 259). In Johnston and Romzek's (1999, 387) words, "typically one or two accountability relationships are operating at any one time. In times of extraordinary events or crises, the other (dormant) types of accountability relationships may be invoked." To study extraordinary events such as the Challenger tragedy, qualitative inquiry, such as case study, is appropriate (Romzek and Dubnick 1987). This also suggests theoretical sampling—the samples are chosen because they are unusually revelatory, extreme exemplars, or opportunities for unusual research access.

Another example of theoretical sampling is in Schwartz and Sulitzeanu-Kenan's (2004) study of the effects of accountability orientations on policy changes after disasters or crises. They first selected Israel and the US for comparison because the two countries share a production-oriented view on accountability but differ in size, political culture, and political administrative system. Within each country, they used three criteria to guide case selection: the crisis was publicly identifiable as a focusing event, production-results values clearly dominated management practice prior to the incident, and a minimum of five years had elapsed since the crisis.

The five issues above help explain why qualitative inquiry has been so important for accountability research. This does not mean all accountability studies must or will be qualitative. After the meaning of accountability is discovered in a particular setting, quantitative measures could be developed to assess the level of accountability. With vast resources and time, quantifiable data about accountability could be collected in multiple times or for a large number of crises. Experiment and survey studies could be used to examine the perceptions and behavioral dynamics among accountability actors. But public administration scholars so far have been primarily interested in questions regarding the meaning, evolution, process, and cause of accountabilities, and such questions invite qualitative methods.

The interests of scholars may change, but meaning, evolution, process, and cause are critical elements for a deep understanding of any social phenomenon. They are real treasures for social science research. Qualitative research is moreover often the first choice for answering questions about which we have no existing knowledge or do not know where to start. When Tsai (2007) asked why Chinese villages, with similar macro-conditions, have variations in governmental provision of public goods, she did not know what the answer might be so she started with two months of preliminary research and eight months of in-depth fieldwork. With interviews and participatory observations she found the treasure: an innovative concept of informal accountability based on encompassing solidary groups and the pursuit of moral standing.

Qualitative Design in Accountability Research: Examples

This section provides examples where different qualitative designs are used to study accountability. The purpose is to illustrate how the research question affects the choice of method, including the sampling and data collection, which, in turn, affects the research outcomes. Greater attention is paid to the more frequently used designs.

Case Study

Case studies are rich, empirical descriptions of particular instances of a phenomenon. Cases are stories, but they are also experiments. A case is an independent analytic unit and can be seen as a distinctive experiment. Multiple cases are discrete experiments that serve as replications, contrasts, and extensions (Yin 1994). Case studies can use a variety of data sources, such as interviews, archival data, survey, ethnographies, and observations. Although some researchers apply the deductive logic and use cases to illustrate theories developed in advance (Yin 1994), most researchers use case studies inductively to build theory. Case studies that build theories are often the most interesting and most impactful in academic research (Eisenhardt and Graebner 2007).

A single case may tell much because conducting a case study is like dissecting a sparrow: Small as the sparrow is, it possesses all its internal organs—small but complete. The Challenger accident is a single case, but it represents a genre of man-made accidents. In Romzek and Dubnick (1987), although the question is why NASA (National Aeronautics and Space Administration) and Morton Thiokol management ignored the engineers' advice and decided to launch the spaceship, the authors attempted to find general lessons about accountability design that would go beyond this accident. To answer this "why" question, the authors delved into congressional reports, news reports, the report of the Presidential Commission on the Accident, and NASA documents. They noticed the professionalization of the Space Program and the politicization and bureaucratization of NASA's accountability, which led to a general lesson: when external institutional pressures take precedence over technical and managerial considerations, problems arise in a professional organization. They inferred that accountability design should fit the task, management strategy, and institutional context.

A single case leaves doubts about generalizability. Do sparrows with different colors and sizes have the same internal organs? We would not know without dissecting at least one sample for each color and size. Comparative case studies are thus designed with multiple cases chosen to represent different conditions. Two classic works provide good examples (Day and Klein 1987; Kaufman 1967). Both are inductive. Kaufman's (1967) *The Forest Ranger* has accountability nowhere in the title, table of contents, or index, but accountability is key to answering the research question: How had the Forest Service successfully produced field behavior consistent with headquarter directives? That is, how had the agency made its field officers accountable? Kaufman realized that in order to understand *how* compliance was actually achieved, the most useful method of inquiry was the approach of the cultural anthropologist: listening to field officers' conversations, visiting their homes, attending their meetings, observing their behaviors, and having conversations about their traditions. The cultural anthropologist approach is time-consuming, so Kaufman could not study a large number of Ranger districts. He deliberately chose five dissimilar districts which together showed almost the full range of Forest Service activities and a wide variety of work conditions. Across the diverse cases Kaufman identified shared patterns.

Similarly, Day and Klein's (1987) research question mandated qualitative inquiry: What is the *meaning* of accountability in practice? Believing accountability is all about the social construction of discourse and criteria about conduct and performance, Day and Klein recognized the need to interview people who were the critical links in accountability systems in order to uncover their perceptions of accountability. Although the authors had developed an analytic framework to help design interview questions, they soon found out that the prepared questions were alien to the respondents and it was better to simply listen to "native" stories. Since accountability is a contextualized process, Day and Klein also noted that the respondents should come from policy arenas that would represent all important and relevant contextual variations. After identifying five contextual factors—direct democratic control, professionalization, service heterogeneity, service complexity, and service uncertainty, they chose five public services to embody variations of all the factors: education, health service, police, social service, and water. Across the arenas, Day and Klein observed some striking common patterns. For example, people saw themselves as being accountable to the "community" at large instead of the lines of constitutional accountability.

In Kaufman (1967) and Day and Klein (1987), the authors had extensive conversations with multiple participants involved in each of the cases, generating original information that would have not otherwise existed (see also Flinders 2001). In other cases, researchers do not conduct first-hand observations or conversations, but use existing information in an attempt to make sense of the information in a new theoretical perspective. An example is Schwartz and Sulitzeanu-Kenan's (2004) study, which asked: *Why* was there policy learning and change after some disasters but not after others? Disasters and crises often generate voluminous reports and investigation, so researchers may rely on existing information. Although the Schwartz and Sulitzeanu-Kenan study was largely inductive, it reviewed previous literature and had some general directions that guided the selection of cases. With theory-informed comparisons, the authors were able to identify some general lessons.

One can also use case studies for deductive research or even add some quantitative flavor or elements into the design. An example is Romzek and Johnston's (2005) case studies on accountability in contracting out. Before the empirical inquiry, the authors had developed an analytical framework and identified potential determinants of accountability effectiveness such as clarity of accountability relationships, suitability of performance measures, ease of performance data collection, and risk retention by the government. When they examined documents and conducted interviews in five cases, they looked for information that enabled them to assign scores (high, moderate, and low) to each of the cases regarding its performance (accountability effectiveness) and each of the pre-identified determinants. Correlating the scores on performance and determinants, the authors were able to show whether the cases support the pre-developed models.

Interview

As a data collection method, interviews can be used in many types of qualitative research, such as case studies and grounded theory analysis. They can be used alone or in combination with other data sources. When used alone to understand the meanings people attribute to their experiences and social worlds, it can be treated as an independent approach as distinct from other qualitative ones. Through interactive conversations, the researcher uses a range of probes and other techniques to obtain a deeper and fuller understanding of the phenomenon with better penetration, exploration, and explanation (Legard, Keegan, and Ward 2003). Good interviews achieve both breadth of coverage across key issues and depth of coverage with each. They are important to discover how a particular group of people think about a particular issue. These people could be making important decisions or represent a particular type of individual.

Interviews are suitable for probing the meaning of accountability as constructed or experienced by actors in their daily life. One example is Acar et al.'s (2008) study of accountability in public–private partnerships. Given little research had been done at the time regarding how participants *view* the functions of accountability in partnerships, talking to the participants seemed to be the logical way to go. The interviewees were asked: What functions and purposes does accountability serve? Why do you think accountability is important? After analyzing the transcripts to find common patterns, categories, and ideas, the authors identified five accountability functions: mapping and manifesting expectations, mobilizing and motivating (ex ante), monitoring and measuring progress and performance, modifying, and mobilizing and motivating (ex post).

There are two important sampling decisions in interviewing. One is the sampling scope: How inclusive or broad should be the target population and sampling frame? In studying accountability in networks, for example, should researchers select interviewees from all types of networks (e.g., information sharing networks and resource exchange networks) and/or from distinct policy areas (e.g., transportation and human services)? Unless the project is generously funded, researchers tend to concentrate on a particular network type or policy area in order to have an in-depth analysis. Acar et al. (2008) focused on partnerships between K-12 public schools and private and/or nonprofit organizations and interviewed various types of actors in such partnerships. Romzek et al. (2012) focused on nonprofit actors in social service delivery networks. Admittedly, as noted in both studies, the choice for depth may limit the external validity of the findings.

Another issue is about sample size: What size is large enough or how do we know we can stop and not interview more people? Interviewing takes time and is not a large-N technique. The sufficient sample size cannot be calculated in advance for interviewing; it must be determined as the analysis progresses. The purpose of analyzing interview data is to find common patterns and categories across interviewees. When the researcher recognizes that adding one or more respondents does not contribute to new patterns or categories, s/he reaches a stage of theoretical saturation and can stop further interviewing. Acar et al. (2008) referred to this saturation principle and stopped at the 38th respondent. The assessment of saturation is obviously subjective and raises the question of credibility. Doubts could fall away if the patterns and categories identified are logical, systematic, and parsimonious. The five accountability functions identified by Acar et al. seem to meet the standard.

Grounded Theory

If interview data are analyzed to induce theory following the procedures of grounded analysis, then the theory derived is a grounded theory—grounded in the everyday experiences of the individuals who have been interviewed or observed in their natural settings. The grounded analysis procedures can be applied to observational data other than interviews, such as field notes, focus group transcripts, archival documents, audio recording, and film. They can be used along with other qualitative approaches such as case studies. There are conflicting models or procedures of grounded analysis (Brower and Jeong 2008), but the one proposed by Strauss (1987) and Strauss and Corbin (1998) is widely used. The core of their procedure includes three successive and iterative coding activities: open coding, axial coding, and selective coding.

Grounded analysis is well-suited to answering "how" and "what" questions: How do actors interact in social settings and how do they make sense of these situations? What are the components or typologies of a social phenomenon or action? What are their implications and boundary conditions? In answering the questions, a new theory or model is proposed. For example, in examining how participants think about the relationship between accountability and governance, Goddard (2005) chose four UK local authorities to ensure variations in size, political party control, service scope, and service stability, followed by interviews over a twelve month period. He then followed Strauss and Corbin's (1998) grounded analysis procedures and provided detailed descriptions on the process, which readers should appreciate because in many accountability studies, as well as in other public administration studies, the authors may simply claim they have followed the procedures without showing how. Reporting the analysis process increases the credibility of the results.

The beauty of grounded theory procedures is that they facilitate emergence of a theory or explanation of phenomena about which we know little or existing knowledge is fragmented. What emerges is not necessarily a causal or an explanatory theory in the strict sense, but it at least reveals the relationships among concepts. What Goddard (2005) derived from his data was the interrelationship of concepts such as governance, accountability, New Public Management (NPM), and budgeting. One interesting finding is that the sense of accountability is more significantly affected by budgeting practices instead of NPM practices.

Romzek et al. (2012) used grounded theory procedures in studying informal accountability among nonprofit network actors. The purposive sample included 22 administrators at 11 nonprofit organizations. Respondents were asked: How do you hold each other accountable? What informal means do you use to demonstrate your sense of obligation to partners? What were your norms and behavioral expectations for the partners? How were inter-organizational conflicts addressed informally? The authors derived a "theory" of informal accountability that integrates some previously fragmented knowledge: the shared norms and facilitative behaviors, the informal system of rewards and sanctions, and the challenges that may undermine informal accountability. The article ends with a diagram that maps the core elements, a practice recommended for grounded analysis (Eisenhardt and Graebner 2007).

Discourse Analysis

Discourse analysis refers to a number of approaches to studying written, spoken, signed language use or any significant semiotic event in social practice. It appeals to researchers for its analytic ability to reveal how institutions and individuals are formed, constructed, and given meaning. Discourse analysis focuses on language and its rhetorical organization, but goes beyond it to explore organized meaning and how knowledge is organized, carried, and reproduced through particular institutional practices (Freshwater 2007). Discourse analysis has variations, with some influenced more by linguistics, post-structuralism, and literary theory, and some more by sociology, psychology, and communications studies.

Discourse analysis could be very valuable for accountability studies. Holding people accountable requires conveying expectations via certain forms of discourse. Giving account means defending or explaining oneself via discourse. As to giving accounts, Scott and Lyman (1968) differentiate between excuses and justifications, each with multiple subcategories. They show that account-giving has five linguistic styles or idiomatic forms—intimate, casual, consultative, formal, and frozen, which should be chosen according to cultural norms and situations. The appropriateness of the style affects the chance of the account being accepted by the other party. Scott and Lyman also identify three strategies for avoiding accounts: mystification, referral, and identity switching. Studying these strategies and linguistic styles would help us understand the accountability relationships and cultural expectations behind them, among others, the way in which people cope and respond to accountability pressures; the way in which institutional legitimacy is maintained; the effects of accountability; and the sense-making in organizations. Almost every accountability question can be approached from this linguistic angle.

So far, however, discourse analysis has not been widely seen in accountability research. O'Reilly and colleagues (2009) provide a rare example. They asked: How do research ethics committees "do" accountability in their decision letters? Discourse analysis was chosen because they wanted to "demonstrate how versions of the world are produced through text" and they were "especially concerned with rhetorical features of text: how the text persuades the reader, and the rhetorical devices drawn upon to get across a particular point of view" (2009, 249). The authors analyzed a sample of 260 letters and uncovered a number of discursive devices and rhetorical strategies used by the committees to justify their decision: drawing attention to the process behind the decision; holding the applicants accountable; referring to expertise among the committee members; and calling upon external authorities to justify. The accountability implications of these tactics were then developed.

QUALITATIVE IN MIXED METHODS

Mixed methods involve collecting, analyzing, and/or interpreting quantitative and qualitative data in a single study or in a series of studies that investigate the same underlying phenomenon. The combination of two approaches offers a better understanding of research problems (Creswell and Clark 2007, 5). The use of two approaches can be parallel/concurrent or sequential. In a concurrent design, qualitative and quantitative data are collected and analyzed about the same time; in a sequential design, one type of data provides a basis for collection of another type. The mixing can be partial or full. A fully mixed design requires the use of both types of method in all research stages. In a partially mixed design, the two types of method are simultaneously used in only one or some research stages. Finally, mixed methods studies may not treat qualitative and quantitative components equally, and one type may play a more important role than the other.

Desirable as they are, mixed methods have not been widely used in accountability research. Tsai's (2007) study on informal accountability in rural China provides an example of sequential design beginning with qualitative and ending with quantitative methods. To understand why Chinese villages with the same formal institutional arrangements and almost the same economic conditions vary significantly in public goods provision, Tsai first spent two months conducting preliminary research in seven different provinces and eight months doing in-depth fieldwork in one set of villages in a southern province. This qualitative stage led to a theory of informal accountability that provided direction for survey design and model testing in the quantitative stage.

Without the interviews and case studies, she could not have observed that local officials provided public goods despite weak formal accountability because encompassing local solidary groups would award them moral standing if they did so. Without the quantitative analysis, it is impossible to know whether the insights are applicable to other Chinese local governments. The two stages validate and triangulate each other.

An excellent example of concurrent mixed-method design is Brandsma's (2010) study on the European Union's (EU) comitology committees—committees that are composed of policy experts representing EU member states. The author's overall question was: "To what extent are committee participants held to account by their superiors at the national level for their input in comitology committees, and how can this be explained and assessed?" (2010, 83). The question was broken down to three descriptive and three explanatory questions. Except the last explanatory question that was answered primarily by interviewing, all other questions were answered by both interview and surveys. The author clearly states that quantitative methods allow for generalization and description across a large number of people, but they are not adequate since the literature on the topic offers too few clues for pre-determining an exhaustive list of survey questions.

FUTURE QUALITATIVE RESEARCH ON ACCOUNTABILITY: TWO CRITICAL ISSUES

Qualitative designs will continue to be used to study accountability. Researchers should integrate qualitative with quantitative designs, improve their credibility, confront the politics of interpretation and back-stage stories, and enhance the authenticity and richness of data reporting. Given space limitation, I focus on two issues.

Theoretical Sensitivity and the Role Of Theory

A popular notion of qualitative designs is to develop theory inductively, but qualitative researchers too often fail to engage important research questions or theorize the questions adequately. In order to go beyond shallow description and develop theory inductively, researchers must be theoretically informed and/or theoretically sensitive to subtleties of meaning embedded in the data. The importance of theoretical sensitivity relates to the role of theory in qualitative research. An extreme position claims that qualitative researchers do not need theory because they should only look for theory from the qualitative data—let the theory come to them. This position is rejected by most researchers because "an open mind is good; an empty mind is not" (Siggelkow 2007, 21). Good qualitative researchers use an iterative process between theory and data. They "begin with a clear research question and must contemplate how extant theory bears on the question" (Brower et al. 2000).

The first-rate qualitative studies on accountability are all informed by existing theories. For example, Schillemans (2012) uses existing knowledge both to identify the research questions and to prepare a framework for guiding the qualitative investigation. For the former, he introduces the concept of horizontal accountability and the debate on accountability deficit. For the latter, he develops an evaluative framework with two dimensions: whether horizontal accountability is a proxy for democratic control and whether it provides learning stimuli. Romzek and Dubnick (1987), before delving into the Challenger case, developed a general framework of public accountability based on source and degree of agency control. Notably, the Challenger accident is not necessarily an accountability case; it led to many academic publications on a range of topics such as decision-making, organizational culture, group dynamics, and communication. Scholars using the same qualitative data come up with different interpretations and theories because they have different theoretical interest and sensitivity. Kaufman's (1967) study shows that even when a cultural anthropologist approach is adopted, the scholar's theoretical sensitivity shapes the theory construction process and outcome.

Existing theories help researchers interpret the results/findings in a way that improves their validity or credibility. In Acar et al. (2008), after forming categories and identifying patterns from the qualitative data, the authors compared the perspectives of practitioners vis-à-vis those of scholars. They showed that the practitioner views were in line with the literature, with added richness and nuances, such as managing expectations is more important than answerability, reciprocal relationship, and learning. They also found something that was not well-studied in the accountability literature—credible commitment—so in the discussion section they made reference to the general public administration literature that emphasizes the concept. Existing theories also helped the authors realize the limitations of their study. Acar et al. recognized that they asked the interviewees to talk about the accountability relationship between schools and the nonprofit/private organizations, so the results did not capture other dimensions of accountability such as political and hierarchical accountability to elected officials and superintendents.

Using previous theories to inform qualitative research does not mean researchers blindly follow the theories. Instead, previous theories serve as a roadmap to be tested. As Brower et al. (2000, 389) suggest, "The researcher should plug theory into the data early and often but should exercise caution to allow the regularities and anomalies in the data to suggest possible theories, rather than force data into theories in ways that obtain a premature closure of meaning." In Acar et al. (2008), before the interviews, the authors noted that the literature had suggested that accountability in network settings may serve functions more to do with identifying expectations, aligning goals, adjusting strategies, assessing implementation, communicating performance, and facilitating learning. However, they note: "Although our literature review led to certain theoretical expectations, the interview was kept as open as possible to let the theory or pattern emerge from the data collection. We intended not to be constrained by a theory...a prior theoretical framework is necessary..., but researchers must keep 'a particular framework from becoming the container into which the data must be poured' (Lather 1986, 267)" (2008, 11).

Since qualitative inquiry is open in nature, the findings do not necessarily conform to the existing theories. Before Romzek and Johnston (2005) started collecting case materials, they had reviewed the literature and identified potential determinants of accountability effectiveness in contracting out. Based on the case evidence, they found support for most of the factors, but observed some surprising findings such as the negative effect of risk shifting. Reporting such surprising findings does not reduce the credibility of the study; rather, it strengthens it.

Sometimes there are competing existing theories and researchers have to match them carefully with the qualitative evidence. Schwartz and Sulitzeanu-Kenan (2004) aimed to find out when disasters or crises are insufficient to produce desirable policy change. They reviewed two lines of literature that offered competing predictions: the policy agenda and policy change theories versus the atrophy of vigilance theory. After carefully examining their comparative cases, they found the American cases supported the expectations prescribed by the policy agenda and policy change theories, but the Israeli cases did not.

Push for Causal Explanation in Real Settings

The insufficient development of causal explanations is a shortcoming of many qualitative studies in public administration generally and accountability research specifically. Most of the studies cited in this chapter try to answer "what" instead of "why" and "how" questions. Even for the few studies that touched on "why" and "how", the causal logic is not always shown in detail. But causal understanding is critical in the world of public administration and policy; it undergirds any rational intervention. "Everyday life is not creatable without a concept of causality" (Argyris 1996). In accountability research, this means asking questions such as: Why was a particular accountability system designed? Why did it produce a negative consequence? How did it happen?

The lack of causal qualitative studies on accountability is, to some extent, not surprising as qualitative methods traditionally were thought of as being able to "describe" and "explore" rather than "explain," a view influenced by the positivist position or the "deductive-nomological" model of scientific explanation. However, since the 1980s, there has been a growing support for the claim that qualitative research, particularly field research, is at least as strong as quantitative research at developing causal explanations (Maxwell 2004). Many people now see quantitative and qualitative methods as having different theories of causality: the variance theory (effects-of-causes and variable analysis) and the process theory (causes-of-effects and the process of interpretation) (Maxwell 2004). Mainstream qualitative researchers do not look for the net effects of a cause among a large number of cases; they document how causes interact to produce an outcome in one or a few cases. That is, they directly investigate the causal processes or mechanisms.

Most of the current accountability studies do not forcefully address causal linkages among constructs, with rare attention to the social mechanisms. Dubnick (2005) once lamented that in both theory and practice the causal relationship between accountability and performance is assumed, not tested or soundly established. The solution, as he correctly sees, is to examine the social mechanisms that link the two constructs. While he suggests experimental designs following Tetlock and colleagues (Lerner and Tetlock 1999; Tetlock 1985), qualitative designs are particularly suitable for uncovering the mechanisms.

The process theory of causality suggests a process approach of research, which analyzes the sequence of events that show how things change over time (George and Bennett 2005). The demonstration of causation requires "a visualizable sequence of events, each event flowing into the next" (Weiss 1994). In particular, narrative and temporal bracketing should be combined because the former helps recognize when and how changes are triggered and the latter helps explain why (Pozzebon and Pinsonneault 2005). This requires data and data reporting that are rich and highly contextualized. This also requires that researchers guard against confirmation bias and look for evidence of observable implications to address alternative explanations.

Participatory action research is another field research method that should be considered. Intensive and long-term involvement helps establish causality because it provides more direct and complete data than any other method. Argyris (2003) argues that this type of research is most appropriate for creating actionable knowledge because the most powerful empirical tests for knowledge are done by making predictions about changing the universe. Currently, many accountability studies are based on practitioner reflections of past events, which are what Argyris (1996) calls science after-the-fact. They fall short in explaining "how to create the conditions and actions in the first place" (1996, 392). In addition, the managerial advice offered in the literature is often not actionable because it neglects the fact that managers do not have the same knowledge, time frame, and ability as the researchers do.

CONCLUSION

Public accountability research will grow in number and rigor. The rigor rests heavily on the methods—whether the methods fit the research question and whether the methods are appropriately executed. Given the five factors identified in this chapter, qualitative methods are very suitable for accountability research. They are particularly valuable if researchers want to find the real treasures: new knowledge, new theories, and new models. Several general lessons should be kept in mind: Ask interesting questions; find rich data; remember the interplay between theory and data; attend to causality; and use mixed methods if possible.

REFERENCES

Acar, M., Guo, C. and Yang, K. 2008. "Accountability When Hierarchical Authority Is Absent." *The American Review of Public Administration*, 38: 3–23.

Argyris, C. 1996. "Actionable Knowledge: Design Causality in the Service of Consequential Theory." *Journal of Applied Behavioral Science*, 32: 390–406.

Argyris, C. 2003. Actionable Knowledge, pp. 423–53 in *The Oxford Handbook of Organization Theory*, eds. H. Tsoukas and C. Knudsen. New York, NY: Oxford University Press.

Boin, A., McConnell, A., 't Hart, P., and Preston, T. 2010. "Leadership Style, Crisis Response and Blame Management: The Case of Hurricane Katrina." *Public Administration*, 88: 706–23.

Brandsma, G. J. 2010. *Backstage Europe: Comitology, Accountability and Democracy in the European Union*. PhD Thesis. Arnhem: Drukkerij Roos en Roos.

Brower, R. S. and Jeong, H.-S. 2008. Grounded Analysis: Going Beyond Description to Derive Theory from Qualitative Data, pp. 823–39 in *Handbook of Research Methods in Public Administration*, eds. K. Yang and G. Miller. New York: CRC Press.

Brower, R. S., Abolafia, M., and Carr, J. B. 2000. "On Improving Qualitative Methods in Public Administrative Research." *Administration & Society*, 32: 363–97.

Courty, P. and Marschke, G. 2007. "Making Government Accountable: Lessons from a Federal Job Training Program." *Public Administration Review*, 67: 904–16.

Creswell, J. W. and Clark, V. L. P. 2007. *Designing and Conducting Mixed Methods Research*. Thousand Oaks, CA: Sage Publications.

Day, P. and Klein, R. 1987. *Accountabilities: Five Public Services*. London and New York: Tavistock Publications.

Denzin, N. and Lincoln, Y., eds. 2000. *Handbook of Qualitative Research*. Thousand Oaks, CA: Sage Publications.

Dubnick, M. and Frederickson, G. 2011. Introduction: The Promises of Accountability Research, pp. xiii–xxxi in *Accountable Governance: Promises and Problems*, eds. M. Dubnick and G. Frederickson. Armonk, New York: M.E. Sharpe.

Dubnick, M. 2005. "Accountability and the Promise of Performance: In Search of the Mechanisms." *Public Performance & Management Review*, 28: 376–417.

Eisenhardt, K. and Graebner, M. 2007. "Theory Building from Cases: Opportunities and Challenges." *Academy of Management Journal*, 50: 25–32.

Ezzamel, M., Robson, K., Stapleton, P., and McLean, C. 2007. "Discourse and Institutional Change: 'Giving Accounts' and Accountability." *Management Accounting Research*, 18: 150–71.

Farrell, C. M. and Law, J. 1999. "Changing Forms of Accountability in Education? A Case Study of LEAs in Wales." *Public Administration*, 77: 293–310.

Flinders, M. 2001. *The Politics of Accountability in the Modern State*. Aldershot: Ashgate.

Freshwater, D. 2007. "Discourse, Responsible Research and Positioning the Subject." *Journal of Psychiatric and Mental Health Nursing*, 14: 111–12.

Gabrielian, V., Yang, K. and Spice, S. 2008. Qualitative Research Methods, pp. 141–68 in *Handbook of Research Methods in Public Administration* (second edition), eds. K. Yang and G. Miller. New York City: CRC Press.

George, A. and Bennett, A. 2005. *Case Studies and Theory Development in the Social Sciences*. Cambridge, MA: MIT Press.

Goddard, A. 2005. "Accounting and NPM in UK Local Government: Contributions Towards Governance and Accountability." *Financial Accountability & Management*, 21: 191–218.

Hummel, R. 1991. "Stories Managers Tell: Why They Are as Valid as Science." *Public Administration Review*, 51: 31–41.

Johnston, J. and Romzek, B. 1999. "Contracting and Accountability in State Medicaid Reform: Rhetoric, Theories, and Reality." *Public Administration Review*, 59: 383–99.

Kaufman, H. 1967. *The Forest Ranger*. Baltimore: The Johns Hopkins Press.

Legard, R., Keegan, J., and Ward, K. 2003. In-Depth Interviews, pp. 138–69 in *Qualitative Research Practice: A Guide for Social Science Students and Researchers*, eds. J. Ritchie and J. Lewis. Thousand Oaks, CA: Sage Publications.

Lerner, J. and Tetlock, P. 1999. "Accounting the Effects of Accountability." *Psychological Bulletin*, 125: 255–75.

Maxwell, J. 2004. "Using Qualitative Methods for Causal Explanation." *Field Methods*, 16: 243–64.

O'Connell, L. 2005. "Program Accountability as an Emergent Property: The Role of Stakeholders in a Program's Field." *Public Administration Review*, 65: 85–93.

O'Reilly, M., Dixon-Woods, M., Angell, E., Ashcroft, R., and Bryman, A. 2009. "Doing Accountability: A Discourse Analysis of Research Ethics Committee Letters." *Sociology of Health & Illness*, 31: 246–61.

Poulsen, B. 2009. "Competing Traditions of Governance and Dilemmas of Administrative Accountability: The Case of Denmark." *Public Administration*, 87: 117–31.

Pozzebon, M. and Pinsonneault, A. 2005. "Challenges in Conducting Empirical Work Using Structuration Theory: Learning from IT Research." *Organization Studies*, 26: 1353–76.

Ritchie, J. 2003. The Application of Qualitative Methods to Social Research, pp. 24–46 in *Qualitative Research Practice: A Guide for Social Science Students and Researchers*, eds. J. Ritchie and J. Lewis. Thousand Oaks: Sage Publications.

Romzek, B. S. and Dubnick, M. J. 1987. "Accountability in the Public Sector: Lessons from the Challenger Tragedy." *Public Administration Review*, 47: 227–38.

Romzek, B. S. and Johnston, J. M. 2005. "State Social Services Contracting: Exploring the Determinants of Effective Contract Accountability." *Public Administration Review*, 65: 436–49.

Romzek, B. S., LeRoux, K., and Blackmar, J. M. 2012. "A Preliminary Theory of Informal Accountability Among Network Organizational Actors." *Public Administration Review*, 72: 442–53.

Schillemans, T. 2012. "Does Horizontal Accountability Work? Evaluating Potential Remedies for the Accountability Deficit of Agencies." *Administration & Society*, 43: 387–416.

Schwartz, R. and Sulitzeanu-Kenan, R. 2004. "Managerial Values and Accountability Pressures: Challenges of Crisis and Disaster." *Journal of Public Administration Research and Theory*, 14: 79–102.

Scott, M. and Lyman, S. 1968. "Accounts." *American Sociological Review*, 33: 46–62.

Siggelkow, N. 2007. "Persuasion With Case Studies." *Academy of Management Journal*, 50: 20–24.

Snape, D. and Spencer, L. 2003. The Foundations of Qualitative Research, pp. 1–23 in *Qualitative Research Practice: A Guide for Social Science Students and Researchers*, eds. J. Ritchie and J. Lewis. London: Sage Publications.

Strauss, A. and Corbin, J. 1998. *Basics of Qualitative Research* (second edition). Thousand Oaks, CA: Sage Publications.

Strauss, A. 1987. *Qualitative Analysis for Social Scientists*. Cambridge, UK: Cambridge University Press.

Tetlock, P. E. 1985. "Accountability: A Social Check on the Fundamental Attribution Error." *Social Psychology Quarterly*, 48: 227–36.

Tsai, L. 2007. "Solidary Groups, Informal Accountability, and Local Public Goods Provision in Rural China." *American Political Science Review*, 101: 355–72.

Weiss, R. S. 1994. *Learning from Strangers: The Art and Method of Qualitative Interviewing*. New York, NY: The Free Press.

Yang, K. 2012. "Further Understanding Accountability in Public Organizations: Actionable Knowledge and the Structure-Agency Duality." *Administration & Society*, 44: 255–84.

Yin, R. 1994. *Case Study Research: Design and Methods* (second edition). Thousand Oaks, CA: Sage Publications.

CHAPTER 11

VISUAL ACCOUNTABILITY

JANE DAVISON

CONTEXT

The Importance of the Visual in Accountability

WE live in a society dominated by visual media, from photographs, film, and television to web pages and social networking sites. In recent decades, accountability mechanisms and manifestations have reflected this accelerated societal trend towards the visual, whether in annual reports, internet usage, organizational presentations, or promotional material. While this "visual turn" has for some time been recognized and researched in the humanities and the social sciences, in the accountability arena researchers, practitioners, and regulators have been slow to awaken to the shift in focus from accountability numbers and narratives to increased visualization of organizational messages. However, there has been a recent blossoming of research interest in the area, such that the visual has been described as the "Watch this space!" field of accountability communication research (Parker 2013).

Visual media are important beyond their ubiquity in contemporary society, where their reach has been assisted by technology and digitalization. Evidence in psychology indicates the power of the visual (relative to that of numbers and words) in cognition and in memory, since the visual appeals to spatial intelligence, and the memory stores forms visually. Visual media can provide framing and impression management and therefore affect decision-making. Visual forms also have the power to carry messages and emotions that lie beyond the capacity of the numbers and narrative text of accountability statements.

Research on the visual in accountability is still at a relatively early stage. Much (although not all) accountability research has tended to focus on the use of visual forms to obscure accountability, through the impression management associated with visual forms such as financial graphs, pictures, architecture, or web pages. These issues are clearly important to the field: In an era when mis-communication and financial scandals have dominated questions of accountability, stakeholders should be alert to the constitutive nature of the visual. However, visual forms may also be put to good use in accountability communication. Financial graphs, when well used, are a highly beneficial way of communicating accounting numbers. Pictures, sketches, and diagrams may usefully fill a gap in the communication of intangibles, which has proved elusive to traditional forms of accounting.

A Brief History of Visual Accountability Research

The early work on the visual in accountability documents in the 1970s and 1980s focused on media that have a direct relationship with accounting numbers, such as financial graphs and schematic cartoon faces. The work on financial graphs has now developed into a substantial corpus (Beattie & Jones 2008), while that on schematic faces has waned, perhaps to be rediscovered in an era where emoticons have now spread into general usage. The only study of representations of accountability in fine art (in medieval Dutch painting and Italian Renaissance art) dates from the 1980s (Yamey 1989). A continued interest in external views of accountability is to be found in analysis of popular film dating from the 1990s. An early study on photographs in annual reports (Tinker and Neimark 1987) examined representations of gender in a 60-year time series of General Motors' annual reports from 1917–76. Pictures and photographs occupy much more space in annual reports than financial graphs, and although they connect less directly with the financial statements, they link more directly with organizations and society through their representations of people, places, and objects, and form an important surround to the accounts. The examination of pictures and photographs was much advanced by a special issue of *Accounting, Organizations, and Society* in 1996 (see Hopwood 1996), and this stream of research has burgeoned since 2000 to include a variety of quantitative and interpretive studies. The field has also widened with the further impetus of a special issue of *Accounting, Auditing, and Accountability Journal* in 2009, to small clusters of work on diagrams, the use of color, visual branding, logos, and architecture. All these areas, including photographs, remain under-researched, but a particularly acute lack of research on web pages should be noted, given the importance of the internet in contemporary accountability communication.

Visual Methods

Overview of Visual Forms and Research Methods

Visual forms relevant to accountability are many and varied, and include:

- static two-dimensional forms, such as pictures, photographs, schematic faces, graphs, charts, diagrams, postal marks, logos, and web pages;

- moving two-dimensional forms such as film, television, video, and interactive web pages;
- three-dimensional forms such as architecture and dress.

Visual methods fall into two broad domains:

- the examination of *pre-existing* visual material;
- the use of *research-generated* visual data as a research tool.

Most of this chapter is about researching visual forms of accountability in *pre-existing* visual material, which is where the majority of work has been directed. There is some comment on using visual forms as a research method, namely the use of research-generated visual data such as in visual elicitation.[1]

Visual methods may be further broadly categorized into:

- empirically-driven approaches, such as visual content analysis (based on pre-existing data) and visual elicitation (based on pre-existing or research-generated material), and
- theoretically-driven approaches, often underpinned by interdisciplinary theory. Theoretical underpinning is rich and varied, stemming from a number of disciplines, such as psychology, social anthropology, philosophy, and art theory.

Visual Content Analysis

Content analysis of visual material in annual reports is the method to which accounting researchers will often instinctively turn, with the advantage of examining data across large samples that may be statistically assessed, in the mould of the "hard" sciences to which much accounting research is allied. Content analysis typically consists of counting numbers of pictures or photographs, and classifying its content into pre-determined categories, such as gender. This method has been used, for example, in a number of gender studies in accountability, examining depictions of gender in annual reports or in film (Bernardi et al. 2005; Dimnik and Felton 2006).

Visual content analysis is, however, not straightforward. Visual material is messy, and does not easily lend itself to quantification. Definitions, boundaries, and content determination are all problematic. What constitutes a picture or photograph? Often visual material is a mix of picture, photograph (or several photographs superimposed one upon another), abstract design, diagram, chart, and text. How should its presence be quantified? The salience of visual material depends upon a number of factors in addition to occurrence, such as the amount of space occupied, prominence of position in a document, repetition, the use of close-ups versus distance shots, or the presence of particular colors. How should the content be classified? The only practical way to attempt to classify the content of a picture is by noting the physical "realities" it purports to represent—the people, places, and things. There are at least three problems with such classifications:

- the constructed nature of the "reality" means that, for example, a "group" picture of a board of directors may have been digitally constructed from separate photographs;
- pictures and photographs can be ambiguous in their representation, and perception lies with the viewer; to counteract such subjectivity, two or more coders may be employed, but this will still not capture the range of interpretations;
- literal "readings" of pictures and photographs are generally the least interesting, and it is the abstract qualities or symbolism which matters. Abstract qualities and symbolism depend even more critically on interpretation, and also on cultural context. Thus, determining whether a given picture or photograph signifies abstract qualities associated with good accountability, such as "control," "independence," or "trust" is extremely problematic. Additionally, symbolism, such as that of the Bradford and Bingley Bank's bowler-hat visual branding, is likely to mean less to an eastern as compared to a western audience, as the cultural context is important.

Visual Elicitation

Visual elicitation is, on the other hand, open to the impressions and subjectivity inherent in the interpretation of the meaning of visual material. Visual elicitation is well-established in sociology and anthropology, and is well-known in management studies and consumer research, but extremely new to accountability research, where there are only a handful of studies (Parker 2009). Visual elicitation may take several forms, but in all cases some form of visual material forms the basis for subsequent structured or semi-structured interview or discussion. Visual data may be generated by the researcher with the express purpose of guiding discussion. Alternatively, research participants may create the data by, for example, taking photographs that capture an aspect of their professional identity as accountants (Warren and Parker 2009), or drawing aspects of their workplace. Visual elicitation may also be stimulated by pre-existing historical or contemporary visual material that arouses views and reactions among research participants. Visual elicitation would seem to be a potentially fruitful avenue for giving focus to the exploration of accountability issues, while recognizing that some caution is advisable with regard to results obtained in this way (Tyson 2009).

Visual Experiments

A more scientific method for gaining research participant response to visual data, often based in theory from psychology, is the use of visual experiments. Here, the researcher has specific hypotheses to test. A visual experiment has three main components, all of which pose certain difficulties.

- A research instrument is constructed, consisting of the visual stimuli being tested plus the means of collecting responses, such as a Likert-scale questionnaire. Constructing a fully robust research instrument is not a straightforward task.
- A setting must be chosen, which may aim to simulate real life, or may be a laboratory-style environment that aims to remove other stimuli; again, the setting can never fully replicate real life, nor is it easy to remove all other stimuli to create a laboratory-style environment.
- Research participants must be invited, who may be paid or unpaid, professionals in a relevant walk of life, or students. Here too, it is problematic engaging participants who will be objective (and therefore unpaid), and of a suitable level of expertise (for example, it may be debatable as to whether MBA students are a good proxy for sophisticated investors, and undergraduates for non-expert investors).

Various aspects of the visualization of financial reporting have been tested experimentally using students as participants. Beattie and Jones (2002) ascertain that the threshold at which viewers perceive a graphical measurement distortion is ten per cent, and conclude therefore that "if financial graphs are to avoid distorting the perceptions of users, then no measurement distortions in excess of 10 per cent should be allowed" (2002, 546). So and Smith (2002) find that color graphics improve decision-making, but only when the information complexity is low and the subjects are female, while Courtis (2004) tests reactions to seven commonly used colors and finds indications that color may not be neutral in financial reporting. Stanton, Stanton, and Pires (2004) give different groups of students different annual reporting documents to see whether they respond more favorably to those containing more impression management material in the form of pictures and narrative material, but find no evidence to support their hypothesis. Townsend and Shu (2010), on the other hand, find with experimental groups of US students that increased "aesthetics" make it more likely that investors will place a higher value on a company, rooted in psychological theory that "opting for a more aesthetic option over a less aesthetic option affirms a person's sense of self" (2010, 7).

Visual Semiotics and Visual Rhetoric

Visual semiotics, originating in arts disciplines and adapted from the "linguistic turn" of critical theory, offers thoughtful modes of analysis that, unlike some of the previous methods considered, attempts to unravel the specific *modus operandi* of the visual image. Influential writers in this area include Roland Barthes, John Berger, W. J. T. Mitchell, and Susan Sontag. While visual semiotics and visual rhetoric are thoughtful approaches, they remain subjective in interpretation, and on a case study basis, albeit guided by theory and carefully argued by reference to evidence from the visual images.

They are ideally, although not exclusively, used by researchers with some experience of working with the methods of interpretive arts disciplines.

Visual semiotics is particularly adaptable to accountability studies as it regards the everyday as being worthy of analysis just as much as "high art," and because it emphasizes the importance of the receiver of an image in creating its meaning. Two works by Roland Barthes are useful in providing universal models that may be used as a framework for the analysis of accountability images: "Rhetoric of the Image" (1982) and *Camera Lucida* (1980), discussed in the next section. In "Rhetoric of the Image," Barthes divides the visual image (taking an advert for Panzani pasta as his point of departure) into two parts: the linguistic (since images frequently contain words, if only as a caption), and the iconic. He argues firstly that the linguistic part of the image "anchors" the often ambiguous meaning of the iconic part of the image. Secondly, he divides the iconic part of the image into "denotation" (description, representation), and "connotation" (suggested meanings, symbolism). Baldvinsdottir et al. (2009) use part of this model, in conjunction with Giddens's work on modernity, in an analysis of the changing professional image of accountants in software adverts, tracking the metamorphosis from a rational responsible professional in the 1970s and 1980s to an "action man" in the 1990s, and a hedonistic individual in the 2000s, with concomitant changes in perceptions of trust.

Visual rhetoric is allied to visual semiotics and similarly aims to unpack the *modus operandi* of the visual image. Rhetoric has its roots in classical times, but visual rhetoric formed an important part of early medieval accounting treatises (Quattrone 2009), whose visual patterns are shown to be linked to thought processes and mental classification, and also to be important mnemonic devices. The study of classical and medieval rhetoric has enjoyed a resurgence in critical theory in recent decades, in the work of Barthes, for example, who advocated mapping linguistic rhetorical figures on to visual images in order to find a "Rhetoric of the Image" (Barthes 1982). Davison (2002) takes the rhetorical figure of antithesis to analyze the contrasting, complex, and interweaving visual messages in Reuters Annual Review 2000, where current investment in new technology is set against Reuters' 150 year reputation in the news and data industry.

A Brief Illustrative Example

A brief example can outline some of the power and challenges of the visual and associated research methods. The front cover of WPP's 2008 annual report and accounts, the major accountability document of the company (marketing communications services), displayed a puzzling painting of a bird in simple but eye-catching shades of brown, red, yellow, and green (see <http://www.wpp.com/annualreports/2008/downloads/WPP_AR08_Full.pdf>). WPP have repeatedly won awards for their annual report design. First reactions on seeing such an image might be: What is it? Do I like it? What is its connection with WPP? And students of accountability might add: What is its relationship with accountability?

Content analysis is not very useful for the analysis of such images beyond gathering general information on the extent of the use of visual images by companies. A content analysis approach would firstly categorize the type of image. Here it is pure visual image apart from the title, and a painting as opposed to a photograph. Then a content analysis would typically measure and record the space occupied by the image (usually as part of a large sample), in this case, almost a full page. But how would its prominence be measured? Thirdly, content analysis would aim to classify the content of the image, often with two coders to mitigate subjectivity. However, herein lies the challenge. We can describe the image as a bird. If we take the trouble to search for a title, on page 185 we discover "Ogalo misterioso," which is Portuguese for "Mysterious Cockerel." How might this be classified? The answer is not at all obvious. In some parts of the world Ogalo is a popular fast-food, but this would clearly be a mis-reading in the case of WPP. Perhaps it might be related to branding? But in precisely what way would this be so? Perhaps it is an environmental message, but again precisely what?

Visual elicitation is potentially more useful in such cases, and could be used in conjunction with selected reader groups to provide much-needed research into reader response to visual images in accountability documents. Using this method, subjective individual views and reactions to the visual image would be actively canvassed. The difficulties here are likely to be the wide range of reactions (for example, a rapid straw poll has elicited common reactions such as "childlike, naive art, tropical colors and patterns, striking, cheerful, 'happy vibes,' aspiring, crowing, confident" to less common reactions such as "natural and organic," "meaningless," and "the fact that the bird is out of proportion with the tree perhaps shows that it is exceeding its expectations as a creature"), without arguments or evidence, and how to summarize such responses. There is also a lack of theory in this area, which adds to the difficulties of how to evaluate reactions.

A *visual experiment* would design a scenario in which to test responses to the image in relation to a specific research question. For example, typical questions might be the extent to which the image influenced readers' reactions to the company's financial performance, to its branding, or to its environmental credentials. Here, a research instrument would be devised which aimed to capture readers' responses, research participants would be engaged, and a setting used, which might be a "laboratory" setting completely removed from other influences or an attempt to replicate a "real world" setting. Experimental work is generally underpinned by work in visual psychology, but there are real practical difficulties in formulating a scientific scenario.

A reading based in *visual semiotics* would typically be based in critical theoretical work and would aim to understand the meaning of the image beyond a description of its content. For example, a Barthesian reading would divide the image into a linguistic element (including the caption) and an iconic element. In the WPP example the linguistic element consists of the captions—the image has been placed in the context of WPP and its "Annual Report," and we know it is a cockerel and has connections with Portuguese. The iconic element would be divided into its denotations, or literal representation, and its connotations. In this example the image denotes a bird. However, it is the connotations that are of more interest. We can all identify with such an everyday creature, and one that has associations with country life, with pride, national emblems (such as the Gallic Rooster), and black magic. We might enjoy the simplicity and naïvety of the painting's style. We might see a symbolic reading that associates the cockerel with WPP's portfolio of brands. On page 184 we also discover the cockerel is a woodcut from the work of an acclaimed Brazilian folk-lore artist, Borges. We are thus enjoined to make a connection between WPP and quality and creativity, and to see WPP's support for the arts in a developing country. On read-ing further into the annual report we discover a series of Borges' woodcuts which all take primitive themes from nature, and might be seen as celebration of the natural environ-ment. If we review a series of WPP's annual reports, we see a strong tradition of promoting the work of a variety of artists in markets important to the company around the world. Visual semiotics brings much-needed theory to the area, but still relies on a subjective reading, albeit a reading that brings associated evidence to support arguments.

Interesting Issues

The Visual Portrayal of Intangibles

Visual media can assist in communicating issues related to accountability. Visual media have a role in portraying intangibles (structural, human, relational) which are not well captured in conventional accounting terms. Intellectual capital statements often take the form of sketches, diagrams, charts, and pictures, as these have been found to be a more effective way of communicating a company's intangible assets (Mouritsen et al. 2001). Branding is not always reflected in the balance sheet (as such expenditure is only capital-ized when brands are purchased rather than internally generated), yet organizations invest huge sums in establishing organizational identity, and much of such branding is inher-ently visual. Davison (2009) explores the role of the quintessentially British bowler hat in the changing fortunes of the Bradford and Bingley Bank, and shows its metamorphosis from anonymous but trustworthy "City gentleman," through a humorous bowler-hatted detective male/female duo, "The Advice Squad," to a colorful and seductive "Ms Bradford and Bingley" reminiscent of the music hall; the changing branding reflects the changing nature of gender in society as well as the need to appeal to a more competitive and deregu-lated global marketplace. Leadership is another intangible regarded as critical for an orga-nization's success, which is excluded from conventional accounting. Visual portraits in annual reports and press releases form important sites of image construction where stake-holders form impressions of the nature of an organization's leadership (Davison 2010).

The Visual Portrayal of Diversity

Diversity is a key issue in contemporary corporate governance, as organizations become ever more accountable for equality of employment opportunity, and as calls are increasingly made for greater diversity of board membership (for example, FRC 2010). The pictures and photographs of annual reports have provided important information regarding diversity, where it has been lacking elsewhere in the reports. Female subordination and stereotyping have been discerned in the study of visual imagery of General Motors (Tinker and Neimark 1987), and in a number of other studies. Stereotyping and inequality regarding both gender and race have been observed in the annual review of Big Four firms (Duff 2011). Companies with a stronger female and/or ethnic minority board presence appear to advertise this fact through pictures of board membership (Bernardi, Bean and Wippert 2005).

Ethical Issues

Ethical issues have been explored with regard to the communication of trust in web-page accounts of Corporate Social Responsibility (CSR); taking a framework from media richness theory, there is evidence that greater trust is associated with "richer" media (photos and video as compared to text) (Cho et al. 2009). Ethical issues have also been explored through interpretive studies drawing on ethical philosophy. Campbell, McPhail, and Slack (2009) draw on Levinas to analyze a rise in human facial representation in annual reports, accompanied by a perceived dehumanization; yet they comment that, paradoxically, the fact of the presence of these faces indicates an Other-interestedness by corporations in addition to their self-interest. Matilal and Höpfl (2009) show how gruesome press photographs of the victims of the Bhopal chemical factory tragedy in India (seen, following Kristeva, as the body and the maternal), contrast with the dry technical accounts of the company's annual report (interpreted as the legalistic and the paternal).

Visual Impression Management

One fundamental issue that has been examined by research is the use of visual media for impression management and the framing of information used for decision-making. Visual devices are voluntary disclosures that generally fall outside standard regulations and full audit procedures, and therefore provide management with considerable scope for impression management. At the same time, management have a duty to shareholders to promote the company's interests and to maximize share value. Impression management has been notably explored in the use of:

- financial graphs
- color, pictures and architecture.

Financial Graphs

Graphs are powerful communication tools that inject color and interest into often drab pages of technical information in annual reports, and are used by the majority of organizations (Beattie and Jones 1992). When well used, they are excellent visual forms for communicating financial information quickly and succinctly. They appeal to our spatial intelligence, enable patterns, comparisons, and trends to be quickly grasped, and are memorable and readily retrievable. Column graphs are the most popular graphical form to convey "financial highlights," the reporting of key performance indicators (typically turnover, profit before tax, earnings per share, and dividend per share); 84 percent of companies have been shown to use column graphs to display such financial indicators. However, financial graphs may be manipulated to give misleading impressions. Graphs may be used selectively, so that only good results (whether by year or by key performance indicator) are graphically highlighted. Graph construction may be tinkered with to give distorted measurements; this may happen through devices such as measurement exaggeration, or the use of broken axes or non-zero axes. In a survey of 240 UK companies, Beattie and Jones (1992) found an incidence of material discrepancy in the graphs of 20 percent of the sampled companies, spread fairly evenly across the key performance indicators. Beattie and Jones (2008) have shown that financial graphs can undermine the neutrality of annual reports, and as a result of their work over a number of years, regulation in the UK now acknowledges the power of graphical representations, and states that care should be taken with their objectivity (Accounting Standards Board 2000).

Color, Pictures, Architecture

Impression management is not restricted to the use of financial graphs. Color "has the ability to impress and to affect moods and behaviour" (Courtis 2004, 265–66), and adding "aesthetics," defined as color and the use of glossy print, makes it more likely that investors will place a higher value on the company (Townsend and Shu 2010). Pictures and photographs may be used to add credibility to a company's annual reports, through imitating a "television epistemology" of entertainment (Graves, Flesher, and Jordan 1996). Pictures have the capacity to convey a company's history and reputation, for example through the reproduction of material from corporate archives, and can thus place current results in a broader context; this could be important to an established company making potentially risky research and development investment that it is obliged by accounting rules to write off in the profit and loss account, thus having a negative impact on profits (Davison 2002). In the charity and NGO sector, pictures and photographs can be used to convey a complex cocktail of accountability messages, ranging from trust and compassion to the dual engagement of many such organizations in the developed and developing worlds (Davison 2007). Architecture too can mould our impressions of an organization. The nineteenth century neo-Baroque Chartered Accountants Hall in London was designed to impress, and to put the relatively new accounting profession on a par with medicine and law (McKinstry 1997). In similar vein, the more recent and striking architecture of the financial sector reflected its exponential growth in the early years of the twenty-first century (McGoun 2004).

A Few Key Contributions

The following discusses a few key contributions that address specific aspects of the particular ways in which visual media function in accountability communication, starting with some studies that discuss the deep-rooted history of the links between the visual and accountability.

Visual Inscriptions and Order in Ancient Egyptian Temples

In the temples of ancient Egypt, pictures are placed alongside numbers and words to record "the ritual of offerings, and the process involved in receiving, weighing and counting them" (Ezzamel 2009, 367). These scenes "construct a 'reality' of an organized and orderly process in imitation of cosmic order, endowing it with religious and administrative legitimacy" (2009, 367–8). Ezzamel observes that the three modes of representation—pictures, numbers, and words—do not completely replicate each other. Pictures are more accessible to an illiterate audience, even if they are composed of denser material open to varying interpretation. The numbers, too, are visual representations that carry patterns and symbolic meaning, linked to order. Ezzamel argues that these highly visualized architectural inscriptions constitute both evidence of the actions of making offerings to the gods by Pharaoh, and serve as records of offerings, and that both these actions connect with the preservation of order: "the action of making the offerings was an exercise in which the Pharaoh discharged accountability to the gods" (2009, 370).

Visual Rhetorical Ordering and Classification in the Italian Renaissance

Quattrone (2009) investigates early Italian accounting treatises from the much later period of the sixteenth century, and explores "how mechanisms of societal accountability intertwine with issues of organizing the minutiae of our daily lives" (2009, 114). He shows, with illustrations, the ways in which visual patterns, from lists to tree diagrams, mould thought patterns. He too argues that visual inscriptions are crucial in "offering clear schematic forms of ordering and organization of thought" (2009, 113), and that such visualization is further linked to the arts of memory and rhetoric. Further, he argues that the visual is not purely representational and record-making, but has the ability to engage and to mobilize.

"Three Ways of Seeing" in Contemporary Annual Reports

The *modus operandi* of the pictures and photographs of contemporary annual reports has been increasingly analyzed. Preston et al. (1996) suggest three "ways of seeing" these visual images. The first way of seeing "views the image as transparently conveying an intended corporate message" (1996, 113)—here images are regarded as a transparent medium of communication, as in the food company PepsiCo's photograph of a Sumo wrestler to symbolize the "Power of Big Brands." The second way of seeing decodes "deeply embedded social significances" (1996, 115), following neo-Marxist aesthetics, and is focused on the ideological content—for example, the portrayal of a new era of high technology on a company's front cover may mask a "pernicious class structure" (1996, 123). The third way of seeing draws on postmodernism to see the constitutive role of images in creating reality, as simulacra become more real than that which they purport to represent.

Visual Portraiture, Business Leadership, and Human Capital

Another model of universal application is that of visual portraiture, formulated by Davison (2010) to highlight the coded ways in which visual images of leadership may be constructed, but equally applicable to portraits of other organizational stakeholders. Human capital is not recognized in conventional accounting, and so these portraits form significant sites for disseminating impressions of leadership. Drawing inspiration from art theory, Davison (2010) devises a model based on four sets of codes: physical, dress, interpersonal, and spatial. Physical codes supply factual information such as gender, ethnicity, and age (although these denominations are increasingly seen as fluid), and of physical attractiveness, known to be linked to success. Dress reflects social and cultural factors, and also organizational codes—for example, more formal dress usually connotes greater status and power, but informality of attire may, on the other hand, be associated with greater creativity. The interpersonal codes of the body language of smiles, hand gestures, and pensive poses reveals feeling and emotion, while group portraits show relationships and status. The spatial codes of portrait settings, and their props and artefacts—typically chairs, tables, mirrors, or symbols of the trade—add further symbolic messages. Campbell et al. (2009) contribute to the discussion of visual portraits by focusing, in the context of employees, on the way a portrait's face and the spectator are organized in relation to each other: the contact may be sideways and indirect, or it may be direct through gaze or outstretched hand; the spectator may be invited to share the view of the employee, or may be entirely distanced. Thus, portraits are not neutral representations, and contribute to our understanding of accountability for human capital at all levels of engagement with the organization.

FINAL THOUGHTS

Visual media are arguably just as important as numbers and words in communicating accountability messages. Yet in the field of accountability, and management studies more broadly, the legitimacy of research taking visual media as either an object or a tool of analysis has been slow to be acknowledged. Visual media have often been regarded as decoration and devoid of content, or at best as transparent representational information. The reality of their essential ambiguity and plurality means that they lend themselves poorly to quantification and thus to generalized analysis across large samples. Finding theory and methods that give appropriate frameworks for visual analysis remains a challenge. Interdisciplinary theory and methods are gradually being adopted, but these can be unfamiliar to scholars in the accountability domain, and based on quite different disciplinary skills and conventions.

Ethical and Legal Hurdles

There are also significant ethical and legal hurdles in conducting and publishing visual research. There are ethical issues of consent before making visual records of people and places, and further issues of confidentiality and anonymity if the material is later published. There are legal matters of copyright and permissions for the reproduction of visual material, which vary internationally. In reproducing annual report photographs in a research paper, for example, it may be necessary to obtain the written permission of the organization, the creator of the image, and any subjects in the image. Reproduction fees can also be costly, and vary according to certain criteria, such as whether or not the material will be available electronically as well as in hard copy, and whether it is to be available in perpetuity. These considerations are time-consuming, not only in fully grasping the issues at stake, but also in the often lengthy and bureaucratic practicalities of locating copyright holders and obtaining their permission.

Yet, the legal and ethical hurdles associated with reproducing visual forms are a sign of the power that is seen to be vested in the visual; while pictures and photographs have been regarded as lightweight ingredients of accountability reports, it may be argued that they are, on the contrary, heavyweight elements (Davison 2007). Visual media are omnipresent and psychologically powerful. They carry messages, and sometimes emotional impact, that lie beyond the capacity of verbal and numerate accountability statements. The role of emotion is also increasingly recognized, whether in studies of organizational workplaces and leadership, or in the irrationality of behavioral finance. The interdisciplinary connections that are necessary to underpin understanding of the *modus operandi* of visual media extend and enrich accountability research by encouraging new ways of working and thinking.

The Rapid Development of the Field

It is for these reasons that, from little interest a decade ago, visual studies in accountability and related management studies have significantly increased in recent years.

There have been a number of recent initiatives by various professional and research bodies and by publishers. The EIASM (European Institute for Advanced Studies in Management) has supported three workshops on aesthetics, art, and management, two workshops on the theme of *Imag[in]ing business*, three on architecture, and a forthcoming workshop on fashion. The UK ESRC (Economic and Social Research Council) has supported the *Building Capacity in Visual Methods* programme. In conjunction with the foundation of the *in*Visio research network (International Network for Visual Studies in Organizations, <www.in-visio.org>), the ESRC has also supported a seminar series and a Researcher Development Initiative to advance visual methodologies in business and management through the development of online researcher/teaching resources focused on various aspects of organizations, including accountability. Routledge have recently commissioned several books on the visual in organizations, for example, Puyou et al. (2011); Bell et al. (2013).

The majority of research has until now been focused on pictures/photographs and on graphs, and the main sources of visual accountability investigated have been annual reports. The UK Financial Reporting Council, with the aid of expert advice from psychology, is addressing the general issue of what it refers to as "clutter" in annual reports (FRC 2011), although visual material is not considered specifically. Yet there is such a wealth of organizational pictorial material, communicating such a wealth of complex accountability messages that the work conducted to date is still in its infancy. Beyond pictures and photographs in themselves, there is an acute need for work on internet-based media such as web pages, video presentations, and social networking sites that have so far been almost totally neglected. Social and environmental reporting makes much use of visual material that similarly remains largely overlooked, with a few exceptions (Cho et al. 2009; Ramo 2011). Other aspects such as logos, sketches, and diagrams present areas of interest. For example, Spira and Page (2011) investigate the use of diagrams (classified into boxes, circles, triangles, and other forms) to communicate aspects of corporate governance and strategy. There is scope for the further development of all these approaches, informed by even greater interdisciplinarity. Much (although not all) accountability research has tended to focus on the use of visual forms to obscure accountability, where it would also be beneficial to highlight the good use to which visual forms may be applied. Such development should bring out the complexities of visual media, and highlight the ways in which they are far more than decoration, or even transparent information, and constitute the potent framing of our thought processes.

NOTE

1. It would be impossible to give details on methods in a short chapter like this, but there is direction to a number of papers where more details on methods can be found, and readers are also directed to the freely available *in*Visio researcher development web pages "*in*spire" at <http://moodle.in-visio.org/>.

References

Accounting Standards Board. 2000. *Year-end Financial Reports: Improving Communication.* Discussion Paper. Milton Keynes: ASB Publications.

Baldvinsdottir, G., Burns, J., Nørreklit, H., and Scapens, R. W. 2009. "The Image of Accountants: From Bean Counters to Extreme Accountants." *Accounting, Auditing & Accountability Journal*, 22: 858–82.

Barthes, R. 1980. *La Chambre Claire.* Paris: Le Seuil.

Barthes, R. 1982. *Rhétorique de l'image in l'obvie et l'obtus.* Paris: Le Seuil.

Beattie, V. A. and Jones, M. J. 1992. "The Use and Abuse of Graphs in Annual Reports: Theoretical Framework and Empirical Study." *Accounting and Business Research*, 22: 291–303.

Beattie, V. A. and Jones, M. J. 2002. "Measurement Distortion of Graphs in Corporate Reports: An Experimental Study." *Accounting, Auditing & Accountability Journal*, 15: 546–64.

Beattie, V. A. and Jones, M. J. 2008. "Corporate Reporting Using Graphs: A Review and Synthesis." *Journal of Accounting Literature*, 27: 71–110.

Bell, A., Schroeder, J., and Warren, S. (eds.). (2013). *The Routledge Companion to Visual Organization.* Oxford: Routledge.

Bernardi, R. A., Bean, D. F., and Weippert, K. M. 2005. "Minority Membership on Boards of Directors: The Case for Requiring Pictures of Boards in Annual Reports." *Critical Perspectives on Accounting*, 16: 1019–33.

Campbell, D., McPhail, K., and Slack, R. 2009. "Face Work in Annual Reports." *Accounting, Auditing & Accountability Journal*, 22: 907–32.

Cho, C. H., Phillips, J. R., Hageman, A. M., and Patten, D. M. 2009. "Media Richness, User Trust and Perceptions of Corporate Social Responsibility." *Accounting, Auditing & Accountability Journal*, 22: 933–52.

Courtis, J. 2004. "Colour as Visual Rhetoric in Financial Reporting." *Accounting Forum*, 28: 265–82.

Davison, J. 2002. "Communication and Antithesis in Corporate Annual Reports: A Research Note." *Accounting, Auditing & Accountability Journal*, 15: 594–608.

Davison, J. 2007. "Photographs and Accountability: Cracking the Codes of an NGO." *Accounting, Auditing & Accountability Journal*, 20: 133–58.

Davison, J. 2009. "Icon, Iconography, Iconology: Visual Branding, Banking and the Case of the Bowler Hat." *Accounting, Auditing & Accountability Journal*, 22: 883–906.

Davison, J. 2010. "(In)visible (In)tangibles: Visual Portraits of the Business Élite." *Accounting, Organizations and Society*, 35: 165–83.

Dimnik, T. and Felton, S. 2006. "Accountant Stereotypes in Movies Distributed in North America in the Twentieth Century." *Accounting, Organizations and Society*, 31: 129–55.

Duff, A. 2011. "Big Four Accounting Firms' Annual Reviews: A Photo Analysis of Gender and Race Portrayals." *Critical Perspectives on Accounting*, 22: 20–38.

Ezzamel, M. 2009. "Order and Accounting as a Performative Ritual: Evidence from Ancient Egypt." *Accounting, Organizations and Society*, 34: 348–80.

FRC. 2010. *The UK Corporate Governance Code.* London: Financial Reporting Council.

FRC. 2011. *Cutting Clutter: Combating Clutter in Annual Reports.* London: Financial Reporting Council.

Graves, O. F., Flesher, D. L., and Jordan, R. E. 1996. "Pictures and the Bottom Line: The Television Epistemology of US Annual Reports." *Accounting, Organizations and Society*, 21: 57–88.

Hopwood, A.G. 1996. Introduction. *Accounting, Organizations and Society*, 21 (1): 55–6.

Matilal, S. and Höpfl, H. 2009. "Accounting for the Bhopal Disaster: Footnotes and Photographs." *Accounting, Auditing & Accountability Journal*, 22: 953–72.

McGoun, E. G. 2004. "Form, Function, and Finance: Architecture and Finance Theory." *Critical Perspectives on Accounting*, 15: 1085–1107.

McKinstry, S. 1997. "Status Building: Some Reflections on the Architectural History of Chartered Accountants' Hall, London, 1889–1893." *Accounting, Organizations and Society*, 22: 779–98.

Mouritsen, J., Larsen, H. T., and Bukh, P. N. D. 2001. "Intellectual Capital and the 'Capable Firm': Narrating, Visualising and Numbering for Managing Knowledge." *Accounting, Organizations and Society*, 26: 735–62.

Parker, L. D. 2009. "Photo-Elicitation: An Ethno-Historical Accounting and Management Research Project." *Accounting, Auditing & Accountability Journal*, 22: 1111–29.

Parker, L. D. 2013. The Accounting Communication Research Landscape pp. 7–25. in *The Routledge Companion to Accounting Communication*, eds. L. Jack, J. Davison, and R. Craig. Oxford: Routledge.

Preston, A. M., Wright, C., and Young, J. J. 1996. "Imag[in]ing Annual Reports." *Accounting, Organizations and Society*, 21: 113–37.

Puyou, F. R., Quattrone, P., McLean, C., and Thrift, N. (eds.) 2011. *Imagining Business: Performative Imagery in Business and Beyond*. Oxford: Routledge.

Quattrone, P. 2009. "Books to be Practiced: Memory, the Power of the Visual, and the Success of Accounting." *Accounting, Organizations and Society*, 34: 85–118.

Ramo, H. 2011. "Visualising the Phronetic Organization: The Case of Photographs in CSR Reports." *Journal of Business Ethics*, 104: 371–87.

So, S. and Smith, M. 2002. "Colour Graphics and Task Complexity in Multivariate Decision-Making." *Accounting, Auditing & Accountability Journal*, 15: 565–93.

Spira, L. F. and Page, M. 2011. *Visualising Corporate Governance and Strategy*. In EIASM (European Institute for Advanced Studies in Management) Workshop on Imagining Business. Segovia, May 2011.

Stanton, P., Stanton, J., and Pires, G. 2004. "Impressions of an Annual Report: An Experimental Study." *Corporate Communications: An International Journal*, 9: 57–69.

Tinker, T. and Neimark, M. 1987. "The Role of Annual Reports in Gender and Class Contradictions at General Motors 1917–1976." *Accounting, Organizations and Society*, 12: 71–88.

Townsend, C. and Shu, S. B. 2010. "When and How Aesthetics Influences Financial Decisions." *Journal of Consumer Psychology*, 20: 452–58.

Tyson, T. 2009. "Discussion of Photo-Elicitation: An Ethno-Historical Accounting and Management Research Project." *Accounting, Auditing & Accountability Journal*, 22: 1130–41.

Warren, S. and Davison, J. 2009. "Visual Perspectives on Accounting and Accountability." *Accounting, Auditing & Accountability*, 22: 845–57.

Warren, S. and Parker, L. D. 2009. "Bean Counters or Bright Young Things? Towards the Visual Study of Identity Construction Among Professional Accountants." *Qualitative Research in Accounting & Management*, 6: 205–23.

Yamey, B. S. 1989. *Art and Accounting*. New Haven and London: Yale University Press.

PART III

ACCOUNTABLE GOVERNANCE

CHAPTER 12

ACCOUNTABILITY AND CONSTITUTIONAL LAW

CAROL HARLOW

MEANINGS AND ORIGINS

THE concept of accountability is well understood by constitutional lawyers and could in some senses be said to comprise the rationale for our discipline. But it is not core terminology within our discipline. Constitutions and constitutionalism are ancient concepts, with a philosophy that runs parallel to, though it may facilitate, accountability. Only a handful of states do not possess a written constitutional text or "Big-C Constitution." Symbolically, the Constitution is a badge of nationhood. It embodies the nation's values, which may or may not include accountability. At a less aspirational level, a constitution provides the framework for government and stands first in the hierarchy of legal norms (Kelsen 1978; Hart 1997).

Accountability, on the other hand, is a relatively modern term with specifically Anglo-American origins; it has indeed been suggested that no exact translation exists in other European languages. Even in English, "accountability" has no single precise meaning. Describing its rapid spread through the English-speaking world, Mulgan (2000, 555) notes how "a word which a few decades ago was used only rarely and with relatively restricted meaning...now crops up everywhere performing all manner of analytical and rhetorical tasks and carrying most of the burdens of democratic 'governance.'" It is in short an "umbrella" term, which rolls up a number of different concepts with variable content.

Accounting and Narrating: An Evolutionary Approach

In the English language, the concept of accountability has two core meanings, each with important constitutional implications. These are best encapsulated in the distinction between the French words "conte" (story or narration) and "compte" (calculation or reckoning). Historically, the association with accounting has the deepest roots. The idea of financial accounting is deeply entrenched in every system of parliamentary government, most notably perhaps in England, where the idea can be traced as far back as Magna Carta (1215). The great legal historian, F. W. Maitland, states that the imposition of any direct tax without the common consent of the realm was "against the very letter of the law" after 1295 (Maitland 1908, 90). Gradually, parliamentary control of the purse strings became a fundamental constitutional principle and a very real check on monarchical executive power. Today the House of Commons, which has achieved sole legislative responsibility for financial matters, scrutinizes all government expenditure on a value-for-money basis through its Public Accounts Committee (PAC). In this work it is supported by the Comptroller and Auditor General, a parliamentary officer, and the National Audit Office. The PAC is the most powerful of parliamentary committees. It can choose the subject of its inquiries, has powers to "call for persons, papers and records" and can subject ministers and witnesses to searching cross-examination. Actors have an obligation to explain and justify expenditure to the PAC and, even if technically it cannot impose sanctions, defaulters can certainly expect to face consequences. In short, the PAC is an authentic accountability forum and stands as a valuable paradigm in the fight for financial accountability that is today a central element in the world-wide search for accountability.

This gradual building up of an accounting process typifies the pragmatic British approach to constitution-making, which so often substitutes history for theory and machinery for principle. But even if Britain had a written Constitution, the powers of this committee would—if they were even mentioned—be only lightly sketched in; a written Constitution is, in other words, a beginning rather than an end. But the role played by control over public expenditure in building a system of parliamentary accountability is nonetheless very widely acknowledged. Strong Appropriations and Budget Committees with similar powers exist in the US Congress. The European Parliament, which started life in 1958 as a seriously under-powered consultative assembly, has used its powers of budgetary control skillfully to build up its powers of scrutiny (Westlake 1998), emerging after the Lisbon Treaty (2009) as virtual co-legislator for the European Union. On the other side of the world in Communist Vietnam, a debate on constitutional amendment opened in the late 1990s with proposals to expand the Legislative Assembly's supervisory and auditing powers over national budgets, to enlarge its staff of professional auditors, and to devolve authority over local budgets to local legislatures (Sidel 2008, 25).

The commonest interpretation of public accountability today is, however, rooted in the simple idea of narration: "giving an account" of events that have taken place or, typically, have gone wrong. In the definition preferred by Bovens (2007a, 450), accountability is a *retrospective* process that obliges an actor (i) to explain and justify his or her conduct (ii) in a forum where questions can be put and (iii) an evaluation made or judgment arrived at. The actor must also expect (iv) to "face consequences." For the public at large, the weight of the definition is likely to fall on the consequences of transgression rather than on explanation; in other words, in common usage, accountability has negative connotations and is closely linked to sanction and punishment.

A more inclusive definition would cover the public accountability of policy-makers in the lawmaking process. This prospective construction is acceptable when applied to a strong representative legislature but less so when used to legitimate one-party governance. Prospective accountability through the participation of civil society in policy-making is closely associated with theories of deliberative democracy, used to legitimate the supranational governance systems that are emerging in the modern world outside any constitutional framework (Cohen and Sabel 1997; Joerges 2002). There is a very real danger that accountability in its core sense of answerability will be undercut by any arrangement that ties potential critics into the policy-making process as partners (Shapiro 2001; Harlow and Rawlings 2007).

Responsibility and Accountability

Responsibility is the British constitutional lawyer's surrogate for accountability. The doctrine of ministerial responsibility to Parliament lies at the heart of the "Westminster model of government," permeating the constitutional system and indispensable to it (Turpin 1994, 110). In numerous constitutions throughout the Commonwealth ministerial responsibility is incorporated as a shared constitutional convention (Smith 2006). Thus the first post-war independence constitution of India (1950) which, in vesting federal executive power in the President (Article 53) follows a US presidential pattern, also stipulates an advisory Council of Ministers, "collectively responsible to the House of the People" (Art. 75 (3)). Nearly fifty years later, the 1996 South African Constitution provided for the "accountability and responsibilities" of ministers who are to be "*responsible* for the powers and functions of the executive assigned to them by the President" and "*accountable* collectively and individually to Parliament" (section 92). This formula seems to distinguish "responsibility," seen as personal and subjective, from "accountability," which is mechanistic.

Similar conflations exist elsewhere. In France, where the word "*responsabilité*" signifies both political responsibility and legal liability, authors seem unable to agree on the meaning and force of the term. Some authors see *responsabilité* as equivalent to the untranslatable Anglo-Saxon word "accountability," others as a non-exportable "English invention" bound up with the character of the British parliamentary system which, as a political aphorism without clear meaning and lacking in legal consequence, cannot be a tenet of the French Constitution (Pouvoirs 2000). Segur (1999) sees a danger that this disagreement is not purely semantic but representative of political indifference in society at large.

In the dual-language European Union, a report from a Committee of Independent Experts, mandated by the European Parliament to investigate alleged corruption in the European Commission, also equated the terms "responsibility" and "*responsabilité*" with the British doctrine of individual and collective ministerial responsibility. There were tremors in Brussels when the Experts spoke of the "growing reluctance among the members of the hierarchy to acknowledge their responsibility. It is becoming difficult to find anyone who has even the slightest sense of responsibility" (Committee of Independent Experts 1999, [4.25]). This celebrated passage imbues the term with moral force. The Experts gave accountability (*comptabilité*) a mechanistic interpretation, though arriving at the important finding that "the principles of openness, transparency and accountability are at the heart of democracy and are the very instruments allowing it to function properly."[1]

Accountability—a Normative Value?

The exact parameters of the doctrine of ministerial responsibility and whether, in the case of individual responsibility, the consequences of default should be resignation, are hotly-debated questions (Finer 1956). Downloading functions and responsibilities to semi-autonomous or executive agencies is a way to undercut the doctrine of ministerial responsibility by severing the essential link between ministers and their departments (Flinders 2004). In this context, the claim has been made that, where operational matters carried out by subordinates are at issue, a minister is "accountable" only in the attenuated sense that s/he has to ascertain the facts, explain them to Parliament and undertake to put matters right. This cunning attempt to avoid "facing the consequences" of departmental error has been strongly resisted—as might be expected—by the British House of Commons, the relevant accountability forum.

The line drawn here marks a step down from a subjective and normative concept of responsibility to a procedural concept of accountability. Some authors, however, see accountability as a normative concept that sets standards for the evaluation of the behavior of public actors (Dubnick 2003). An accepted British textbook (Turpin and Tomkins 2007, 13) recently called accountability "a liability or obligation attaching to those invested with public powers or duties"—a role normally assigned to responsibility—claiming it also as "a leading principle" of the British constitution. It has been suggested too that the "checks-and-balances" Constitution of the United States creates an expectation of accountability that establishes it as a constitutional virtue (Bovens 2007b). It is hard to resist the conclusion that accountability has reached the status of a near universal "good governance" principle, approximating in value to the foundational principle of the rule of law (Harlow 2011).

Key Constitutional Concepts

Three concepts in particular take the place of accountability in constitutional theory: the rule of law, which is the foundational principle for every western legal order; the constitutional doctrine of separation of powers; and the notion of "constitutionalism," which embodies the idea of limited government. While none of these is precisely an account-ability principle, each in its own way provides a framework within which accountability can flourish.

Rule of Law Doctrines

In its simplest form, the rule of law—like accountability, a highly contestable term—requires no more and no less than that all members of society, the rulers not excepted, are subject to and must observe the law. To this purely formal principle further pro-cedural requirements may be attached; the law must be clear enough to allow citizens to plan their lives; criminal law must not be retrospective, etc. (Hayek 1944). As pro-pounded by the great constitutional writer Albert Venn Dicey (1959, 187–96), the core of the rule of law in the English constitution is the "idea of legal equality, or of the universal subjection of all classes to one law administered by the ordinary courts." To this central theme Dicey adds the rule against retrospective criminality and the fact that civil liber-ties are embodied in case law rather than a written Bill of Rights—by no means a crucial prerequisite for the rule of law. This is a highly procedural definition.

An alternative, though equally procedural, interpretation of the maxim is embod-ied in the German ideal of the *Rechtsstaat*,[2] closely associated with the philosophy of Immanuel Kant (1724–1804) and the jurisprudence of Hans Kelsen (1881–1973). The *Rechtsstaat* is a "constitutionalist" state in which public power is constrained by law; the "legislature is bound by the constitutional order, the executive and the judiciary by law and right" (Art. 23 of the *Grundgesetz* or Basic Law). It is also a state regulated by clearly formulated rules arranged hierarchically; the laws are to be definite and not retroac-tive and all official acts must be clearly reasoned. The *Rechtsstaat* is in short a "juridi-fied" or "rule of rules" state in which law governs the administration and regulates social relationships (Teubner 1988). The *Rechtsstaat* embodies transparency: it enables citi-zens to know the basis on which public power is exercised and check that there is lawful authority for what has been done. It also embodies accountability; from constitutional level downwards, the acts and decisions of public authorities are subject to evaluation. Reasoned decision-making is a powerful accountability tool; decisions can be tested against the yardstick of their reasoning and reviewed for proportionality by indepen-dent courts.

These are procedural or "thin" definitions of the rule of law, which purport to be value-free. Whether this can ever be so is highly contentious. The Kantian *Rechtsstaat* is relatively value-free in the sense that it is based on reason and not on natural law—a nineteenth-century preference shared by the English philosopher, Jeremy Bentham. In fact it is an embodiment of liberal rationalism in which the rule of law is itself a liberal value. This places liberals in a dilemma. Thin definitions of the rule of law allow sub-stantive irrationality and inequality to flourish within a framework of formal legality, a contradiction in terms exemplified in real life by the German Nazi or South African apartheid regimes. The paradox has fuelled demands to "thicken" the rule of law by incorporating substantive elements. In 1959, for example, the International Commission of Jurists signed the Declaration of Delhi at a Congress composed of lawyers from 53 countries. This significant text, signed as new states were emerging from a colonial past, presaged the coming dominance of the human rights movement. But the Declaration associated the rule of law principle not only explicitly with the infant human rights movement but also with democratic government, arguing that government should be subject to limitations on its lawmaking powers and that discriminatory laws or laws curtailing civil and political freedoms should be outlawed. Arguably, this is to overload the rule of law, asking of it work it was not designed for. There is then a danger, as Raz (1977) puts it, that in seeking to encapsulate a complete social and political philosophy within a single principle, liberals will deprive the rule of law of any useful role independent of their dominant philosophy. It is surely better to say, as the Treaty of European Union does, that the state "is founded on the values of respect for human dignity, freedom, democracy, equality, the rule of law and respect for human rights" than to assert that the absence of democratic institutions is a violation of the rule of law.

The argument over "thick" and "thin" definitions has not gone away. A political dimension is involved: economic liberals favor thin definitions with the emphasis on enforceability and access to courts; human rights lawyers naturally prefer thick definitions that include democratic values and human rights. There may also be a cultural divide; a recent study of twelve Asian countries found differing interpretations of the rule of law in each society as well as conflicting visions within each (Peerenboom 2004). A "thin" version of the rule of law in the sense of a formal legal system guaranteeing a measure of legal security certainly obtains in China and the government has lately committed to a "thickened" version that takes account of its socialist values and state-centered economy (Peerenboom 2002). But the "thick" rule of law is essentially a modern western construct, closely connected with liberal democracy; whether it can flourish in a different political context remains to be seen.

Separation of Powers

The basic principle of the separation of powers doctrine is simple: no one branch of government should be entrusted with all the functions and powers of government. The so-called "triadic" interpretation, which identifies three essential state functions (lawmaking, implementation, and adjudication) and allocates them to three separate bodies (legislature, executive, and judiciary), owes its popularity to Montesquieu's celebrated treatise, *De l'Esprit des Lois*, published in 1748. The French variant of the doctrine, in place since the revolutionary constitution of 1791, adheres strictly to this model, allocating to each organ of government the plenitude of powers necessary properly to carry out its function (Troper 1980). This complete separation of functions led at first to a serious lack of accountability in the French state, since a law of 1790 decreed that neither the state nor public servants individually could be held liable for wrongdoing in a civil or criminal court. It took almost a century to evolve a judicial section of the Council of

State within the executive branch of government sufficiently powerful to hold the executive to account, and a further century before legislation could be invalidated on grounds of unconstitutionality.[3]

Separation of powers comes, however, with many variant interpretations, of which the most influential has undoubtedly been the "checks-and-balances" approach of the US Constitution. In the influential *Federalist Papers*,[4] James Madison felt it necessary to defend the constitutional draft of 1787 against criticism that it breached the principle of separation of powers. His argument was that, "unless these departments be so far connected and blended as to give to each a constitutional control over the others, the degree of separation which the maxim requires, as essential to a free government, can never in practice be duly maintained" (Federalist Papers 1788, Nos. 47 and 48). We must remember that the US Constitution was not at first concerned specifically with either accountability or democracy, though both were later to emerge as significant constitutional values. Dedicated to "the blessings of Liberty," it was designed to prevent excessive concentrations of power. It adopts a dual strategy of federalism and "checks-and-balances" as protections against excess of power. Presidential power is limited by the need to turn to Congress for both legislation and resources; congressional power is limited by a presidential right of veto; states' rights will be protected by the Senate, which represents them, and by the courts.

In contrast to the "Westminster model," which locks government and Parliament tightly together, the US model offers a strong, unitary executive presidency, separate from Congress.[5] The President appoints "Heads of Department" to a Cabinet together with all policy-making officials, who must be confirmed by the Senate; they are responsible to the President, who may dismiss them (though this is notably difficult to achieve). Today, when much administration is carried out by independent executive agencies, these too are responsible to the President, though his powers of control are limited. Congress retains ultimate control over this powerful executive through its legislative powers; through the budget, a perennial source of dispute; through the machinery of report; through the Senate's powers to confirm presidential nominations to public appointments; and, at the end of the day in the case of the President, through impeachment. However, as Tushnet observes (2009, 96–109), in modern America party politics can render this powerful presidency virtually impotent.

Judicial Independence

A weighty factor in the American "checks-and-balances" equation has been the emergence of a strong and highly independent court system with the renowned Supreme Court at the apex. As Tocqueville (1863) observed in the early nineteenth century, it is to courts that citizens in this highly litigious society turn first to protect their liberties. The Supreme Court first established its power of constitutional review in *Marbury v. Madison* (1803) and state courts also have authority to decide constitutional questions. This has raised questions of judicial accountability and ascendancy, engendering fierce debate amongst American constitutional lawyers (Bickel 1962; Ely 1980; Shapiro 1988).

While the US model has promoted legal accountability through courts, Parliament is the principal accountability forum in the Westminster model—though in Canada the balance has possibly shifted with the passage of the Charter of Rights and Freedoms in 1982. Typically, however, the Westminster family of governments is less concerned with formal separation than with judicial independence, guaranteed most strongly in the Australian Constitution, which prohibits delegation of the judicial function. Again, a Justice of the Supreme Court of India cannot be removed from office except by an order of the President passed after an address in each House of Parliament, supported by a majority of the total membership of that House and by a majority of not less than two-thirds of members present and voting. This guarantee has empowered a confident Supreme Court unafraid to intervene in policy matters—for example, by allowing the growth of a vital public interest law movement (Iyer 2008). The stance of the judiciary during the Indian Emergency (1975-1977), when Mrs. Gandhi governed with emergency powers, led to legislation that reduced the power of the Supreme Court and State High Courts to pronounce on the constitutional validity of laws.[6] This unhappy episode highlights the relevance of judicial independence to the contemporary quest for accountability. Under the influence of the United Nations and other international organizations, most states are at least theoretically committed to the principle of judicial independence. Thus China committed to judicial independence when it joined the World Trade Organization (Mei-Ying Hung 2004). More precisely, the Basic Law of the Hong Kong Special Administrative Region, which emerged from a common law tradition, couples a list of the rights and freedoms of its residents with a specific chapter detailing the safeguards for judicial independence. Those who violate rights should be accountable to forums that can enforce rights and provide redress.

Constitutionalism

The importance of a Big-C Constitution as a limiting device, in the sense of a single written instrument specifying the structure of public power, has long been recognized. McIlwain (1940, 16) noted that written constitutions, "creating, defining and limiting governments" had become "the general rule in almost the whole of the constitutional world" and that "foundational constitutionalism" in the sense that directly relates the legitimacy of government to a written constitution, had come to dominate constitutional thinking. To a century that had seen society devastated by two World Wars and had suffered the excesses of fascistic and totalitarian authoritarianism, constitutionalism, with its liberal democratic origins and claims to afford limitations on power, undoubtedly had its attractions. One of the first steps of the occupying powers (the US, UK, and France) in rehabilitating Germany after World War II was to draft the Basic Law that became the *Grundgesetz für die Bundesrepublik Deutschland*, approved in 1949. Article 20 established the Federal Republic of Germany as a parliamentary democracy and federal republic with a separation of powers structure and set out basic institutional principles characteristic of a liberal democratic constitution:

(i) The Federal Republic of Germany is a democratic and social federal state.
(ii) All state authority is derived from the people. It shall be exercised by the people through elections and other votes and through specific legislative, executive, and judicial bodies.
(iii) The legislature shall be bound by the constitutional order, the executive and the judiciary by law and justice.

The *Grundgesetz* set in place the powerful Constitutional Court (*Bundesverfassungsgericht*) as guardian of the Constitution and its fundamental rights, and made an unequivocal commitment to the inviolability and inalienability of human rights. Latterly, those few states without this type of "Big C Constitution" have come under continual pressure to bring their heterogeneous constitutional arrangements under the umbrella of a codified constitution. Under German influence, the infection has spread to supranational level with the campaign for a European Union Constitution, culminating in a Constitutional Treaty—a constitution for, but not of, the people—drafted by a Constitutional Convention, which was to see its labors rejected in popular referenda.

Contemporary interpretations of constitutionalism have "thickened" the concept. Today it has morphed into "liberal constitutionalism" to include foundational principles that govern apparently clear constitutional texts. Thus, faced with a difficult interpretative question concerning the constitutional right of Quebec to secede from the Canadian federation, the Canadian Supreme Court decided in the *Quebec succession reference* case (1998) against a literal interpretation of the text, choosing to rely instead on "supporting principles and rules" that supposedly made up the "unwritten constitution": i.e., federalism, democracy, the rule of law and constitutionalism and respect for minorities. This is a common judicial practice. The French Council of State devised general principles to fill the gap left by the absence of a Bill of Rights in the Constitution of the Fifth Republic (Letourneur 1951). The Court of Justice of the European Communities (ECJ) followed suit in the seminal case of *van Gend en Loos* (1963) with general principles of European Community law, which could be "constitutionalized" and so help to establish its primacy.

Constitutionalism, Culture, and Redress

In his much misunderstood definition of the rule of law, Dicey (1959, 197) made the important point that rights and guarantees without remedies are futile. He contrasted the common law rights that "pervaded" the English constitution with those catalogued in a continental-style of Bill of Rights. In making this point he has been accused of insularity but Dicey well understood what he was saying. He stated clearly that the "merely formal distinction" is of no account; "Liberty is as well secured in Belgium as in England." What mattered was the provision of adequate remedies for violation, which had, in the historical English constitution, been built up over the years since Magna Carta.

The guarantees of a written constitution are minimal and certainly inadequate to secure accountability. The Weimar Republic possessed a Constitution that remained in force from 1919-1945 but it was generally regarded as a "dead parrot" once Adolf Hitler had ascended to the Chancellorship in 1933. The 1936 Constitution of the USSR guaranteed gender and racial equality and freedom of religion of citizens (Ch. 10, Arts. 122–24) but this was not the experience of individual citizens. Thus the security of a constitution depends first, as Dicey insisted, on powerful forms of redress but secondly on a *culture* of constitutionalism. This truth was underlined by E. S. Corwin (1981, 47) when he described the US Constitution as extorted from a reluctant people and spoke of formal ratification as "a not especially propitious commencement." But Corwin emphasized the "transforming miracle" that occurred once the US Constitution came into effect. There was "a blind worship" of its principles, which accounted for its success. Despite criticism and reform, replacement has never been seriously suggested.

The very success of the US Constitution has contributed to the spread of the constitutionalist ideal. Its institutions have been borrowed by later constitution-makers— Germany, Japan, Nigeria, and many other post-war constitutions owe much to the US model—and its value-system has been widely disseminated throughout the modern world. The seed is fertile but without the constitutional culture, growth has often been stunted. Transplanted constitutional doctrines may operate very differently in a different political culture. Japanese constitutionalism is rooted in Western thought, with borrowings from Prussia, France, Germany, and Britain. Executive power is vested in a Cabinet and the doctrine of collective ministerial responsibility has been deliberately transplanted from Westminster with the provision that the Prime Minister and several Cabinet Ministers must be a member of the Diet. But this has not proved enough to ensure accountability. There is a very strong bureaucratic culture in Japan; the Prime Minister has not in practice emerged as a strong leader and political supervision is insufficiently strong. Consequently, the political agenda has remained in the hands of a powerful bureaucracy. The balance is tilted further by the lack of a culture of individual judicial responsibility, with a judiciary strongly supervised hierarchically (Miyazawa 1994). The result is a feeble system of judicial review from courts that lack effective mandatory remedies (Matsui 2011). Accountability, as French theorists suggest (see Pouvoirs, above), is largely a matter of culture.

Constitutionalist dogma offers a three-fold argument in favor of written constitutions, all with roots in the period of the Enlightenment. The first is an argument for legitimacy. From Magna Carta to the European Convention, Bills of Rights have lent a special sanctity to rights, making it hard for government to override them. A Big-C Constitution testifies—or ought to testify—to popular support. A Constitution should not be the end product of government draftsmen, of an elite, or of colonial rulers; it must be of the people, by the people, for the people. It must demonstrate that "individuals have entered into a compact with each other to produce a government: and this is the only mode in which governments have a right to arise, and the only principle on which they have a right to exist" (Paine 1969). The second argument concerns rationality; a Constitution represents a Hamiltonian effort at "establishing good government from reflection and choice" (Federalist Papers 1788, No. 1). The third is an argument for transparency; a written text makes "deliberative democracy" possible during constitution-making. It facilitates understanding of the system of governance and allows citizens to identify their rights. None of these is precisely an argument for accountability, though each might make an important contribution to it.

State of the Art: Globalization and The Human Rights Movement

In an influential essay optimistically entitled "The Rise of World Constitutionalism," Bruce Ackerman (1997) opined that "the Enlightenment[7] hope in written constitutions was sweeping the world." Ackerman's main objective was to draw attention to the insular and narrow focus of American constitutional writing; "constitutionalism" to Americans meant no more than the iron grip of the 1778 text. He hoped for wider horizons. But if his main purpose was to encourage American openness to a wider constitutional debate, Ackerman's article also highlighted a thematic shift. The world was going global and constitutional scholarship would have to follow suit.

That liberal constitutionalism moved on to an international plane was largely due to the rapid spread of the human rights movement. This was in turn facilitated by the post-World War II adoption of human rights charters and conventions—notably the European Convention on Human Rights (1950) and International Covenant on Civil and Political Rights (1966)—which began to move individual rights and liberties outside the framework of national Bills of Rights into supranational space. Of 106 national constitutions written since 1985, all contain a charter of rights and all but five established a mode of rights review so that "those who once claimed to possess sovereignty in their respective legal systems—national lawmakers and states—now govern with judges" (Stone Sweet 2011, 122). Human rights texts provided support for the independence of the judiciary. Judicialized procedural due process rights are also widely accepted to be fundamental rights; they are beginning to be adopted even in China where the concept of due process is entirely foreign (He 2010).

Transnational courts, such as the European Court of Human Rights, gained power and legitimacy from human rights texts, emerging as extra-territorial accountability forums. Principles developed in national systems were uploaded by transnational courts to form transnational legal orders and downloaded to national systems (Slaughter 2004). For example, proportionality testing is a powerful accountability tool in the hands of judges. The proportionality principle, that acts of public authorities must be appropriate, necessary, and proportionate, started life as a central principle of

German constitutional law (Alexy 2002); today it has transmuted into a constitutional doctrine accepted almost globally (Stone Sweet and Matthews 2008). As transnational courts began to play the principal role in the "constitutionalization" of human rights law, assuming the role of an international lawmaker, the law/democracy controversy assumed a new dimension. Today the debate rages everywhere where judges possess a human rights jurisdiction or powers of constitutional review, and the contribution of American theorists mentioned earlier has resonance far beyond the English-speaking world (Waldron 2006).

Liberal constitutionalism also assumed an extra-territorial dimension. Universalism crept on to the agenda in the shape of a systematized "cosmopolitan law" that would entrench a "liberal universal sovereignty" and universal legal order based on a universally recognized crystallization of constitutional principles, policed by transnational and constitutional courts (Held 2010). Claims are made for a universal "humanity law" (Teitel 2011). A "global administrative law" based on American principles would, it is argued, contribute to the accountability machinery (Stewart 2005).

Challenges to the constitutional settlements that emerged during the nineteenth and twentieth century today come from above and below. At sub-national level, minority groupings clamor for recognition and claim rights of self-determination. As federal Canada struggled to resolve the problem of Quebec sovereignty, Czechoslovakia broke in two, and the Belgian federation teetered towards collapse, sheltered by its membership of the European Union. There was much interest in federal or quasi-federal solutions (Burgess and Gagnon 1993). The 1978 Spanish Constitution experimented with "autonomous communities" while "asymmetrical devolution" forestalled the break-up of the United Kingdom. Further demands for fragmentation—which may or may not receive federal solutions—are likely as increased prosperity in India and China brings calls for further democratization. The case for localism is in part a request for accountability. Regionalism, on the other hand, arguably decreases accountability, as real power leaches upwards and sideways to multi-national enterprises and supranational organizations.

Theories of supranational constitutionalism were tested in the crucible of the European Communities, as it staggered through treaty-making stages towards a "Constitution for Europe." For constitutional lawyers, however, Europe presented the opportunity for cultural interchange, bringing together scholars from different constitutional cultures with the common purpose of analyzing and fostering the new regime. New ideas, rooted in the post-modernist political philosophy of Jürgen Habermas and stimulated by the seminal work of Joseph Weiler (1991; 1999) began to appear as lawyers came together to discuss the character of this unique transnational regime. German scholarship has been to the forefront, with substantial contributions to the theorizing of European constitutional law. It may be that the strong constitutionalist movement has peaked with the draft Constitutional Treaty, repudiated in national referendums. Inspired by Germanic jurisprudence, constitutionalism remains alive; in the world of fragmentation that followed Lisbon, however, subsidiarity has come on to the agenda and doctrines of legal pluralism gained new credence (Krisch 2010).

Significant gaps in accountability at supranational level are becoming evident. These need to be explored (Grant and Keohane 2005). Utopian theories of world constitutionalism need to be evaluated against empirical research. Take the case of agencies, an ingenious way, as argued above, for national governments to evade accountability and parliamentary scrutiny. At the supranational level, where "agencification" is advancing very rapidly, there is much theorizing around the idea of democratic deficit but little empirical research into the way agencies actually function (Busuioc 2010) or indeed to the accountability of international institutions more generally. Constitutional law has tended to download responsibility for machinery to administrative law, its junior and less theoretical partner, while the work of theorizing the concept of accountability has been left to political scientists. In many ways this is appropriate. At the end of the day it may be that accountability is essentially a political concept—or even a convenient fiction. The era of constitutionalism may be past or the age of accountability may be passing. Constitutions are however likely to endure.

Notes

1. In the reforms that followed, it was an attenuated form of accountability that figured in the list of good governance principles promoted by the Commission (European Commission, 2001:10) and has since predominated.
2. French terminology distinguishes these two conceptions in the phrases 'règne de la loi' and 'état de droit' or 'l'état légal'.
3. The Constitutional Council (CC), established by the 1958 Constitution, rules on the constitutionality of proposed laws at the suit of senators or members of the assembly. Since 2010, citizens may also raise the question of constitutionality before a court, which can then refer the point to the CC.
4. *The Federalist Papers*, a debate between Alexander Hamilton, John Jay, and James Madison in preparation for the Constitutional Convention, were published in 1788 and are now available online from the Library of Congress.
5. Note that, in 1787, when the US Constitution was drafted, Ministers of the Crown did not sit in the English Parliament.
6. The Forty-second Amendment of the Constitution of India Act 1973 justified on the ground that "Parliament and the State Legislatures embody the will of the people and the essence of democracy is that the will of the people should prevail" was modified in 1974 by the Forty-third and Forty-fourth Amendment of the Constitution of India Acts.
7. The Enlightenment was an early eighteenth century European intellectual movement embracing thinkers such as Spinoza, Locke, Newton, Montesquieu, Rousseau, Voltaire, and Adam Smith, which sought reform through rationalism and science.

References

Ackerman, B. 1997. "The Rise of World Constitutionalism." *Virginia Law Review*, 83: 771–97.
Alexy, R. 2002. *A Theory of Constitutional Rights*. Oxford: Oxford University Press; originally published 1984.

Bickel, A. 1962. *The Least Dangerous Branch*. New York: Bobbs-Merrill.

Bovens, M. 2007a. "Analysing and Assessing Accountability: A Conceptual Framework." *European Law Journal*, 13: 447–68.

Bovens, M. 2007b. "New Forms of Accountability and EU-Governance." *Comparative European Politics*, 5: 104–20.

Burgess, M. and Gagnon, A. 1993. *Comparative Federalism and Federation*. Toronto: University of Toronto Press.

Busuioc, M. 2010. *The Accountability of European Agencies: Legal Provisions and Ongoing Practices*. Delft: Eburon.

Cohen, J. and Sabel, C. 1997. "Directly Deliberative Polyarchy." *European Law Journal*, 3: 313–42.

Committee of Independent Experts, First Report on Allegations of Fraud, Mismanagement and Nepotism in the European Commission. Brussels, 15 March 1999.

Corwin, E. S. 1981. *Corwin on the Constitution*, ed. R. Loss. Ithaca and London: Cornell University Press.

Dicey, A. V. 1959 edn. *Introduction to the Study of the Law of the Constitution*, ed. E. C. S. Wade. London: MacMillan.

Dubnick, M. 2003. "Accountability and Ethics: Reconsidering the Relationships." *International Journal of Organization Theory and Behavior*, 6: 405–41.

Ely, J. H. 1980. *Democracy and Distrust: A Theory of Judicial Review*. Cambridge, Mass.: Harvard University Press.

European Commission, White Paper on European Governance. COM (2001) 428 final (OJ 2001, C287, p.1).

Federalist Papers. 1788. eds. A. Hamilton, J. Jay, J. Madison. Available online at Library of Congress.

Finer, S. E. 1956. "The Individual Responsibility of Ministers." *Public Administration*, 34: 377–96.

Flinders, M. 2004. "Distributed Public Governance in Britain." *Public Administration*, 82: 883–909.

Grant, R. and Keohane, R. 2005. Accountability and Abuses of Power. *World Politics American Political Science Review*, 99: 29–43.

Harlow, C. and Rawlings, R. 2007. "Promoting Accountability in Multi-Level Governance: A Network Approach." *European Law Journal*, 13: 542–62.

Harlow, C. 2011. Accountability as a Value for Global Governance and Global Administrative Law, pp. 167–85 in *Values in Global Administrative Law*, ed. G. Anthony. Oxford: Hart Publishing.

Hart, H. L. A. 1997 edn. *The Concept of Law*, eds. P. Bulloch and J. Raz. Oxford: Clarendon Press.

Hayek, F. A. 1944. *The Road to Serfdom*. London: Routledge.

He, H. 2010. The Dawn of the Due Process Principle in China, pp. 382–402 in *Effective Judicial Review*, ed. C. Forsyth. Oxford: Oxford University Press.

Held, D. 2010. *Cosmopolitanism: Ideals and Realities*. Cambridge: Polity Press.

International Commission of Jurists. 1966. *The Rule of Law and Human Rights: Principles and Definitions*. Geneva: International Commission of Jurists.

Iyer, V. 2008. The Supreme Court of India, pp. 121–68 in *Judicial Activism in Common Law Supreme Courts*, ed. B. Dickson. Oxford: Oxford University Press.

Joerges, C. 2002. "Deliberative Supranationalism: Two Defences." *European Law Journal*, 8: 133–51.

Kelsen, H. 1978. *The Pure Theory of Law*. Berkeley: University of California Press.

Krisch, N. 2010. *Beyond Constitutionalism: The Pluralist Structure of Postnational Law*. Oxford: Oxford University Press.

Letourneur, M. 1951. "Les principes généraux dans la jurisprudence du Conseil d'Etat." *Etudes et Documents*, p. 19.

Maitland, F. W. 1908. *Constitutional History of England*. Cambridge: Cambridge University Press.

Matsui, S. 2011. *The Constitution of Japan: A Contextual Analysis*. Oxford: Hart Publishing.

McIlwain, C. H. 1940. *Constitutionalism: Ancient and Modern*. Ithaca: Cornell University Press.

Mei-Ying Hung, V. 2004. "China's WTO Commitment on Independent Judicial Review: Impact on Legal and Political Reform." *American Journal of Comparative Law*, 52: 77–132.

Miyazawa, S. 1994. Administrative Control of Japanese Judges, pp. 263–81 in *Law and Technology in the Pacific Community*, ed. P. Lewis. Boulder: Westview.

Mulgan, R. 2000. "'Accountability': An Ever-Expanding Concept?" *Public Administration*, 78: 555–73.

Paine, T. 1969. *Rights of Man*, ed. H. Collins. Harmondsworth: Penguin Books; originally published 1791.

Peerenboom, R. 2002. *China's Long March Toward Rule of Law*. Cambridge: Cambridge University Press.

Peerenboom, R. 2004. Varieties of Rule of Law, pp. 1–55 in *Asian Discourses of Rule of Law*, ed. R. Peerenboom. Los Angeles: University of California Press.

Pouvoirs. 2000. No. 92, Special Issue. *La Responsabilité des Gouvernants*.

Raz, J. 1977. "The Rule of Law and its Virtue." *Law Quarterly Review*, 93: 195–211.

Segur, P. 1999. "Qu'est-ce que la responsabilité politique?" *Revue de droit public*, 6: 1599–623.

Shapiro, M. 1988. *Who Guards the Guardians? Judicial Control of Administration*. Athens: University of Georgia Press.

Shapiro, M. 2001. "Administrative Law Unbounded." *Indiana Journal of Global Legal Studies*, 8: 369–77.

Sidel, M. 2008. *Law and Society in Vietnam: The Transition from Socialism in Comparative Perspective*. New York: Cambridge University Press.

Slaughter, A. M. 2004. *A New World Order*. Princeton: Princeton University Press.

Smith, D. E. 2006. Clarifying the Doctrine of Ministerial Accountability as it Applies to the Government and Parliament of Canada. *Restoring Accountability: Research Studies*, 1. Commission of Inquiry into the Sponsorship Program and Advertising Activities (The Gomery Inquiry).

Stewart, R. B. 2005. "US Administrative Law: A Model for Global Administrative Law?" *Law and Contemporary Problems*, 68: 63–108.

Stone Sweet, A. and Mathews, J. 2008. "Proportionality Balancing and Global Constitutionalism." *Columbia Journal of Transnational Law*, 47: 73–165.

Stone Sweet, A. 2011. The European Court of Justice, pp. 121–54 in *The Evolution of EU Law*, eds. P. Craig and G. de Búrca. Oxford: Oxford University Press.

Teitel, R. G. 2011. *Humanity's Law*. Oxford: Oxford University Press.

Teubner, G. 1988. Juridification: Concepts, Aspects, Limits, Solutions, pp. 3–48 in *Juridification of Social Spheres*, ed. G. Teubner. Berlin: de Gruyter.

Tocqueville, A. de. 1863 edn. *Democracy in America*. Cambridge, Mass.: Sever and Francis; originally published 1831.

Troper, M. 1980. *La séparation des pouvoirs et l'histoire constitutionnelle française*. Paris: Librairie générale de droit et de jurisprudence.

Turpin, C. and Tomkins, A. 2007 edn. *British Government and the Constitution.* Cambridge: Cambridge University Press.

Turpin, C. 1994 edn. Ministerial Responsibility, pp.109–54 in *The Changing Constitution*, eds. J. Jowell and D. Oliver. Oxford: Clarendon Press.

Tushnet, M. 2009. *The Constitution of the United States of America.* Oxford: Hart Publishing.

Waldron, J. 2006. "The Core of the Case Against Judicial Review." *Yale Law Journal,* 115: 1346–406.

Weiler, J. H. H. 1999. *The Constitution of Europe.* Cambridge: Cambridge University Press.

Westlake, M. 1998. The Style and the Machinery: The Role of the European Parliament in the EU's Legislative Processes, pp. 137–47 in *Lawmaking in the European Union*, eds. P. Craig and C. Harlow. Dordrecht: Kluwer Law International.

CHAPTER 13

ACCOUNTABILITY IN PUBLIC ADMINISTRATION

B. GUY PETERS

BETWEEN EXPERTISE AND CONTROL

RECONCILING the permanence and expertise of the public bureaucracy with political control is a persistent problem for any political system. This problem of accountability is more acute in democratic regimes (Etzioni-Halevey 1983) and the potential conflict between democracy and bureaucracy remains a continuing or increasing challenge to contemporary democratic systems (Flinders 2011). The potential conflict between the political and the administrative is, however, also a concern even in autocratic regimes. Any political leader will want to ensure that the remainder of the political system will follow his or her policies, and that the policies as implemented will be the same as those enacted by legislatures or political executives. At the same time those leaders will want to utilize the expertise of the career bureaucracy in both making and executing public policies.

Maintaining any desired relationship between legislation and implementation is difficult given the amount of delegation involved in the administrative process (Huber and Shipan 2002; Horn 1995). Even if public administrators are attempting to comply perfectly with legislation there are enough decisions that must be made in the process of implementation that there can easily be "policy drift." Further, in many instances the bureaucratic organization may not want to comply perfectly during implementation, having its own priorities and its own conceptions of what constitutes good policy in its domain (Goodsell 2011). Therefore, there must be some means of holding these organizations and their members accountable for their actions and for deviations from policy intentions.

The need for accountability in public administration, however, extends beyond simply ensuring that policies are implemented as intended. There are, for example, increasing demands for efficiency in the public sector, and more generally for improved policy performance. In addition, there are also an increasing number of stakeholders to whom public organizations must answer for their actions. Therefore, accountability is an increasingly complex and difficult concept for public administration, and also becomes more difficult to ensure (Mulgan 2000; Considine 2002). And beyond those issues corruption is endemic in many countries and intentional and unintentional abuse of administrative authority occurs in all societies. Therefore, in considering accountability it is crucial to build systems that are sufficiently robust to detect and punish malfeasance while at the same time permitting the administrative process to proceed efficiently and effectively.

DIMENSIONS OF ACCOUNTABILITY

As noted, accountability has become more complex but even without the additional complexity there are several dimensions to this concept. In the study of public administration these dimensions are sometimes used interchangeably, but it is important to consider the implications of these different dimensions, and also their possible conflicts. Accountability is referenced very frequently in both academic and more popular discourse, and it is therefore crucial to be very clear concerning what exactly is meant by the term.

Who and What?

A first question about accountability is who is involved, and what sort of actions are being considered, particularly considered in terms of the control of inappropriate actions (see Table 13.1).[1] Understanding the issues involved in accountability requires first finding the nature of the administrative errors, and then finding some means of correcting them (Adams 2009; Chan and Rosenbloom 2010). In general those errors may be of three types. The first, and perhaps the most common, is that administrative actors do what they are intended to do, but do it poorly or inefficiently. While this may constitute a problems for the clients of the program, and a political problem for the minister

Table 13.1 Accountability issues in public administration

	Poor Performance	Excessive	Action	Inaction
Individual				
Organization				

involved, it is primarily a managerial problem that can be addressed by better supervision, training, or improving processes.

The second, and more difficult, type of error is when public sector actors exceed their legitimate authority. Perhaps the most commonly cited example of this type of behavior is the use of excessive force by the police and other security services. Likewise, businesses complain about regulators being excessively zealous in their enforcement of the laws. Somewhat paradoxically, the application of excessive rules and procedures may actually be a way to prevent action (Dubois 2010; Auyero 2012). Correcting this type of error requires designing methods of control within the organization, as well as means for those harmed by the excessive actions to gain redress.

The third, and perhaps most difficult, form of error by public sector actors is inadequate action, or no action at all. While the police may sometimes act too aggressively, they are also at times accused of not responding adequately to calls from poorer or minority neighborhoods. Likewise, individual public servants may choose to shirk rather than engage in the active exercise of their responsibilities (Brehm and Gates 1997). While businesses may be concerned about the perceived zeal of regulators, environmentalists may be concerned about what they consider a lack of enthusiasm for the task.

Finally, any of these three types of error may be performed by an individual civil servant or by a public organization. These differences in the actors, just as is true for the different types of error, may require different types of remedy or better yet different types of prevention. Enforcing accountability on an organization is a more difficult undertaking than is dealing with individual malfeasance or nonfeasance. Many remedies for the individual miscreant are available within an organization itself, while attempting to enforce accountability on an entire organization generally requires the involvement of other organizations within the executive branch or perhaps the application of political pressures. Further, malfeasance by individuals may be random or episodic, while malfeasance by an organization is more likely to be systematic.

Accountability Per Se

In a strict sense accountability refers to the requirement that an actor, be it an individual or an organization, render some account of their actions to an independent authority. Further, accountability also implies that the independent authority to whom the account is rendered will have some capacity to enforce remedies for any perceived failures on the part of the individual or the organization that is found wanting. This reporting may be routinized, as when organizations must table an annual report, or it may arise when it is suspected that there is a problem that must be addressed.[2] In either case, however, the process of accountability involves some external actor and some hierarchical controls.

There are a huge number of instruments available for political and judicial officials to enforce accountability, some of which are described below when discussing hierarchy.

While legislatures have been the center of this form of accountability, the courts have also been central, although their role varies according to the administrative traditions of different countries (Painter and Peters 2010). Also, governments have created a number of autonomous organizations designed to impose controls over the public sector, whether financial (various audit organizations) or the conduct of public officials. These organizations may also involve citizens directly, as is the case for many police complaints organizations.[3]

Responsibility

Responsibility is another term that is sometimes used interchangeably with accountability. However, while accountability implies some external controls, responsibility involves internalized means of control (Bovens 1998). Responsibility is a more individually oriented concept of how to control the behavior of the public bureaucracy. Individual civil servants are assumed to be responsible either to the law or to individual codes of ethics, and may therefore be placed into conflict with their nominal political masters who may require them to undertake actions that civil servants consider inappropriate.

While the norm of responsibility is very appealing, the practice may be more difficult (DeLeon 2004). For senior public servants with substantial power of their own and good career prospects outside government, standing on legal or moral principles is relatively easy. Responsibility becomes more difficult, however, for employees at the bottom of their hierarchies. In the extreme we can see the young soldier being given an order that he or she believe violates military law and understand the courage it would take to refuse.[4] Few public employees are acting *in extremis* like that but the principle of accountability is the same.

Responsiveness

Responsiveness is also used as a means of describing the need to exercise some control over public administration, especially from a democratic perspective. Public administration is meant to be responsive to the political leaders of their organizations, given that those political leaders have some form of mandate to legitimate their actions. Likewise, as public servants, members of public organizations should also respond to their clients, and to the public more generally. And as the making and delivery of public policies increasingly involves a range of social actors (Torfing et al. 2012) there are additional demands for responsiveness to those stakeholders in the process (Considine 2002).

The demands for responsiveness may present the greatest problems for the "street level bureaucrats" who actually meet with clients (Meyers and Vorsanger 2012). These civil servants face demands from their organizations and from the law for implementing the law in particular manner, but at the same time confront clients who have needs and demands that may exceed the legal possibilities. In some instances these lower echelon employees have become advocates for their clients within the organization, seeking to provide greater benefits. In other cases, they appear to have taken the side of the organization and its rules.

Given the importance of responsiveness in individual public servants, and especially those at the bottom of the organizational pyramid, the rather hoary but yet significant concept of representative bureaucracy becomes relevant for accountability. One means of making administration responsive to the working class, or to ethnic minorities, or to women, is to include those individuals within the bureaucracy itself (Selden 1997). The assumption, although not always supported with evidence, is that civil servants will be more responsive to the demands of citizens like them than they are to other groups.

The responsiveness of bureaucracies to their immediate stakeholders and to their clients does present, however, another problem for democracy. If one ideal of democracy is inclusiveness and equality then making public organizations responsive to only a limited number of individuals and interests appears to lessen that inclusiveness substantially. This narrowed inclusiveness can be justified in part by those groups being involved being differentially affected by the programs but there still does appear some democratic problem with this version of accountability. Similarly, emphasizing representative bureaucracy may imply that civil servants recruited from minority communities would favor that community rather than apply laws equally. This behavior would be responsive in some senses but certainly deny the equality sought in most governments.

The development of various forms of "network governance" (Sørensen and Torfing 2008) manifests a somewhat paradoxical version of this inclusion problem. Much of the justification for these network structures has been to overcome the deficiencies of representative democracy and to make government more responsive and inclusive. In practice, however, the limited inclusiveness within networks may make them even less democratic than representative institutions built on the norm of one person, one vote (see Davies (2012) for a very particular critique).

Conflicts

The three alternative conceptions of accountability discussed above are all important as means of enforcing controls over the bureaucracy. They are all important, but they do not necessarily all agree on how to cope with administrative error, and there is therefore the potential for conflict. For example, a civil servant may be given an order by his or her minister (*responsiveness*) that he or she believes to be illegal (*responsibility*). How can this conflict be resolved? Or a public organization may be required by parliament or its minister (*accountability, responsiveness*) to make policies that it believes are inappropriate or wasteful (*responsibility*). Again, how can this apparent conflict be resolved?

There are, unfortunately, few simple answers for resolving conflicts among the fundamental dimensions of accountability. Some governments have attempted, for example, to provide civil servants some protection from being personally responsible for following commands from ministers if they point out their objections (Heintzman 2013). Others attempt to remove some organizations that may have to make politically difficult decisions from direct ministerial control so that they may make decisions on the basis of expertise or professional criteria. Despite the protections that may be built into the system, these remain vexing problems for administrative systems that are at once attempting to respond to the criteria of responsibility and responsiveness, both of which have some place in democratic governance.

These conflicts also point to the famous debate between Herman Finer and Carl J. Friedrich over the essence of accountability. This debate occurred in the shadow of World War II, and the recognition that a defense of "just following orders" no longer appeared acceptable. On the one hand Finer (1940) argued that the only way to enforce accountability was to have clear rules and clear mechanisms of oversight so that any malfeasance within bureaucracy could be detected and punished. Friedrich (1940) on the other hand, argued that no amount of control could protect against individuals or organizations that did not have the appropriate values. Such control amounted to an infinite regress of control—*qui custodiet ipsos custodes*—and therefore the only real protection against malfeasance was the training of public servants and the inculcation of values into the public service.

The discussion of "neutral competence" and "responsive competence" in American public administration (Rourke 1992) represents another classic argument in public about the conflicts surrounding accountability in the public sector. On the one hand, public administration scholars and practitioners have praised the norm of neutrality for civil servants, implying that they would be responsible to the law and implement it *sine irae ac studio*. On the other hand, however, part of their task also is to serve the government of the day and provide that government with the capacity to implement their own priorities while in office.

The conflict between neutral and responsive competence is far from an American peculiarity, and arises in most administrative systems. It may arise especially in cases such as South Africa where there is some sense that government should compensate people for past injustices (Cameron 2009) through differential access to employment. These issues may even arise in non-democratic regimes where public officials are under pressure from citizens to deliver public services while at the same time facing pressure from their political masters to conform to party controls (Tsai 2007).

This conflict between neutrality and responsiveness is also manifest in most parliamentary systems as the increasing politicization of the civil service tends to undermine neutrality and emphasize political mechanisms for accountability. The evidence on the continuing politicization of administration is now extensive (Vanhoonacker and Neuhold 2013) although the evidence about its impact is less clear. That said, several governments are attempting to find mechanisms to restore the balance between civil service neutrality and responsiveness to political leaders (Aucoin 2012).

INSTRUMENTS FOR ACCOUNTABILITY

Like many arguments about fundamental issues in governance, both sides of the Friedrich–Finer debate have substantial merit. That may be true intellectually, but in practice governments have placed their money with the Finer side of the argument and built a range of instruments to attempt to control the actions of public servants. They have invested relatively less time and energy in training about values, although almost all civil service systems now do have a code of conduct of some sort. The characteristic response of the public sector has been to implement mechanisms for oversight, in part because citizens appear to prefer these to rather vague statements about ethics and values.

This simple dichotomy between formal institutions to enforce accountability and values as a base of accountability is, however, perhaps insufficient to capture the variety of ways in which accountability is now enforced. The continuing growth of alternative means of enforcing accountability represents in part the ingenuity of institutional designers, but also reflects the increasing complexity of the manner in which the public sector performs its tasks. The increasing number of instruments used for accountability further reflects the move away from "command and control" instruments in the public sector generally (Salamon 2001) toward softer and more collaborative instruments.

One useful scheme for categorizing instruments of accountability was developed by Hood and his colleagues (2004). This scheme does not include mechanisms based on values and ethics, but it does demonstrate the changing forms of instruments employed to detect malfeasance and punish it, and also mechanisms used to attempt to improve performance within the public sector. Much of the argument implicit in this analytic scheme is that the public sector would work better for citizens if instead of being concerned with detecting and punishing error, it could develop means of minimizing the occurrence of those errors.[5]

Hierarchy

The dominant mechanism for addressing issues of accountability remains hierarchy. The assumption in democratic governments is that civil servants within a public organization are accountable to their superiors within the organization, and that as a whole they are accountable to their minister, and that the minister is accountable to parliament (Day and Klein 1987).[6] This chain of accountability is assumed to function in part through the instrument of public law, and in part because politicians (especially those of the opposition party or parties) have an incentive to expose malfeasance on the part of the bureaucracy.

Although this chain of connections running up to the parliament remains the conventional statement about accountability, there are other hierarchical mechanisms for enforcing accountability. Administrative law, and in some instances other aspects of law,[7] constitutes a major complement to parliamentary methods for enforcing accountability. The clearest example of the use of legal instruments for accountability comes from the Napoleonic administrative tradition (Ongaro 2010) and the reliance on institutions such as the *Conseil d'Etat* to confirm the legality of administrative actions ex ante.

The dependence on law for accountability varies markedly across political systems. As noted above, within Europe the systems derivative from the Napoleonic tradition rely more on law than do others (Ziller 2012). Similarly, administrative systems in Latin America have depended heavily on law for controlling civil servants and for managing many aspects of governing. This legalism in administration has tended to undermine the pursuit of efficiency in public administration, and to produce rather classic examples of the displacement of goals (Nef 2012).

Thirdly, although generally associated with the legislature, auditing represents another major approach to hierarchical controls over the bureaucracy. The auditing role in accountability has been enhanced because these organizations now emphasize performance accounting rather than strict financial accounting (Leeuw and Rist 1994). While maintaining financial probity is certainly important in the public sector, the accounting organizations also now assess how well the organizations are performing their tasks. As discussed in more detail below, performance has become central to accountability and exercising control over the public bureaucracy and auditing organizations have played a major role in this transformation (Peters 2007).

All of these hierarchical methods involve the use of some form of authority to control the bureaucracy. The assumption underlying all these mechanisms is that the ability to detect and punish individuals and organizations is sufficient to produce compliance. This hierarchical approach may well produce results but it also may produce resistance from within the organizations and require further instruments for compliance. Again the Friedrich argument (see above) about the need to inculcate values into the administrative system has relevance, given that control through training and values may be more efficient than controls through hierarchical oversight and enforcement.

Mutuality

A second generic mechanism for enforcing accountability depends upon civil servants and public organizations watching each other. At its simplest, this form of accountability can be seen when policemen patrol in pairs. In part this is for safety but it is also a means of controlling their behavior—one watches the other. As Friedrich might be quick to point out this would do no good if both are corrupt or abusive, but in general people are less likely to act illegally or immorally if they are with others, especially their peers.

In public administration this principle of mutuality can be enacted by creating parallel structures within the public sector. The extreme version of this has been the utilization of parallel party and government hierarchies in Communist regimes. In democratic regimes, the increasing politicization of public administration has been associated in some countries with the development of parallel hierarchies, one political and one civil service that watch each other warily. Inspectorates that have been common in Napoleonic regimes, and increasingly prevalent in other systems, also involve setting one group of civil servants to watch another. Prefectoral systems also involve one set of civil servants watching another, although in these systems and inspectorates the power of the groups involved is asymmetric. Finally, all departments and large agencies in the US federal government have an inspector general, a public employee charged with controlling "fraud, waste and abuse" within his or her organization (Apaza 2011).

The mechanism of mutuality for controlling public servants involves building a certain amount of redundancy into the public sector. Redundancy is usually considered wasteful and an appropriate target for reorganization, but duplicate organizations may also be functional for both accountability and for the performance of some public tasks (Landau 1969). For purposes of accountability, redundancy provides means of enforcing controls over one part of the administrative system through organizations and actors that might be capable of performing the same tasks as those of the target of accountability. The question for institutional designers therefore is whether the benefits of enhanced accountability outweigh the costs associated with redundancy.

In contemporary mechanisms for service delivery the multiple actors involved may constitute another form of mutualism. The multiple stakeholders involved in contemporary policy may provide opportunities for one group to be monitoring the others involved. When there are, for example, private sector stakeholders involved in partnerships then they are constantly monitoring the behaviors of their partners, and vice versa (Forrer et al. 2010). If indeed these are partnerships in which the actors involved depend upon each other, then the partners have a great deal to gain from watching one another.

Although mutualism is an important mechanism for accountability in partnerships it depends upon the participants having relatively equal powers over the other. In less-developed systems where local civil society actors may be dependent upon international organizations, or perhaps on government, then ensuring mutual accountability is more difficult (Blescu and Young 2009). If the civil society organizations are dependent financially upon the international organization, or a national aid organization, they have difficulty in being an equal stakeholder that can exercise mutual controls.

Competition

Competition represents another means of enforcing accountability in the public sector. This method moves the furthest away from traditional hierarchical forms of accountability, and depends on methods that are closer to the market than to formal bureaucratic controls. Competition is perhaps less useful for the larger organizations within the public sector, but it is useful for individual service-providing organizations such as schools and hospitals. Although the participants in the process may not conceptualize it as such, these organizations are competing to be the best performing organizations. The assumption is therefore that the desire to succeed in such real or contrived competitions will make these public organizations perform as well as possible—much as they would be assumed to do in market competition—and will place pressure on managers to drive their organizations to continuous improvement.

One of the additional virtues of competition as an instrument for accountability is that it is a more continuous activity than many forms of hierarchical accountability. While having an issue raised in parliament tends to happen infrequently for any but the most controversial organizations, competition may occur on an almost daily basis. This then means that organizations and individuals in the public sector must be constantly cognizant of competitive pressures for improvement.

As a mechanism for accountability, competition depends to a great extent upon making the performance of public organizations public, generally through the media. On a regular basis the performance of schools on standardized tests, for example, will be made public with the assumption that the parents of pupils in the poorly-performing schools will exert pressure on school leaders and teachers to perform better. Or, in the United States, in "No Child Left Behind" the students in poorly-performing schools could leave and go to a better school and have that movement funded by the school district.

Competition represents one means of utilizing performance management for purposes of accountability. Traditional forms of accountability, especially those relying upon parliamentary means, often expose rather minor bureaucratic errors but which can be used to embarrass the sitting government. The use of performance measures, and with that, competition, is more focused on the extent to which public organizations and the individuals within them reach established goals, with those goals being measured quantitatively. These measures also allow a focus on improvements over time rather than being only discrete assessments at a single time.

Although the idea of performance management appears very useful for accountability, it depends heavily on the capacity to measure performance effectively. Not only is it difficult to validate measures for many of the most important activities of government, but once they are in place the actors being subjected to performance measurement will find ways to avoid and to "game" the measures, and are thus able to deflect some of the pressure that might be applied to them. Even in relatively simple versions of competition as an accountability instrument there is some need to be able to define clearly the criteria on which the competition is being waged, and that measurement represents the "Achilles heel" of the performance as accountability movement (Radin 2006; Bannick and Ossewaarde 2012).

This mechanism for accountability also depends in part on the mobilization of the population. One assumption of competition is that if the population understands that their local schools or hospitals are not performing well they are then willing to do something about any perceived deficiencies. In such a perspective effective accountability depends upon a participatory culture and mechanisms available for citizens to participate effectively. These mechanisms are of course lacking in authoritarian regimes (but see Keane 2011) and clientelistic systems may prevent citizens from being effective complainers. Even in more developed systems, the clients of public programs may have some trepidation about complaining about their treatment by the bureaucracy (Hicken 2011).

Contrived Randomness

The final dimension of accountability discussed by Hood and his colleagues depends upon random assessment and intervention by some external actor. This might be considered a variant of the hierarchical approach, given that the actor intervening in the random fashion is almost invariably in a hierarchical relationship with the actor being assessed. Some other actor, for example the media, may be considered as acting in this manner, but the most effective means of using this mechanism involves using actors that have some capacity to impose a sanction on organizations or individuals being assessed. That said, the actors involved in mutualism could also be involved in random assessment of the behaviors of their associates.

Contrived randomness can be seen operating most often in auditing. Although public organizations generally have a regular audit cycle, there may be random checks to forestall larger problems in the annual audit, or simply to keep the organization cognizant of its need for fiscal probity. Other random inspections of schools, prisons, nuclear facilities, and the like represent attempts to ensure that high standards are maintained at all times, and not just at the time of scheduled inspections.[8] The use of inspectorates and other mechanisms for oversight are increasingly important components of "regulation inside government" (Hood et al. 1999; Downe and Martin 2007) and having these organizations in place provides opportunities for random evaluations and control.

SUMMARY AND CONCLUSIONS

Holding the bureaucracy accountable is a crucial activity for democratic political systems. As many elements of conventional forms of democracy tend to become weakened—the decline in voting and in political party membership for example—then accountability becomes even more crucial for democratic government (Peters 2012). Fortunately, changing patterns of administration with greater involvement of stakeholders have provided alternative mechanisms for promoting accountability, albeit with some challenges of their own.

These new mechanisms for accountability join a host of other interpretations and instruments of administrative accountability. On the one hand, this jumble of instruments provides a rich menu for those who would attempt to control the administrative system. On the other hand, however, the multiple means and multiple meanings can create uncertainty and confusion both for the bureaucracy and for citizens. If these different instrumentalities provide different answers then can there be said to be any real answer to the accountability question?

Although some 70 years old at this time of writing, the Friedrich–Finer debate on accountability remains as relevant as it ever was. In some ways the Friedrich position is being strengthened by the increasing emphasis in government, and in society more generally, on transparency. The increasing demands for transparency in law, combined with the activity of the media, place public servants (and politicians) increasingly under a microscope. In such settings an internal compass guiding their actions may be essential. The importance of many of the formal mechanisms for detecting error may be reduced because so much of government is now more visible, and it may therefore be appropriate to consider supporting greater individual responsibility in governing.

Much of the discussion of accountability has been in terms of enforcement and even punishment. While that certainly has been the tradition in the efforts to control the public bureaucracy, it is not the only possible use of the instruments described above. Monitoring the activities of these organizations also provides a good deal of information that can be used to improve their performance. Whether this is done through formal performance management methods or through less quantitative ways, accountability provides opportunity for learning. The learning opportunities are often forgotten in the rush to find and punish errors, but more effective governments will learn from any errors detected through the various accountability processes.

NOTES

1. See Peters (2010) for a more extended discussion.
2. These two circumstances are referred to as "police patrol" and "fire alarm" styles of accountability. See McCubbins and Schwartz (1984).
3. At the extreme, various versions of "truth and reconciliation" commissions especially in African countries have attempted to expose wrongdoings, if not to issue sanctions.
4. Although certainly different in many respects from others, the military are public employees and must be held to the same (or perhaps higher) standards of accountability.
5. Any organization, and especially any organization performing complex tasks, will have some level of error in its operations. The question therefore is how to minimize those errors rather than merely punish the offenders.
6. This same basic idea may be applied in non-democratic regimes as well, with the proviso that the parliament may not be accountable to the people in the same way assumed in democracies. Most non-democratic regimes have legislative bodies to maintain the illusion that they are indeed democratic.
7. In the United States and to some extent other common law countries the regular courts can be used to address malfeasance or real harms (torts) produced by the public sector. Sovereign immunity can be an impediment, but not an absolute barrier, to the use of law for accountability.
8. Also, Kaufman (1962) pointed out how random movement of personnel may also be used to enforce probity among those employees.

REFERENCES

Adams, G. B. 2009. *Unmasking Administrative Evil*. Armonk, NY: M.E. Sharpe.
Apaza, C. R. 2011. *Integrity and Accountability in the Department of Homeland Security and the Inspector General*. Burlington, VT: Ashgate.

Aucoin, P. 2012. "New Political Governance in Westminster Systems: Impartial Public Administration and Management Performance at Risk." *Governance*, 25: 177–99.

Auyero, J. 2012. *Patients of the State: The Politics of Waiting in Argentina*. Durham, NC: Duke University Press.

Bannink, D. and Ossewaarde, R. 2012. "Decentralization: New Modes of Governance and Administrative Responsibility." *Administration & Society*, 44: 595–624.

Blescu, M. and Young, J. 2009. *Partnerships and Accountability: Current Thinking and Approaches Among Agencies Supporting Civil Society Organizations*. London: Overseas Development Institute.

Bovens, M. A. 1998. *The Quest for Responsibility: Accountability and Citizenship in Complex Organizations*. Cambridge: Cambridge University Press.

Brehm, J. and Gates, S. 1997. *Working, Shirking and Sabotage: Bureaucratic Response to a Democratic Public*. Ann Arbor: University of Michigan Press.

Cameron, R. G. 2009. "New Public Management Reforms in the South African Public Service: 1999–2009." *Journal of Public Administration*, 44 (4.1): 910–42.

Chan, H. S. and Rosenbloom, D. H. 2010. "Four Challenges to Accountability in Contemporary Public Administration: Lessons from the United States and China." *Administration & Society*, 42: 11–33.

Considine, M. 2002. "The End of the Line? Accountable Governance in the Age of Networks, Partnerships and Joined-Up Government." *Governance*, 15: 21–40.

Davies, J. S. 2012. *Challenging Governance Theory: From Networks to Hegemony*. Bristol: Policy Press.

Day, P. and Klein, R. 1987. *Accountabilities*. London: Tavistock.

DeLeon, L. 2004. On Acting Responsibly in a Disorderly World: Individual Ethics and Administrative Responsibility, pp. 351–62 in *The Handbook of Public Administration*, eds. B. G. Peters and J. Pierre. London: Sage.

Downe, J. and Martin, S. 2007. "Regulation Inside Government: Processes and Impacts of Inspection of Local Public Services." *Policy & Politics*, 35: 215–32.

Dubois, V. 2010. *The Bureaucrat and the Poor: Encounters in a French Welfare Office*. Aldershot: Ashgate.

Etzioni-Halevy, E. 1983. *Bureaucracy and Democracy: A Political Dilemma*. Boston: Routledge and Kegan Paul.

Finer, H. 1940. "Administrative Responsibility in Democratic Government." *Public Administration Review*, 1: 225–50.

Flinders, M. 2011. "Daring to be a Daniel: The Pathology of Politicized Accountability in a Monitory Democracy." *Administration & Society*, 43: 385–419.

Forrer, J., Kee, J. E., Newcomer, K. E., and Boyer, E. 2010. "Public-Private Partnerships and the Public Accountability Issue." *Public Administration Review*, 70: 475–84.

Friedrich, C. J. 1940. Public Policy and the Nature of Administrative Responsibility, pp. 3–24 in *Public Policy*, eds. C. J. Friedrich and E. S. Mason. Cambridge: Harvard University Press.

Goodsell, C. T. 2011. *Mission Mystique: Belief Systems in Public Agencies*. Armonk, NY: M.E. Sharpe.

Heintzman, R. 2013. Establishing the Boundaries of the Public Service: Toward a New Moral Contract pp. 85–138, in *Governing: Essays in Honour of Donald J. Savoie*, eds. J. Bickerton and B. G. Peters. Montreal: McGill/Queens University Press.

Hicken, A. 2011. "Clientelism." *Annual Review of Political Science*, 11: 281–310.

Hood, C., James, O., Peters, B. G., and Scott, C. 2004. *Controlling Modern Government: Variety, Commonality and Change*. Cheltenham: Edward Elgar.

Hood, C., James, O., Scott, C., Jones, G. W., and Travers, T. 1999. *Regulation Inside Government: Waste Watchers, Quality Police, and Sleaze Busters*. Oxford: Oxford University Press.

Horn, M. J. 1995. *The Political Economy of Public Administration*. Cambridge: Cambridge University Press.

Huber, J. D. and Shipan, C. R. 2002. *Deliberate Discretion: The Institutional Foundation of Bureaucratic Authority*. Cambridge: Cambridge University Press.

Kaufman, H. A. 1962. *The Forest Ranger*. Baltimore, MD: The Johns Hopkins University Press.

Keane, J. 2011. Monitory Democracy?, pp. 212–35 in *The Future of Representative Democracy*, eds. S. Alonso, J. Keane, and V. Merkel. Cambridge: Cambridge University Press.

Landau, M. 1969. "Redundancy, Rationality and the Problem of Duplication and Overlap." *Public Administration Review*, 29: 346–58.

Leeuw, F. L. and Rist, R. C. 1994. *Can Governments Learn? Comparative Perspectives on Evaluation and Organizational Learning*. New Brunswick, NJ: Transaction Publishers.

McCubbins, M. and Schwartz, T. 1984. "Congressional Oversight Overlooked: Police Patrols Versus Fire Alarms." *American Journal of Political Science*, 26: 165–79.

Meyers, M. and Nielsen, V. L. 2012. Street Level Bureaucracy, pp. 305–16 in *The Handbook of Public Administration* (second edition), eds. B. G. Peters and J. Pierre. London: Sage.

Mulgan, R. 2000. "Accountability: An Ever-Expanding Concept?" *Public Administration*, 78: 555–73.

Nef, J. 2012. Public Administration and Public Sector Reform in Latin America, pp. 642–58 in *The Handbook of Public Administration* (second edition), eds. B. G. Peters and J. Pierre. London: Sage.

Ongaro, E. 2010. *Public Management Reform and Evaluation: Trajectories of Administrative Change in Italy, France, Greece, Portugal and Spain*. Cheltenham: Edward Elgar.

Painter, M. and Peters, B. G. 2010. *Administrative Traditions and Administrative Reform*. London: Routledge.

Peters, B. G. 2007. Performance-Based Accountability, pp. 15–32 in *Performance Accountability and Combating Corruption*, ed. A. Shah. Washington, DC: The World Bank.

Peters, B. G. 2010. *The Politics of Bureaucracy*. Sixth edition. London: Routledge.

Peters, B. G. 2012. Bureaucracy and Democracy, pp. 235–54 in *Bureaucracy and Accountability in Modern Democracies*, eds. J. Pierre and J-M. Eymeri Douzanes. London: Routledge.

Radin, B. A. 2006. *Challenging the Performance Movement: Accountability, Complexity and Democratic Values*. Washington, DC: Georgetown University Press.

Rourke, F. E. 1992. "Responsiveness and Neutral Competence in American Bureaucracy." *Public Administration Review*, 52: 539–46.

Salamon, L. M. 2001. Introduction, pp. 3–23 in *Handbook of Policy Instruments*, ed. L. M. Salamon. New York: Oxford University Press.

Selden, S. C. 1997. *The Promise of Representative Bureaucracy: Diversity and Responsiveness in a Government Agency*. New York: M.E. Sharpe.

Sørensen, E. and Torfing, D. 2008. *Theories of Democratic Network Governance*. Basingstoke: Macmillan.

Torfing, J., Peters, B. G., Pierre, J., and Sorensen, E. 2012. *Interactive Governance: Advancing the Paradigm*. Oxford: Oxford University Press.

Tsai, L. L. 2007. *Accountability Without Democracy: Solidary Groups and Public Goods Provision in Rural China*. Cambridge: Cambridge University Press.

Vanhoonacker, S. and Neuhold, C. 2013. *Politicization of the Public Service*. Basingstoke: Macmillan.

Ziller, J. 2012. The Continental System of Administrative Legality, pp. 323–32 in *The Handbook of Public Administration* (second edition), eds. B. G. Peters and J. Pierre. London: Sage.

CHAPTER 14

....

ACCOUNTABLE CIVIL SERVANTS

....

JOHN UHR

CIVIL SERVICE ACCOUNTABILITY

....

DEBATES over "accountable civil servants" reflect deeper disputes over the place of the civil service in power-sharing arrangements in modern systems of governance (Du Gay 2002; Rohr, Rosenbloom, and Schaefer 2010). This chapter acknowledges many important dimensions of civil service accountability relating to core issues in public management arising from power-sharing arrangements: traditional arrangements with power shared between government ministers and career officials, as found in almost all forms of representative government; modern arrangements with power shared between official bureaucracies and approved non-state actors, illustrated in important ways in the international provision of foreign aid by most wealthy contemporary governments; and post-modern arrangements with power shared between bureaucrats and disapproved-of activists, such as influential global whistle-blower Julian Assange.

In each case of power-sharing there are debates over appropriate norms of civil service accountability, close and compliant when working with law-abiding governments but distant and fractious when working with Assange-like whistle blowers. Fundamentally important are the constitutional implications of different practical ways of designing and managing systems of public administration. Resolution of contemporary debates over the "public" accountability of increasingly "privatized" aspects of public administration will not occur until the disputing parties come to some agreement over the public roles of a civil service (Mulgan 2000; Radin 2006; Bovens 2007). This resolution has to take note of the many roles of civil services: as primary provider or as contract manager of public services, including advisory and regulatory services in such core constitutional policies as nationality and citizenship which, because they do so much to define what we mean by "the public," appropriately rest outside the responsibility of contracted service providers. Analysts note the many roles of *informal* accountability as power holders negotiate networks of obligation outside the formal architecture of governance (Romzek, LeRoux and Blackmar 2012; Yang 2012; see also Romzek in this handbook).

THE ANALYTICAL FRAMEWORK: WEBER AND WILSON

The anxieties are new but the analytical frameworks are well-rehearsed (Mulgan 2003). Perhaps the most influential is Max Weber's (1864–1920) doctrine of the values of technical expertise and political neutrality promoted by career civil services, separate from the values of popularity and political partisanship cultivated by elected politicians. The Weberian idea is that modern government assumes bureaucrats will act accountably under the direction of elected politicians whose own professional accountability is tested by public confidence. Bureaucratic and political accountability work differently: civil services learn to accept accountability to the government of the day for their procedural integrity (as Weber said: "eliminating…love, hatred, and all purely personal, irrational, and emotional elements"), while politicians accept that their own accountability is tested by wider, not always well-informed, public discourse about their political performance (Weber 1994, 216). For Weber, debates over civil service accountability focus on "the rules" for rational public administration while disputes over political accountability depend on heated political debate and quite personalized electoral competition among political elites.

Empirically, distinctions between administration and politics are imprecise. Weber's separation of the two worlds of administration and politics is an "ideal-type" arrangement, intended to minimize politically active bureaucracy by reorienting the civil service to the cold rationality of "reasons of state." Weber knew that modern society would never fully replicate this neat model of governance: some bureaucrats would play politics while some politicians would play administration. Even well-managed non-politicized bureaucracies would still "collide with" the political class which distrusts administrative independence, sharply critiqued by US pioneer of public administration, Woodrow Wilson (1856–1924), as "an offensive official class" preoccupied by "arbitrariness or class spirit" (Weber 1994, 220–1; Wilson 1966, 35–6). For Wilson (1966, 39), "practical statesmanship must come first, closet doctrine second." The main solution to internally active politics within bureaucracy is external political accountability. Representative democracy opposes rule by an unrepresentative bureaucracy, with modern democracies domesticating bureaucracy through burdens of political accountability to the government of the day.

Weber could see what Wilson could also see, that the civil service is administratively supreme in running the modern state but does that difficult job best when it subscribes professionally to something like a "policy/administration dichotomy". Politicians decide public policy and the civil service administers or implements that policy with technical excellence, using what Wilson (1966, 29) called "unpartisan" and "businesslike" skills or what Weber (1994, 214) termed "purely technical superiority," such as "speed, unambiguity, knowledge of the files, continuity, discretion, unity, strict subordination, reduction of friction and of material and personal costs." For instance, state revenue officials do not prescribe rates of taxation but work out technically competent ways of securing taxes from individuals and organizations following the formal authority of legislation and government policy. So too, international civil services do not determine treaties or declare conflicts between their nation and others, but professionally craft international relationships to promote the policies, and punish the partners, determined by government.

CIVIL SERVICE ACCOUNTABILITY IN PRACTICE: WHITEHALL AND WINSTON CHURCHILL

One influential exemplar of a professional civil service is "Whitehall," the name given to the British civil service as the non-political substructure of "the Westminster system" of parliamentary government (Hennessy 1990). The term "Westminster" typically takes precedence over "Whitehall" because the civil service is considered accountable to "the government of the day," comprising the party or parties possessing the confidence of Parliament, to whom the governing ministry is itself accountable. This system of cabinet government includes a large number of ministers, each exercising the primary demands of accountability over civil service agencies under their allocated responsibility. *Collective* ministerial responsibility refers to the governing ministry's accountability to Parliament for its confidence and continuity in office. *Individual* ministerial responsibility refers to each minister's accountability to Parliament for political management of his or her ministerial role, including leadership of the allocated civil service agencies. Seen from the perspective of the ordinary civil servant, the minister individually and the ministry collectively hold the reins of accountability, exercising formal authority over the bureaucracy and taking formal responsibility before Parliament for the performance of that bureaucracy. To use traditional Whitehall language, civil servants are "anonymous and invisible" for most public purposes, taking whatever official responsibilities are given to them by ministers, to whom almost all of their professional accountabilities are owed.

That, at least, is a traditional theory of civil service accountability favored by career officials. The reality is considerably less tidy, with competing lines of accountability cross-hatching the bureaucracy with many pressure points. For the most part, the system carries on well despite discrepancies between the idealized expectations of ministerially-based accountability and the realized expectations of competing accountabilities. An outstanding example of non-compliance with standard expectations relates to Winston Churchill, perhaps Britain's most esteemed political leader in modern times. During most of the 1930s, Churchill was out of favor with his own governing party, holding no ministerial office and serving as a non-ministerial backbencher, with no official authority or rights over the civil service (Gilbert 2004). Churchill's major policy cause was to bypass the wishful-thinking of "appeasement" by restoring British re-armament in the face of the rising threat from the Nazi regime in Germany.

Churchill repeatedly showed that the British government's claims about defense preparedness were faulty and misleading. His main fear was that public opinion was being misled by inaccurate government information. To cut through the government-induced public complacency, Churchill needed more accurate information on Nazi war preparations and British unpreparedness to respond. The source was close at hand: during the 1930s, increasing numbers of civil servants (including serving military officers) became covert providers of government information to Churchill. Some leaked confidential information, others handed over copies of government documents, some prepared their own written briefing papers, others briefed Churchill personally but secretly (Gilbert 2004). All turned to Churchill, persuaded that their accountability to the government of the day was conditional rather than categorical. Even the cabinet secretary, Sir Maurice Hankey, initially lent his private support, secretly praising Churchill for demonstrating public leadership that the government could not muster. Others, like the Foreign Office's Ralph Wigram, went much further, meeting and briefing Churchill frequently, sometimes with the acquiescence of top officials. Churchill was later to praise Wigram for "his courage, integrity of purpose, high comprehending vision" and to honor him as "the epitome of courage and farsightedness" (Gilbert 2004, 107, 173, 267–8).

Standing back from the fascinating details of this case study, we can see that it all turns on competing interpretations of "the public interest" and on how different officials understand loyalty to "the State." In the British context, and across the Westminster-derived world generally, traditional concepts of "officers of the crown" have always had the potential to separate out accountabilities owed to "the government" and to "government" as such. If "the state" is an abstract concept which is difficult to operationalize, then "the crown" can work more concretely in those constitutional monarchies (in and beyond Westminster) where an idealized accountability to the crown can limit aspects of accountability owed to the ministry, itself conceptualized traditionally as "the crown's advisers" (Rohr 2002, 29–31). These opaque constitutional conventions are rarely replaced by transparent public law. The conventions remain as relevant markers of disputed accountability, as can be seen in the debates surrounding "the Ponting affair", that 1980s repeat of the 1930s Churchill saga. Ponting was yet another Defense official who broke ranks and followed in his predecessors' footsteps by briefing parliamentary representatives, in this case about the Thatcher government's misleading public information about the Falklands War (Bovens 1998, 146–8; Rohr 2002, 31–4; Hennessy 1990, 344–5, 352, 602). The Thatcher government brought the full force of legal accountability against Ponting, only to watch a jury acquit him in the belief that civil servants do indeed have higher obligations to help parliament hold governments accountable. After that horse had bolted, the UK civil service hierarchy reformulated its own professional code of conduct to re-state the traditional doctrine that civil servants owe their primary duty of accountability to the government of the day: a doctrine later reshaped by the Blair government when modernizing this along with many other aspects of civil service organization (Hennessy 1990, 363, 378, 671).

Balancing Internal and External Accountability

Accountability is one of those "good things" now sparking debate over whether contemporary political systems can have too much accountability for their own good. The debate illustrates how far we are from a scholarly consensus on the precise details of an accountable civil service (Flinders 2011; Tetlock 2011; Dubnick 2011; Papadopoulos 2012). As we shall see, the real debate is not over accountability as such but over competing balances of *public* accountability. For most purposes, public accountability of civil services means external accountability to legitimate representatives of the public: legislators and political executives. Public accountability also reaches to the press and mass media as an important medium of accountability, including the burdens of publicity associated with civil service media exposure (Philp 2009, 33–4). Frameworks of legal accountability are equally important but for our purposes in this chapter we view legal accountability as one expression of public accountability typically put in place by the legislature to promote officials' adherence to the rule of law. Other chapters in this handbook provide more detailed examination of legal accountability in general and its place in democratic governance.

Far removed from legal forms of public accountability are forms of *internal* accountability. For nearly all practical purposes, most civil services rely heavily on frameworks of internal accountability, with the rule of hierarchy protecting many mandated public values such as selection, remuneration, and promotion all based on merit (Savoie 2004, 2–4). In most cases, these important operational forms of internal accountability are subject to external review: by the courts in the event of a legal challenge over compliance with the rule of law; and by politicians in the legislative and executive branches in the event of challenges over compliance with other public expectations of civil service conduct. Both forms of accountability are important. *Internal* accountability is important as one valuable way of "letting the managers manage" and of honoring the day-to-day professional autonomy of the civil service within the framework of the rule of law. *External* accountability is important in setting legal and political limits on bureaucratic autonomy within the framework of constitutional government, which in most systems of representative democracy allows the public voice to feed into government formulations of the public interest.

We can see the public value of external accountability by briefly considering other forms of internal accountability. Even the most zealous advocate of bureaucracy (literally: "rule by bureau") envisages a system of internal accountability within the bureaucratic system to check the power of wayward bureaucrats or zealous bureaucracy. Systems of paternalism ("father knows best") help us see where bureaucracy and accountability might meet, with ruling power placed in the hands of those convinced they know what is in the interests of the ruled, procedurally as well as substantively. For understandable reasons, democratic civil services are associated with constitutional norms quite removed from paternalism, which is a traditional pre-democratic form of accountability. Even advocates of pure bureaucracy would concede that bureau-power, like all other forms of power, could be abused to harm important public interests. The root problem could be mistakenness as much as malice, with advocates of accountability hoping that adequate checks might protect against both mischiefs: lack of relevant public knowledge as well as lack of public commitment. So too, at the other extreme of formal ruling typologies, it is possible to imagine that even anarchic systems of self-government (anarchy literally means "rule-less") leave open the possibility that self-rulers could mistakenly fail to protect their own self-interests. Thus every trace of paternalism reflects a belief that accountability can be a spur to greater responsibility among those held to account.

Mention of the companion concept of "responsibility" helps us here. The real issue for civil services operating in systems of modern representative government is how to devise systems of accountability which promote two desirable core qualities: public *service* that is properly *civil*. To anticipate a longer argument: An accountable civil service is one which is true to its constitutional responsibilities as a civil as distinct from government (or military or party political) service. The trick with accountability is that a proper civil service is separate from *but not independent of* "the government." It is separate because the constitutional value it embodies is of public administration under the direction but not the domination of established political interests. In contrast to traditional concepts of military service, the civil service is not an extension of the political executive ready to "do battle" with the executive's declared enemies. The business of the civil service is public administration under the rule of law, in contrast to the military service operating under the rule of war, at least when engaged in its core business.

Accountability in both of its forms (internal and external) is thus important because it is a means to promote the end of official responsibility. But to relate forms of accountability to the substance of responsibility is only to identify the terms in a classic debate over an accountable civil service that can be traced back to the influential Friedrich–Finer debates over the constitution of democratic governance (Woll 1966, 221–75; Mulgan 2000, 557; Jackson 2009). Carl Friedrich promoted a version of inner professional accountability as best suited to the promotion of official responsibility, against the damage done to capacities for responsible bureaucratic discretion by intrusive external accountability wielded by political power-holders. Herbert Finer defended a traditional rule-of-law perspective in which officials were held accountable to the legislature for their part in implementing executive programs of government. Friedrich defined official responsibility in terms of the exercise of professional discretion to give effect to the mandate of the political executive in contrast to Finer's version of legislative supremacy in which official responsibility was subject to whatever limits the legislature deemed appropriate. Neither advocate opposed accountability as the primary means of regulating the bureaucracy; both promoted the end of a duly responsible civil service; yet neither yielded to the opponent's model of official responsibility. Friedrich articulated values of internal professional responsibility against Finer's values of external political responsibility.

A core concept in dispute here is delegation, particularly when accountability is seen as linked to potential sanctions (Flinders 2009). Many analysts of accountability narrow it down to explanations of suspect relationships likely to lead to disciplinary sanctions. This approach, however, leaves out relationships with other forms of sanctions, such as adverse media publicity (Philp 2009, 34–6, 43–4). Friedrich, and especially Finer, both appreciated that accountability to institutions which lack power to discipline misconduct is part of the democratic agenda of public accountability relevant to civil services. Friedrich sketches out a model of delegation from the political to the bureaucratic executive, empowering officials to exercise discretionary judgment in implementing the government's public mandate. Finer follows a different model of delegation, interposing the legislature between the sovereign public and the government, reminding officials of the mandate enjoyed by the legislative branch to hold the government itself accountable. The missing term in this debate is "responsive" to which I will return in the last section of this chapter. The idea is an important implicit value in this classic debate, with Finer fearful that Friedrich will make the bureaucracy unduly responsive to sectional interests either already influencing the political executive or about to be privileged through their "client access" to the bureaucracy's management of programs directed to their sector. For his part, Friedrich is apprehensive that Finer will make the bureaucracy unduly responsive to the many competing sectoral interests dominating different parts of the elected legislature.

HOW IS CIVIL SERVICE ACCOUNTABILITY UNDERSTOOD AND IMPLEMENTED?

Analysts of civil services have difficulty knowing exactly how accountability is understood by civil services and officials themselves. This difficulty is not due to any shortage of words about accountability generated by civil services, most of which have published an impressive library of official documents proclaiming their devotion to the value of accountability, external as well as internal, political as well as legal (Mulgan 2003). The trick is to know what this profusion of public administration orthodoxy really means for those whose conduct is being described, "normalized," and regulated. We noticed earlier that the UK civil service greatly increased its explicit attention to codes of accountability in the wake of the Ponting affair, when the bureaucratic hierarchy felt that its traditional system of internal accountability was under new threat. The steady global expansion of the ethos of "New Public Management" (NPM) since the 1980s has brought new formulations into professional prominence, but it is far from clear that traditional informal codes of inner accountability have been replaced by the new nostrums of network governance and "stakeholder accountability" (Chan and Rosenbloom 2010). The conventional orthodoxy espoused by leading civil services proclaim new charters of accountability which balance requirements of political accountability to "the government" for compliance with policy mandates with new obligations of managerial accountability to stakeholders (clients, funders, partners, and so on) for compliance with "results-oriented" administrative practices. Contemporary governance is quite messy: "increasingly pluricentric, multilevel, networked, hybrid," with a prevailing "fluid nature" (Bovens, Schillemans, and 't Hart 2008, 239). We can see some of the ways that civil service systems try to balance these competing burdens of accountability before stepping back to report ways in which analysts try to assess and evaluate the practical effect of emerging frameworks of accountability.

Again, British debates can help. The standards of accountable civil service over the recent NPM years have largely emanated from the civil service itself, with carefully crafted doctrines about the role of career bureaucrats as non-politicized (but politically responsive) instruments of the political executive. This example is a realistic acknowledgement that the ministry confers a range of public responsibilities on the bureaucracy while retaining primary carriage of parliamentary and wider public accountability for the conduct of government. That is, the bureaucratic hierarchy demonstrates its traditional role as provider of governance advice to "the government" even about the accountability burdens which the ministry bears on behalf of the civil service. In this approach, accountability works as a way of managing expectations, more than by black-letter regulation of official conduct (Willems and Van Dooren 2011, 508). In practice of course, the structure of public expectations is generally far from watertight, in part because the political executive is itself split between leading members of cabinet who value consolidated power, especially when explaining and justifying government performance, and lesser ministers who appreciate the countervailing value of "letting the managers manage" processes of public accountability when government agencies need to respond to accusations of maladministration or incompetence.

Another gap in the structure of public expectations emerges from the rise of specialist external accountability agencies, such as the influential British body, the Committee on Standards in Public Life, which illustrates the trend towards holding the career civil service more openly accountable along with all other powerful components of British government. The Committee's use of regular surveys of public attitudes helps recast the "public" dimension of public accountability through reinforcement of the need across government to meet higher community expectations of accountability as the central or core principle in the Committee's charter list of public standards.[1]

RELEVANT ISSUES AND PROBLEMS

My focus has been on constitutional roles and responsibilities performed by civil services. Frankly, most commentary moves quickly on from these regime-value preoccupations to explore a wide range of more urgent (although not necessarily more important) issues in policy implementation. Over the past several decades, most western nations have reduced the size of the core public service by selling off many government-owned enterprises or by contracting-out services to non-government providers supervised by a smaller core of government regulators and performance-scrutineers. The tendency is that many governments now employ fewer civil servants than previously, even when governments are paying more in government services directed through alternative service delivery arrangements. The current international agenda of challenges facing civil service accountability includes some acknowledgement of the need for constitutional anchorage of regimes of civil service accountability. More important, however, are challenges of power-sharing in policy implementation: power shared between the bureaucracy and selected (by open competition or by discretionary contract) non-government service providers (Chan and Rosenbloom 2010, 24–7). These challenges are especially acute in the area of service delivery to government-designated priority clients: in many cases, recipients of what was traditionally regarded as welfare (but is now regarded as temporary "workfare"), but also included are business recipients of government assistance in critical sectors of the economy such as manufacturing where employment prospects are, for many countries, under threat of increasingly intense global competition.

A clear example of this type of accountability literature is a Canadian article on "the dialectics of accountability" (Aucoin and Heitzman 2000). The term "dialectics"—which others refer to "logics" (Bovens, Schillemans, and 't Hart 2008, 226)—here refers to the important public value emerging from the checks and balances of competing doctrines of accountability with creative tension capable of generating progress in public appreciation of accountable government. Of particular note is the importance of "reform" captured in the title and the dominating theme of this influential article. If there is one predominating international "issue" facing accountability, it is the nature of properly "reformed" accountability. Some leading students of accountability are now distancing themselves from this "reformist narrative," the "reformist aspiration," and "reformist agendas" with this "obsession with accountability" (Dubnick 2011, 705–6). The standard reformist view is that government structures generally are reform-ready, perhaps over-ready; and that structures of public administration are in need of overhaul and experiment as we search for a contemporary model of an accountable civil service that is fit for purpose in the novel circumstances of twenty-first century governance.

As is well known, the recent rhetoric of administrative reform certainly predates this turn-of-the-century rendition by Aucoin and Heitzman, deriving historically from the public management (or "managerialist") innovations of western governments in the 1970s and 1980s, when "public administration" was transformed into "public management" (Kettl 2005, 1–40). The initial phase of this reformist period brought forth "accountability for results" (or "accountability for performance") as a new standard against which to measure civil service performance, replacing traditional forms of procedural ("by the book") accountability. Aucoin and Heitzman provide an influential model of accountability in three parts: *control* against misuse of authority; *assurance* of due compliance with standards; and the newly emerging model of "learning in pursuit of *continuous improvement* in governance and public management." It is this third part which captures the current era of accountability reform, with its emphasis on efforts "to reinvent both political behavior and political culture as essential to a larger reinvention of government" (Aucoin and Heitzman 2000, 53; Gregory 1998, 522–7; Bovens, Schillemans, and 't Hart 2008, 232).

STANDARDS AND PROCEDURES

What standards are relevant when external analysts attempt to evaluate practices of accountability (Bovens 2007, 462–7)? We can see from the above that practices of civil service accountability should be measured against norms of "an accountable civil service." We can also note that many governance actors, including contracted service providers, can and do weigh in with hard-nosed assessments of the accountability expected of them by the civil service and of the civil service's own accountability. What holds for those hired by government holds even more for those in government doing the hiring; politicians and their growing armies of partisan staff also undertake assessments of civil service accountability, including those potentially awkward arrangements (such as terms and conditions of paid employment, travel allowances, office management procedures) which call on officials to hold political office-holders accountable. The classic cross-over agency between these internal governance actors and the more analytical world of external actors is the office of state audit where so much of the really detailed hard work assessing government performance occurs (Bovens 2007, 456). State auditors are themselves civil servants, with their own distinctive accountability obligations befitting their status as mediators between the political executive and the legislature. Given that state auditors can act on their own initiative in reviewing civil service performance, we should take note that an "accountable civil service" is hard to conceive in the absence of a powerful and well-resourced state audit function. How competently and productively they carry out their functions depends in turn on how well they satisfy their own accountability scrutineers.

There is a rich intellectual agenda emerging in the field of accountability evaluation. Here we focus on those parts that relate most immediately to civil service structures. Until quite recently, analysts were primarily interested in *vertical* accountability: hierarchical relationships of account between bureaucratic subordinates and political superiors (Bovens 1998, 79–92). Older schools of evaluation dealt mainly with issues of compliance by bureaucrats with the formal and informal "rules and regulations" shaping political expectations. Later schools of evaluation have begun to deal with Aucoin and Heitzman's third domain by attempting to measure bureaucratic contributions to relevant public dialogue over government performance generally. Thus, the earlier world of evaluation has now been joined by interest in *horizontal* and *diagonal* accountability: horizontal referring to relationships of account across governmental institutions where power and answerability is shared (not necessarily equally) by the participating institutions; and diagonal referring to relationships of account between different institutions which get drawn into shared arrangements through emerging governance networks (Bovens 2007, 460). Governance systems can blend forms of accountability, so that vertical and horizontal can exist side by side, raising interesting research questions about the positive value of over-engineered or "redundant accountability" (Schillemans 2010). Predictably, evaluation researchers have only little more success measuring horizontal than diagonal accountability—as we move from horizontal to diagonal forms of accountability, we move further away from the simply hierarchical world where designated authorities control carefully specified delegations of power to subordinate entities. Moreover, we span social sectors, bringing together business and civil society interests working in many different styles of partnership with "the government." Problems of "complexity and heterogeneity" abound; for example, one estimate of non-profit accountability includes "some ninety different components," each measurable but not in any obvious commensurate way (Chandler and Dumont 2010).

What standards do external analysts look to when trying to evaluate "accountability in the shadow of hierarchy" (Schillemans 2008)? The "hierarchy" refers to the power of political office-holders to "hire and fire" senior favorites who administer agencies. Remember that the task is to evaluate accountability performance in terms of relationships of account, which means that analysts have to assess the effectiveness of the account *receivers* as well as the account *givers*. When evaluating vertical accountability, this implies examination of the conduct of political authorities as they deliberate over what balance of rewards and punishments are merited in specific circumstances. But non-vertical forms of accountability lack this concentrated authority, so much so that many cases include debate and contest over exactly who has "the upper hand" when seeking to modify the conduct of the many players with legitimate parts to play in the governance process. It is only quite recently that governments looked to non-government entities to help with policy innovation and program implementation, but this has grown so quickly that governments have now emerged as prominent external stakeholders in many non-government, particularly not-for-profit, entities (Chandler and Dumont 2010). Evaluation therefore tends to become a broad-gauge assessment of the policy and administrative judgment exercised by the different interests as they share public power. For instance, public–private partnerships pose acute problems for civil servants responsible for managing the accountability agenda, which can be separated into six or so quite distinctive dimensions, each calling for expert independent assessment: risk, costs and benefits, political and social impacts, expertise, collaboration, performance measurement (Forrer, Kee, Newcomer, and Boyer 2010). Civil servants have roles in managing each of these dimensions, but there is no one model about how their own accountability can be informed by competing judgments over so many dimensions of governance.

Inspired in part by theories of deliberative democracy, some analysts argue that the way forward is to assess accountability proactively rather than reactively, in terms of "operative deliberative processes" inherent in practices of public administration (Khademian 2010; Dubnick 2011, 707–9; Philp 2009, 44–5; Mulgan 2000, 569–70). Evaluators of horizontal relationships "stress their relevance to organizational learning, not the possibilities for ministerial control" (Schillemans 2008, 190). The challenge facing evaluators is to move beyond charting the power dynamics at work in any set of governance relationships and to assess the contribution all interests make to the formation of what I will term a sustainable "public judgment" about policy process and substance. This is no easy task when we consider the developing nature of governance as "a highly dynamic iterative pattern of give and take, a kind of marathon dance of accountability" (Dubnick and Frederickson 2009, 156). Where earlier students of accountability relied on concepts of "the public interest" (vividly illustrated in our Churchill case study), contemporary students tend to use this different benchmark about "public judgment" which derives less from the analyst's own normative concept of the public interest and more from empirical evidence of the public sustainability of the outcomes (including procedural outcomes) arising from the governance process. Evaluators are interested in measuring the extent to which horizontal accountability "stimulates the learning capacity of agencies" so that they, together, can strengthen the deliberative interaction of agencies sharing public power (Schillemans 2008, 190; Savoie 2006, 19–22; Philp 2009, 40–1). An important test is wider community acceptability of such policy partnerships, separate and distinct from immediate political acceptability by "the government."

RESEARCH AGENDA

The starting point for reflection on a research agenda is the need for more cross-national comparative studies of civil service accountability. Specialists in "comparative public administration" who note the prominence of studies of "reform and accountability" in the field, identify three important benefits of comparative analysis: first, overcoming reliance on parochial perspectives based on single-nation studies; second, generating cross-national generalizations; and third, located between these two benefits, better specification of national differences (Seibel 2010). Chan and Rosenbloom (2010) have taken a lead by charting the many differences between China and the United States, each illustrating a distinctive model of modernization, with China more "statist" than the market-inclined United States. The world provides many additional examples of nationally distinctive modes of governance, most adapting in their way to global trends towards agreed international standards, even to the point of generating transnational civil services managing national compliance with emerging accountability accords in trade and commerce, investment, immigration, and tourism in addition to the traditional challenges of war and peace and the emerging challenges of human rights and international development.

Related aspects of intergovernmental affairs are federalism, multilevel government and administrative decentralization. The pressing question is to what extent can national-level civil servants be held accountable for government performance in federal systems? (Radin 2002, 41–58; 2006, 153–82; 2011). Federalism and its related division of powers arrangements deserve fresh research attention, partly to correct old misconceptions about flawed accountability and partly to record new practices of accountability in the context of decentralized governance. Federalism was long regarded as too prone to "buck-passing," with the result that dispersals of power became excuses for (or even justifications of) "hollowed out" accountability, with elaborate formal structures hiding the lack of substantive accountability by officials. But few contemporary governments can manage without resorting to federal arrangements involving multiple layers of civil services sharing accountability for the governance process. Older forms of federalism start out with notions of shared sovereignty which sometimes lead to attempts to separate accountability neatly along vertical lines, with subnational units answering for some policy areas and the national unit for others. Newer versions of federalism often privilege the national center of power but balance this against substantial delegations of power and also accountability to local areas.

A related research topic flagged earlier is "responsiveness": when push comes to shove, to what interests and institutions and ideas do civil servants feel themselves primarily responsive, regardless of the formal architecture of accountability (Du Gay 2002; Savoie 2004, 16–17; Mulgan 2000, 566–9)? If mechanisms of accountability are measured in terms of their impact on a responsible civil service, then where does "responsiveness" fit in to the framework of accountable and responsible governance? Lest we incline too quickly to a view of politically docile civil services, we should first ask about the place of internal professional norms in structuring regimes of responsiveness. Further, what views about "responsiveness" emerge from the courts as the constitutionally-mandated non-political branch of government acting as arbitrators of accountability? Finally, what evidence can persuade "accountability zealots" that their measures of official responsiveness to performance targets are measures of bureaucratic docility as much as measures of good policy outcomes (Tetlock 2011, 699–702)?

Finally, the requirements of "social accountability" require closer examination (Bovens 2007, 457). This term refers to the forms of accountability which governance entities encounter when processes of "civic engagement" bring civil society actors into fora of public policy and administration. A 2005 policy paper by the World Bank put social accountability on the international governance agenda, usefully supplying future researchers with goals and benchmarks for consideration when evaluating the reality against the promise of this new field of accountability. As with other forms of accountability, social accountability can be preoccupied with administrative process or policy substance or a blend of both. The issue here is where civil services feature in any of these forms. Thus far, studies of social accountability have tended to examine administrative process in developing countries where social accountability has been beneficial in bringing greater public accountability to the bureaucracy. Once again, students of social accountability have seen the potential of this and other unconventional forms of accountability to "reform" traditionally closed or impervious public sectors. An important research priority is whether similar routines of civic engagement can open up new accountability dimensions in civil services in developed countries.

Honoring the Reactivity of Accountability and the Initiative of Responsibility

So many of the terms of reference for this chapter reflect Weber's original interests. Unfortunately, one of those interests not properly covered has been the capacity of civil services to elude their accountability to legislatures, often using threats of national security to confine their accountability to their immediate political ministers. Weber is one of the first analysts to puncture this resilient form of bureaucratic politics (Weber 1994, 233–5).

I have argued that the topic of accountable civil servants is best examined by reference to debate over the constitutional roles and responsibilities of civil services. Role definition is rarely an easy task because many competing accountabilities can threaten officials. For instance, our early case study about Churchill can be revisited, noting that when encouraging public servants to provide him with confidential information, Churchill used to advise valued defense officers "that loyalty to the State must come before loyalty to the Service" (Gilbert 2004, 177). Competing official roles vary according to changing understandings of a polity's constitutional system, even in quite developed systems like Canada (Savoie 2006, 271–4). One powerful model featured in many global examples of modernizing governance is the constitution of representative government, including many varieties of representative democracy. Yet even across the subset of systems of representative democracy we encounter expert anxiety not only about *underdone accountability* ("accountability gaps" and "accountability deficits"), but also about *overdone accountability* ("multiple accountability disorders," "accountability paradoxes," "accountability overkill," "accountability bias," and "informal accountability") (see also Mulgan's and Halachmi's chapters in this handbook). Both sets relate to perceived dysfunctions in accountability, all of which can be applied to civil services. In this first set, civil services can be viewed as part of the problem of insufficient reach of public accountability over contemporary governance. In the second set, civil services can also be viewed as part of the problem of what we might term "compromised conditionality": delegating power to other governance actors which is hedged in with onerous burdens of formal accountability, so much so that the forms of reporting and account-giving crowd out innovative uses of public power (Mulgan 2003; Yang 2012).

What holds for government contractors, also holds for government officials. As we learn when things go wrong in government, accountable public officials are not necessarily responsible governance actors, despite all their due compliance with the terms and conditions of the power delegated to them. We risk returning to the beginning if we think of accountability as a creed of governance based on "a fundamentalist faith" nurturing accountable but not necessarily responsible civil servants. Helping civil servants to honor not only the *reactivity* of accountability but also the *initiative* of responsibility remains a major challenge facing democratic governance (Dubnick 2011, 709–10; Philp 2009, 36–8; Rohr, Rosenbloom, and Schaefer 2010).

NOTE

1. See: <www.public-standards.gov.uk>.

REFERENCES

Aucoin, P. and Heitzman, R. 2000. "The Dialectics of Accountability for Performance in Public Management Reform." *International Review of Administrative Sciences*, 66: 45–55.

Bovens, M. 1998. *The Quest for Responsibility*. Cambridge: Cambridge University Press.

Bovens, M. 2007. "Analysing and Assessing Accountability." *European Law Journal*, 13: 447–68.

Bovens, M., Schillemans, T., and 't Hart, P. 2008. "Does Public Accountability Work?" *Public Administration*, 86: 225–42.

Chan, H. S. and Rosenbloom, D. 2010. "Four Challenges to Accountability in Contemporary Public Administration." *Administration & Society*, 42: 11s–33s.

Chandler, G. and Dumont, G. 2010. "A Non-Profit Accountability Framework." *Canadian Public Administration*, 53: 259–79.

Du Gay, P. 2002. "How Responsible is 'Responsive' Government?" *Economy and Society*, 13: 461–82.

Dubnick, M. J. and Frederickson, H. G. 2009. "Accountability Agents." *Journal of Public Administration Research and Theory*, 20: i125–i141.

Dubnick, M. J. 2011. "Move Over Daniel: We Need Some 'Accountability Space.'" *Administration & Society*, 43: 704–16.

Flinders, M. 2009. "Theory and Method in the Study of Delegation." *Public Administration*, 87: 955–71.

Flinders, M. 2011. "Daring to be a Daniel." *Administration & Society*, 45: 595–619.

Forrer, J., Kee, J. E., Newcomer, K. E., and Boyer, E. 2010. "Public-Private Partnerships and the Public Accountability Question." *Public Administration Review*, 70: 475–84.

Gilbert, M. 2004. *Winston Churchill: The Wilderness Years*. London: Pimlico.

Gregory, R. 1998. "Political Responsibility for Bureaucratic Incompetence." *Public Administration*, 76: 519–38.

Hennessy, P. 1990. *Whitehall*. London: Fontana Press.

Jackson, M. 2009. "Responsibility versus Accountability in the Friedrich-Finer Debate." *Journal of Management History*, 15: 66–77.

Kettl, D. 2005. *The Global Public Management Revolution*. Second edition. Washington: Brookings Institution Press.

Khademian, A. M. 2010. "Organizing in the Future." *Public Administration Review*, 70: s167–s69.

Mulgan, R. 2000. "'Accountability': An Ever Expanding Concept?" *Public Administration*, 78: 555–73.

Mulgan, R. 2003. *Holding Power to Account*. Basingstoke, UK: Palgrave Macmillan.

Papadopoulos, Y. 2012. "Daring to be a Daniel." *Administration & Society*, 44: 238–52.

Philp, M. 2009. "Delimiting Democratic Accountability." *Political Studies*, 57: 28–53.

Radin, B. A. 2002. *The Accountable Juggler*. Washington: Congressional Quarterly Press.

Radin, B. A. 2006. *Challenging the Performance Movement*. Washington: Georgetown University Press.

Radin, B. A. 2011. "Federalist." *Public Administration Review*, 71: s128–s34.

Rohr, J. 2002. *Civil Servants and Their Constitutions*. Lawrence, KS: University of Kansas Press.

Rohr, J., Rosenbloom, D. H., and Schaefer, D. 2010. "Recovering, Restoring and Renewing the Foundations of American Public Administration." *Public Administration Review*, 70: 621–33.

Romzek, B., LeRoux, K., and Blackmar, J. M. 2012. "A Preliminary Theory of Informal Accountability Among Network Organizational Actors." *Public Administration Review*, 72: 442–53.

Savoie, D. J. 2004. "Searching for Accountability in a Government Without Boundaries." *Canadian Public Administration*, 47: 1–26.

Savoie, D. J. 2006. "The Canadian Public Service has a Personality." *Canadian Public Administration*, 49: 261–81.

Schillemans, T. 2008. "Accountability in the Shadow of Hierarchy." *Public Organization Review*, 8: 175–94.

Schillemans, T. 2010. "Redundant Accountability." *Public Administration Quarterly*, 34: 300–37.

Seibel, W. 2010. "Beyond Bureaucracy". *Public Administration Review*, 70: 719–30.

Tetlock, P. E. 2011. "Vying for Rhetorical High Ground in Accountability Debates." *Administration & Society*, 43: 693–703.

Weber, M. 1994. Parliament and Government in Germany, pp. 130–271 in *Weber: Political Writings*, eds. P. Lassman and R. Speirs. Cambridge: Cambridge University Press.

Willems, T. and Van Dooren, W. 2011. "Lost in Diffusion?" *International Review of Administration Sciences*, 77: 505–30.

Wilson, W. 1996. The Study of Administration, pp. 15–41 in *Public Administration and Policy*, ed. P. Woll. New York: Harper Torchbooks.

Woll, P. 1966. *Public Administration and Policy*. New York: Harper Torchbooks.

World Bank Institute 2005. *Social Accountability in the Public Sector*. Washington: World Bank.

Yang, K. 2012. "Further Understanding Accountability in Public Organizations." *Administration & Society*, 44: 255–84.

CHAPTER 15

....

ACCOUNTABLE NETWORKS

....

ERIK HANS KLIJN AND JOOP F. M. KOPPENJAN

NETWORKS AND ACCOUNTABILITY

IN public administration theory and practice, it is increasingly acknowledged that many processes of decision-making, policy implementation, and service delivery in the public sector take place within so-called governance networks (Osborne 2010; Sørensen and Torfing 2007; Provan and Kenis 2008). The concept of governance refers to the horizontal interactions by which autonomous yet interdependent actors coordinate their actions (Pierre 2000; Rhodes 1997). Governance networks can be defined as "more or less stable patterns of social relations between mutually dependent actors, which form around a policy program and/or cluster of means and which are formed, maintained and changed through series of games" (Koppenjan and Klijn 2004, 69–70). These networks emerge out of a necessity to interact. They can be consciously designed in the sense that actors deliberately interact and structure their interactions with organizational arrangements and rules. Often, however, governance networks result from spontaneous interactions and gradually emerging rules and arrangements (Hanf and Scharpf 1978; Marsh and Rhodes 1992; Laumann and Knoke 1987).

Although actors are required to interact because of resource dependencies, they often find it hard to coordinate their interactions by themselves. Interactions within the network may produce sharp conflicts about, for instance, the distribution of the costs and benefits of a solution. The diverging or conflicting perceptions of actors regarding the nature of the problem(s), the desired solution(s), or the appropriate arrangements to be used, can result in major obstacles to attempts to achieve mutually acceptable outcomes. Conscious efforts to enhance coordination are usually referred to as network management or meta-governance (Agranoff and McGuire 2003; Koppenjan and Klijn 2004; Meier and O'Toole 2007; Sørensen and Torfing 2007).

Governance networks emerge from efforts to increase the effectiveness of public policies and service delivery in situations of interdependencies. Accountability is not an underlying concern in these efforts. From an accountability perspective, networks can be considered problematic. It is difficult to hold actors accountable for outcomes that are realized by various actors collaborating in processes that are opaque and hard to assess. Nevertheless, there is a growing need to hold networks accountable in order to enhance the legitimacy of the governance networks that increasingly dominate the public administration landscape.

We define *accountability* as the extent to which actors (accounters: those rendering accounts) are held accountable for their behavior and performance by other actors (accountees: those to whom account is rendered). The *accountability process* is the process by which an accounter renders account to an accountee. We call the procedures, instruments, and arrangements by which account is given, *accountability mechanisms*. In order to render account, *standards* are needed about what is considered accountable behavior and performance. These standards may be derived from goals, but also from expectations regarding appropriate behavior and rules, reflecting norms and values (Bovens, Goodin, and Schillemans in this volume; Koliba et al. 2010). The nature of accountability can be *vertical*, establishing accountable behavior to superiors and actors higher in the hierarchy, or *horizontal*, establishing accountable behavior among and towards stakeholders in the network (see Bovens et al. in this volume).

As shown later in more depth, the accountability of governance networks is problematic given the complications that occur regarding accounters, accountees, accountability mechanisms, and accountability standards.

FORMS OF ACCOUNTABILITY IN NETWORKS

In the classical representation of policymaking and public service delivery, accountability—at least in the ideal model—is for the most part clear. Elected politicians are responsible for setting policy and can be held accountable by voters in elections. Bureaucratic accountability—public servants being held accountable by their superiors—is arranged by hierarchy and strict bureaucratic rules (and the primacy of politics). Now, on the one hand, all these forms of accountability are the same in the situation where policymaking and service delivery takes place in networks. Or as Considine (2002, 23) remarks: "Courts still wish to see the letter of the statute honored and due process followed. Parliaments still expect detailed, descriptive reports which name and shame programs. Citizens groups still press ministers and civil servants to take responsibility for public programs, even if the programs are delivered by contractors." Thus in networks also, most of the well-known accountability mechanisms (bureaucratic rules, political representation, etc.) and accountable behavior (normal professional behavior) are still required and in place, but they function in a different setting of a "shared power world" and are partly replaced or supplemented by other mechanisms of accountability or accountable behavior. An example is when public officials engage in networks to achieve policy goals. They then become network managers who try to achieve a package of goals that satisfy various stakeholders. Thus, what a network manager is actually doing is exploring a workable substantial solution for a policy problem that can satisfy as many stakeholders as possible (see Koppenjan and Klijn 2004; Agranoff and McGuire 2003). Because such a manager finds himself in a position of interdependency, he is not able to force a solution in the network through a top-down decision-making process. This situation consequently changes both the accountability mechanisms by which he works and his accountable behavior.

Types of Networks and Accountability

Networks can take different forms. Part of the confusion in the literature on networks, and certainly on accountability, relates to this. For instance, in the US, network scholars are less occupied with issues such as democracy and accountability than European authors (Sørensen and Torfing 2007). This may result from the fact that the US literature deals with service delivery networks in which a clear decision of a political body results in the contracting out of a service to a lead organization that coordinates the parties involved in the delivery of public services (Provan and Kenis 2008; Meier and O'Toole 2007). European scholars often focus on complex decision-making among a variety of public and private parties that meet in various arenas and whose relations are not formally arranged (Rhodes 1997). The loosely coupled nature of networks may lead to less formally organized accountability and less clear standards to which actors can be held accountable.

So, the form that accountability takes depends on the type of network with which we are dealing. In general, more tightly organized networks have a more clearly arranged accountability structure since a lead organization or a network administrative organization acts as accounter towards a political or administrative accountee (see also Provan and Kenis 2008). Loosely coupled networks often do not have such an arrangement. It also makes a difference whether politicians or governments are part of a network, or whether they initiate and meta-govern the networks (for instance by organizing joined-up services or decision-making for policy implementation). If they are part of the network or govern the network hands-on, accountability relationships may become blurred. If they set clear standards for the operation of the network up front and govern the network according to these standards, conditions for accountability are more favorable.

Types of Accountability in Networks

A network manager initiating an urban restructuration process, involving citizen/tenant groups, private investors, shop owners, and municipal departments, is still accountable to his superior in the bureaucracy and to his elected officeholder (say the city alderman). Now, however, he is also accountable for his behavior to the other actors in the network, which might be for instance citizen groups that are in discussion about possible negative effects on their existing houses of new dwellings; and he is subject to different account-ability mechanisms that may or may not be more or less formally laid down. Standards such as fair play in negotiations suddenly enter the process as accountability mechanisms. So the fact that networks encompass a larger number of actors creates extra accountabil-ity mechanisms and the need for other accountable behavior; but it also of course makes the accountability more complicated. Because more actors are involved whose behavior can be held accountable and various different accountability mechanisms are concur-rently present, accountability, in terms of both accountability mechanisms and account-able behavior, becomes more complicated or even conflictive (see Koliba et al. 2010). An example of the latter is the many forms of interactive policymaking in which citizens are invited to policymaking processes. In this way, forms of direct participative democ-racy with its accountability mechanisms, where citizens and other stakeholders have a direct say in decisions, are introduced within representative democratic procedures. As empirical research into these processes shows, this can cause sharp clashes (Klijn and Koppenjan 2000; Edelenbos 2005). Table 15.1 presents a brief overview of the main differ-ences in accountability between a classical situation and a network situation.

Bureaucratic accountability in classical decision-making processes is fairly straight-forward. Public managers are accountable to their superiors. Although this account-ability remains as well as the accountability to previously established political goals (performance and performance indicators), public officials in network situations may encounter other more horizontal mechanisms of accountability. A common character-istic of networks is that often the involved actors have to reach agreement on goals (or even more often packages of goals) during the process. This means that public officials who operate in networks at a certain juncture have to comply with these agreed goals. There might even be tensions between the goals agreed in the network for which net-work members will be held accountable and the political goals of elected officeholders for which civil servants are also accountable.

Legal accountability, in principle, as is clear from Table 15.1, is not very different in networks than it is in classical policymaking. So the European rules for public authori-ties tendering out services or products do not differ as between a traditional setting, where government tenders a product after deciding in detail what the requirements are, and a network setting, for instance if the desire is to create a public–private partnership. Sometimes, however, it is more difficult to determine who is responsible for outcomes. If public and private actors form an alliance, generally called public–private partnerships, it is for instance not always exactly clear who is responsible for policy and outcomes.

Norms of *professional accountability* and *social accountability* also are affected when public officials find themselves in networks or even managing networks. Newman (2004) observes that public servants operating as managers in network-like situa-tions try to construct different meanings of accountability to cope with the new situ-ation of interdependence. On the one hand, they emphasize hierarchy and classical values such as viewing themselves as public servants and not as policy advocates. On the other hand however, they stress that working in networks implies being challenging

Table 15.1 Types of accountability in classical and network situations

Type of accountability	Classical policymaking	Network
Bureaucratic accountability (to principals, superiors by means of bureaucratic rules, and primacy of politics)	Vertical accountability to higher officials (and eventually political officeholders) along clearly hierarchical lines Accountability to politically established goals (performance)	Besides vertical accountability, other forms of accountability are established, since public officials have to give account to other stakeholders as formally laid down in covenants, contracts, or other mutual agreements Accountability to horizontally established goals agreed upon by involved actors
Legal accountability (to legal bodies)	Public organization responsible for its actions (administrative law and/or private law)	Legal accountability is in some cases (public–private partnerships) more complex because actors have joint responsibility for products, outcomes, or services
Professional accountability (peers and professional bodies)	Professional norms of bureaucrats (neutrality and service to the public cause) and others	Normal professional rules still apply (for civil servants and others), but new professional codes may emerge relating to new roles in networks Like professionalism in the sense of following norms of good conduct in interactions and negotiations The idea of professionalism can change
Social accountability (to societal stakeholders)	Social accountability takes place by public announcement of decisions and transparency of the democratic process Media attention	Need and pressure for more extensive accountable behavior to involved stakeholders by public servants (360 degree accountability) Media attention
Political/democratic accountability (to political forums, representative bodies)	Primacy of politics (elected politicians are responsible for policy content) accountable to electorate (voting) Mainly vertical accountability	Additional accountability to involved stakeholders in the network (participation rules **can** create accountability to a new political forum—an audience of citizens and others—that goes beyond the representational bodies) Vertical accountability is expanded by (informal or formal) horizontal forms of accountability

and creative and that in their behavior they try to be accountable to the stakeholders (who can be actors in the network, clients of services provided by the network, etc.). They also emphasize that national standards of policy (and policy goals) have to be met, and this can be seen as creating tensions between various forms of accountable behavior: towards the classical bureaucracy, towards national goals (to deliver performance), and towards stakeholders involved in the process.

Within governance networks, various accountability mechanisms and standards for accountable behavior and performance co-exist. Of course, accountability becomes more complicated in networks than in traditional policymaking and public services delivery. This is especially visible in the dimension of *democratic accountability*.

Networks and Democratic Accountability

In relation to accountability issues in networks, most attention by far in the literature has focused on the tension between the vertical forms of accountability characteristic of representational democracy and the more horizontal forms of democratic accountability that seem to be becoming more dominant in networks (see Klijn and Skelcher 2007; Sørensen and Torfing 2007).

There appear to be two positions in this debate. From the first perspective, the emergence of networks threatens the classical democratic institutions and their forms of accountability. This arises because if various societal actors are involved in the formulation (and implementation) of policy goals, as is the case in governance networks, the primacy of politics is challenged in one way or another (Klijn and Skelcher 2007). This tension is also confirmed by empirical research (Klijn and Koppenjan 2000; Edelenbos 2005; Skelcher, Mathur, and Smith 2005).

In the network literature however, one can also find another position. Networks attempt to organize other, more horizontal and informal forms of accountability (in addition to the formal political accountability of officeholders). In this way, various stakeholders have the opportunity to become actively involved in processes of decision-making and implementation, thereby bringing in both new standards for accountability (direct accountability to participating citizen groups) and new accountable behavior that arises out of this for officials (see Sørensen and Torfing 2007). The large number of publications on interactive decision-making, collaborative governance, interactive governance, etc. (Klijn and Koppenjan 2000; Edelenbos 2005; Ansell and Gash 2008; Torfing and Triantafillou 2011) is evidence of this trend towards new accountability mechanisms and behavior. The fact that tensions arise between the two forms of accountability is not so much a confirmation that governance networks and their horizontal accountability mechanisms are hard to combine with representational democracy, but rather an indication that adequate arrangements to combine both horizontal and vertical accountability mechanisms are lacking.

ACCOUNTABILITY PROBLEMS IN NETWORKS: A SHORT OVERVIEW

The emergence of governance networks is an answer to complex policy problems where actors are interdependent and need one another's resources to achieve solutions.

Networks result not from efforts to be accountable, but from efforts to be effective. Firstly, performance in networks depends upon the joint actions of various actors, making it hard to establish who is accountable for what and to whom. Furthermore, networks may be closed, involving only actors who have crucial resources and keeping others out. Next, networks are often under-institutionalized: they are guided by informal ways of doing and lack clearly defined goals, performance, or procedures. These characteristics underlie many of the accountability problems of governance networks. These problems are now discussed in more detail.

The Number of Accounters: The Problem of Many Hands

Governance networks are not devoid of accountability mechanisms or standards. Each participant within a network is still accountable to his/her own mother organization: civil servants to bureaucracy and democracy, politicians to their constituency, professionals to their peers, private participants to their CEOs and shareholders, pressure groups to their boards and member councils. Accountability becomes problematic because within governance networks various actors co-produce networks outcomes. As a result, the "problem of many hands" arises. In collaboration it is hard to establish the contribution of each participant. Consequently, the existing vertical accountability mechanisms become less effective. Public administrators will resist being held responsible for performance for which they are dependent upon others. Interdependencies can be used by network actors to shrink responsibilities, blaming others for failure. Furthermore, the various accountability mechanisms are focused on the goals, norms, and values of the specific organizations involved. Because of this fragmented accountability structure, it may be that no one holds the network to account for its overall performance. This may jeopardize the performance of the network as a whole, due to a lack of incentives to achieve synergies that go beyond the goals of individual network members (Provan and Kenis 2008). It may also lead to the production of negative network externalities—e.g., shifting the cost or risks of collaboration to third parties—since none of the involved actors are held accountable for the effects produced by the network as a whole (Bovens et al. this volume; Koliba et al. 2010).

The Closedness of Governance Networks

Because networks are vehicles for solving policy problems or arranging service delivery, they are often relatively closed. In many instances, only actors whose resources are considered critical are included. This is not a new observation. Since the start of network research, authors have emphasized the closed nature of networks (Rhodes 1997). Recent conceptualizations of networks stress that networks are more inclusive and often deliberately try to include a wide variety of groups (see Edelenbos 2005; Ansell and Gash 2008; Torfing and Triantafillou 2011). This may result in growth in the number and variety of accountees. From an accountability perspective this can be a problem. Network actors may find it hard to render account to these various publics, who not only judge them according to different standards, but often also speak another language or follow different accountability rhythms. Despite the opening up of networks, empirical research shows that participation often remains limited (see for instance Marcussen and Torfing 2007). Networks often arrange accountability to the group of stakeholders that are known and included, but accountability to external stakeholders (social accountability) is poorly organized. Decisions are not made in a transparent way. Insofar as information is available to outsiders, it is difficult to assess because of its specialized nature.

The media are often mentioned as a pressure to enhance social accountability because they communicate policy and political events to a wider public and are traditionally seen as the "watchdog of democracy" (see Bennett 2009). However, many authors have argued that the media, because of growing competition and commercialization (and the need to attract advertising and thus many readers/viewers), have changed the nature of news provision (see Bennett 2009). The media tend to emphasize conflicts and make the news more personal and dramatic. Although quite some evidence exists for this claim (see Patterson 2000 for instance) and these biases certainly can have consequences for the accuracy of the information provided, it remains a question whether biased news really is a threat to the so-called watchdog function.

Korthagen (2011), looking at the media attention on five complex decision-making processes around environmental issues, shows that media biases are strongly connected to opposition groups (environmental organizations, citizen groups that oppose government plans). Thus, the media spotlight increases in the event of groups (citizen groups, environmental groups) criticizing government plans. In such cases, media attention can frame the story as a conflict and dramatize it by associating the government plans with concrete damage to individual life (citizens) or nature; this fits in the media logic of framing stories as conflict, personalized, and so forth. Therefore, although media biases are present, they also provide an instrument for opposition groups to enter the decision-making arena (because the story is framed in conflict terms that are attractive to the media) and thus create opportunities for countervailing power or the watchdog function. In that sense, the media can contribute to enhancing accountability by providing more transparency and opening up networks despite their biased news production.

The Problem of Under-Institutionalization and Hybridity

As stated above, governance networks have emerged or are designed as efforts to increase the effectiveness of public decision-making, policy implementation, or service delivery, without accountability being a major concern therein. Often, governance networks have developed hardly any rules about conduct or accountability. Skelcher, Mathur, and Smith (2005), for instance, observe that partnerships and networks in the UK seem to be mainly preoccupied with performance. They conclude that "few partnerships have institutionalized practices to ensure transparency and openness in their operation" (2005, 585). In particular, little attention is being given to rules of public access (social accountability) and membership conduct (professional accountability). The literature on collaborative governance and interactive decision-making that looks at the participation of citizens in governance processes comes to similar conclusions (see Klijn and Koppenjan 2000; Sørensen and Torfing 2007; Edelenbos 2005; Ansell and Gash 2008). Thus, networks often are under-institutionalized and, if rules and structures are provided, they are aimed at performance rather than at creating accountability. Insofar as accountability mechanisms are present, it may be that, because of the presence of various accountees, mechanisms become mixed. The hybridity of accountability mechanisms that results from this may give rise to uncertainty, confusion, or shrinking (Koliba et al. 2010). In the next section, this phenomenon is further discussed with reference to the tension between vertical and horizontal democratic accountability.

The Lack of, and Confusion Over, Accountability Standards

In classical policymaking processes, accountability is achieved by measuring outcomes of decisions by standards of performance criteria. Civil servants and others have to account for outcomes, and these are judged against political decisions taken earlier and/or the goals of a specific policy program. In networks, this is slightly more difficult, as has been observed in the network literature (see Koppenjan and Klijn 2004). Not only are more actors involved with different goals, thus making it more complicated to establish for which goals accountability should be provided, but also goals are often not established at the beginning but emerge in the negotiation process. Thus, it is more difficult to assess the results for which actors are to be held accountable. Because performance and the goals to be achieved are the result of negotiation, it is difficult to hold the actors, including elected politicians, completely accountable for them. Also, actors see different, sometimes conflicting, performance requirements and have to improvise. So, network managers engaged in integral service delivery may need to cope with national performance indicators, while at the same time coping with their need to be responsive to citizens, stakeholders, and their home organization (for instance the local municipality). As Newman (2004) shows, there may be significant tensions between these demands. This means that accountable behavior in a network context is partly constructed in the process as a consequence of performance (indicator) demands, professional norms, and the need to involve stakeholders (see also Acar, Guo, and Yang 2008).

DESIGNING ACCOUNTABILITY MECHANISMS FOR GOVERNANCE NETWORKS

Within governance networks, various accountability mechanisms as well as standards for accountable behavior and performance co-exist. At first sight, this might lead to optimism regarding the potential for accountability in networks: Vertical accountability is not simply hollowed out; rather, within networks, the various accountability mechanisms potentially might reinforce one another. However, this variety also causes accountability problems. It may result in confusion, mechanisms may be incompatible or undermine each other, and it may well be that they do not cover all network activities: There may be black spots (compare Willems and Van Dooren 2011). In order to enhance the accountability of networks, these problems need to be addressed. A first step may be to make accountability mechanisms and accountability standards more explicit. This step may be followed by attempts to complement, change, or replace them. One way to do this is to deliberately (re-)design and (re-)negotiate rules for interactions in networks. In the network literature, this is referred to as "process design" or—if these efforts aim at more fundamental changes of rules in networks—as "institutional design" (De Bruijn et al. 2010; Koppenjan and Klijn 2004). Acknowledging that the opportunities to realize these design efforts are limited and dependent on the context and the support of other actors within and outside the network, we now discuss some design options for strengthening horizontal accountability in networks. Since horizontal accountability is limited and will supplement but not replace vertical accountability, below we will also reflect on ways to reconcile vertical accountability with the horizontal nature of governance network practices.

Designing Horizontal Accountability of Governance Networks

Process design implies the design of an architecture that will initiate and guide the interaction of actors participating in the interaction process. This process architecture specifies the actors that are supposed to participate, the agenda, the resources available, the activities with their projected chronology and timeline, the role division and rules, and the institutional arrangements that will facilitate the interaction. The process design can be seen as a set of rules that the actors agree upon and that will guide their interactions (De Bruijn et al. 2010).

Elaborating on the potential set of institutional rules, Ostrom (1990; see also Koppenjan and Klijn 2004) suggests that these rules may specify:

- positions (which roles are available)
- boundaries (exit and access rules)
- scope (delineation of activities)
- the use of information
- the division of authority
- way of decision making and conflict regulation (decision rules)
- division of costs, benefits, and risks
- rules regarding products and codes of behavior.

The process design provides the governance network with both accountability mechanisms and accountability standards. It offers the opportunity to specify accounters and accountees, procedures by which accounters render account—including the information rules to be followed—the standards specifying the behavior and performance required, and the rules that apply when these requirements are not met or need to be amended. Although in practice processes within governance networks often emerge and there are no explicitly agreed process rules, a consciously designed and agreed upon process design may make rules explicit, thus providing the conditions for accountability. The process design performs an internal function: guiding interactions among participants within governance network processes by providing internal transparency. It provides the standards and mechanisms for actors to hold one another accountable for the way they behave, perform their tasks, and achieve results. Also, it performs an external function in signaling to their environment what the process is about and how the network will behave, thus providing external transparency and legitimacy. These rules can consequently play an important role in social accountability processes in which network actors give account of their behavior and performance to the outside world, be they citizens, users, stakeholders that do not actively participate, inspectorates, governments, or media.

The architecture of the process is not self-executive. Therefore, the quality of process management is important. Process management fulfills a constituting role with regard to the drafting of the process design and with regard to its implementation, fine-tuning, monitoring, and updating. This requires a competent, independent management with sufficient resources and acceptable both to participants in the process and to the outside world (Edelenbos 2005; Koppenjan and Klijn 2004).

The quality of the accountability of a governance network will be further enhanced by the presence of institutional provisions that safeguard its openness and commitment to be held accountable. These may be horizontal accountability arrangements such as benchmarking, certification, societal reports, self-evaluations, peer group assessments, and assessments by users and stakeholders (Bovens 2006; Sørensen and Torfing 2007).

Process design results in the institutionalization of rules, positions, and relationships of actors, thus contributing to the institutionalization of the network. Consequently, no watershed exists between attempts at process design and at institutional design aimed at the conscious adaptation of the institutional characteristics of networks. Insofar as these design attempts are aimed at enhancing the accountability of networks, they may be ways to create more accountable networks. However, horizontal accountability does not replace vertical accountability and may, for instance, obstruct traditional forms of democratic accountability. Involving citizens in the preparation of proposals for physical planning projects may certainly contribute to the transparency, accountability, and legitimacy of these projects vis-à-vis stakeholders. This may, however, make it harder for elected politicians to reject these proposals, although they may have good reasons to do so—for instance because the projects will produce negative effects elsewhere, or give rise to wider concerns about public values or interests that are not taken into account. Therefore, in addition to enhancing horizontal accountability, ways to reconcile horizontal network processes and vertical accountability have to be considered. We now discuss this issue.

Designing Vertical Accountability of Governance Networks

The logic behind governance networks is that they provide flexibility and connect stakeholders with essential resources. Introducing strong vertical oversight and accountability will probably destroy most of the strong assets of governance networks. Nevertheless, within governance, vertical accountability needs to be arranged, since politicians and bureaucratic superiors remain important accountees and since horizontal accountability mechanisms have their limitations from a normative point of view (e.g. problems with representativeness).

Therefore, an important question is how vertical accountability mechanisms can be designed or strengthened in such a way that they do not hinder or disturb the governance network processes, while complementing and reinforcing horizontal accountability mechanisms.

In order to hold network actors accountable, politicians should take the complexities, interdependencies, and dynamics that characterize governance network processes into account. The *complex nature* of problems and policies with which governance networks deal makes it hard to formulate goals or frameworks ex ante. Politicians should be aware of their limited resources, their limitation in understanding the implications of policies, and the delicate set of values involved. The *dependencies* of government in governance networks make it hard to simply impose preconditions on actors. Negotiation and deliberation are required. The *dynamics* make it hard to set goals and frameworks up front and to stick to these conditions without regularly reconsidering and adapting them to new insights and changed circumstances. Flexibility, ongoing deliberation, and learning by both politicians and network actors are needed (Aucoin and Heintzman 2000; Considine 2002; Acar, Guo, and Yang 2008).

Since in practice accountability relationships between politicians and network actors are mostly implicit, governed by unshared expectations and informal rules, designing vertical accountability mechanisms includes arranging these relationships in an explicit way. Building on the requirements specified above, this design might include rules that respect the following principles:

- Address complexity by information processing. In order to overcome information setbacks, politicians should be informed on policy initiatives in a timely manner. This may require their participation in processes of policy formation within governance networks. Expectations about their roles should be made explicit, e.g. clarifying that participation does not automatically lead to the acceptance of outcomes. This rule will allow politicians to take an independent stance in the process of decision-making about goals and frameworks.

- Address complexity by accepting multiple standards and indicators. Holding governance networks accountable requires the specification of a framework of goals and requirements to guide the process. Given the complexity of problems and policies, goals and frameworks that will be used to hold governance networks accountable should not be restricted to one dimensional output or outcome indicators. On the other hand, "mushrooming" of indicators, or the exclusive use of qualitative intentions to act rather than quantitative result obligations, should be prevented, as these could give network actors the opportunity to shrink from accountability (De Bruijn 2007; Carter 1989). Here, a delicate balancing act is needed. Requirements should not be restricted to outcome indicators, but should also specify standards regarding accountable behavior within networks and what constitutes an accountable process.

• Address interdependencies by negotiating frameworks. Taking an independent stance does not mean simply imposing a framework on network actors. Rather, it seems sensible to negotiate such a framework, thus providing network actors with an incentive to give information on what they consider to be important goals and preconditions, creating opportunities to fine-tune conditions, and creating commitment to the accountability process. Of course, this does not exclude the possibility of using the shadow of hierarchy in these negotiations.

• Address interdependencies of accounters to other parties. Rules to guide the accountability process may include an agreement on the loose coupling of performance and sanctioning. If the "comply or explain" rule is accepted, room for deliberation is created while commitment is maintained. Explicitly introducing the right to explain helps to prevent blame games and generates conditions for learning (De Bruijn et al. 2010).

• Address dynamics by accepting adjustments. Given the dynamic nature of governance network processes, goals and preconditions cannot be set up front and remain unchanged during the process. They need to be readjusted and updated during the process (compare Van Kersbergen and Van Waarden 2004). In order to prevent the process from becoming non-binding, rules have to be formulated that stipulate the conditions under which the framework can be adapted. The "comply or explain" and exit rules are examples of such rules.

• Address dynamics by flexibility of accountees. Furthermore, by introducing practices such as public hearings at certain points in the governance network process, e.g., when impasses block these processes, politicians might bypass the problem of outdated ex ante policy frameworks and information overload, and invite participants to inform them, so that they can make an informed and tailor-made intervention in the horizontal process that will be considered legitimate by network actors and the outside world. However, this requires politicians to be committed to the governance network process and to refrain from attempts to realize electoral gains. Although there are known examples of these types of interventions, it is far from sure that they will be possible in any given situation (compare Koppenjan, Kars, and Van der Voorst 2011).

RESEARCH THEMES

When public policies and public services are decided upon and delivered in networks, accountability becomes more complicated than in case of traditional policymaking within government. In networks, various actors from within and outside government are involved, co-producing policies and services; this makes it hard to answer the question of who is accountable for what and to whom.

Accountability problems may relate to the relative closedness of networks towards elected politicians and bureaucratic superiors and towards the outside world: stakeholders, third parties, and the media. Accountability problems may also relate to the informal and loosely coupled nature of networks that lack clear accountability mechanisms and standards. Accountability problems may also result from the fact that the involvement of various actors from different domains and organizations entails the bringing together of various forms of horizontal and vertical accountability. This leads to complex accountability patchworks that are badly understood, encompass incompatible components, leave things uncovered, provide opportunities for shirking and opportunistic behavior, or result in confusion.

Despite these observations, there is no need for pessimism. Attempts to establish accountable networks can build on the various existing accountability mechanisms and standards. On the other hand, trying to change existing mechanisms and standards may prove more difficult than simply introducing new ones. The major challenge is to make existing accountability mechanisms and standards explicit and to initiate joint processes of design aimed at reconciling them. This difficult task is made even more difficult by the lack of research into accountability networks so far. The accountability mechanisms that are present in networks, the standards that are used, the roles that accounters and accountees fill, and the ways actors deal with accountability problems as identified in this contribution, are largely *terra incognita* and remain an important and actual research challenge. When it comes to governance networks, the research on accountability has only just started.

References

Acar, M., Guo, C., and Yang, K. 2008. "Accountability When Hierarchy is Absent: Views from Public-Private Partnership Practitioners." *American Review of Public Administration*, 38: 3–23.

Agranoff, R. and McGuire, M. 2003. *Collaborative Public Management: New Strategies for Local Governments*. Washington, D.C.: Georgetown University Press.

Aucoin, P. and Heintzman, R. 2000. "The Dialectics of Accountability for Performance in Public Management Reform." *International Review of Administrative Sciences*, 66: 45–55.

Ansell, C. and Gash, A. 2008. "Collaborative Governance in Theory and Practice." *Journal of Public Administration Research and Theory*, 18: 543–71.

Bennett, W. L. 2009. *News: The Politics of Illusion*. Eighth Edition. New York: Pearson Longman.

Bovens, M. A. P. 2006. *Analyzing and Assessing Public Accountability: A Conceptual Framework*. European Governance Papers, No. C-06-01. Retrieved from <http://dspace.library.uu.nl/handle/1874/234842>.

Carter, N. 1989. "Measuring Government Performance." *Political Quarterly*, 59: 369–75.

Considine, M. 2002. "The End of the Line? Accountable Governance in the Age of Networks, Partnerships and Joined-Up Service." *Governance*, 15: 21–40.

De Bruijn, J. A. 2007. *Managing Performance in the Public Sector*. London/New York: Routledge.

De Bruijn, J. A., ten Heuvelhof, E. F., and in 't Veld, R. J. 2010. *Process Management: Why Project Management Fails in Complex Decision Making Processes*. Heidelberg: Springer.

Edelenbos, J. 2005. "Institutional Implications of Interactive Governance." *Governance*, 18: 111–34.

Hanf, K. and Scharpf, F. W., eds. 1978. *Interorganizational Policy Making*. London: Sage.

Kersbergen, K. and Van Waarden, F. 2004. "Governance as Bridge Between Disciplines." *European Journal of Political Research*, 43: 143–71.

Klijn, E. H. and Koppenjan, J. F. M. 2000. "Politicians and Interactive Decision-Making: Institutional Spoilsports or Playmakers?" *Public Administration*, 78: 365–87.

Klijn, E. H. and Skelcher, C. K. 2007. "Democracy and Governance Networks: Compatible or Not? Four Conjectures and Their Implications." *Public Administration*, 85: 1–22.

Koliba, C., Meek, J. and Zia, A. 2010. *Governance Networks in Public Administration and Public Policy*. Boca Raton, F.L.: CRC Press/Taylor and Francis.

Koppenjan, J. F. M., Kars, M. and Van der Voort, H. 2011. Politicians as Meta-Governors: Can Metagovernance Reconcile Representative Democracy and Network Reality?, pp. 129–48 in *Interactive Policy Making, Metagovernance and Democracy*, eds. J. Torfing and P. Triantafillou. Colchester, U.K.: ECPR Press.

Koppenjan, J. and Klijn, E. H. 2004. *Managing Uncertainties in Networks: A Network Approach to Problem Solving and Decision-Making*. London: Routledge.

Korthagen, I. 2011. *The Soft Side of Hard News: The Biased Journalistic Construction of Complex Decision Making*. Paper presented at Netherlands Institute of Government Conference. Rotterdam: 1–2 December 2011.

Laumann, E. O. and Knoke, D. 1987. *The Organizational State: Societal Choice in National Policy Domains*. Wisconsin, W.I.: University of Wisconsin Press.

Marcussen, M. and Torfing, J., eds. 2007. *Democratic Network Governance in Europe*. Cheltenham: Edward Elgar.

Marsh, D. and Rhodes, R. A. W., eds. 1992. *Policy Networks in British Government*. Oxford: Clarendon Press.

Meier, K. and O'Toole, L. J. 2007. "Modeling Public Management: Empirical Analysis of the Management-Performance Nexus." *Public Administration Review*, 9: 503–27.

Newman, J. 2004. "Constructing Accountability: Network Governance and Managerial Agency." *Public Policy and Administration*, 19: 17–33.

Osborne, S. P. 2010. *The New Public Governance: Emerging Perspectives on the Theory and Practice of Public Governance*. London: Routledge.

Ostrom, E. 1990. *Governing the Commons: The Evolution of Institutions for Collective Action*. Cambridge: Cambridge University Press.

Patterson, T. E. 2000. *Doing Well and Doing Good: How Soft News and Critical Journalism Are Shrinking the News Audience and Weakening Democracy—and What News Outlets Can Do About It*. Boston, M.A.: Joan Shorenstein Center on the Press, Politics and Public Policy, Kennedy School of Government, Harvard University.

Pierre, J., ed. 2000. *Debating Governance: Authority Steering and Democracy*. Oxford: Oxford University Press.

Provan, K. G. and Kenis, P. 2008. "Modes of Network Governance: Structure, Management, and Effectiveness." *Journal of Public Administration Research and Theory*, 18: 229–52.

Rhodes, R. A. W. 1997. *Understanding Governance: Policy Networks, Governance, Reflexivity and Accountability*. Buckingham/Philadelphia: Open University Press.

Skelcher, C., Mathur, N. and Smith, M. 2005. "The Public Governance of Collaborative Spaces: Discourse, Design and Democracy." *Public Administration*, 83: 573–96.

Sørensen, E. and Torfing, J., eds. 2007. *Theories of Democratic Network Governance*. Cheltenham: Edward Elgar.

Torfing, J. and Triantafillou, P., eds. 2011. *Interactive Policy-Making, Meta-Governance and Democracy*. Colchester: ECPR Press.

Willems, T. and Van Dooren, W. 2011. "Lost in Diffusion? How Collaborative Arrangements Lead to an Accountability Paradox." *International Review of Administrative Sciences*, 77: 505–30.

....

CHAPTER 16

ACCOUNTABILITY AND CITIZEN PARTICIPATION

....

BODIL DAMGAARD AND JENNY M. LEWIS

INVOLVING CITIZENS IN ACCOUNTABILITY: WHY AND HOW?

IN democracies, electoral participation is the prime vehicle for making policy makers accountable to citizens. However, criticism has been mounting that electoral participation alone does not adequately fulfill this purpose and it has been argued that additional and direct channels of citizen participation in accountability are needed (e.g. Young 2000; Fung and Wright 2003). The potential for accountability gains by focusing on incorporating citizen perspectives and knowledge using more direct modes appears obvious, but it is much less clear how this can be done in meaningful ways. There have been surprisingly few systematic examinations of how citizen involvement might be integrated with accountability concerns despite the large scholarly interest in both issues. In particular, little has been achieved in describing how accountability mechanisms involving citizens might be designed so as to make the functioning of public services more accountable. Without the appropriate structures and processes in place, attempts to increase such participation might simply increase the level of activities that *appear* to make public services more accountable, without altering the fundamental dynamics between the governors and the governed.

In this chapter we set out to provide an analytical framework that will help to measure citizen participation in accountability beyond the fundamental mechanism of parliamentary elections. The normative premise is that citizen involvement in direct accountability mechanisms expands the notion of accountability as a virtue, as discussed by the editors of this volume in the introductory chapter. The virtue of participatory accountability mechanisms is not merely the accountability processes in and of themselves, but their participatory content and their democratic potential.

Just as accountability as a virtue rests on a number of core arguments, so does participation as a virtue. Granting citizens voice and exit options, it is argued, enhances responsiveness (a democratic argument) as well as improves policy accuracy and appropriateness (efficiency and effectiveness arguments). The increased demand for these desirable outcomes takes place against a background of new modes of governing that since the 1970s have spread around most of the Western world—New Public Management (NPM) and network governance. These both make substantial yet very different normative claims about citizen involvement. NPM thinking promotes the idea that citizens should be regarded as *consumers* or *customers* who have real choices available to them, and are able to make informed decisions about which services they use (Hood 1991). These consumers are seen to have the power to voice their concerns about public services, although mainly to exit to other services if those they are using are not performing as they should. Both exit and voice can point to underperformance, but voice provides information about the reasons for this, while exit only indicates a performance problem (Hirschman 1970; see also Dowding and John 2012). An exit-based mode of governing potentially gives greater influence to those receiving public services as people who can expect that their needs will be satisfied (like customers in a market).

In contrast, network governance casts citizens as potential *partners*. Departing from the observation that no one actor has the capability to reach desired policy outcomes alone (Kooiman 1993; 2003; Rhodes 1997), a large number of public and private actors are called upon to contribute to the policy process. As monolithic government organizations have been broken up into smaller units and many different actors have become involved in public service provision, space has been created for a potential expansion in the role for citizens in governing. They now have more opportunities to become engaged through a number of different channels, because the system provides more opportunities for non-state actors to become involved. Over the last decade there have been many deliberate attempts to engage a range of partners, including citizens, in new governance arrangements. Citizens as partners are not limited to exit options—they have voice options too.

Both of these new normatively grounded ideal typical roles for citizens—as consumers (in NPM) or as partners (in network governance)—have a range of possibilities attached. Both the more competitive (but not learning) relationship underlining the exit options of consumers in the NPM view, and the more collaborative (and learning) relationship supposed in the voice options of partners in the network governance view, allow citizens to oblige a public service actor to explain and justify his or her conduct. They can: "pose questions and pass judgment, and the actor may face consequences" (Bovens 2006, 9). Hence, either mode of governing might shift power to citizens, but equally neither of them might, depending on what participation actually entails in any specific case. This situation calls for an analytical framework which is able to assess what is actually going on; i.e. a framework not designed to capture arguments about participatory accountability as a virtue, but designed to evaluate empirical cases of accountability where citizen participation is included.

In this chapter we offer an analytical framework sensitive to the quality of citizen participation, which is measured in terms of transferred power from the governors to the citizens, and in terms of the degree to which citizens have access to accountability measures. We do this by combining Arnstein's (1969) classic ladder of participation with a focus on citizen participation in regard to *bureaucratic accountability*, centered on efficiency and learning (cf. Bovens et al. 2008). The learning aspect of bureaucratic accountability stressed by Bovens and his colleagues requires an exploration of how citizen participation—hailed in other organizational contexts for its contribution to learning (Fischer 2000)—may be combined with accountability. We leave aside the democratic and constitutional aspects of accountability (cf. Bovens et al. 2008) in order to create a framework that is both useable and not too complicated to apply to specific examples, in order to assess the level of citizen participation in accountability within them. Besides, new forms of citizen participation vis-à-vis democratic aspects of accountability is already a well-trodden field of research (e.g. Fung 2001, 2004; Fung and Wright 2003; Sørensen and Torfing 2005; Esmark 2007; Agger and Löfgren 2008). In addition, the constitutional aspects are less crucial for our purposes, because they essentially refer to procedures and structures of access which distract attention from the substance of the contribution of citizens.

Our focus is on situations where the actual effects of citizen participation can be observed and judgments about the characteristics of their participation can be made. The framework emerging from this combination allows us to assess the features of a given example of participatory accountability in terms of the quality of the participation and the extent of the accountability measures. We proceed by first presenting Arnstein's ladder of participation, then introducing our framework for assessing participatory accountability. This is followed by a discussion of some of the key tensions arising from incorporating the participation of citizens into the concept of accountability. These are too numerous to enumerate here, so we have chosen to focus on just four of them—the tension between accountability holders and holdees, the tension between the level of power and the scope of the issues, the tension between citizens' accountability at the individual and the collective level, and the tension that is generated by stretching the concept of accountability well beyond its original meaning, to include citizen participation. The chapter is wrapped up in a conclusion which discusses the usefulness of the framework and the need for expanding the concept of accountability from within its more traditional boundaries, if we are to view citizen participation as an important aspect of accountability. We use the term "citizen" throughout the chapter to refer to those who are governed. In the examples used in the section on tensions, we follow the use of the original authors and refer to "clients."

The Ladder of Participation

Beginning from the bottom up, Arnstein's first two rungs on the ladder are manipulation and therapy. She classifies both of these as non-participation, contrived as substitutes for genuine participation, where those with power attempt to educate or cure the participants. Manipulation occurs in cases where participants are placed on rubberstamp committees or advisory boards, or empty types of participation such as "information gathering" and "public relations." Therapy refers to cases where citizens are engaged in activities which are meant to educate them and divert them from the important issues.

The third rung on the ladder is informing, and the fourth is consultation. Citizens may hear and be heard at these two tokenistic levels, but they lack the power to have their views taken seriously by those who make the decisions. Participation here is a restricted step towards full participation, because the exchange occurs essentially from officials to citizens (for example, through the news media, pamphlets, and posters) and citizens have no negotiating power. Meetings can also be used in this way, and consultation can also be tokenistic when participants' ideas are not taken into account. Attitude surveys, neighborhood meetings, and public hearings can all be used in this manner. Placation (the fifth rung) is a higher level of tokenism where participants do have some degree of influence. Citizens can advise, but they have no right to decide. When boards include very few citizens, and their rights and responsibilities are ill-defined and unclear, participation is limited and decisions are made by the many (or elsewhere).

Partnership is the sixth rung of the ladder and here citizens begin to have genuine decision-making powers, as they can negotiate and engage in trade-offs. When there is "an organized power-base in the community to which the citizen leaders are accountable" (Arnstein 1969, 221), and where they have resources, this can be effective. Genuine partnerships in Arnstein's classification are those in which the citizens can initiate plans as well as work on them. As her language signifies, it is only beginning at this level that citizens are on a footing that means they can hold officials to account.

Delegated power and citizen control are the top two rungs of Arnstein's ladder. Here, the participants either have a majority of decision-making seats or full managerial control: "citizens hold the significant cards to assure accountability of the program to them" (1969, 222). An alternative model of delegated power is for separate groups of citizens and officials to meet in parallel, but with citizens holding veto power over decisions. Full control, the top rung of the ladder, is where citizens can govern a program, be in full charge of policy and management, and negotiate the conditions under which others may change them. There is real accountability at these two levels of participation.

Arnstein's paper was written at the height of the community development movement in the US and reflects the particular concerns in that country at that time. Four decades later and outside the American context, we argue that Arnstein is a useful foundation for several reasons. First, her ladder has become a classic statement on citizen participation and is still widely referred to. Second, although her examples are about a different time, the basic dynamics of what she is describing are fairly universal. It is about those people who traditionally are not involved in governing being included in some manner. Third, her ladder provides a classification which demonstrates the many and significant gradations of participation with a convincing description of the differences between them. Although there have been some more recent variations on her classification (for example, Connor 1988; Bruns 2003), the basic elements of it remain. Fourth, the governance changes over the last four decades outlined earlier have made a classification of participation even more useful.

Arnstein's premise that the best outcome is citizen control can sit comfortably with the NPM governing mode, where customers are able to demand what they want in a (quasi-) market. However, citizen power takes on other connotations viewed from the perspective of network governance, because the end-goal of the engagement of citizens in policy making is not citizens' control over the state but the *collaborative* effort to produce a given output. The sharp division between the governors and the governed implicit in Arnstein's thinking becomes fuzzy under network governance and the ultimate goal of citizens' power *over* the state makes less sense as this implies power over the citizenry itself. Or phrased differently: Participatory governance makes citizens appear on both sides of the equation as both holders and holdees of accountability. Some scholars have already proposed solutions to this Gordian knot, e.g. Esmark (2007), who from a post-liberal democracy perspective argues for tying accountability to representatives of functional interest groups that serve as account holders. While identifying functional interest groups and assuring their representatives access to accountability measures may be part of a solution in some cases, we argue that a further assessment of the nature of the problem is needed to discover and explore other workable solutions. To this end we turn to our analysis of participatory governing and accountability.

A FRAMEWORK FOR CITIZEN PARTICIPATION IN ACCOUNTABILITY

One way to build an analytical framework designed to examine the quality of participatory accountability is to combine Arnstein's ladder of participation and her notion that citizen participation is measured by the redistribution of power from the powerful to the powerless (i.e. citizens) with Bovens's (2006) above-cited definition of accountability. Doing so allows for an assessment at one point in time of participatory accountability in empirical settings according to the degree that citizens are enabled to oblige an accountee to explain or justify his or her conduct, pose questions and pass judgment, and define and apply possible consequences. The framework of participatory accountability presented here includes an implicit recognition of participation as a virtue. While Arnstein would probably only classify the top three rungs of her ladder as genuinely representing cases where governors can be held to account by citizens, the partnerships and co-production that exist in many contemporary governing situations have led us to view levels further down as also providing (limited) accountability. And, as we shall see, participatory accountability at the highest levels poses specific tensions to the notion of accountability.

Table 16.1 presents our framework of citizen participation in accountability, which consists of five levels. The bars have been set slightly differently to Arnstein's, whose rungs have been included in the table for comparison. Beginning from the lowest level,

Table 16.1 Five levels of citizen participation in accountability

Levels of participation and descriptions of accountability activities *Italics indicate forward looking activities*		Arnstein's ladder of participation	
Joint ownership	*Set the agenda (policy making)* *Define correction/innovation to ensure effectiveness and responsiveness* • Define and apply consequences • Pass judgment (full range) • Pose specific questions	Citizen control	Citizen power
Collaboration	*Impact the agenda (services delivered)* • Pass judgment (full range) • Pose specific questions	Delegated power	
Advice	*Impact the setting or change the standards monitored* • Pass judgment (limited range) • Pose specific questions	Partnership	
Involvement	Monitor the processes • Pose specific questions	Placation	Tokenism
	Discuss the issues (place at the table) • Pose general questions	Consultation	
"Education"	Receive information • One-way communication	Informing	
	Subjects of persuasion • Non-participation	Therapy	Non-participation
	Subjects of misinformation • Non-participation	Manipulation	

"*Education*"—notably in inverted commas—represents the case in which citizens passively receive information from the account giver. This information may be purposefully misleading, targeted to cause acceptance (persuasion), or objectively trustworthy. However in each of these three cases, there are no related channels or forums in which the citizens may react to the information given except on the individual level by exiting as discussed above (see Bosman et al. 2008 for an example). The *participatory* aspect of such account giving is therefore insignificant and contains no aspect of learning through citizen involvement. It is however worth noting that accountability measures in this category may be essential on other dimensions; performance measures used for organizational steering or statistics available for scrutiny by policy analysts or journalists are obvious examples often made public through statistical services hosted by national, regional, and local governments or directly by the delivering agencies.

Involvement is the second level in this framework. At this level the accountability measures include a forum in which citizens have access to discuss the information given, monitor processes at their own initiatives, and pose either general or more specific questions that the account giver would be obliged to answer. There are plenty of examples of accountability at this level, for instance when parents in school boards are invited to debate a school's budget, but have no—or at least only indirect—influence on the number of pupils in each class and the hiring and firing of staff, not to mention curriculum priorities and pedagogical approaches. The limited direct powers granted to citizens (the parents in this example) in these situations may contribute in an important way to accountability, by showing popular (parental) backing to a chosen (school) policy. Many providers of public services would dread a situation in which such backing was absent, regardless of the lack of formal powers involved. Studies on the activities of UK school governing boards (for example, Farrell 2005) suggest however that the participation of these boards rarely exceeds what in our framework would amount to the involvement level.

For the third level—*advice*—informal means of influence are exchanged for more formal powers. At this level, citizens are actively participating in holding account givers to account by posing specific questions on performance, and are granted the formal power of passing judgment. What is more significant regarding the participatory aspect is that at this rung citizens are able to have an impact on the setting of the services delivered and contribute to making decisions on which standards should be used to measure and monitor services. Judging from a general overview of the performance measurement literature, citizens are noticeably absent when it comes to the processes of selecting permanent key performance measures. It is not unusual, continuing with the school board example, that the parents on the board may decide to ask for new types of information on an ad hoc basis, such as the pupils' grade point averages (perhaps categorized by subjects, or cross-checked with different teachers, or compared to other schools) or how many pupils continue on and to which type of further education. The demand for some of these indicators will be tied to specific one-time circumstances while others may signal a new concern on part of the parents and will become part of a new standard set of indicators monitored.

Collaboration, the fourth level, is where judgment on policy outcomes and performance is now jointly in the hands of the participating citizens and the service. The major difference between this level and *advice* lies in the ability of citizens to influence the policy agenda and change the services delivered. Citizens in such schemes are co-responsible for determining which services are being produced. This means that the judgments passed on the outcomes will include judgments on issues that the citizens themselves have participated in formulating. Continuing with the school analogy, at this level the citizens would be able to have input to decisions on the choice of pedagogical approaches, in collaboration with the teachers. The set-up and functioning of citizen participation in Chicago elementary school boards examined by Fung (2001; 2004) is an example of the type of collaboration we would find at the fourth level.

As we reach the fifth and final level, which we have labeled *joint ownership*, the inseparability between the account holders and account holdees becomes a prime characteristic. At this level participating citizens not only pose questions and pass judgment but also define and apply possible sanctions; i.e. play a part in all aspects of holding someone to account. But at this level citizen participation also concerns formulating and deciding future policies in a broad sense as well as pinpointing correctional and/or innovative steps on specific issues and services. The parents in our school example are now in a position to hire and fire teachers and change the curriculum if they are unhappy with the performance of the school, or if they want to see a different set of priorities in place. The term "joint ownership" points to using voice to suggest improvements. This is not because the exit option excludes learning per se—providers of public services may well become aware of models of services that do not work and change behavior as a reaction to exit. Rather, the new behavior resulting from voice will come from direct involvement by the recipients of the service, rather than simply the providers' interpretation of what exit indicates about their services. What is intriguing at this level is that, by their involvement in policy making, the participating citizens appear on both sides of the accountability equation both as account givers and account holders. While policy making and the delivery of public services through joint ownership are on the rise, most of these examples do not have, or have only superficially, built-in accountability measures. One British example of joint ownership is the Caterham Barracks Community Trust (CBCT)—used by Bovaird (2007) as an example of "community governance." A complex participatory and deliberative process led to the production of a "local view" of how a former military area could be regenerated into affordable housing and subsequently the actual regeneration process was overseen by the CBCT. The trust itself is being held accountable by a number of individual and organizational charitable trustees drawn from the community.[1]

TENSIONS IN PARTICIPATORY ACCOUNTABILITY

Our analytical framework reveals a number of questions and tensions at the various levels of citizens' participation in accountability, particularly the topmost one, as well as with the framework itself. We devote the remainder of the chapter to a discussion of four of the most obvious tensions arising, with some tentative first steps towards formulating possible means for easing them. The first tension concerns the dual role of participating citizens, functioning as both account holders and holdees and possible ways of living with the inherent paradox of this. The second deals with the scope of the issues to which an actor may be held to account by participating citizens. We discuss and question the apparent inverse relationship between citizens' power to hold an actor to account and the scope of the issues covered by the account mechanism. The third tension is that of distinguishing between citizens as individuals or as part of a community and its implications for accountability measures. Finally, we address the problem of the stretching of the notion of accountability that consideration of some forms of citizen participation seems to imply.

Being Holder and Holdee at the Same Time: Keeping Oneself to Account?

At the three highest levels of our framework (joint ownership, collaboration, and advice) we implicitly accept that learning is part of accountability, and so more backward-looking notions of accountability are transformed into forward-looking policy-making activities. Learning from audits, complaints, and other accountability mechanism inherently implies framing the problem in new ways and formulating new solutions. Learning from participatory accountability activities implies that the involved citizens take part not only in setting and applying sanctions ex post, but in framing problems and conceiving ways to tailor, correct, and improve inadequate performance and service delivery ex ante.

Involving citizens as co-designers or co-producers of public services also makes citizens co-responsible and it becomes impossible to make a clear distinction between those who govern and those who are governed. This inseparability has consequences for Arnstein's notion of citizen control and likewise for our notion of citizen power, since citizens in the role of "those who are governed" are asked to exercise control over themselves as governors. Here we have a dilemma. If we reject measures that fall short of transferring powers to the citizens (as held by Arnstein) when modeling citizen involvement, we "limit [...] the potential for sharing experience, knowledge and the harnessing of multiple perspectives inherent in successful user involvement" as Tritter and Callum (2006, 166) warn. Yet if we introduce measures along these lines, how are the involved citizens kept accountable?

In fact, a number of measures—which appear to be gaining popularity—aim to deal with this dilemma. Drawing on ideas that align with Teubner's (1983; 1993) work on reflexive law, thoughts on self- and meta-governance (e.g. Sørensen and Triantafillou 2011; Torfing et al. 2012), and coined more specifically by Fung (2001; 2004) as "accountable autonomy," cases of citizen participation are increasingly being met with a variety of requirements that on the one hand seek to empower participants and enhance self-governing capacities, and on the other hand seek to promote and assure self-restraining and self-regulating capacities. A delicate dance results from such efforts aimed at tapping into the energy and knowledge that comes with citizen participation, while at the same time securing certain standards and steering the participation. Requirements established to boost accountability of participatory governing can be both procedural and substantial. Obliging citizens to reflect upon their involvement in a given co-governing situation once a year would be an example of a procedural measure, which could be further adapted to make the participants reflect on specific issues (e.g. finances, outcomes, user satisfaction, etc.). Another example of a procedural measure would be to require that co-governing boards and similar groups document the way in which deliberation processes are conducted. Fung (2001; 2004) provides an example of Chicago school boards along these lines. Importantly, these accountability measures do not decide on particular outcomes. They are similar to means used to further corporate social responsibility (Barnard, Deaking and Hobbs 2004; Buhmann 2011) which admittedly are not precisely an issue for citizen participation, but they do share common features regarding the accountability issues.

Scope of Participatory Accountability

A second issue that arises from our analytical framework concerns the question of *what* the participating citizens may hold a public service provider to account for. By definition, as we ascend through the levels of participation, the involvement of citizens increases, but what happens to the scope of the issues dealt with?

Empirical examples of participatory accountability measures appear to indicate that as we ascend the ladder, the *scope* of the issues to which citizens in client panels and the like may hold an actor to account appears to narrow. Hence, citizens may be able to pose questions, pass judgment as well as define and apply possible consequences, and even to define correctional or innovative steps to ensure effectiveness and responsiveness and set the broader policy agenda—but for increasingly narrow issues. Linhorst, Eckert, and Hamilton (2005) provide an illustration of this trade-off in a study of client participation in a psychiatric hospital. Their study uncovers a number of formal and informal means of client participation most of which enable clients to discuss general issues and to pose general and specific questions about the services offered at the hospital. These measures, albeit broad in scope, did not provide clients with direct power to sanction anyone or to change any procedures. Yet one measure—a performance improvement system—did actually provide clients (in collaboration with staff) with powers to decide on specific hospital policies and operating procedures. However, the issues treated under this measure were very narrow in scope, e.g., dealing with scheduling clients' medical appointments and improving safety measures for clients and staff working in the hospital's warehouse (2005, 25). Another example is the recent significant widening of complaint issues for Danish public healthcare patients. Earlier, complaints could only be related to the malpractice of a named individual while since 2010 complaints may concern erroneous treatment following inadequate planning, coordination, or communication. This amounts to malpractice by the whole *system* and not by a specific individual (Conradsen 2011). However, as Conradsen shows, patients are excluded from the forums in which corrective measures are discussed and decided upon.

A few empirical examples do not document a trend, yet we have found no empirical example in which the extent of accountability measures (the power of the citizens) is not inversely related to the scope of the issues for which an actor can be held to account. While such an inverse relationship is neither surprising nor alarming in itself, it does raise some questions. One is who is to determine whether an issue is "big" or "small." Elderly citizens participating in a board governing an aged care home may be granted substantial power on issues of staffing and investments, yet really only be fully interested in the quality of the food and coffee. More broadly this leads to question about Arnstein's fundamental premise that citizens—always—want more power and influence. Supposing that the elderly in the example are granted power to decide on the quality of food and drinks, what should make them invest time and efforts in participating in governing issues when the risk of being blamed as co-responsible for unpopular decisions is likely to be larger than any gratitude from their peers (their constituency)?

Citizens as Individuals or Collective Entities

Arnstein perceives citizens as part of collective entities such as neighborhoods, parents' associations, and farmers' cooperatives and citizen power is implicitly understood as a transfer of power to collective entities composed of citizens. Yet in empirical examples of participatory accountability citizens as collective entities are most typically found on the lower rungs of participation, where their powers are limited to that of being informed or, at best, being able to pose general questions to the account giver. Citizen boards seldom hold the power to impose sanctions, define correctional steps, and so on, except perhaps on very limited issues as discussed just above.

However, inspired by new public management thinking, steps have been taken in many areas and in many countries that grant the individual power to pose sanctions on a service provider in the form of exit options. Voucher systems have enabled parents to have a choice of school for their children (at least in theory, see Mumm 1993); the elderly have increasingly been granted a choice between providers of elderly care and experiments have been undertaken with "individual budgeting" leaving decisions with the elderly recipients on what, where, and when to buy services (Newman et al. 2008); the sick may have their choice of hospital (even in some cases private or foreign) even when these services are paid for by public funding. While exit is the ultimate sanction against a service provider, our analytical framework does not catch that kind of individual power and is clearly skewed towards collective participation by citizens.

The discussion of individual versus collective citizen participation in accountability measures poses a dilemma that is ultimately a political one. The methodological individualism inherent in NPM thinking suggests the construction of accountability measures granting powers (particularly exit powers) to the individual, supposing future development to be driven by competitive forces reacting upon the aggregated behavior by individuals. The notion of interdependence between actors embedded in network governance suggests the construction of accountability measures granting powers to collective entities of citizens supposing future development to be driven by voice and collaboration.

As accountability measures, voice and collaboration involve a time span that does not exist in the binary exit option. Thus, while individual exit options may be considered a very powerful accountability tool, in the long run repeated collaboration and voicing—even on lower rungs of the participatory accountability ladder—may potentially lead to more influence over how and under which conditions public services are provided, particularly if and when choice is not a real option (Mumm 1993; Farrell and Jones 1999).

Accountability with Citizen Participation—Stretched Too Far?

As Mulgan (2000) described, the concept of accountability seems to be an ever-expanding one. His description of this includes that it has been expanded in four ways beyond its traditional meaning of calling actors to account. The first of these is that it is now applied to internal agonizing rather than external reckoning, and shifts the focus to the individual responsibility of officials. The second is its meaning as institutional mechanisms for controlling officials' behavior, which is centered on control rather than accountability as one means for enforcing control. The third and fourth ways that accountability has been expanded are more relevant to the current discussion. These are that it now includes making officials responsive to their political masters and to public wishes by means other than simply calling them to account (voice), and that it also stands for a democratic dialogue with citizens where no one is being called to account (Mulgan 2000).

Accountability as responsiveness to elected politicians implies an accounting to the public through accounting to their directly elected representatives. Accountability as responsiveness to clients of services is analogous to private firms being sensitive to consumer demands, and renders agencies directly accountable to the public. Mulgan argues that both of these confuse the notion of accountability with popular demands. Making services more responsive provides incentives for providers to consider the wishes of their clients, but while this may improve services, it does not necessarily mean that they have become more accountable. In a competitive market, consumers can exit to an alternative provider, but rarely do they have an opportunity to voice what they would rather have.

The fourth extension of accountability to incorporate a notion of dialogue refers to seeing accountability as a dialectical activity where officials have to answer, explain, and justify their actions in open discussion and debate (Mulgan 2000). It has therefore come to be seen as linked to deliberative democracy where officials are forced to engage in some form of dialogue with the public. However, there is a key difference between accountability and deliberative democracy, in that there is an unequal relationship of superior and subordinate, where the latter takes direction from the former, in the core meaning of accountability. "The dialogue of accountability occurs between parties in an authority relationship and can only be understood in the context of that relationship" (Mulgan 2000, 570). He concludes that both analytical clarity and citizens' rights might be better served by keeping the concept of accountability within tighter limits.

The implications of this for an examination of accountability and citizen participation appear to be in opposition to using Arnstein's upper rungs of the ladder as representing accountability. This is partly a difference in focus: Arnstein was not writing about accountability but about citizen power. The concern here is with the role of citizens in accountability, rather than citizen control over the state. However, it is also a more substantive difference in creating a framework for accountability that is explicitly focused on participation by clients of services or citizens more broadly. But this provides a significant clue about why there are so few examples of citizen participation in accountability at the level of joint ownership. It is new and difficult territory for both governors and citizens. It also appears to be rife with contradictions when it is set against more common views of accountability that see a clear distinction between accountors and accountees. Pollitt's (2003, 89) claim that all definitions of accountability agree that it is about "a relationship in which one party, the 'accountor', recognizes an obligation to explain and justify their conduct to another, the 'accountee'," is in contrast with Behn's (2001) notion that accountability is now much more complicated than this dyadic relation. Yet even Behn does not include citizens in his list of those that people are now accountable to—bosses, subordinates, peers, team members, customers, and suppliers. We conclude that the concept of accountability must necessarily be stretched if citizen participation is to be genuinely included within it.

Using the Framework of Citizen Participation in Accountability

By integrating Arnstein's ladder of citizen participation with more current concerns about accountability and involvement, we have created a framework for classifying types of citizen participation in accountability. The five broad levels outlined—from education (least participation) through involvement, advice, collaboration, and finally, joint ownership (most participation)—provide a means for categorizing specific examples of service delivery and the participation of citizens, on a scale which considers the scope of participation by citizens in accountability. Some examples illustrate how this might be used, but only the inclusion and analysis of many more examples (which is beyond the scope of this chapter) will provide a true test of the utility of this framework.

However, we also hope that this framework is not just useful, but also logically sustainable as a means for deciding what kind of participation is actually in place in any specific example of public service delivery, and how much accountability this implies. For this to be the case, it is necessary to extend the notion of accountability beyond one that renders it as necessarily an authority relationship as some argue, to one where it is at least hypothetically possible for the governors and the governed to be joint owners. Again, we emphasize that empirical testing of this framework with a range of contemporary examples should yield evidence about whether this is over-stretching the concept of accountability, or an essential step to take if the idea of citizen participation is to be taken seriously.

Note

1. see <www.caterhambarracks.org.uk/Membership.html>.

REFERENCES

Agger, A. and Löfgren, K. 2008. "Democratic Assessment of Collaborative Planning Processes." *Planning Theory*, 7: 145–64.

Arnstein, S. 1969. "A Ladder of Citizen Participation." *Journal of the American Planning Association*, 35: 216–24.

Barnard, C., Deakin, S., and Hobbs, R. 2004. *Reflexive Law, Corporate Social Responsibility and the Evolution of Labour Standards: The Case of Working Time*. ESCR Centre for Business Research Working Paper, No. 294. University of Cambridge.

Behn, R. 2001. *Rethinking Democratic Accountability*. Washington, DC: Brookings Institution.

Bosman, R., Bours, G. J. J. W., Engels, J., and de Witte, L. P. 2008. "Client-Centred Care Perceived by Clients of Two Dutch Homecare Agencies: A Questionnaire Survey." *International Journal of Nursing Studies*, 45: 518–25.

Bovaird, T. 2007. "Beyond Engagement and Participation: User and Community Coproduction of Public Services." *Public Administration Review*, 67: 846–60.

Bovens, M. 2006. *Analysing and Assessing Public Accountability: A Conceptual Framework*. European Governance Papers (EUROGOV), No. C-06-01. Retrieved from <http://dspace.library.uu.nl/handle/1874/234842>.

Bovens, M., Schillemans, T., and 't Hart, P. 2008. "Does Public Accountability Work? An Assessment Tool." *Public Administration*, 86: 225–42.

Bruns, B. 2003. *Water Tenure Reform: Developing an Extended Ladder of Participation: Politics of the Commons*. In RCSD (Regional Center for Social Science and Sustainable Development) Conference, *Articulating Development and Strengthening Local Practices*. Chiang Mai, Thailand, 11-14 July 2003.

Buhmann, K. 2011. "Reflexive Regulation of CSR: A Case Study of Public-Policy Interests in EU Public-Private Regulation of CSR." *International and Comparative Corporate Law Journal*, 8: 38–76.

Connor, D. D. 1988. "A New Ladder of Citizen Participation." *National Civic Review*, 77: 248–57.

Conradsen, I. M. 2011. "The End of Administrative Appeal? The Case of the Danish National Agency for Patients' Complaints and Patients' Rights". *Proceedings of the Annual Meeting of Permanent Study Group for Law And Public Administration*, eds. D. C. Dragos, F. Lafarge and P. Willumsen. Bucharest: Editura Economica.

Dowding, K. and John, P. 2012. *Exits, Voices and Social Investment: Citizens' Reaction to Public Services*. Cambridge: Cambridge University Press.

Esmark, A. 2007. Democratic Accountability and Network Governance: Problems and Potentials, pp. 274–96 in *Theories of Democratic Network Governance*, eds. E. Sørensen and J. Torfing. Basingstoke: Palgrave MacMillan.

Farrell, C. M. 2005. "Governance in the UK Public Sector: The Involvement of the Governing Board." *Public Administration*, 83: 89–110.

Farrell, C. M. and Jones, J. 1999. "Evaluating Stakeholder Participation in Public Services—Parents and Schools." *Policy & Politics*, 28: 251–62.

Fischer, F. 2000. *Citizens, Experts and the Environment: The Politics of Local Knowledge*. Durham, NC: Duke University Press.

Fung, A. 2001. "Accountable Autonomy: Toward Empowered Deliberation in Chicago Schools and Policing." *Politics & Society*, 29: 73–101.

Fung, A. 2004. *Empowered Participation: Reinventing Urban Democracy*. Princeton: Princeton University Press.

Fung, A. and Wright, E. O. 2003. *Deepening Democracy: Institutional Innovations in Empowered Participatory Governance*. London: Verso.

Hirschman, A. O. 1970. *Exit, Voice, and Loyalty: Responses to Decline in Firms, Organizations, and States*. Cambridge, MA: Harvard University Press.

Hood, C. 1991. "A Public Management for All Seasons?" *Public Administration*, 69: 3–19.

Kooiman, J., ed. 1993. *Modern Governance: New Government-Society Interactions*. London: Sage.

Kooiman, J. 2003. *Governing as Governance*. London: Sage.

Linhorst, D., Eckert, A., and Hamilton, G. 2005. "Promoting Participation in Organizational Decision Making by Clients with Severe Mental Illness." *Public Health*, 50: 21–30.

Mulgan, R. 2000. "'Accountability': An Ever Expanding Concept?" *Public Administration*, 78: 555–73.

Mumm, P., ed. 1993. *Parents and Schools: Customers, Managers or Partners?* London: Routledge.

Newman, J., Glendinning, C., and Hughes, M. 2008. "Beyond Modernisation? Social Care and the Transformation of Welfare Governance." *Journal of Social Policy*, 34: 531–57.

Pollitt, C. 2003. *The Essential Public Manager*. Maidenhead: Open University Press.

Rhodes, R. A. W. 1997. *Understanding Governance: Policy Networks, Governance, Reflexivity and Accountability*. Buckingham: Open University Press.

Sørensen, E. and Torfing, J. 2005. "The Democratic Anchorage of Governance Networks." *Scandinavian Political Studies*, 28: 195–218.

Sørensen, E. and Triantafillou, P., eds. 2011. *The Politics of Self-Governance*. Farnham: Ashgate.

Teubner, G. 1983. "Substantive and Reflexive Elements in Modern Law." *Law & Society Review*, 17: 239–86.

Teubner, G. 1993. *Law as an Autopoietic System*. Oxford: Blackwell.

Torfing, J., Peters, B. G., Pierre, J., and Sørensen, E. 2012. *Interactive Governance: Advancing the Paradigm*. Oxford: Oxford University Press.

Tritter, J. Q. and McCallum, A. 2006. "The Snakes and Ladders of User Involvement: Moving Beyond Arnstein." *Health Policy*, 76: 156–68.

Young, I. M. 2000. *Inclusion and Democracy*. Oxford: Oxford University Press.

CHAPTER 17

ACCOUNTABILITY AND MULTI-LEVEL GOVERNANCE

YANNIS PAPADOPOULOS

WHAT IS MULTI-LEVEL GOVERNANCE?

COOPERATION in policy-making among governmental levels as well as between public and non-public actors is described as a shift from "government" to "governance." "Governance" in this rather narrow meaning refers to a process of formulating or implementing collectively binding decisions by *networks* involving public actors (politicians and administrators) together with non-public actors of different natures (firms, interest representatives and stakeholders, and experts): "Fundamentally, a network can be defined as a group of goal-oriented interdependent but autonomous actors that come together to produce a collective output (tangible or intangible) that no one actor could produce on its own" (Isett et al. 2011, 161). Instead of hierarchical steering by the state, deliberation, bargaining, and compromise-seeking are the main *modi operandi* in governance networks.

With "downward" devolution and decentralization, and the "upward" Europeanization or, more broadly, internationalization of policy-making, governance is today frequently coupled to "multi-levelness," a characteristic that one encounters first in federalist systems divided into different levels of government. This means that policy-making requires the cooperation of distinct governmental levels (local, subnational/regional, national, European, transnational), in what one might be tempted to call, rather, multi-level gov-ern*ment*. But particular policies such as European Union (EU) structural and regional policies exemplify multi-level gover*nance*, as they are based on both the cooperation of public actors across levels *and* on cooperation with non-public actors in partnership forms.[1] The emphasis of the concept of multilevel governance is, thus, on the growing importance of horizontal and vertical interdependence between policy-making actors, especially in the context of European and transnational integration (Bache and Chapman 2008, 398). An illustration of the combination of "multi-levelness" and network governance is provided by the fact that subnational governments have an interest in showing to national and supranational authorities that they stand close to civil society actors to prove the authenticity of their representational claims (Piattoni 2009, 174).

Blanco et al. (2011, 304) note that the literature on governance networks "conceives the spread of networks and partnerships as part of a strategy to open up decision-making processes to interest groups and to citizens themselves." The present chapter explains, however, why such a spread can have an impact on the democratic accountability of decision-makers that is not necessarily positive. Accountability is viewed here, in line with the definition provided by the editors of this handbook, as a social mechanism: a relation in which an agent can be held to account by another agent and face consequences (see also Bovens 2007). Democratic accountability in representative government is the accountability of decision-makers to the electorate. The normative attractiveness of this form of accountability relies on the existence of a direct line upward from "we the people" to government and downward from government to society (Hupe and Edwards 2012). However, with multi-level governance, this kind of straightforward relationship is undermined. This chapter seeks to identify the properties of multi-level governance that can be responsible for that and concludes that accountable multi-level governance should not be equated with democratic government.

THE PROBLEMATIC "DEMOCRATIC ANCHORAGE" OF NETWORK FORMS OF GOVERNANCE

Networks can be analytical constructs that researchers use as a metaphor to describe the more or less dense relations linking a set of individual or organized actors. Although the metaphorical use of the "network" concept has been criticized (Dowding 1995), multi-level networks involved in policy-making are empirically detectable (Slaughter 2004). They range from networks composed of administrative actors in charge of informal negotiations between governmental units belonging to distinct decisional levels in federalist systems (Bolleyer 2009) to formalized networks of regulators in a supranational polity such as the European Union, associating national regulatory authorities with EU-level actors (typically members of the Commission or a European agency).[2]

According to Sørensen and Torfing (2009),[3] the democratic anchorage of network forms of governance should be ensured if they display the following attributes:

- control by elected politicians
- accountability of actors participating as representatives of collective interests

- possibility of critical scrutiny and contestation by stakeholders
- broad inclusiveness and procedural fairness.

Such a democratic anchorage of multi-level forms of governance should not be taken for granted. An obvious reason is that multi-level settings may involve the supra- or transnational level, characterized by a deficit of democratic accountability.[4] However, it can also be hypothesized that a number of other reasons also undermine the democratic accountability of multi-level governance, and they are presented below.[5]

The Cooperative Logic of Multi-Level Negotiations

Hooghe and Marks (2003) distinguish between two types of multi-level governance. Type I governance has a strong resemblance to federalism: it refers to the dispersion of authority to general-purpose, non-intersecting, and durable jurisdictions. Type II governance presents a picture that is more complex and fluid. Governance functions are performed by a vast number of jurisdictions that are task-specific, may overlap with each other, and tend to be flexible to adjust to problem-solving imperatives. Types I and II are not exclusive: Formal institutions of government create special-purpose bodies to carry out particular tasks such as water provision, public transportation, health care, etc. Usually, it is the growth of Type II multi-level governance bodies that leads to concerns with regard to democratic accountability (Bache and Chapman 2008). Type I governance is part of the circuit of representative democracy, whereas Type II governance, which is more network-like, tends to be decoupled from it, most notably because it tends to escape control by elected politicians (see also Koppell in this volume).

However, even Type I governance impacts democratic accountability, although it remains governance by elected politicians. In spite of the formal division of competencies between decisional levels, several competencies overlap across them, and the resources for effective policy-making must be pooled from different levels as well. Interdependence entails the risk of mutual vetoes leading to suboptimal agreements on the lowest common denominator: the "joint decision trap" problem (Scharpf 1988). This problem can be overcome if the involved elected governments display a cooperative attitude (Benz 1998). However, this weakens their democratic accountability: Mutual deliberation and negotiation are possible only if those involved are not tightly constrained by the demands of their democratic "principals" (citizens or parliaments). These problems due to the extension of the chain of delegation are amplified by the fact that intergovernmental negotiations are prepared by administrators who can enjoy considerable discretion too.

Further, even democratically accountable governments will be only accountable on paper for their participation in intergovernmental policy coordination if the account-holders lack information. Only those who are close to negotiators are aware of the meanders of intergovernmental negotiations and, because several actors are involved in often opaque negotiated decision-making, it is also hard to decipher who is responsible to what degree for which part of what (Considine and Afzal 2011, 376). This is the well-known "problem of many hands" (Thompson 1980) or "paradox of shared responsibility" (Bovens 1998, 45–52): It becomes easier to evade justifications for poor performance because actors can engage in "blame-shift games" (Hood 2007, 200).

On the other hand, the relevant literature has also identified the reverse problem, which is caused by insufficient network pluralism. Networks may be subject to closure, and their members are likely to collude, erect barriers to outsider control and participation (Lord 2004, 114), and resort to self-serving "club-type rulemaking" (Koppell 2010, 172). Network pluralism is, thus, a variable; a classic distinction is between closed and cohesive "policy communities" and more open and fluid "issue networks" (Marsh and Rhodes 1992). There is, however, a trade-off. Pluralism remedies problems of imperfect representation, but it may aggravate problems of accountability due to the dilution of responsibility. Finally, participants in negotiations are themselves caught in an accountability dilemma: They must satisfy multiple account-holders with different preferences. "Multi-levelness" can be a resource for playing one level against another (Putnam 1988), but it is a constraint as well. Even actors who are directly subject to the control of their electorates are, in reality, subject to multi-level accountability—they must account for their actions not only to their constituencies but also to their negotiation partners. The latter constraint can be expected to prevail whenever democratic "principals" (citizens but also MPs) lack information that makes them vigilant (see below). Furthermore, even if accountability holders are able to open up the "black box" of negotiations, their representatives therein can still justify shifts in their preferences through the need to consider claims and menaces made by their partners.

The Weak Visibility of Governance Networks

Visibility is a necessary condition for accountability: If the account-holders are not informed about the actions of the accountees, they will lack sufficient information to evaluate these actions in a reflexive manner.[6] Apart from the aforementioned "problem of many hands," basically two factors make what happens in policy networks hardly visible to outsiders: the lack of formalization of networks and the privatization of some governance activities (with policy-making power conferred to actors who are not the "usual suspects," i.e., public office-holders).

The lack of network visibility is not always deliberate, but sometimes activities within networks remain opaque to facilitate the achievement of compromise. Public accountability may be inimical to compromise-seeking, which may require that interactions within networks take place behind closed doors. Publicity entails the risk of favoring "plebiscitary reason" (Chambers 2004), and public accountability to voters or to the rank-and-file may inhibit solutions that cannot be easily "sold" to them. Therefore, "informalization" strategies may be preferred by policy-makers to avoid public scrutiny. However, even formalized networks may not be visible to a broad public: How many consumers are aware that standards affecting their daily life are formulated, for instance, in entities such as the non-governmental International Standardization Organization (ISO)? In the field of transnational standard-setting, the ISO has developed more than 16,000 standards (Prakash and Potoski 2010, 75) and accounts for about 85% of all international product standards (Büthe and Mattli 2010, 456). ISO comprises about 180 technical committees, 550 subcommittees, and 2,000 working groups involving several thousand representatives selected by national organizations, mostly from industry. Although ISO standards are voluntary and the organization has no formal capacity to enforce them, countries increasingly adopt this form of "soft" law. ISO is best described as a global network

> ... comprising hundreds of technical committees from all over the world and involving tens of thousands of experts representing industry and other groups. The institutional backbone of these networks is formed by private sector standards bodies at the national level. Domestic bodies are thus part and parcel of the international institutional architecture. (Mattli and Büthe 2003, 4)

Similar problems of lack of visibility affect the practice of the International Accounting Standards Board (IASB). The IASB is a private organization directed and financed by the International Accounting Standards Committee Foundation, a private company registered in the U.S. state of Delaware and funded by voluntary contributions. Most of them come from the "Big Four" global accountancy firms, which also monitor the implementation of accounting standards. This private organization has now become the de facto global regulator of accounting standards and, in the European Union alone, more than 7,000 companies have started using IASB standards (Perry 2009). Each IASB standard requires endorsement by the EU Commission, and this form of public recognition is reversible. However, the Commission bases its endorsement decisions on regular advice from another private organization: the European Financial Reporting Advisory Group (EFRAG), which is "an umbrella network of organizations representing European employers, banks, accountancy professions, insurers, stock exchanges and financial analysts" (Perry and Nölke 2006, 576).

Even if politicians' conduct has nowadays become the object of increased (and feared) media scrutiny and politicians adjust their behavior to media "dramaturgy" (Hajer 2009), the day-to-day practice of multi-level governance is immune to "(self-)mediatization" and to the scrutiny of "monitory" (Keane 2009) bodies. The media usually do not display any interest in multi-level governance—they cannot produce meaningful and sellable "news" out of it—and neither do journalists possess enough expertise to delve into it. For instance, two case studies on the EU Open Method of Coordination showed that the media did not play the watchdog role that is expected of them (De la Porte and Nanz 2004, 277). The lack of accountability is not necessarily due to a lack of public accounts. In their case study of structural funds policy in South Yorkshire, Bache and Chapman (2008, 413) find that, even if reports are provided, problems arise in getting the account-holders to understand the explanations provided in them. Either because the reporting documents are too complex or because there is no interest in them, the public sphere that is necessary for accountability is absent from multi-level governance. Even if it has been argued that we live in the era of "audience" democracy (Manin 1997), in the sphere of multi-level governance, the production and reception of "communicative discourse" is, rather, the exception to the rule (Schmidt 2006).

The Weak Coupling of Networks with the Democratic Circuit

If decisions are prepared by policy networks, the legislative function of parliaments is affected; if they are implemented by them, it is their control function that is weakened. As a result, one can speak of a "loosening grip of representative democracy on acts of governing" (Bekkers et al. 2007, 308). Network governance is not the only factor possibly driving toward what has been characterized as a process of "deparliamentarization" (Von Beyme 2000) or, more radically, of "post-parliamentary" democracy (Benz 1998), but it is considered to contribute to that trend. Is this causal relationship correct?

There are few empirical studies of the democratic anchorage of governance networks, and even fewer are comparative in their scope. Skelcher et al. (2011) find cross-country variation and identify the type of democracy (majoritarian or consensus) as well as the varying strength of voluntary associations as contextual factors (elements of the democratic *milieu*) affecting the degree of anchorage. A comparative study of three policy sectors in seven European democracies (Kriesi et al. 2006) concludes that state agents are the most powerful group in policy networks and that their influence is stronger than the influence of political parties, which are the traditional sources of preference aggregation and policy formation. Another comparative study (Bache and Olsson 2001), focusing on EU structural funds policy that is considered the prototypical case of multi-level governance (Marks 1996), shows that elected officials participated in partnership bodies in Sweden but not in the United Kingdom; this made hardly any difference however because, even in Sweden, the influence of politicians was negligible.[7] Skelcher (2007, 2009) finds that elected politicians remained very much absent from UK public–private partnerships, whose members were primarily accountable to their organizations and to the local community. However, parties were much more present in partnerships in Flanders (De Rynck and Voets 2006) and, based on a case study of structural funds policy in South Yorkshire, Bache and Chapman (2008, 409–10) provide a more differentiated account of the influence of elected local councilors. The scattered empirical evidence is so far inconclusive.

In any case, too tight a coupling of networks with the circuit of *politique d'opinion* (Leca 1996) can be problematic as well, because policy networks can then be instrumentalized by governmental or other partisan actors to the detriment of problem-solving (*politique des problèmes*).[8] Hence, one should seek to optimize rather than maximize the degree of coupling between policy networks and the representative circuit, although the definition of the optimal point might remain controversial. A crucial issue in terms of influence is who is in charge of "meta-governance"; that is, the governance of governance networks themselves. According to Torfing (2007, 13), this task is largely delegated to the administration, which usually makes the decisions regarding the design of

networks (taking, for example, the form of working groups and the like), their participants, their attributions, the framing of issues on their agenda, and their management.
This argument received punctual confirmation by Skelcher et al. (2005), who found
that public administrators played an important role in network design in the United
Kingdom. Is this a problem with respect to accountability?

Members of the administration are subject to vertical accountability to their political superiors, and the latter are subject to democratic accountability through the risk of
electoral sanctions. However, the length of the chain of delegation combined with the
magnitude of administrative discretion can make the accountability chain (running in
the reverse direction from the delegation chain) fictitious again. In addition, depending
on their views about democracy, "managers-as-designers" may be more or less sensitive
to issues of democratic control (Jeffares and Skelcher 2011). Technocratic traits seem,
thus, discernible in multi-level governance;[9] yet it is impossible to assess whether they
are more pronounced than in traditional forms of policy-making.

Even if governance networks are dominated by technocrats and elected politicians
are physically marginalized, it may well happen that networks operate in the shadow
of democratically authorized institutions, which would thus exert an indirect influence on their outputs. This would be an illustration of the "law of anticipated reactions"
(Friedrich 1937): If networks operate under the Damoclean sword of rejection of their
outputs by democratic institutions that are in charge of their formal ratification, then
there are strong incentives for network members to internalize the preferences of these
institutions. This, however, may be challenged. Parliamentary assemblies may have the
formal right to overrule decisions formulated in networks or to supervise how decisions
are implemented, but it is questionable whether this represents a credible threat. One
may legitimately raise doubts as to whether MPs have sufficient time and expertise to
exert effective oversight.

Auel (2007), for instance, found considerable variation in the ability of national
parliaments to control the executive when it is involved in European policy-making.
Interestingly, parliaments are more influential if they succeed in becoming involved in
informal negotiations with the government. They must then adopt opaque practices,
and this implies a trade-off: Governments are more accountable to parliaments on EU
matters if the latter exercise their control function outside public scrutiny, but this causes
prejudice regarding the accountability of parliamentary action to the citizenry. There is
no reason why Auel's conclusions on classic intergovernmental decision-making in the
EU would not apply equally (if not more) to the even less visible practice of multi-level
governance. Raunio (2007, 169) refers, for instance, to evidence on the Open Method
of Coordination, according to which "national parliaments have not scrutinized OMC
documents in the same way as they process EU laws."

It can be expected that the more multi-level governance is uncoupled from representative government, the higher the risk that the accountability process is undermined by
attribution errors in the assignment of responsibilities. Thanks to media attention, elected
officials are highly visible targets for sanctions without necessarily being at the core of
policy-making in the complex processes of network governance. The effectiveness of the

democratic feedback loop is thus reduced: The retrospective evaluation of office-holders on the grounds of their policy achievements and the prospective evaluation of candidates for office on the grounds of their pledges become fictitious. The incumbent parties are held responsible for political decisions whose formulation or implementation at least partly escapes their control, and candidates standing for election make promises that structurally they will not be in a position to fulfill because, once in power, they will have to negotiate with other influential actors. Since networks deliver a variety of outputs—among others, decisions, standards, or merely knowledge (Marcussen and Olsen 2007, 286)—the accountability gap is more alarming if authority to issue binding decisions is (even plainly de facto) conferred on networks than if networks offer only advice.

The Deficient Democratic Accountability of Network Members

The problem of deficits in the collective democratic accountability of policy networks as organizational entities can be aggravated by the fact that the individual accountability of the actors involved in them may be deficient as well.

The only network actors that are directly accountable to the citizenry are elected politicians, but they are not necessarily key players, and even if they are, their action in networks lacks visibility, as already mentioned. As also noted, politicians sometimes delegate much of their power to members of the bureaucracy, who are only indirectly accountable to the citizenry due to the lengthy chain of delegation. This is even more the case in the administrative structure of the European Commission or in the case of the proliferating autonomous regulatory agencies. As for experts participating in networks, to be credible they must convince their audience about their independence. Thus, they are not bound by a delegation relationship, and they are accountable only to their professional community, a form of "peer" accountability "based on mutual monitoring of one another's performance within a network of groups, public and private, sharing common concerns" (Goodin 2003, 378). This "social accountability regime," with the risk of loss of reputation as the main sanctioning mechanism, differs from the traditional accountability regime in public governance based on the legally codified threat of electoral sanctions for politicians and the equally codified threat of administrative sanctions for members of bureaucracies (Mashaw 2006).

Representatives of interest groups and NGOs are accountable only to limited constituencies such as donors or their members.[10] This is accountability neither to the general public nor to the communities affected by NGO action. NGOs act as "surrogates" (Mansbridge 2003) for the populations whose well-being is of concern to them,[11] but the latter cannot sanction them if they are not satisfied with them. If representation is not based on ex ante formal authorization, it requires at least the ex post consent (if only tacit) on behalf of those allegedly represented: "a plausibly democratic perspective must surely lead to the view that those targeted as constituents by a claimant should have a chance to respond and to assess the claim" (Saward 2010, 148). However, no procedures are foreseen with the purpose of subjecting self-proclaimed representatives to a test of recognition of their claims by their constituencies. When an organization legitimizes itself by claiming to represent the public interest, its (external) accountability to such a diffuse reference group becomes nebulous. Furthermore, many organizations do not escape the problems of elitism that reduce the internal accountability of their leaderships to the rank-and-file (if any). For instance, in spite of recent efforts to regulate the conditions of access to EU policy-making, NGOs involved in it often lack adequate internal democratic structures, and their supporters do not manifest a will to monitor their action (Warleigh 2006; Saurugger 2008). In the case of UK local partnerships, board members expressed puzzlement when the topic of their accountability was raised: "respondents reported feeling that they had a free hand to do what they thought was best when on the partnership board and tended only to report back to their nominating body when they thought it necessary" (Skelcher 2009, 171).

Private corporations, which are also sometimes present in network forms of governance, are primarily accountable to their shareholders: This poses again the problem of lack of external accountability as these firms are not accountable to those who are affected by their externalities (workers, residents in neighboring areas, etc.). To be sure, firms are accountable to consumers through the market, and NGOs, for instance, threaten with boycotts those among them that are reluctant to comply with social or environmental standards. Nevertheless, neither internal (through shareholder action) nor external (through public opinion alerts) pressures seem to have a significant positive effect on corporate responsibility with respect to social or environmental concerns (Vogel 2005), and even if such effects are produced, they depend on the degree of market competition, the type of issue or company involved (highly visible brands are more vulnerable to pressure), or the existence of strong social expectations on firms to behave in a normatively acceptable way (Graz and Nölke 2008, 4–5). Ultimately, the market accountability regime also differs from that of public governance (Borowiak 2011, 127–49).

The Pressure toward Interdependence Accountability

It may finally be conjectured that the more network members are emancipated from "principals" with whom they would be in a delegation relation, the more accountability dilemmas (see above) will be resolved to the benefit of "peer" accountability. This also requires network homogeneity: The extent to which a feeling of "common fate" or an *esprit de corps* develops within networks is an empirical matter, but if such a feeling develops, then it is likely that network participants become primarily accountable to their network partners in soft and horizontal accountability relations. In this kind of "interdependence" accountability (Scott 2000, 50–2), the fear of "naming and shaming" is expected to yield disciplining effects because "free riders" or unreliable actors risk loss of reputation in the network, and their partners will not continue to trust them in the future or might even ostracize them (Scott 2006, 180). Finally, such pressure is stronger if the network is consolidated and small. According to the *Gesetz des Wiedersehens* (Luhmann 1973, 39), trust-generating behavior is favored by one's anticipation that one will regularly face one's peers and be confronted with accountability demands by them.

This soft form of mutual accountability can operate to the benefit of the common good only if network members share strong public-minded values or if they are sufficiently representative of social pluralism.[12] Networks should also consider the interests of weak actors or of actors whose preferences do not coincide with the network's "mainstream" orientation. This is, however, challenged by two bodies of literature, each focusing on distinct limits to pluralism. First, the literature on collective action (Olson 1982) emphasizes strategic behavior by "insiders" whose interest lies in using benefits from participation in arenas of power as exclusive ("club") goods and in externalizing the costs generated by their choices ("rent-seeking" behavior). Second, the literature on deliberation reveals that the lack of cognitive variety in deliberative settings—overly-intense ties between participants and, as a result, too strong a sense of community—can lead to closure and to "enclave deliberation" (Sunstein 2001). This impedes learning based on critical scrutiny, which is necessary for the effectiveness of accountability mechanisms and requires, in a sense, mutual trust not to be blind. There is hardly any empirical research dealing with those matters in multi-level governance settings, so it is not possible to say whether rent-seeking or "groupthink" is widespread. However, a more fundamental critique of horizontal peer accountability is that it should not be considered a functional equivalent of vertical democratic accountability. Mutual learning by policy-makers is quite another objective of accountability than popular control by "policy-takers," and control *in* the network does not substitute for control *of* the network.

A Divorce between Power and Accountability?

"Power and accountability have been divorced, if not de jure so de facto and we now need to assess what this means for democratic governance," writes Pierre (2009, 592) in a piece on transformations of governance. The amplitude of the accountability gap is an empirical matter that depends upon quite a number of factors. To a large extent, the proliferation of sites of authority in multi-level governance is matched by the proliferation of control mechanisms (Grant and Keohane 2005), leading "to a more diversified and pluralistic set of accountability relationships" (Bovens 2007, 110). The emergence of complex accountability regimes may be viewed as an adaptation to the complexities of network governance. Multi-level accountability networks are, for instance, established between "monitors" such as courts or ombudsmen, thus involving the European Court of Justice or the European ombudsman together with their national counterparts (Harlow and Rawlings 2007). Are such complex regimes efficient in their disciplining function? Competing hypotheses can be formulated, and again, more empirical research is needed to have a clearer view.

Mechanisms of "comprehensive" accountability are, to a large extent, replaced by "compartmentalized" modes of issue accountability (Tsakatika 2007). Scott (2000, 57) refers to mechanisms that "are in tension with one another, in the sense of having different concerns, power, procedures, and culture, which generate competing agendas and capacities." The extent to which multiple accountability forums have divergent preferences, if they communicate with each other and coordinate their action, should be carefully scrutinized. Overall, it can be expected that being watched by multiple controllers will produce a disciplining effect because redundancy improves control (Scott 2000), and the pluralism of critical perspectives brought about by a diversity of accountability forums is welcome. In addition, redundancy provides multiple venues to account-holders and increases their blackmailing potential by making the environment of decision-makers less predictable. However, being placed under the scrutiny of "too many eyes" may also induce risk-averse behavior and blame-avoidance strategies on behalf of the controlled. Furthermore, surveillance by too many eyes may lead, in the end, to fatalism or indifference, as it increases the randomness of control (Hood 1998). In short, how actors will behave in a context of indeterminacy may well be indeterminate, too. The situation is complicated by the fact that some of the accountability mechanisms at work are of the "soft" type: non-codified, operating through social pressure or through stigmatization in the public sphere, etc. Are they, perhaps, toothless? The efficiency of "hard" sanctions is disputed in the literature on cooperative forms of governance, yet the efficiency of "soft" sanctions has not been established either. Accountability "forums" with no formal right to sanction are "weak" publics (Fraser 1993): They can influence the governance processes by informing actors with a sanctioning capacity about their views, but their own judgment is not authoritative.

Quite another question is that of the relationship of the complex accountability regime of multi-level governance with democracy. Network forms of governance are considered problematic both from a liberal point of view because of their frequent lack of formalization and from a democratic point of view, emphasizing the necessity of popular control (Dryzek 2010, 122–4). Many accountability mechanisms in multi-level governance perform different functions (such as ensuring learning) than mechanisms of democratic accountability, which aim at ensuring responsiveness, and should thereby make citizens confident that their preferences (input) are reflected in the production of decisions that affect them (output). Hence, the divorce in multi-level governance is not so much between power and accountability as a whole, but, rather, between power and *democratic* accountability.

Accountability forums in multi-level governance may well not include democratic "principals" such as elected officials (not to mention ordinary citizens)—think about peer accountability. The relationship between accountability and representation is thereby loosened; Those who control network outputs ex post are not necessarily the same as those who formulate ex ante mandates to networks. In addition, accountability forums may be weakly accountable—think of organized civil society actors acting as "surrogate" accountability-holders—and accountability relations may lack transparency themselves—think again about peer accountability that best functions in closed networks. Therefore, the emergence of alternative forms of accountability in multi-level governance can be no remedy for the erosion of democratic accountability. Rubenstein (2007, 631) correctly maintains that "standard" (democratic) accountability is superior to its different surrogates, which should be viewed as no more than second-best alternatives. In spite of the proliferation of accountability mechanisms and of the normative discourse on accountability as a virtue, accountable governance is no synonym for democratic government.

NOTES

1. See, for instance, the case of regional Monitoring Committees, which are deliberative bodies supervising the operation of EU Structural Funds (Kamlage 2008). See also the "Open Method of Coordination" (Kröger 2007), based on policy goals agreed upon between the governments of EU member states and followed by policy recommendations adopted in deliberations between national experts and EU officials, whose implementation may require the cooperation of subnational and non-public actors as well.
2. See, for instance, Martens (2008).
3. See also Löfgren and Agger (2007) and the criteria developed by Mathur and Skelcher (2007) for the assessment of the democratic quality of network governance. For example, the "Governance Assessment Tool," which contains indicators of transparency and external accountability for multi-level partnerships (Skelcher 2007).
4. For a differentiated analysis of the accountability of various EU institutions, see Bovens et al. (2010).
5. See also Papadopoulos (2011).
6. This problem of "hidden action" and "hidden information" has been emphasized by the "principal–agent" theory of delegation (see, among many others, Lupia 2003).
7. See also the analysis based on Scandinavian data in Olsson (2003).
8. On cases from France and Germany, see, respectively, Taiclet (2006) and Auel (2006), and on the United Kingdom compared with smaller European states, see Skelcher et al. (2011).
9. See also the role of technocrats as described by Bache and Chapman (2008, 410–2).
10. For an analysis of different forms of NGO accountability depending on NGO type and NGO interactions with their environment, see Ebrahim (2007).
11. Rubenstein (2007, 625) distinguishes "surrogate accountability" from "mediated standard accountability." In the latter, accountability-holders delegate the tasks of surveillance or sanction to an agent (for instance, to courts), whereas such delegation does not exist in surrogate accountability.
12. A similar condition is posed by Chambers (2004) when she refers to the moral necessity for deliberations *in camera* to be respectful of the public interest ("public reason").

REFERENCES

Auel, K. 2006. Multilevel Governance, Regional Policy and Democratic Legitimacy in Germany, pp. 44–62 in *Governance and Democracy. Comparing National, European and International Experiences*, eds. A. Benz and Y. Papadopoulos. New York: Routledge.

Auel, K. 2007. "Democratic Accountability and National Parliaments: Redefining the Impact of Parliamentary Scrutiny." *European Law Journal*, 13: 487–504.

Bache, I. and Chapman, R. 2008. "Democracy Through Multilevel Governance? The Implementation of the Structural Funds in South Yorkshire." *Governance: An International Journal of Policy, Administration, and Institutions*, 21: 397–418.

Bache, I. and Olsson, J. 2001. "Legitimacy Through Partnership? EU Policy Diffusion in Britain and Sweden." *Scandinavian Political Studies*, 24: 215–37.

Bekkers, V., Dijkstra, G., Edwards, A., and Fenger, M. 2007. Governance and the Democratic Deficit: An Evaluation, pp. 295–312 in *Governance and the Democratic Deficit*, eds. V. Bekkers, G. Dijkstra, A. Edwards, and M. Fenger. Aldershot: Ashgate.

Benz, A. 1998. Postparlamentarische Demokratie? Demokratische Legitimation im kooperativen Staat, pp. 201–22 in *Demokratie—eine Kultur des Westens?* ed. M. Th. Greven. Opladen: Leske & Budrich.

Blanco, I., Lowndes, V., and Pratchett, L. 2011. "Policy Networks and Governance Networks: Towards Greater Conceptual Clarity." *Political Studies Review*, 9: 297–308.

Bolleyer, N. 2009. *Intergovernmental Cooperation: Rational Choices in Federal Systems and Beyond*. Oxford: Oxford University Press.

Borowiak, C. T. 2011. *Accountability and Democracy: The Pitfalls and Promise of Popular Control*. Oxford: Oxford University Press.

Bovens, M. 1998. *The Quest for Responsibility*. Cambridge: Cambridge University Press.

Bovens, M. 2007. "New Forms of Accountability and EU-Governance." *Comparative European Politics*, 5: 104–20.

Bovens, M., Curtin, D., and 't Hart, P. 2010. *The Real World of EU Accountability: What Deficit?* Oxford: Oxford University Press.

Büthe, T. and Mattli, W. 2010. Standards for Global Markets: Domestic and International Institutions, pp. 455–76 in *Handbook on Multi-level Governance*, eds. H. Enderlein, S. Walti, and M. Zürn. Cheltenham: Edward Elgar.

Chambers, S. 2004. "Behind Closed Doors: Publicity, Secrecy, and the Quality of Deliberation." *The Journal of Political Philosophy*, 12: 389–410.

Considine, M. and Afzal, K. A. 2011. Legitimacy, pp. 369–85 in *The SAGE Handbook of Governance*, ed. M. Bevir. London: Sage.

De la Porte, C. and Nanz, P. 2004. "The OMC: A Deliberative-Democratic Mode of Governance? The Cases of Employment and Pensions." *Journal of European Public Policy*, 11: 267–88.

De Rynck, F. and Voets, J. 2006. "Democracy in Area-Based Networks: The Case of Ghent." *American Review of Public Administration*, 36: 58–78.

Dowding, K. 1995. "Model or Metaphor? A Critical Review of the Policy Network Approach." *Political Studies*, 43: 136–58.

Dryzek, J. S. 2010. *Foundations and Frontiers of Deliberative Governance*. Oxford: Oxford University Press.

Ebrahim, A. 2007. Towards a Reflective Accountability in NGOs, pp. 193–222 in *Global Accountabilities: Participation, Pluralism, and Public Ethics*, eds. A. Ebrahim and E. Weisband. Cambridge: Cambridge University Press.

Fraser, N. 1993. Rethinking the Public Sphere: A Contribution to the Critique of Actually Existing Democracy, pp. 109–42 in *Habermas and the Public Sphere*, ed. C. Calhoun. Cambridge, Mass.: MIT Press.

Friedrich, C. J. 1937. *Constitutional Government and Politics*. New York: Harper.

Goodin, R. E. 2003. "Democratic Accountability: The Distinctiveness of the Third Sector." *European Journal of Sociology*, 44: 359–93.

Grant, R. W. and Keohane, R. O. 2005. "Accountability and Abuses of Power in World Politics." *American Political Science Review*, 99: 29–44.

Graz, J.-C. and Nölke, A. 2008. Beyond the Fragmented Debate on Transnational Private Governance, pp. 1–26 in *Transnational Private Governance and its Limits*, eds. J.-C. Graz and A. Nölke. London: Routledge.

Hajer, M. 2009. *Authoritative Governance: Policy Making in the Age of Mediatization*. Oxford: Oxford University Press.

Harlow, C. and Rawlings, R. 2007. "Promoting Accountability in Multilevel Governance. A Network Approach." *European Law Journal*, 13: 542–62.

Hood, C. 1998. *The Art of the State: Culture, Rhetoric, and Public Management*. Oxford: Clarendon Press.

Hood, C. 2007. "What Happens when Transparency Meets Blame-Avoidance?" *Public Management Review*, 9: 191–210.

Hooghe, L. and Marks, G. 2003. "Unraveling the Central State, but How? Types of Multi-level Governance." *American Political Science Review*, 97: 233–43.

Hupe, P. and Edwards, A. 2012. "The Accountability of Power: Democracy and Governance in Modern Times." *European Political Science Review*, 4: 177–94.

Isett, K. R., Mergel, I. A., LeRoux, K., Mischen, P. A., and Rethemeyer, R. K. 2011. "Networks in Public Administration Scholarship: Understanding Where We Are and Where We Need to Go." *Journal of Public Administration Research and Theory*, 21 (suppl. 1): 157–73.

Jeffares, S. and Skelcher, C. 2011. "Democratic Subjectivities in Network Governance: A Q Methodology Study of English and Dutch Public Managers." *Public Administration*, 89: 1253–73.

Kamlage, J.-H. 2008. Assessing the Legitimacy of European Regional Policy: The Interplay of Civil Society and State Actors in Sweden and Germany, pp. 185–207 in *Civil Society Participation in European and Global Governance*, eds. J. Steffek, C. Kissling, and P. Nanz. Basingstoke: Palgrave.

Keane, J. 2009. *The Life and Death of Democracy*. New York: W.W. Norton and Co.

Koppell, J. G. S. 2010. *World Rule: Accountability, Legitimacy, and the Design of Global Governance*. Chicago: The University of Chicago Press.

Kriesi, H., Adam, S., and Jochum, M. 2006. "Comparative Analysis of Policy Networks in Western Europe." *Journal of European Public Policy*, 13: 341–61.

Kröger, S. 2007. "The End of Democracy as We Know it? The Legitimacy Deficits of Bureaucratic Social Policy Governance." *Journal of European Integration*, 29: 565–82.

Leca, J. 1996. La "gouvernance" de la France sous la Cinquième République. Une perspective de sociologie comparative, pp. 329–65 in *De la Ve République à l'Europe*, eds. F. d'Arcy and L. Rouban. Paris: Presses de Sciences Po.

Löfgren, K. and Agger, A. 2007. How Democratic are Networks Based on Citizen Involvement?, pp. 29–49 in *Tensions Between Local Governance and Local Democracy*, eds. J. Franzke, M. Boogers, J. M. Ruano, and L. Schaap. The Hague: Reed Business.

Lord, C. 2004. *A Democratic Audit for the European Union*. Basingstoke: Palgrave.

Luhmann, N. 1973. *Vertrauen—Ein Mechanismus der Reduktion sozialer Komplexität*. Stuttgart: Enke.

Lupia, A. 2003. Delegation and its Perils, pp. 33–54 in *Delegation and Accountability in Parliamentary Democracies*, eds. K. Strøm, W. C. Müller, and T. Bergman. Oxford: Oxford University Press.

Manin, B. 1997. *Principles of Representative Government*. Cambridge: Cambridge University Press.

Mansbridge, J. 2003. "Rethinking Representation." *American Political Science Review*, 97: 515–28.

Marcussen, M. and Olsen, H. P. 2007. Transcending Analytical Cliquishness with Second-Generation Governance Network Analysis, pp. 273–92 in *Democratic Network Governance in Europe*, eds. M. Marcussen and J. Torfing. Basingstoke: Palgrave.

Marks, G. 1996. Exploring and Explaining Variation in EU Cohesion Policy, pp. 388–422 in *Cohesion Policy and European Integration: Building Multi-Level Governance*, ed. L. Hooghe. Oxford: Oxford University Press.

Marsh, D. and Rhodes, R. A. W., eds. 1992. *Policy Networks in British Government*. Oxford: Clarendon Press.

Martens, M. 2008. "Administrative Integration Through the Back Door? The Role and Influence of the European Commission in Transgovernmental Networks within the Environmental Policy Field." *Journal of European Integration*, 30: 635–51.

Mashaw, J. L. 2006. Accountability and Institutional Design: Some Thoughts on the Grammar of Governance, pp. 115–56 in *Public Accountability: Designs, Dilemmas and Experiences*, ed. M. W. Dowdle. Cambridge: Cambridge University Press.

Mathur, N. and Skelcher, C. 2007. "Evaluating Democratic Performance: Methodologies for Assessing the Relationship between Network Governance and Citizens." *Public Administration Review*, 67: 228–37.

Mattli, W. and Büthe, T. 2003. "Setting International Standards: Technological Rationality or Primacy of Power?" *World Politics*, 57: 1–42.

Olson, M. 1982. *The Rise and Decline of Nations: Economic Growth, Stagflation, and Social Rigidities*. New Haven: Yale University Press.

Olsson, J. 2003. "Democracy Paradoxes in Multi-Level Governance. Theorizing on Structural Fund System Research." *Journal of European Public Policy*, 10: 283–300.

Papadopoulos, Y. 2011. Accountability and Multi-Level Governance: More Accountability, Less Democracy?, pp. 102–21 in *Accountability and European Governance*, eds. D. Curtin, P. Mair, and Y. Papadopoulos. New York: Routledge.

Perry, J. 2009. *Goodwill Hunting: Accounting and the Global Regulation of Economic Ideas*. PhD dissertation. Free University Amsterdam.

Perry, J. and Nölke, A. 2006. "The Political Economy of International Accounting Standards." *Review of International Political Economy*, 13: 559–86.

Piattoni, S. 2009. "Multi-Level Governance: A Historical and Conceptual Analysis." *Journal of European Integration*, 11: 163–80.

Pierre, J. 2009. "Reinventing Governance, Reinventing Democracy?" *Policy & Politics*, 37: 591–609.

Prakash, A. and Potoski, M. 2010. The International Organization for Standardization as a Global Governor: A Club Theory Perspective, pp. 72–101 in *Who Governs the Globe?* eds. D. D. Avant, M. Finnemore, and S. K. Sell. Cambridge: Cambridge University Press.

Putnam, R. D. 1988. "Diplomacy and Domestic Politics: The Logic of Two-Level Games." *International Organization*, 42: 427–60.

Raunio, T. 2007. National Parliaments and the Future of European Integration: Learning to Play the Multilevel Game, pp. 158–76 in *Democratic Dilemmas of Multilevel Governance*, eds. J. DeBardeleben and A. Hurrelmann. Basingstoke: Palgrave.

Rubenstein, J. 2007. "Accountability in an Unequal World." *The Journal of Politics*, 69: 616–32.

Saurugger, S. 2008. "Interest Groups and Democracy in the European Union." *West European Politics*, 31: 1274–91.

Saward, M. 2010. *The Representative Claim*. Oxford: Oxford University Press.

Scharpf, F. W. 1988. "The Joint-Decision Trap: Lessons From German Federalism and European Integration." *Public Administration*, 66: 239–78.

Schmidt, V. 2006. *Democracy in Europe: The EU and National Polities*. Oxford: Oxford University Press.

Scott, C. 2000. "Accountability in the Regulatory State." *Journal of Law and Society*, 27: 38–60.

Scott, C. 2006. Spontaneous Accountability, pp. 174–91 in *Public Accountability. Designs, Dilemmas and Experiences*, ed. M. W. Dowdle. Cambridge: Cambridge University Press.

Skelcher, C. 2007. Democracy in Collaborative Spaces: Why Context Matters in Researching Governance Networks, pp. 25–46 in *Democratic Network Governance in Europe*, eds. M. Marcussen and J. Torfing. Basingstoke: Palgrave.

Skelcher, C. 2009. "Fishing in Muddy Waters: Principals, Agents, and Democratic Governance in Europe." *Journal of Public Administration Research and Theory*, 20: 61–75.

Skelcher, C., Mathur, N. and Smith, M. 2005. "The Public Governance of Collaborative Spaces: Discourse, Design and Democracy." *Public Administration*, 83: 573–96.

Skelcher, C., Klijn, E.-H., Kübler, D., Sørensen, E., and Sulivan, H. 2011. "Explaining the Democratic Anchorage of Governance Networks." *Administrative Theory and Praxis*, 33: 7–38.

Slaughter, A.-M. 2004. *A New World Order*. Princeton: Princeton University Press.

Sørensen, E. and Torfing, J. 2009. "Making Governance Networks Effective and Democratic Through Metagovernance." *Public Administration*, 87: 234–58.

Sunstein, C. 2001. *Republic.com*. Princeton: Princeton University Press.

Taiclet, A.-F. 2006. Governance, Expertise and Competitive Politics: The Case of Territorial Development Policies in France, pp. 63–80 in *Governance and Democracy: Comparing National, European, and International Experiences*, eds. A. Benz and Y. Papadopoulos. London: Routledge.

Thompson, D. F. 1980. "Moral Responsibility of Public Officials: The Problem of Many Hands." *American Political Science Review*, 74: 905–16.

Torfing, J. 2007. Introduction: Democratic Network Governance, pp. 1–22 in *Democratic Network Governance in Europe*, eds. M. Marcussen and J. Torfing. Basingstoke: Palgrave Macmillan.

Tsakatika, M. 2007. "A Parliamentary Dimension for EU Soft Governance." *Journal of European Integration*, 29: 549–64.

Vogel, D. 2005. *The Market for Virtue: The Potential and Limits of Corporate Social Responsibility*. Washington, DC: The Brookings Institution Press.

Von Beyme, K. 2000. *Parliamentary Democracy: Democratization, Destabilization, Reconsolidation, 1789–1999*. Basingstoke: Palgrave.

Warleigh, A. 2006. Making Citizens from the Market? NGOs and the Representation of Interests, pp. 118–33 in *Making European Citizens*, eds. R. Bellamy, D. Castiglione, and J. Shaw. Basingstoke: Palgrave.

CHAPTER 18

ACCOUNTABLE INTERNATIONAL RELATIONS

MICHAEL GOODHART

A VERY BRIEF HISTORY OF ACCOUNTABLE INTERNATIONAL RELATIONS

INTERNATIONAL relations has traditionally referred to relations among states. It has a long history; efforts to constrain the behavior of states and to hold their leaders accountable are ancient, predating the modern states system itself. Until recently, these efforts were primarily focused on the definition, interpretation, and enforcement of international law, understood as natural law, treaty law, and as a common law of nations binding on all states. Achieving accountability through international law has always been complicated by the lack of robust enforcement mechanisms, however. Sovereign states routinely ignore or even flout international law when it is in their interest to do so. Only when powerful states decided to enforce international law was there any semblance of accountability in international relations as traditionally understood. War, the threat of war, and sanctions were its blunt instruments.

In the nineteenth century, the horrors of modern warfare prompted a significant shift in thinking about international accountability. The first of what are now called the Geneva Conventions, ratified in 1864, marked an attempt to codify international law with respect to the treatment of sick and wounded soldiers and of civilians tending to them. Interestingly, it enjoined signatories to recognize and respect the right of a new international organization, the Red Cross, to care for the sick and wounded without molestation from any party. Following the First World War, the League of Nations marked another significant advance in the institutionalization of accountability in relations among states—at least on paper. The League was created to preserve peace, resolve international disputes, and regulate states' behavior in areas from labor to the treatment of ethnic minorities.

Following the Second World War (and the implicit failure of the League), international resolve to achieve collective security and ensure accountability among states was redoubled, as evidenced in the strength of the influential but short-lived world federalist movement (Cabrera 2011). Meanwhile, the League was reincarnated and reinvigorated in the form of the United Nations (UN), whose Security Council and human rights instruments were intended to put teeth into international standards of accountability. At the same time, a number of powerful international governance organizations (IGOs) were created—the IMF and World Bank were the most prominent—to promote international economic and financial stability and facilitate cooperation. Much like the League before it, the UN was quickly paralyzed by great power rivalry, defanging the Security Council and turning human rights into an ideological cudgel.

Two significant developments have sparked the recent explosion in demands for more accountable international relations. The first is the spectacular increase, since the 1970s, in global governance, along with related changes in the quantity and quality of transnational activity generally (see Zürn 2005, 143–4). Global governance regimes reflect states' desire to gain or reassert control in domains where trans-border flows of various kinds limit domestic policy and regulatory reach. The growth in global governance, in turn, both reflects and hastens the ongoing expansion and intensification of interdependence, especially economic interdependence.

The other crucial development was the end of the Cold War, which rendered demands for accountable international relations somewhat less implausible. In the absence of superpower rivalry, political space opened up for coordination and cooperation where none had previously existed. This change also inaugurated an unprecedented consensus on human rights that, however fissiparous, provides a common framework for scholars theorizing the normative implications of interdependence and global governance and a common vocabulary for citizens and activists articulating demands for constraints on the exercise of power.

International relations refers both to relations among states and to the discipline dedicated to the study of these relations. Scholars in that field have taken to calling their field and their object of study "world politics," in recognition that global governance and economic interdependence signify not just a scalar increase in relations but a transformation in the nature of those relations. IGOs, as their name suggests, are creatures of states. They are governed by representatives of states, and much of their authority is delegated to them by states.[1] States use IGOs to defend and promote their own interests, and on the whole global governance arrangements reflect the balance of power among states. Thus global governance remains very much a matter of inter-national relations.

At the same time, some IGOs enjoy significant autonomy from their principals; a small but growing number, most notably the WTO, can sanction member states against their will. In addition, some IGOs have the authority to alter their rules and even the scope of their authority without the unanimous consent of their members or signatories; the International Criminal Court (ICC) is one example. Non-governmental organizations (NGOs) as well as a more amorphous global civil society also play a significant role in holding states and IGOs to account. The upshot is that there is no neat analytic distinction or clear empirical difference between international relations and what is sometimes called transnational politics or global governance. I use the term "world politics" interchangeably with "international relations" as a way of reminding readers of these complications.

HOLDING STATES AND LEADERS TO ACCOUNT

International treaties signed in the wake of the Second World War criminalized genocide, torture, war crimes, and other crimes against humanity and further developed international humanitarian law. These treaties form the cornerstone of an international legal system, anchored in the UN, that is committed to upholding human rights (see Smith 2009). In addition, regional human rights mechanisms, especially the European Court of Human Rights (ECHR), have evolved into powerful and respected institutions for upholding international law. Long dismissed as ineffective because they lack enforcement power, such mechanisms are viewed by scholars today in a different light. International legal and political theorists now recognize that coercive enforcement is not synonymous with effectiveness and that there are several distinctive models of effective enforcement at the global level (Alter 1998; Cassel 2001; Helfer and Slaughter 1997; Jacobson and Ruffer 2003).

The end of the Cold War renewed the prospect of more concerted international action to deter violations of international law and to hold states and leaders accountable for their behavior toward other states and toward their own citizens. During a brief period of "new world order" in the 1990s, the UN Security Council played an active role in this effort; its reversal of Iraq's invasion of Kuwait and establishment of the International Criminal Tribunals for the former Yugoslavia (ICTY) and for Rwanda (ICTR) marked a significant departure from past practice and echoed the early post-war activism represented by the UN police action in Korea and the Nuremberg and Tokyo tribunals. This activism quickly receded into a renewed stalemate, however, and by the end of the 1990s NATO, failing to win Security Council approval, intervened in Kosovo on its own authority, triggering a profound debate about the merits of the NATO action and about intervention generally (see Holzgrefe and Keohane 2003).

Outside the UN system, efforts to end impunity for genocide, war crimes, and crimes against humanity progressed rapidly in the 1990s along several parallel fronts. In October 1998, Augusto Pinochet, former Chilean general and dictator, was arrested in London on UK warrants issued at the request of a Spanish judge who had charged the general with an array of crimes committed during his rule, including recognized international crimes such as torture. The complexities of the case are beyond this essay's scope, but the decision by the UK's Law Lords that Pinochet could not claim immunity from prosecution for such crimes as a head of state set a path-breaking precedent (see Byers 2000). This case echoed other legal developments, including the development and advocacy of principles of universal jurisdiction for serious crimes under international law (Macedo 2001)[2] and the growing use of the Alien Tort Claims Act in American courts to prosecute individuals for crimes that violate the law of nations or international treaties to which the United States is a party (Malanczuk 1997).

International efforts to end impunity and deter bad behavior also took a quantum leap forward with the establishment of a permanent international criminal tribunal, the International Criminal Court (see Schabas 2011). Some 120 states are signatories to the Rome Statute, which grants the Court secondary jurisdiction in cases where states parties are involved (as perpetrators or victims) or when cases are referred to it by the UN Security Council (UN General Assembly, 1998). While the Court is established by treaty among states, it came into being thanks largely to the efforts of an impressive international coalition of civil society organizations that pushed for its ratification and played a key role in the negotiation of the Rome Statute (Glasius 2006).

Powerful states have also made increasing use of sanctions as a tool of accountability—and coercion. There has been a great deal of debate about whether sanctions are effective and whether they impact the right people (see Drezner 1999). "Smart" sanctions are designed to target rulers while sparing citizens, but economic sanctions—the most potent weapon in the sanctions arsenal—necessarily affect the entire population. When utilized by IGOs, by the UN, or by states acting in concert, the legitimacy of sanctions becomes a salient (and quite controversial) problem.

All of these mechanisms—courts, treaties, sanctions, tribunals, and legal doctrines supported by and through institutions of the UN, along with occasional Security Council authorization of military intervention—together form a web of international accountability arrangements designed to hold states and rulers accountable for their behavior. Yet increasingly, the debate about accountability in world politics is focusing elsewhere, on decisions and policies originating in global governance regimes.

ACCOUNTABLE GLOBAL GOVERNANCE

While the criminal behavior of states and leaders remains a pressing concern, contemporary discussion of accountability in international relations highlights a somewhat different problem: what many critics perceive as a lack of legitimacy in world politics. Scholars and activists hope that achieving greater international accountability will bestow or impose legitimacy upon global governance arrangements and upon the expanding variety of transnational actors whose activities affect people all over the world (cf. Koenig-Archibugi 2010, 1146). This critique is directed primarily at IGOs— especially international financial institutions like the IMF, the WTO, and the World Bank. It is also frequently leveled at transnational corporations (TNCs).[3]

This demand for accountability is in some respects quite puzzling. As Grant and Keohane (2005) argue, there is no shortage of accountability in world politics today. They identify seven mechanisms—hierarchical, supervisory, fiscal, legal, market, peer, and public reputational mechanisms—through which transnational power-wielders are held to account. In particular, they maintain, IGOs are among the most accountable actors in world politics (2005, 37). Yet many critics seem to view IGOs, TNCs, and other actors as illegitimate *despite* their rather extensive accountability.

This paradox points to the central problem of accountability in world politics: Many actors are viewed as illegitimate because they are not *democratically* accountable— accountable to the people whose lives they shape and constrain or to the people in whose names or on whose authority they ostensibly act. The World Bank and IMF are highly accountable, but they are not democratically accountable; TNCs are highly accountable, but they are not democratically accountable. The concern with democratic accountability has grown alongside the increasingly political character of international relations, as exemplified in the mushrooming impact of decisions and policies made by IGOs. While democratic accountability is just one form of accountability, it is the form most closely associated with political legitimacy and thus the one most ardently desired by critics of existing global governance arrangements.

Calls for democratic accountability in world politics create a conundrum for scholars and activists alike, as increasing the democratic accountability of transnational actors and global governance regimes has proven difficult and controversial. Democratic accountability has traditionally referred to the right of citizens to hold their rulers to account; Held (1996, 88–9) describes it as entailing that rulers "must be held accountable to the governed through political mechanisms . . . which give citizens satisfactory means for choosing, authorizing and controlling political decisions." Models of democratic accountability link these particular mechanisms quite closely with political legitimacy, a link forged in democratic notions of popular sovereignty or rule by the people.

These models have proven difficult to replicate globally because there is no democratic institutional architecture for realizing accountability on a global scale. Cosmopolitan democrats have therefore called for the creation of political structures to subject transnational actors to a form of global democratic constitutionalism (Held 2004; Archibugi 2008)—a sort of return to world federalist proposals. Such projects have proven controversial, however, because many scholars and practitioners, among them many friends of democracy, doubt whether extending democratic mechanisms in this way is possible or even desirable (Dahl 1999). Skeptics cite monumental practical obstacles (Keohane 2006, 5) and deep theoretical reservations about the normative underpinnings of such global arrangements (Goodhart 2007; Kymlicka 1999).

Some scholars have even warned that theoretical ideals of democracy are inappropriate for assessing global governance arrangements (Moravcsik 2004; Zweifel 2002). Similarly, pluralists like Keohane (2006) and Nye (2001), who see the danger of unaccountable governance, have called for greater attention to non-democratic accountability mechanisms as instruments for taming abuses of power in world politics. To continue to hope for democratic accountability, on this view, will lead to disappointment and distract from other means of constraining power and limiting its abuse. Yet critics lament that these other means have so far failed to stem even the worst abuses of power or to confer much legitimacy upon world politics.

An example can help to clarify what is really at issue here. Consider the World Bank, where policy is set by the President and by a 188-member Board of Governors, which includes representatives from each member state. Routine operations are overseen by 25 Executive Directors, five of whom are appointed by the five largest shareholders, while the remaining 20 are appointed or elected by the other members. Fiscal accountability is ensured by the shareholders (member states), who enjoy voting rights weighted to reflect their contributions. Clearly, the Bank is very highly accountable.

It has nonetheless been a target of intense criticism concerning its role in promoting structural adjustment (Stiglitz 2002) and concerning many specific policies and decisions—perhaps most famously its support for the construction of large dams in the Narmada Valley and elsewhere (Khagram 2002). Responding to pressure and criticism from civil society groups, the Bank has recently undertaken efforts to achieve greater social accountability (World Bank 2009). It supports reforms that make government officials more accountable at home, and it has adopted policies designed to make itself more responsive to the needs and interests of those whose welfare it ostensibly promotes. Mostly these reforms involve greater consultation with local residents and groups affected by particular projects funded or overseen by the Bank, though the use of Poverty Reduction Strategies (begun in 1999) is intended to give countries and citizens a more direct role in guiding anti-poverty measures (APSA 2012, 16).

This example highlights the problem with alternative accountability mechanisms. As Grant and Keohane (2005, 37) put it, discussing IGOs: "The problem is not a lack of accountability as much as the fact that the principal lines of accountability run to powerful states, whose policies are at odds with those of their critics, and which may or may not themselves be fully democratic." The difficulty, then, is not that alternative mechanisms of accountability are ineffective in international relations, but that their effectiveness actually undermines political legitimacy by bolstering the influence of powerful actors and interests (cf. Steffek 2008, 53ff.).

Part of the confusion about these questions stems from a more general confusion regarding the meaning and usage of the term accountability. In the literature the term is used both to denote certain processes or mechanisms and to designate a particular political virtue (Bovens 2010). The *process* of accountability typically refers to the arrangements through which accountability-holders monitor and sanction power-wielders. The scholarly emphasis on processes of accountability is primarily descriptive and fairly narrow, referring to social mechanisms, institutional relations, and the post hoc effectiveness of sanctioning (Bovens 2010, 948). When scholars describe IGOs as accountable, they are using the term in this sense.

The *virtue* of accountability is more complex; it refers to normative considerations, including the standards of accountability and their use in evaluating the behavior of various agents (Bovens 2010, 947). As Grant and Keohane (2005, 29) argue, "accountability...implies that some actors have the right to hold other actors to a set of standards, to judge whether they have fulfilled their responsibilities in light of those standards, and to impose sanctions if they determine that those responsibilities have not been met."[4] When invoked as a virtue, accountability refers specifically to compliance with *democratic* standards—or with closely related ones like transparency, responsibility, participation, and deliberation (Bovens 2010, 949).

The association of the virtue of accountability with specifically democratic standards explains why many transnational actors appear illegitimate despite being subject to highly effective processes of accountability. The failure of alternative mechanisms of accountability to confer legitimacy upon international relations results from the non-democratic standards of accountability those mechanisms typically uphold.

Insisting on the distinction between processes and virtues of accountability clarifies that the public or political legitimacy that many activists and scholars have hoped accountability would bring to world politics is not a general feature of all processes of accountability but specifically a function of democratic accountability. The distinctive and legitimacy-conferring characteristics of democratic accountability lie not in the design or effectiveness of its mechanisms but rather in the standards that democratic accountability upholds.

VIRTUES OF DEMOCRATIC ACCOUNTABILITY

The core idea of democratic accountability is that the people are entitled to hold their rulers to account. On this model, standards of accountability collapse into the notional "will of the people," translated more or less directly (at least in theory) through the mechanisms of election, representation, public opinion, and so on, into law and policy. If the mechanisms are working properly, the question of standards is completely elided; the standard is simply conformity with the will of the people.

In thinking about how to translate models and modalities of democratic accountability to the transnational context, scholars have naturally focused on the question of *who* is entitled to hold power-wielders to account. That is, they have emphasized the *process* of democratic accountability. This approach has not been terribly fruitful, because in world politics, the logic of democratic accountability breaks down. The familiar democratic mechanisms don't and can't work globally because their legitimacy turns out to have less to do with the mechanisms themselves than with certain distinctive features of the Westphalian state: First, the symmetry and congruence between citizens and rulers and between the laws and policies rulers make and their constituents (Held 1995, 224); second, the peculiar status of the people, whose standing as a source of democratic legitimacy is a function of its taken-for-grantedness (Goodhart 2011; 2007).

Identifying democratic standards of accountability independently from the mechanisms with which they are commonly associated, advances the debate on accountable international relations in three related ways. First, it shifts scholarly attention from processes of accountability to the virtues or values of accountability appropriate for world politics. Second, in doing so it indicates how scholars and activists might bridge the gap between the highly developed mechanisms of accountability in world politics and lingering worries about the lack of legitimacy of global governance arrangements. Finally, a standards-or values-based approach to democratically accountable international relations captures the intuitions underlying some of the most innovative developments in the transnational practice of accountability today, at once benefitting from their insights and helping to put them on a clearer normative and conceptual footing.

I shall remark on the first two points only briefly. Determining appropriate democratic standards of accountability for world politics might seem daunting. International practice, however, suggests that there is broad (if not always deep) consensus that human rights provide appropriate standards to which transnational actors should be held. This consensus is evident in the critical vocabulary employed by critics and by NGOs and other groups working for greater accountability (Macdonald and Macdonald 2006); it is equally evident in the rhetoric of powerful transnational actors themselves—even if this rhetoric is merely the homage of vice to virtue. There are also good historical and normative reasons for linking democracy and human rights closely together (Goodhart 2005; Gould 2005; Habermas 1996). Finally, human rights standards are widely recognized as legitimate in assessing the behavior of states and leaders and are well-established in international legal and institutional practice.[5]

Once a democratic standard is identified, it becomes possible to think about its application and implementation through a wide range of mechanisms. An advantage of disentangling standards from processes of accountability is that it shows how existing mechanisms of accountability in world politics might be turned to democratic ends through the application of democratic standards. The typical assumption is that particular mechanisms of accountability entail certain standards—that market mechanisms, for instance, entail profit as the standard to which power-wielders are held.

This is not, however, a logical necessity. All sorts of mechanisms might be used to uphold democratic standards, assuming that accountability-holders are willing to adopt them. Admittedly, it is a stretch to imagine that powerful actors—states, shareholders—would voluntarily adopt and implement democratic standards of accountability. The point is simply to stress that the aim of activists and scholars interested in greater accountability in world politics need not be to re-establish "democratic" mechanisms of accountability on a global scale. Other accountability mechanisms, including some not yet imagined, might suffice.

FOUR INNOVATIONS IN GLOBAL ACCOUNTABILITY

The third point deserves somewhat more attention. How does the standards-based approach to accountable international relations conform to existing practices? What can it tell us about the normative and conceptual grounding of those practices? Four examples—accountability in governmental networks, global administrative law, surrogate accountability, and global civil society—illustrate the complementarities between the standards-based approach and recent theoretical and practical innovations in accountability.

Transgovernmental Networks

Slaughter has written persuasively about the significant and growing role played by networks of government officials in world politics and the importance of ensuring that these networks are accountable. She recognizes that the lack of accountability is an easy charge to make against transnational governmental networks of the kind she studies and one that requires a response. Specifically, she acknowledges that such networks can reasonably be criticized for their lack of transparency, for their potential domination by industry or other interests or experts, for circumventing or undermining domestic political processes, for being unrepresentative, for allowing foreign influence on judicial decision-making to affect domestic law, and for replicating or magnifying power asymmetries in world politics (Slaughter 2004b, 219–30). These complaints are typical of complaints about global accountability deficits generally. They also illustrate how governmental networks blur the boundary between international relations and global governance.

Slaughter's solution is two-pronged. She proposes a range of mechanisms to ensure that officials enmeshed in such networks remain accountable at home, through strategies including recognition and visibility of their dual roles and domestic deliberation about appropriate standards for participation in transnational networks (Slaughter 2004b, 231–44; 2004a, 163). She also identifies five norms or principles that might serve as "ground rules" for how networks of this kind could operate. The most important of these, in her view, is deliberative equality, which refers to inclusion, fairness in negotiations, and so on (Slaughter 2004a, 176). Other important international norms include legitimate difference (pluralism), positive comity (dialogue over deference), checks and balances, and subsidiarity (Slaughter 2004a, 163). These norms are informed by the work of political philosophers, by domestic constitutional principles, and by emerging global practices. They reflect the "values of equality, tolerance, autonomy, interdependence, liberty, and self-government" (Slaughter 2004b, 31).

Adherence to these norms would make transgovernmental networks—and by implication, international relations and global governance arrangements of all kinds—more just and more legitimate. Slaughter is a skeptic about global democracy, but recognizes that the "new world order" requires legitimacy and that this legitimacy would be enhanced through greater accountability. Her reluctance to embrace global accountability mechanisms seems rooted in uncertainty about how to define democratic accountability in the global context (Slaughter 2004b, 218), a concern that echoes the familiar preoccupation with the identity of the accountability-holders. Still, in its advocacy of global constitutional norms or principles, her proposal militates in the direction of the proposal for accountability to democratic standards advanced here. That framework helps to clarify and bolster her contention that accountability to (democratic) norms might increase the legitimacy of global governance arrangements.

Global Administrative Law

A related approach to accountability in the global context comes from proponents of global administrative law (GAL). GAL refers to the set of "principles, procedures, and review mechanisms that are emerging to govern decision-making and regulatory rule-making" (Kingsbury et al. 2004, 2). It comprises administration and regulation undertaken by IGOs, transnational networks of government officials, regulators working under the auspices of treaties, hybrid intergovernmental-private arrangements, and private institutions with regulatory functions (2004, 8). Global administration represents a distinct space or sphere characterized by its autonomy, the increasing power of its decision makers, and the scope of their influence; it is thus important to recognize its importance and to further develop novel and appropriate principles and mechanisms of accountability to govern this space and the decisions made within it (2004, 13).

GAL appeals to many scholars because it achieves juridification in world politics without relying on authorization by a global parliament or enforcement through a world state. The standards that typify GAL—transparency, participation, and review—will not necessarily make global governance more democratic, but they will make it more reasoned (Chesterman 2008, 40). Indeed, proponents of GAL acknowledge the democratic deficits that plague global governance, but conclude that GAL cannot, on its own, fill them. This is primarily owing to the lack of a "convincing" global theory of democracy that would replicate domestic models of democracy globally (Kingsbury et al. 2004, 35; cf. Chesterman 2008, 44). Such worries wrongly conflate democratic accountability with democracy, ignoring that greater democratic accountability might be achieved without the complete democratization of world politics (Goodhart 2011).

One way this might be achieved is by expanding the principles on which GAL is based. While transparency, participation, and review are certainly democratically desirable, they need not exhaust the standards that global administrative law might uphold. Indeed, a human rights standard would do a lot to inform the design and assessment of specific conceptualizations and implementations of each of those principles. In addition, it might push administrative law beyond pure proceduralism by establishing substantive limits on rule- and policy-making.

It would also align with the expanding jurisprudence of forums like the ICC and ECHR, helping to reinforce global standards of accountability for behavior and decision-making. While the specific mechanisms and procedures for ensuring compliance with a democratic GAL would no doubt vary, they would surely require the institutionalization of meaningful opportunities to deliberate, influence, and contest rules and policies—measures that go a step or two beyond the consultative reforms, discussed earlier, undertaken by the World Bank (cf. Bohman 2004; Goodhart 2008).

Surrogate Accountability

The final examples to consider concern so-called surrogate accountability (following Rubenstein 2007). Surrogate accountability refers to the process of third parties taking a role in the accountability process—either by setting standards of accountability, finding and interpreting information, or imposing sanctions (2007, 617). It becomes necessary or relevant because of asymmetries of power in world politics, which sometimes make it impossible for accountability-holders to carry out these functions on their own (or to do so effectively). These asymmetries can be balanced, in part, when third parties act in behalf of accountability holders in holding power-wielders to account. Weak states or communities often cannot exercise accountability over powerful states or IGOs whose decisions directly affect them even when their right to do is widely recognized. In such cases, NGOs or other surrogates might act in their behalf.

Rubenstein points out that this form of accountability entails certain risks, as the surrogates are not themselves accountable to the accountability-holders in whose behalf they act. She argues that surrogates can be evaluated normatively on the basis of how well they substitute or stand in for accountability holders (2007, 627), gauging how democratic or representative the surrogates are. New research by Koenig-Archibugi and Macdonald (2012) finds that the type of surrogate and the institutional features of proxy accountability mechanisms play a significant role in determining how closely surrogate standards of accountability track accountability-holders' interests and preferences.

Macdonald and Macdonald (2006) investigate what they call non-electoral accountability, which is characterized as an adaptation to the disaggregated, dispersed, and decentralized forms of power and functional and jurisdictional differentiation typical of globalization. When power is organized this way, they argue, traditional electoral mechanisms of (democratic) accountability are ineffective and inappropriate ways of ensuring political control over the exercise of power. By "reverse engineering" democratic elections, they show that these mechanisms have the function and purpose of establishing political control over any agents of power (state or nonstate) that jeopardize people's enjoyment of their democratic entitlements (2006, 93)—roughly, their human rights, including especially economic rights, as well as autonomy and equality (2006, 95). Having distilled this democratic standard, they look at new mechanisms of accountability that serve as alternate mechanisms for democratic control of power.

While not exactly a form of surrogate accountability, their approach also recognizes that democratic accountability need not rely on a direct correspondence between those entitled to hold power to account and those who do the work of holding power to account. Using examples of activist campaigns in the global garment industry, they show how non-electoral mechanisms allow those whose democratic entitlements are directly threatened by power to reassert some political control by invoking and acting to protect their human rights (Macdonald and Macdonald 2006).

Studies of surrogate accountability highlight that ensuring a voice or a connection to those who are immediately impacted by the exercise of power remains crucial to the legitimacy of alternate accountability mechanisms. While democratic norms provide general standards of accountability, they also inform the creation of mechanisms to allow for deliberation, influence, and contestation, as discussed earlier.

Global Civil Society

Surrogate accountability and accountability to democratic standards help to answer questions about the role of global civil society (GCS) as a mechanism of *democratic* accountability. Numerous scholars have rightly lauded GCS for its achievements and potential for taming power (see e.g., O'Brien et al. 2000; Scholte 2004). Moreover, GCS embodies for many scholars and activists a democratic ethos and structure. Yet critics have raised serious concerns about NGOs, for example, pointing out that they speak for others, often without their explicit authorization. In addition, NGOs and other actors in GCS do not formally represent those on whose behalf they advocate (they are not elected), and their values and priorities do not necessarily reflect those of most or even of many people. Moreover, many NGOs and other segments of civil society actively promote undemocratic aims and ideals (Bob 2012; cf. Chambers and Kopstein 2001).[6]

Accountability to democratic standards helps to clarify how and why GCS might be a mechanism of democratic accountability. When NGOs and other actors advocate democratic standards of accountability, when they act as good surrogates according to the normative criteria discussed here, they can promote democratic accountability. Likewise, networks of government officials and global administrative law can also be vehicles of democratic accountability. Skeptics have been too quick to dismiss the possibility of democratically accountable international relations. This is good news for scholars and activists committed to the idea that world politics might be made more legitimate through becoming more (democratically) accountable.

Conclusion

International relations can refer both to the interactions among states and to interactions and transactions involving their delegates, including the IGOs that wield increasing power and authority in world politics. Befitting a world in which interdependence was comparatively low and autonomy comparatively high (Zacher 1992), accountability in international relations was historically conceived as a matter of holding states and their leaders to account for their behavior. Natural and international law established norms governing how states might treat their citizens and rules to govern the international system. It is in this tradition that modern human rights and humanitarian law evolved, giving rise to a range of legal doctrines and institutions designed to deter and punish atrocious behavior by states and rulers.

The expanding importance of global governance has raised new concerns related to accountability in our increasingly interdependent world, concerns about the accountability of policy- and decision-making at the global level. These concerns are driven by doubts about the legitimacy of existing global governance arrangements. Democracy is the gold standard for legitimacy in decision-making, but it has proven difficult to determine how democratic accountability might be achieved globally. This chapter outlined a case for accountability to democratic (human rights) standards and showed how this approach confirms and explains several important trends in recent international practices of accountability.

As global interdependence grows, accountable behavior and accountable decision-making will become ever more important. Strengthening the web of accountability for bad behavior and developing new mechanisms for increasing the legitimacy of decision-making using democratic standards are thus urgent scholarly and political priorities.

ACKNOWLEDGMENTS

I am very grateful to Leslie Marshall for her research on this project, and to the editors for their patience and helpful suggestions.

NOTES

1. On the distinction between *international* and *global* governance organizations, see Koppell, this volume.
2. Serious crimes include (1) piracy; (2) slavery; (3) war crimes; (4) crimes against peace; (5) crimes against humanity; (6) genocide; and (7) torture.
3. I do not discuss TNCs further here, though much of my argument applies to them; see Koppell and Leader in this volume for further discussion.
4. Philp (2009, 31–3) notes that the sanction might be linked to the failure to give an account or to the contents of the account, an important distinction.
5. See Goodhart (2011, 57–8) for a response to common objections to human rights standards.
6. For a general discussion of accountability issues in GCS see Brown and Moore (2001); Cavill and Sohail (2007); Kaldor (2003).

REFERENCES

Alter, K. J. 1998. "Who Are the 'Masters of the Treaty'"? European Governments and the European Court of Justice." *International Organization*, 52: 121–47.

APSA. 2012. *Democratic Imperatives. Innovations in Rights, Participation, and Economic Citizenship.* Report of the Task Force on Democracy, Economic Security, and Social Justice in a Volatile World. Washington, DC: APSA.

Archibugi, D. 2008. *The Global Commonwealth of Citizens: Toward Cosmopolitan Democracy.* Princeton: Princeton University Press.

Bob, C. 2012. *The Global Right Wing and the Clash of World Politics.* Cambridge: Cambridge University Press.

Bohman, J. 2004. "Constitution Making and Democratic Innovation: The European Union and Transnational Governance." *European Journal of Political Theory,* 3: 315–37.

Bovens, M. 2010. "Two Concepts of Accountability: Accountability as a Virtue and as a Mechanism." *West European Politics,* 33: 946–67.

Brown, L. D. and Moore, M. H. 2001. "Accountability, Strategy, and International Nongovernmental Organizations." *Nonprofit and Voluntary Sector Quarterly,* 30: 569–87.

Byers, M. 2000. "The Law and Politics of the Pinochet Case." *Duke Journal of Comparative and International Law,* 10: 415–42.

Cabrera, L. 2011. Introduction: Global Institutional Visions, pp. 1–20 in *Global Governance, Global Government: Institutional Visions for an Evolving World System,* ed. L. Cabrera. Albany: State University of New York Press.

Cassel, D. 2001. "International Human Rights Law in Practice: Does International Human Rights Law Make a Difference?" *Chicago Journal of International Law,* 2: 121–35.

Cavill, S. and Sohail, M. 2007. "Increasing Strategic Accountability: A Framework for International NGOs." *Development in Practice,* 17: 231–48.

Chambers, S. and Kopstein, J. 2001. "Bad Civil Society." *Political Theory,* 29: 837–65.

Chesterman, S. 2008. "Globalization Rules: Accountability, Power, and the Prospects for Global Administrative Law." *Global Governance,* 14: 39–52.

Dahl, R. 1999. Can International Organizations Be Democratic? A Skeptic's View, pp. 19–36 in *Democracy's Edges,* eds. I. Shapiro and C. Hacker-Cordón. Cambridge: Cambridge University Press.

Drezner, D. W. 1999. *The Sanctions Paradox.* Cambridge: Cambridge University Press.

Glasius, M. 2006. *The International Criminal Court: A Global Civil Society Achievement.* London: Routledge.

Goodhart, M. 2005. *Democracy as Human Rights: Freedom and Equality in the Age of Globalization.* New York: Routledge.

Goodhart, M. 2007. "Europe's Democratic Deficits Through the Looking Glass: The European Union as a Challenge for Democracy." *Perspectives on Politics,* 5: 567–84.

Goodhart, M. 2008. "Human Rights and Global Democracy." *Ethics and International Affairs,* 22: 395–420.

Goodhart, M. 2011. "Democratic Accountability in Global Politics: Norms, not Agents." *Journal of Politics,* 73: 45–60.

Gould, C. C. 2005. *Globalizing Democracy and Human Rights.* Cambridge: Cambridge University Press.

Grant, R. W. and Keohane, R. O. 2005. "Accountability and Abuses of Power in World Politics." *American Political Science Review,* 99: 29–43.

Habermas, J. 1996. Popular Sovereignty as Procedure, pp. 463–490 in *Between Facts and Norms. Contributions to a Discourse Theory of Law and Democracy.* Cambridge, MA: MIT Press.

Held, D. 1995. *Democracy and the Global Order: From the Modern State to Cosmopolitan Governance.* Stanford: Stanford University Press.

Held, D. 1996. *Models of Democracy*. Stanford: Stanford University Press.

Held, D. 2004. "Democratic Accountability and Political Effectiveness from a Cosmopolitan Perspective." *Government and Opposition*, 39: 364–91.

Helfer, L. P. and Slaughter, A.-M. 1997. "Toward a Theory of Effective Supranational Adjudication." *Yale Law Journal*, 107: 273–391.

Holzgrefe, J. L. and Keohane, R. O. (eds.) 2003. *Humanitarian Intervention: Ethical, Legal, and Political Dilemmas*. Cambridge: Cambridge University Press.

Jacobson, D. and Ruffer, G. B. 2003. "Courts Across Borders: The Implications of Judicial Agency for Human Rights and Democracy." *Human Rights Quarterly*, 25: 74–92.

Kaldor, M. 2003. "Civil Society and Accountability." *Journal of Human Development*, 4: 5–27.

Keohane, R. O. 2006. "Accountability in World Politics." *Scandanavian Political Studies*, 29: 75–87.

Khagram, S. 2002. Restructuring the Global Politics of Development: The Case of India's Narmada Valley Dams, pp. 206–30 in *Restructuring World Politics. Transnational Social Movements, Networks, and Norms*, eds. S. Khagram, J. V. Riker, and K. Sikkink. Minneapolis: University of Minnesota Press.

Kingsbury, B., Krisch, N. and Stewart, R. B. 2004. *The Emergence of Global Administrative Law*. IILJ Working Paper, No. 2004/1. Global Administrative Law Series, NYU School of Law.

Koenig-Archibugi, M. 2010. "Accountability in Transnational Relations: How Distinctive Is It?" *West European Politics*, 33: 1142–64.

Koenig-Archibugi, M. and Macdonald, K. 2012. "Accountability-by-Proxy in Transnational Non-State Governance." *Governance*, DOI: 10.1111/j.1468-0491.2012.01609.x

Kymlicka, W. 1999. Citizenship in an Era of Globalization: Commentary on Held, pp. 112–26 in *Democracy's Edges*, eds. I. Shapiro and C. Hacker-Cordón. Cambridge: Cambridge University Press.

Macdonald, T. and Macdonald, K. 2006. "Non-Electoral Accountability in Global Politics: Strengthening Democratic Control within the Global Garment Industry." *European Journal of International Law*, 17: 89–119.

Macedo, S. (ed.) 2001. *The Princeton Principles on Universal Jurisdiction*. Princeton: Program in Law and Public Affairs, Princeton University.

Malanczuk, P. 1997. *Akehurst's Modern Introduction to International Law*. New York: Routledge.

Moravcsik, A. 2004. "Is There a "Democratic Deficit" in World Politics? A Framework for Analysis." *Government and Opposition*, 39: 336–63.

Nye, J. S. 2001. "Globalization's Democratic Deficit: How to Make International Institutions More Accountable." *Foreign Affairs*, 80: 2–6.

O'Brien, R., Goetz, A. M., Scholte, J. A., and Williams, M. 2000. *Contesting Global Governance. Multilateral Economic Institutions and Global Social Movements*. Cambridge: Cambridge University Press.

Philp, M. 2009. "Delimiting Democratic Accountability." *Political Studies*, 57: 28–53.

Rubenstein, J. 2007. "Accountability in an Unequal World." *Journal of Politics*, 69: 616–32.

Schabas, W. A. 2011. *An Introduction to the International Criminal Court*. Cambridge: Cambridge University Press.

Scholte, J. A. 2004. "Civil Society and Democratically Accountable Global Governance." *Government and Opposition*, 39: 211–33.

Slaughter, A.-M. 2004a. "Disaggregated Sovereignty: Towards the Public Accountability of Global Government Networks." *Government and Opposition*, 39: 159–90.

Slaughter, A.-M. 2004b. *A New World Order*. Princeton: Princeton University Press.

Smith, R. K. M. 2009. Human Rights in International Law, pp. 26–45 in *Human Rights: Politics and Practice*, ed. M. Goodhart. Oxford: Oxford University Press.

Steffek, J. 2008. "Public Accountabiilty and the Public Sphere of International Governance." *Ethics and International Affairs*, 24: 45–68.

Stiglitz, J. E. 2002. *Globalization and Its Discontents*. New York: Norton.

UN General Assembly. 1998. "Rome Statute of the International Criminal Court (Last Amended 2010)." The Hague (Netherlands): International Criminal Court.

World Bank. 2009. *Social Accountability*. Retrieved from <http://web.worldbank.org/WBSITE/EXTERNAL/TOPICS/EXTSOCIALDEVELOPMENT/EXTPCENG/0,,contentMDK:2050 9424~menuPK:1278120~pagePK:148956~piPK:216618~theSitePK:410306,00.html>.

Zacher, M. W. 1992. The Decaying Pillars of the Westphalian Temple: Implications for International Order and Governance, pp. 58–101 in *Governance Without Government: Order and Change in World Politics*, eds. J. N. Rosenau and E.-O. Czempiel. Cambridge: Cambridge University Press.

Zürn, M. 2005. Global Governance and Legitimacy Problems, pp. 136–63 in *Global Governance and Public Accountabillity*, eds. D. Held and M. Koenig-Archibugi. Oxford: Blackwell Publishing.

Zweifel, T. D. 2002. "Who is Without Sin Cast the First Stone: The EU's Democratic Deficit in Comparison." *Journal of European Public Policy*, 9: 812–40.

PART IV

ORGANIZATIONAL
ACCOUNTABILITY

CHAPTER 19

....

ACCOUNTABLE PUBLIC SERVICES

....

BARBARA S. ROMZEK

PUBLIC SERVICES AND ACCOUNTABILITY

....

GOVERNMENTS provide many public services to their residents, such as national defense, public health, safety and welfare, to name a few categories.[1] The past 30 years have involved a significant increase in the types of organizational arrangements used by governments to deliver public services (Salamon 2002; Warner and Hefetz 2008). While direct delivery of public services by government workers remains the most common arrangement, alternative delivery strategies play a substantial role in public services. These alternatives include two-party contracts between public and private or nonprofit entities (Brown and Potoski 2003; Johnston and Romzek 2010) and intergovernmental collaborations (Thurmaier and Wood 2002; Duggan and Green 2008; US Government Accountability Office 2012). The more complex arrangements include multi-party and multi-sector collaborations that can include public–private partnerships (Hodge and Greve 2005) and networks of service providers (Romzek et al. 2012).

This variety of administrative arrangements for public service delivery reflects different institutional designs, managerial approaches, and administrative tasks. The combination of administrative diversification for government services and focused political agendas on government accountability has fostered "an increasingly dense and aggressive accountability industry" (Flinders 2001, 595–96). Accountability is necessarily contextually based, and these delivery arrangements will vary in the opportunities and challenges they present for achieving accountability.

FORMAL AND INFORMAL ACCOUNTABILITY

Accountability can be pursued through formal structures and processes as well as informal interpersonal dynamics. Formal accountability uses explicit performance standards and reporting relationships, such as hierarchy, external oversight, deference to staff expertise, and responsiveness to stakeholders (Romzek 2000). Informal accountability derives from implicit norms and unofficial performance expectations individuals have of each other; it works through informal interpersonal dynamics rather than official reporting relationships (Koliba et al. 2011; Romzek 2011).

Formal accountability arrangements typically identify in advance sources of authority, performance expectations, reporting requirements, accountability mechanisms, and the range of potential consequences. Hierarchy and external auditing are the most time-honored examples of formal accountability. These are most evident in performance management strategies which emphasize measurable outcomes and summary assessments, such as benchmarks, scores, or report cards that allow for comparison. Deference to expertise typically is used in situations where discretion and specialized knowledge are essential, for example, when complex judgments are needed to determine strategies for programs and/ or clients which require tailored outcomes, e.g., environmental remediation or health care. Accountability based on responsiveness to key stakeholders, such as elected officials and service recipients, is a long-standing strategy that is increasingly popular. Citizen or client surveys for feedback and/or assessment, often measuring satisfaction with services, are popular examples emphasizing responsiveness. While the preponderance of formal accountability mechanisms is based upon vertical reporting relationships (scrutiny by internal or external authority), accountability can be built into horizontal relationships, as reflected in memoranda of agreement, contracts, or partnerships among independent entities. Formal horizontal arrangements involve written agreements that stipulate relationships, responsibilities, and consequences of performance between independent parties who agree to cooperate.

Informal accountability emerges from interpersonal interactions that are based upon shared goals and implicit shared norms of interaction. Over the course of repeated interactions individuals in official and unofficial groups develop informal norms, expectations, and patterns of behavior as group members (Ostrom 2000). These interpersonal interactions give rise to shared norms, discretionary behaviors, unofficial monitoring, and informal rewards and/or sanctions conferred by individuals operating in the shared service arena (Romzek et al. 2012).

Informal accountability can manifest in vertical accountability relationships, for example receiving unofficial rewards and/or sanctions based upon meeting (or failing to meet) the informal expectations of one's supervisor or funding authority regarding job performance. Informal accountability plays an even more significant role in institutional arrangements involving horizontal relationships, e.g., in intergovernmental

agreements, partnerships, and collaborative networks, where service providers cooperate and interact in pursuit of a shared goal and where reputational consequences, such
as loss of respect among peers, are important sanctions. For example, in a network of
service providers, network organizations typically have a shared goal and/or shared
clients, and network actors find the need to collaborate to accomplish their service
delivery goals.

Both formal and informal accountability present challenges. Formal accountability
relationships in the public sector embody a range of challenges: multiple stakeholders
(O'Connell 2005), multiple and often conflicting performance expectations (Page 2004),
multiple and overlapping accountability relationships (Romzek 2000; Koliba et al. 2011),
difficulty measuring performance (Radin 2006), and uneven implementation of consequences (Romzek and Johnston 2005). While the institutional contexts and structures
will differ, these challenges are present in varying degrees in the different service delivery arrangements.

Informal accountability challenges based on institutional features include goal
conflict, competition and turf battles, as well as financial pressures. As is true for formal accountability, the manifestation of these challenges will vary by context, but
the general dynamics are present in most service delivery cases. Individual interpersonal dynamics encounter challenges due to staff turnover (which disrupts relationships), communication gaps, failures of initiative, differences in perspectives
based upon hierarchical position, and tensions between the operation of formal and
informal accountability (Koliba et al. 2011; Romzek et al. 2013). This last challenge,
tension between formal and informal accountability, is an example of having "too
much" of what is presumably a good thing. In such instances the different accountability arrangements can work at cross purposes and undermine the overall process of achieving answerability for performance. Sometimes formal monitoring can
undermine informal accountability. For example, trust is a cornerstone of informal
accountability, yet the need for formal reporting in social services contracts often
undermines the degree of trust in informal interpersonal relationships (Almqvist and
Hogberg 2005).

DIRECT SERVICE DELIVERY

Direct delivery involves services produced internally by a government agency, delivered by public employees, using public funds, and subject to government supervision
and financial protocols. Direct service delivery varies around the globe; but typically
governments directly provide services for "public goods," e.g., services which provide
shared benefits to all and which cannot be withheld from those who do not pay for
them.[2] Examples of such services include national defense, law enforcement, and
public parks. National governments tend to provide direct services in areas such as
national security, public health, transportation, postal services, and social services.

Local and regional governments typically provide directly a wide range of services, such as public safety, public health, roads, street lighting, neighborhood parks, as well as water, sewers, and public transit. Local governments in particular are likely to retain direct production for services that are difficult to measure and have high transaction costs (Brown and Potoski 2003), such as the operations of airports and child welfare services.

Accountability arrangements in direct delivery tend to rely on formal supervision and oversight, emphasizing reporting to authority about whether performance expectations were met. Performance goals can be specified as inputs (e.g., staffing), processes (appropriate use of funds), outputs (number of cases processed), or outcomes (changes in community health indicators). Outputs are most often the focus of performance because of the ease of developing measurable objectives. A popular example is the use of satisfaction ratings from key stakeholders, typically elected officials and clientele (Heikkila and Isett 2007). The current popularity of measuring outputs leads to performance indicators such as the number of citizens or clients served, timeliness of response to service requests, work productivity, and overall customer satisfaction.[3]

Informal accountability is also at work in direct service provision—even in the most hierarchical organization. The process emerges from individuals embedded in social networks and exercising significant discretion with regard to rules and procedures (Maynard-Moody and Musheno 2000). Informal accountability in direct service arrangements is reflected in the kinds of facilitative behaviors and rewards most people have observed, such as helping a co-worker during a rush period. The classic negative examples of informal accountability are instances where groups voluntarily restrict productivity by "working to rule" due to social network influences.

The strengths of accountability in direct service delivery lie in the potential for consensus on definitions of performance and clear chains of responsibility and reporting relationships. Some direct services, e.g., trash collection or filling potholes, lend themselves to clear specification of performance expectations and relatively straightforward measurement of performance. Efforts by the New York City police department to tackle crime fighting in a systematic way emphasized this approach; it decentralized authority and emphasized performance measurement and dissemination of results to all relevant police units (O'Connell 2001).

Direct service delivery for more complex services presents accountability challenges due to the difficulty of specifying and measuring performance (Radin 2006). Not all services lend themselves to objective measures of outputs or outcomes, as an example, mental health. Another challenge relates to identifying true costs of service delivery (a pre-requisite to knowing if services are delivered efficiently); this difficulty rests with the frequent pattern of public organizations relying on departmental cross-subsidies.

There are a number of alternatives to direct delivery of public services. Most alternative delivery arrangements are reflected in formal agreements, e.g., legislative authority, contracts, memoranda of understanding (MOU), and partnerships. These typically specify formal accountability practices; informal accountability emerges out of the repeated interactions of individuals working within the service arena. The discussion that follows addresses the accountability dynamics that tend to be present in these broad categories of delivery alternatives.

CONTRACTING

Contracting for service delivery is one of the most widely used and long-standing alternatives to direct provision by governments. It reflects a strong political sentiment that markets offer important discipline in costs and greater opportunities for accountability. The most straightforward contracts typically involve two parties, with the government agency serving as the principal and another organization acting as the agent, e.g., a government entity contracting with a private or nonprofit provider for housing services (Sclar 2000).

National governments tend to contract for health and social services, food services, and transportation (Osborne and Brown 2005; Pollitt 2011). At the turn of the twenty-first century, the vast majority of services contracted by local governments in the US were for trash collection and ambulance services (Dilger et al. 1997). The range of contracted services at the local level has expanded to include a wider variety of essential services such as sanitation, transportation, public safety, and social services (Brown and Potoski 2003).[4]

Formal accountability in contracts is built upon carefully written agreements that anticipate incentives in contract design, and specify in advance performance expectations, performance measures, monitoring relationships and consequences (Johnston and Romzek 2010). Typically, contracting involves a mix of several different accountability relationships, relying heavily on external oversight and performance measurement (reporting, auditing), deference to the expertise of contractors, and responsiveness to key stakeholders, with appropriate adaptations (Brown et al. 2006; Page 2004; Romzek and Johnston 2005).

These formal accountability relationships are supplemented by informal accountability dynamics which develop over time, especially when contracts require on-going adjustments over the course of the contract (Romzek et al. 2012). Shared norms, such as trust and reciprocity, are key variables in such situations. Facilitative behaviors, such as renegotiating terms of the contract when not required to do so, lead to increased trust and reciprocity, which in turn increase motivation to comply with performance expectations.

The strengths of accountability regimes used in contracting lie in government's ability to specify performance expectations in contract language and the flexibility to switch providers if contractor performance is not acceptable. The expectation is that the discipline of the market (the presence of competitors who could be alternative providers) enhances contractor accountability because contractors anticipate they could lose the contract if they do not perform well.

The challenges to effective accountability practices in contracting reside in the difficulty contracting principals have in specifying performance, developing good performance measures, and collecting reliable performance data (Lambright 2008). Once these are accomplished, there are still the transaction costs associated with managing contracts and the difficulty developing effective accountability strategies (Johnston and Romzek 2010; Joaquin and Greitens 2012).

Governments generally do an inadequate job managing and monitoring contractor performance, identifying transaction costs, and imposing sanctions. In fact, research shows that local governments do more monitoring of their in-house service delivery than their contracted services (Marvel and Marvel 2007). Sometimes the difficulty imposing sanctions is due to a lack of alternative providers (Johnston and Girth 2012) and other times due to a lack of political will (Romzek and Johnston 2005).

COLLABORATION

While the predominant service delivery arrangements are direct delivery and contracts, there are a number of more complex public service delivery arrangements that fall under the broad label of collaboration: partnerships, intergovernmental collaborations, and networks. These categories of delivery alternatives are not exclusive. For example, public–private partnerships and many collaborations are based upon contractual agreements. Others involve memoranda of agreements for services that vary in complexity and degrees of interdependence among service providers. There are complex collaborations within the public sector and across public, private and nonprofit sectors; some arrangements are formally organized in networks and partnerships, others are more loosely structured collaborations. The common denominator for these endeavors is that a government agency arranges for a multi-party organizational entity to provide a public service.

Collaborations are often initiated through some official action when the services to be provided are complex and delivery requires expertise beyond that available within one organization (Emerson et al. 2012). Collaborations tend to emphasize greater integration of program services across multiple agencies, typically with the goal of achieving economies of scale and tapping specialized capacities. Collaborations involve multiple organizations in coordinated activities where no single organization is in charge, collaborators interact as peers, and cooperation is the basis for successful performance. All collaborations have some component of shared goals, which is the basis for the interaction, and involve some sharing of resources, e.g., effort, funding, or professional knowledge.

Collaborations occur in a wide range of areas; examples include emergency management, environmental services, public health, social services, and transportation. Collaborators often share authority. Monitoring activities can take the form of both formal accountability, through monitoring and documenting performance, and informal accountability through facilitative behaviors and informal rewards and sanctions.

Partnerships

Partnerships reflect a popular collaboration option. While public–private partnerships are most often seen in public infrastructure projects and services (Forrer et al. 2010), they have also been used to provide public services. Partnerships for service delivery that cross sector boundaries (public, private, and nonprofit) typically involve the direct participation of a nongovernmental organization in a venture with a public agency. Partnerships can facilitate innovation and tap the unique expertise and efficiencies available in the nongovernmental sectors (Hodge and Greve 2005).

Partnerships usually are rooted in contractual relationships; but they rarely embody simple principal–agent relationships. Instead they involve joint production of services or products, represent relationships on relatively equal terms, and can vary in locus of control, sources of funding, and ownership. Cross-sector partnerships typically involve long-term commitments and a pooling of experience and expertise. They often have significant capital funding requirements associated with the degree of assumed risk and tend to involve financial and organizational arrangements where both the sectors can benefit (Teisman and Klijn 2002; Hodge and Greve 2005). Typically partners contribute funds or services in exchange for certain rights or future income.

Non-contractual partnerships between governments and nonprofit organizations involve frequent exchanges of information, sharing of volunteers, and joint recruitment of staff. The most robust partnerships are in the areas of arts and culture, public safety, and emergency response, with public safety and emergency response partnerships having greater longevity.

By design, partnerships emphasize horizontal, mutual accountability relationships usually in formal agreements that specify roles, responsibilities, rights, and risks. To the extent that partnerships are based in contracts or memoranda of understanding, the formal accountability dynamics noted in the earlier discussion of contracts apply. Formal accountability of partnerships is enhanced with clear specification at the outset of each partner's roles, responsibilities, performance expectations, and assumed risks, with stipulation of potential consequences for results (rewards and/or sanctions), such as shared return on investments and partner options when one party fails to meet its responsibilities in the joint endeavor. Partnerships must address complex and sometimes conflicting expectations, and balance pressures related to "myriad public demands: cost-effectiveness, risk sharing, innovation, reliability, timeliness, stakeholder participation, transparency, and security" (Forrer et al. 2010). Informal accountability emerges in partnerships through the development of reciprocal relationships among partners, where "everyone is simultaneously both an agent and a principal, holding each other accountable for achieving the missions for which the partnership is formed ... [In such instances] the monitoring and measuring function of accountability is more about improving the performance of the partnership through negotiation and learning than about 'answerability' or 'control' of public bureaucracies by elected politicians" (Acar et al. 2008, 15). From an accountability perspective, the advantage of partnerships rests with the shared roles and risk, complementary expertise, and organizational capacities.

The strength of accountability in partnerships rests on the clarity of the agreements, the ability to identify the separate responsibilities and contributions of the partners, and the trust and reciprocity that foster informal accountability. Partnership accountability is best assured and assessed when incentives are properly aligned, transaction costs and benefits clearly identified, expertise is appropriately deployed, performance is effectively measured, arrangements enable trust to develop, and risks are shared appropriately (Goldsmith and Eggers 2004; Forrer et al. 2010).

The challenges of accountability of partnerships relate to project governance, financial transparency, risk, and performance measurement. Accountability can be difficult to achieve due to a lack of independent evaluators, difficulties getting performance data (e.g., due to contract complexity, secrecy, and the like), poor evaluation design (lack of rigorous data, poor definition of outcomes), as well as use of inappropriate measures of discount rates, risk transfers, and net benefits (Hodge and Greve 2007). These can arise, in part, due to the reluctance of private sector organizations to share confidential information with public sector monitors (Forrer et al. 2010).

Intergovernmental Collaboration

Intergovernmental collaborations are common among national, regional, and local governments in areas such as health and human services, coastal zone management, and emergency management. Popular mechanisms include interagency agreements, interagency collaborator positions, joint program efforts, working groups, task forces, commissions, and lead agencies. Several national governments have used interagency collaborations to expand clients' access to a range of public services through electronic means by providing a single point of contact for citizens and clients to access a multitude of government services.[5] This has been the case to varying degrees in Australia, Canada, France, Ireland, Singapore, and the United Kingdom (Duggan and Green 2008).

Interlocal agreements are one variation on intergovernmental collaboration; they typically entail horizontal links between cities and vertical links across city, county, and regional governments (Thurmaier and Wood 2002). A majority of cities and counties in the US report at least one interlocal agreement (Agranoff 1989).[6] Often such agreements involve one government delivering services to residents in neighboring governmental jurisdictions, with the level of collaboration being fairly minimal; many are fairly straightforward contracts. The range of services provided through such venues is large, including public safety, road maintenance, emergency response, water and sewer, transit services, legal and accounting services.

Accountability for intergovernmental service delivery arrangements varies depending on the level of government and nature of the service provided. For national governments the emphasis has been on formalized reporting to hierarchical superiors and oversight bodies based on mandated service standards and performance metrics (Duggan and Green 2008; Radin 2006). Traditional accountability strategies used within organizational boundaries can be a source of tension in intergovernmental arenas when individuals must balance expectations of one's "home" agency with those of the collaborative entity.

The challenge of accountability for service delivery is even more complicated when multi-party collaborations are used, especially in networks that cross sector lines. Such circumstances increase the chances of goal conflict, turf battles, and fiscal constraints. Efforts to address these often emphasize collaborative discussion of performance standards. Accountability in social services for children and families in two American states (Georgia and Vermont) relied on a formal committee to measure core results and indicators, to set clear targets for local collaboratives to use to focus their efforts and track indicators (Page 2003). Local governments report a lack of formal monitoring of performance of interlocal collaborations (Thurmaier and Wood 2002; Brown and Potoski 2003; Jaoquin and Greitens 2012). One reason for this may be the higher levels of trust and reciprocity among interlocal collaborators who often share a common professional orientation; these shared norms are key components of informal accountability.

The strength of accountability in intergovernmental collaborations rests in the shared institutional culture, clarity of performance standards and reporting relationships, complementary capacities and expertise, and deference to discretion and expertise of workers (Page 2004). The shared culture is reflected in the fact that local governments are more comfortable collaborating with other governments than with private or non-profit entities; they report higher levels of trust (Brown and Potoski 2003).

Intergovernmental collaborations face all of the usual challenges of traditional forms of service delivery as well as the challenges of coordinating the actions of several organizations with different authority structures, expertise, and service delivery protocols (Moynihan 2005). These challenges include specifying performance expectations and identifying a performance measurement system that reflect interdependent performance measures and, *joint* contributions, and yield data that are understandable (Pollitt 2011).

Challenges to effective accountability in interagency collaborations include mission conflicts, turf protection over mission and resources, as well as incompatible procedures, processes, data, and technology. A key challenge arises because collaborations rarely have one organization that is in complete control, hence there is a tendency for confusion over authority and leadership. This can lead to tensions over who needs to answer to whom, and the potential for disagreement about which results to measure (Page 2004). In such collaborations, informal accountability dynamics can help bridge any gaps of leadership and organizational culture by emphasizing shared norms of trust, reciprocity, and respect for partners' institutional turf (Romzek et al. 2012); trustworthy behavior yields informal accountability rewards. In essence, informal accountability can fill the gaps that arise in formal accountability.

Networks

Networks are a common mechanism for multi-sector collaboration; they are "structures of interdependence involving multiple organizations...where one unit is not merely the formal subordinate of the others in some larger hierarchical arrangement" (O'Toole 1997, 45). A distinguishing characteristic for collaboration within networks is the interdependence of outcomes. In the service delivery arena, networks often emerge in response to a two-party contract between a government agency and a lead nongovernmental organization, with the former acting as the sole buyer of services and the latter taking the lead to create the network to meet the capacity needs for service delivery (Milward and Provan 2006; Romzek and Johnston 2005). This strategy has been widely used by many state and local governments working across many service sectors, including economic development, fire response and prevention, disaster relief, parks and recreation, and a wide range of social and human services.

Formal accountability arrangements in collaborative networks are typically based in contracts or memoranda of agreement. As such, networks have similar accountability features to those discussed earlier for contracts. Formal accountability is built into foundational agreements that specify roles, responsibilities, performance expectations, outcomes, and consequences. Often networks adopt a portfolio of success metrics that relate to inputs as well as outputs at both network level and agency levels. The details of performance metrics frequently are subject to further negotiation and adjustment as the network members gain experience delivering the service.

The strengths of formal accountability mechanisms in collaboration rest in the clarity in membership, decision making (rules), and parameters for action and conflict resolution that formal agreements can provide. Explicit formal performance expectations and formal mechanisms to monitor, evaluate, and report results can be set up in advance, such as stipulating that lead agencies report out what they have accomplished, including data trends. For example, formal accountability processes can reinforce collaborative efforts through agencies' strategic and annual performance plans when they establish complementary goals and strategies and use performance reports to account for collaboration results. Individual accountability for collaborative efforts can be reinforced in performance management systems that establish individual goals for collaboration (US Government Accountability Office 2005). For example, the US federal government has incorporated performance expectations for individuals with collaboration responsibilities that specify the individual will identify one "partner agency" program objective and incorporate it into their own personal performance goals. In other words, the agencies explicitly identify the goal of working across an organizational boundary and evaluate individuals according to these expectations.

The strength of informal accountability in networks lies in the interpersonal dynamics that reinforce and reward common goals and generate significant opportunities for unofficial mechanisms to develop for rewarding and/or punishing members who violate rules and norms or defect on commitments (Ostrom et al. 2000). In effective networks, informal norms and interorganizational dynamics lead to the development of reciprocal relationships and a sense of partner accountability that can generate informal rewards (Page 2004; Romzek et al. 2012). While informal accountability can be present within a single organization, its significance is greatly magnified by the current widespread use of third-party service delivery arrangements, especially collaborative networks.

A basic accountability challenge in networks is managing institutional competition and the tension between unity of effort and pursuit of separate organizational goals (Saz-Carranza and Ospina 2011). Other challenges derive from the lack of well-defined hierarchy and difficulties discerning unique institutional and/or individual responsibility. In designing performance expectations one must balance specificity and flexibility: the need to articulate performance expectations precisely and clearly enough to foster effective performance and allow sufficient flexibility to enable network actors to use discretion and innovate where appropriate. Challenges based on informal interpersonal dynamics include a lack of common organizational culture, staff turnover that disrupts informal collaborative networks, and tensions between formal and informal accountability mechanisms.

FUTURE OF RESEARCH AND PRACTICE ON PUBLIC SERVICES ACCOUNTABILITY

Regardless of the administrative arrangement, the fundamental motivation behind all strategies for public sector accountability is to ensure that services are provided in ways that are consistent with the governmental values of equity, responsiveness, transparency, and probity. Accountability for public services is a complicated endeavor, with providers facing multiple stakeholders, diverse expectations, and complex implementation protocols. Achieving accountability is challenging even when reporting relationships are the most straightforward, e.g., based on two parties in a hierarchical reporting relationship operating under objective performance standards. These accountability challenges are even more complex when public services are delivered through contracts, partnerships, intergovernmental collaborations, or networks.

Governments have made many well-intentioned efforts to design effective accountability systems for the delivery of public services. The result is a tangled web of accountability that relies on a wide array of vertical and horizontal relationships based on formal processes and informal dynamics. Some accountability types complement each other, others work at cross purposes. Conventional wisdom characterizes this tangled web of accountability as "red tape." But the reality is that an administrative process which one actor perceives as a barrier to efficient operation (red tape) is often perceived by another as a valid accountability mechanism that provides a useful check against inappropriate behavior.

Experience has shown that there are some fundamental dynamics and best practices that apply in most instances, with appropriate adaptations to institutional context.

The fundamental administrative reality is that accountability is never cost free. Formal accountability typically involves extra administrative steps, documentation, and oversight; at the very least, there are transaction costs associated with the supervision and monitoring that are essentials of accountability. For example there are often high costs to develop, collect, and interpret quality performance data. When these steps are effective, the result is greater accountability and the cost is usually defensible. In most instances there are tradeoffs between efficiency and accountability; this tradeoff is the price of accountability. There is also a price for ineffective accountability arrangements, involving both transaction costs as well as the cost of inefficiencies, poor performance, misplaced efforts, or fraud. These are the costs that often lead to frustrations and cynicism among service providers and stakeholders.

Long experience has provided a fairly clear idea of how government should and can go about achieving accountability in direct service delivery. The empirical questions tend to focus on whether the result is effective accountability. The widespread and increasing use of alternative delivery methods raises several issues that warrant further research. Clearly, in many instances government can retain responsibility and accountability when alternative delivery arrangements are used. But to do so requires extra attention to governmental values of equity, responsiveness, transparency, and probity. One valuable area of inquiry would explore the complexities of accountability when the boundaries of inherently governmental responsibilities are stretched (or breached), such as when alternative arrangements involve nongovernmental entities in programs that can impact civil rights or liberties. Another valuable area of inquiry would explore the interaction of the multitude of formal and informal accountability arrangements, and identify conditions under which these different approaches reinforce or undermine each other. A third area of inquiry relevant to the use of alternative delivery strategies would focus on the role of front-line employees in advancing or undermining accountability.

Best Practices

It is important to remember that accountability is contextually bounded. Political, legal, socioeconomic, environmental and other dimensions influence accountability for service delivery (Emerson et al. 2012). While each service delivery strategy has unique challenges, several best practices that enable effective accountability are listed below. One key overarching challenge for effective accountability is to align accountability arrangements with the institutional context, management strategy, and service delivery design, and to strive to achieve a strategic balance among the different types of accountability, especially between bureaucratic and collaborative strategies (Koliba et al. 2011). A second key challenge is to recognize and build upon both formal processes and informal accountability dynamics for maximum effectiveness (Romzek et al. 2012). More focused best practices relate to clarity of design of the service delivery initiative, the goals of the activity, as well as the participants, performance, and culture of collaboration.

Design: Ensure that the design of service delivery arrangements clearly specify each party's roles, rights, risks, and rewards. When third party alternatives are used, provide orientation that clarifies cultural assumptions on both sides of the arrangements. Develop good evaluation design and performance measures from the outset, with clarity as to which entity is responsible for collecting data and which is responsible for monitoring and evaluating performance.

Stakeholders: Identify all key stakeholders. Recognize staff as key stakeholders and manage to minimize turnover of key staff (provide recognition). Recognize client or end-user interests and perspectives to better design delivery strategies and get regular feedback on performance.

Goals: Clearly specify service goals. Identify shared goals among collaborators and recognize the value of common goals. Identify contributions to joint goals.

Performance expectations: Clearly define performance expectations in advance. Recognize the existence of multiple expectations and any potential conflicts among them. Ensure all parties to the service delivery protocol (whether direct delivery or through contract, partnership, or collaboration) know how their roles contribute to the service delivery goals.

Management capacity: Within the responsible governmental entity, develop an in-house management capacity to monitor service delivery arrangements, whether direct delivery or contract, partnership or collaboration. This capacity includes the ability to calculate the full transaction costs into the assessment of cost of service delivery and a willingness to renegotiate service delivery arrangements based upon experience with initial service delivery protocols. Develop evaluation and feedback sessions to help agency managers apply lessons learned to subsequent service delivery areas. Joint training and measurement of contributions to joint goals can facilitate accountability.

Monitor performance: Identify performance measures and collect reliable performance data that are appropriately aligned with service goals (inputs, process, outputs, or outcomes). Identify separate and joint contributions of partners and, collaborators. Build service delivery standards, including collaborative goals, into agency and individual performance reviews. Recognize, value, and reward informal facilitative behaviors. Provide feedback.

Cultivate collaborative culture: Cultivate norms of trust and reciprocity and transparency. When a multi-agency arrangement, emphasize cooperation and inclusiveness, be sure to provide an orientation to third party providers to clarify culture and expected norms as well as performance expectations. Cultivate trust and reciprocity, and effective and consistent communication. Share information through frequent and robust communication. Maximize staff stability to sustain interpersonal relationships. Create low cost opportunities for personal interaction and idea sharing.

Hold accountable: Impose rewards and /or sanctions as warranted. This is often one of the steps omitted.

Public services are delivered using a variety of organizational arrangements, with an increasing emphasis in the past several decades on third-party delivery. This increased reliance on alternative delivery arrangements reflects an interest in capturing greater efficiencies and expertise of other organizational entities. Accountability is always challenging for service delivery, whether those services are delivered directly by a government agency or by third parties. Elements of vertical and horizontal accountability relationships are embedded within formal structures and offer both opportunities and challenges to effective answerability for performance. Interpersonal dynamics, which are the basis for informal accountability relationships, can complement or work at cross purposes to formal accountability arrangements. The resulting tangled web of both formal and informal accountability relationships presents both opportunities and challenges to service delivery. The best practices noted above, when applied to the unique institutional arrangements of the service delivery strategy, can help maximize the chances of eliciting effective accountability.

Notes

1. For example, governments have typically provided direct services for passports, road construction and maintenance, street lighting, vehicle driver licenses, motor vehicle registrations, transportation, public safety (e.g., police, fire, traffic control, and emergency management), solid waste collection, tax assessment, water treatment, education, recreation, and social services (e.g., health and welfare). The International City Management Association identifies 64 different services offered by cities in their study of government services (Brown and Potoski 2003; Warner and Hefetz 2008).

2. Economists refer to these terms as "nonexcludable" and "nonrivalrous" (Sclar 2000). The former refers to the fact that the provided service is shared by all; it is impossible to prevent others from enjoying the benefits. The latter refers to the fact that providing the service to one individual does not does not diminish the availability of the same service to others.

3. For example, in the UK, departments develop three-year Public Service Agreements that set out their priority objectives and develop formalized service standards; Australia is developing service delivery metrics based upon user satisfaction levels, level of connected government, efficiency, and capacity improvements; and the US has a performance-reporting regime emphasizing performance metrics and outcome-based results of federal agencies service delivery efforts (Duggan and Green 2008). The US federal government created two performance management initiatives, the legislatively-originated Government Performance and Results Act (in 1993) and the executive branch's Program Assessment Rating Tool (2001); both sought to link program performance to budgets (Radin 2006). The US Social Security Administration (SSA) uses various measures of performance, including targets for claims processing and claims pending, work productivity, customer wait times at field offices, and overall customer satisfaction with service delivery (US Government Accountability Office 2009, GAO-09-511T).

4. One of the more comprehensive approaches to contracting is used by the City of Centennial, Colorado; it has embraced the concept of contracts for public services as the "first" option in its philosophy of service delivery, using direct service delivery only when contracting is deemed to be unfeasible.

5. For example, the "Service Canada" delivers over 50 different programs and services on behalf of 15 federal departments and agencies, including employment insurance, pensions, old age security, national phone service, and student loans (Duggan and Green 2008, 46–7).

6. Formal and informal interlocal agreements are used in many functional areas, including public safety, public works (road, infrastructure, sanitary sewer, storm water improvement), utilities, law enforcement (police, fire, emergency response), recreation, support services (purchasing and bidding, tax administration, contractor licensing, financial management), public health, and bond issues (Thurmaier and Wood 2002).

References

Acar, M., Guo, C. and Yang, K. 2008. "Accountability When Hierarchical Authority is Absent." *American Review of Public Administration*, 38: 3–23.

Agranoff, R. 1989. Managing Intergovernmental Processes, pp. 131–47 in *Handbook of Public Administration*, ed. J. Perry. San Francisco: Jossey-Bass.

Almqvist, R. and Hogberg, O. 2005. Public-Private Partnerships in Social Services: The Example of the City of Stockholm, pp. 231–56 in *The Challenge of Public-Private Partnerships: Learning from International Experience*, eds. G. Hodge and C. Greve. Northampton, MA: Edward Elgar.

Brown, T. L. and Potoski, M. 2003. "Transaction Costs and Institutional Explanations for Government Service Production Decisions." *Journal of Public Administration Research and Theory*, 13: 441–68.

Brown, T. L., Potoski, M., and Van Slyke, D. 2006. "Managing Public Service Contracts: Aligning Values, Institutions and Markets." *Public Administration Review*, 66: 323–31.

Dilger, R. J., Moffett, R. R. and Struyk, L. 1997. "Privatization of Municipal Services in America's Largest Cities." *Public Administration Review*, 57: 21–26.

Duggan, M. and Green, C. 2008. *Transforming Government Service Delivery: New Service Policies for Citizen-Centered Government*. Somers, NY: IBM Global Social Segment.

Emerson, K., Nabatchi, T. and Balogh, S. 2012. "An Integrative Framework for Collaborative Governance." *Public Administration Research and Theory*, 22: 1–29.

Flinders, M. 2001. *The Politics of Accountability in the Modern State*. Aldershot: Ashgate.

Forrer, J., Kee, J. E., Newcomer, K. E., and Boyer, E. 2010. "Public Private Partnerships and the Public Accountability Question." *Public Administration Review*, 70: 475–84.

Goldsmith, S. and Eggers, W. D. 2004. *Governing by Network: The New Shape of the Public Sector*. Washington, DC: Brookings Institution.

Heikkila, T. and Isett, K. R. 2007. "Citizen Involvement and Performance Management in Special Purpose Governments." *Public Administration Review*, 67: 238–48.

Hodge, G. and Greve, C., eds. 2005. *The Challenge of Public-Private Partnerships: Learning from International Experience*. Northampton, MA: Edward Elgar.

Hodge, G. and Greve, C. 2007. "Public-Private Partnership: An International Performance Review." *Public Administration Review*, 67: 545–58.

Joaquin, M. E. and Greitens, T. J. 2012. "Contract Management Capacity Breakdown? An Analysis of U.S. Local Governments." *Public Administration Review*, 72: 807–16.

Johnston, J. M. and Girth, A. M. 2012. "Government Contracts and 'Managing the Market': Exploring the Costs of Strategic Management Responses to Weak Vendor Competition." *Administration & Society*, 44: 3–29.

Johnston, J. M. and Romzek, B. S. 2010. The Promises, Performance, and Pitfalls of Government Contracting, pp. 369–420 in *The Oxford Handbook of American Bureaucracy*, ed. R. F. Durant. Oxford: Oxford University Press.

Koliba, C. J., Mills, R. M. and Zia, A. 2011. "Accountability in Governance Networks: An Assessment of Public, Private, and Nonprofit Emergency Management Practices Following Hurricane Katrina." *Public Administration Review*, 71: 210–20.

Lambright, K. 2008. "Agency Theory and Beyond: Contracted Providers' Motivations to Properly Use Service Monitoring Tools." *Journal of Public Administration Research and Theory*, 19: 207–27.

Marvel, M. K. and Marvel, H. P. 2007. "Outsourcing Oversight: A Comparison of Monitoring for In-House and Contracted Services." *Public Administration Review*, 67: 521–30.

Maynard-Moody, S. and Musheno, M. 2000. "State Agent or Citizen Agent: Two Narratives of Discretion." *Journal of Public Administration Research and Theory*, 10: 329–58.

Milward, H. B. and Provan, K. G. 2006. *A Manager's Guide to Choosing and Using Collaborative Networks*. Washington, DC: IBM Center for the Business of Government.

Moynihan, D. P. 2005. *Leveraging Collaborative Networks in Infrequent Emergency Situations*. Washington, DC: IBM Center for the Business of Government.

O'Connell, L. 2005. "Program Accountability as an Emergent Property: The Role of Stakeholders in a Program's Field." *Public Administration Review*, 65: 85–93.

O'Connell, P. E. 2001. *Using Performance Data for Accountability: The New York City Police Department's CompStat Model of Police Management*. Washington, DC: IBM Center for the Business of Government.

Osborne, S. P. and Brown, K. 2005. *Managing Change and Innovation in Public Service Organizations*. New York: Routledge.

Ostrom, E. 2000. "Collective Action and the Evolution of Social Norms." *Journal of Economic Perspectives*, 14: 137–58.

O'Toole, L. 1997. "Treating Networks Seriously: Practical and Research-Based Agendas in Public Administration." *Public Administration Review*, 57: 45–52.

Page, S. 2004. "Measuring Accountability for Results in Interagency Collaboratives." *Public Administration Review*, 64: 591–606.

Page, S. 2003. "Entrepreneurial Strategies for Managing Interagency Collaboration." *Journal of Public Administration Research and Theory*, 13: 311–40.

Pollitt, C. 2011. Performance Blight and the Tyranny of Light? Accountability in Advanced Performance Measurement Regimes, pp. 81–97 in *Accountable Governance: Problems and Promises*, eds. M. J. Dubnick and H. G. Frederickson. Armonk, NY: M.E. Sharpe.

Radin, B. 2006. *Challenging the Performance Movement: Accountability Complexity and Democratic Values*. Washington, DC: Georgetown University Press.

Romzek, B. S. 2011. The Tangled Web of Accountability in Contracting Networks: The Case of Welfare Reform, pp. 22–41 in *Accountable Governance: Problems and Promises*, eds. M. J. Dubnick and H. G. Frederickson. Armonk, NY: M.E. Sharpe.

Romzek, B. S. 2000. "Dynamics of Public Sector Accountability in an Era of Reform." *International Review of Administrative Sciences*, 66: 21–44.

Romzek, B. S. and Johnston, J. M. 2005. "State Social Services Contracting: Exploring the Determinants of Effective Contract Accountability." *Public Administration Review*, 65: 436–49.

Romzek, B. S., LeRoux, K. and Blackmar, J. 2012. "A Preliminary Theory of Informal Accountability among Network Organizational Actors." *Public Administration Review*, 72: 442–53.

Romzek, B. S., LeRoux, K., Johnston, J., Blackmar, J., Kempf, R., and Piatak, J. S. 2013. "Informal Accountability in Multisector Service Delivery Collaborations." *Journal of Public Administration Research & Theory*, doi: 10.1093/jeopart/mut027.

Salamon, L. M. 2002. *The Tools of Government: A Guide to the New Governance*. Oxford: Oxford University Press.

Saz-Carranza, A. and Ospina, S. M. 2011. "The Behavioral Dimension of Governing Interorganizational Goal-Directed Networks: Managing the Unity-Diversity Tension." *Journal of Public Administration Research and Theory*, 21: 327–65.

Sclar, E. D. 2000. *You Don't Always Get What You Pay For: The Economics of Privatization*. Ithaca: Cornell University Press.

Teisman, G. R. and Klijn, E. H. 2002. "Partnership Arrangements: Governmental Rhetoric or Governance Scheme?" *Public Administration Review*, 62: 197–205.

Thurmaier, K. and Wood, C. 2002. "Interlocal Agreements as Overlapping Social Networks: Picket-Fence Regionalism in Metropolitan Kansas City." *Public Administration Review*, 62: 585–98.

U.S. Government Accountability Office. 2005. *Results-Oriented Government: Practices That Can Help Enhance and Sustain Collaboration Among Federal Agencies*. Washington, DC: GAO-06-15, October.

U.S. Government Accountability Office. 2009. *Social Security Administration: Further Actions Needed to Address Disability Claims and Service Delivery Challenges*. Washington, DC: GAO-09-511T, March.

U.S. Government Accountability Office. 2012. *Managing for Results: Key Considerations for Implementing Interagency Collaborative Mechanisms*. Washington, DC: GAO-12-1022, September.

Warner, M. E. and Hefetz, A. 2008. "Managing Markets for Public Service: The Role of Mixed Public-Private Delivery of City Services." *Public Administration Review*, 68: 155–66.

CHAPTER 20

ACCOUNTABILITY AND NEW PUBLIC MANAGEMENT

PER LÆGREID

THE WAVE OF NPM REFORMS

THIS chapter aims to link the rise of public accountability to the wave of New Public Management (NPM) reforms that has swept through most advanced democratic administrations in recent decades. One primary characteristic of NPM is the adoption by public organizations of the management and organizational forms used by private companies. This challenges two traditional doctrines of public administration: first, that public-sector organizations are "insulated" from the private sector, and second, that they operate in accordance with a precise set of rules limiting the freedom of public officials (Dunleavy and Hood 1994). In contrast, the NPM movement prescribes that the formal organization of the public and private sectors should be similar and that managers in public-sector organizations should have discretion in their daily work. NPM has produced a shift from a bureaucratic ethos of office to a managerial regime.

The main components of NPM are disaggregation, competition, and use of incentives (Dunleavy et al. 2006). NPM is about hands-on professional management, explicit standards of performance, a greater emphasis on output control, and private-sector management techniques. It also advocates splitting up public organizations through horizontal and vertical specialization, contract management and market orientation, an increased emphasis on service orientation and user participation, and cost-cutting. NPM is supposed to score high on managerial autonomy and ex post control and low on policy autonomy and ex ante control. NPM has sought to separate policy-making more clearly from policy administration and implementation. Policy-makers make policy and then delegate its implementation to managers and hold them accountable by contract.

NPM reforms have a mixed theoretical foundation. The first set of ideas comes from economic organization theory and focuses on contracts, economic performance, and market solutions. The second set of ideas comes from the managerialist school of thought, which focuses on the primacy of managerial principles in the bureaucracy. The tensions arising from the hybrid character of NPM results from the contradiction between the centralizing tendencies inherent in contractualism and the devolutionary tendencies of managerialism. NPM is something of a hybrid, advocating both decentralization (let the managers manage) and centralization (make the managers manage). NPM thus prescribes both more autonomy and more central control at the same time.

NPM ideas have been implemented to different degrees, at different paces, and with differing emphases on the various elements of the reform package in different countries and sectors (Christensen and Lægreid 2011a). One can discuss whether NPM has led to a convergence of administrative systems, yet there is much to suggest that ideas and policy programs resemble one another more than the corresponding practices do. In this chapter we will not address variations in NPM directly, but discuss NPM effects on accountability more generally and also comment on different sequences of NPM and post-NPM reforms.

ACCOUNTABILITY AND NPM

The quest for stronger accountability was a driver of many NPM reforms. A key premise was that with effective vertical managerial accountability better performance would follow (Boston and Gill 2011). Still the relationship between accountability and performance is contested and it is becoming increasingly clear that we have to operate with a multi-dimensional accountability concept going beyond hierarchical accountability.

The NPM reforms have complicated the already broad notion of accountability in the public sector (Mulgan 2003). It is important to recognize the various dimensions of accountability, the complex context of public accountability, and the multiple overlapping accountability relations of administrative reform (Romzek 2000; Behn 2001). Rather than reducing or increasing accountability, NPM implies a transfer from one set of accountability relationships to another (Olsen 2010). Regarding *who* is accountable, the NPM reforms tend to concentrate more on individual accountability and less on collective accountability. The NPM reforms focus on individual managerial accountability, whereby each person acts for him- or herself within strategic guidelines according to his or her own self-interest and is personally accountable for the results.

Concerning accountability *for what*, one can distinguish between accountability for processes and procedures, such as fairness, equity, and impartiality; accountability for finances; and accountability for performance and results (Behn 2001). NPM reforms have tended to change the accountability focus from processes and compliance with rules and input (finances) to output and results. More traditional notions of accountability, such as accountability for fairness and for processes, have been challenged by notions of increased efficiency, competition, and cost effectiveness.

In considering *why* accountability is rendered, a distinction can be drawn between vertical mandatory accountability and horizontal voluntary accountability relationships. NPM tends to supplement the vertical mandatory accountability relationship with more voluntary horizontal accountability arrangements such as social accountability to customers and users of public services as well as market-based forms of accountability. Instead of being integrated elements of responsible, collective public bodies, public administrators are supposed to be autonomous and entrepreneurial and pay attention to signals they receive from their clients or customers. This raises the question of whether NPM reforms based on the ideas of customer service, competition, and contracting may not weaken civic responsibility, commitment and political equality, and accountability even if some aspects of service are improved. Agentification and corporatization tend to reduce the importance of political signals and political control and make it more difficult to balance institutional autonomy and accountability (Christensen and Lægreid 2002).

Tensions

There is a tension in NPM between political accountability and managerial accountability (Day and Klein 1987). Political accountability has the specific aim of making political leaders systematically responsive to popular wishes and involves dialogue and debate about what should be done (Goodin 1999). Managerial accountability is a more neutral, technical exercise involving book-keeping and evaluation of whether tasks are being performed efficiently and effectively. Under NPM, accountability is based on output, competition, and contractual relations and thus represents a departure from the old public administration, where various forms of accountability were based on input, processes and procedures, hierarchical control, legality, and trust (Christensen and Lægreid 2002).

NPM challenged the traditional principle of ministerial responsibility that focused attention on elected officials assumed to be accountable for all that went on under their jurisdiction. Under NPM administrative executives are held more directly responsible for their performance and the work of their agency (Barberis 1998; Dubnick 2005). A major objective of NPM reforms is the improvement of public-sector performance through forms of accountability involving more direct connections between the providers and users of public services. The role of political accountability has been reduced and the exposure of the manager has been increased.

Under NPM, politicians are supposed to be "chief executives" and assume a strategic role, formulating general goals and assessing results without being involved in single cases and day-to-day business and implementation (Pollitt and Bouckaert 2011). Civil servants, on the other hand, are supposed to operate as managers or entrepreneurs in agencies at arm's length from politicians and to be held accountable through incentives and performance systems. The problem is that both politicians and civil servants find it difficult to practice these roles. The question arises of whether executive politicians are willing or able to adopt the role of strategic managers envisaged for them by NPM. For politicians, operating solely as strategic goal formulators is problematic. They would prefer to be involved in the details of implementation and in single cases. Civil servants, for their part, tend to lose a sense of a unified public service, and increasing the distance between them and the political executive tends to reduce responsiveness and accountability. There is also some ambiguity in much of the rhetoric around accountability insofar as some executive politicians have used the new politics/administration split to redefine policy weaknesses as managerial failures. This enables politicians to offload accountability when things go wrong (Pollitt and Bouckaert 2011).

NPM reforms have generated a renewed tension between flexibility and political accountability. How to guarantee political accountability when politically sensitive questions are left to experts in autonomous agencies is a matter of concern. Taking as an example the Prison Service and the Child Support Agency in the UK, Barberis (1998) reveals that NPM reforms have widened the accountability gap and he argues for the need to reconstruct the traditional doctrine of ministerial responsibility, allowing for a measure of direct accountability among civil servants.

There is also a tension in NPM between the need for greater managerial discretion and autonomy on the one hand and the need for a greater degree of managerial accountability and control on the other. NPM focuses primarily on strengthening managerial accountability, which requires a clear assignment of responsibility for action, a clear statement of goals, and a focus on results and performance in relation to outputs. Increasing devolution, fragmentation, "out-sourcing," marketization, and "business process engineering," all of which are prescribed by NPM reforms, will make a model of strictly hierarchical accountability from the top less easily applicable (Bovens 1998). Generally managerial accountability works best in the least political, or politically salient, areas of public service.

Another tension is between managerial accountability and attempts to reduce the burden of internal scrutiny and paperwork. Stronger managerial accountability often implies that operational managers have to provide data on performance indicators, quality improvement schemes, or performance audits (Pollitt and Bouckaert 2011). This has been variously labeled as re-bureaucratization, an audit explosion, increased regulation inside government, or target overload.

There is also a trade-off between managerial accountability and increased effectiveness (Pollitt and Bouckaert 2011). When managers concentrate on specific output, they often tend to ignore outcomes and to stress efficiency rather than effectiveness. When managers focus on outcome and effectiveness it is hard to hold them accountable, partly because of the problem of attributing outcome to actual behavior and actions by individual organizations and partly because of difficulties of timing. Outcome is difficult to link to annual accountability assessment because it often manifests itself over extended time periods. Often accountability systems tend to favor output because it is easier to measure, easier to hold someone accountable for, and less costly to monitor. Thus NPM tends to focus excessively on output.

Although new interpretations of accountability have proliferated, older interpretations have not disappeared. NPM has had an impact on accountability, but bureaucratic policy-making in central government does not seem to be a forum where such features are particularly noticeable (Page 2010). Ministerial accountability is still a highly pervasive medium of accountability and politics tend to trump performance. Ministerial responsibility remains fundamental (Flinders 2001). Page (2006) reveals that overseers and supervisors now monitor compliance with fewer procedures and measure more outcomes. But beyond this generalization, sweeping claims about changes in accountability are difficult. Managerial accountability varies from one reform program to another and there is a complex mixture of political, legal, professional, hierarchical, and market accountability. There is no consistent pattern of change across accountability relations.

Dilemmas

What we see instead is the co-existence of different and partly contradictory interpretations of administrative accountability, which create potential dilemmas and contradictions for the individual civil servant. This is in line with the layering argument advanced by March and Olsen (1995, 174). Traditional *Rechtstaat* accountability relationships are still important but have now been supplemented by newer NPM accountability relations producing accountability dilemmas and tensions for civil servants. Without a classical Weberian model in place focusing on rules, legality, impartiality, due process, ethical capital, and public ethos, NPM reforms run into trouble. Thus NPM is not an alternative to Weberianism, and a strong Weberian ethos in the public administration is needed to make it work (Pierre and Rothstein 2010).

NPM prescribes market accountability, implying the ability to recognize and accommodate market signals. The population is seen as a collection of consumers and customers focusing on individual benefits whose relationship with the government is primarily commercial rather than political. At the same time, public–private partnerships and networks have made accountability relations more ambiguous (Olsen 2010). The NPM movement has pushed accountability downwards by holding out the promise of improved performance (Schillemans and Bovens 2011). In a study of five Dutch agencies the latter focus on the benefits of accountability redundancies and argue that multiple accountability relations may be suitable for an increasingly pluralistic approach to governance. But there is also a danger that the existence of tangled accountability relationships in welfare reforms designed to enhance the contract networks of service providers will make it difficult to identify which agency or actor is responsible for which outcomes (Romzek 2011).

Generally NPM reforms challenge the sovereign hierarchical state model based on a chain of delegation from political principals to subordinate agents and corresponding traditional concepts of accountability. It is also a challenge to go beyond the static typologies of different accountability relations and to reveal the accountability-related processes and dynamics that NPM reform processes produce. Such reform processes normally represent unstable, unsettled polities and unexpected situations that go beyond the more stable routine situations and business as usual (Olsen 2013). In such situations accountability processes affect the actual exercise and control of authority, power, and responsibility, and the question of who shall have the right and capacity to call to account, to question and debate the information given, and to face judgment and consequences becomes a more open one.

NPM has produced a more fragmented and autonomous public sector, which is accountable not only as a tool for elected political leaders. Public-sector organizations have been given increased discretion not only with regard to administrative and technical issues but also in policy issues, and they have become political actors that not only address their political principals but also have multiple relationships to society (Lægreid and Verhoest 2010). Thus one of the biggest flaws in the NPM reforms is the dichotomy between policy-making and management (Kettle 2006), which proves problematic when put into practice. Most of the premises that guide administrative behavior seldom reach the attention of political executives and citizens. The problem with this hierarchical principal–agent approach to political, administrative, and managerial accountability is that it assumes a clear division between politics and administration. In practice, however, much of the work of the public administration is political and this tends to blur the politics/administration divide and make administrative and managerial accountability more difficult and demanding. This means that we have to go beyond the hierarchical principal–agent approach to accountability and allow more dynamic multi-dimensional accountability relationships.

PERFORMANCE AND ACCOUNTABILITY

Various NPM initiatives were based on the assumption that enhanced accountability would improve performance. But the empirical evidence that this has happened is inconclusive (Lægreid and Verhoest 2010) and evidence of whether performance measurement leads to better accountability is scarce (Dooren, Bouckaert, and Halligan 2010; Van de Walle and Cornelissen in this volume). The relationship between accountability and performance is characterized by tensions, ambiguities, and contradictions, and more responsibility for performance does not lead to more accountability for performance (Bouckaert and Halligan 2008). Behn (2001) claims that there is an accountability dilemma and argues that performance audit tends to focus more on compliance than on performance, often homing in on small errors, and is biased towards hierarchy and punishment and hence tends to undermine public trust. Dubnick (2005) argues that the idea that accountability increases performance has been accepted without careful scrutiny and he claims that there is an "accountability paradox" in which more accountability actually diminishes organizational performance.

Thiel and Leeuw (2002) focus on unintended consequences of performance measurement often linked to minimal accountability requirements. They reveal a "performance paradox" implying a weak correlation between performance indicators and performance itself. One of the perverse effects of performance measurement is gaming (Hood 2006). Thus there is a tension between performance and accountability, and more accountability does not necessarily produce better government (Bouckaert and Peters 2002). The tension between the requirements of accountability and those of effective executive action is a classic dilemma of public administration. Thus we cannot rely on the assumption that accountability improves performance. Rather than acting as a driver of improved performance, accountability tends to slow down improvements. In reform situations there is often disagreement about what constitutes improvement and for whose benefit improvements are made, which makes the relationship between performance and accountability even more blurred.

Rather than trying to resolve the question of whether or not accountability enhances performance, researchers should concentrate on determining under which circumstances different types of accountability can have an overall positive effect (Behn 2001). Accountability can involve both benefits and negative consequences. Steets (2010) distinguishes between three negative impacts: First, agents are often held accountable for adherence to multiple and sometimes contradictory standards. In such situations accountability demands can have a paralyzing effect on organizations and produce "multiple accountabilities disorder" (Koppell 2005). Second, accountability mechanisms generate costs. To monitor activities requires substantial efforts. Third, accountability can hamper flexibility, innovation, and entrepreneurial behavior. Generally, the dysfunctional behavioral effects of performance measurement are caused by manipulation either of the measurement process or of the organizational output (Dooren, Bouckaert, and Halligan 2010).

The NPM reforms emphasize performance and results. But the challenge is not only to permit public managers to produce better results but also to provide accountability to a democratic electorate. Pollitt (2011) examines critically the contested proposition that performance management systems will improve agency accountability to citizens and political representatives. Using two case studies—the UK's National Health Service and the World Bank's World Governance Indicators—he concludes that the measurement of performance has not enhanced political accountability. But some researchers also reject the assumption that accountability necessarily has either positive or negative consequences. Aucoin and Heintzman (2000) claim that improving accountability arrangements does not necessarily improve performance, but the proposition that performance can improve in the absence of improved accountability cannot be sustained. Accountability is seen as a tool to strengthen a government's learning capacity. Increased horizontal accountability of executive agencies might increase organizational learning but not democratic control (Schillemans 2011).

Another study by Radin (2011) examines the Government Performance and Result Act and the Program Assessment Rating Tool in the USA. She argues that these two major efforts to apply performance measurements in US federal agencies focus almost exclusively on bureaucratic accountability and fail to address the complexity of the American political system. She claims that if promises of accountability are to be fulfilled then accountability mechanisms need to be adapted to the complex political environment in which they are expected to operate. Chan and Rosenbloom (2010) analyze challenges that NPM reforms in USA and China face with respect to maintaining bureaucratic, legal, and political accountability. They conclude that similar reforms might lead to different results in terms of performance and accountability. Thus to meet the promises of accountability cultural and contextual factors need to be taken into consideration.

The Ambiguity of Accountability under NPM

There is often a trade-off between accountability and the increased flexibility and entrepreneurship of NPM reforms. But this is not necessarily always the case (Deleon 1998). Different accountability mechanisms are appropriate in different circumstances depending on the type of problem they are designed to handle. Accountability is thus not inconsistent with administrative reform; Neither entrepreneurial behavior nor increased discretion for professional managers needs to result in diminished accountability. Rather than asking whether government officials are more accountable or less after NPM reforms, one should focus on what kind of accountability the participants perceive as appropriate (Romzek 2000). Emphasizing outcomes and outputs at the expense of input and processes does not necessarily mean more or less accountability. Rather it means that different accountability relationships should be addressed. Accountability in a multi-functional public sector means to be responsible for the achievement of multiple and often ambiguous objectives.

The emergence of NPM reforms thus seems to have made accountability a more ambiguous and complex issue (Thomas 1998). By highlighting the importance of people as consumers and playing down their role as citizens, NPM has introduced the dual accountability of civil servants to politicians and consumers. The role of political leaders is also ambiguous under NPM: Elected officials have a role as strategists in defining the long-term goals of the public sector and assessing the results, but at the same time they are expected to give considerable discretion to operative agencies. The ambiguity of responsibility becomes especially clear when things go wrong (Gregory 1998). NPM reforms have led to a fragmentation of the public sector, and the acceptance of political responsibility by ministers has been attenuated and political accountability undermined (Christensen and Lægreid 2002).

NPM argues for more business efficiency and accountability for performance without paying much attention to political accountability and accountability for fairness (Behn 2001). A preoccupation with efficiency tends to overvalue the need for managerial accountability rather than promoting political accountability. Efficiency is no guarantor of good political and social judgment, which is essential in securing genuine political accountability and legitimacy in a democracy (Gregory 1998). The pursuit of managerial accountability can exact a price in the shrinkage of a sense of political accountability.

There is a built-in inconsistency in NPM. The reformers claim to empower customers, free managers, and strengthen political control, but these three things are difficult to achieve simultaneously (Pollitt and Bouckaert 2011). Regarding the standards of accountability, it is important to realize that the objectives, norms, and roles of public governance are different from those of the private sector. What distinguishes public governance from private-sector management is its accountability for a unique set of public missions and norms such as representation, equality, equity, fairness, impartiality, integrity, justice, and citizenship. There is also a need to re-examine the tendency to view citizens as customers because the concept of customer as used in the marketplace is devoid of the entitlements or rights associated with citizenship. The success of market-oriented accountability is dependent on citizens having sufficient resources to make their preferences felt in the market and on the perfect realization of the notoriously unrealistic conditions that characterize the economist's "ideal market" (Goodin 1999).

NPM, Accountability, and Appropriateness

NPM tends to downplay the collective and integrative aspects of the state and to emphasize the aggregative aspects (March and Olsen 1989). It represents a shift in focus concerning accountability, from a broadly defined public interest to a more narrowly defined set of personal interests. It is a paradox that while one goal of NPM is to open public administration to the public, it may ultimately reduce the level of democratic accountability and lead to the erosion of the public nature of public service (Haque 2001).

NPM reforms have shifted the balance from input democracy and input legitimacy to output democracy and output legitimacy (Peters 2011). This is due to more direct contact between the public administration and the public resulting from modern reforms based on devolution, fragmentation, and increased user-orientation and legitimation of choices in terms of results, performance, and effectiveness. In the light of this NPM reforms can be seen as a shift from a type of democracy that was chiefly concerned with the legitimacy of its decisions—and therefore focused on processes, representativeness, and legality—to a greater preoccupation with the effective implementation of decisions.

The output model focuses more on managerial accountability and ex post judgment of performance and assigns a narrower customer or consumer role to users where the main emphasis is on individual rights and choices. It does not answer the question of how atomized actors making choices in a market can contribute to creating a stable and responsible democratic system. The new output role in this model is mainly about service delivery and direct contact with the civil service. It may be seen as non-political or even anti-political (Frederickson 1996).

A customer-oriented system poses problems of democratic accountability. The pressure to be responsive to service consumers tends to run counter to the government's obligation to be accountable to the public at large through its elected representatives. This may weaken commitment, political equality, and accountability even if some aspects of service are improved. A political theory is needed that can explain how applying customer service techniques and tools to government and giving civil servants more authority to make policy decisions about the results they produce and how they produce them is consistent with democratic accountability (Behn 2001).

Post-NPM and Accountability

Over the past decade this NPM model has been challenged by post-NPM reform measures characterized by an increased focus on integration, networks, and horizontal coordination as well as by a rediscovery of bureaucracy and a renewed emphasis on the rule of law and stronger central government capacity (Christensen and Lægreid 2007). The result is increased complexity and the development of hybrid organizational forms. In a multi-functional public sector goals are often conflicting and imprecise. Accountability in such a system means being answerable to different stakeholders and for the achievement of multiple and often ambiguous objectives. Thus the accountability relations tend to become shared resulting in unclear accountability lines (Boston and Gill 2011).

Autonomization produced problems of political accountability since arm's length agencies were harder for ministers to control, yet in most cases if they did unpopular things, it was still the minister who got the blame from the media and the public. This was one reason why joined-up and whole-of-government initiatives were launched.

A managerial concept of democracy might weaken civic responsibility, engagement, and political equality and enhance the role of administrators and managers (Christensen and Lægreid 2002). Post-NPM reform measures are supposed to handle some of these challenges by moving the reforms away from output democracy and aggregative political processes and toward a greater emphasis on input democracy and integrative political processes. A new generation of post-NPM reforms has emerged more concerned with central political capacity, coordination, and how public administration can be made more politically accountable (Christensen and Lægreid 2007). And tendencies toward re-bureaucratization have generated a new interest in administrative and political accountability (Olsen 2010).

One challenge facing civil service systems in the second generation of reform is balancing the demand for flexibility and accountability. A main concern arising from agencification and regulatory reforms is how to make agencies independent and at the same time accountable—upwards to politicians, horizontally to other agencies, and downwards to consumers and regulatees (Scott 2000). The autonomy of regulatory agencies from government may lead to agency capture, creating problems of democratic accountability and to accountability deficit.

The question of accountability is also closely related to power relations. Increased agencification often means transferring power from political executives to managers, and technocrats are emerging as highly influential bureaucrats enjoying broad institutional autonomy. One observation is that power relations seem to be changing faster than accountability relations (Christensen and Lægreid 2002). The political leadership often finds itself in situations where it has responsibility without the corresponding power and control. Conversely, many of the autonomous agencies may gain more power without necessarily becoming more accountable. In a situation where more and more public services are being provided by semi-autonomous agencies and private-sector bodies, government executives are increasingly being held accountable for performance standards that are difficult to impose on third parties (Frederickson and Frederickson 2006). The trend in the second generation of reforms to strengthen the center can be seen as an effort to reduce such accountability problems and to bring political accountability to the fore once again (Roberts 2011).

Challenges for Further Research

Major administrative reforms such as NPM have to be assessed in relation both to governance representativeness and to governance capacity (Christensen and Lægreid 2011b). The first concern is closely related to political accountability and focuses on measures designed to give citizens more influence—in other words, by introducing mechanisms that allow their attitudes and opinions to be represented in the policy-making process. The second concern has a bearing on administrative accountability, efficiency, and to what degree social developments are affected by government decisions and public policy programs. A main challenge is to find organizational forms that enhance both the representativeness and the capacity of governance. In practice this is a tall order. There might be a trade-off between integrity and requirements for accountability on the one hand and effective service delivery on the other hand. NPM reforms have weakened political accountability and strengthened managerial and social accountability, but this transformation is by no means a panacea for the ills of contemporary democracy (Peters 2011). Generally there is a need for more systematic knowledge about the effects of different accountability arrangements on the quality of government and democracy..

We are facing compound welfare state reforms that are held accountable to different forums. NPM reforms have not replaced the old public administration but merely supplemented it and produced more complex and hybrid organizational forms. Instead of choosing between different accountability mechanisms we have to treat them as supplementary and complementary in a mixed political order that combines and blends different modes of governance (Olsen 2010). We have revealed a multiple accountability regime in which the different accountability mechanisms do not substitute for each other (Schillemans 2008) but are redundant rather than segregated (Scott 2000). A new accountability regime with more complex, dynamic, and layered accountability forms is emerging. A key challenge is how to handle hybrid accountability relations embedded in partly competing institutional logics. It is often claimed that such different conceptions of accountability might undermine organizational effectiveness. But that might not always be the case (Schillemans and Bovens 2011). Multiple accountabilities may be appropriate solutions for an increasingly pluralistic governance system. Accountability is about managing diverse and partly conflicting expectations (Romzek and Dubnick 1987). Calling officials to account means inviting them to explain and justify their actions within a context of shared beliefs and values, which implies a dialogue between officials and those to whom they are accountable.

In a liquid state with a fluid, complex, flexible, semi-autonomous, and fragmented polity one has to go beyond the traditional forms of political accountability to close the "accountability gap" that has emerged in the aftermath of NPM reforms (Flinders 2012). We have to rethink democratic accountability in ways that resonate with the new reality of modern governance systems. Just to reinstall conventional hierarchical principal–agent accountability relations is problematic in the current more fluid state.

There is a mutual relationship between accountability and NPM reforms. Administrative reform processes represent unsettled, dynamic, and unexpected situations. Often the reform agents have limited power and also weak means–end knowledge regarding the impacts of the reforms. They face different contextual constraints when formulating and implementing reforms, and their ability for rational calculation regarding effects is limited. This implies that the NPM reforms may affect accountability relations but also that different accountability relations may influence how the reforms work in practice. Thus we need to go beyond the static classification of different accountability relations and also study the dynamic relationships between reforms and accountability and how the reforms also affect the interplay between different accountability relationships. We also need to supplement the hierarchical principal–agent approach of delegation and vertical channels of accountability with analyses of how multiple and hybrid accountability relations interact and change over time.

We must go beyond the instrumental flavor of accountability and the focus on principal–agent relations and also include the logic of appropriateness and accountability mechanisms that espouse intrinsic values such as integrity, democratic legitimacy, justice, and fairness (March and Olsen 1995; Dubnick and Frederickson 2011). Roberts (2002) argues for keeping public officials accountable through use of public dialogue in order to address "wicked problems." Thus a multi-dimensional accountability approach is needed to handle accountability in a pluralistic political-administrative system. Comparative studies of NPM could be used to assess the changes it has brought in accountability arrangements surrounding public managers in different countries, different policy areas, on different administrative levels, and over time.

References

Aucoin, P. and Heintzman, R. 2000. "The Dialectics of Accountability for Performance in Public Management Reform." *International Review of Administrative Science*, 66: 45–55.

Barberis, P. 1998. "The New Public Management and a New Accountability." *Public Administration*, 76: 451–70.

Behn, R. 2001. *Rethinking Democratic Accountability*. Washington: Brookings Institution Press.

Boston, J. and Gill, D. 2011. Working Across Organizational Boundaries: The Challenges for Accountability, pp. 213–47 in *Future State: Directions for Public Management in New Zealand*, eds. B. Ryan and D. Gill. Wellington: Victoria University Press.

Bouckaert, G. and Peters, B. G. 2002. "Performance Measurement and Management: The Achilles Heel in Administrative Modernization." *Public Performance and Management Review*, 25: 359–62.

Bouckaert, G. and Halligan, J. 2008. *Managing Performance: International Comparisons*. London: Routledge.

Bovens, M. 1998. *The Quest for Responsibility*. Cambridge: Cambridge University Press.

Chan, H. S. and Rosenbloom, D. H. 2010. "Four Challenges to Accountability in Contemporary Public Administration: Lessons from the United States and China." *Administration and Society*, 42: 11–33.

Christensen, T. and Lægreid, P. 2002. "New Public Management: Puzzles of Democracy and the Influence of Citizens." *Journal of Political Philosophy*, 10: 267–96.

Christensen, T. and Lægreid, P. 2007. "The Whole-of-Government Approach to Public Sector Reform." *Public Administration Review*, 67: 1057–64.

Christensen, T. and Lægreid, P. 2011a. *The Ashgate Research Companion to New Public Management*. Aldershot: Ashgate.

Christensen, T. and Lægreid, P. 2011b. "Democracy and Administrative Policy: Contrasting Elements of NPM and Post-NPM." *European Political Science Review*, 3: 125–46.

Day, P. and Klein, R. 1987. *Accountability: Five Public Services*. London: Tavistock Publishers.

Deleon, L. 1998. "Accountability in a 'Reinvented' Government." *Public Administration*, 76: 539–58.

Dooren, W. van, Bouckaert, G. and Halligan, J. 2010. *Performance Management in the Public Sector*. London: Routledge.

Dubnick, M. 2005. "Accountability and the Promise of Performance: In Search of Mechanisms." *Public Performance and Management Review*, 28: 376–417.

Dubnick, M. J. and Frederickson, H. G. 2011. Introduction: The Promises of Accountability Research, pp. xiii–xxxii in *Accountable Governance. Problems and Promises*, eds. M. J. Dubnick and H. G. Frederickson. New York: M.E. Sharpe.

Dunleavy, P. and Hood, C. 1994. "From Old Public Administration to New Public Management." *Public Money and Management*, 14: 9–16.

Dunleavy, P., Margetts, H., Bastow, S., and Tinkler, J. 2006. "New Public Management Is Dead: Long Live Digital-Era Governance." *Journal of Public Administration Research and Theory*, 16: 467–94.

Flinders, M. 2001. *The Politics of Accountability in the Modern State*. Aldershot: Ashgate.

Flinders, M. 2012. *The Liquid State and Accountable Governance: Insights from the Coalition Government's "Public Bodies Reform Agenda" in the United Kingdom*. In ASPA (The American Society for Public Administration) Annual Conference, *Redefining Public Service Through Civic Engagement*. Las Vegas, 2–6 March 2012.

Frederickson, D. G. and Frederickson, H. G. 2006. *Measuring the Performance of the Hollow State*. Washington, DC: Georgetown University Press.

Frederickson, H. G. 1996. "Comparing the Reinventing Movement with the New Public Administration." *Public Administration Review*, 56: 263–70.

Goodin, R. E. 1999. Accountability—Elections as One Form, pp. 2–4 in *The International Encyclopedia of Elections*, ed. R. Rose. Washington, DC: Congressional Quarterly.

Gregory, R. 1998. "Political Responsibility for Bureaucratic Incompetence: Tragedy at Cave Creek." *Public Administration*, 76: 519–38.

Haque, M. S. 2001. "The Diminishing Publicness of Public Service Under the Current Mode of Governance." *Public Administration Review*, 61: 65–82.

Hood, C. 2006. "Gaming in Targetworld: The Targets Approach to Managing British Public Services." *Public Administration Review*, 66: 515–21.

Kettle, D. 2006. "Modernising Government: The Way Forward—A Comment." *International Review of Administrative Science*, 72: 313–17.

Koppell, J. G. S. 2005. "Pathologies of Accountability: ICANN and the Challenge of 'Multiple Accountabilities Disorder.'" *Public Administration Review*, 65: 94–108.

Lægreid, P. and Verhoest, K. 2010. *Governance of Public Sector Organizations: Proliferation, Autonomy and Performance*. London: Palgrave Macmillan.

March, J. G. and Olsen, J. P. 1989. *Rediscovering Institutions*. New York: Free Press.

March, J. G. and Olsen, J. P. 1995. *Democratic Governance*. New York: Free Press.

Mulgan, R. 2003. *Holding Power to Account: Accountability in Modern Democracies*. London: Palgrave Macmillan.

Olsen, J. P. 2010. *Governance Through Institution Building*. Oxford: Oxford University Press.

Olsen, J. P. 2013. "The Institutional Basis of Democratic Accountability." *West European Politics*, 36 (3): 447–73.

Page, E. C. 2010. "Accountability as a Bureaucratic Minefield: Lessons from a Comparative Study." *West European Politics*, 33: 1010–29.

Page, S. 2006. "The Web of Managerial Accountability." *Administration and Society*, 38: 166–97.

Peters, B. G. 2011. Responses to NPM: From Input Democracy to Output Democracy, pp. 361–74 in *The Ashgate Research Companion to New Public Management*, eds. T. Christensen and P. Lægreid. Aldershot: Ashgate.

Pierre, J. and Rothstein, B. 2010. Reinventing Weber: The Role of Institutions in Creating Social Trust, pp. 405–16 in *The Ashgate Research Companion to New Public Management*, eds. T. Christensen and P. Lægreid. Aldershot: Ashgate.

Pollitt, C. 2011. Performance Blight and the Tyranny of Light? Accountability in Advanced Performance Measurement Regimes, pp. 81–97 in *Accountable Governance. Problems and Promises*, eds. M. J. Dubnick and H. G. Frederickson. New York: M.E. Sharpe.

Pollitt, C. and Bouckaert, G. 2011. *Public Management Reform*. Third edition. Oxford: Oxford University Press.

Radin, B. 2011. Does Performance Measurement Actually Improve Accountability?, pp. 98–110 in *Accountable Governance. Problems and Promises*, eds. M. J. Dubnick and H. G. Frederickson. New York: M.E. Sharpe.

Roberts, A. 2011. *The Logic of Discipline*. Oxford: Oxford University Press.

Roberts, N. 2002. "Keeping Public Officials Accountable Through Dialogue: Resolving the Accountability Paradox." *Public Administration Review*, 65: 511–26.

Romzek, B. 2000. "Dynamics of Public Accountability in the Era of Reform." *International Review of Administrative Sciences*, 66: 21–44.

Romzek, B. 2011. The Tangled Web of Accountability in Contracting Networks: The Case of Welfare Reform, pp. 22–41 in *Accountable Governance: Problems and Promises*, eds. M. J. Dubnick and H. G. Frederickson. New York: M.E. Sharpe.

Romzek, B. and Dubnick, M. 1987. "Accountability in the Public Sector: Lessons from the Challenger Tragedy." *Public Administration Review*, 47: 227–38.

Schillemans, T. 2008. "Accountability in the Shadow of Hierarchy: The Horizontal Accountability of Agencies." *Public Organization Review*, 8: 175–94.

Schillemans, T. 2011. "Does Horizontal Accountability Work? Evaluating Potential Remedies for the Accountability Deficit of Agencies." *Administration and Society*, 43: 387–416.

Schillemans, T. and Bovens, M. 2011. The Challenges of Multiple Accountabilities: Does Redundancy Lead to Overload?, pp. 3–21 in *Accountable Governance: Problems and Promises*, eds. M. J. Dubnick and H. G. Frederickson. New York: M.E. Sharpe.

Scott, C. 2000. "Accountability in the Regulatory State." *Journal of Law and Society*, 76: 539–58.

Steets, J. 2010. *Accountability in Public Policy Partnerships*. London: Palgrave Macmillan.

Thiel, S. van and Leeuw, F. L. 2002. "The Performance Paradox in Public Sector." *Public Performance and Management Review*, 25: 267–81.

Thomas, P. G. 1998. The Changing Nature of Accountability, pp. 348–93 in *Taking Stock: Assessing Public Sector Reforms*, eds. B. G. Peters and D. J. Savoie. Quebec: Canadian Centre for Management Development.

Van de Walle, S. and Cornelissen, F. 2014. Performance Reporting, pp 441–455 in *Oxford Handbook of Public Accountability*, eds. M. Bovens, R.E. Goodin, and T. Schillemans. Oxford: Oxford University Press.

CHAPTER 21

ACCOUNTABILITY AND THE NONPROFIT SECTOR

STEVEN RATHGEB SMITH

MULTI-LAYERED ACCOUNTABILITY

ACCOUNTABILITY in the context of nonprofits is multi-layered and complicated (Barber 2001; Goodin 2004; Ebrahim 2009; Benjamin 2008; LeRoux 2009; Smith 2010; Kearns 2012). Nonprofits are expected to be accountable to a variety of stakeholders including public and private funders, individual donors, the community at large, their board of directors, the users of their programs, and third party accrediting bodies. Many nonprofits also provide difficult-to-evaluate services, so it is a challenge to discern if nonprofits are actually achieving their mission and program goals. Many nonprofits are small without large staffs and resources for accountability compliance. Despite the community roots of many nonprofits, many do not have extensive citizen participation in governance or program implementation. Most accountability regimes tend to focus on legal, financial, and programmatic concerns rather than citizen engagement; thus one of the key attractions of nonprofits is often neglected in the push by public and private funders for more accountability.

A FRAMEWORK FOR UNDERSTANDING NONPROFIT ACCOUNTABILITY

Legal Accountability

In terms of legal accountability, nonprofits are incorporated and sanctioned by their government according to specific regulations and laws (Kearns 2012; Simon, Dale, and

Chisholm 2006). Great variation exists around the world in the legal requirements for incorporation of nonprofits which also makes a tremendous difference in the accountability expectations.

In the US, nonprofits are incorporated at the state level and the federal Internal Revenue Service (IRS) recognizes incorporated nonprofits under the tax-exempt code in the federal corporate income tax law. The tax-exempt category includes a wide variety of different types of organization—from charitable purpose organizations to social clubs to unions and trade associations. Only charitable organizations incorporated in the US are eligible for tax deductible contributions from individual and corporate donors. Other types of nonprofit organization are tax-exempt from corporate income taxes, property and sales taxes (in most jurisdictions). In the US, the IRS has specific guidelines for eligibility for tax-exempt status which includes, for example, a charitable mission, to be incorporated as a 501(c) (3) organization, and appropriate by-laws (Simon, Dale, and Chisholm 2006). Historically, the IRS has not exercised stringent legal control on the formation of nonprofit organizations. The number of nonprofit charitable organizations now exceeds one million, so extensive oversight is simply impossible. More fundamentally the US has historically been committed to relatively low barriers to entry for individuals and groups interested in forming nonprofits. It is quite straightforward and simple to create a nonprofit charitable institution.

In many other countries, the legal requirements for the formation of a nonprofit are quite stringent, creating much higher barriers to establishment. Tax deductibility of charitable gifts is also quite limited in many countries, reducing the incentive to form a nonprofit. In some countries, nonprofits engaged in advocacy often are subject to constant surveillance and detailed reporting requirements. In Russia, for example, President Putin signed legislation in July 2012 that requires NGOs that receive foreign funding to register as "foreign agents." These NGOs are also subject to detailed financial audits and twice-yearly reporting requirements to the state (BBC News 2012). In Turkey, NGOs are required to register with the Ministry of the Interior and specifically report foreign grants, although the reporting stipulations are not as onerous as in Russia (ICNL 2012). China often establishes NGOs as essentially arms of the state, thus they are often called GONGOs (Government Organized NGOs). They are then subject to tight oversight and monitoring from the state (Wu 2003).

In the US, the UK, Canada, Australia, and many European countries, the legal tradition has been to encourage advocacy through nonprofit organizations so the oversight evident in Russia, Turkey, China and other countries is not considered necessary or appropriate. Nonetheless, governments have striven to insure compliance with the nonprofit corporate structure for larger organizations with sizable budgets. A key distinguishing feature of the nonprofit corporate structure, especially for charitable institutions, is that the staff and board of directors of a nonprofit organization shall not distribute the "profits" of the organization to its owners. This "non-distribution constraint" is embedded in the laws regulating nonprofit organizations (Hansmann 1980). This non-distribution constraint can be violated through self-dealing between the typically volunteer board and the organization or through related party transactions.

Excessive salaries paid to the executives of a nonprofit organization can also be a way of evading the non-distribution constraint.

The legal regulation of the non-distribution constraint has become more complicated in recent years with the increased pressure for nonprofits to generate earned income and establish corporate partnerships (Smith 2012; Cordes and Steuerle 2009; Crutchfield and Grant 2008). The former includes many different and varied strategies: creating a for-profit subsidiary and raising revenue from fees such as technical assistance, tuition, or the sale of goods and services. This interest in earned income is part of a broader interest in social enterprise and social entrepreneurship. Many of these social enterprises have hybrid structures combining elements of nonprofit and for-profit organizations (Light 2007; Dees 1996). But the new hybrid legal forms raise new and more complex regulatory issues for government officials since the boundaries between nonprofit and the for-profit sector are less clear. Further, it complicates the accountability concerns of the board of directors. Typically, the board of a nonprofit is guided by the social mission of the organization but social enterprises are guided by the so-called "double bottom-line" to nonprofit governance as the board and staff strive to achieve both social goals and financial returns.

The governance of nonprofits is thus distinctly different from for-profit organizations. The latter are accountable to their shareholders, who are also the owners. Nonprofits do not have shareholders or owners with a legal claim on the revenues or assets of the organization. For nonprofits, ownership is less clear than in for-profits; a nonprofit board of directors is, however, accountable to the general public (due to the tax preferences extended to nonprofits) and as such can be considered the "surrogate" owners of the nonprofit. As detailed by Kearns (2012), the board of directors of a nonprofit have three types of obligation: 1) a duty of obedience to faithfully implement the mission; 2) a duty of care to perform their board responsibilities with prudence, care, and due diligence; and 3) a duty of loyalty to place the interests of the organization above their own personal interests.

Government regulators have tended to operate on the assumption that nonprofit boards will usually strive to uphold these obligations. For small, all-volunteer, nonprofits such as a local neighborhood association or self-help group, this board governance issue is usually not a serious problem since the organization does not have any significant budget or substantial responsibilities. However, agencies with multiple programs, large government contracts, and/or hybrid for-profit/nonprofit structures require more sophisticated boards of directors who can provide firm strategic guidance to the agency, especially since the staff of the agency may have priorities that are not in the best long-term interest of the nonprofit.

Importantly, the governance of many nonprofits does not include formal members. Most nonprofit charitable organizations in the US for example are not membership organizations; the board is instead self-perpetuating with the current board nominating and electing new board members. Yet, certain types of nonprofit organizations in the US are membership organizations where the members elect the board. These nonprofits include large national environmental organizations such as the Sierra Club, neighborhood associations, self-help organizations, and many trade associations and social clubs.

Many nonprofit organizations begin as informal groups of people who are passionate about a particular cause or issue such as preventing delinquency; training the disadvantaged for the labor market; saving endangered species; or achieving better equity and social justice. These informal groups do not have legal incorporation and tend to operate by consensus or as a "committee of the whole." Little distinction exists in the beginning between the leadership and the members of the organization, even in situations where a chair or director's position exists. These organizations also do not have any formal legal accountability since they are unincorporated, although individual members of the organizations could be potentially liable for the actions of the group or the association. Informal groups are often propelled to seek legal incorporation—and hence greater accountability to outside stakeholders, including government—by the desire to shield individual members from personal liability as well as the prospect of obtaining more resources through public and private grants. Most public and private funders will not award grants to organizations lacking formal tax-exempt status. Donors are also less likely to give to unincorporated groups since a donor will not receive a tax deduction unless the organization is incorporated.

Given the roots of nonprofits in informal groups, legal incorporation (and thus legal accountability) means that nonprofits many have to restructure their own internal accountability. A board of directors needs to be created, officers need to be appointed or elected, and the constraints of legal incorporation including limitations on political advocacy and lobbying may require organizations to change their mission, especially if they were created purely as advocacy organizations. These internal changes can present knotty challenges for the governance of nonprofits, since after incorporation many nonprofits may retain many of the staff and volunteers from the initial informal group.

In sum, legal accountability in the context of a nonprofit can be straightforward or potentially complex. For small organizations, potential accountability problems regarding mission, finances, and the law are less likely given the lack of revenue and acutely targeted mission of most of these organizations. But as the scale and scope of the organization increases, legal accountability can become more challenging.

Financial Accountability

With greater complexity, another type of accountability—financial accountability—is also more daunting (see Kearns 2012). Grass-roots organizations often receive small cash and in-kind donations which do not require formal and sophisticated accounting rules and audits by outside accounting firms are too expensive and usually unnecessary. Informal groups have so little money that any donations or revenue are simply collected and put in a savings or checking account to be disbursed at a later time. Also, the fiduciary role of the leaders of these informal groups is personal rather than organizational. Since these organizations tend to have relatively little money, the leaders of the organization often focus on its mission and purpose rather than on revenue development. A classic example might be a self-help group with no revenue whatsoever and a fluctuating membership. The objective of supporting each other and people with similar concerns takes precedent over a focus on the finances.

But legal incorporation requires a shift among the leaders of the organization. Nonprofits in the US above $50,000 need to report their finances to the IRS, even if only in relatively rudimentary form. This information is then available on the web for any citizen to view. This transparency can promote greater due diligence among nonprofits, even those relatively small organizations. As nonprofits grow and obtain public and private grants, they are then required to adopt more conventionally-accepted accounting standards, including audited financial statements. Indeed, many public and private funders increasingly require audited financial statements from their grantees. For nonprofits with government contracts, agencies also need to conform to government expectations pertaining to the allocation of costs within the agency's budget. This effort entails careful oversight of agency spending to ensure that public funds are being spent in accordance with government rules. Effective monitoring also requires an ongoing investment by the agency in data collection and reporting. Overall, government funding is associated with the professionalization of an agency as an adaptive response to the prospect or receipt of government funding (Hwang and Powell 2009; Smith and Lipsky 1993). The increasing competitiveness of the government contracting environment tends to encourage this professionalization since many agencies do not have access to significant private resources as alternatives to those from government.

Financial accountability has two other key components. First, agencies, once incorporated, need to put in place internal controls to protect the agency against fraud and embezzlement. The board of directors of a nonprofit need to demonstrate, as a condition of exercising its fiduciary role, that it has reasonable control over the organization's finances and does not allow unethical or illegal activity to occur. Failure to have appropriate internal controls could potentially leave board members and/or the staff of an agency legally liable for any debts incurred from this inappropriate activity.

Second, nonprofits have historically been rated, at least in part, by funders and charitable rating agencies such as the Wise Giving Alliance and Charity Navigators on the percentage of their total revenue devoted to fundraising costs. For instance, a traditional benchmark has been that a nonprofit should devote no morethan 40 percent of its revenue to fundraising costs with the remainder devoted to program costs. The concern is that donors need to know that their scarce charitable dollars are going to deliver programs and reach the intended beneficiaries rather than simply pay the salaries of agency fundraisers. Some agencies also hire external fundraisers who work for for-profit firms. This issue has been a most pronounced concern among public regulators, private foundations, and private donors in the US, since many other countries do not have the same history of charitable donations.

State regulators have tried without success to limit the amount a nonprofit can spend on fundraising expenses, primarily because of legal rulings by the US Supreme Court. Thus, charity rating services such as Charity Navigator have instead promoted self-regulation by nonprofits by rating and evaluating nonprofits on their fundraising expenses ratio and essentially urging citizens to avoid donations to agencies with high fundraising expenses. Other organizations, such as the United Way, the federated fundraising organization that provides grants to local nonprofit service organizations, has also promoted low fundraising costs and many local United Way chapters have urged keeping fundraising costs to 15 percent.

Fundraising ratios, though, bear little or no relationship to the outcomes of an organization's programs. Further, many observers of the nonprofit sector have noted that the emphasis on fundraising ratios has tended to promote a lack of needed investment in the administrative infrastructure of local organizations, as agencies are pressured by their funder to keep costs low (Barber 2001; Light 2004).

More generally, professionalization of the administrative infrastructure of a nonprofit may be related to the life-cycle of the organization (Oster 1995; Light 2004). As they evolve and mature, agencies necessarily need to put in place different financial systems in order to sustain their operations. The financial accountability of a small informal, all-volunteer, self-help group will be very different than what is expected of a large, complex, human service agency with multiple revenue sources and government contracts. More generally, the growth in new nonprofit organizations in many countries means that many nonprofits are evolving into more mature organizations, requiring new financial accounting, while at the same time government regulators strive to ensure that the regulatory regime can effectively monitor a larger and more complex universe of nonprofit agencies.

The Growing Focus on Accountability for Performance

Since the mid-1990s, performance expectations for nonprofits, especially agencies providing public services, has risen in scope and intensity for several reasons. The "reinventing government" movement sparked much greater interest in improving the performance of public services (Osborne and Gaebler 1992). This movement and the related New Public Management (NPM) also encouraged policymakers to adopt more market-based strategies for addressing public problems such as contracting with private nonprofit and for-profit agencies (Hood 1991; Phillips and Smith 2010). Social policy reform legislation in countries such as the UK and the US embodied this shift in management thinking by requiring performance-based contracts in fields such as child welfare, welfare-to-work, and workforce development (Heinrich and Choi 2007; Phillips and Smith 2010; Smith 2010; Alcock 2012).

The fiscal and debt crisis also encouraged many government officials to adopt various performance management strategies to target services and ensure scarce funding was allocated to the most effective organizations. Many private funders including leading national foundations reinforced this trend by their own performance management expectations. Indeed, government funding agencies and many private foundations, especially the larger foundations with significant grant portfolios, now require the use of performance management strategies by their nonprofit grantees. These higher expectations have led nonprofits to adopt an array of performance-oriented strategies including benchmarking, balanced scorecards, logic models, and social return on investment.

Benchmarking entails an effort to compare a specific nonprofit organization (or set of agencies) with other similar organizations. It has its roots in the for-profit management world where companies are often compared on various measures, including profitability (Letts, Ryan, and Grossman 1999). The attraction of benchmarking is that it offers nonprofits a mechanism for them to assay their organization's performance on important issues such as administrative costs, the efficiency of their fundraising operations, and client placement rates. Benchmarking offers a strategy for program improvement and greater accountability, even in the absence of specific outcome data which is often lacking for many nonprofit programs.

In recent years, countless nonprofit agencies have used benchmarking. But benchmarking tends to be most helpful with easy-to-obtain information such as number of administrators, membership levels, and the amount of donations. More complex and elusive measures such as client placement rates are more difficult to benchmark for logistical and practical reasons. And, many nonprofit staff forcefully argue that program outcomes like placement rates are less susceptible to comparison given the sometimes dramatic differences in the social, economic, and political context of local nonprofits.

Another performance management strategy embraced by many nonprofits is the balanced scorecard, a strategic planning tool that seeks to integrate financial, programmatic, operational, and mission-related objectives (Kaplan 2002). Thus, a nonprofit agency can strive to create a more efficient and effective organization while at the same time remaining faithful to its mission. More competition for funding and the fiscal crisis has placed pressure on nonprofits to be more "business-like" or commercial (Kearns 2012; Smith 2012; Eikenberry and Kluver 2004). The balanced scorecard requires integration of the social goals of the nonprofit into the overall priority-setting process of the organization. Despite its holistic approach to organizational strategy, the balanced scorecard tends to focus on measurable indicators of costs and program utilization and thus it is not widely used to consider the citizenship- and community-building role of nonprofits although it potentially could be used to address these issues. Also, the measurement of actual program impact through the balanced scorecard approach is challenging given the difficulty of obtaining relevant outcome data due to the expense and the elusive long-term effects of many nonprofit programs.

Another tool for achieving greater performance accountability is a "logic model." Indeed, many public and private funders now require nonprofit grant and contract applicants to develop a logic model as part of their grant application. A logic model is basically a performance strategy that forces nonprofits to map the entire "production process" for their programs, from the initial inputs such as staff and resources, to the long-term programmatic outcomes (Hatry 2006). In so doing, logic models hold the promise of focusing nonprofits on better performance and the resource and infrastructure ingredients of high performance even if nonprofit staff and volunteers do not have the information on their ultimate long-term outcomes. For funders, logic models are a strategy to hold nonprofits accountable for the implementation of their grant programs. And, funders could sanction a nonprofit that falls short of its intended service delivery model after a contract or grant was awarded.

In the US, logic models have certainly caught the attention of nonprofits nationwide. Arguably their greatest value is on the "front-end" of service implementation. Ideally, the process of creating a logic model should engage a broad spectrum of a nonprofit agency's staff and volunteers in thinking about impact and outcomes. This extensive involvement can then help with the refinement of strategy and help nonprofits executives win the support of agency stakeholders for program goals and direction. However, the goal of logic models as a strategy to drive better outcomes and help funders select the most effective agencies for funding remains quite problematic. Logic models tend to focus on programmatic performance and generally do not engage the agency in thinking about governance or citizen and community relationships.

One other performance accountability strategy designed with nonprofits and their difficult-to-evaluate programs in mind is the Social Return on Investment (SROI). Too often, nonprofit programs, especially social welfare and health programs, are evaluated quite narrowly and thus may not appear to demonstrate significant value for the community. SROI is designed to overcome this problem through a more inclusive approach to thinking about costs and benefits which consider the savings to society of nonprofit services. For example, a person's employment due to job training and placement by a nonprofit would produce long-term savings (i.e. benefits) for society that should be considered when evaluating the impact of a nonprofit program (Javits 2008).

Like other performance management initiatives, SROI focuses on programmatic impact rather than governance and community benefits such as citizen engagement. SROI is also quite complicated in practice so its adoption within the nonprofit sector has been fairly limited, although the conceptual framework employed in SROI has encouraged funders and nonprofits to approach social impact more inclusively and to be rigorous and data-driven in thinking about costs and benefits.

In recent years, the pressure on nonprofits to achieve improved accountability has been reinforced by rating agencies and private funders. For example, charity rating services such as Charity Navigator have revised their rating standards to include specific criteria on the evaluation of outcomes. Nonprofits are now evaluated on the extent to which they demonstrate that they are seriously incorporating an outcome orientation in their organizations. The Better Business Bureau, the Independent Sector, and Guidestar have joined together to develop a "Charting Impact" project to encourage an outcome orientation among nonprofits. The National Center for Charitable Statistics at the Urban Institute has also developed an online tool called PerformWell to offer nonprofits advice and information on performance management strategies.

Leading foundations are also emphasizing outcomes in the funding policies. The Acumen Fund is a nonprofit that strives to achieve a positive impact through its grants by combining an outcome and market orientation (Ebrahim and Rangan 2010). This "impact investing" approach has been supported by large national foundations such as the Bill and Melinda Gates Foundation, the Skoll Foundation, the Omidyar Network, the Hewlett Foundation, and the Obama administration through the Social Innovation Fund (SIF) and other federal funding programs.

The impact investing approach is an attempt to reframe accountability for nonprofits. A long-time concern of many funders has been that it is difficult to evaluate nonprofit programs and many donors give to nonprofits more because they are sympathetic with the mission of the agency than its proven results. Consequently, funders and scholars have proposed a "venture philanthropy" approach to investing in nonprofit organizations (Letts, Ryan and Grossman 1999). Like venture capitalists who invest in start-up organizations and are very focused on start-up performance, advocates of venture philanthropy, including impact investing, argue that funders should only invest in nonprofit organizations who are taking outcomes seriously. Nonprofits with proven outcomes should attract additional public and private resources.

THE DILEMMAS OF NONPROFIT ACCOUNTABILITY

The changing landscape of accountability for nonprofits has created nettlesome dilemmas for the nonprofit especially as it pertains to the engagement of citizens, the responsiveness to their community of interest, their role as advocates in the policy process, and societal expectations on their citizenship responsibilities. This section discusses these dilemmas in detail.

The Challenge of Community Representation and Engagement

The importance of nonprofits as policy advocates and sites of community engagement has received broad attention from scholars, policymakers, and nonprofit leaders in recent years (Goodin 2004; Bovaird 2007; Sirianni 2009; Smith 2010). Significantly, Putnam (1993; 2000) in his well-known work on social capital argued that voluntary associations provide an opportunity for individuals to develop cooperative social networks—or social capital—that can be the basis for community action, more empowered citizens, safer neighborhoods, and higher levels of economic development. The effectiveness and sustainability of community organizations is thus related substantially to their levels of social capital—organizations with higher levels of trust will be quicker to respond to internal and external challenges; outside funders will be more likely to give grants and contracts; and citizens will be more likely to be satisfied with these organizations (and their government).

The value of voluntary organizations as sites of citizen engagement and participation was echoed by Skocpol (2003), whose detailed research on large federated national non-profit organizations, such as the American Red Cross and the YMCA, led her to con-clude that national organizations at one time played a key role in mobilizing citizens and fostering political participation and community engagement. To her, many national nonprofit organizations lost their membership and community focus as they profes-sionalized and placed greater emphasis on fund-raising from individuals and founda-tions. The resultant loss of citizen participation weakened the representative role of these organizations and played a major contributing role to the decline in political and citizen engagement in the United States.

By implication, the research of Putnam and Skocpol suggests that the big increase in nonprofit service agencies (which typically lack formal membership) has inadvertently created major obstacles to citizen engagement because the community "space" previ-ously occupied by membership organizations is now populated with service agencies. To be sure, many of these service agencies initially began their organizational lives as informal community groups with deep engagement by local citizens and committed to a "community of interest" (Smith and Lipsky 1993). A group of neighborhood activists might start an intervention program for at-risk youth in their community with small in-kind and cash donations, their entire focus on service to the local community. Or leaders in the local Latino community might start a program for Latino youth. Typically, these local citizens are not initially providing a highly professionalized service and their measures of success tend to fit with their understanding of their mission and the com-munity's needs. Over time, these informal groups may obtain government grants or contracts whereupon the expectations of government may be at variance with the focus of these nonprofit service organizations on their community of interest.

The potential for a mismatch between a nonprofit's community of interest orientation and the expectations of public and private funders has been growing due to the prolif-eration of new accountability regimes (Ospina, Diaz, and Sullivan 2002). This poten-tial conflict can be especially severe in circumstances of performance contracting when the performance measures may be imposed with little input from the nonprofit orga-nization. Thus, performance contracting regimes may be structured so that it makes it difficult for nonprofit organizations to provide services in a way compatible with their original understanding of their mission. Moreover, evidence suggests that government contracts can further distance an agency from its users and community. Contracts cre-ate a connection between the agency and government administrators, so the agency naturally tends to focus on the preservation of funding levels and the possibility of addi-tional contracts. Advocacy on behalf of the agency tends to be directed toward goals that are specific to agency funding and regulations rather than more general social policy issues or specific concerns related to users (such as improved housing or better access to accessible transportation) (Mosley 2013; Smith and Lipsky 1993).

Nonprofits may also face conflicting and contradictory pressures regarding collabo-ration and competition at the local level. Nonprofit staff and volunteers are embedded in local professional and social networks. Given the relative scarcity of public and private resources, strong incentives for collaboration can exist. Cooperation among agencies can reduce administrative costs and help build an integrated, more effective response to local social problems such as economic development or affordable housing. But the current environment of competition and market-based strategies complicates the ability of nonprofits to work together and engage citizens in a collaborative problem-solving process at the local level (Goodin 2004; Smith 2010; Kearns 2012).

Meeting Expectations of Street-Level Practice

More reporting, improved financial management, and a greater outcome orientation are now characteristic of the accountability expectations of nonprofit agencies (Brodkin 2008; Ebrahim 2009; Smith 2010; Benjamin 2008; LeRoux 2009). These important goals raise critical issues for the staff and volunteers—the so-called street-level workers—in nonprofit organizations (Lipsky 2010). Street-level workers in nonprofits may originally be oriented toward serving their community of interest with maximum responsiveness, given budget and logistical constraints (Smith and Lipsky 1993; Ospina, Diaz, and Sullivan 2002). For informal organizations, the staff (often volunteers) may have been quite close to local citizens, and, moreover, many staff and volunteers are attracted to nonprofits because of their passion for the purpose and mission of the organization. An ideal type of nonprofit dependent upon philanthropic resources and voluntarism would give these street-level workers broad discretion to achieve the mission of the organizations and serve the community and local citizens. Accountability tends to be to their own norms based upon their backgrounds and professional training as well as the "process" accountability that required monitoring and reporting the way in which services were delivered such as the number of client visits, expenditure categories, and staff to client ratios. Adherents of the New Public Management (NPM) have argued that this inattention to outcomes needs to be rectified through the imposition of new performance standards. Many of these new standards, especially various forms of performance management, can limit the discretion of the street-level workers in nonprofits in order to focus them on specific outcome targets.

The restriction on discretion is manifest in a variety of ways: 1) a focus on narrow performance targets rather than a more holistic approach to a specific person receiving service; 2) a reorientation of street-level workers toward programs and services with measurable outcomes; and 3) a shift toward services with a likelihood of success (either programmatic or financial). In an era of scarce resources, street-level workers in nonprofits (as well as the agency board and leaders) often lack the independent resources to preserve the autonomy of volunteers and staff. The result can be an inexorable shift toward the accountability expected by external funders and away from the insights and wisdom of street-level workers.

To be sure, street-level workers in nonprofits are not without resources to evade or ignore programmatic performance targets since the staff and volunteers may know how to comply with performance regulations without sacrificing their own programmatic objectives. However, this effort is arguably more difficult in a fiscally scarce environment with more competition for funding. Many nonprofit agencies have also endured reductions in staffing creating a more intense and demanding job situation with staff and volunteers expected to achieve more results with less staffing; in these circumstances, street-level workers may be poorly positioned to exercise their own discretion on behalf of agency clients and their communities. This situation may be inadvertently reinforced by the board of directors who face pressure to raise revenue and exercise caution in governing the agency, so they may not challenge inappropriate regulations or performance expectations due to concern for the possible negative consequences to the agency of disrupting relationships with important funding entities.

TOWARD A BROAD APPROACH TO ACCOUNTABILITY

The capacity of nonprofits to promote civic engagement and responsiveness to local communities can be bridged but it requires a rethinking of the current approach to accountability to encompass a more holistic understanding of the value of nonprofits and their contributions to local communities. In general, active engagement of users in agency governance or operations tends to be rare among nonprofit organizations providing public services, unless mandated by law. Instead, nonprofit organizations with the most active user involvement tend to be self-help and/or advocacy organizations. Yet, countertrends related to participation are apparent throughout the world. The debt and fiscal crisis has forced many agencies to seek donations and political support from their communities. Many agencies are much more active in seeking political support to restore lost funding, protect existing contracts, or obtain new contracts. The widespread interest in earned income activities and corporate partnerships has pushed nonprofits to create new opportunities for the community to support the agency financially. For instance, special event dinners for the local agency for the homeless are a way of engaging the local citizenry through financial support and at least a subset of these individuals will then be engaged in the agency through volunteering on an ongoing or periodic basis. Greater structural complexity including ad hoc and advisory committees for specific purposes, such as fund-raising or strategic planning, encourages more community engagement and consultation. Indeed, many community agencies operating service programs have learned out of necessity to be more consultative with the community because they are offering programs that require community assent and cooperation.

The mind-set about accountability among policymakers needs to change. Too often, policymakers view the role of nonprofits very narrowly. Government administrators could instead encourage more community participation and engagement through regulations and indirect and direct support and technical assistance (also, Wichowsky and Moynihan 2008). Government administrators could encourage agencies to employ an array of participation methods: board representation slots where appropriate, advisory groups comprised of community members to advise the agency on strategic priorities and/or service-related concerns, community input meetings including focus groups, surveys of community members, participation by the nonprofit service agency in other community activities or associations, and community co-production on planning and governance (see Bovaird 2007; Alford 2009).

In particular, hospitals in the US are now required to report their "community benefit" spending. This concept holds promise as a potential model for thinking more broadly about accountability. Community benefit spending for hospitals can include mission-related services such as home or hospice care, and community-building activities such as partnerships with the local schools, local economic development, sponsorship of charity events such as walk-a-thons, and health education and promotion activities. This broader framework for evaluating community benefit for nonprofit hospitals points toward the need to think about the relationship between nonprofit organizations, their users, and their communities when approaching accountability (Gray and Schlesinger 2009).

In short, nonprofits can be sites of vibrant civic engagement and community governance, and providers of valuable local services. Contemporary accountability regimes tend to emphasize organizational maintenance, competition, entrepreneurship, and sustainability. To be sure, civic engagement in the governance and operations of local nonprofits can be time-consuming, albeit very worthwhile for the agency and the community. And it can be especially daunting for smaller nonprofits without substantial staff and volunteer capacity.

To achieve accountability and citizen engagement, nonprofits need to consult with many stakeholders and think comprehensively and strategically about their mission. Extensive consultation with stakeholders can help build community support which can be especially helpful in the current environment of scarce resources. Input from the community and the street-level workers in nonprofits can also improve the accountability process and help promote the development of effective measures of nonprofit accountability, including for program outcomes. This effort can also promote long-term sustainability by attracting public and private resources and enhance organizational legitimacy and credibility. This broad effort is not easy given the pressure to achieve outcomes as well as the lack of funding. However, this comprehensive approach to accountability will help nonprofits to achieve program efficiency and effectiveness. As a result, the evolving role of nonprofits in society will be enhanced and strengthened while promoting more active engagement in the community.

ACKNOWLEDGMENTS

The author is very grateful for comments on earlier drafts of this chapter from Putnam Barber, Robert Behn, Tony Bovaird, Robert Goodin, and Donald Moynihan. Excellent research assistance was also provided by Staci Goldberg-Belle.

References

Alcock, P. 2012. *The Big Society: A New Policy Environment for the Third Sector?* Third Sector Research Centre Working Paper, No. 82. Birmingham, UK: University of Birmingham.

Alford, J. 2009. *Engaging Public Sector Clients: From Service-Delivery to Co-production.* London: Palgrave MacMillan.

Barber, P. 2001. *Accountability: A Challenge for Charities and Fundraisers.* New Directions for Philanthropic Fundraising, No. 31. San Francisco: Jossey-Bass.

BBC News. 2012, 21 July. *Russia: Controversial NGO Bill Becomes Law.* Retrieved from <http://www.bbc.co.uk/news/world-europe-18938165>.

Benjamin, L. M. 2008. "Bearing More Risk for Results: Performance Accountability and Nonprofit Relational Work." *Administration & Society,* 39: 959–83.

Bovaird, T. 2007. "Beyond Engagement and Participation: User and Community Co-Production of Public Services." *Public Administration Review,* 67: 846–60.

Brodkin, E. Z. 2008. "Accountability in Street-Level Organizations." *International Journal of Public Administration,* 31: 317–36.

Cordes, J. J. and Steuerle, C. E., eds. 2009. *Nonprofits and Business.* Washington: Urban Institute.

Crutchfield, L. R. and Grant, H. M. 2008. *Forces for Good: The Six Practices of High-Impact Nonprofits.* San Francisco: Jossey-Bass.

Dees, J. G. 1996. *The Social Enterprise Spectrum: Philanthropy to Commerce.* Boston: Harvard Business School Publishing.

Ebrahim, A. and Rangan, V. K. 2010. *Acumen Fund: Measurement in Impact Investing (A).* HBS Case Collection, 310-11. Harvard Business School.

Ebrahim, A. 2009. "Placing the Normative Logics of Accountability in 'Thick' Perspective." *American Behavioral Scientist,* 52: 885–904.

Eikenberry, A. M. and Kluver, J. D. 2004. "The Marketization of the Nonprofit Sector: Civil Society at Risk?" *Public Administration Review,* 64: 132–40.

Goodin, R. 2004. *Democratic Accountability: The Third Sector and All.* Paper presented to Seminar Series on "Institutional Analysis of Law, Politics, and Society." SUNY Buffalo Law School.

Gray, B. and Schlesinger, M. 2009. "Charitable Expectations of Nonprofit Hospitals: Lessons from Maryland." *Health Affairs,* 28: w809–w21.

Hansmann, H. B. 1980. "The Role of Nonprofit Enterprise." *Yale Law Journal,* 89: 835–901.

Hatry, H. P. 2006. *Performance Measurement: Getting Results.* Second edition. Washington, DC: Urban Institute.

Heinrich, C. J. and Choi, Y. 2007. "Performance-based Contracting in Social Welfare Programs." *American Review of Public Administration,* 37: 409–35.

Hood, C. 1991. "A Public Management for All Seasons." *Public Administration,* 69: 3–19.

Hwang, H. and Powell, W. W. 2009. "The Rationalization of Charity: The Influences of Professionalism in the Nonprofit Sector." *Administrative Science Quarterly,* 54: 268–98.

International Center on Nonprofit Law (ICNL). 2012. *NGO Law Monitor: Turkey.* Retrieved from <http://www.icnl.org/research/monitor/turkey.pdf.>.

Javits, C. I. 2008. *REDF's Current Approach to SROI.* San Francisco: The Roberts Foundation.

Kaplan, R. S. 2002. *The Balanced Scorecard and Nonprofit Organizations.* Boston: Harvard Business School.

Kearns, K. P. 2012. Accountability in the Nonprofit Sector, pp. 587–615 in *The State of Nonprofit America,* ed. L. M. Salamon. Washington, DC: Brookings.

LeRoux, K. 2009. "Managing Stakeholder Demands: Balancing Responsiveness to Clients and Funding Agencies in Nonprofit Social Service Agencies." *Administration & Society*, 41: 158–84.

Letts, C. W., Ryan, W. P. and Grossman, A. 1999. *High Performance Nonprofit Organizations: Managing Upstream for Greater Impact*. New York: Wiley.

Light, P. C. 2004. *Sustaining Nonprofit Performance: The Case for Capacity Building and the Evidence to Support It*. Washington, DC: Brookings Institution.

Light, P. C. 2007. *The Search for Social Entrepreneurship*. Washington, DC: Brookings.

Lipsky, M. 2010. *Street-Level Bureaucracy*. New York: Russell Sage Foundation.

Mosley, J. 2013. "The Beliefs of Homeless Service Managers About Policy Advocacy: Definitions, Legal Understanding, and Motivations to Participate." *Administration in Social Work*, 37: 73–89.

Osborne, D. and Gaebler, T. 1992. *Reinventing Government*. New York: Plume.

Ospina, S., Diaz, W., and O'Sullivan, J. F. 2002. "Negotiating Accountability: Managerial Lessons from Identity-Based Nonprofit Organizations." *Nonprofit and Voluntary Sector Quarterly*, 31: 5–31.

Oster, S. 1995. *Strategic Management of Nonprofit Organizations*. New Haven: Yale University Press.

Phillips, S. and Smith, S. R. 2010. *Governance and Regulation in the Third Sector: International Perspectives*. London: Routledge.

Putnam, R. D. 1993. *Making Democracy Work*. Princeton, NJ: Princeton University Press.

Putnam, R. D. 2000. *Bowling Alone*. New York: Simon and Schuster.

Simon, J., Dale, H. and Chisholm, L. 2006. The Legal Framework of the Nonprofit Sector, pp. 243–66 in *The Nonprofit Sector: A Research Handbook*, eds. W. W. Powell and R. Steinberg. New Haven: Yale University Press.

Sirianni, C. 2009. *Investing in Democracy: Engaging Citizens in Collaborative Governance*. Washington, DC: Brookings Institution Press.

Skocpol, T. 2003. *Diminished Democracy: From to Management in American Civic Life*. Norman: University of Oklahoma Press.

Smith, S. R. and Lipsky, M. 1993. *Nonprofits for Hire: The Welfare State in the Age of Contracting*. Cambridge, MA: Harvard University Press.

Smith, S. R. 2010. "Nonprofits and Public Administration: Reconciling Performance Management and Citizen Engagement." *American Review of Public Administration*, 40: 129–52.

Smith, S. R. 2012. Social Services, pp. 192–228 in *The State of Nonprofit America*, ed. M. Salamon. Washington, DC: Brookings Institution Press.

Wichowsky, A. and Moynihan, D. P. 2008. "Measuring How Administration Shapes Citizenship: A Policy Feedback Perspective on Performance Management." *Public Administration Review*, 68: 908–20.

Wu, F. 2003. "Environmental GONGO Autonomy: Unintended Consequences of State Strategies in China." *The Good Society*, 12: 35–45.

CHAPTER 22

ACCOUNTABLE CORPORATE GOVERNANCE

SHELDON LEADER

INTERNAL AND EXTERNAL PERSPECTIVES ON THE CORPORATION

IT might seem surprising that a book dedicated to issues of *public* accountability should contain a chapter on corporations, institutions that are primarily private. This becomes understandable, however, as society watches such public functions as the operation of hospitals, schools, and prisons pass into the hands of private owners/operators. This in turn has generated a concern about corporate power per se. In the private sector, companies making products ranging from shoes to computer software have the power to control peoples' working and consuming lives, and in some cases can be strong enough to dictate some of a government's policy priorities. The internal processes for reaching decisions in these corporations, as well as the external impacts flowing from such decisions, are properly the concern of society as a whole.

To whom, and for what, should the modern commercial corporation be accountable? How can corporate governance be structured so as to deliver a satisfactory answer to this question? At first glance, there is little new in this enquiry. We know that companies are not allowed to pollute, to falsify accounts, or to pay workers less than the legal minimum wage. These and many other measures are designed to make the company a more responsible citizen. The search for improved corporate accountability, one might conclude, is of this kind. There is nothing new or fundamental at stake here, either in terms of governance or in terms of challenges to the traditional rationale and legitimacy of the commercial enterprise.

We can call this an external perspective on corporate accountability. That is, the company faces the society outside of it, and is accountable to the latter for the damage it does. However, there is another way of taking our initial questions. They might aim at a shift in internal perspective, reaching inside the corporation and changing its constitution, its objectives, and the principles conferring legitimacy on it. This in turn can produce a shift in those to whom the entity is accountable, and a shift in what it is obliged to do for them. It is this internal perspective that allows us to raise such questions as should employees be entitled to direct representation on the Board of Directors alongside shareholder representatives? If yes, should they also be entitled to a share in company profits on an equal basis with shareholders? Should the company properly take responsibility for the impact of its working practices on the family lives of its employees? Of course there are similar questions to ask about others, apart from employees, who are affected by what a company does.

This shift to an internal perspective can be accompanied by important shifts in the more classical questions about external accountability. We know, for example, that a pharmaceutical company must not injure health with its products, but should it be held accountable if it refuses to sell a drug at a price that will give access to a cure for a serious disease to the population of an impoverished country?

In what follows we will look at the issues about accountability that arise from these questions, questions that begin with challenges to the traditional organizing principles for the modern commercial company.

STRUCTURES OF GOVERNANCE AND SITES OF POWER

It might help first to identify the sites of power, and the rules relating to them, within the typical private enterprise. The classical model, subject to modifications in particular companies, structures the body in the following way. Those who supervise the functioning of the company are the Board of Directors. Those who manage the company day-to-day are answerable to the Board, and the Board itself is answerable to the company's shareholders. The shareholders, like citizens in a democracy, typically have the right to vote the Board in or out of power but do not have managerial authority. In some countries, the supervisory function of the Board of Directors is carried out by an organ, the Supervisory Board, which is separate from the Managerial Board.[1] The latter is answerable to the former. In other countries there is only one tier of authority, the Board of Directors, and some of those who manage the company day to day also sit on it, such as the Chief Executive Officer (CEO).[2] The CEO, as well as other directors with managerial functions, are answerable to the whole Board of which they are members. Finally, there is the category of employee. Employment is a distinct legal link to the company—often via a contract stipulating terms and conditions of work and statutory protection against different forms of unfair treatment at work, ranging from gender discrimination through to an abusive dismissal.

Any single individual can occupy one or more of these roles. She might be a member of the Board, Chief Executive Officer, employee, and shareholder. Her interests will be different in each role, though they also overlap. This divergence and overlap becomes more salient when these roles begin to come apart and locate in different individuals: A salient example is the employee who is not part of the executive nor a shareholder.

The shareholders, directors, managers, and employees are usually not personally liable for the company' debts on loans, awards of damages against it, or for fines it has to pay. These remain the responsibility of the company alone. The only exception will be if the relevant individuals go beyond the limits for appropriate functioning in their roles, and engage in, for example, crimes, or transactions in bad faith. Shareholders are, under the famous doctrine of limited liability, also immune from suit against them personally for e.g. debts or fines owed by their company.

Many companies, especially larger ones, organize themselves into a cluster of legally separate enterprises, sometimes known as a corporate group. In the simplest model, a parent company owns all of the shares of several subsidiary companies. As a shareholder, the parent company benefits from the general principle of limited liability. Its subsidiaries are treated by law as separate companies and their obligations not to pollute, collaborate in human rights abuse, etc., remain with them and do not extend to the parent. Recent developments in social accountability are leading to the laws of several countries making inroads into this limited liability for parent companies, a point that will be considered below.

In asking *where* power typically resides within the organization, it is important to distinguish two kinds: managerial and supervisory power. Most corporate law regimes around the world allocate a supervisory role to the non-executive members of the Board of Directors, and, in turn, to the shareholders. Non-executive members of the Board are not to be involved in the day-to-day running of the company but instead supervise it from a distance, considering serious failures in day-to-day management and acting accordingly. Management, in turn, is precisely the locus of initiatives, reversals of policy, decisions to price goods or services, etc., that make up its executive function. The main corporate law regimes are careful to exclude those exercising supervisory functions from undue interference with managerial functions. Shareholders, for example, may pass resolutions telling management what they want them to do, but if management is convinced that this is bad for the company the law will back them up as they refuse to follow those resolutions. The only fallback for the shareholder is removal of the director or, in extreme cases, of the whole Board.

The famous split between ownership and control arises from this basic premise of corporate law. Managerial power is allowed to develop on its own because it is seen as a distinct function, with distinct prerogatives, from those of the Board or of shareholders. When this is coupled with a relatively large and diffuse set of shareholders, the latter are frequently unable to check management in the way they are formally entitled to. Those who want, in the name of greater social accountability, to widen the representation on the Board so that it reflects the interests of groups other than shareholders are sometimes frustrated to find that their inroads into company policy are equally limited. They sit some distance from daily decision making and are structurally not able to influence it as much as they would like. Nevertheless, this is an important dimension of potential accountability. At the same time, as will be seen, there is a place for closer participation of a wider group of stakeholders in the *exercise* of managerial power. As an important additional feature of governance, this carries its own challenges, as will be seen.

Legitimacy

In whose interests should the company operate? There are two well-known approaches to an answer. They are endorsements of certain stakeholder interests grounded on a theory of property, and endorsements grounded on a theory of citizenship. In order to avoid begging key questions, we can deploy this broad category, "stakeholder," to refer to all of those who have an interest in benefiting from or avoiding damage by company activity, and treat the owner of shares in the company as a species of this wider genus.

Stakeholders as Property Holders

Some argue that the company should serve the interests of those having property rights that it must respect. This is a perspective sometimes shared by those who support and by those who oppose the idea that the company exists to satisfy the interests of its shareholders. In favor of shareholder dominance it is claimed that the shareholder invests his or her property as an engagement with an uncertain future, and that this risk carries the right to what remains of revenue after costs are deducted.

Some of those who disagree, wishing to secure a position for other stakeholders alongside shareholders, simply widen this form of reasoning. Margaret Blair (1995, 239), for example, argues that stakeholders are "all parties who have contributed inputs to the enterprise and who, as a result, have at risk investments that are highly specialized to the enterprise." Employees take risks with their productive lives by investing time and effort in the company. Furthermore, they often invest in developing firm-specific skills that are unique to a given enterprise and not easily left behind. It follows that there is no reason to give the interests of any investor of any particular form of capital any particularly privileged place as compared with that of any other species of investor. The company exists to serve the interests of all of them.

Stakeholders as Citizens

A distinct way of challenging the dominance of shareholder interests is to attack the root of the idea that property rights per se provide privileged interests to which the corporation is to be accountable. The company, it is argued, has an essentially social purpose. As the Belgian government put the point, the company "...is an element of society which must contribute to society as a whole." (Council of Ministers 1997). The stakeholder arrives here not via his position as an investor of property, but via his or her general rights as a citizen.

This is a view sometimes based on the observation that the modern corporation has separated control from ownership. It can be seen as early as Marx's (1920) claim that the abolition of private property in the means of production was not the primary task of socialism, since that abolition had already taken place at the hands of capitalism. As capitalism matured, he argued, production would escape the control of the nominal owners of the corporation and fall into the hands of distant managers. As Karl Renner (1949, 220) expressed the point, the property in the share "...has become so estranged from the owner that he must consult the newspaper to get information about its position." The distance of the laborer from control over his product—his alienation—is paralleled by the distance of the investor of funds from control over his stake.

On this approach, there is a crucial transformation that needs to take place in thinking about corporate accountability. Labor is not to step into the shoes of the shareholder and become the set of interests that it is the mission of the company to benefit. Instead, society steps into the breach. It removes shareholders' claim to "...a social surplus product by individuals who fulfil no social function" (Renner 1949).

We also find this claim that the corporation is a social institution in the influential work of Berle and Means. They argued that shareholders in large companies often hold "passive property...in shares of stock or bonds," while managers hold "active" property, controlling "the plant, good will, and organization which make up the actual enterprise." Passive property must, they argued, "...yield before the larger interests of society." They envisaged a time—not via expropriation but rather by evolution—when the interests of shareholders in maximal profits would give way to the wider community demanding of corporate management that it balance the need for "fair wages, security to employees, reasonable service to their public, and stabilization of business" (Berle and Means 1932, 347).

The practical upshots of these two perspectives are quite different. Where the first approach would add a limited number of stakeholders—those who had made investments of their property in the enterprise—the second argument adds a much wider list, made up of the members of the wider society in which the corporation is located—and their representatives. This approach is willing to place on company boardrooms representatives of consumer groups, environmental pressure groups, representatives of local commerce, along with trade union and works council members.[3]

Problems

We need to ask how much help is provided by these two ways of arguing for stakeholder rights when hard choices have to be made between such options as changing the location of a factory and preserving local employment; between increasing wages and putting more resources into investment in technology, etc.

The difficulty with these two approaches is that each obscures the way in which these decisions are to factor in accountability to society. The problem with the property-based strategy is that it only allows into the magic circle of corporate priorities those individuals who have taken risks with their resources—with their finance or with their working lives—and who have treated this resource as a form of investment which expects its fair return. But the meeting ground between those affected on the one hand, and the use and abuse of company power on the other, is larger and more complex, often calling on factors that have little to do with who has taken a risk with their property. Corporate decisions about plant location or investment in technology benefit some and injure others. How is the injury to be balanced against the benefit conferred? To whom, within the group of people concerned, should management be accountable if they get the answer wrong? Is the group which is entitled to complain of an injury different from the group entitled to demand that the company benefit them? There are at least three sets of interests that figure here:

a) There are those to whom, because of certain interests they have, management is *ultimately* accountable. These can be called its sovereign stakeholders. The word 'sovereign' here designates not only the state or other supreme authority. In the private sector it also designates those with the final say over who governs the enterprise, and for which purpose. The Board of Directors is often elected and can be removed by this group, much as the electorate can install and remove a political leader. In the company, the shareholder has classically been given these powers, but is heavily contested for a place at the table by other candidates, such as employees who are sometimes given votes to elect or remove their representatives on the Board (as in the German system, supra n. 1).

b) There are those to whom management is *strategically* accountable, or strategic stakeholders. In failing to attend to the interests of this group a miscalculation might be made about the best way to further the company's purposes. Satisfying the interests of shareholders in paying a dividend might, on some occasions, provide the best fit with these purposes, but at other times it might make more sense to prefer raising wages substantially at the expense of dividends. It is all a question of what yields the optimal functional result for the company.

c) There are those to whom management is *equitably* accountable. These deserve not to have their basic interests in their health, job security, property, right to privacy, etc. injured. Some of these equitable interests arise from background entitlements, such as human rights, while other such entitlements arise within the constitution of the company, as happens when a minority of shareholders claim a right that management not treat them unfairly by e.g. weakening their claim to influence or revenue that the majority enjoys.

The company is properly held accountable along these three distinct lines. The notion of a fair return for risk taken with one's property does not help us to locate the interested

parties on one or more of the axes. We will look more closely at how we can work positively with these axes after a consideration of the citizenship theory.

The citizenship theory fares no better. Here, to recall, the starting point is the notion
of the company as a social institution. On this approach, a parallel can be drawn
between the obligations of the state towards society and the obligations of the corporation towards that society. Note how this runs together the third concern, for equitable
accountability, with the first, for ultimate accountability. Assume that Mr. Jones, qua
citizen, is among those to whom his local town council is ultimately accountable via the
ballot box. Assume as well that the council's waste management policy risks negligently
polluting Mr. Jones's land. It makes sense, in a democracy, that Mr. Jones's use of his
right to vote should reflect his concern about his wrongly damaged property. The first
and third lines of accountability should be linked. Turning to a company, however, this
linkage is less certain. If Mr. Jones's land is vulnerable to pollution by a private company,
or a worker controlled cooperative, it does not follow that his particular interest in preventing that damage should underpin giving him a right to vote to appoint or remove
the company's or cooperative's directors. It should give him a right to protest against
the possible damage and to sue if it occurs, but the right to vote for members of the
board would not normally be part of the package. The damage being done to him by the
company must certainly be prevented, but it does not follow that this concern should
be enough to entitle him to a say about who should run the company and what its objectives should be. This would be true even if we assume that the company is limited to
operating within the same geographical boundaries as does the town council. The third
species of corporate accountability does not automatically link up with the first.

ANOTHER LOOK

If the foregoing analysis is correct, then we need to change the question: "whose interests is it the duty of the company to serve?" This creates a false set of options, asking for a
choice between categories of person, the alternatives offered being shareholders or some
wider set of constituents such as employees or members of local communities affected
by corporate decisions. Instead, the difference between interests which are properly
dominant in the corporate agenda and those which are secondary or even irrelevant is
not a difference connected to distinct types of person, but arises out of the quality of the
interests themselves. People may and do share in a range of these interests in overlapping and diverging ways.

Strategic Interests

If the company is to be strategically accountable, satisfying this requirement might be in
tension with the requirement that it also be equitably accountable. A decision that best

promotes the purpose of, for example, making shoes at a profit might call for restructuring the enterprise in a way that prejudices women more than men. The corporate law of most countries builds in room for these strategic considerations. But in taking such strategic decisions, the law usually rejects *automatic* priority to be given to shareholders on every occasion when their demands compete with those of, say, employees. Even in those regimes which assign long-term primacy to shareholders, these systems recognize that good strategy might well call for raising wages rather than paying higher dividends in order to keep the company functioning effectively. Indeed, the law in most jurisdictions is clear that management would violate its fiduciary duty to promote the company's best interests if it were to give blanket priority to shareholder demands across all of its decisions.[4]

Equitable Interests

Those shaping the social accountability of the company might well take the view that equity must take precedence over strategy in certain situations. This is particularly strong as a potential motive when human rights enter into the picture. If a pharmaceutical company is pressed by a state to sell certain medicines at a loss in order to fight HIV/AIDS, the company may be called on to do this out of a direct concern to help the state to fulfill the right of its subjects to adequate health care, and not by appealing to the company's strategic motivation to maintain its public image for the sake of its long term gain. There are those who argue that strategic accountability is all that legitimately concerns the company's directors, and should always trump equitable accountability. At most, says this position, the satisfaction of a human rights demand (for example for improved housing or medical care) should be treated as a company's responsibility only if this is not incompatible with its ability to meet its strategic goal of making a profit.[5] This position is contested by those who argue that the company should be willing to concede a limitation on its strategic objectives in favor of equitable demands—if selling the medicines at a loss yields no longer term gain in public opinion, so be it, says this view. The loss should still be borne (see e.g., Global Issues 2002).

One can go further. It is legitimate to ask how *much* of a loss should be borne by a company in order to satisfy these equitable demands. There are those who are only willing to tolerate marginal inroads into profitability, so bringing them close to those totally devoted to the company's strategic objectives who tolerate no inroads into corporate profit at all. There are others, however, who argue that adequate accountability here requires the company to make much greater sacrifices. It would, on this view, be right to require the company to allocate its available resources to satisfying the human right in question and to cease being required to do so only when and if the company reaches the point of itself no longer being viable as a commercial entity.

In testing this limit to accountability, it is important to keep in mind the distinction between avoiding *damage* to a basic right, such as the right to life that can be threatened from negligent management of work places, and acting to *improve* satisfaction of a basic right via providing inexpensive medicines to the gravely ill. If a company cannot afford to keep a workplace safe, then arguably it should be allowed to go bankrupt. On the other hand, if it cannot afford to provide the medicines at a loss without itself going broke, then there is arguably greater room for it to compromise on its improvement of access to its medicines.

This is an area in which corporate power and corporate responsibility can come apart. Recall that the parent company stands in relation to a subsidiary as shareholders do to their company: There is limited liability. This allows the parent company of a pharmaceutical group, for example, to claim that its subsidiary is an independent company, for which the parent is not responsible. In fact, the latter often sets and supervises the policies of the former far more closely than does a typical body of shareholders. The result is that a subsidiary supplying medicines in our example might claim that it is close to insolvency when this may be because its resources are regularly transferred to the parent well before any litigation arises. This leaves it in a position to claim that it does not have the resources to provide the medicines at a loss.

This insulation of parent companies from social accountability is coming under pressure for reform, some of it initiated by important judicial decisions that narrow the gap between legal fiction and reality. For example, Royal Dutch Shell has claimed that, as parent company in the Shell Group, it has no duty of care in making sure that its subsidiary in Nigeria implements group environmental guidelines. However, the English Court of Appeal has decided (in a case not involving Shell, but likely to affect it in the future) that parent companies do have this duty of care, and this principle is likely to spread to other leading jurisdictions of concern to multinationals (Essex Business and Human Rights Project 2012, Section II).[6]

Sovereign Interests

Those to whom the corporation is ultimately accountable, be they shareholders or employees or others, are in this position because of a particular sort of interest they have which is distinct from those which are strategic or equitable. Strategic interests, if served, help the fulfillment of a corporate purpose; equitable interests deserve respect on their own merits, detached from, and a potential constraint on, corporate purposes. A sovereign interest, by way of contrast, is in *defining* a corporate purpose rather than simply seeing it well served strategically, or pursued equitably. This is what is at stake when, for example, employees of a pharmaceutical company press it to add to its objectives the provision of hospital facilities for poorer countries, or campaign for their automobile manufacturing employer to make vehicles that are affordable by the least well-off part of the population. If these efforts were successful, in any given case, then the added corporate purposes legitimately take priority over the simple profitability of the company; they are now part of the reason the company exists in the first place.

The creation or change of a private company's objectives is traditionally a matter for ultimate control by shareholders.[7] This is usually based on the notion that they own the company, and so flows from the property theory described earlier. However, the other half of that property theory examined might come into its own at this point, serving to widen the group of sovereign stakeholders. If, say, a group of employees have invested their efforts for some years in a particular company, does this entitle them to a say, via their representatives on the Board, in defining what the company exists to do? It is true that they have not been present at the beginning, when the company was set up and the decisions about its objectives were taken by its initial owners. But should this make a difference? Most shareholders in companies have arrived well after its founding, but this does not lessen their rights to press for redefinition of company purposes. Why then should this matter for employees? If employees are allowed to share in this sovereign role, why not other stakeholders, such as members of the community in which the enterprise is located? If we agree to admit them, does this take us back to the proposition examined earlier that the company is essentially a social institution, and as such fully accountable to society? These are areas for legitimate debate about the locus of *sovereign* interests. This debate, however, should not be allowed to set the terms on which a socially accountable company serves *strategic* or *equitable* interests. These remain distinct considerations, and damage is done if sovereign stakeholders take the place of strategic and equitable ones. Distinct elements of governance must match distinct lines of accountability.

LINKING ACCOUNTABILITY AND THE ELEMENTS OF CORPORATE GOVERNANCE

If these three types of interest, strategic, equitable, and ultimate, are each to be satisfied, what implications do these distinct directions of accountability have for corporate governance?

Corporate Governance and Strategic Interests

The advance of a company's basic purposes cannot be left to the control of any single set of stakeholders. Shareholders are not better placed than employees to indicate how well a company's objective is served by a particular planned strategy. It could easily frustrate the company's objectives if shareholders were automatically to be paid a dividend rather than pay any increase in salary; the reverse could also be true. All depends on the circumstances, showing which of the strategies is most appropriate.

The decision is therefore ultimately a managerial one. However, while the decision is of this type, this does not imply that management may operate without the participation of all relevant stakeholders. These stakeholders, participating in the *formulation* of corporate strategy, do not play a supervisory role, as they might elsewhere in the company.

Instead they provide vital information about the impact of any given plan of action on corporate objectives. Works councils exist for this reason. They are set up as consultative bodies within companies, and express the views of employees about the corporate wisdom of one course of action rather than another. They often sit alongside the trade union, which can help with strategic decisions but is better placed to serve equitable interests more forcefully via collective bargaining. It is the union which typically negotiates with the company, causing it to compromise on its objectives to some extent in order, say, to avoid a strike. That is not something that an in-company works council is equipped to do. Other bodies, such as representatives of environmental interests, or of the interests of the local community or of small businesses, can also provide a better informed picture of the strategic impact of any given decision.

It is important to improve a company's accountability to society via strengthening the governance of its strategic decisions. Management's choices about whether to move production to another country, or to tighten the monitoring of employee performance, can backfire if those making them are not adequately informed about the true impact on the people who are meant to bring about the hoped-for results. However, participation in strategic decisions is no substitute for participation in decisions affecting equitable interests, such as human rights. Those who become part of a company's internal strategic decision-making process are often shocked and frustrated at their inability to persuade the company that its choice of strategy is a poor one because of the damage it will do to society, independently of whether it improves profitability.

Corporate Governance and Equitable Interests

The participation by stakeholders that is meant to defend equitable concerns is different in kind from that which is concerned to help with strategic interests. Consider a mining company that plans an access road to one of its installations in a poor country. It might, as many do, have a choice between building the road some distance from nearby villages, or using existing roads through the villages. Assume that the former solution will be considerably more expensive than the latter. If it does go through the villages, however, dust will be generated, with effects on health, particularly for children and older people (on this type of problem see Amnesty International United Kingdom 2005). What should it do? Strategically, the answer depends on which solution will do least to harm its reputation, together with the consideration of being as cost-efficient as possible. Equitably, the matter looks different. Protecting the interest in health has independent weight. It would call for governance via an external body, such as the state or an international authority with power for example to revoke project loans for failures to respect the basic rights of local populations.[8] That would satisfy the supervisory arm of governance. However, there is the participatory arm as well. Here, those representing the local population in our example should have the right to intervene at an early stage in project design to make sure that planners are aware of the health risks and have time to choose alternative routes. The fault in much corporate accountability in this area arises from the fact that companies are willing to consult about the social impact of their projects only once basic decisions on these matters are taken, leaving consultation with those affected at the margin. This goes against the spirit of certain key human rights requirements, such as the right of indigenous peoples that relocation will not take place without their free, *prior*, and informed consent (UN Declaration on the Rights of Indigenous Peoples, Article 10).

When the location of a project in one place rather than another means that local populations are threatened with ejection from their homes or farms or destruction of sites of vital importance to their identity, their equitable concerns to resist are vulnerable to being swallowed by the strategic way in which priorities are defined.[9] Equitable concerns cannot be solely entrusted to a corporation's *method* of taking account of them—however much the enterprise may be of good faith, and however strongly it endorses the need to be socially responsible, there is little to induce it on its own to give priority to equity over strategy (cf. Leader 2005; 2006). Currently this is a problem with Afghanistan's effort to inject wider social concerns into the operations of mining corporations. On the one hand, its draft Minerals Law requires a company to carry out mining in a way that interferes as little as possible with the rights of any lawful occupant of the surface land, such as a farmer.[10] The company is entitled to pursue its strategic priorities, but must adjust them so as to do least damage to the equitable interests of the population at large. However, elsewhere in the same statute the reverse is the case: The company's strategic interests take automatic priority over equity. For example, those entitled to farm the surface land retain their right to use water (a key human right) but only on condition that they do not interfere with the company's right to carry out exploration activity.[11] If there are no effective external regulators of corporate activity in Afghanistan, then the enterprise itself—however clear its commitment to social responsibility—will favor the spirit behind the second part of the law over the first.

While participants in strategic decisions should not be called on to *negotiate* with the company, pressing it to move away from its commitment to long-term profit in order to give more room for the defense of human rights or the environment, negotiation is appropriate in the defense of equitable interests. It is the domain of bargaining backed with the pressure of strikes, pickets, local population boycotts, or other forms of protest. It is also the domain for state regulation, and as such is a crucial and distinct channel of social accountability.

Corporate Governance and Sovereign Interests

Those with sovereign interests are entitled to have the last word in answering the question, what is this particular company here for? Should we bring it to an end? Should we change course fundamentally? The mechanisms for reaching such decisions are well-developed in corporate organization, via the Board of Directors and ultimately the shareholders. What is missing is an appropriately *wider* set of sovereign stakeholders to occupy the positions of sovereign control. To occupy a position of sovereign control, however, gives the holder more than power over the definition of group purposes. It also confers, as has been seen, the power to decide who will exercise supervisory power in the Board of Directors, and via accountability to the Board, control over managerial power. A threat to adequate social accountability lies here. It is too easy for management to turn their accountability to the Board into a formality, and for the Board in turn to manipulate bodies of shareholders. Apart from well-informed institutional holders of shares such as pension funds or ethical investment funds, most individual shareholders have little idea of relevant facts other than as the company presents them. For this reason, any viable program to increase social accountability of the company must continue to encourage NGO's and allied bodies to become shareholders so as to be able to press points of view and provide information that would otherwise be missing.

AGENDA: WAYS OF APPROACHING RELATIVE PRIORITIES

Challenges to the legitimacy of the modern corporation are not new. New, however, is the spread of agreement on the need for strong social accountability even among corporations themselves. A steadily increasing number of major enterprises publicly acknowledge that they can have an impact on human rights, and provide detailed accounts of the steps they take to avoid damaging them. This plateau of consensus, however, is the point of departure for fundamental conflict over the precise meaning of that social commitment. It is here that concrete solutions need to be worked out, and these in turn depend on further fundamental work concerning the basic principles structuring power lying beyond the state.

If the arguments advanced here are valid, then we need to move away from one starting point in analysis and towards another. We cannot begin by asking to whom the corporation should be accountable: shareholders, employees, or members of the community. Instead we need to start by asking just what the objective of accountability is, and to what extent this objective serves strategic, equitable, or sovereign interests. It is not possible to further all of these demands at once. Trade-offs have to be worked out. This can divide apparent allies; some employees may align themselves with the company's strategic decision to outsource a branch of its activity, while others might resist this in order to protect—equitably—their jobs. One shareholder might endorse a merger for strategic reasons that the company advances, while another shareholder in the same company may see that the merger will lead to withdrawal of plant from a local community with disastrous effects on equitable concerns. What has to be worked out are ways of approaching relative priorities among these types of interest. With that in hand, one can begin to address the question, to whom is the company properly held accountable?

NOTES

1. The leading example is that of larger German companies (Schulten and Zagelmeyer 1998).
2. As in the UK (see e.g. Institute of Directors 2010).
3. For an elaboration of these points, on which the foregoing paragraphs draw, see Leader (1999) passim.
4. "There is nothing in company law to prevent directors having regard to other interests if they judge reasonably and in good faith that to do so is conducive to the health of the company. Indeed, for directors not to give appropriate weight to all the company's key relationships may well be a breach of their fiduciary duty" (Royal Society of Arts and Manufacturing 1995, 12).
5. "... Responsible business is not a trade-off between people, planet and profit" (Business in the Community 2011).
6. Shell has made this argument before the Netherlands judiciary, which has so far narrowed the principle formulated in Chandler's case, though the matter is on appeal. <https://www.milieudefensie.nl/english/shell/oil-leaks/courtcase/press>.
7. In some companies, the Board of Directors can have this power, but it is ultimately up to the shareholders to accept or reject the change.
8. These sanctions can in principle be imposed by e.g. the World Bank's International Finance Corporation for breach of its project standards imposed as conditions for making the loan. <http://www.ifc.org>. The IFC's effectiveness is questioned by some human rights defenders (see e.g., Bretton Woods Project 2006).
9. The problem is acute in the mining industry in various parts of the world. See Internal Displacement Monitoring Centre: "While an estimated 25 million people are displaced worldwide by conflict, the number of people uprooted by development projects is thought to be much higher."
10. Cf. Draft Minerals Law of 2012, Art 42 (2) (a) and Art 42 (1) (a). Retrieved from <http://mom.gov.af/Content/files/Mineral_Law_Consultation_English.pdf>.
11. Ibid Section 52 (1) (5). On the prerogatives of mining companies over water supplies under the draft law, see Global Witness, *A Shaky Foundation? Analysing Afghanistan's Draft Mining Law* (2013) p. 12

REFERENCES

Amnesty International United Kingdom. 2005. *Contracting out of Human Rights. The Chad-Cameroon Pipeline Project*. London: Amnesty International UK.

Berle, A. A. and Means, G. C. 1932. *The Modern Corporation and Private Property*. New York: Macmillan.

Blair, M. 1995. *Ownership and Control: Rethinking Corporate Governance for the Twenty-First Century*. Washington DC: Brookings Institute.

Bretton Woods Project. 2006. *Barrage of Criticism Over IFC Safeguards Review*. Retrieved from <http://www.brettonwoodsproject.org/art-538524>.

Business in the Community. 2011. *The Business Case for being a Responsible Business*. Retrieved from <http://www.bitc.org.uk/resources/publications/cr_business_case.html>.

Council of Ministers. 1997. *Les Societes Anonymes Autonomes*. Note, Section 1(3).

Essex Business and Human Rights Project. 2012. *Corporate Liability in a New Setting: Shell and the Changing Legal Landscape for the Multinational Oil Industry in the Niger Delta.* Colchester, UK: University of Essex.

Global Issues. 2002. *Profit over People.* Retrieved from <http://www.globalissues.org/article/51/corporations-and-human-rights#Profitoverpeople>.

Institute of Directors. 2010. *Corporate Governance Guidance and Principles for Unlisted Companies in the UK.* Retrieved from <http://www.iod.com/MainWebSite/Resources/Document/corp_gov_guidance_and_principles_for_unlisted_companies_in_the_uk_final_1011.pdf>.

Internal Displacement Monitoring Centre. *Development-Induced Displacement.* Retrieved from <http://sinope.activeweb.fr/8025708F004BE3B1/(httpInfoFiles)/C753862FA2CF8B7CC1257115004752ED/$file/Protection%20from%20module%20handout%20development%20displacement.pdf>.

Leader, S. 1999. "Participation and Property Rights." *Journal of Business Ethics,* 21: 97–109.

Leader, S. 2005. Collateralism, pp. 53–67 in *Global Governance and the Search for Justice,* ed. R. Brownsword. Oxford and Portland, OR: Hart Publishing.

Leader, S. 2006. "Human Rights, Risks, and New Strategies for Global Investment." *Journal of International Economic Law,* 9: 657–705.

Marx, K. 1920. *Capital: Volume III.* Translated by E. Untermann. Chicago: Charles H. Kerr and Co.

Renner, K. 1949. *The Institutions of Private Law and their Social Functions.* London: Routledge.

Royal Society of Arts and Manufacturing. 1995. *Tomorrow's Company.* London: RSA.

Schulten, T. and Zagelmeyer, S. 1998. *Board-Level Employee Representation in Europe.* Retrieved from <http://www.eurofound.europa.eu/eiro/1998/09/study/tn9809201s.htm>.

For Further Reading

Anghie, A. 2005. *Imperialism, Sovereignty and the Making of International Law.* Cambridge, UK: Cambridge University Press.

Clapham, A. 2006. *Human Rights Obligations of Non-state Actors.* Oxford: Oxford University Press.

De Schutter, O. 2006. *Transnational Corporations and Human Rights.* Oxford and Portland, OR: Hart Publishing.

Deva, S. 2012. *Regulating Corporate Human Rights Violations: Humanizing Business.* London/New York: Routledge.

Frynas, J. and Scott, P., eds. 2003. *Transnational Corporations and Human Rights.* New York: Palgrave.

Jägers, N. 2002. *Corporate Human Rights Obligations: In Search of Accountability.* Antwerpen: Intersentia.

Joseph, S. 2004. *Corporations and Transnational Human Rights Litigation.* Oxford and Portland, OR: Hart Publishing.

Leader, S. 1995. Private Property and Corporate Governance, pp. 85–113 in *New Perspectives in Company Law,* ed. F. Patfield. London: Graham and Trotman.

Leader, S. 2001. "The Reach of Democracy and Global Enterprise." *Constellations,* 8: 538–53.

Muchlinski, P. 2007. *Multinational Enterprises and the Law.* Second Edition. Oxford: Oxford University Press.

Nystuen, G., Follesdal, A., and Mestad, O. 2011. *Human Rights, Corporate Complicity and Disinvestment.* Cambridge: Cambridge University Press.

Sullivan, R., ed. 2003. *Business and Human Rights: Dilemmas and Solutions.* Sheffield, UK: Greenleaf Publishing Ltd.

UN Guiding Principles on Business and Human Rights. 2012a. *The Interpretive Guide.* Retrieved from <http://www.business-humanrights.org/Home>.

UN Guiding Principles on Business and Human Rights. 2012b. *The Ruggie Principles.* Retrieved from <http://www.business-humanrights.org/Home>.

Zerk, J. 2006. *Multinationals and Corporate Social Responsibility: Limitations and Opportunities in International Law.* Cambridge: Cambridge University Press.

Important Websites

The following are some website links that you should consult from time to time to keep up with recent developments.

- Business and Human Rights Resource Centre, available at <http://www.business-humanrights.org/Home>.
- Office of the UN High Commissioner for Human Rights (Business and Human Rights section), available at <http://www.ohchr.org/EN/Issues/Business/Pages/BusinessIndex.aspx>.
- Website of Prof. John Ruggie, Special Representative of the Secretary General on Human Rights and Transnational Corporations and Other Business Enterprises, available at <http://www.business-humanrights.org/SpecialRepPortal/Home>.
- Amnesty International, Business and Human Rights webpage, available at <http://www.amnesty.org/en/business-and-human-rights>.
- International Commission of Jurists, Expert Legal Panel on Corporate Complicity in International Crimes, available at <http://www.business-humanrights.org/Updates/Archive/ICJPaneloncomplicity>.
- International Centre for Settlement of Investment Disputes, available at <http://icsid.worldbank.org/ICSID/Index.jsp>.
- International Finance Corporation, available at <www.ifc.org>.
- European Bank of Reconstruction and Development, available at <http://www.ebrd.com/pages/homepage.shtml>.
- Inter-American Development Bank, available at <http://www.iadb.org/en/inter-american-development-bank,2837.html>.

CHAPTER 23

ACCOUNTABLE GLOBAL GOVERNANCE ORGANIZATIONS

JONATHAN G. S. KOPPELL

UNDERSTANDING THE ACCOUNTABILITY CHALLENGE IN GLOBAL GOVERNANCE

ACCOUNTABILITY debates over global governance organizations have a rich and compelling history. What is at stake is often significant; even if the organization seems obscure and narrowly-focused, the potential to impact a global audience is ever-present. Before engaging the matter of accountability and offering examples of global governance to illustrate key points, I hope to impress upon the reader a core argument of this chapter. Accountability in global governance is really about legitimacy. What is the basis of these organizations' role in promulgating global rules of the game—in health and human rights, in trade and development, in shipping and communications, and so on? Accountability will be discussed at length, and parsed into its constituent components, but it will ultimately be linked to concerns that global governance organizations lack the democratic legitimacy on which, according to political theory, all modern rulemaking authority must rest.

The actions of global governance organizations have an impact on a vast number of lives, but they are not guided by the legal and political rules, or even the organizational norms of a nation in the way that democratic domestic governance organizations are guided. This peculiarity is owed to the very nature of their role. Global governance organizations seek to create rules and norms that stretch beyond nation-states. The earliest entities sought to do so for technical reasons. The International Telecommunications Union and Universal Postal Union were creating rules, starting in the mid-nineteenth century, to govern activities that literally superseded the power of a single nation. At the turn of the twentieth century, the forerunner of the World Intellectual Property

Organization emerged in response to the reality of global trade and the need for an international system of patent and trademark protection that crossed borders. Facilitating transnational activity and limiting abuses made possible by the division of authority along national boundaries was thus an initial goal. This purpose still animates many international rule-makers, but contemporary global governance organizations do not only seek to prevent abuse, they are also established to create and implement rules in pursuit of collective goals. The World Health Organization sets standards that help control the spread of pandemic diseases, for instance. The Forest Stewardship Council, a less well-known nongovernmental rule-maker, has emerged as a force in the forest management sector where intergovernmental efforts proved ineffectual. The Council runs certification programs that attempt to balance the economic needs of individual countries and the environmental sustainability of the entire planet.

In these and every other instance of global governance, members of global governance organizations—be they national governments or corporations—are ceding rule-making power to another entity. Given this reality and the significance of the issues before global governance organizations (GGOs), it is no wonder that critics and advocates alike have raised questions as to their accountability. It is not only that GGOs tackle issues that many of us care deeply about, it is precisely that they are writing rules limiting what nations, firms, and individuals can do, a role normally reserved for elected representatives of sovereign nations. Sometimes, firms—and certainly individuals—are totally unaware of it. Arnold's (2005, 314) example of the World Trade Organization's (WTO) potential rules governing the accountancy profession are a good case in point:

> …[the ruling] encroaches on a wide range of policy matters from issues that define the professional knowledge base (such as educational qualifications and the content of professional examinations) to decisions about who can own accounting firms, and what services accounting firms can offer. The accounting profession as a whole is largely unaware that these questions, which are traditionally regarded as domestic policy issues, have been discussed and, in some cases decided, in closed meetings of WTO committees and without broad consultation with the various constituencies that are affected.

Accountability questions *can be* more intense for global governance organizations with a seemingly weak or limited reach to governments. Ironically, the debates over these GGOs can be less visible to the general public because so many appear obscure and narrowly tailored. The Basel Committee on Banking Standards creates rules intended to establish baseline standards for the safe operation of financial institutions and has very limited national representation, inviting only members from the wealthiest countries (Barr and Miller 2006). Most readers had probably never heard of the Basel Committee, at least until after 2007 when the global financial crisis revealed that the scope of its authority is much broader than its membership. The Internet Corporation for Assigned Names and Numbers (ICANN) is another GGO, this one nongovernmental, operated by private sector engineers and other technical experts from around the world, but under the terms of an unusual exclusive contract with the U.S. government (Mathiason 2009). The fact that the U.S. government developed and owned the original backbone of the internet, particularly its root servers, provided control that was delegated to ICANN. To put it mildly, the legitimacy of this control is questioned frequently, notwithstanding ICANN's fairly limited mandate: governing the domain name system. It is no wonder that ICANN faces numerous, serious, accountability challenges (Koppell 2005).

WHAT GGOs DO AND HOW THEY ARE DESIGNED TO DO IT

International organizations are created to perform a number of significant functions outside of rule-making, each of which presents unique and complex accountability challenges (Balboa forthcoming; Hammer and Lloyd 2011). The Red Cross, CARE International, and other organizations that provide aid to disaster victims worldwide, collectively handle billions of dollars from individuals and governments and must be accountable for how these funds are spent (Kerlin and Thanasombat 2006). Production in transnational corporations raises accountability questions related to the impact on the environment, labor practices, safety standards, and other global ethical concerns (Koenig-Archibugi 2004). As one can imagine, public and private organizations that promulgate rules dictating decisions across whole industries are held to account for very different reasons than are foreign aid and profit-seeking production. For that reason it is helpful to distinguish rule-making from other organizational functions. Classification schemes for organizations tend to focus on ownership (government or nongovernment), goals (profit or nonprofit), or jurisdiction (international, national, local). Peculiarly, they have generally not been divided by *function* as this table does.

Table 23.1 offers some common functions performed by governmental and nongovernmental international organizations. They are the production of goods, such as

Table 23.1 Typology of international organizations

Primary functions of international organizations	Mostly governmental	Mostly non-governmental
Production of goods and infrastructure	World Bank	Habitat for Humanity International; Landesa
Service provision	North Atlantic Treaty Organization; World Health Organization	International Committee of the Red Cross; TEACH for All
Mobilization of interests		Greenpeace; Amnesty International
Governance	World Trade Organization; European Union	International Accounting Standards Board; The Forest Stewardship Council

computers and bridges; the provision of services like health care and religious content; the mobilization of interests, including advocacy and awareness-raising; and global rule-making. Of course functions are often blended in organizations and so they defy strict classification. Similarly, the attributes of many organizations are blended, making them more or less connected to governments, a continuum where one end represents organizations with no direct public involvement or mission and, the other represents multilateral organizations established and run by appointed government officials. For example, the World Bank, although multifaceted, is heavily involved in infrastructure projects around the world. Whereas it was established by treaty with the consent of many nations, Habitat for Humanity builds houses, employs workers, and recruits volunteers globally, but is connected to governments tangentially through grants.

Governance is about creating processes and structures that constrain and regulate behavior (Peters 1995). The function of rule-making is used here in a way similar to what Majone (1997) calls "regulatory" governance. The regulatory infrastructure guiding Europe is created by the mostly public (government) entity, the European Union (EU). The International Accounting Standards Board (IASB), on the other hand, was created by private individuals in several industries, making it a mostly "private" organization. But its rules regarding the financial industry guide the behavior of banks and individuals around the world. It makes more sense to use the terms governmental and non governmental when referring to sector and that is the protocol followed from here. The examples and empirical work referred to throughout this chapter are based on organizations that actively attempt to order the behavior of actors on a global scale. They span a range of industries and many are very nearly self-contained governments with narrow subject focuses. Therefore, their organizational designs are concerned with representation, participation, and other features commonly associated with democratic governments.

Even with our focus primarily on global rule-making (i.e. governance) organizations, there is considerable variation in organizational structure. Indeed, we will identify three different models of global governance by considering four areas of organizational design—structure, rule-making process, adherence, and interest group participation—and aggregating the results to create clusters of similar entities. This is different from the most common way of dividing up the population of organizations which typically focuses on sector (governmental or nongovernmental) as the driver of design choices—but it is an imperfect predictor, making clear the need to get beyond this simple dividing mechanism. Each set of variations in the design of GGOs is discussed here with a number of examples to illustrate.[1]

Structure essentially captures the design of participation in the organization, by members and professional staff, including things like rights and responsibilities, the power division among members, and the balance of power between members and staff. Traditional GGOs represent one cluster of choices and Hybrid GGOs represent another (see table 23.2). One hallmark of Traditional GGOs is that the full membership of the organization is geographically representative, but they choose a subset of members to govern in an intermediate council. On the other end of the spectrum are

Table 23.2 Organizational design

Organizational design feature	Design Choices	
Structure	**Traditional** representative and hierarchical	**Hybrid** non-representative and decentralized
Rule-making	**Forum** formal process that allows informal obstruction	**Club** consensus-based process with flexibility
Adherence	**Conventional** legal, regulatory means	**Composite** market-based "sanctions"
Interest group participation	**Global Concertation** blend of pluralist and corporatist relationships	

non-representative GGOs that do not have a membership at all. They are governed by individuals, often drawn with the intent to mimic some geographic and industry-based representation, but still enabling maximum responsiveness to up-and-coming key players. The International Labour Organization (ILO) exemplifies the traditional representation structure, delegating the agenda-setting and policy decisions regarding workplace rights to an intermediate council called the Governing Body. The hybrid structure is illustrated by ICANN. ICANN, discussed in the introduction, has the reverse set up from ILO. It includes aspects of representation, but it comes in the specialized task forces, the Address Supporting Organization being one of those specialized bodies. What really sets ICANN apart is that the specialized bodies are not drawn from some larger, overarching representative membership.

GGOs from the government sector, like the ILO, typically adopt the traditional model and those from the private sector adopt a hybrid model, reflecting the expectations of a governmental body to adhere to norms associated with democratic governance. A similar prioritization is seen in the choice of system for apportioning influence and the internal bureaucratic system, both of which are components of structure. That is, traditional GGOs from the government sector maintain equal voting power—one nation, one vote to reaffirm national sovereignty—and a hierarchical staff arrangement, while hybrid GGOs maximize responsiveness to key players with decentralized decision-making arrangements. That is not to say that there are no anomalies. The traditional GGO type contains its fair share of nongovernmental organizations. The Forest Stewardship Council, for example, is characterized as a traditional organization notwithstanding features that differentiate it from classic governmental GGOs (most obviously the membership of nongovernmental entities).

Approaches to *rule-making*, on the other hand, are not as clearly predicted by sector and do not divide as neatly as the variation in structure. Nevertheless, two types can be distinguished and, like structure, one resembles the Western domestic tradition and the other incorporates less traditional rule-making ideas. They are forum and club types, respectively. Rule-making is the process for drafting and approving treaties, standards, and regulations. It varies in the level of formality, method for concluding a decision period, and other factors. Forum rule-making types favor government sector norms in that their rule-making follows a formalized process but that emphasizes political over technical considerations. To conclude a decision-making period, a supermajority vote is formally permissible, but consensus is often sought to satisfy legitimacy expectations. Interestingly, the ambiguity of "consensus" makes it easier for key parties to halt undesirable outcomes, representing an interesting safeguard for members concerned about deleterious rules emerging from a GGO.

The club approach to rule-making is more informal, technocratic and designed to facilitate harmony among participants. While less driven by formal requirements delineated in procedural requirements, the club approach still ensures protection of core members' interests. Two leading standard-setting bodies in the world, the International Organization for Standardization (ISO) and the International Electrotechnical Commission (IEC), follow the forum model. ISO covers standards from sewing machine equipment to information technology. Procedures for their collaboratory work with the IEC are carefully laid out in the ISO/IEC Directives where they specify instructions to ensure consistency but allow for relatively unstructured work among group members.

A third area of design is *adherence*. The challenge of compelling adherence to agreed rules is a hallmark feature of GGOs, dramatically differentiating them as a distinct class of entities from nation-states. Most have no ability to enforce anything and must rely on their agents—governmental or industry members of the organization—who themselves often delegate (formally or informally) implementation authority. This creates a nested principle–agent problem for adherence. GGOs use a variety of tools, both to motivate the agent and to compel adherence from the agent ultimately targeted: the regulated entities. There are two types of adherence models based on the tools used and whether the dominant adherence agent is a governmental entity. They are Conventional and Composite GGOs. In short, conventional types tend to rely on tools associated with regulations that come with legal sanctions or denial of some privilege when violated. Composite types rely on market mechanisms to compel adherence, where "sanctions" derive from business decisions or engagement mechanisms. Suspending membership, for example, is one engagement-related mechanism. Publicizing the noncompliant status of an entity is another mechanism, one that was very effective in getting Toronto, Canada and several Chinese cities to comply with World Health Organization guidelines during the SARS epidemic (BBC 2003). Surprisingly, governmental GGOs are fairly evenly distributed across the two types, and although nongovernmental GGOs do tend toward the composite type, sector is still a weak predictor of adherence type.

A final element of organizational design for GGOs is the *integration of interest groups*, a key issue to understanding any policy-making process and certainly one with significant explanatory power in global governance. Commercial interests tend to dominate most but not all GGOs. Yet sector does not predict the pattern of organized interests with much precision. Initial exploration into interest group patterns within GGOs used the familiar concepts of pluralism and corporatism, the former describing an open access relationship between interest groups and GGO members and the latter describing ongoing, coordinated collaboration between the two. Ultimately, it is more accurate to say GGOs blend the two, a participation strategy labeled Global Concertation. Global Concertation is defined by competition and integration of interests into the GGO process, general dominance of commercial interest over civil society due to resource disparities, and emphasis on firm-level behavior as the ultimate targets to change. Internet, technology-related, and environmental policy domains especially see the most persistent set of public interest groups, while others, such as the International Maritime Organization, have stronger industry interest group collaboration. Global Concertation describes the preponderance of GGOs and interest group participation. Its most unusual contribution to thinking about interest groups in a global context is that the model places GGOs in direct competition with interest groups. GGOs often act as pseudo-trade organizations, aggregating member preferences and organizing them. Because they internalize negotiations with companies and national delegations, GGOs have a natural advantage over industry-bound interest groups and seem to crowd them out at the international level.

Tensions in GGO Accountability

All this sorting of GGOs based on their design serves a purpose relevant to our goal in this chapter. It helps explain the accountability problem in global governance organizations. From the variation in structure, we can draw important insights into the accountability pressures on global rule-making bodies. Even with laudable goals, and their impressive ability to clear political and technical hurdles, they seem doomed to confront continued accountability failures. This is because accountability requires every GGO to implicitly make a number of promises—control, fairness, integrity, and legitimacy—that are difficult to meet concomitantly (Dubnick and Frederickson 2011). But dig just below the surface and you will likely uncover a multiplicity of intended meanings and varied expectations based on governmental or nongovernmental status that makes the challenge much more formidable. The lack of conceptual clarity has also presented roadblocks to theory-building in organizational and political sciences. And, as a number of international relations scholars have sought to resolve the accountability challenge for the network of GGOs competing and collaborating within issue areas, the multiplication of accountability definitions and conceptions has only increased (Held and Koenig-Archibugi 2005; Grant and Keohane 2005; Mattli and Büthe 2011; Rosenau 2007).

The accountability framework presented below draws on previous frameworks and is intended to organize conceptions of accountability in a way that is applicable to government and nongovernmental organizations, and therefore across the range of GGOs. Five vital dimensions to the concept of accountability are identified in the literature.

Table 23.3 Conceptions of accountability

Conception of Accountability	Key Determination
Transparency	Did the organization reveal the facts of its performance?
Liability	Did the organization face consequences for its performance?
Controllability	Did the organization do what the principal ordered?
Responsibility	Did the organization follow the rules?
Responsiveness	Did the organization fulfill expectations?

The value of the five-part typology is that it does *not* offer a new comprehensive definition, but rather makes explicit the inherent tensions within the very idea of accountability—a key reason why the problem of accountability in global governance is to be managed, not resolved. The five dimensions of accountability are transparency, liability, controllability, responsibility, and responsiveness. Table 23.3 shows all five, with the critical question that underlies each. For each dimension of accountability there is a question to be asked of an organization or individual to determine its accountability in that sense.

Transparency and liability are the foundations on which other expectations of accountability rest. Several scholars start dissecting the problem of accountable GGOs with the requirements of transparency and liability (Stiglitz 2003; Grant and Keohane 2005). Lack of transparency and minimal liability are the clearest deficits of unaccountable organizations. They are the first accountability mechanisms to be remedied when gross violations of organizational norms make newspaper headlines. Transparency ensures that an organization reveals the facts of its performance. After the EU Commission collectively resigned, based on 140 pages revealing its fraud, corruption, and mismanagement, transparency became the modernization mantra of the next commission (Wille 2010). The European Transparency Initiative was launched in 2005 with a series of reforms to make publicly available information on use of funds, commissioner interaction with interest groups, and more. And accountability did not stop there. Whereas the European Parliament (EP) relied on political pressure to achieve the resignation of all 20 members, the reforms ensured liability would be less precarious in the future. Now the EP can request the resignation of individual commissioners via the Commission President, forcing each to face consequences for unethical behavior. Liability need not rise to the level of dismissal and criminal charges to be effective. Civil servants are held liable through performance reviews and organizations face budget cuts as punishment for missing performance targets. The point is that the person or organization face consequences for their action.

Transparency and liability are largely straightforward and complementary means to evaluate the degree of organizational accountability. Where tensions tend to arise is among the three substantive dimensions of accountability: controllability, responsibility and responsiveness.

Accountability is often equated with control, particularly in the domestic context of government agencies. Backed by the theoretical tradition of scholars like Wilson (1887) and Goodnow (1900), many public administration studies have tackled questions of bureaucratic control, essentially focusing on whether the bureaucracy did what the principal ordered. It is not always apparent that being accountable in the controllability sense is a good thing (Romzek and Dubnick 1987; Radin and Romzek 1996; Romzek 1996; Romzek and Ingraham 2000).

In the international context, controllability creates a serious challenge because it is often unclear to whom the organization should be accountable. Nongovernmental GGOs suffer unique accountability tensions because there is little legal clarity on who controls them and often little agreement on who should control them. The IASB experience following the financial crisis is a good case. When IASB devised new financial reporting standards that were to be adopted independently in countries around the world, the outlook for their uptake and increased accountability was positive. This was partly because the IASB's system of due process for designing standards had made it a model of transnational governance (Mattli and Büthe 2011). Nonetheless, conflict and concern over the degree of control held by private actors in the organization led to significant restructuring in 2009 (Richardson and Eberlein 2011). To assuage the accountability fears of the U.S., Japan, and other powerful countries, IASB created a Monitoring Board composed of government authorities and gave it oversight and appointment authority over the Trustees of the organization. Governmental GGOs do not escape controllability conflicts. The WTO for example includes member countries from the full range of economic development. They are, theoretically, collectively in control but divergent interests in trade policy lead to different perceptions of accountability. On one side, WTO standard-setting in the accounting business (i.e. the *Disciplines on Domestic Regulation in the Accountancy Sector*) is viewed as unduly influenced by industry and determined in closed committee meetings, while on the other negotiations are seen as unnecessarily protracted and the standards as too limited in their reach (Arnold 2005).

Bureaucrats are further constrained by laws, rules, and norms that seemingly supersede a principal's orders. This is called responsibility-type accountability and asks simply, did the organization follow the rules? It is a core, if not prosaic source of accountability described by public law principles (Moe and Gilmour 1995). To hold an organization culpable for a transgression it is necessary to have rules in place (Mattli and Büthe 2011). The U.N.'s Human Rights Council recently adopted a Code of Conduct for Special Procedures to clarify expectations of the human rights monitors so that compliance mechanisms could be built around those rules (Alston 2011). Responsibility extends beyond formal rules to informal norms and professional standards that guide a significant amount of behavior. Professional standards are a key element of the alternative notion of accountability articulated by Friedrich (1940) in his debate with Finer (1941). Accountable bureaucrats should not simply follow orders, Friedrich argues, but should use their expertise constrained by professional and moral standards. Indeed, conflict between responsibility and controllability left the U.N.'s Code of Conduct mired in controversy for years, as certain countries believed the code would reduce the monitors' independence and effectiveness and other countries believed it would increase their control over arbitrary targeting of regions for investigation (Alston 2011).

The last dimension of accountability is responsiveness. Responsiveness is used here to differentiate an organization's attention to the needs of its constituents (or clients) from attention to the orders of hierarchical principals. Sometimes the word "responsiveness" is conflated with control, but upward accountability (i.e. doing what the principal ordered) needs to be assessed separately from outward accountability (i.e. responsiveness to clients) in GGOs because they often create intractable tension for organizations trying to satisfy both. The World Bank has seen controllability and responsiveness clash when, for instance, the U.S. and other member states demand control while NGOs and other interests groups pressure the Bank for greater attention to the demands of recipient nations and their citizens who are most affected by Bank policies (Grant and Keohane 2005). Even this is fraught, as it is uncertain whether organized groups, like environmental groups that lobby the Bank to discontinue a dam-building program and better preserve habitats in developing countries, actually speak for the people in a said country and, if not, whether they themselves constitute an important constituency (Fox and Brown 1998). No matter how one comes down on such questions, clearly the imperatives of responsiveness push toward a quite different accountability than control or responsibility.

ORGANIZATIONAL DESIGN AS RESPONSE TO ACCOUNTABILITY AND LEGITIMACY

The inherent tensions between accountability expectations mean that organizations acting to increase their accountability along one dimension may inescapably reduce it along another. In the past, I have referred to this organizational predicament as MAD, multiple accountabilities disorder (Koppell 2005). GGOs that manage a balance can maintain themselves as effective rule-making organizations over the long run, despite the fact that they are often the groups that suffer the loudest accountability criticisms (Grant and Keohane 2005). The balance struck by an organization is not typically determined by the calculus of organizational leaders but rather is embedded in the organizational design choices of the GGO. Indeed, the great variation in the design of international governing organizations is explained as a response to the same challenge: Governing organizations must satisfy divergent accountability expectations. Pulling together the different options for organizations regarding the structure, rule-making, adherence, and interest group participation described in table 23.2, three models of global governance and their ability to satisfy responsibility or responsiveness expectations can be distilled:

Classical GGO model: The classical model is defined by a high likelihood of choosing a traditional structure (e.g., representative), a forum-style of rule-making (e.g., formalized decision rule), and conventional-type adherence mechanisms (e.g., formally coercive). No type of interest group participation is strongly associated with the classical model, although corporatism is more likely than concertation or pluralism. Most governmental GGOs follow this model, including the well-known World Health Organization and Universal Postal Union. Their emphasis on administrative procedures reveals a preference for maximizing responsibility type accountability.

Cartel GGO model: GGOs adopting a cartel model are strongly associated with a hybrid structure (e.g., geographically distributed), club-style rulemaking (e.g., consensus-driven decision "rule"), conventional adherence mechanisms, and a corporatist model of interest group participation. This is the least common model chosen, but includes some of the most influential and controversial GGOs, such as the World Trade Organization. The cartel's ability to circumvent or create procedures on the fly maximizes responsiveness to critical stakeholders.

Symbiotic GGO model: Symbiotic GGOs are defined by their strong association with forum rule-making, composite adherence mechanisms, and concertation interest group interaction. They are equally likely to choose a traditional or hybrid structure. As a result, market mechanisms play a significant role in adherence schemes and interest groups tend to align into spheres of authority, as described by Rosenau (2007). The symbiotic model is most likely to include young, headline-making GGOs, such as the International Accounting Standards Board and the Forest Stewardship Council. Being the most common model, it also contains its fair share of governmental groups such as the World Intellectual Property Organization.

So each model allows a different accountability balance to be struck, but the question that still remains is why they strike the balance they do. How does the balance they chose allow them to survive and remain effective over the years? I argue that the answer is that they are balancing the need for legitimacy and authority to secure participation, acceptance, and adherence to the rules they produce (Koppell 2010). The authority and legitimacy to govern must to be understood as distinct concepts when applied to international organizations. Indeed, GGOs are distinctive governing bodies precisely because of the propensity for the requirements of legitimacy and authority to conflict rather than being mutually reinforcing as is often the case. Why do people submit to authoritative organizations and individuals? One of the most broadly accepted reasons for obedience is that the organization or person wielding power is perceived to be legitimate (Franck 1990). Nonetheless one need only think of any number of authoritative regimes in history, totally bereft of democratic legitimacy, to see the two are distinct. We acknowledge the authority of organizations lacking in legitimacy.

Some scholars of international relations have suggested that the solution to the accountability conundrum for global governance organizations lies in a differentially formulated definition that takes into account the distinctiveness of the context and demands. So a global governance organization could be characterized as "accountable" if it met some notion of the concept that we would likely deem unsatisfactory in the domestic context (Grant and Keohane 2005). This is a worthwhile approach in that it is realistic about what is and is not possible in the world of global governance where authority is sometimes delegated by states and sometimes not, to take one observation offered by Grant and Keohane.

And this is a major issue. Even in the clearest cases, the bases of legitimacy and authority within a sovereign nation cannot be transferred wholesale into the international context; there is no consensus either on how to make the transfer piecemeal (Bernstein 2004). Normative legitimacy, in the domestic context, demands equality of representation, due process, and participation (among other virtues). At the same time, however, GGOs must also make good on the promised output. Put simply, the state of affairs must be better *with* the organization than before it (Buchanan and Keohane 2006).

This could be called legitimacy but it is far from the normative notions we typically think about in the nation-state. Rather this is a pragmatic basis of legitimacy or what I would characterize as authority without normative legitimacy, authority based on the self-interested calculation by the governed that the potential costs of disobedience outweigh the gains (Wrong 1988). For example, the United States accepts the authority of the World Trade Organization, even when it rules against American interests because U.S. policymakers have determined that maintaining an international trade regime is in the national interest. Any member of a global governance system might walk away from a GGO at the point the calculation scales are tipped. The core demand of pragmatic authority then, is to make the institutionalization of power in the interests of the governed.

If a nation, company, or individual walks away from a GGO—particularly one whose participation is central to the effectiveness of that organizations—it denies the organization authority, even if the organization continues to satisfy the normative legitimacy demands of governance. Authority is buttressed by legitimacy in some GGOs, such as the International Civil Aviation Organization. In many other cases, however, GGOs face the danger of a downward spiral between pragmatic authority and normative legitimacy losses because core demands of the two are in conflict. The organization must pay special attention to the interests of key players, which simultaneously violates systems of due process, equal representation, and other normative expectations of legitimacy (Buchanan and Keohane 2006). But push too far on interest-based authority and the organization undermines any foundation of legitimacy. The tyranny of the strong is limited because when the less-powerful actors walk away, it limits widespread adoption of rules and thus the value proposition for anyone to participate in the organization.

These choices between legitimacy and authority that translate to organizational effectiveness are most commonly experienced as accountability failures (Koppell 2010). This is somewhat unfair because it might be more accurately seen as an emphasis on one form of accountability over another. With its emphasis on fidelity to principles regarding representation and process, meeting the demands of legitimacy in GGOs calls for *responsibility*-type accountability. Granting special deference to key players as a means of building authority would be seen as *responsiveness* in accountability terms. Failures of responsibility-type accountability directly undermine normative legitimacy, while failures of responsiveness-type accountability are experienced as losses of pragmatic authority.

The three models identified through empirical examination and sorting of GGOs thus should be seen as institutionalization of these prioritizations. The classical model is familiar and accepted as legitimate, with representation on the basis of geography and equality of voting, for example. Authority is a less dominant concern but nonetheless classical GGOs ensure they offer responsiveness to key members through safety valves in the rule-making system that assure the possibility of waylaying an undesirable outcome and weak adherence mechanisms. The cartel and symbiotic models offer alternative management strategies that both build authority at the expense of legitimacy. The cartel model does so through structure, by severely limiting membership. Conversely, GGOs adopting the symbiotic model are less constrained by structure and more able to build participation around interested constituencies. The rule-making process is more accessible and the adherence mechanisms stronger because rule adoption and implementation often occur through governments. But as composite adherence systems suggest, adherence by industry is flexible until it gets to the point of state adoption. All this is to the end of maximizing responsiveness.

Although the expectations of responsibility and authority have partly to do with expectations of the governmental versus nongovernmental sector, other considerations of the day-to-day function of the GGO may also help explain why normative legitimacy concerns come to trump authority concerns or viceversa. The "public-ness" of their main purpose, for example, matters to model choice, and is not perfectly correlated with sector. Public-ness has to do with the extent to which an organization services the public interest. Analysis of global governance organizations suggest other variables also drive the model choice, including the degree to which the rule-making subject matter is technical, the nature of the coordination promoted by the rule, and the nature of the organizations' membership.

Agenda

Global governance organizations will only play more important roles in a continually globalizing world. Satisfying demands for accountability will remain vital to their success which means it is critical to understand the tensions therein. As has been shown in this chapter, GGOs face accountability demands on at least five fronts and the expectations associated with each often come in conflict, making the proper course of action ambiguous for any GGO. Specifically, one of the most common tensions for GGOs is between responsibility for the normative expectations of democratic rules and procedures, and responsiveness to the interest-based expectation of stakeholders. GGOs appear to be structurally configured to manage this tension (and others) with biases toward legitimacy or authority demands influenced by multiple contextual variables. In this sense, there is no "solution" per se to the GGO accountability challenge. Rather there are only more or less successful management strategies and these will vary by circumstances.

Introducing this tensions framework in this chapter is intended to enhance the debate regarding the accountability of global governance organizations by separating the varied dimensions of accountability from each other. Doing so does not resolve the conflicts but laying them bare is a step forward. It forces critics and designers of global rule-making regimes to confront the tradeoffs inherent in global governance. And it may indeed set the stage for new solutions to some of the accountability conflicts described in these pages.

Technological innovations have already altered the dynamics of global governance and will likely continue to do so. The ubiquity of the internet has dramatically increased the transparency of the global rulemaking process such that the process of drafting global standards is more accessible to more people every day. This does not necessarily mean that more parties have *access* and *influence* in decision-making, but clearly it is easier for all interested parties to maintain awareness of governance processes. Not surprisingly, ICANN was among the first entities to truly grapple with this reality given the nature of the organization's constituencies and it has not always been a smooth process with one of the organization's elected directors even suing for access to documents that were not made available.

In the past, formal guarantees of access and openness were somewhat hollow given the huge investment of resources required to participate. The average citizen or non-corporate interest group simply couldn't afford to fly halfway around the world for meetings even if they were free to attend. Such procedural guarantees are more meaningful in the contemporary context. Again, this does not make global governance any easier. Like the argument that open meetings laws make compromise in the halls of government more difficult, increased transparency may make global governance more challenging. And, as noted earlier, it may have the unintended consequence of pushing rule-making to venues where the expectations for *responsibility*-type accountability are reduced.

Technological changes have implications beyond the rulemaking process. The mechanics of tracking adherence to nongovernmental rule-makers have evolved significantly, for example, in the area of natural resources (Auld et al. 2010). Certificates for sustainable forestry, organic coffee products, and recycled electronic waste are some of the GGO programs growing in popularity precisely because technology makes it easier for members to be held liable for noncompliance. Technology also improves transparency so that member industries can verify the data and criteria GGOs use to make their decisions. This changes the calculus of global governance significantly because it suggests that seemingly soft adherence regimes can be more robust. Thus one might logically accept more compromise in the rule-making process—offering safety valves where necessary—with the knowledge that the associated adherence regime will have some real bite. In the absence of such robust "enforcement," one might opt for the sanctity of the rule-making process, reasoning that generating the most demanding standard is optimal if only for aspirational purposes. Again, understanding the trade-offs is critical to understanding the implications of technological shifts.

Moving forward, the accountability challenge for global governance organizations will never be static. Not only will the environment in which each organization operates change, the organizations themselves will evolve. Although not emphasized in this chapter, one implication of the "tensions" approach outlined here is that the demands on and resources of every organization evolve over time. But again the implications are uncertain. In the early days of an organization, some might argue that normative legitimacy is particularly important. On the other hand, gaining the buy-in of a few key parties is arguably most crucial in the establishment phase. Once a GGOs is established as the undisputed rule-maker in a given domain, even the most influential member may find it difficult to resist undesirable outcomes and yet the pressures for greater accountability will surely rise. Understanding the dynamics of GGO accountability across time—as organizations age and evolve—is a central priority for students of global governance.

NOTE

1. This analysis is based on extensive interviews and cluster analysis of 25 global governance organizations; see Koppell (2010) for a full description of the study.

REFERENCES

Alston, P. 2011. "Hobbling the Monitors: Should U.N. Human Rights Monitors be Accountable?" *Harvard International Law Journal*, 52: 563–648.

Arnold, P. J. 2005. "Disciplining Domestic Regulation: The World Trade Organization and the Market for Professional Services." *Accounting, Organizations and Society*, 30: 299–330.

Auld, G., Cashore, B., Balboa, C., and Bozzi, C. 2010. "Can Technological Innovations Improve Private Regulation in the Global Economy?" *Business and Politics*, 12 (3): Article 9.

Balboa, C. M. Forthcoming. The Accountability and Legitimacy of International Non-Governmental Organizations in *The NGO Challenge for International Relations Theory*, eds. W. E. DeMars and D. Dijkzeul.

Barr, M. S. and Miller, G. P. 2006. "Global Administrative Law: The View from Basel." *European Journal of International Law*, 17: 15–46.

BBC. 2003, May 27. *Toronto Back on WHO SARS List*. Retrieved from <http://news.bbc.co.uk/2/hi/americas/2939136.stm>.

Bernstein, S. 2004. *The Elusive Basis of Legitimacy in Global Governance: Three Conceptions*. Institute on Globalization and the Human Condition Working Paper Series, No. GHC 04/2. Hamilton, ON: McMaster University.

Buchanan, A. and Keohane, R. O. 2006. "The Legitimacy of Global Governance Institutions." *Ethics & International Affairs*, 20: 405–37.

Dubnick, M. and Frederickson, G. 2011. Introduction: The Promises of Accountability Research, pp. xiii-xxxii in *Accountable Governance: Problems and Promises*, eds. M. Dubnick and G. Frederickson. Armonk, NY: M.S. Sharpe.

Finer, H. 1941. "Administrative Responsibility in Democratic Government." *Public Administration Review*, 1: 335–50.

Friedrich, C. J. 1940. Public Policy and the Nature of Administrative Responsibility, pp. 3–24 in *Public Policy*, ed. C. J. Friedrich. Cambridge, MA: Harvard University Press.

Fox, J. A. and Brown, L. D, eds. 1998. *The Struggle for Accountability: The World Bank, NGOs and Grassroots Movements*. Cambridge, MA: MIT Press.

Franck, T. M. 1990. *The Power of Legitimacy Among Nations*. New York: Oxford University Press.

Goodnow, F. J. 1900. *Politics and Administration: A Study in Government*. New York: Macmillan.

Grant, R. W. and Keohane, R. O. 2005. "Accountability and Abuses of Power in World Politics." *American Political Science Review*, 99: 29–43.

Hammer, M. and Lloyd, R. 2011. *Pathways to Accountability II: The 2011 Revised Global Accountability Framework: Report On the Stakeholder Consultation and the New Indicator Framework*. London: One World Trust.

Held, D. and Koenig-Archibugi, M. 2005. *Global Governance and Public Accountability*. Malden, MA: Blackwell.

Kerlin, J. and Thanasombat, S. 2006. *The International Charitable Nonprofit Subsector: Scope, Size, and Revenue*. Policy Brief. Washington, DC: The Urban Institute.

Koenig-Archibugi, M. 2004. "Transnational Corporations and Public Accountability." *Government and Opposition*, 39: 234–59.

Koppell, J. 2005. "Pathologies of Accountability: ICANN and the Challenge of 'Multiple Accountabilities Disorder.'" *Public Administration Review*, 65: 94–108.

Koppell, J. 2010. *World Rule*. Chicago, IL: The University of Chicago Press.

Mathiason, J. 2009. *Internet Governance: The New Frontier of Global Institutions*. New York: Routledge.

Mattli, W. and Büthe, T. 2011. *The New Global Rulers: The Privatization of Regulation in the World Economy*. Princeton, NJ: Princeton University Press.

Majone, G. 1997. "From the Positive to the Regulatory State: Causes and Consequences of Changes in the Mode of Governance." *Journal of Public Policy*, 17: 139–67.

Moe, R. C. and Gilmour, R. S. 1995. "Rediscovering Principles of Public Administration: The Neglected Foundation of Public Law." *Public Administration Review*, 55: 135–46.

Peters, B. G. 1995. Introducing the Topic, pp. 3–19 in *Governance in a Changing Environment*, eds. B. G. Peters and D. J. Savoie. Montreal: McGill-Queen's University Press.

Radin, B. A. and Romzek, B. S. 1996. "Accountability Expectations in an Intergovernmental Arena: The National Rural Development Partnership." *Publius*, 26: 59–81.

Richardson, A. J. and Eberlein, B. 2011. "Legitimating Transnational Standard-Setting: The Case of the International Accounting Standards Board." *Journal of Business Ethics*, 98: 217–45.

Romzek, B. S. and Dubnick, M. J. 1987. "Accountability in the Public Sector: Lessons from the Challenger Tragedy." *Public Administration Review*, 47: 227–38.

Romzek, B. S. 1996. Enhancing Accountability, pp. 97–114 in *Handbook of Public Administration*, ed. J. L. Perry. San Francisco: Jossey-Bass.

Romzek, B. S. and Ingraham, P. W. 2000. "Cross Pressures of Accountability: Initiative, Command, and Failure in the Ron Brown Plane Crash." *Public Administration Review*, 60: 240–53.

Rosenau, J. N. 2007. "Governing the Ungovernable: The Challenge of a Global Disaggregation of Authority." *Regulation & Governance*, 1: 88–97.

Stiglitz, J. E. 2003. "Democratizing the International Monetary Fund and the World Bank: Governance and Accountability." *Governance: An International Journal of Policy, Administration, and Institutions*, 16: 111–39.

Wille, A. 2010. "Political-Bureaucratic Accountability in the EU Commission: Modernising the Executive." *West European Politics*, 33: 1093–116.

Wilson, W. 1887. "The Study of Administration." *Political Science Quarterly*, 2: 197–222.

Wrong, D. H. 1988. *Power, its Forms, Bases and Uses.* Chicago, IL: University of Chicago Press.

PART V

ACCOUNTABILITY
MECHANISMS

CHAPTER 24

....

ELECTIONS

....

MARK N. FRANKLIN, STUART SOROKA, AND
CHRISTOPHER WLEZIEN

ELECTIONS AND ACCOUNTABILITY

....

ACCOUNTABILITY in representative democracies centers on elections, which provide voters with the means to directly check sitting politicians. Voters can re-elect the incumbents or throw them out, letting others take the reins of government control. It is a retrospective mechanism—it takes into account what sitting politicians have done during their time in office. This ability to reward and punish politicians after the fact provides an important incentive to those politicians to continue to take account of what the public wants once they are in office. Of course, this presumes that politicians are interested in re-election, which in most cases seems a foregone conclusion.

That elections serve as important accountability mechanisms in representative democracies is evident in a vast body of work on empirical democratic theory, certainly from *The Federalist Papers* (Hamilton, Madison, and Jay 2008 [1788]) onward. The richness of the literature on electoral accountability comes at a cost, however. Ideas about and definitions of electoral accountability vary from one body of literature to another. There is, as a result, a certain degree of ambiguity in the conceptualization and study of electoral accountability. One aim of this chapter is to draw together and contrast the different bodies of literature that speak to the issue.

Let us start with an important caveat: elections are very blunt instruments for holding politicians to account (Key 1961, 459). They retain or reject sitting politicians but they do not clearly signal what voters did or did not like. Citizens typically get just one opportunity to vote in nation-wide elections every four years or so; and that vote is supposed to capture their reactions to a whole host of policies, across all domains, over an extended period. It is, as a consequence, very difficult to know what it is exactly that elections are rewarding or punishing. Indeed, the result may have more to do with the choices on offer. For instance, the public may give the government an additional term in office not because they like what the government is doing but because the alternatives are worse. Scholars of elections may know what caused the election to go the way it did, but it is not at all clear that the winners (and losers) of elections actually have and use this information. And without a clear signal, the interpretation of the election outcome may be socially (and/or politically) constructed.[1] The critical point is this: Electoral accountability may be a central component of representative democracy, but it can often be both unclear and ineffective.

That said, electoral accountability *is* indeed one of the central elements of representative democracy; and the accumulated literature on the subject is quite voluminous. The chapter begins by addressing certain general issues in electoral accountability: (a) what it means and how we might best characterize it, and (b) two views of electoral accountability, in terms of the Responsible Party Model (RPM) and the thermostatic model (TM) of opinion–policy relationships. We then turn to (c) the details of electoral accountability, namely, the ways in which electoral accountability varies as a function of institutions and actors. The end result is a picture of the varied conceptions, fundamental importance, and limited scope of electoral accountability in modern democratic government.

What is Electoral Accountability?

As is clear from previous chapters in this handbook, there are many forms of accountability. In normal English usage, the word means no more than giving an account, being "answerable" in Goodin's (2000) terms. In one sense, then, government accountability has much in common with the contemporary notion of "freedom of information"—the ability of citizens to demand and receive details of any and all (or most) aspects of government affairs. Elections are one means of informing citizens about government policies and performance. More importantly, they make governments directly answerable to voters.

Political parties are central to electoral accountability. Elections focus directly on political parties, after all, deciding whether the leases of those in government will be renewed. The opposition parties also matter: They provide choice, and the competition between parties in and out of government provides voters with important information (see esp. Manin et al. 1999). Of course candidates themselves can matter as well, depending on the electoral system. Competition makes it possible for voters to evaluate the sitting government's performance, as well as the viability of available alternatives.

The results of elections may be positive or negative for governing parties. Positive evaluations may result in a government being confirmed in office for a further term, but the positive evaluation is no less an exercise in accountability than a negative evaluation would have been. Moreover, even negative evaluations may not result in a government being replaced, for instance if the only available alternative is judged worse by voters. So the failure to replace a poorly-performing government does not tell us that the government was not held accountable. And, as a consequence, the extent to which accountability has consequences for the quality of democratic governance is not captured simply by the tendency for a poorly-performing government to be replaced—accountability has to be assessed in some other way.

In what other ways can we evaluate accountability, then? Considerations of what it is that voters do on Election Day are of primary importance. Do they base their judgments on the policies government parties undertake? Or do they focus more on conditions, such as the economy, which may or may not reflect what elected officials do? Political institutions also are important. Do they make it easier or harder for voters to identify which party is responsible for government decisions? Do they effectively translate approval (disapproval) into government control? Are there other ways than re-electing governments, or not, by which the preferences of voters can both guide the behavior of governments, and hold those governments accountable for their actions?

TWO VIEWS OF ELECTORAL ACCOUNTABILITY

The Responsible Party Model

Classic accounts of electoral accountability focus on the idea of governing parties being judged according to how responsibly they have fulfilled their electoral promises (Schattschneider 1950; Ranney 1951). This very simple model applies best to the archetypal British system, namely, one that concentrates power in the hands of single-party governments. The idea is that parties running for (re-)election promise that, if granted a legislative majority, they will enact certain desired policies. At the next election they are held responsible for the policies enacted. If those policies were in accord with promises and worked well, the governing party is expected to be rewarded with a new lease on government power. If a government reneged on its promises, or if the resulting policies did not have the expected effects, a governing party might be replaced by another party judged more likely to enact valued policies.

The expected outcome of the Responsible Party Model (RPM) is to give rise to a system in which governments (or rather, governing parties) have a strong incentive to produce policies that "look like" the policies preferred by those who vote for them. So the extent to which the RPM is found to operate in practice can be assessed by discovering what policies are preferred by voters, by legislators and by governments, and seeing how well these preferences match. The closer the match all the way up the chain, the more representative governments will be seen to be.

The RPM also gives rise to the notion of a government "mandate," bestowed by voters who select the party whose policies they prefer, with the expectation that it will enact those policies. And the model focuses on elections as the source of policy change. It assumes that between elections a governing party does its best to fulfill its mandate and that voters, at the next election, will judge the party on the basis of how well it has done so.

The RPM is very clean and clear, to be sure. Like most "ideal types," however, it is more useful in theory than in practice. Consider that, while it is premised on the development of representative government in Britain, it does not adequately capture even the British case. Also like most ideal types, considering some of the model's weaknesses can be illuminating.

To begin with, the theory does *not* provide a means for determining what is and is not part of the government's mandate. It also does not explicitly address what happens if a problem arises during the period between elections (a puzzle mentioned by Key 1961, 413). And it pays no attention to any policies or performance problems that are not the subject of election promises. It is not policy- or performance-oriented, but promise-oriented. It also gives no attention to the question of how responsibility would be allocated between parties that were jointly members of a coalition government. Perhaps even more importantly, the theory pays no attention to the role of challenging parties other than to see them as "waiting in the wings" for their turn at government should the ruling party or parties be rejected by voters. There are, in short, a good number of regular features of modern representative government that are not adequately captured by the RPM; and it is, as a consequence, of limited use for understanding electoral accountability.

Moreover, some large disjunctions are seen in practice between expectations derived from the RPM and the way governments and governing parties are treated at elections. Quite often we see parties re-elected that manifestly failed to live up to campaign promises and—even more surprisingly—quite often we see parties defeated that performed exactly as they promised. Since the responsible party model provides no means for anticipating the circumstances under which failures will be forgiven or successes go unrewarded, these theoretical deficiencies further undermine the attractions of this model to contemporary scholarship.[2] There is however an alternative model of public responsiveness and accountability, both at and between elections.

The Thermostatic Model

It was long ago pointed out by Karl Deutsch in his *The Nerves of Government* (1963) that government policy-making requires regular attention to consequences, both anticipated and otherwise. Only by paying close attention to the way policies work in practice can policymakers fine tune them effectively. One of the ways in which policymakers can learn about the consequences of their policies is by means of grassroots reactions communicated through party and administrative channels. Another is by means of public opinion polls. In these and other ways, politicians need to take account of public opinion as a source of feedback regarding policy implementation.

For public opinion to serve this function two requirements must be fulfilled. First, policymakers must be motivated to take account of it. Though policymakers are often motivated by the desire to "make good policy," which provides incentives to take account of at least some types of public reactions, the threat of electoral sanction (and hence electoral accountability) replaces the question "what is good policy?" with the question "what do voters want?" This makes voters the final arbiters of what will be considered good policy.

The second requirement for thermostatic representation is that voters know what governments are doing. This does not mean that individuals need to be well informed about what policymakers actually do. A large body of research demonstrates that individuals are not well informed on such matters (e.g., Delli Carpini and Keeter 1996; Kuklinski and Quirk 2000). It does require that the public (in the aggregate) has sufficient information about what is happening in areas it considers important. If this condition is fulfilled, people would adjust their relative preferences – their support for more or less policy – in response to changes in policy (Wlezien 1995): downward in response to increases in policy and vice versa. This not only underscores the incentive for policymakers, it provides the raw material—reasonably well-informed preferences—that policymakers can effectively respond to, or "represent."

Opinion and policy thus are intimately related in the Thermostatic Model but in a fashion that is quite different to what is proposed by the Responsible Party Model. In the Thermostatic Model public preferences change, partly due to changes in the underlying preferred levels of policy and party due to changes in policy itself. If policymakers respond to public preferences, therefore, they will bring policy more in line with what the public wants and the public will prefer less policy change.[3] The extent to which dynamic representation is taking place can be assessed by estimating the length of time it takes for the policies of governments to come into alignment with public preferences: The shorter the time-gap between demand and supply, other things being equal, the more responsive governments will be seen to be. Some scholars refer to this as the "efficiency" of democratic governance (Soroka and Wlezien 2010).

This Thermostatic Model of dynamic representation yields different expectations from the Responsible Party Model because it explicitly takes into account changing public preferences (Wlezien 1995; 2004). There are four primary differences. First, governments that fail to fulfill their promises may not be punished if public demand for the policy in question has waned or been fulfilled in some other way. Second, governments that succeed in carrying out their promises may not be rewarded if they continue to propose more of the same after public demand in that area has been met. Third, such governments, even if they stop proposing more of the same policy and turn their attention to other things, may still not be rewarded if those other things are policy areas in which some other political party has a relative advantage. And, fourth, governments can be held accountable for failure to address exogenous change in policy demand occurring between elections.

Exogenous change in policy demand may sound far-fetched, but in practice it is not uncommon. Consider 9/11, or the onset (and evolution) of the 2008 financial crisis.

There are numerous other less dramatic but still substantial "shocks." Second, even where the need for policy in a particular area has remained the same, the salience of that policy area can change, perhaps reflecting what is happening in other domains (Wlezien 2005). For example, in the wake of 9/11 concerns about various social welfare issues received less public attention in the US. In the thermostatic model, such changes in issue salience can be directly reflected in policy.[4]

So the Thermostatic Model has a number of advantages over the Responsible Party Model when it comes to thinking about electoral accountability. In the first place (a) it is policy- and performance-oriented, as is required where accountability is concerned, whereas the RPM does not call for or require a governing party to be held accountable for its performance while in office, unless it made promises that it violated. Then (b), the thermostatic model does not focus exclusively on elections as the mechanism for ensuring changes in the activities (policies) for which governments will be held accountable. Governments are assumed to respond to a continuous stream of information about how their policies are being assessed. Moreover, (c) because the model does not require the replacement of government parties in order for there to be change in the activities for which governments are held accountable, there is no particular problem if those governments are coalition governments. Finally, and relatedly, (d) the thermostatic model does not require certain election outcomes that may not occur in practice (that a government remains in office even as it fails to produce desired policy does not necessarily signal a lack of electoral accountability). It is the fact of elections rather than their outcomes that matters for dynamic representation.[5]

The fact of elections is *absolutely critical*, however. Even in a revised view of accountability, where reactions to policy are not limited to election promises or election campaigns, elections are the mechanism (threat) that encourages responsiveness on the part of governments, and that turns public assessments of accountability into action, i.e., rewards or penalties for past behavior (see Adams 2012). Of course, dynamic representation should work best where accountability is most evident. This brings us to our next topic.

VARIATIONS IN ELECTORAL ACCOUNTABILITY

Our discussion of accountability has thus far taken place at 30,000 ft. We have considered some general issues in discussions of electoral accountability. In this section, we focus on the details.

Electoral accountability quite clearly varies across political-institutional contexts. We regard this variation as a function of (a) institutions, and (b) actors. On the one hand, political institutions can structure the focus and ease of electoral accountability. On the other hand, electoral accountability is largely dependent on the actors within those institutions—on the behavior of voters, politicians, and the mass media.

Institutions

Surely the most important institutions where electoral accountability is concerned are electoral institutions. The major difference on this dimension is between majoritarian and proportional systems (though there is of course a lot of variance within each of these broad categories). The impact that these different systems have on the connection between votes cast at elections and seats won in legislatures is well understood (Duverger 1972; Lijphart 1999; Cox 1987). Less well understood are the other effects that electoral systems may have on accountability, through the impact that electoral systems have on the structure of party systems and governments.

The main effect of electoral systems on accountability follows from the fact that the focus of accountability in single-member plurality (SMP) systems typically is the individual representative, and the focus in a proportional (PR) system typically is the political party.

Whether the role of parties in SMP systems is to increase or decrease the potential for electoral accountability is unclear. On the one hand parties serve as a useful information shortcut for voters who need to understand where their prospective representatives stand on issues, or what their incumbent representatives did since the last election. This is of course equally true in proportional systems. But whereas proportional systems allow voters to reward and penalize parties directly (i.e., on the ballot, where votes are typically for parties), majoritarian systems provide a more tenuous link between voters and parties by requiring voters to elect individual representatives. In Parliamentary SMP systems this generally amounts to rewarding and penalizing parties but, to the extent that voters focus on candidates for legislative office, accountability shifts towards those representatives and away from parties, creating a clear problem when it comes to holding parties accountable for policymaking. Among mature democracies this problem may be most evident in the United States.

That said, proportional systems are not without their own problems. Proportional systems allocate seats in the parliament in proportion to votes cast for each party, providing better representation in the legislature for an electorate containing a diversity of different opinions. But opinion diversity is such that PR is likely to give rise to more than two parties and, for that reason, it is not very likely to yield a single-party government. So the better representation provided by PR in terms of matching parties to preferences comes along with increasing indeterminacy as to which parties will be included in the resulting government. In PR systems, government formation normally becomes a separate step in the political process beyond the direct control of voters. This has serious consequences where accountability is concerned, making it more difficult to hold parties accountable for their performance in office.

The critical point for the time being is that majoritarian and proportional systems point electoral accountability in two quite different directions; and so the effectiveness of each electoral system in producing electoral accountability becomes the product of a host of other institutional factors such as party financing, party discipline, legislative procedures, and (in PR systems) the prevalence of pre-electoral pacts that can refocus election campaigns from parties to governments. As a consequence, important questions arise as to the behavior to be expected of voters. Should voters focus on representatives or on parties? If the latter, should they hold all governing parties accountable for all government decisions? Or is accountability for certain decisions best directed at one party in particular? Both systems have the potential to diffuse "clarity of responsibility," making it harder to hold governments accountable—though the way in which obfuscation can occur is different in each system.

In short, neither SMP nor PR systems may be clearly better where electoral accountability is concerned. Note that this observation that *both* SMP and PR are problematic where accountability is concerned conflicts somewhat with what has become a standard view in the literature on electoral systems and representation. We see that view, captured in work by Lijphart (1999) and Powell (2000), roughly as follows. Majoritarian systems produce strong, single-party governments that tend to take positions off to the left or right of the average voter. Proportional systems, in contrast, necessitate governance through coalitions, which tends to encompass ideologically middling parties. This brings the government closer to the median voter and produces better representation.

There is a small but growing body of work that suggests otherwise, however (Blais and Bodet 2006; Golder and Stramski 2010). This work finds little difference in the match between the positions of citizens and public policy across majoritarian and proportional systems. Powell's (2011) own very recent research shows much the same, and highlights the importance of party systems. Research on dynamic policy representation (Soroka and Wlezien 2010; Wlezien and Soroka 2012) further suggests that proportional systems may not be highly responsive to changing public opinion. Indeed, where differences in dynamic representation do exist, they appear to point to the success of majoritarian systems. Why is this the case? One possibility is that coalition governments are less able to react to changing circumstances between elections because (inter-party) coordination is more difficulty and costly (Wlezien and Soroka 2012). This partly reflects the increased transaction costs but also the constraints posed by coalition agreements. Another is that SMP systems provide greater electoral incentives to governments. Because they tend to produce single party governments, SMP systems clarify the locus of (party) responsibility for voters, which makes reward and punishment more likely. On top of this, because a shift in the Election Day vote has more consequence for political control in majoritarian systems, governments there have more reason to pay close attention to changing public preferences.

These recent nuanced findings seem to conflict with what Powell (2000) refers to as the "two visions" of democracy: where PR produces good representation along with poor accountability, and SMP systems provide good accountability along with poor representation. But in that work Powell was thinking in terms of a match between the attitudes of the electorate and the attitudes of representatives and governments—and this match (sometimes called "congruence") does seem to be worse in majoritarian systems. Evidence of good representation in majoritarian systems, by contrast, comes mainly from studies of dynamic responsiveness. So accountability and representation need not be at odds, depending on the type of representation, and it ultimately may be that dynamic representation is strongest in systems that provide high levels of accountability.

Clarity of responsibility has been an especially prominent theme in the literature on federalism, or vertical decentralization; this is of course another dimension of political institutions with important implications for electoral accountability. The focus in the existing literature is on the reduced ability of voters to hold governments accountable when it is not clear which government did what. There is a good deal of work focused on economic voting—one variant of electoral accountability—and research suggests that voters' tendencies to penalize and reward governments for economic conditions is decreased in federal systems (e.g., Anderson 2006; Anderson 2000; Leyden and Borrelli 1995; Lowry, Alt, and Ferree 1998; Powell and Whitten 1993). Some research focuses on policy as well and finds, similarly, that people confuse the actions of multiple (and over-lapping) governments (Wlezien and Soroka 2011). However, note that there is some evidence that voters are able to correctly assign responsibility when voting even in highly federal regimes (see, e.g., Arceneaux 2006; Schneider and Jacoby 2003; Cutler 2004; 2008). To be clear: there may be situations in which federalism produces better representation (e.g., when there is a need for regional variation), but electoral accountability is invariably reduced in any federal system in which the responsibilities of different levels of government overlap. Consider also "second order election" theory, focused mainly on the European context, in which both subnational and EU (European Union) elections are regarded as being driven mainly by national domestic politics. This perspective reflects a similar concern with the complications that vertical decentralization poses for accountability (see, e.g., Marsh 1998; Hix and Marsh 2007).

Other electoral/political institutions matter as well. In fact, we have thus far ignored what is perhaps the most commonly-identified institution in the empirical literature on electoral accountability, namely, term limits. Term limits have a very clear impact on politicians' re-election incentives: When a sitting politician is prevented by a term limit from being re-elected there is a greatly-reduced incentive to be responsive to voter demands. Not surprisingly, this is what studies find (e.g., Besley and Case 1995; Alt et al. 2011; Ferraz and Finan 2011; for a recent review, see Ashworth 2012).

Still, we want to emphasize here that term limits are just one of the institutions important to variance in electoral accountability. Even where all politicians are subject to reward and penalty in the next election, electoral accountability is the product of a host of institutional factors, including electoral systems, party systems, horizontal and vertical decentralization, as well, of course, as term limits.

Actors

The impact of institutions on electoral accountability is in large part a product of the behavior of actors within the political system. Here we focus on three sets of actors: first and foremost, voters, but politicians and journalists as well.

Voters define the terms of accountability. They decide whether to reward or punish elected officials and the basis for doing so. We have focused this chapter on policy, but our assessments depend on what voters actually do and whether and how policy matters. Political scientists have learned a great deal about what voters do on Election Day. We know why they line up in support of or in opposition to governments in particular election years. We also know why electoral preferences shift from year to year. This would appear to have important implications for what governments do.

Party attachment is of special importance. It is the leading determinant of vote choice in countries where it is possible to distinguish the two.[6] It also conditions electoral accountability. If commitment to party is strong, there is little basis for electoral accountability, particularly where such commitments differentiate a single party from all others, which would seem to make change particularly unlikely. Under such conditions, voters would not judge politicians on the basis of policy or other things. They would vote for their parties regardless of the actions of those parties. Importantly, research shows commitments to party changing over time. The change may not be dramatic, but it is palpable; that is, party preferences are not fixed. It also is important that people do not always vote for their most preferred parties. This allows other things to matter on Election Day.

Policy also is an important determinant. Much research shows that people's issue preferences structure their votes, and this finding suggests that sitting governments actually are held accountable for the decisions they take. While the large body of individual-level evidence is suggestive, what matters most to accountability are aggregate election outcomes—they dictate who wins and provide signals for elected officials. Erikson, MacKuen, and Stimson (2002) have conducted the most powerful work, focusing on the US. They show that the public's policy preferences structure the aggregate vote for president (and Congress), and that politicians' positions also matter. There are similar findings (based on ideological rather than policy positions) for the UK (Hakhverdian 2012). In short, the public tends to choose the candidate that best represents their positions. This implies that elections serve the purposes of accountability. Even to the extent governments represent changing public preferences between elections, the elections themselves also help correct disjunctures between what the public wants and what it is getting.

Other, non-policy factors also matter on Election Day. The state of the economy is the usual suspect, and much research demonstrates a connection between it and the vote. Research also reveals significant institutional effects (Duch and Stevenson 2008; Brug, Eijk, and Franklin 2007; Powell and Whitten 1993). Economic prosperity is not the only type of performance that is consequential to the vote. Research shows that other aspects of security are important, including international and domestic peace. These so-called valence issues actually may be increasing in importance, particularly in those countries where party commitments are weakening (Kayser and Wlezien 2011).[7]

Politicians also are critical to electoral accountability. We know that the availability of information is of fundamental importance. This does not happen magically. Politicians "prime" issues, and provide competing "frames" for political debates. Vavreck (2009), for instance, demonstrates that the economy impacts the vote only because of what politicians do during election campaigns. By priming their advantage, politicians make the economy come to matter to voters; if not primed, it does not come to matter, at least not as much. The campaign serves to bring home the economic (and other non-economic) fundamentals of the election (see Erikson and Wlezien 2012).

Finally, the mass media play an important role. Unless voters have information, after all, electoral accountability is impossible. Press freedom is fundamental. Media competition is as well. Without some level of freedom and competition, media systems may not provide the information required to effectively evaluate elected officials or their opposition. Of course, the mass media do not matter just for electoral accountability; they matter for accountability more generally.

ELECTORAL ACCOUNTABILITY MATTERS

Elections make politicians pay attention to what the public wants and reflect public demands in their policies and performance. But accountability varies across institutional settings, across the things that politicians do and across the times at which they do those things. Policy and performance matter more to election outcomes with proximity to Election Day, with clarity of responsibility, and with the extent of electoral and party competition. Only competitive elections in high clarity countries yield good accountability, and then only in regard to items that voters focus on. However, the threat of such elections also promotes dynamic representation of the public's policy preferences even at times far removed from elections. And the notion of representative democracy without electoral accountability, however imperfect, is hard to imagine. Effective representative democracy requires a regular opportunity for voters to reward or penalize governments for their performance.

Elected officials do not completely control the things that matter to voters in the voting booth, however. This is especially true for aspects of performance such as the economy (policy scholars commonly refer to these as "outcomes"). To the extent that voters hold governments accountable for aspects of performance beyond direct governmental control, elections can become much like a game of musical chairs (Achen and Bartels 2002).[8] Things are somewhat different for policy—while the impact of what governments do upon taking office may not be felt immediately, the policy is observable. And it may be that changes in the control of the economy, owing, for instance, to globalization, have increased the importance of policy in other areas (Hellwig 2008).

The fact that voters reward or punish politicians based on things over which those politicians have limited control is another reason to be concerned about the efficiency of electoral accountability. However, this does not mean that politicians have no incentive to represent the public's policy preferences. As we have seen, public opinion and government policy do matter on Election Day and with real consequences for the ideological disposition of governments (also see Dalton et al. 2012). In short, even an inefficient mechanism can work. Electoral accountability, inefficient as it may be, is both a critical, and in many instances an effective, element of representative democratic governance.

This is not to say that there aren't other concerns. One is the possibility that voters (or the consequences of voter decisions) are deliberately misdirected by government manipulation of the electoral system, for example, by gerrymandering. Governments can also manipulate other "rules of the game," for example, by calling a referendum in the hopes of overcoming an adverse decision in a nation's legislature.

Much research on electoral accountability remains to be done. We see two areas worth particular attention. The first is the debate about the relative merits of SMP versus PR systems. As discussed above, some of the most influential work in the literature on comparative democratic institutions was very clear about the merits of PR (e.g., Lijphart 1999) but subsequent empirical work raises questions about the generalizability of those ideas (Blais and Bodet 2006; Wlezien and Soroka 2012). Not only may PR systems fail to improve the quality of representation; they also may make accountability more problematic. We do not really know, however. Researchers are only part-way through what should be a careful empirical investigation into the various merits and difficulties with SMP and PR systems where representation and accountability are concerned.

The second area for future work focuses on the way in which political behavior varies across institutional contexts. The literature on vote choice has exploded in recent years, spurred on in part by election studies around the world (many coordinated through the Comparative Studies of Electoral Systems project). We only have a partial sense of how the voting calculus changes from one institutional context to the next, however; and we do not really understand the ways in which voters hold governments, or parties, or politicians to account for past behaviors and campaign promises. There are some evolving new research agendas, to be sure. Some examples include Roy's (2011) work on voters' use of information across varying electoral-institutional contexts, and Naurin's (2011) work on whether parties keep, and are held accountable for, election promises. But understanding the relative merits of political institutions for electoral accountability clearly requires a more complete consideration of differences in how voters behave across a variety of institutional contexts.

ACKNOWLEDGMENTS

We thank Mark Bovens, Robert Goodin, Markus Kruezer, and Thomas Schillemans. Mark Franklin would like to acknowledge assistance from the Netherlands Institute for Advanced Studies in the Humanities and Social Sciences who provided ideal working conditions for finishing this chapter.

NOTES

1. In particular, politicians may claim mandates for certain policies even if not supported by the public. On this, and on mandate politics generally, see Grossback et al. (2006).
2. Though note that such results also may point to other non-policy causes of election outcomes, e.g., the economy, which we consider below.
3. The exact match between how much policy the public wants and actually gets is difficult to empirically assess (see Soroka and Wlezien 2010).
4. See Jones (1995); Franklin and Wlezien (1997); Wlezien (2004); Jones et al. (2009); Jennings and John (2009); Soroka and Wlezien (2010) on the importance of salience in policymaking and responsiveness.
5. However, the Thermostatic Model does lead to predictions regarding election outcomes that have been found to be fulfilled in the United States—the only polity where this link has been investigated explicitly (see Erikson et al. 2002; Boelstad 2011).
6. In parliamentary systems it has been found hard to distinguish attachment from support; it also appears as though voters can hold multiple party identifications in multiparty systems. In such systems many scholars accordingly prefer to talk of "propensity to vote" as a measure of how strongly individuals are committed to certain parties (see, e.g., Eijk et al. 2006; Weisberg 1999).
7. There may be important differences in how policy and valence issues impact elections. Research shows that voter reactions to the economy focus mostly on *change* and especially recent events (Hibbs 1987; Achen and Bartels 2002; Kayser and Wlezien 2011; Erikson and Wlezien 2012), which makes sense since earlier events often will have been largely the responsibility of the previous government. When reacting to policy, by contrast, voters appear to consider the state of policy, which is the sum of policy changes over a much more extended period.
8. The mechanism appears to be the misdirection of political blame, i.e., politicians blaming the government for things beyond its control.

REFERENCES

Achen, C. and Bartels, L. 2002. *Blind Retrospection: Electoral Responses to Droughts, Flu, and Shark Attacks.* In APSA (American Political Science Association) Annual Meeting. Boston, 29 August – 1 September 2002.

Adams, J. 2012. "The Causes and Electoral Consequences of Party Policy Shifts in Multiparty Elections: Theoretical Results and Empirical Evidence." *Annual Review of Political Science*, 15: 401–19.

Alt, J., Bueno de Mesquita, E., and Rose, S. 2011. "Disentangling Accountability and Competence in Elections. Evidence from US Term Limits." *Journal of Politics*, 73: 171–86.

Anderson, C. 2000. "Economic Voting and Political Context: A Comparative Perspective." *Electoral Studies*, 19: 151–70.

Anderson, C. D. 2006. "Economic Voting and Multilevel Governance: A Comparative Individual-Level Analysis." *American Journal of Political Science*, 50: 449–63.

Arceneaux, K. 2006. "The Federal Face of Voting: Are Elected Officials Held Accountable for the Functions Relevant to Their Office?" *Political Psychology*, 27: 731–54.

Ashworth, S. 2012. "Electoral Accountability: Recent Theoretical and Empirical Work." *Annual Review of Political Science*, 15: 183–201.

Besley, T. and Case, A. 1995. "Does Electoral Accountability Affect Economic Policy Choices? Evidence from Gubernatorial Term Limits." *Quarterly Journal of Economics*, 110: 769–98.

Blais, A. and Bodet, M. A. 2006. "Does Proportional Representation Foster Closer Congruence Between Citizens and Policymakers?" *Comparative Political Studies*, 39: 1243–62.

Boelstad, J. 2011. "Dynamic Representation Voting: Presidential Elections in Light of New Policy Data." *PS: Political Science and Politics*, 45: 44–50.

Brug, W. van der, Eijk, C. van der, and Franklin, M. 2007. *The Economy and the Vote*. New York: Cambridge University Press.

Cox, G. W. 1987. *The Efficient Secret: The Cabinet and the Development of Political Parties in Victorian England*. Cambridge: Cambridge University Press.

Cutler, F. 2004. "Government Responsibility and Electoral Accountability in Federations." *Publius: The Journal of Federalism*, 34: 19–38.

Cutler, F. 2008. "One Voter, Two First-Order Elections?" *Electoral Studies*, 27: 492–504.

Dalton, R., Farrell, D., and McAllister, I. 2012. *Political Parties and Democratic Linkage: How Parties Organize Democracy*. Oxford: Oxford University Press.

Delli Carpini, Michael X. and Scott Keeter. 1996. *What Americans Know about Politics and Why It Matters*. New Haven, Conn: Yale University Press.

Deutsch, K. W. 1963. *Nerves of Government*. New York: The Free Press.

Duch, R. and Stevenson, R. 2008. *The Economic Vote*. New York: Cambridge University Press.

Duverger, M. 1972. Factors in a Two-Party and Multiparty System, pp. 23–32 in *Party Politics and Pressure Groups: A Comparative Introduction*, ed. M. Duverger. New York: Thomas Y. Crowell.

Easton, D. 1965. *A Framework for Political Analysis*. Englewood Cliffs, NJ: Prentice-Hall.

Eijk, C. van der, Brug, W. van der, Kroh, M., and Franklin, M. 2006. "Rethinking the Dependent Variable in Electoral Behavior: On the Measurement and Analysis of Utilities." *Electoral Studies*, 25: 424–47.

Erikson, R. and Wlezien, C. 2012. *The Timeline of Presidential Elections: How Campaigns Do (and Do Not) Matter*. Chicago: University of Chicago Press.

Erikson, R., MacKuen, M., and Stimson, J. 2002. *The Macro Polity*. Cambridge: Cambridge University Press.

Ferraz, C. and Finan, F. 2011. "Electoral Accountability and Corruption: Evidence from the Audits of Local Governments." *American Economic Review*, 101: 1274–1311.

Franklin, M. and Wlezien, C. 1997. "The Responsive Public: Issue Salience, Policy Change, and Preferences for European Unification." *Journal of Theoretical Politics*, 9: 347–63.

Golder, M. and Stramski, J. 2010. "Ideological Congruence and Electoral Institutions." *American Journal of Political Science*, 54: 90–106.

Goodin, R. E. 2000. *Accountability: Elections as One Form: The International Encyclopedia of Elections*. Washington, DC: Congressional Quarterly Press.

Grossback, L. J., Peterson, D. A., and Stimson, J. A. 2006. *Mandate Politics*. Cambridge, MA: Cambridge University Press.

Hakhverdian, A. 2012. "The Causal Flow between Public Opinion and Policy: Government Responsiveness, Leadership, or Counter Movement?" *West European Politics*, 35: 1386–1406.

Hamilton, A., Madison, J., and Jay, J. 2008. *The Federalist Papers*. Oxford: Oxford University Press; originally published 1788.

Hellwig, T. 2008. "Globalization, Policy Constraints, and Vote Choice." *The Journal of Politics*, 70: 1128–41.

Hibbs, D. 1987. *The American Political Economy*. Cambridge: Harvard University Press.

Hix, S. and Marsh, M. 2007. "Punishment or Protest? Understanding European Parliament Elections." *Journal of Politics*, 69: 495–510.

Jennings, W. and John, P. 2009. "The Dynamics of Political Attention: Public Opinion and the Queen's Speech in the United Kingdom." *American Journal of Political Science*, 53: 838–54.

Jones, B. D. 1995. *Reconceiving Decision-Making in Democratic Politics: Attention, Choice, and Public Policy*. Chicago: University of Chicago Press.

Jones, B. D., Baumgartner, F., Breunig, C., Wlezien, C., Soroka, S., Foucault, M., Francois, A., Green-Pedersen, C., Koske, C., John, P., Moretensen, P. B., Varone, F., and Walgrave, S. 2009. "A General Empirical Law of Public Budgets: A Comparative Analysis." *American Journal of Political Science*, 53: 855–73.

Kayser, M. and Wlezien, C. 2011. "Performance Pressure. Patterns of Partisanship and the Economic Vote." *European Journal of Political Research*, 50: 365–94.

Key, V. O. 1961. *Public Opinion and American Democracy*. New York: Knopf.

Kuklinski, J. H., and Quirk P. J. 2000. "Reconsidering the Rational Public: Cognition, Heuristics, and Mass Opinion," pp. 153–182 in *Elements of Reason*, A. Lupia, M. McCubbins and S. Popkin, eds. Cambridge: Cambridge University Press.

Leyden, K. M. and Borrelli, S. A. 1995. "The Effect of State Economic Conditions on Gubernatorial Elections: Does Unified Government Make a Difference?" *Political Research Quarterly*, 48: 275–300.

Lijphart, A. 1999. *Patterns of Democracy: Government Forms and Performance in Thirty-Six Countries*. New Haven: Yale University Press.

Lowry, R. C., Alt, J. E., and Ferree, K. E. 1998. "Fiscal Policy Outcomes and Electoral Accountability in American States." *American Political Science Review*, 92: 759–74.

Manin, B., Przeworski, A. and Stokes, S. 1999. Elections and Representation, pp. 29–54 in *Democracy, Accountability, and Representation*, eds. A. Przeworski, S. Stokes, and B. Manin. Cambridge: Cambridge University Press.

Marsh, M. 1998. "Testing the Second-Order Election Model after Four European Elections." *British Journal of Political Science Research*, 32: 211–23.

Naurin, E. 2011. *Election Promises, Party Behaviour and Voter Perceptions*. Hampshire: Palgrave MacMillan.

Popkin, S. L. 1991. *The Reasoning Voter: Communication and Persuasion in Presidential Campaigns*. Chicago: University of Chicago Press.

Powell, G. B. and Whitten, G. 1993. "A Cross-National Analysis of Economic Voting: Taking Account of the Political Context." *American Journal of Political Science*, 37: 391–414.

Powell, G. B. 2000. *Elections as Instruments of Democracy: Majoritarian and Proportional Views*. New Haven: Yale University Press.

Powell, G. B. 2011. Party Polarization and the Ideological Congruence of Governments, pp. 197–213 in *Citizens, Context, and Choice. How Context Shapes Citizens' Electoral Choices*, eds. R. J. Dalton and C. J. Anderson. Oxford: Oxford University Press.

Ranney, A. 1951. "Toward a More Responsible Two-Party System: A Report of the Committee on Political Parties." *American Political Science Review*, 45: 488–99.

Roy, J. 2011. "Information Heterogeneity, Complexity and the Vote Calculus." *Journal of Elections, Public Opinion and Parties*, 21: 29–56.

Schattschneider, E. E. 1950. "Toward a More Responsible Two-Party System: A Report of the Committee on Political Parties." *American Political Science Review Supplement*, 44: 1–99.

Schneider, S. and Jacoby, W. G. 2003. "Public Attitudes Toward the Policy Responsibilities of the National and State Governments: Evidence from South Carolina." *State Politics and Policy Quarterly*, 3: 246–69.

Soroka, S. N. and Wlezien, C. 2010. *Degrees of Democracy*. New York: Cambridge University Press.

Vavreck, L. 2009. *The Message Matters: The Economy and Presidential Campaigns.* Princeton, NJ: Princeton University Press.

Weisberg, H. 1999. Political Partisanship, pp. 681–729 in *Measures of Political Attitudes,* eds. R. John, P. Shaver and L. Wrightsman. San Diego: Academic Press.

Wiener, N. 1961. *Cybernetics, or Control and Communication in the Animal World.* New York: Wiley.

Wlezien, C. and Soroka, S. 2011. "Federalism and Public Responsiveness to Policy." *Publius: The Journal of Federalism*, 41: 31–52.

Wlezien, C. and Soroka, S. 2012. "Political Institutions and the Opinion-Policy Link." *West European Politics*, 35: 1407–32.

Wlezien, C. 1995. "The Public as Thermostat: Dynamics of Preferences for Spending." *American Journal of Political Science*, 39: 981–1000.

Wlezien, C. 2004. "Patterns of Representation: Dynamics of Public Preferences and Policy." *Journal of Politics*, 66: 1–24.

Wlezien, C. 2005. "On the Salience of Political Issues." *Electoral Studies*, 24: 555–79.

CHAPTER 25

···

HIERARCHY

···

MARK D. JARVIS

Hierarchical Accountability

···

AMONG accountability mechanisms, hierarchy, or more specifically hierarchical accountability, sits at an odd nexus. Despite being the most commonly known and long-standing mechanism of accountability, hierarchical accountability is also commonly criticized as an anachronism; a relic of a bygone era of democratic governance and public administration dominated by command and control approaches.

In theory, those at the top of the hierarchical "chain of command" delegate authority to those subordinate to them while at the same time holding these subordinate actors accountable for their decisions, behavior and performance in exercising this delegated authority. These superior–subordinate relationships cascade down the chain all the way from citizens, as the ultimate superiors at the top, to "street-level" bureaucrats who are responsible for implementing public policies and programs. In this way, hierarchy establishes the democratic current that runs throughout contemporary systems of public governance and administration, linking the various actors, organizations, and institutions that make up the core features of democratic systems of governance (Strøm 2000). Through the electoral process, citizens are thus able to ensure democratic control over the various actors who play a role in the institutions of representative democratic governance. For this reason, many regard hierarchical accountability as *the* most important mechanism of accountability. For instance, Bovens (2005, 190) notes that hierarchy is most often the primary form of accountability in public organizations and underpins most other types of accountability (e.g., political).

The critique of anachronism holds that hierarchical accountability has been outpaced by the speed of reform and broader evolution in the way we govern ourselves, rendered incompatible with the complexity that characterizes contemporary public organizations and the realities of the way advanced democracies are governed (Scott 2000, 42; Considine 2002). Under the Westminster system, for example, it is said to be unrealistic to expect a minister of a department to know, and be responsible for, all the relationships encompassed within his or her portfolio, let alone anything about the actual operations (Aucoin and Jarvis 2005; Bovens 2005). Some critics of hierarchical accountability suggest simply replacing this approach with what they see as more appropriate mechanisms of accountability, while others suggest sharply adapting or supplementing it to cope with changing realities on the ground (see Behn 2001; Schillemans 2008).

DEMOCRATIC CHAIN OF COMMAND

Across both parliamentary and presidential systems, public governance and administration relies on delegation and accountability. While the design and nature of delegation practices and systems may differ across and within jurisdictions, both parliamentary and presidential systems are based on the assumption that government business is most efficiently and effectively conducted when authority is delegated extensively to different actors or groups of actors to carry out aspects of the governance and administration of public affairs. Representatives who are directly elected by citizens exercise public authority in the legislative and executive branches of government—the power of the state—on behalf of citizens, rather than in their own right. In turn, these elected representatives also delegate authority, creating additional hierarchical relationships and a chain of delegation running from voters down to those civil servants who support the development and carry out the implementation of public policy. As depicted in Figure 25.1, this chain consists, at a minimum, of four relationships in the parliamentary system. Authority is delegated: "1) from voters to elected representatives; 2) from legislators to the executive branch, specifically to the head of government (the prime minister); 3) from the head of government (prime minister) to the heads of different executive departments; and, 4) from the heads of different executive departments to civil servants" (Strøm 2000, 267).

A similar depiction can also be used to highlight the basic features of the hierarchical chain for a presidential system (see Figure 25.2) with voters electing representatives at three different levels who confer authority on subordinate political and departmental actors.

Given the way that public authority is conferred from a superior authority to a designated body or individual in these systems, accountability, so the argument goes, is critical to ensuring that this authority is exercised in what is deemed to be a suitable manner, defined differently by different actors involved in the democratic system. Strøm (2000, 267) described this as "a corresponding chain of accountability" that runs in the reverse direction: "An agent is *accountable* to his principle if (1) he is obliged to act on the latter's behalf, and (2) the latter is empowered to reward or punish him for his performance" [emphasis in the original]. In this way hierarchical accountability—where a superior has delegated authority to a subordinate and is able to hold that actor to account for the use

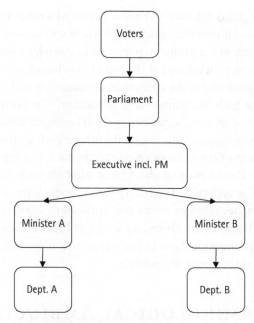

Note: Adapted from Strøm (2000).

FIGURE 25.1 Basic features of hierarchical chain in parliamentary systems

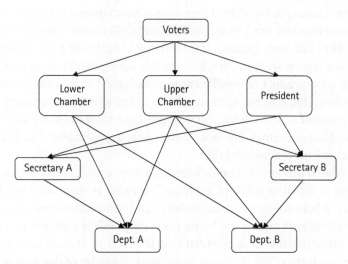

Note: Adapted from Strøm (2000).

FIGURE 25.2 Basic features of hierarchical chain in presidential systems

of that authority—is a guard against the abuse of power. Moreover, in this model, a super-ordinate is accountable for everything done by his subordinates on his authority, which provides a clear solution to the problem, pervasive in complex bureaucracies, of "many hands". With the exception of citizens at the top of the chain and the very bottom rung of civil servants, everyone else in the core chain of delegation and hierarchical account-ability plays the role of both "accountee" and "accountor." The bottom rungs of the civil service do not play this dual role, because they do not delegate authority to anyone, and thus are not superiors to anyone. Citizens, on the other hand, are the ultimate sovereigns in the democratic process. Only citizens are not accountable to a superior power.

It should be made clear here that the figures used above both oversimplify these respective systems of governance. The reality is that both systems are complex hierar-chies,[1] involving a broader range of actors and institutions—and superior–subordinate relationships—in addition to the central structure of hierarchy depicted. The result is that many, if not most, individuals or organizations are accountable to more than one superior for different authorities they exercise.

Terminological Ambiguity

A review of the literature addressing hierarchical accountability leaves some fundamen-tal conceptual questions unanswered. Do all of the superior–subordinate relationships along the democratic chain qualify as hierarchical mechanisms of accountability? What is the key distinction that sets hierarchical accountability apart from other mechanisms of accountability? The contributors to the literature to date have not been entirely clear.

At least three factors seem to contribute to this ambiguity. First, in part, this confu-sion is simply a by-product of insufficient terminological care in the literature. This is seen in the use of different but easily conflated terms to refer to different or even the same mechanisms of accountability. For example, Grant and Keohane (2005, 36) use the terms "hierarchical accountability" and "supervisory accountability" to distinguish two different mechanisms of accountability.

A second related problem is that different efforts to establish typologies of account-ability operate at different levels of analysis. The result is that particular hierarchical accountability relationships or arrangements can be simultaneously classified differ-ently. While sub-classifications are by no means a problem unto themselves—indeed they can be quite helpful—it is essential that the level of classification be explicit to avoid further confusion. The two most prominent examples of this sort of typological distinction are intra- vs. inter-organizational accountability relationships and political vs. bureaucratic/administrative accountability. For example, Bovens (2005, 204) dif-ferentiates himself from Romzek and Dubnick (1998), Behn (2001), and Pollitt (2003) by emphasizing the intra-organization nature of accountability to superiors for public managers, in contrast to the other authors' characterization of these relationships as bureaucratic or hierarchical accountability. Hierarchy, as an accountability mechanism, can operate both within and across organizational boundaries as well as political or bureaucratic levels depending on the specific hierarchical relationship and actors who are obliged to provide an account and to whom the account is due. Different authors may have good reasons for drawing the distinctions they have introduced, but the manner in which these distinctions have been drawn often contributes to ambiguity within the literature. At times, this results from not making sufficiently clear the reasoning that underpins these discrepancies or explaining how new typologies relate to existing ones, adding complexity rather than reducing it.

Third, there are also some legitimate debates in the literature as to the defining characteristic that differentiates hierarchical accountability from other accountability mechanisms. For example, Romzek (2000, 23–4) only associates a subset of superior–subordinate relationships that entail "close supervision of individuals who have low work autonomy" with the concept of hierarchical accountability (see also Dicke and Ott 1999, 505). This excludes a range of important superior–subordinate relationships.

Seldom, if ever, is delegated power completely unencumbered (Wilson 1989, 149). Rules or laws, in addition to other less formal constraints such as regulations or social norms, often establish boundaries on how delegated authority can or cannot be used. Nevertheless, delegation entails that authority is assigned or conferred, formally or informally, from a superior to a subordinate. The key is that delegation of authority actually allows the subordinate to exercise discretion as to how to use that authority. Romzek provides an excellent example of this in the touchstone examination of accountability in the wake of the Challenger tragedy. In their classic study, Romzek and Dubnick (1987, 233) describe how, notwithstanding the intensification of "hierarchical reporting relationships," managers and supervisors held considerable discretion, not just in determining what information was shared with more senior officials, but also for decision-making. As they describe: "responsibility for specific aspects of the overall program was transferred to supervisors at lower levels in the reporting hierarchy, and the burden for giving the go ahead to launch decision makers shifted from the engineers and experts towards those supervisory personnel" (1987, 233).

In those cases where the subordinate has no discretion, the division of labor does not actually entail delegation. There is no discretion in the exercise of authority to be held to account for. Rather, the superior–subordinate relationships Romzek (2000), describes are comprised of the rote assignment of tasks, including the specification of how those tasks are to be performed. Aucoin and Jarvis (2005, 34) argue, "where there is no delegation at all, superiors retain full accountability because their subordinates are expected to act only as instructed."

THE KEY DISTINCTION: DIRECT DELEGATION

This chapter endorses a broad conception of hierarchy as a mechanism of accountability. While it recognizes the value of typologies that seek to further classify sub-*types* of accountability mechanisms, it maintains that the fundamental feature that sets hierarchy as a mechanism of accountability apart from other mechanisms transcends these further breakdowns.

Bovens, Goodin, and Schillemans describe in Chapter 1 of this volume a number of key questions useful for understanding—and differentiating—accountability mechanisms that have been central to the accountability literature: *Who is accountable? To what forum are they accountable? For what are they accountable? How?* The fundamental feature of hierarchical accountability mechanisms, as described earlier, is the delegation of authority from superior to subordinate and commensurate accountability from subordinate to superior. In this way, hierarchy crystalizes responsibility on a single accountable individual or actor for the performance of a task or tasks in light of the performance expectations attached to the performance of those tasks.[2] The relationship between the subordinate and the superior—the accountable actor and the forum to whom the account is due—speaks to who is accountable to whom and for what, while allowing for variations in the specific ways that account-giving and scrutiny occur. Most importantly, the superior–subordinate relationship makes the obligation to provide an account clear—the accountability forum to whom the account is due is in a place of direct and immediate authority over the accountable actors for the authority they have conferred upon them.

This distinction speaks to where hierarchy as a mechanism of accountability derives its legitimacy. This clear line of authority and accountability underpins both the obligation to provide an account to the forum and the forum's authority to scrutinize and question the account, as well as to form a judgment about the actor's actions, decisions, and/ or performance and impose sanctions as he or she sees fit (sanctions being seemingly more common than rewards: see Behn 2001). That is, the accountability forums associated with hierarchical accountability afford their legitimacy from the direct authority— and power—they hold in the context of an existing superior–subordinate relationship between the two parties. This remains whether that accountability interaction occurs within or across organizational boundaries, or at the political or bureaucratic level. In contrast, accountability forums associated with other types or mechanisms of accountability derive their legitimacy from an array of considerations, such as laws and administrative regulations, professional codes and obligations, or broader social pressures.

As Mulgan (2000, 559) notes: "this deference to superiors is a familiar feature of accountability within bureaucracies and other hierarchical organizations." As per Weber's (1968, 957) bureaucratic "ideal-type," the central characteristics of public bureaucracies include appointed officials charged with carrying out clearly defined responsibilities that accord with their competencies under clear rules in a "monocratically" organized structure, where each level is subject to control by the level above it in a continuous hierarchy. That being said, Weber (1968, 957) held that "the principle of hierarchical office authority" is not a unique feature of public bureaucracies, arguing instead that it "is found in all bureaucratic structures: in state and ecclesiastical structures as well as in large party organizations and private enterprises. It does not matter for the character of bureaucracy whether its authority is called 'private' or 'public.' "

While hierarchical accountability may be common to both private and public organizations, precise comparisons of the nature of hierarchy in both are difficult given key differences between the broad categories of organizations. For example, private corporations of a same/similar size as traditional government departments/bureaucracies are rare. Further, accountabilities tend to be less ambiguous in private corporations and other organizations. As Wilson's (1989, 131, 316) classic study *Bureaucracy* notes, it is not just that organizational goals are clearer and easier to measure in the private than in the public sector, though they often are, but also that goals tend to be more singular, whereas in the public sector, even when an actor or organizational unit has measureable, clear objectives, they tend to have to balance a range of contextual goals as well.

VARIATIONS ON A MECHANISM

Central to a mechanistic understanding of accountability are the institutional arrangements through which an individual or organizational unit can hold another to account (see Bovens 2010). In the case of hierarchy, this encompasses relationships between superior and subordinate actors where an individual in a position of direct and immediate authority delegates authority to another actor, whether formally or informally, and, in turn, holds that actor to account for the exercise of the delegated authority ex post facto.

Given the number of different hierarchical accountability relationships that exist within democratic governments, and the differences in the nature of those relationships, it is no surprise that there is a range of variations of this accountability mechanism. Institutional arrangements can, of course, vary by jurisdiction. That said, the basic variants of hierarchical accountability for the core relationships along the chain of command (as depicted in Figures 25.1 and 2) are similar across jurisdictions. Table 25.1, below, provides an overview of the more common hierarchical accountability arrangements. Hierarchical accountability mechanisms range from standard periodic elections and more populist recall referenda that allow citizens to dismiss democratically elected representatives whose performance they are dissatisfied with, through to ongoing formal and informal performance feedback given to civil servants by their administrative superiors behind closed doors.

While not all of the forms of hierarchical accountability listed in Table 25.1 are found in all jurisdictions, empirical research suggests that there is considerable convergence both over time and across jurisdictions in the evolution of at least some hierarchical accountability mechanisms. Hierarchy is perhaps most highly associated with civil service bureaucracies. While there have been limited empirical investigations of the actual practice of hierarchical accountability among civil servants, the research that has been undertaken has pointed to a few core variations of this mechanism. For example, in Kaufman's (1967, 198) classic study *The Forest Ranger*, he richly describes the key role mechanisms of hierarchical accountability—extensive reporting to, and inspections

Table 25.1 Variations of hierarchical accountability

Accountable Actors	Hierarchical Accountability Mechanisms
Elected representatives	• Elections • Recall referenda
Executive/government (collective accountability)	• Votes of confidence in the government • Formal oral questions from the opposition in Parliament put to the government for ministers' response • Scrutiny by parliamentary/congressional committees (including of legislation and/or budgets) • Reviews of the administration of particular statutes by members of legislatures • Annual reports to legislatures on departmental plans and performance prepared by departments and agencies
Heads of executive departments (e.g., ministers) (individual accountability)	• Prime minister/president's assessment of the performance and actions of individual ministers/secretaries and appointees • Formal oral questions from the opposition in Parliament regarding ministers' decisions, actions and/or performance • Scrutiny of ministers/secretaries' decisions, actions and/or performance by legislative committees
Top level civil servants	• Minister/secretary's assessment of performance and actions • Assessment of body or individual responsible for appointment of top civil servants • Formal performance measurement-based appraisals • Scrutiny by other agencies or forums that are sources of directly delegated authority (e.g., financial or staffing authorities delegated directly by statute or some agency or body)
Middle and lower civil service ranks	• Internal ongoing formal and informal performance feedback given by their administrative superiors • Formal performance measurement-based appraisals

by, superiors; informal feedback; and performance reviews and assigned performance ratings—play among a broader range of integrating techniques, in achieving what he describes as "voluntary conformity," notwithstanding the considerable discretion and autonomy rangers actually held and the highly decentralized organizational nature of the forest rangers program (e.g., the great physical distance between many superiors and subordinates). Similar descriptions run throughout Wilson's (1989) *Bureaucracy*, and the cases examined therein, and are also consistent with Romzek and Dubnick's (1987, 233) description of the rise of emphasis on "hierarchical reporting relationships" (although they do not provide the same level of detail).

While these classic studies of hierarchy span the last half-century and are concentrated in the United States, the hierarchical accountability approaches they describe are consistent with findings from more recent research. Jarvis (2012, 14) describes how ongoing, informal feedback that most often occurs behind the closed doors of a superior's office alongside annual or semi-annual formal performance reviews comprise the primary mechanisms of accountability among the hierarchical relationships between working, managerial, and executive-level civil servants in Canada, Australia, and the Netherlands. This is not to say there has been no evolution within the various forms of hierarchical accountability. For example, Jarvis (2012, 8) also documents the changing nature of reporting and investigations. Superiors are less dependent on self-reporting by subordinates due to the central role information technology has played in the establishment of various control systems (e.g., document and budget tracking systems, online agendas, computer-use monitoring programs) that also allow for post facto scrutiny of the decisions and behavior of lower-level officials.

Further, even where there is convergence in the basic mechanisms of hierarchical accountability, there are often distinctions and nuances in design and implementation across jurisdictions. For example, while all advanced democracies involved some form of elections, the exact nature of elections differs across, and within, parliamentary and presidential systems on key matters like who citizens actually cast votes for and how votes translate into the selection of the representatives who act on their behalf. First-past-the-post electoral systems where citizens vote only for their local constituency representatives, who then in turn collectively select the government, are used in the Westminster parliamentary systems in Britain for elections to the House of Commons and in Canada at both the federal and provincial levels. In contrast, the other Westminster parliamentary systems in Australia and New Zealand and a number of other non-Westminster parliamentary systems such as the Netherlands, use forms of proportional representation that rely on different approaches to indicating voter preferences for representatives and parties. Only in some presidential systems do citizens directly elect the chief executive, usually referred to as the president.[3] All of these variations have important implications for the hierarchical accountability relationships between citizens and their elected representatives.

Formal performance assessment/management processes focused on individual civil servants are utilized in most jurisdictions. Recent interviews with officials in the Netherlands, Canada, and Australia, suggest that the general approach to performance assessments is consistent across all three countries (Jarvis 2012, 15). It is based on a periodic (rather than episodic) cycle of assessment that begins with setting expected results to be achieved in the coming year and subsequent meetings to determine whether the expected results have been achieved. Performance indicators in all three jurisdictions include a mix of behavioral and programmatic or policy outputs and outcomes. Differences between, and within, the jurisdictions, include: the number of meetings; the nature of performance ratings, whether qualitative (e.g., exceeded expected results) or quantitative (e.g., a numerical scale); whether and how information from the assessments is fed up the hierarchical chain; and, whether annual assessments are tied to financial benefits such as bonuses at the executive levels or pay increments. The interviews also suggest that the Australian approach is considerably more systematic (Jarvis

2012, 15). The style and nature of the content and assessment approach is more consistent within, and across, departments. There is also more emphasis in linking individual performance to unit and departmental level business plans in Australia.

As Wilson (1989, 302, 307) illustrates, national hierarchical arrangements can differ in nature across the culture of different countries (e.g., individual vs. organizational focus; formal vs. informal communications; rigid vs. flexible hierarchy). In addition to differences in form, there can also be variations in the substance of what individuals are held to account for via the same or similar mechanisms (for example, see Aucoin and Heintzman 2000; Bovens, Schillemans, and 't Hart 2008; and Jarvis 2009 on the different purposes of accountability). In part these variations are also due to broader issues of institutional design across countries or sub-national jurisdictions.

Another thing that should be noted about the variations of hierarchical accountability is that, overwhelmingly, the specific mechanisms are not exclusive to hierarchy. In actual practice, most of these variations can be, and are, conjoined with other mechanisms or models of accountability. For example, as discussed, for most civil servants, annual performance agreements are among the most common formal variant of hierarchical accountability. Yet, clearly the system of annual performance agreements and assessments is also an extension or form of performance measurement (see Van de Walle and Cornelissen in this handbook) and administrative accountability.

Strengths and Weaknesses

The principle strength of hierarchy as a mechanism of accountability is the same characteristic that distinguishes it from other mechanisms of accountability: the direct line of delegation and accountability between accountor and accountee. This provides two widely recognized primary benefits: greater clarity and greater sanctioning authority.

While there is some risk of overstating the lucidity of hierarchical accountability relationships, the direct relationship makes clear—at least in theory if not always in practice—who should be accountable (the individual to whom authority was delegated) to whom (the individual or body who delegated the authority) and for what (how that authority was subsequently exercised, including how lower ranks were held to account where further delegation occurred). In this way, hierarchical accountability should allow for the identification of accountability gaps, by tracing where authority is actually transferred, formally or informally, and whether appropriate corresponding reciprocal accountability arrangements are put into place and enacted. Where no accountability arrangements have followed the delegation of authority, or the mechanisms of accountability that have been put into place are not effective, an accountability gap can be said to exist (Bovens, Schillemans, and 't Hart 2008, 229).

In addition to providing clarity, hierarchy, based on direct delegation of authority, grants superiors the legitimacy to scrutinize, question, and pass judgment on the account, and—perhaps most importantly—levy sanctions or grant rewards, as they see fit. Some studies that acknowledge the limits of hierarchy also recognize that the "the relatively 'weak' mechanisms" affiliated with horizontal accountability "gain in influence through their connection with hierarchical powers," while allowing that stronger mechanisms are not necessarily always the most influential (Schillemans 2008, 191). This point is often made in relation to alternative or distributed governance arrangements like arm's length agencies or networked management approaches. It should be noted though that just because these agencies are at least notionally removed from direct interference in deciding how to accomplish the tasks they are assigned does not mean they are not hierarchically accountable to some forum. Depending on their statutory basis, they are usually accountable to the minister of the portfolio to which they belong or to Parliament via the minister for their use of resources or failure to accomplish their assigned tasks or other matters of maladministration or malfeasance.

Notwithstanding these benefits, it is also the case that hierarchical accountability does suffer some weaknesses. While the range of specific variations discussed above are all of course subject to their own specific fragilities, a number of more general points on the limits of hierarchy can also be made. First, as a point of caution, notwithstanding the simplicity of hierarchical accountability, it does not automatically follow that the actual practice of holding individuals to account is as straightforward. For example, the intervening relationships between those at the upper echelons of the chain of command and those towards the bottom add greater distance and make it particularly difficult to assemble all the necessary information to adequately hold individuals to account (Day and Klein 1987; Aucoin and Jarvis 2005; Bovens 2005).

In addition, it should go without saying that these hierarchical relationships do not occur in isolation. They are "nested" in a wider set of relationships and this affects the content and dynamics of these superior–subordinate relationships and any associated accountability processes. This can, for instance, limit the willingness of superiors to engage in scrutiny and to demand information. These problems are further exacerbated by other behaviors like blame-shifting or avoidance (Hood 2002). Challenges such as these can limit the capacity of hierarchical accountability arrangements to secure control and address wrongdoing or poor performance (Bovens 2005, 191).

Second, many of the specific variations of hierarchical accountability suffer from a lack of transparency, especially below the level of the minister. This reflects what Bovens (2005, 190) refers to as the "one for all" approach to accountability where: "processes of calling to account start at the top. The rank and file do not appear before that external forum but hide behind the broad shoulders of the minister . . . who, at least in dealings with the outside world, assumes complete responsibility and takes all the blame." In an era where the demand for transparency seems to be increasingly rising, notwithstanding potential perverse effects (see Grimmelikhuijsen 2012), it seems inconceivable that civil servants can continue to be held to account, nearly exclusively, without public or political scrutiny if accountability is not just to be done, but seen to be done. Indeed, there are signs that this is already breaking down with politicians questioning civil servants directly in a number of jurisdictions (Barberis 1998, 453; Aucoin and Jarvis 2005, 48; Bovens 2005, 197; Jarvis 2009, 535).

Third, as alluded to earlier, legitimate questions as to the goodness of fit of hierarchical accountability mechanisms do exist. These questions are largely driven from two realities. First, not all bodies are intended to be subject to, or reflective of, direct hierarchical control. Most prominently, much has been written on agencification—the rise of executive agencies, largely in the wake of the New Public Management. These organizational structures have been deliberately established to operate at "arms-length" from direct ministerial or government management or control, creating a gap in accountability for their operation up the chain of command (Aucoin and Bakvis 1988; Pierre and Peters 2000). The same holds for partnership arrangements (Howard and Phillips 2012). Second, most subordinate actors or bodies engage with a range of stakeholders who are not their immediate superiors or principals. Notwithstanding this lack of a clear, direct line that characterizes superior–subordinate relationships, these stakeholders may desire or merit holding public actors to account in their own right through participatory structures and more networked forms of governance (Peters 2010, 211). For example, while citizens sit as sovereigns at the apex of the democratic chain of command, citizens have no direct authority over the street-level bureaucrats they may encounter in accessing public services and may demand more direct means of accountability (Mulgan 2000, 568; 2003; Pollitt 2003). Further, especially as one moves away from more traditional accountability purposes, such as democratic control or assurance, to other objectives, such as organizational learning, feedback from a broader range of individuals rather than only an immediate superior can be beneficial—or even essential—to improving performance or policy (Aucoin and Heintzman 2000). Accountability creates feedback information with which public organizations may learn how to improve their conduct.

As Schillemans (2011, 388) notes, both the perceived disjuncture between the heightened independence of a range of alternative governance arrangements and the superior–subordinate relationships at the core of hierarchical accountability, as well as the range of actors who crowd the organizational fields of public sector organizations, have given rise to a range of alternative modes of accountability that can be grouped as *horizontal* forms of accountability. Many of these are discussed in subsequent chapters.

A RESEARCH AGENDA

The importance of hierarchical accountability is clear: In contemporary systems of governance, citizens do not govern directly. Instead, they rely on elected representatives to exercise power on their behalf. In turn, these elected representatives further delegate authority to appointed officials who help governments develop and implement public policy. Hierarchical accountability—the direct superior–subordinate relationships in which the former delegates authority directly to the latter and then seeks to hold them to account for the exercise of that delegated authority—instills the opportunity for those who delegate authority, starting with citizens, to maintain democratic control down the chain of command. Relationships along the chain can be both intra- and inter-organizational, and operate at political and bureaucratic levels. Without an effective system of accountability those to whom authority is delegated would be able to exercise power without regard to the wishes of the democratic sovereigns: citizens.

That being said, hierarchical accountability is not without its challenges. A failure to address the lack of transparency associated with hierarchical accountability, or the exclusionary nature of focusing solely on direct superiors over other actors—including citizens—will continue to feed the perspective that hierarchy is archaic and outmoded. This will continue to undermine the relative importance that many observers and scholars place on hierarchical accountability. Notwithstanding the privileged position hierarchical accountability has conventionally enjoyed in the literature, a significant research agenda beckons. This is the case primarily for three reasons. First, the rise in emphasis on more networked or distributed governance models in public governance and administration has, naturally, been mirrored by a growing body of literature on newer, more pluralistic accountability relationships that increasingly are viewed as being at the fore of contemporary governance, as well as the dilemmas that they pose. This seems to have led to a diminishing amount of research focused on hierarchical accountability. This shift in focus to more horizontal, mutual, and competitive performance-focused accountability approaches threatens to obscure the continuing evolution of hierarchy as an important mechanism of accountability.

Second, where research has addressed hierarchical accountability it has overwhelmingly focused on either the political level, often considering the ability or effectiveness of Parliament holding governments or their ministers to account, or on very top level civil service officials, focusing on the political–bureaucratic interface. Little research has focused directly on accountability in the lower linkages of the hierarchical chain, including internal civil service accountability below the level of top civil service officials. While some tend to be dismissive of the importance of these arrangements, believing that "real power" is concentrated nearly exclusively at upper echelons, others have recognized the importance of the hierarchical accountability interactions that occur within organizations at these lower levels as "the *sine qua non* for the other, external forms of public accountability" (Bovens 2005, 187). To the degree that some attention has been paid, it has concentrated almost exclusively on specific work arrangements (e.g., the complexities of accountability for horizontal initiatives), or the use of specific instruments (e.g., performance reporting), or as a limited aspect of a discussion of broader management reform. More attention is required here.

Finally, while the literature to date in the field of public accountability has established a strong theoretical basis for understanding accountability, broadly it suffers a dearth of empirical research (Bovens, Schillemans, and 't Hart 2008; Jarvis and Thomas 2012). There is a range of descriptive and critical research questions that demand shifting gears. While some preliminary research has been done that compares hierarchical accountability practices in a limited number of jurisdictions, greater empirical knowledge is required about convergence and divergence in the occurrence and operation of hierarchical accountability instruments in different jurisdictions. This will require a large-scale study that combines quantitative and qualitative approaches. Other questions that require answering include:

- Are hierarchical accountability mechanisms effective in holding civil servants and elected officials to account?
- Are there particular contexts under which hierarchy is more and less effective (e.g., purposefully "flat" organizations)?
- Within the context of hierarchical accountability, which types of rewards and punishments provide effective incentives to change behavior and bring about improvement in performance?
- What are the unintended consequences of hierarchical accountability and how might these be addressed (e.g., demoralization, lack of trust)?
- How do internal and external oversight bodies augment and detract from traditional models of hierarchical models of accountability?
- Under what conditions does hierarchy easily adapt to conjoin with other mechanisms of accountability?

The answers to these questions will only be determined through ongoing, robust, comparative empirical examination that relies on varied and innovative research designs and techniques required to gather evidence on how accountability processes serving different purposes actually work in different domains. A small number of studies are now slowly emerging in this tradition across accountability mechanisms (see for example, Schillemans 2007; Busuioc 2010; Brandsma 2010) that can serve as a model for this work.

ACKNOWLEDGMENTS

THE author gratefully acknowledges the invaluable comments and assistance of Herman Bakvis, Paul Thomas, Mark Bovens, Thomas Schillemans, Lawrence Buhagiar, Anne White, and Stephen Saideman in strengthening this chapter. The author alone is responsible for the analysis and conclusions drawn, including any errors.

NOTES

1. In contrast, in simple hierarchies each subordinate in the superior–subordinate relationship is accountable to only one superior, allowing that each superior may have more than one subordinate, regardless of how many levels there may be in the hierarchy.
2. Ideally, though likely rarely in practice, this is based on agreed–upon expectations and with commensurate authority and resources to fulfill those obligations. This of course raises

critical questions as to who decides whether such authority and resources are adequate to the task assigned.

3. Even in the United States, citizens do not directly elect the president. Notwithstanding the common perception, in casting their ballots voters are actually electing the members of an Electoral College, who *then* in turn elect the president.

REFERENCES

Aucoin, P. and Bakvis, H. 1988. *The Centralization-Decentralization Conundrum*. Halifax, NS: The Institute for Research on Public Policy.

Aucoin, P. and Heintzman, R. 2000. "The Dialectics of Accountability for Performance in Public Management Reform." *International Review of Administrative Sciences*, 66: 45–55.

Aucoin, P. and Jarvis, M. 2005. *Modernizing Government Accountability: A Framework for Reform*. Ottawa: Canada School for Public Service.

Barberis, P. 1998. "The New Public Management and a New Accountability." *Public Administration*, 76: 451–70.

Behn, R. D. 2001. *Rethinking Democratic Accountability*. Washington: Brookings Institution.

Bovens, M. 2005. Public Accountability, pp. 182–208 in *The Oxford Handbook of Public Management*, eds. E. Ferley, C. Pollitt, and L. E. Lynn. New York: Oxford University Press.

Bovens, M. 2010. "Two Concepts of Accountability: Accountability as a Virtue and as a Mechanism." *West European Politics*, 33: 946–67.

Bovens, M., Schillemans, T., and 't Hart, P. 2008. "Does Public Accountability Work? An Assessment Tool." *Public Administration*, 86: 225–42.

Brandsma, G. J. 2010. *Backstage Europe: Comitology, Accountability and Democracy in the European Union*. Doctoral dissertation. Utrecht University.

Busuioc, M. 2010. *The Accountability of European Agencies: Legal Provisions and Ongoing Practices*. Delft: Eburon.

Considine, M. 2002. "The End of the Line? Accountable Governance in the Age of Networks, Partnerships, and Joined-Up Services." *Governance: An International Journal of Policy, Administration, and Institutions*, 15: 21–40.

Day, P. and Klein, R. 1987. *Accountabilities: Five Public Services*. London: Tavistock.

Dicke, L. and Ott, J. S. 1999. "Public Agency Accountability in Human Services." *Public Productivity and Management Review*, 22: 502–16.

Grant, R. and Keohane, R. 2005. "Accountability and Abuses of Power in World Politics." *American Political Science Review*, 99: 29–43.

Grimmelikhuijsen, S. G. 2012. *Transparency and Trust: An Experimental Study of Online Disclosure and Trust in Government*. Doctoral dissertation. Utrecht University.

Hood, C. 2002. "The Risk Game and the Blame Game." *Government and Opposition*, 37: 15–37.

Howard, C. and Phillips, S. 2012. Moving Away from Hierarchy: Do Horizontality, Partnerships, and Distributed Governance Really Signify the End of Accountability?, pp. 314–41 in *From New Public Management to New Public Governance*, eds. H. Bakvis and M. D. Jarvis. Montreal: McGill-Queens University Press.

Jarvis, M. D. 2009. "The Adoption of the Accounting Officer System in Canada: Changing Relationships?" *Canadian Public Administration*, 52: 525–47.

Jarvis, M. D. 2012. *The Black Box of Bureaucracy: Interrogating Accountability in the Public Service*. In CPSA (Canadian Political Science Association) Annual Conference. Edmonton, 15 June 2012.

Jarvis, M. D. and Thomas, P. 2012. The Limits of Accountability: What Can and Cannot Be Accomplished in the Dialectics of Accountability?, pp. 271–313 in *From New Public Management to New Public Governance*, eds. H. Bakvis and M. D. Jarvis. Montreal: McGill-Queens University Press.

Kaufman, H. 1967. *The Forest Ranger: A Study in Administrative Behavior*. Washington: RFF Press.

Mulgan, R. 2000. "'Accountability': An Ever-Expanding Concept?" *Public Administration*, 78: 555–73.

Mulgan, R. 2003. *Holding Power to Account: Accountability in Modern Democracies*. Houndmills: Palgrave/MacMillan.

Peters, B. G. 2010. "Bureaucracy and Democracy." *Public Organization Review*, 10: 209–22.

Pierre, J. and Peters, B. G. 2000. *Governance, Politics and the State*. London: MacMillan Press.

Pollitt. C. 2003. *The Essential Public Manager*. London: Open University Press/McGraw-Hill.

Romzek, B. 2000. "Dynamics of Public Sector Accountability in an Era of Reform." *International Review of Administrative Sciences*, 66: 21–44.

Romzek, B. and Dubnick, M. 1987. "Accountability in the Public Sector: Lessons from the Challenger Tragedy." *Public Administration Review*, 47: 227–38.

Romzek, B. and Dubnick, M. 1998. Accountability, pp. 6–11 in *International Encyclopedia of Public Policy and Administration. Vol. 1*, ed. J. Shafritz. Boulder, CO: Westview Press.

Schillemans, T. 2007. *Verantwoording in de Schaduw van de Macht: Horizontale Verantwoording bij Zelfstandige Uitvoeringsorganisaties*. Den Haag: Lemma.

Schillemans, T. 2008. "Accountability in the Shadow of Hierarchy: The Horizontal Accountability of Agencies." *Public Organization Review*, 8: 175–94.

Schillemans, T. 2011. "Does Horizontal Accountability Work? Evaluating Potential Remedies for the Accountability Deficit of Agencies." *Administration and Society*, 43: 387–416.

Scott, C. 2000. "Accountability in the Regulatory State." *Journal of Law and Society*, 27: 38–60.

Strøm, K. 2000. "Delegation and Accountability in Parliamentary Democracies." *European Journal of Political Research*, 37: 261–89.

Weber, M. 1968. *Bureaucracy: Economy and Society*. New York: Bedminster Press.

Wilson, J. 1989. *Bureaucracy: What Government Agencies Do and Why They Do It*. New York: Basic Books.

CHAPTER 26

··

ACCOUNTING AND AUDITING

··

CHRISTIE HAYNE AND STEVEN E. SALTERIO

Accomptare

··

Accountability gains its original meaning from the discipline of accounting (Bovens 2006). Indeed, according to some scholars accountability and accounting share the same etymological roots in the Latin word "*accomptare*" (to account) (Oldroyd 1995). Accountability has grown from those roots to having a diversity of meanings (Bovens 2006) but the core idea is still the provision of an account for actions to others who have some right to require the provider make an account. Financial statements provide one means of public accountability common to all entities: public sector, not-for-profit or third sector, publicly traded corporations, or private limited companies, albeit it is confined to providing a financial account with limited qualitative elaborations in what are known as the footnotes to the financial statements. Further, depending on the type of entity under consideration (i.e., for-profit vs. government/not-for-profit), those to whom an account is to be rendered have relatively little authority to probe beyond the account presented. Given that those rendering an account may wish to put "their best face" on in the accounts, accountants acting as auditors are employed to check those accounts and hence provide external creditability through certification or audit opinion on the accounts.

Given the limited nature of the financial accounts rendered, it follows that stakeholders demand information beyond the financial such as environmental accounting and corporate social responsibility accounting. These and other diverse areas have been enumerated as areas in which accountability is critical. This chapter reflects this move to expand accountability beyond the sometimes perceived as narrow role of financial accounts.

In this chapter we examine public accountability in the context of financial accounting and auditing by addressing two questions. First, what are the relationships of public accountability facilitated by financial accounting and auditing? Second, what is the current state of research on public accountability in financial accounting and auditing, including calls for expansion of accounts beyond their historical focus on the financial? This review requires us to look at the "big picture" of the role of financial statements (including accounts beyond financial) in acts of public accountability as well as the micro roles of accountability practices and pressures on individuals involved in providing and attesting to accounts, whether financial or other.

PUBLICLY ACCOUNTABLE ENTITIES

In this section we set the institutional context for how financial accounts and certification thereof are used as a mechanism of public accountability across various entities. We discuss mainly for-profit business entities (which include "private companies" and "publicly traded corporations") but identify differences in entities that derive their funding from donations (i.e., not-for-profit or third sector entities) or are funded by taxation (i.e., governmental entities).

The Nature of the Accountability Problem

In many societies for-profit business started out with what is known as the proprietorship model where the owner-manager was directly and personally responsible for all of the activities of the entity. As businesses grew more complex and capital needs grew larger than what any one person or small group could manage, the concept of a limited liability company was developed where "owners" (i.e., shareholders) only risked their initial investment. While at first, limited liability companies had relatively few investors (in the low hundreds), the concept was expanded to allow large numbers of investors through markets to purchase shares resulting in a pool of owners/shareholders and other stakeholders (e.g., creditors, donors for not-for-profits, taxpayers for governments) separate from managers. This separation of ownership and control creates what has been called the classic agency problem.

An agency relationship is one where a principal/owner contracts an agent/manager to perform services on their behalf. The owner delegates some decision-making authority to the agent, but it is unlikely that the agent's actions to maximize his/her own utility will always align with the principal's interests. The agency theory argument focuses on two sources of agency costs: moral hazard (i.e., the likelihood that an agent will shirk due to his/her effort not being observable by the principal and attempting to provide the principal with a false report to cover up the lack of effort) and adverse selection (i.e., where the agent knows more about the current conditions or future prospects of an entity than its external stakeholders and hence has an informational advantage that can be used to falsify reports to the principal). See Scott 2011, Ch. 9 for a detailed exposition.

This owner–manager relationship in agency theory allegedly parallels the relationship between shareholders and managers of publicly traded companies: Owners of public companies are unable to observe management effort and act with much less information than managers have so there are incentives for managers to shirk or behave opportunistically. This principal–agent relationship in a publicly traded company is not that different from relationships in government/not-for-profit organizations. These organizations are also managed by agents who are responsible for acting on behalf of their respective principals: donors and voting public.

Governance refers to a variety of mechanisms intended to impact or constrain executive decision-making when there is a separation of ownership and control (Larcker, Richardson, and Tuna 2007). Various governance mechanisms offer potential remedies to reduce the inefficiencies that arise from moral hazard and adverse selection. Examples of such mechanisms include independent boards of directors, large institutional shareholders, and market mechanisms—all of which allow managers to be displaced if performance is not acceptable (Larcker, Richardson, and Tuna 2007).[1] The nature and extent of accountability between the various internal and external stakeholders of an organization is a key issue for which financial accounting statements are seen as a response.[2]

The Actors in the Financial Accounting Accountability Relationship

Figure 26.1 suggests there are two main groupings of actors, those in the governmental and not-for-profit sectors and those in the for-profit corporate sector that are affected by the state legal apparatus (e.g., statute law and court decisions) and a state-endorsed regulatory structure.

Figure 26.1 shows, in accordance with democratic ideals, that the public and its elected representatives are the source of all public accountability pressures. These accountability pressures are enacted in the laws that provide the state with institutional means to oversee governmental/not-for-profit entities as well as for-profit corporations (especially publicly traded corporations).

RELATIONSHIPS OF ACCOUNTABILITY FOR PUBLICLY TRADED CORPORATIONS

Table 26.1 describes the various ways of providing financial accountability, albeit the first and the last are the two most researched areas.

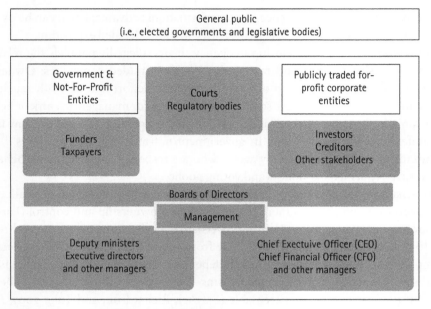

FIGURE **26.1** Actors and their accountabilities

Table 26.1 Means of accountability employed by boards of directors to various publics

- Financial Statements (all entities)
- Annual Reports (Management Discussion and Analysis (MD&A) of results is required for-profit publicly traded corporations; rest of annual report is voluntary for all entities but most, except the smallest, provide one)
- Internal Control over Financial Reporting Certification (for-profit publicly traded corporations)
- Tax information forms (not-for-profit organizations)
- Corporate social and environmental reporting (voluntary for all entities)
- Auditors reports:
  - Annual Financial Statement Audit (all entities, some not-for-profits that meet a size test are not required but recommended)
  - Auditor's Report on Internal Control over Financial Reporting (for-profit publicly traded corporations traded on US stock exchange based anywhere in the world that meet a size test)
- Value for money audits (mainly governmental entities)

Publicly traded for-profit corporations (hereafter "public companies") are owned by shareholders who notionally elect Boards of Directors (see right hand side of Figure 26.1). Boards theoretically "run" the corporation through hiring, firing, and compensating managers who have talent to run the corporation in a competitive capitalist economy. The Board is intended to be an oversight body representing the owners (Anand 2004). However, research shows management teams, especially the Chief Executive Officers (CEOs), are the drivers of corporate governance especially in cases

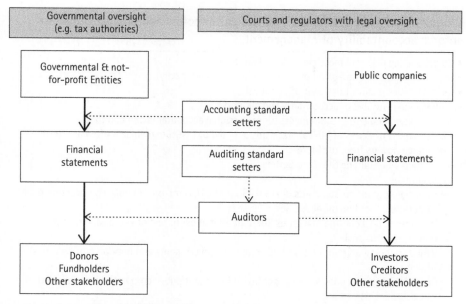

FIGURE **26.2** Interactions among governance actors

where the public company has a large number of widely dispersed shareholders none of whom has a controlling interest in the company (Cohen, Krishnamoorthy, and Wright 2002; 2010).

The environment of public accountability for public companies includes courts and other regulatory bodies mandated by government—see top right of Figure 26.2 and Table 26.2. Figure 26.2 describes graphically how the two focal accounts examined in this chapter (i.e., financial accounting statements and audit reports over the financial statements) are employed by the actors to respond to accountability pressures.

In this chapter we leave aside courts, as with the exception of the USA, where there is a very active private citizen use of courts to enforce investor rights, courts elsewhere tend to focus on government enforcement of the laws that apply to corporations. In most countries, securities commissions are the principal government body charged with the responsibility to oversee regulation of securities traded in their respective country. Although the powers and responsibilities of securities commissions vary between countries, generally, these agencies set and enforce the rules for their stock exchange(s) and the financial (and other) reporting requirements for listed companies.

Laws (e.g., Securities Acts of 1933 and 1934 in the USA) require public companies to provide to their shareholders audited financial statements that have been approved by the Board of Directors (see right hand column of Figure 26.2) to provide financial accountability to their shareholders.[3] These laws recognize that the Board and management have different interests which may also differ from those of shareholders, hence public companies are required to provide assurance that the financial statements are truthful. Specifically, an audit of the financial statements is intended to provide

Table 26.2 Mechanisms to aid in boards of directors and broader public to enforce accountability of management

- Courts and legal system more generally (all entities)
- Securities regulators (for-profit publicly traded corporations only)
- Tax authorities (mainly not-for-profit entities)
- Professional institutes of accountants and auditors
  - Examination and entry requirements for professional accountants and auditors
  - Enforcement of Codes of Ethical Standards adopted by institute members often as a result of delegated powers from the State
- Accounting and Auditing Standard Setters
  - Accounting:
    - Financial Accounting Standards Board (FASB in the USA for-profit public corporations, private corporations, not-for-profit entities)
    - International Accounting Standards Board (IASB in most of rest of world for-profit publicly traded corporations)
    - Various national accounting standard setters for governments and not-for-profit entities
  - Auditing:
    - Public Company Accounting Oversight Board (for-profit public corporations traded on USA stock exchanges)
    - International Auditing and Assurance Standards Board (for-profit public corporations in the rest of the world and NOT traded on USA stock exchange, not-for-profit entities)
    - Various national audit standard setters for government auditing

shareholders and other users with reasonable assurance that the information contained therein is free from material misstatement according to measurement standards denoted historically as "GAAP" (generally accepted accounting principles). De facto, auditors are appointed by an organization's management team, even in countries where de jure auditors are appointed by the shareholders or boards of directors. However, recent corporate reforms have emphasized that the Board needs to take charge of the selection of auditors although the effectiveness of this requirement is questionable (Anand 2004; Anand and Maloney 2004).

The existence of standards for accounting (GAAP) and for how to audit those accounts (known as "GAAS"—generally accepted auditing standards) necessitates defining the role of standard-setters. As one commentator states "Standard setters define the accounting language that management uses to communicate with the firm's external stakeholders" (Healy and Whalen 1999, 366).[4] Governments also create regulatory authorities or agencies to regulate the audit practices of public accountants. In the US, the Securities and Exchange Commission is the regulatory body that appoints the members of the Public Company Accounting Oversight Board (PCAOB) that creates auditing standards and carries out quality inspections of audit work by the audit firms (PCAOB 2011). This is a rather recent development in common-law countries that has at its genesis the US Sarbanes-Oxley Act (SOX) of 2002. Because of the creation of the PCAOB, other countries around the world have adopted similar oversight structures for public company auditors (e.g., Canadian Public Accountability Board in Canada).

Relationships of Accountability for Government/ Not-For-Profit Organizations

Up to this point, the description of the relationships of accountability has focused primarily on public companies. We now focus briefly on the differences in relationships of accountability for the government/not-for-profit sectors as seen on the left hand side of Figure 26.2. Government and not-for-profit organizations are required by the non-distribution constraint to use any surplus (revenues in excess of expenditures in a period) in subsequent periods to achieve their mission. Some countries give not-for-profits the choice as to whether they incorporate or not, and this decision affects the extent of accountability expected from not-for-profits since incorporating makes a not-for-profit a legal entity. As a legal entity, not-for-profits are treated like and expected to be accountable in ways more analogous to a public company. Like public companies, not-for-profit organizations are also obliged to follow accounting standards in providing their accountability reports, albeit in recent years there has been a tendency to develop sector-specific standards for government and not-for-profit entities.

While public accounting firms often supply audit services to not-for-profit entities and government corporations, government accounts themselves are frequently audited by officers of the national legislative body.[5] Towards the bottom left hand side of Figure 26.2, notice that government/not-for-profit organizations are accountable to the public, but more specifically, to voters and donors. Compared to the accountability demanded of public companies by the public (i.e., shareholders and other stakeholders), government/not-for-profit organizations are not subject to market discipline for their products/services (i.e., they do not have to be profitable), nor are they subject to shareholder discipline (i.e., not-for-profit funders cannot sell their interest to third parties nor be taken over in a hostile takeover). Due in part to the accountability requirements of governments to their taxpayers, a specialized type of auditing has grown up around the audit of government operations known variously as "value for money," "performance auditing," or "efficiency auditing."[6] A value-for-money audit investigates whether the government received "good value" for the funds expended (English, Guthrie, Broadbent, and Laughlin 2010; NAO 2011; Radcliffe 1997; 1998), that is, providing an account of the economy, efficiency, and effectiveness of funds expended (Radcliffe 1997).

MACRO EMPIRICAL RESEARCH IN ACCOUNTING AND AUDITING ON ACCOUNTABILITY

Defining accountability in the business world, at least as far as financial accountability goes, and examining public accountability in research is complicated by several critical questions: "accountability by who?," "accountability to whom?," "accountability for what?," and "accountability how?" The question of to whom public companies are accountable and what it is they are accountable for are paramount within the macro level research on public accountability.

There is a long history of theoretical debate about who public companies are accountable to within the business and accounting literatures that dates back at least to the 1930s (e.g., Berle (1931) versus Dodd (1932)) and that continues to the present day (e.g., Schweiker (1993) versus Shearer (2002)). This debate is far from over as others continue to theorize about the question of accountable to whom.

Accountability to whom

We begin with Sinclair (1995) whose research shows that "accountability to whom?" depends on the context of the entity. She finds that government executives/managers are caught up in a web of five different versions of the question "accountable to whom?" The first three are well known: political accountability represents a public servants' authority to act on behalf of elected representatives, though the public servant is actually directly accountable to the minister; public accountability represents public servants' direct accountability to the public; and managerial accountability describes the responsibility a supervisor has to monitor a subordinate's transformation of resources into outputs. The other two forms of accountability Sinclair identifies are professional accountability which reflects one's sense of duty as a member of a professional group, and personal accountability which reflects a person's fidelity to their own conscience. The CEOs' descriptions contained contradictions over language, attitude, and feelings: when talking about accountability and being held accountable, they described each accountability with structural discourse and personal discourse. These discourses make sense of the problematic ways in which CEOs think about and experience different forms of accountability. Sinclair shows that through their CEOs, organizations are accountable to a variety of groups yet only have one language through which to do most of their accounting, the financial accounts.

In the not-for-profit sector O'Dwyer and Unerman (2008) examine the Irish section of a non-governmental organization (NGO), Amnesty International, to highlight the unfortunate consequences of increasing accountability. Historically, Amnesty International sought to provide accountability to a wide range of stakeholders. Amnesty recognized a need for and sought heightened accountability because of increased competition for donor funding, to garner additional credibility, and also to protect and legitimize their name. Amnesty's desire for increased accountability resulted in what Roberts (1991) coins hierarchical accountability where the balance of power in a relationship is not equal. At the expense of holistic accountability, Amnesty International began to privilege high-net-worth donors. This focus on powerful donors narrowed the objectives Amnesty was able to pursue and consequently constrained or altogether eliminated some of the organization's social and environmental pursuits. Because identifying all potential beneficiaries of Amnesty's work was impossible, it was much easier for the NGO to focus on upward accountability to donors that hold significant economic and political power over Amnesty.

In public companies and more generally the for-profit sector, Gibbins and Newton (1994) show that for public accountants (i.e., auditors) the answer to the question "accountable to whom?" leads to many possible responses. Via survey data they empirically demonstrate that demands for accountability can stem from different types of relationships, for example, social, contractual, and hierarchical (e.g., supervisor/subordinate) including the relationship with the corporation that hires them to audit their financial accounts. These various demanders of accountability might neither agree with what is to be accounted for nor how it is to be accounted for as each source of accountability exerts varying degrees of pressure, and accountants' perception of the degree of pressure also varies.

Accountable for What

In the for-profit sector the most straightforward answer to the question "accountable for what?" is the provision of financial statements. The production and certification of financial statements also shares an advantage on the surface that it appears to be a uniform means of accountability that is consistent across all sectors. Accounting information appears to enable accountability at a distance; accounting resolves problems of trust and divergent interests that physical distance and organizational hierarchy create (Roberts and Scapens 1985). Accounting negotiates and defines significant events, communicates and enforces expectations, and enacts power relations (Roberts 1991).

Roberts (1991) theorizes accounting as a vehicle or medium that is enacted in the network of accountability in Figures 26.1 and 26.2. The traditional view (Benston 1982) has accounting as a neutral and objective set of techniques that passively and accurately report organizational results. An alternative account of accounting is that it becomes implicated in social and organizational processes such that the mere fact of rendering an account also transforms what it is purporting to measure and represent (Roberts 1991).

While accounting and accountants are called upon to broaden the set of public accountabilities of the public company, including such behavior in financial accounts is argued to be difficult because (1) measuring social benefits is very complex and (2) reporting social costs that result from public companies' behavior would also be hard to measure (Benston 1982). Of course, there are alternatives to financially incorporating socially responsible behavior in the financial reports of an organization. Instead, non-financial summaries of socially responsible activities can be detailed (e.g., corporate social reporting), or information releases other than publications of financial statements can be employed (Gray 1992).

Cooper and Owen (2007) evaluate the state of corporate social reporting by examining the contents of social/sustainability reports. The researchers focus on nominees of the 2003 ACCA UK Sustainability Reporting Awards, and as a result they select 12 companies whose reports are considered to be leading-edge. Cooper and Owen report that some companies showed initiative by hiring external specialists to guide the Corporate Social Reporting (CSR) steering committees and to collect input and concerns from various stakeholder groups. However, in a strong analogy of the control that management has over the audit function (see the discussion in the micro section next), rather than having the stakeholders appoint the consultants, the consultants are appointed by management, they report to management, and the discussion forums developed by the steering committees are not linked back to corporate decision-making. Thus, rather than having CSR reporting embedded within the corporate decision-making apparatus, it remains isolated from those "more important" operating decisions with financial overtones. Cooper and Owen concluded that they did not come across any examples where stakeholder concerns surpassed shareholder concerns, and so they were skeptical about whether any of the stakeholder consultations influenced accountability at all. Their analyses suggested therefore that the increase in social reporting seemed to be mainly rhetoric instead of enhanced public accountability.

Instead of focusing on reports separate from the financial accounts, Gray (1992) takes a closer look at the implications of accounting for the environment and provides some suggestions on how existing financial accounting practices might account for environmentalism. Conceptually, Gray challenges the reductionist quality of traditional economic theory where environmental issues are considered an externality and thus insignificant in accounting practice. Gray makes a case for the environment as an "internality" (as opposed to traditional economic dogma that corporate effects on the environment are an "externality" that corporations do not get charged for) and argues for social accounting where accountability, community, and environment are key tenets. A wide range of opportunities for environmental accounting exist: compliance and ethical reports/audits; waste and energy reports/audits; environmental budgets; environmental impact assessments; environmental and social reports/audits; and environmental asset accounting and maintenance (Gray 1992).

The two studies just reviewed only consider the consequences of non-financial reporting within the organization, but the consequences external to the organization are also important. To date, this is a relatively under-researched topic, but one that seems to be increasing in attention. Moneva and Cuellar (2009) show that while financial environmental disclosures result in market valuation, non-financial environmental disclosures do not. Similarly, in a sample of Swedish companies, Hassel, Nilsson, and Nyquistc (2005) find that environmental investments represent increased costs; environmental performance had a negative effect on firm earnings and market value. Contrary to these findings, research also shows that the perception of corporate sustainability shifted from a costly waste to a future investment from 2003 to 2010 while the perception of sustainability reporting lost its positive effects detected in 2007 and 2008 (Lopatta and Kaspereit 2011).

Performance Accountability

Accountants and accounting-like requirements (e.g., standards) are often deeply implicated in organizations being held accountable for performance in other ways than financial. For example, Neu (2006) reports on the effect of one Canadian provincial government's performance accountability requirements on its education system.

Rather than focusing on dollars and cents, schools and school boards were required to account for the results they achieved relating to targets set by the government, in order to receive continued funding—accordingly, the government changed the required type, amount, and flow of information. The new accounting and account-ability requirements focus on whether schools are using resources to their greatest potential, comparing actual results to government-determined expectations (e.g., analogous to accounting standards), identifying any necessary improvements, and reporting this information to a much larger network. Increasing the accountabil-ity mechanisms (e.g., reporting education test results on the Alberta Learning web-site[7]) creates a normalizing gaze (grounded in Foucauldian theory; see Foucault 1979; Macintosh 1994) that Neu claims reconstituted the public space of education by shifting power, reorganizing social groups, and introducing new ways of talking and behaving. A new industry was borne from these changes (e.g., school performance rankings), and schools allegedly became more efficient in their allocation/use of resources (Neu 2006).

Performance accountability outside the financial statements is also practiced in the public company realm. Similar to the normalizing gaze noted in Neu (2006), Roberts, Sanderson, Barker, and Hendry (2006) report disciplinary effects that arise when chief executives and finance directors meet with fund managers and institutional investors. Normally, the interaction between companies and investors occurs over distance via documents, so financial statements serve as the key accountability mechanism. Face-to-face meetings offer a different accountability pressure and provide an opportunity for investors to hold managers accountable for different things. Investors may hold manag-ers accountable by posing a variety of questions to "test" managerial ability about such subjects as the familiarity of managers with their organization, with the industry and the markets; whether they have a united strategic vision; whether they follow through on their intentions; and whether they are operating on behalf of shareholders or in their own self-interest (Roberts et al. 2006; Gaved 1997).

Roberts et al. (2006) find these meetings serve as a critical form of accountability between companies and investor representatives. The company's executives undergo an intense amount of preparation and rehearsal so that they are prepared to answer ques-tions carefully, and, more importantly, so that any answers they provide tell the same story among different executives. Although the scrutiny results in high levels of anxiety among company managers, it is an opportunity for investors to see management tell their story and paint a picture of their firm. In these meetings, managers are constituted by being seen and investors have a rare opportunity to test their understanding of the company rather than have to depend only on financial statements and other public information. The key theme Roberts et al. (2006, 286) suggest they uncovered in the analysis of these meetings is that they are an exercise of disciplinary power: "Only in the face-to-face meetings do executives encounter directly their vulnerability to the inves-tors' gaze and it is this [Roberts et al.] would argue that enforces the weight of normal-izing judgement."

Summary of Macro Level Research in Accounting and Auditing

Throughout the discussion of macro level research, we have demonstrated that a clear answer does not exist to the question of to whom entities in the for-profit sector are accountable. The same inconclusiveness is found in the discussion of what it is that these entities should provide accounts about. Yet despite this inconclusiveness, the macro level research has informed those studying accountability about the production and certification of financial accounts as well as the potential means to expand those accounts to areas of increasing relevance to society, such as corporate social responsibility and environmental accounting.

MICRO EMPIRICAL RESEARCH

Accountability research in accounting and auditing at the micro level focuses on the underlying rationale for why the audit exists and under what conditions the auditor's report over the financial statements can actually add value to this accountability activity of management. This relationship can be seen in the bottom right hand corner of Figure 26.2. This research draws again extensively on agency theory to motivate its investigations. Another stream of micro research on accountability focuses on how accountability relationships within the audit firm, and between the audit firm and those who pay for its services, leads to higher quality auditing, hence higher quality accountability reports by the managers to the stakeholders. This research draws heavily on the work of Tetlock (1983) and his analysis of the various pressures that can result in enhanced or hindered accountability among parties. The focus in this stream of research is therefore the individual auditor and his/her interaction with the audit firm, auditing standards, and accounting standards as seen in the center column of Figure 26.2.

Enhancing the Quality of Financial Statements to Serve as Accountability Reports

A classic solution to the agency problem is that the principal (i.e., the Board on behalf of the shareholders) offers a relatively low wage contract to the agent (i.e., the managers) assuming that the agent will engage in value-reducing activities by taking advantage of informational problems associated with moral hazard and adverse selection. Being rational actors, managers seek to find ways to increase their compensation. Theoretical research suggests that a monitor, or an auditor (see Watts and Zimmerman 1986, Ch. 13 for a summary of this early research), will be hired to independently verify the claims of the agent (i.e., management) to the stakeholders of an entity as long as the monitoring costs are less than the increase in the value of the firm due to a reduction in agency costs. Hence, the argument is that managers will voluntarily engage an independent auditor to attest to their reports as long as they can share in the increased value of the firm resulting from the audit report creating an endogenous demand for auditing without regulation.

For reasons that are not altogether clear, albeit largely historical (Chow 1993), the current institutional setting has the managers hire, fire, and compensate the auditors, the very people that are supposed to render an independent opinion about the quality of managers' accountability reports to third parties (Knechel, Salterio, and Ballou 2007, Ch. 2). While legal form, especially since 2002 with the passage in the USA of SOX (2002), may have an independent committee of the board of directors or indeed the shareholders as the group formally hiring, firing, and compensating the auditor (Anand 2004), because management has to work with the audit firm they retain a dominant voice in "recommending" the hiring, firing, and compensation of the auditor (Fiolleau, Hoang, Jamal, and Sunder 2013). Further, before the recent passage of SOX (and of many equivalent rules and regulations around the world) audit firms were free to sell virtually any service they wanted to their audit clients on a consulting basis except where it led them to audit their own work (e.g., auditors could not be the book-keepers for a firm they audited). These non-audit services came to represent a very large portion of the revenues of audit firms, often equaling and on occasion dwarfing the size of the audit fee (Frankel, Johnson, and Nelson 2002). The question then arose whether the auditor was truly an independent monitor of the management's accountability reports. Finally, given the much higher profit margins for such consulting services and the inside track that the audit firm often had in landing such consulting contracts, audit firms had begun in the 1970s to "low ball" the price charged for the audit in order to gain this inside track on the more profitable consulting services (DeAngelo 1981).

The classic research definition (as opposed to a professional code of ethics definition) of auditor independence in accounting was proposed by DeAngelo (1981). She defined independence as whether auditors, after discovering a material misstatement in the financial statements made by managers, will report the misstatement to the principals. Her theoretical analysis suggested that, holding all else equal, larger audit firms will produce higher quality audits as they have more to lose in terms of both fees and clients if it is discovered that they are not independent and have not reported material misstatements. This finding holds in her analysis even in the presence of high non-audit services fees and low-balling the price of the audit in order to obtain the inside track on these consulting engagements.

An extensive empirical literature has evolved to examine the effects of audit and non-audit fees as proxies for the extent of auditor independence from management (Francis 2004; 2011). The typical study in this research stream relates the fee data to some measure of the quality of the manager's financial reporting after controlling for various determinants of audit fees that are unrelated to auditor independence concerns (e.g., firm size, the amount of debt, etc.). With limited exceptions (Frankel et al. 2002), most large-scale studies of hundreds to thousands of firms failed to find any significant association between fees to auditors and the quality of financial reporting, suggesting that the current institutional arrangement is not problematic (Francis 2004). In recent years, however, research has focused on settings where management is motivated to produce a false report (i.e., when the firm is facing potential bankruptcy) and these studies are beginning to find associations between fees to auditors and management's financial reporting quality (Blay and Geiger 2013). Indeed, Blay and Geiger (2013) suggest that the audit fee being paid by the firm to the auditor (or more precisely the anticipation of future audit fees) is just as likely to lead to auditors allowing lower financial reporting quality by managers as non-audit fees.

Individual Auditor Accountability Pressures

The assumption made in DeAngelo (1981) is that all audit firms could develop technology that would lead to an equal likelihood of detecting material misstatements in managers' financial reports. Other researchers realized however that auditors are people and that people can be motivated (and demotivated) to perform audits with higher degrees of likelihood of detecting material misstatements. These researchers drew on the seminal work of Tetlock (1983) to examine both the positive and negative effects of interpersonal accountability pressure on individual auditors given how the audit firm is organized, the relationship with managers they are reporting to, and the interactions they have as professionals with standards.[8]

Gibbins and Newton (1994) validated the assumption that auditors believed themselves to be accountable to many people. Indeed, the hierarchical structure of an audit firm with its intensive multiple reviews of auditors' working papers (i.e., the evidence they collect about whether the financial statements are misstated) has been described by some accounting researchers as one giant accountability-inducing organization (Rich, Solomon, and Trotman 1997). In addition, there are pressures from the accounting profession and latterly from regulators of that profession to ensure that professional auditing and accounting standards (produced by various standard-setters) are met via third-party inspection of the quality of the audit work on individual audits (DeFond 2010). Finally, there is accountability to the management of the entity as noted above; the auditor is paid by the management of the entity that hires them to carry out the audit. Hence, the auditor is enmeshed in a matrix of accountability relationships that may have very different effects on how the auditor performs his or her work.

Kennedy (1993; 1995) explicitly developed a framework for debiasing auditor's judgments that concluded that process accountability would lead to reductions in auditor biases that were effort- or motivation-related and demonstrated this with respect to the recency bias (Hogarth and Einhorn 1992). As audit researchers were well-versed in the heuristics and biases paradigm (Tversky and Kahneman 1974) it was natural that they investigate whether the hierarchical accountability in an audit firm led to better performance in the collection and interpretation of audit evidence. Researchers therefore explored the limits of accountability to improve auditor judgments in various settings (e.g., collectability of amounts owed to the firm, likelihood of bankruptcy, etc.), who they were held accountable to (e.g., the attitude of the superior in the audit firm who was reviewing their work, client management, etc.) and with respect to a variety of biases that had been documented to affect auditor judgments (e.g., time pressure, dilution effect, recency effect, etc.) (Turner 2001; Glover 1997; Hoffman and Patton 1997; Asare, Trompeter, and Wright 2000; Cohen and Trompeter 1998). On the whole, the research found that accountability was an important force in auditor performance but that it frequently interacted with the setting and was not necessarily effective on all biases. Further, it seemed that auditors would tailor their position to whomever was salient in the scenario as the one they should be accountable to, including client management.

A second phase of research in this area focused on when and where accountability might be effective in improving auditor performance by examining factors that might mediate its effectiveness (e.g., auditor knowledge, problem-solving ability, and task complexity as in Kao (1999)) and when accountability itself might mediate the effectiveness of other forces at work in the auditor's world (Tan, Ng, and Mak 2002). As the most recent decade ended, researchers were circling back to the original finding in Gibbins and Newton (1994). Bagley (2010) found that auditors experience increased negative affect from their work as the complexity of the accountability pressures grows with multiple and not completely consistent actors that the auditor is being held accountable to. Interestingly, she only found performance differences on relatively routine tasks whereas the more complex judgmental tasks were not affected by the multiple accountabilities or the increased negative affect attributed to them.

Summary of Micro Level Research in Accounting and Auditing

Micro levels of research in accounting and auditing reflect themes explored elsewhere in this book, issues related to agency theory at the individual actor level and to social psychology research on accountability. These studies allow us to understand how "independent" directors have come increasingly to rely on auditors to be an "independent from management" source of information in carrying out their governance activities, while at the same time the auditor, by being held to account by the management of companies via audit fees and appointment practices, struggles to provide this "independent" account to directors. Furthermore, this struggle plays out within the audit firm itself as it seeks to deal with pressure from client management to keep the audit fee low while at the same time an opposite demand by regulators for "higher quality" auditing adds pressures to do more audit work at a higher cost. Furthermore, at the individual auditor level, accounting and auditing researchers have demonstrated once again that context matters and while accountability theories from social psychology are important motivators of the research, one cannot simply expect that the same results demonstrated in the psychology lab will be found in the applied audit context.

CONCLUDING COMMENTS

While much progress has been made in research on public accountability in accounting and auditing, there is little doubt that much remains to be done. Ever increasing stakeholder demands, changing standards and regulation, lobbying by activist groups, and other influences ensure accountability as a topic ripe for further investigation.

Further, while we document that diverse accountability pressures on individual auditors are not new (cf. Gibbins and Newton (1994) report on research carried out twenty years or more ago), the results of these conflicting pressures are only beginning to be understood by researchers. It is unclear to us whether regulators, standards setters, and indeed the third parties who rely on financial accounts to make decisions, understand the myriad of possible effects that these demands for accountability have on the accountants who produce and the auditors who certify such information. At a time when many question the ability of accountants to produce and certify financial accounts, the techniques and formats of auditing and accounting appear to be taken as unproblematic in the calls to extend the underlying principles of these reports to domains beyond the financial.

Indeed, over the last decade, the explosion of an "audit society" (Power 1997) indicates that "audit" has taken on many new guises and forms, many of which are far removed from the financial statement audit (e.g., audits of internal control, risk, performance measurement). During the same period, corporate failures such as Enron have surfaced and shaken the public's faith in the assurance provided by audit services. Cases like Enron might well be signals that financial audit needs substantial rethinking, not so much as to the practices but rather as to the motivations of those who practice it. In other words, are the incentives of the auditors too closely aligned with those of management instead of with those stakeholders that the account is to be rendered to? Similar issues are bound to unfold as researchers explore further the implications of the expansion of the "audit society" in empirical research (Free, Salterio, and Shearer 2009) that features settings with similar institutional arrangements.

To conclude, we have attempted to sensitize the reader to a set of macro studies on public accountability in accounting including the incentives of managers to commit fraud and auditors to report honestly; the inherent conflicts of interests in having, in most cases, the auditor being hired, compensated, and even fired by the reporting entity, let alone more obvious conflicts of interest over the auditor providing non-audit services that he/she then audits; and how notions of accountability determine what the entity accounts for and how such accountabilities are enacted. Further, we have discussed and evaluated micro-related research on public accountability mainly focusing on how the auditor can be made a more effective actor in facilitating the public accountability of various entities through accountability pressures within the hierarchical audit firm.

Notes

1. To detail an example further, since ownership and control is separated, shareholders must rely on boards of directors to represent their interests, and so the board is responsible for overseeing the governance guidelines and policies of publicly held companies. It is suggested that over time, boards become so dominated by the management of an organization that their oversight role becomes ineffective and executives end up with substantive authority (Berle and Means 1932).

2. External stakeholder groups include shareholders, debt holders, creditors, suppliers, and customers. In contrast, internal stakeholders include the board of directors, executives, and other employees.

3. Companies must prepare four key financial statements: a statement of financial position, comprehensive income, changes in equity, and cash flows (the first three are more commonly known as a balance sheet, income statement, and retained earnings). Audited financial statements are made public at least annually in a company's annual report which includes a variety of other information (e.g., CEO's report, auditor's report) although more frequent reporting in cases without an audit may be called for (e.g., quarterly in the U.S.A., semi-annually in most European countries). The annual report contains the Management Discussion and Analysis (MD&A) that offers a narrative account of how the company has performed in the eyes of management. Further, the financial statements are supplemented with "notes" that provide readers with details of the accounting policies chosen, the particulars of certain computations, alternative ways of measurement, and more detail about some of the line items on the financial statements.

4. Until recently, standards for accounting and auditing were a local phenomenon varying from country to country with local standard setters devising and disseminating their own set of unique standards. Recently, there has been a significant adoption of international accounting and auditing standards (Deloitte 2011; IFAC 2010).

5. Auditors General in many British Commonwealth countries and the General Accounting Office in the USA are two examples of what have become known collectively as Supreme Audit Institutions. See <http://www.intosai.org/>.

6. See the Comprehensive Auditing Foundation at <http://www.ccaf-fcvi.com>.

7. See <http://education.alberta.ca/admin/testing.aspx>.

8. It is interesting to note that Tetlock himself actually was briefly involved in audit judgment research on accountability. See Buchman, Tetlock, and Reed (1996).

References

Anand, A. I. 2004. "Shareholder Isolation and the Regulation of Auditors." *The University of Toronto Law Journal*, 54: 1–44.

Anand, A. I. and Maloney, N. 2004. "Reform of the Audit Process and the Role of Shareholder Voice. Transatlantic Perspectives." *European Business Organizations Law Journal*, 5: 223–92.

Asare, S. K., Trompeter, G. M., and Wright, A. M. 2000. "The Effect of Accountability and Time Budgets on Auditors' Testing Strategies." *Contemporary Accounting Research*, 17 :539–60.

Bagley, P. L. 2010. "Negative Affect. A Consequence of Multiple Accountabilities in Auditing." *Auditing: A Journal of Practice and Theory*, 29: 141–57.

Benston, G. J. 1982. "Accounting and Corporate Accountability." *Accounting, Organizations and Society*, 7: 87–105.

Berle, A. A. 1931. "Corporate Powers as Powers in Trust." *Harvard Law Review*, 44: 1049–59.

Berle, A. A. and Means, G. C. 1932. *The Modern Corporation and Private Property*. New York: The MacMillan Company.

Blay, A. D. and Geiger, M. A. 2013. "Auditor Fees and Auditor Independence. Evidence from Going Concern Reporting Decisions." *Contemporary Accounting Research*, 30: 579-606.

Bovens, M. 2006. *Analysing and Assessing Public Accountability: A Conceptual Framework.* European Governance Papers, No. C-06-01.

Buchman, T. A., Tetlock, P. E. and Reed, R. O. 1996. "Accountability and Auditor's Judgments About Contingent Events." *Journal of Business Finance and Accounting,* 23: 379–98.

Chow, C. 1993. "The Impacts of Regulation on Bondholder and Shareholder Wealth. The Case of the Securities Acts." *The Accounting Review,* 58: 485–520.

Cohen, J. R. and Trompeter, G. M. 1998. "An Examination of Factors Affecting Audit Practice Development." *Contemporary Accounting Research,* 15: 481–504.

Cohen, J., Krishnamoorthy, G., and Wright, A. 2002. "Corporate Governance and the Audit Process." *Contemporary Accounting Research,* 19: 573–94.

Cohen, J., Krishnamoorthy, G., and Wright, A. 2010. "Corporate Governance in the Post-Sarbanes-Oxley Era: Auditors' Experiences." *Contemporary Accounting Research,* 27: 751–86.

Cooper, S. M. and Owen, D. L. 2007. "Corporate Social Reporting and Stakeholder Accountability. The Missing Link." *Accounting, Organizations and Society,* 32: 649–67.

DeAngelo, L. E. 1981. "Auditor Independence, 'Low Balling,' and Disclosure Regulation." *Journal of Accounting and Economics,* 3: 113–27.

DeFond, M. L. 2010. "How Should the Auditors Be Audited? Comparing the PCAOB Inspections With the AICPA Peer Reviews." *Journal of Accounting and Economics,* 49: 104–108.

Deloitte. 2011. *Use of IFRS by jurisdiction.* Deloitte Global Services Limited—IAS Plus. Retrieved from <http://www.iasplus.com/country/useias.htm#?>.

Dodd, E. M. 1932. "For Whom Are Corporate Managers Trustees?" *Harvard Law Review,* 45: 1145–48.

English, L. M., Guthrie, J., Broadbent, J., and Laughlin, R. 2010. "Performance Audit of the Operational Stage of Long-Term Partnerships for the Private Sector Provision of Public Services." *Australian Accounting Review,* 20: 64–75.

Fiolleau, K. J., Hoang, K. J., Jamal, K., and Sunder, S. 2013. "How Do Regulatory Reforms To Enhance Auditor Independence Work in Practice?" *Contemporary Accounting Research,* 30: 864-890.

Foucault, M. 1979. *Discipline and Punish. The Birth of the Prison.* New York, NY: Vintage Books.

Francis, J. R. 2004. "What Do We Know About Audit Quality?" *The British Accounting Review,* 36: 345–68

Francis, J. R. 2011. "A Framework for Understanding and Researching Audit Quality." *Auditing: A Journal of Practice and Theory,* 30: 125–52.

Frankel, R. M., Johnson, M. F. and Nelson, K. K. 2002. "The Relation between Auditors' Fees for Non-Audit Services and Earnings Management." *The Accounting Review,* 77: 71–105.

Free, C., Salterio, S., and Shearer, T. 2009. "The Construction of Auditability. MBA Rankings and Assurance in Practice." *Accounting Organizations and Society,* 34: 119–40.

Gaved, M. 1997. *Closing the Communications Gap. Disclosure and Institutional Shareholders.* London: The Institute of Chartered Accountants in England & Wales.

Gibbins, M. and Newton, J. D. 1994. "An Empirical Exploration of Complex Accountability in Public Accounting." *Journal of Accounting Research,* 32: 165–86.

Glover, S. M. 1997. "The Influence of Time Pressure and Accountability on Auditors' Processing of Nondiagnostic Information." *Journal of Accounting Research,* 35: 213–26.

Gray, R. 1992. "Accounting and Environmentalism: An Exploration of the Challenge of Gently Accounting for Accountability, Transparency and Sustainability." *Accounting, Organizations and Society,* 17: 399–425.

Hassel, L., Nilsson, H., and Nyquistc, S. 2005. "The Value Relevance of Environmental Performance." *European Accounting Review*, 14: 41–61.

Healy, P. M. and Whalen, J. M. 1999. "A Review of Earnings Management Literature and its Implications for Standard Setting." *Accounting Horizons*, 13: 365–83.

Hoffman, V. B. and Patton, J. M. 1997. "Accountability, the Dilution Effect, and Conservatism in Auditors' Fraud Judgments." *Journal of Accounting Research*, 35: 227–37.

Hogarth, R. M. and Einhorn, H. J. 1992. "Order Effects in Belief Updating. The Belief-Adjustment Model." *Cognitive Psychology*, 24: 1–55.

IFAC. 2010. *Basis of ISA Adoption by Jurisdiction*. International Federation of Accountants. Retrieved from <http://www.ifac.org/about-ifac/membership/compliance-program/basis-isa-adoption>.

Jensen, M. and Meckling, W. 1976. "Theory of the Firm. Managerial Behavior, Agency Costs, and Ownership Structure." *Journal of Financial Economics*, 3: 305–60.

Kao, A. 1999. "Accountability Effects on Auditors' Performance. The Influence of Knowledge, Problem-Solving Ability, and Task Complexity." *Journal of Accounting Research*, 37: 209–23.

Kennedy, J. 1993. "Debiasing Audit Judgment with Accountability. A Framework and Experimental Results." *Journal of Accounting Research*, 31: 231–45.

Kennedy, J. 1995. "Debiasing the Curse of Knowledge in Audit Judgment." *The Accounting Review*, 70: 249–73.

Knechel, R., Salterio, S., and Ballou, B. 2007. *Auditing. Risk and Assurance*. Third edition. Cincinnati, OH: Thomson Southwest.

Larcker, D. F., Richardson, S. A., and Tuna, I. 2007. "Corporate Governance, Accounting Outcomes, and Organizational Performance." *The Accounting Review*, 82: 963–1008.

Lopatta, K. and Kaspereit, T. 2011. *The Value Relevance of Corporate Sustainability and Sustainability Reporting in Europe*. Working paper, available at <http://papers.ssrn.com/sol3/papers.cfm?abstract_id=1976224>.

Macintosh, N. B. 1994. *Management Accounting and Control Systems. An Organizational and Behavioral Approach*. Chichester: John Wiley & Sons.

Moneva, J. and Cuellar, B. 2009. "The Value Relevance of Financial and Non-Financial Environmental Reporting." *Environmental and Resource Economics*, 44: 441–56.

NAO. 2011. *Assessing Value for Money (VFM)?* National Audit Office. Retrieved from <http://www.nao.org.uk/successful-commissioning/successful-commissioning-home/general-principles/value-for-money/assessing-value-for-money/>.

Neu, D. 2006. "Accounting for Public Space." *Accounting, Organizations and Society*, 31: 391–414.

O'Dwyer, B. and Unerman, J. 2008. "The Paradox of Greater NGO Accountability: A Case Study of Amnesty Ireland." *Accounting, Organizations and Society*, 33: 801–24.

Oldroyd, D. 1995. "The Role of Accounting in Public Expenditure and Monetary Policy in the First Century AD Roman Empire." *Accounting Historians Journal*, 22: 117–29.

PCAOB. 2011. *Mission, Structure and History*. Public Company Accounting Oversight Board. Retrieved from <http://pcaobus.org/About/History/Pages/default.aspx>.

Power, M. 1997. *The Audit Society: Rituals of Verification*. Oxford: Oxford University Press.

Radcliffe, V. S. 1997. Competing Rationalities in 'Special' Government Audits: The Case of NovAtel." *Critical Perspectives on Accounting*, 8: 343–66.

Radcliffe, V. S. 1998. "Efficiency Audit: An Assembly of Rationalities and Programmes." *Accounting, Organizations and Society*, 23: 377–410.

Rich, J.S., Solomon, I., and Trotman, K.T. 1997. "The Audit Review Process: A Characterization from the Persuasion Perspective." *Accounting, Organizations and Society*, 22: 481–505.

Roberts, J. 1991. "The Possibilities of Accountability." *Accounting, Organizations and Society*, 16: 355–68.

Roberts, J. and Scapens, R. 1985. "Accounting Systems and Systems of Accountability: Understanding Accounting Practices in their Organizational Contexts." *Accounting, Organizations and Society*, 10: 443–56.

Roberts, J., Sanderson, P., Barker, R., and Hendry, J. 2006. "In the Mirror of the Market: The Disciplinary Effects of Company/Fund Manager Meetings." *Accounting, Organizations and Society*, 31: 277–94.

Schweiker, W. 1993. "Accounting for Ourselves: Accounting Practice and the Discourse of Ethics." *Accounting, Organizations and Society*, 18: 231–52.

Scott, W. R. 2011. *Financial Accounting Theory*. Sixth edition. Toronto: Prentice Hall.

Shearer, T. 2002. "Ethics and Accountability. From the For-Itself to the For-the-Other." *Accounting, Organizations and Society*, 27: 541–73.

Sinclair, A. 1995. "The Chameleon of Accountability: Forms and Discourses." *Accounting, Organizations and Society*, 20: 219–37.

Tan, H. T., Ng, T. B., and Mak, B. W. 2002. "The Effects of Task Complexity on Auditors' Performance. The Impact of Accountability and Knowledge." *Auditing: A Journal of Practice & Theory*, 21: 81–95.

Tetlock, P. E. 1983. "Accountability and Complexity of Thought." *Journal of Personality and Social Psychology*, 45: 74–83.

Turner, C. W. 2001. "Accountability Demands and the Auditor's Evidence Search Strategy: The Influence of Reviewer Preferences and the Nature of the Response (Belief vs. Action)." *Journal of Accounting Research*, 39: 683–706.

Tversky, A. and Kahneman, D. 1974. "Judgment under Uncertainty: Heuristics and Biases." *Science*, 185: 1124–31.

Watts, R. L. and Zimmerman, J. L. 1986. *Positive Accounting Theory*. Englewood, NJ: Prentice-Hall.

CHAPTER 27

··

PERFORMANCE REPORTING

··

STEVEN VAN DE WALLE AND FLOOR CORNELISSEN

PERFORMANCE REPORTING: WHAT IT IS AND WHERE IT COMES FROM

··

THERE is a trend to making more and more public sector performance information publicly available, both to politicians through performance reporting, and to citizens through rankings, websites, and performance reports. The assumption is that performance reporting makes public organizations more accountable: Citizens can collectively consult league tables and decide about whether they want to continue using the service. The ultimate punishment for poor performance is an abandonment of the service and a transfer to an alternative provider. Politicians and boards can use performance information to decide about budget allocations, appointments, or emergency measures.

The gradual shift to New Public Management (NPM) from the mid-1980s meant a change in public sector accountability. The introduction of various ex post mechanisms to account for performance supplemented traditional ex ante legal mechanisms. What is generally meant by an accountable public sector in this context is a public sector that is answerable for its performance (Romzek 2000; Hyndman and Anderson 1998). This means that organizations' accounting systems were joined by a series of non-financial reporting systems (Dubnick 2005, 385–6), and that performance was added as a key organizational value. Rather than concentrating on controlling the use of public authority and providing assurance of abiding by rules and values in public spending, accountability mechanisms increasingly came to be seen as mechanisms facilitating improvement of public services (Aucoin and Heintzman 2000; Bovens, Schillemans, and 't Hart 2008). The focus of accountability systems also changed through an increasing importance of external accountability (i.e. to citizens) and a shift from process to output and outcome.

Accountability, or "being called to account for one's actions" (Mulgan 2000, 570), gradually came to be defined as demonstrating one's performance. This new approach to account-giving—accountability for performance—required explicit standards of performance (Behn 2001). By defining accountability as being answerable for performance, it would obviously be necessary to produce performance information. Subsequent decades thus saw an increase in performance management systems, often (misleadingly) labeled and branded as accountability systems (Radin 2006). They were not just supposed to work as naming and shaming mechanisms, but through providing information these performance management systems would contribute to a learning process and in this way improve performance (Bovens, Schillemans, and 't Hart 2008). An increase in transparency and thus accountability is an important goal in itself and the mere possibility of holding organizations accountable for their actions is considered to be highly valued by the public (Mayne 2007; Werner, and Asch 2005).

WHAT MAKES ACCOUNTING FOR PERFORMANCE DIFFERENT?

The effects of accounting for performance extend beyond the mere provision of information to facilitating a different style of decision-making. Through better performance information, public organizations would learn more about their own performance. Providing politicians and boards with detailed sets of performance metrics, it was thought, would support them in holding public officials, departments, front-line delivery bodies, and autonomous agencies to account, and help them to take better decisions. Furthermore, such information would help to maintain a healthy level of knowledge-based trust between principals and agents (Van de Walle 2010).

Citizens would be able to use performance information to put pressure on public services and politicians and to make better-informed choices when using public services (Van de Walle and Roberts 2008). In the new "performance management doctrine," the nature of accountability would be changed, both for the public, by making government actions transparent (external accountability), and for elected officials by reducing information asymmetries (internal accountability) (Moynihan 2008, 10–11, 35). The key mode of such transparency was through making performance information available to policy makers and to the wider public. It was assumed that through these two pressures, from citizens and from politicians and boards, greater accountability would lead to increased performance (Dubnick 2005).

Whereas traditional accountability about the performance of public services to citizens was mediated through elected bodies (DeLeon 1998), citizen-oriented reforms introduced a direct accountability relationship between (individual) citizens and public services through making performance information publicly available and through introducing complaints mechanisms, ombudsmen, etc. Democratic accountability mediated through elected bodies was partly replaced by direct accountability to users, and by accountability organized by the central government through an elaborate system of targets and monitoring systems (Greener 2009, 51–8). The former shift fits within a broader shift from vertical to horizontal accountability (Bovens 2005). This change also meant that individual civil servants and individual services could now also be called to account.

THE EFFECTS OF PERFORMANCE REPORTING ON ACCOUNTABILITY AND DECISIONS

Despite the high-minded rhetoric about accounting for performance, reality is less accommodating. Performance measurement, performance management, and performance-based accountability are generally connected in theory, but less so in practice (Thomas and Winnipeg 2007). Process-based accountability continues to dominate practice. One reason for this failure is that "accountability for results is possible only where goals are clear, and accountability for process is possible only where there is general agreement as to which processes are the most (or the only) appropriate ones—the 'best practices', in management vernacular" (DeLeon 1998, 546). This is less than straightforward in a policy context. Accountability is often used as a solution to all sorts of organizational problems, and the link between performance information and accountability has become highly embedded in organizational rhetoric (Dubnick 2005). The real question is: Do these accountability mechanisms work (Bovens, Schillemans, and 't Hart 2008), and does publishing of performance information lead to more accountability and hence better performance?

In this chapter we mainly concentrate on two accountability relations mainly affected by an increased availability of performance information: accountability to citizens by making performance information publicly available and accounting to politicians by providing them with performance metrics about the organization. Both topics are receiving increasing attention in the literature (Van Dooren and Van de Walle 2008). Providing politicians and citizens with more performance information has been the answer to improving accountability, but do these two groups actually use performance information in taking decisions?

IS PERFORMANCE INFORMATION USED IN POLITICAL DECISION MAKING?

Politicians wanting to control large and complex public services need easily accessible information to take decisions. This desire for more and better information in the policy and budgeting cycle has found expression in various initiatives, all based on very rational approaches to policy-making and budgeting (Thomas and Winnipeg 2007). In order to improve public accountability, many public organizations produce considerable amounts of performance information. Such provision of information fits well within the principal–agent logic whereby the agent is requested to provide information that helps the principal to steer the agent and make the agent accountable. Principals, in a public sector context mainly politicians, are thus assumed to use the available performance information to hold the agent accountable. Without such performance information, an information deficit and information asymmetry prevent the politicians from exercising control. Surprisingly, studies analyzing whether politicians actually use such performance information are relatively scarce (Pollitt 2006), and we have only recently seen an increase in empirical research into the topic.

Evidence for the Limited Use of Performance Information

The link between performance measurement and decision making and between performance metrics and accountability is often assumed. Researchers, however, are very skeptical about the usefulness of performance indicators (Askim 2009; Laegreid, Roness, and Rubecksen 2006). Academic interest in the "use" of (performance) information has so far been rather limited (Pollitt 2006, 41). Much of the evidence on whether the information coming from performance measurement is actually used in decision-making is anecdotal (De Lancer Julnes, and Holzer 2001), and opinion on whether performance measurement actually matters for decisions is divided (Ho 2005, 18; Askim 2009).

We have seen a growing number of studies of how politicians use performance information (Ho 2005; Bogt 2004; Johnsen 2005; Brun and Siegel 2006). A common finding in this research is that politicians often do not value the performance information. Pollitt focused on the use of performance reports by end-users, and the evidence he reviewed "suggests that evaluation and performance reports and audits are seldom highly valued by politicians or citizens" (Pollitt 2006, 38). Aldermen in the Netherlands use performance information infrequently, and do not always see much value in the available information (Bogt 2004). Pollitt reviewed evidence that indicated that Auditor General's reports in Canada were not read in their entirety by Canadian Members of Parliament (MPs) and that performance information is not really used in budgeting decisions in the US (Pollitt 2006). In decision-making, political considerations and performance information are used (Heinrich 1999), but we know little about their respective weight, and about the contextual factors that influence this selection.

Yet, before discarding performance information because it is not used by politicians anyway, we need to recognize that most studies focused on instrumental use. Politicians may not pick up performance reports, "read them carefully and then set out directly to apply their findings to the reformulation of policy or the better management of programmes" (Pollitt 2006, 49), but this does not mean performance information is not used at all. Politicians use various ways to collect information, and the use of information may be less formalized than what the existence of performance reports or league tables suggests. Decision-makers often find little use in performance indicators and instead prefer to rely on personal interactions with civil servants (Bogt 2004). Politicians normally engage in "problemistic search" and seek out supplementing sources of information, rather than just relying on one predefined set of information (Cyert and March 1963).

One of the most extensive initiatives to study the use of performance information by local politicians can be found in Norway, where several authors have studied this phenomenon as part of a large-scale project (Askim 2009; Johnsen 2005). Johnsen (2005) studied the use of non-mandatory performance measurement in political institutions in Norwegian local government. Askim (2009; 2008) studied local politicians' use of performance information in Norway, with a focus on these politicians' needs and abilities. Some of his findings were "that use of performance information increases with a politician's rank within the polity; that the politicians with the highest education make the least use of performance information; that polity size has a positive effect on use; and that different factors matter in distinct ways in different phases of policymaking."

Differences in Performance Information Use

Performance information is more embedded in some sectors than in others, and also the use of performance information in decision-making differs between policy sectors, partly because of a longer data-use tradition, or because of the different nature of evidence in these fields (Askim 2005). Van Dooren (2004) found similar differences across policy domains in the use of indicators in a study of parliamentary questions in the Belgian Parliament. In an encompassing study in Switzerland, Frey and Widmer (2011) found that performance information was used to varying degrees between different and within single policy fields. In a study among local councilors in Norway, use of performance information seemed to be especially relevant for councilors within the sectors of elderly care, administrative affairs, and education (Askim 2007). Others found large differences in patterns of use of performance information depending on organizational culture (Moynihan 2005, 204) and country (Pollitt et al. 2010). This is in line with more general studies on the use of evidence in policymaking (Davies, Nutley, and Smith 2000, 3; Nutley and Webb 2000, 14).

A second set of explanations focuses on the skills and resources required to use performance information. The complexity of performance information and the costs involved in using and understanding it can pose a barrier for politicians. Pollitt suggested that to politicians, speed and to-the-point information are most useful, whereas the trend in performance evaluation seems to be an increasing complexity of information. As a result, performance evaluation remains the domain of experts and managers, and not politicians—or citizens (Pollitt 2006). Availability of time may also explain differences between national research findings (Askim 2009). In their study of the influence of performance information on legislative reforms in Switzerland, Frey and Widmer (2011) found that the use of information is positively associated with the strength of the performance information, as measured by the information's credibility, certainty, and consistency.

The Effect of Performance Information on Accountability

A surprising finding from these studies is that the availability of performance information changes information asymmetries, but not always in the expected direction. Rather than seeing parliaments get a stronger role in the political game through the increased possibilities for holding the government to account, parliaments actually appear to lose out in the information war. Johnson and Talbot (2007) looked at the extent to which the UK parliament is able to use performance information to hold the government to account, and found that "On balance it would seem that it is parliament rather than the executive which is currently most challenged by the PSA and other performance policy reports." (2007, 130). Marnoch (2010) found similar effects among Scottish MPs, where the executive was also seen to have a monopoly on policy information, because "Political issues have become more difficult to conceptualize and are consequently increasingly positioned beyond the policy competence of parliamentarians operating outside of government with its knowledge-handling capacities." (2010, 2). In an earlier study he already stated that MPs often use performance information in an act of self-positioning, for instance by challenging the integrity of the performance information. Additionally, parliamentarians "generally fail to develop a sufficiently sophisticated appreciation of what performance means in order to hold government to account." (2010, 22).

There are differences in how politicians use performance information. Marnoch looked at health committees in Scotland, Northern Ireland, and Wales and found that the political position of the health committee members influences their use of performance information. In the Scottish case, committee members who belonged to the parties in government and who were promoted to the ministerial office had used performance information less often than their colleagues (Marnoch 2010). These findings imply that those politicians closest to the center of power and the executive use less performance information and that use of formal performance information is higher among those politicians suffering the most from information asymmetries. Askim (2009), on the other hand, found that in Norwegian municipalities, politicians closer to the apex of power used more performance information. From an accountability perspective, one would expect backbenchers to compensate for the information asymmetry by using large amounts of performance information, yet Askim found that it was frontbenchers in municipal councils who made more use of performance information. An exception was the mayor, who used far less performance information. Councilors using more performance information also had much contact with citizens and municipal employees, thereby further increasing information asymmetry. Possible explanations for this finding could be either that backbenchers are unaware of the information asymmetry, that the costs for them to retrieve performance information are too high, or that they just feel they don't need performance information as much as frontbenchers do. Finally, Askim also found that higher-educated and more experienced councilors appear to use less performance information than their colleagues.

DO CITIZENS USE PERFORMANCE INFORMATION?

Performance reporting is also directed at citizens. Accounting for performance towards citizens is closely related to what is generally labeled the choice agenda, and more recently the personalization agenda. Well-informed and benefit-maximizing citizens are searching for ways to consume public services that correspond to their wishes. They will thus choose between a variety of services offered by an equally large variety of public, non-profit, and private organizations, and change supplier when these services underperform. Publicly available performance indicators assist citizens in making informed choices (Le Grand 2007, 84). Through publishing performance indicators in easily accessible formats and platforms, public services give account of their performance. We will argue in this chapter, as we have done earlier, that such an approach presupposes that citizens actually use such performance information, and that this information plays a central role in citizens' choice behavior.

Public sector reforms, especially from the early 1990s on, gave citizens more say in public services. Early changes concentrated mainly on giving citizens more voice as customers, through allowing them to file complaints or to go to an ombudsman. Greater transparency facilitated such voice, and the publication of performance metrics was just one of the expressions of such increased transparency. A second set of innovations focused on giving citizens more choice, ultimately allowing them to exercise their exit option (Paul 1992; Meijer and Schillemans 2009; Besley and Ghatak 2003). Here as well, performance information was regarded as a central requirement for such exit to be able to function. It was assumed that citizens, after consulting various performance metrics, would choose between a range of public, non-profit, and private service providers (Van de Walle and Roberts 2008; Le Grand 2007). We have thus seen a sharp increase in publicly available performance information. This information is not limited to annual reports or publicly available performance reports. Rankings and league tables have also become a common feature, especially in the health and education sectors, but also elsewhere. Quite often, such performance information is not created by the organizations themselves, but supplied through various mediators, such as interests groups, consumer associations, or news media.

While generally regarded as a logical next step in NPM-style reforms of public services, few reflected about the assumptions of human behavior behind the voice and choice agenda (Clarke et al. 2007). The assumed mechanism behind making performance information available to citizens was that citizens are autonomous decision-makers (Le Grand 2007) and would 1) actually consult performance information before making a decision on which school, hospital, or social service provider to use, and 2) would use this information to change their behavior. Because the phenomenon of publishing performance information in a format that is easy to use for citizens is relatively new, the evidence about whether it is actually used is limited. In this section we provide an overview of recent findings in two sectors. Schools and hospitals are two types of institutions with which many citizens have direct experience. They deliver services in an area where citizens expect high quality, and choice is also relatively easy in these sectors.

Accountability through Publishing School Performance Data

Education is one of the public services where a substantial amount of performance information is publicly available, at different levels, from kindergartens to primary and secondary schools to higher education and universities. This information includes a variety of data, generally available at the level of individual schools and universities, and often offered to the public through a system of rankings and league tables. It includes national test results, research output, university application success rates, etc. This information is offered to inform parents or students in order to facilitate them in making a conscious and well-informed choice of institution. It also assists voice processes by making it easier for parents to see how well their child's school is doing. It is generally assumed that parents and students do use this information, and there is indeed substantial evidence that additional information—that is, new information that actually contributes to citizens' knowledge about the quality of an educational institution—does have an effect on the choice that is made. For this effect to occur however, it is important that this information can easily be retrieved and interpreted. By readily presenting this type of information parents were thought to be relieved of the necessity to perform an extensive search in order to compare schools, and thus face much lower decision-making costs (Hastings and Weinstein 2008). At the same time, schools are being forced to perform well if they do not want to be shamed publicly and lose pupils.

Despite the emphasis that has been placed on school performance, though, other factors have been found to be at least equally important in choice behavior, notably distance to the school (Hastings and Weinstein 2008). The additional costs on choice imposed by distance appear not to outweigh school quality as indicated by indicators. One study, in which school quality information was published in a national newspaper (and, subsequently, in several regional newspapers as well), found that students did use quality information, but that they were willing to travel no more than an additional 200 meters to attend a better performing school (Koning and Wiel 2010). Similar studies have focused on the effects of university league tables on university choice (Gunn and Hill 2008).

Accountability Through Publishing Hospital Performance Data

Another area which has seen a sharp increase in publicly available performance information is healthcare. Just as was the case with education, the effects of publishing performance information on choice behavior are mixed. Some studies show a clear effect on patient choice. One such example is about consumers' choice of fertility clinics in the United States. The study found a clear relationship between the publication of clinics' performance information and the choice by consumers of certain clinics (Bundorf et al. 2009).

In other sectors, the effects of public performance metrics on patients' choice seem to be more limited or even absent. Reviews of previous studies on the effects of quality information on consumer choice of both health plans and health care providers in the US found modest but significant effects (Harris and Buntin 2008; Kolstad and Chernew 2009). Jin and Sorensen (2006) correct for the effects of prior known information on patients' decision-making, and find that quality rankings can have a significant additional influence on health plan choice. The number of patients actually using such information, however, was relatively low in the latter study. In German hospitals, although the measured effects were relatively small, the publication of performance information did result in changes in patients' choices: Hospitals with above average quality turn out to be chosen more often than worse scoring hospitals, and worse scoring hospitals are populated mostly by patients living in the direct vicinity of that hospital (Sauerland and Wübker 2008). What's more, hospitals making their performance information public also receive more inquiries from prospective clients. Analysis of the effects of performance information on choice needs though to take availability of alternatives into account. Patients do not necessarily pick the hospital closest to their residence (see Le Grand (2007, 101) for an overview of evidence), yet Stevenson (2006) looked at nursing homes and found the absence of choice to be a factor limiting the effect of publishing performance information.

In contrast to the German study on hospital choice mentioned above, a similar study in the Netherlands found that patients do not seem to use quality information for choosing their hospital. Lako and Rosenau (2009) found that most Dutch patients rely on their General Practitioners' (GP) advice when picking a hospital instead. Of 31 percent of patients that did choose their hospital in this study, 14 percent indicated that the hospital's reputation was the main reason for this, and the hospital's location was also found to be an important factor in decision-making. Reputation and other peoples' opinions of health care institutions appear to be an important factor in making decisions, putting published performance information well behind GPs' and acquaintances' opinions as a factor determining patient choice (Lako and Rosenau 2009). Patients have indicated that they had more confidence in their GPs than in formal rankings, especially if they knew their GPs well (Harris and Buntin 2008; Marshall et al. 2000).

ACCOUNTING FOR
PERFORMANCE: TAKING STOCK

Did Accounting for Performance Deliver What It Promised?

Performance information takes a central role in public sector reforms. From a principal–agent perspective it is seen as a tool to assist politicians and boards in holding public service managers (and the government) to account. Towards citizens, performance information is presented as a tool assisting them in making informed choices between public services and in holding public sector workers and politicians accountable.

The review of the literature revealed overall a relatively limited role for performance information. At best, performance information was just one of many elements influencing decisions, and its importance should not be overestimated. Further evidence showed inequalities in the use of performance information, suggesting that increasing the availability of performance information in order to improve accountability relations is not a neutral tool. Yet, the evidence is relatively mixed. In the case of politicians' use of performance information, some studies suggest that performance information helps some politicians to correct for their relative information deficit. Yet other studies suggested that an increased availability of performance information may in fact lead to a widening gap between those who are informed and those who aren't. In this case, performance information does little to change accountability processes, and probably only reinforces existing processes.

Evidence is also mixed on the effects of making performance information available to citizens on their ability and willingness to make informed choices. Even though critics have suggested that making performance information publicly available will mainly benefit highly-educated citizens, the effects do not seem to be that straightforward. Rather, there appear to be important differences between types of public services, and the situation within which choices need to be made. Even though the added value of performance information in citizens' choice behavior has generally been assumed in public service reforms, there are relatively few studies about how citizens actually choose public service providers. If there is one thing that clearly emerges from the literature, then it should be that the importance of performance information is relatively limited in this choice process.

The Effect of New Accountability Mechanisms on Equity

Critics of the choice agenda and the related provision of choice-facilitating performance information have repeatedly pointed at the fact that making evidence-based choices is difficult and therefore likely to privilege well-educated citizens and citizens in higher socio-economic classes. Choice has been described by its critics as a *middle class obsession*, even though the evidence on choice behavior does not seem to confirm this conviction (Le Grand 2007). Studies do indeed show mixed effects of choice on disadvantaged groups. Koning and Wiel (2010) looked at the effects of publishing school quality data on school choice, and found no differences in responses to performance information between socio-economic groups. Many studies on school choice reveal that it is travel time to school rather than the performance information provided that determines choice. Publishing performance information to facilitate choice therefore only influences choice if there is ample choice of high quality schooling in the neighborhood (Hastings and Weinstein 2008). If no such choice is available, it is likely to be only those parents with more resources who will make a deliberate decision to move their children further afield.

There is a similar debate in relation to hospital choice. Here, the main argument is that health information might be too complicated to assist citizens in making informed choices, and that therefore it will mainly be well-educated citizens who use such information. In settings where most service users are young, wealthy, and more highly educated, and the services not acute, such as fertility clinics, there is a clear effect of publicly available performance information on clinic choice (Bundorf et al. 2009). A review of patient choice in the National Health Service (NHS) found that citizens with higher education were more likely to use performance information in choosing a health care provider (Fotaki et al. 2008). In a Dutch study, higher-educated patients did not indicate considering their GP's advice as important as other, less-educated patients, which indicates different approaches by different subgroups. However, quality information was not mentioned as a factor of influence on their choice and, in addition, findings no longer proved significant after multivariate analysis (Lako and Rosenau 2009). Other studies find that higher education probably does increase both the response of patients to quality information and the awareness of such information in general. Apart from education, other factors also lead to differences in the use of performance information in making choices. Some studies found that females and ethnic minorities value health care quality information more (Harris and Buntin 2008; Kolstad and Chernew 2009). In contrast, Schneider and Epstein (1998) in their study on the influence of cardiac surgery performance information on cardiac patients' hospital choice found that men seemed somewhat more likely to be aware of hospital performance rankings than women. Their findings furthermore strongly suggested factors such as age, level of education and health status as influencing such awareness. Length of sickness period and income level also seemed to play a role here.

Internal Effects of Accounting for Performance

Public managers and public organizations change their behaviors to anticipate external reactions to their published performance outcomes. The performance management literature is divided about whether performance information and performance measurement actually lead to better quality services, and has given considerable attention to dysfunctional effects (Werner and Asch 2005; Smith 1995). Such dysfunctional effects range from excessive attention for what is easily measurable, over a fixation on targets and indicators, to outright gaming. In the latter, public organizations deliberately underperform in order to avoid higher targets in a subsequent year.

A result is that performance metrics may crowd out other processes of priority setting in organizations. Such metrics have also become increasingly important in the evaluation of personnel. A failure to achieve (internally or externally) defined targets is then a reason to deny promotion or to terminate employment. Success in achieving targets brands one as a good manager and greatly facilitates job transfers.

Measuring performance is by definition a conservative undertaking. Good measurement systems and well-functioning performance accountability systems only operate in stable environments with a great deal of standardization (Meijer 2005). Diverging from the norm or standard is risky for an organization, because it results in lower performance—as measured by the standard. While performance reporting may indeed increase accountability and stimulate organizations to improve, it may at the same time stifle more far-reaching innovation and stimulate risk avoidance through strong homogenizing tendencies. While the logic behind the introduction of performance reporting systems suggested more democratic types of accountability systems where individual users would be able to hold organizations to account, this standardization seems to suggest a shift of power to the standard-setters. These can be central government, professional bodies, consumer organizations, or news media. Within organizations, this may mean a greater importance for management and organizations' technostructures, to the detriment of the power of professionals. A related effect is that accountability requirements have been found to be very bureaucratic and resource-consuming (Gregory 2003). Finally, the easy availability of a wide range of performance metrics may facilitate attack politics, where performance information is not in the first place used for accountability or improvement purposes, but to launch attacks on organizations or persons through a selective use of data (Flinders 2011). Performance information is then not used to make a balanced assessment but only to support pre-existing structures and attitudes. Yet the question remains whether this really is a departure from other forms of accountability, or only a change in the arguments and tools.

References

Askim, J. 2005. *Explaining Variations in Embeddedness of Performance Information Among Local Government Politicians.* In EGPA (European Group for Public Administration) Annual Conference. Bern, 31 August – 3 September 2005.

Askim, J. 2007. "How Do Politicians Use Performance Information? An Analysis of the Norwegian Local Government Experience." *International Review of Administrative Sciences*, 73: 453–72.

Askim, J. 2008. Determinants of Performance Information Utilization in Political Decision Making, pp. 125–39 in *Performance Information in the Public Sector: How It is Used*, eds. W. Van Dooren and S. Van de Walle. Basingstoke: Palgrave Macmillan.

Askim, J. 2009. "The Demand Side of Performance Measurement: Explaining Councillors' Utilization of Performance Information in Policymaking." *International Public Management Journal*, 12: 24–47.

Aucoin, P. and Heintzman, R. 2000. "The Dialectics of Accountability for Performance in Public Management Reform." *International Review of Administrative Sciences*, 66: 45–55.

Behn, R. D. 2001. *Rethinking Democratic Accountability*. Washington, DC: Brookings University Press.

Besley, T. and Ghatak, M. 2003. "Incentives, Choice and Accountability in the Provision of Public Services." *Oxford Review of Economic Policy*, 19: 235–49.

Bogt, H. J. ter. 2004. "Politicians in Search of Performance Information? Survey Research on Dutch Aldermen's Use of Performance Information." *Financial Accountability & Management*, 20: 221–52.

Bovens, M. 2005. Public Accountability, pp. 182–208 in *The Oxford Handbook of Public Management*, eds. E. Ferlie, L. E. Lynn and C. Pollitt. Oxford: Oxford University Press.

Bovens, M., Schillemans, T., and 't Hart, P. 2008. "Does Public Accountability Work? An Assessment Tool." *Public Administration*, 86: 225–42.

Brun, M. E. and Siegel, J. P. 2006. "What Does Appropriate Performance Reporting for Political Decision Makers Require? Empirical Evidence from Switzerland." *International Journal of Productivity and Performance Management*, 55: 480–97.

Bundorf, M. K., Chun, N., Goda, G. S., and Kessler, D. P. 2009. "Do Markets Respond to Quality Information? The Case of Fertility Clinics." *Journal of Health Economics*, 28: 718–27.

Clarke, J., Newman, J., Smith, N., Westmarland, L., and Vidler, E. 2007. *Creating Citizen-Consumers: Changing Publics and Changing Public Services*. London: Sage.

Cyert, R. M. and March, J. G. 1963. *A Behavioral Theory of the Firm*. Englewood Cliffs, NJ: Prentice-Hall.

Davies, H., Nutley, S., and Smith, P. 2000. Introducing Evidence-Based Policy and Practice in Public Services, pp. 1–11 in *What Works? Evidence-Based Policy and Practice in Public Services*, eds. H. T. O. Davies, S. Nutley and P. Smith. Bristol: The Policy Press.

De Lancer Julnes, P., and Holzer, M. 2001. "Promoting the Utilization of Performance Measures in Public Organizations: An Empirical Study of Factors Affecting Adoption and Implementation." *Public Administration Review*, 61: 693–708.

DeLeon, L. 1998. "Accountability in a 'Reinvented' Government." *Public Administration*, 76: 539–58.

Dubnick, M. 2005. "Accountability and the Promise of Performance: In Search of the Mechanisms." *Public Performance & Management Review*, 28: 376–417.

Flinders, M. 2011. "Daring to be a Daniel: The Pathology of Politicized Accountability in a Monitory Democracy." *Administration & Society*, 43: 595–619.

Fotaki, M., Roland, M., Boyd, A., McDonald, R., Scheaff, R., and Smith, L. 2008. "What Benefits Will Choice Bring to Patients? Literature Review and Assessment of Implications." *Journal of Health Services Research & Policy*, 13: 178–84.

Frey, K. and Widmer, T. 2011. "Revising Swiss Policies: The Influence of Efficiency Analyses." *American Journal of Evaluation*, 32: 494–517.

Greener, I. 2009. *Public Management: A Critical Text*. Basingstoke: Palgrave Macmillan.

Gregory, R. 2003. Accountability in Modern Government, pp. 557–68 in *Handbook of Public Administration*, eds. B. G. Peters and J. Pierre. London: Sage.

Gunn, R. and Hill, S. 2008. "The Impact of League Tables on University Application Rates." *Higher Education Quarterly*, 62: 273–96.

Harris, K. M. and Buntin, M. B. 2008. *Choosing a Health Care Provider: The Role of Quality Information*. Robert Wood Johnson Foundation.

Hastings, J. S. and Weinstein, J. M. 2008. "Information, School Choice, and Academic Achievement: Evidence from Two Experiments." *Quarterly Journal of Economics*, 123: 1373–1414.

Heinrich, C. J. 1999. "Do Government Bureaucrats Make Effective Use of Performance Management Information?" *Journal of Public Administration Research and Theory*, 9: 363–93.

Ho, A. T. 2005. "Accounting for the Value of Performance Measurement from the Perspective of Midwestern Mayors." *Journal of Public Administration Research and Theory*, 16: 217–37.

Hyndman, N. S. and Anderson, R. 1998. "Performance Information, Accountability and Executive Agencies." *Public Money and Management*, 18: 23–30.

Jin, G. Z. and Sorensen, A. T. 2006. "Information and Consumer Choice: The Value of Publicized Health Plan Ratings." *Journal of Health Economics*, 25: 248–75.

Johnsen, A. 2005. *Determinants of Non-Mandatory Performance Measurement in Norwegian Local Government: A Comparison of Political, Economic and Sociological Explanations*. In EGPA (European Group for Public Administration) Annual Conference. Bern, 31 August – 3 September 2005.

Johnson, C. and Talbot, C. 2007. "The UK Parliament and Performance: Challenging or Challenged?" *International Review of Administrative Sciences*, 73: 113–31.

Kolstad, J. T. and Chernew, M. E. 2009. "Quality and Consumer Decision Making in the Market for Health Insurance and Health Care Services." *Medical Care Research and Review*, 66: 28S–52S.

Koning, P. and Wiel, K. van der. 2010. *Ranking the Schools: How Quality Information Affects School Choice in the Netherlands*. Den Haag: CPB Discussion Paper 150.

Laegreid, P., Roness, P. G. and Rubecksen, K. 2006. "Performance Management in Practice: The Norwegian Way." *Financial Accountability and Management*, 22: 251–70.

Lako, C. J. and Rosenau, P. 2009. "Demand-Driven Care and Hospital Choice: Dutch Health Policy Toward Demand-Driven Care. Results from a Survey Into Hospital Choice." *Health Care Analysis*, 17: 20–35.

Le Grand, J. 2007. *The Other Invisible Hand: Delivering Public Services Through Choice and Competition*. Princeton: Princeton University Press.

Marnoch, G. 2010. *"The Better We Are Watched the Better We Behave": Are Devolved Parliaments Providing a Better Window for Oversight?* In PSA Specialist Group Conference, *British and Comparative Territorial Politics*, Oxford: 7–8 January 2010.

Marshall, M. N., Shekelle, P. G., Leatherman, S., and Brook, R. H. 2000. "The Public Release of Performance Data: What Do We Expect to Gain? A Review of the Evidence." *Journal of the American Medical Association*, 283: 1866–74.

Mayne, J. 2007. Accountability for Program Performance: A Key to Effective Performance Monitoring and Reporting, pp. 157–76 in *Monitoring Performance in the Public Sector, Future Directions from International Experience*, ed. J. Wholey. New Jersey: Transaction Pub.

Meijer, A. and Schillemans, T. 2009. "Fictional Citizens and Real Effects: Accountability to Citizens in Competitive and Monopolistic Markets." *Public Administration and Management—An Interactive Journal*, 14: 254–91.

Meijer, A. 2005. "Vreemde Ogen Dwingen: Maatschappelijke Controle in de Publieke Sector." *Bestuurskunde*, 14: 25–31.

Moynihan, D. P. 2005. "Goal-Based Learning and the Future of Performance Management." *Public Administration Review*, 65: 203–16.

Moynihan, D. P. 2008. *The Dynamics of Performance Management: Constructing Information and Reform*. Washington, DC: Georgetown University Press.

Mulgan, R. 2000. "'Accountability': An Ever-Expanding Concept?" *Public Administration*, 78: 555–73.

Nutley, S. and Webb, J. 2000. Evidence and the Policy Process, pp. 13–41 in *What Works? Evidence-Based Policy and Practice in Public Services*, eds. H. T. O. Davies, S. M. Nutley, and P. C. Smith. Bristol: The Policy Press.

Paul, S. 1992. "Accountability in Public Services: Exit, Voice and Control." *World Development*, 20: 1047–60.

Pollitt, C. 2006. "Performance Information for Democracy: The Missing Link?" *Evaluation*, 12: 38–55.

Pollitt, C., Harrison, S., Dowswell, G., Jerak-Zuiderent, S., and Bal, R. 2010. "Performance Regimes in Health Care: Institutions, Critical Junctures and the Logic of Escalation in England and the Netherlands." *Evaluation*, 16: 13–29.

Radin, B. A. 2006. *Challenging the Performance Movement: Accountability, Complexity, and Democratic Values*. Washington, DC: Georgetown University Press.

Romzek, B. S. 2000. "Dynamics of Public Sector Accountability in an Era of Reform." *International Review of Administrative Sciences*, 66: 21–44.

Sauerland, D. and Wübker, A. 2008. *Wie Qualitätsinformationen die Krankenhauswahl beeinflussen: Eine empirische Untersuchung*. Lahr: WHL Diskussionspapier no. 15.

Schneider, E. C. and Epstein, A. M. 1998. "Use of Public Performance Reports: A Survey of Patients Undergoing Cardiac Surgery." *Journal of the American Medical Association*, 279: 1638–42.

Smith, P. 1995. "On the Unintended Consequences of Publishing Performance Data in the Public Sector." *International Journal of Public Administration*, 18: 277–310.

Stevenson, D. G. 2006. "Is a Public Reporting Approach Appropriate for Nursing Home Care?" *Journal of Health Politics, Policy and Law*, 31: 773–810.

Thomas, P. G. and Winnipeg, M. 2007. *Why Is Performance-Based Accountability So Popular in Theory and Difficult in Practice? World Summit on Public Governance. Improving the Performance of the Public Sector*. Taipei City, 1–3 May 2007.

Van de Walle, S. and Roberts, A. 2008. Publishing Performance Information: An Illusion of Control?, pp. 221–6 in *Performance Information in the Public Sector: How It is Used*, eds. W. Van Dooren and S. Van de Walle. Basingstoke: Palgrave Macmillan.

Van de Walle, S. 2010. New Public Management: Restoring the Public Trust Through Creating Distrust?, pp. 309–20 in *Ashgate Research Companion to New Public Management*, eds. T. Christensen and P. Laegreid. Aldershot: Ashgate.

Van Dooren, W. and Van de Walle, S. 2008. *Performance Information in the Public Sector: How It is Used*. Basingstoke: Palgrave Macmillan.

Van Dooren, W. 2004. "Supply and Demand of Policy Indicators: A Cross-Sectoral Comparison." *Public Management Review*, 6: 511–30.

Werner, R. M. and Asch, D. A. 2005. "The Unintended Consequences of Publicly Reporting Quality Information." *Journal of the American Medical Association*, 293: 1239–44.

CHAPTER 28

....

PERFORMANCESTAT

....

ROBERT D. BEHN

ACCOUNTING FOR TARGETED PERFORMANCE

PUBLIC executives are accountable for a myriad of responsibilities that can be organized into three categories (Behn 2001, 6–10). Public executives are accountable for:

(1) **Finances:** For the probity with which they deploy public funds, as established by the rules of budgeting and accounting.
(2) **Fairness:** For the integrity with which they treat employees, vendors, and citizens, as established by the rules for hiring and promoting employees, for selecting and dealing with vendors, and for interacting with citizens.
(3) **Performance:** For achieving public purposes, as established (but only very broadly) by an agency or program's authorizing legislation.

Governments have established multiple and detailed rules for what public executives should do to ensure that they handle taxpayer funds with probity and for what public executives should do to ensure that they treat employees, vendors, and citizens fairly. Yet, there exist almost no rules for what public executives should do to ensure that they achieve public purposes.

This creates the "accountability bias" (Behn 2001, 12–14). Because the rules of accountability for finances and fairness are very explicit, those who are in the accountability-holding business—even if they seek to hold public executives accountable for performance—focus on these first two concerns. If an "accountability holdee" has violated the rules for finances or for fairness, the "accountability holder" has a clear case.

But for what kinds of performance should a public executive be held accountable? Maybe the legislature has established an explicit performance target—a specific result to be produced by a specific date. Then, if the public executive and his or her organization fail to achieve the defined target, someone could be held accountable. But who? Should it be the executive who failed to mobilize people to achieve the target? Should it be the legislature that failed to provide the executive with the resources necessary to achieve the target? Or should it be the collaborators, whose work is necessary to achieve the target, but whose commitment to the task was less than enthusiastic? It isn't obvious. Indeed, in many situations, the locus of responsibility could be quite debatable.

Accountability for performance is qualitatively different from accountability for finances or fairness.

PERFORMANCE AUDITS AND THE AUDIT EXPLOSION

The fundamental difference between the clear nature and specific mechanisms of accountability for finances and fairness and the ambiguity in the meaning of accountability for performance has not, however, deterred the accountability holders. Those officials responsible for holding public executives accountable for finances and fairness—accountants, auditors, inspectors general—have become entrepreneurial. They have launched a variety of efforts to expand their portfolio to include accountability for performance.

In the United Kingdom, the result has been what Power (1994; 2005) calls "the audit explosion." The official accountability holders no longer conduct only financial and fairness audits. To their professional repertoire they have added "performance audits". Today, any self-respecting government auditor has his or her own performance-auditing unit.

There is, however, not only a conceptual difference between auditing finances and auditing performance. There is also an operational difference. A financial audit is based on expectations for behavior that reflect generally accepted political norms that have been well-codified in law and regulation. These rules tell public mangers the purposes and activities for which they can and cannot spend money. They define theft (and other forms of misappropriation), establish specific expectations, and provide the bases for a financial audit.

The same applies to auditing for fairness. There are generally accepted political norms that have been well-codified in law and regulation. These rules tell public managers how they should and should not treat employees, vendors, and citizens. They define fairness, establish specific expectations, and provide the bases for a fairness audit.

For performance, however, what is the equivalent of the rules for finances and fairness? Who has set what expectations for performance for which the auditors can check? What are the bases for a performance audit?

The US Government Accountability Office (GAO), in its "Yellow Book," establishes *Government Auditing Standards*. In it, GAO (2011, 18) says that the objectives of a performance audit "vary widely and include assessments of program effectiveness, economy, and efficiency; internal control; compliance; and prospective analyses [about the future]." That's quite a broad list; indeed GAO lists 32 different examples of "performance audit objectives." Thus, GAO's list gives the performance auditor a lot of room to maneuver. Most importantly—and most troubling—it permits the auditors to establish their own, personal standards for what does or does not constitute good performance.

When it comes to determining what performance targets a public agency should achieve, legislatures are quite allergic to specificity. After all, by proposing an explicit performance target to be achieved, a legislator can easily alienate allies who have different performance priorities. Moreover, once a legislature has created a specific result to be achieved, it will find itself under pressure to provide the resources (money, staff, flexibility) necessary to achieve this result. Yet, without such specificity—without explicit performance targets—how can an independent auditor evaluate an agency's performance?

COMPARED WITH WHAT?

Accountability begins with an evaluation. To hold a public agency accountable for finances, or fairness, or performance, the accountability holders first have to evaluate its work: How well did the agency do in handling public funds with probity? How well did the agency do in treating employees, vendors, and citizens with integrity? How well did the agency do in achieving its purposes?

Moreover, all evaluations require a comparison. Whether the accountability holders are concerned about finances, or fairness, or performance, they need a basis of comparison. Indeed, every evaluation begins with the basic question: "Compared with what?" (Poister 2004, 112; Behn 2008a). For finances and fairness, this basis of comparison is the established rules: Did the agency comply with the rules?

For performance, however, what is the basis of comparison? To evaluate a public agency's performance, an evaluator—be that a citizen or an auditor—requires some kind of explicit statement about what the agency is supposed to accomplish. Specifically, to do any performance evaluation—to determine whether an agency is performing well—the evaluator must make three choices.

First, the evaluator must choose a purpose. What public purpose is the agency supposed to achieve? For example, the purpose of a city's health department might be "to protect and foster the health of the city's citizens and visitors."

Second the evaluator needs to make this conceptual purpose operational by selecting the specific aspects of performance on which to focus—specific dimensions of performance that need to be improved and thus that need to be measured. These are the organization's "performance deficits"—the places along its value chain (from inputs to processes to outputs to outcomes) where it needs to make some significant improvements (Behn 2006b).

For example, how should the city's citizens or auditors measure the health department's performance? Should it measure the number of citizens who got sick last year? The number of people who got sick from food poisoning in the city's restaurants? The number of children vaccinated for measles? The number of health-code violations that city inspectors issued to restaurants? The number of citizens who are obese? The number of innovative regulations that the health commissioner issued for newly identified health problems that have yet to be effectively controlled? In choosing what to measure, the organization's executives are choosing what performance deficits they think should be fixed next.

In the abstract, this choice is not obvious. It depends upon the specific city's specific circumstances. If a large number of citizens (is a large number 2,000, or 200, or 20, or 2?) have contracted food poisoning from the city's restaurants, the health commissioner may need to focus on this performance deficit. Alternatively, if all organizations are fully complying with the city's entire health code, maybe the commissioner should seek to make people healthier by improving personal behaviors that the department cannot regulate but only encourage.

Third, having chosen how to measure performance, the evaluator needs to choose a standard of comparison: With what criterion should this year's measured performance be compared?

For example, should the agency's performance be compared with the performance of other, similar agencies in other, similar jurisdictions? Unfortunately, these agencies will never be identical. They may have started from a higher or lower base. If last year other health departments had many fewer cases of food poisoning from restaurants, do they provide an appropriate basis of comparison? These other agencies may have had different performance deficits and thus chosen to focus their energies on other aspects of citizen and visitor health.

Or, maybe this year's achievements should be compared with last year's. If so, what should count as a success?[1] If the department reduced the cases of food poisoning by five percent, is this a success? Given that the health department does not directly *produce* citizens without food poisoning, what should count as poor, good, or superior performance?

To establish accountability for performance, there exists a wide variety of purposes, measures, and criteria. And all of the officially-authorized or self-appointed accountability holders will argue that they—and they alone—have identified the correct ones.

The demands of accountability for finances and fairness may be strict, but they are official, clear, and widely accepted. Moreover, the accountability holdees have a simple, proven strategy for success: Follow the rules. If the rules are clear and not contradictory, and the agency follows them, it cannot get into trouble. When, however, it comes to accountability for performance, there are no rules. Every accountability holder can invent his or her own purpose, measures, and comparative criteria.

Pity the poor public executive. The rules for accountability for performance are undefined, conflicting, constantly changing, and enforced by empires of umpires, each of whom refuses to recognize the legitimacy of the others. When it comes to performance, the accountability holdees never have it easy.

THE PERFORMANCE-TARGET ETHIC

Still, public executives are not completely at the whims of these competing claims for performance accountability. Rather than live in fear that a new accountability holder will invent some new performance purpose, or performance measure, or performance standard, they could embrace their own accountability (Moore 1995, 273–82, 352, 387). They could establish their own basis by which they and others could compare their performance—their own performance basis for which they are willing to be accountable.

To do this, public executives need to make the same three choices. They need to articulate a clear purpose for their agency. They need to establish specific performance measures by which to judge progress against their performance deficits. And they need to create specific performance targets: specific results to be achieved by a specific date.

For example, if food poisoning is a serious problem, the director of a municipal health department might decide to make reducing these illnesses a key purpose. To do so, however, the health director has an obligation to do more than deliver the customary speech proclaiming that "we will vigorously attack the immoral restaurant owners and close them down." The commissioner also needs to establish both a way to measure progress and to set a specific target for next year (and perhaps for several years).

In making these three choices, the department director creates a basis of comparison. These choices answer the "compared with what?" question.

For the evaluation of a public agency, there exist many possible bases of comparison. For citizens, however, the most useful standard may be the agency's own—provided that the agency's executive has actually established one. Thus, citizens (and legislators, journalists, and auditors) need to create a performance-target ethic: "We expect our elected and appointed executives to establish specific, meaningful performance targets" (Behn 2008b). Such a norm—not a rule, but an expectation[2]—would ensure that all public executives will answer the "compared with what?" question by creating specific purposes, performance measures, and performance targets. Then, citizens would have a clear way to judge whether their jurisdiction or agency was performing well. Then there would exist a clear basis for evaluating the performance of a jurisdiction or agency and thus for establishing its accountability for performance.

THE DANGER AND THE OPPORTUNITY

By specifying purpose, measures, and targets, public executives create a specific basis for performance accountability. This is dangerous. The members of the jurisdiction's or agency's leadership team have told the world what they will accomplish, and they should not be surprised when the world holds them to it. They can no longer complain about the performance standard to which they are being held. They themselves have created that standard, and the world will reasonably expect that they will achieve their target—and thus further their purpose.

The leadership team could, of course, decide not to specify a purpose, or measures, or targets. Doing so will not, however, eliminate their accountability for performance. It will merely delegate to others—who have their own purposes, measures, and targets—the basis for their accountability. They will still be evaluated. They will still be accountable. No longer, however, will they be able to influence the basis of this evaluation and accountability. This is even more dangerous.

Moreover, by specifying their purpose, measures, and targets, the leadership team creates a specific cause with which to mobilize resources and motivate people. For as Hackman (1986, 102) observes: "People seek purpose in their lives and are energized when an attractive purpose is articulated for them." A public organization—almost by definition—has an attractive purpose, perhaps several. By clearly and repeatedly articulating this specific purpose (or purposes), the leadership team can motivate people.

Performance targets are also motivating. Individuals and teams both perform better if they are given specific targets to achieve and provided with feedback on their progress (Latham, Borgogni, and Petitta 2008; Latham and Pinder 2005; Locke and Latham 1984; 2004). About evidence accumulated over four decades by Locke, Latham, and their colleagues on the effect of "goal setting" on organizational performance, Duncan (1989, 172) reports: "No other motivation technique known to date can come close to duplicating that record."

Yes: Specifying purpose, measures, and targets is dangerous. But these also create a powerful opportunity to produce significant improvements in performance.

CompStat to CitiStat to PerformanceStat

In 1994, the New York City Police Department (NYPD), under the leadership of Commissioner William Bratton and Deputy Commissioner Jack Maple, created CompStat—a leadership strategy focused on reducing crime. Bratton's targets were quite specific: reduce crime by 10 percent in the first year, by 25 percent by the end of the second year, and by 40 percent over three years (Bratton and Knobler 1998, 202, 194). And, indeed, compared with the baseline of 1993, crime did drop. NYPD reduced crime by 12 percent in 1994, and by 27 percent by the end of 1995. Over three years, however, the reduction was "only" 36 percent.[3]

Since then, numerous police departments, primarily in the US (Weisburd et al. 2004) and Australia (Chilvers and Weatherburn 2004; Mazerolle, Rombouts, and

McBroom 2007), have created their own version of CompStat. Further, other public agencies in New York City, and then elsewhere, created their own adaptations that could be labeled "AgencyStat." For example, in 1998, to improve its performance in moving welfare recipients to employment, the New York City Human Resources Administration created JobStat. In 2005, the Los Angeles Department of Public Social Services established DPSSTATS to improve its own performance. In 2011, the US Department of Housing and Urban Development created HUDStat and the Federal Emergency Management Agency launched FEMAStat.

In 2000, Martin O'Malley, the new mayor of Baltimore created the original CitiStat (Behn 2007). Since then, other cities (primarily in the US) have created their own version (Behn 2006a). Indeed, some US counties and states have created what could, along with CitiStat, be called "JurisdictionStat."

The word "PerformanceStat" (Behn 2008c; Behn 2014) covers all of these similar (but never identical) leadership strategies for improving performance in public agencies and government jurisdictions.

THE PERFORMANCESTAT LEADERSHIP STRATEGY

What, however, is this PerformanceStat? What are the core leadership principles and key operational components that are shared by these various efforts to improve performance? Here is a definition:

> A jurisdiction or agency is employing a PerformanceStat performance strategy if, in an effort to achieve specific public purposes, its leadership team persists in holding an ongoing series of regular, frequent, integrated meetings during which the chief executive and/or the principal members of the chief executive's leadership plus the director (and the top managers) of different subunits use current data to analyze specific, previously defined aspects of each unit's recent performance; to provide feedback on recent progress compared with targets; to follow-up on previous decisions and commitments to produce results; to examine and learn from each unit's efforts to improve performance; to identify and solve performance-deficit problems; and to set and achieve the next performance targets. (Behn 2014)

To employ a PerformanceStat strategy, the leadership team must, indeed, choose purpose, measures, and targets. But they must do more—much more. The purpose, measures, and targets establish what is to be accomplished. They provide the basis for performance accountability. They are not, however, sufficient for success. An effective PerformanceStat leadership strategy includes a number of leadership activities designed to actually achieve these targets and thus their underlying purposes.

Thus, besides purpose, measures, and targets, the design of a PerformanceStat leadership strategy needs to include other components about which the leadership team must make key operational choices and engage in essential leadership practices:

- Data: What kind of current performance data does the organization need to collect?
- Analysis: How can the organization analyze these data so as to identify performance deficits and improvements?
- Meetings: How and when will who conduct what kind of regular, frequent, integrated meetings with whom in the room?
- Feedback: How and who will provide feedback on progress compared with the targets?
- Operational Capacity: Who will build the necessary organizational capabilities (including the ability for central staff and operational units to analyze the data)?
- Follow-Up: Who will employ what kind of follow-up approach to keep everyone focused on the decisions made at the meetings: the problems identified, the solutions proposed, and the commitments made?
- Persistence: How will the leadership team ensure that it does not get distracted but remains focused on performance and results?

This is not, however, a mere mimicking of other CompStats, CitiStats, and PerformanceStats. Indeed, the leadership team needs to think seriously about how it should adapt the principles and components of the strategy to its own situation and to accomplish its own purposes.

As the long definition and the detailed list of leadership practices suggests, PerformanceStat is complex. Nevertheless, underlying this strategy are a number of principles that can help a leadership team keep itself focused on what it needs to do to achieve its targets and purposes. Specifically, by employing—with creativity and diligence — its own PerformanceStat, the members of the leadership team will:

- Focus on eliminating or mitigating their current *performance deficit(s)* that are inhibiting their ability to achieve their targets and purposes.
- *Identify, collect*, and *analyze* current (not last year's historic) data that relate to these purposes and targets, that can help reveal whether or not performance is improving, and that can provide some insight into the changes and differences in performance.
- Establish a routine and rhythm to their effort to produce results through an on-going series of *regular, frequent, integrated meetings* during which they and subunit managers will *analyze their data*, probe both successes and failures for lessons and insights, offer *feedback* on progress, *follow up* on past commitments, look to *learn* what is (and isn't) working (and to foster organizational learning

between meetings), and discuss what slight adjustments or major transformations they need make to their existing performance tactics.

- Help ensure that every unit and every individual *persists* in their collective dedication to improving performance and producing results.

These various leadership practices can motivate people to work with creativity, energy, and dedication to achieve the purposes and targets.

ROUTINE OR REVOLUTION?

All this hardly looks revolutionary. Almost all management books describe almost all of these principles and components. Shouldn't we expect that public executives will automatically do these things? What makes PerformanceStat different? Why does it deserve our attention?

In the abstract, nothing. In the operation, everything. For the PerformanceStat potential comes not from any individual component of the strategy but from their creative combination—from the energy and diligence with which the leadership team adapts these principles and implements these components. Public executives who have developed an effective PerformanceStat strategy are not doing so as a sideline. For them, it is not just another management fad. They are dedicated to using their own PerformanceStat to ensure that their organization improves performance, produces results, achieves its targets, and thus accomplishes its purposes.

PerformanceStat is different because the organization's leadership team is prepared to accept accountability for its performance. Moreover, these executives are prepared to employ a variety of leadership and management principles to produce significant results. As Bratton has been wont to tell mayors: "If you have a police chief that can't get crime down, get yourself a new police chief" (Buntin 2007, 30).

A STRATEGY, NOT A SYSTEM

An effective PerformanceStat leadership strategy consumes time—the most valuable resource of a leadership team. That is why PerformanceStat has been adopted (and adapted) by fewer governmental jurisdictions and public agencies than its accomplishments would suggest. Indeed numerous jurisdictions and agencies have launched their own PerformanceStat only later—as the time commitment became more expensive and thus more obvious—to lose their enthusiasm. They postpone a meeting, cancel a few, then suspend them all. And certainly their subordinates aren't complaining. Who wants to be questioned about some managerial inadequacy in front of superiors, peers, and subordinates? Eventually, these nascent PerformanceStats atrophy and—without even an Eliotian whimper—disappear.

Why? Because those who sought to employ this strategy for improving performance mistook it for a "system." Given how various PerformanceStats have been described, this error is easy to make: CompStat has been described as a "strategic control system" (Jannette 2006, 1; Dabney 2010, 30). Baltimore's CitiStat has been called a "data-driven, strict accountability performance measurement system" (Jannette 2006, 8), "a data-driven management system" (Perez and Rushing 2007, 3), and "a simple operations management tool," "a database system," and "an accountability tool" (Economy League of Greater Philadelphia 2007). For example, Buffalo's CitiStat has been described as a "computerized accountability system" (Meyer 2006).

It is very seductive to think of PerformanceStat — of any CompStat or CitiStat — as a "system." The word "system" suggests that there exists a simple set of technical procedures. Furthermore, it suggests that any organization that simply follows these procedures properly will produce marvelous results. Indeed, the word "system" suggests that you can easily install it in your own organization, push the start button, and walk away. Everything will work smoothly and efficiently—all on automatic pilot.

Unfortunately, PerformanceStat doesn't work that way. It is not close to being as mechanistic as the word "system" implies. It is a leadership strategy, and as such requires active, attentive, dedicated leadership.

Still, because so many people throw the "system" word around so carelessly, many government organizations, in their effort to establish their own PerformanceStat, miss something important — often many somethings. Although numerous organizations have widely publicized that they too have something with the ***Stat suffix, too many of these claims are incapable of realizing the full PerformanceStat potential. They have missed something important. They have ignored the intangible but indispensable role of "leadership".

The system concept is based on the implicit assumption that the organization is the proper unit of analysis. It is the *organization* that has to get the *system* right. Actually, the proper unit of analysis is the leadership team. Too many people, when they seek to understand PerformanceStat, seek to catalog the visible and explicit components of the system. Instead, they need to appreciate the subtle and tacit practices of the leadership team. Any jurisdiction or agency may, indeed, have faithfully copied every piece of some "performance model"; yet the resulting system will contribute little to results without real—constant and consistent—leadership.

Making this "Leadership" Operational

"Leadership" is a buzz word—a fuzzy word. What does it really mean? For PerformanceStat, what is the leadership part?

It is not that complex. And it is certainly not charisma. Rather, it involves a number of essential responsibilities of almost any public executive—certainly of any public executive who seeks to improve performance. These responsibilities require little technical training, but they may require a lot of mentoring, experimentation, and learning. For unless the executive has already accumulated a wide range of managerial and leadership experiences, and unless the executive has been fortunate enough to have been coached by some observant, savvy, and thoughtful tutors, he or she will need to learn a number of new leadership practices.

The leadership practices required to make a PerformanceStat strategy work are quite operational. Nevertheless, they need to be implemented with creativity and subtlety. Here are several of the most important:

- Emphasizing the Purpose: What exactly is the organization trying to accomplish? In too many public-sector organizations, this is never explained clearly and succinctly, let alone with conviction. Yes, there may be a mission statement posted on the wall, but who pays attention? Only if the members of leadership team keeps reiterating their purpose—in both their words and in their behavior—will others take it seriously.

- Establishing Targets: To improve performance, an organization needs not only performance measures with which to assess progress but also targets with which to judge success. Without a target, there is no standard for success. This is why establishing a target is a leadership responsibility. Those who are establishing the organization's standard of success are—by definition—the organization's leaders.

- Providing Feedback: This looks easy. Tell people what they are doing wrong and what they are doing right. But few people like being told that their performance is inadequate. Explaining clearly in what ways performance is inadequate and thus what needs to be fixed—with the necessary urgency, yet without sounding overly critical—is an essential practice that requires an intricate balance. Conversely, complementing people on what they have accomplished while also explaining what needs to be done next is another subtle yet essential leadership practice.

- Conducting the Follow-Up: This appears to be nothing more than asking the question: "Did you get it done?" Doesn't every leader do this? Still, effective leaders can frame questions—in both words and tone—to establish concern, urgency, and focus, without being either too critical or too casual. This follow-up—asking specific questions of specific individuals about specific assignments—creates responsibility. It establishes what Latané, Williams, and their colleagues call "identifiability" (Williams, Harkins, and Latané 1981; Williams et al. 1989). Williams, Harkins, and Latané (1981, 303) observe that "when individual outputs are always identifiable (even in groups), people consistently exert high levels of effort, and if their outputs are never identifiable (even when alone), they consistently exert low levels of effort."

- Recognizing Accomplishment: To the accountability holdees, there exist two distinct possibilities: "When they do something good, nothing happens. But when they screw up, all hell can break loose" (Behn 2001, 3). To improve performance, however, an organization's leaders needs to do more than punish failure. They also need to reward success in a way that is proportional to the success. Often, this needs to be little more than recognition that is appropriate for the accomplishment. For in any organization, recognition conveys status. Consequently, the opportunity to earn recognition, and thus status, can motivate many people.

- Reproving the Recalcitrant: Still, not everyone will quickly sign up to improve their own performance. And the malingerers' deleterious behavior can easily convince the tentatively industrious that their efforts are not valued. So "why bother?" This leadership practice requires more subtlety than recognizing accomplishment. Fortunately, persistently asking questions in a quasi-public meeting—in front of not just superiors but also peers and subordinates—is often an effective way to discipline the recalcitrant, uncooperative, and incompetent.

- Fostering Learning: How can everyone in an organization learn and employ the tactics, strategies, and knowledge of a subunit that has achieved its targets? Helping these "positive deviants" (Spreitzer and Sonenshein 2004) to identify, describe, and explain the source of their success is never easy—particularly when a lot of the knowledge that underlies this success is strictly tacit.

- Running a meeting: This hardly sounds like a *leadership* practice. Running a meeting is a very prosaic task. Every day, in every work place, in every corner of the planet, people run meetings. Yet, what do these meetings accomplish? How many are productive? How many help to produce results? Conducting a meeting that helps an organization to improve performance is a skill—a rather uncommon leadership skill. Indeed, the meeting—more than the data or the analysis—is at the center of the PerformanceStat strategy. For it is at the meeting, with key people present, that the leadership team has the opportunity to emphasize the purpose, establish targets, provide feedback, conduct the follow-up, recognize accomplishment, reprove the recalcitrant, and foster learning.

- Sustaining Persistence: In any organization—particularly in a governmental jurisdiction or public agency—this is not easy. The world is full of problems, and most have acquired their own, well-organized constituency that seeks to push its problem to the top of every priority list. Effective public executives learn how to deal politely with these would-be accountability holders while keeping their organization focused on their public purpose, their performance deficits, and their performance targets.

None of these leadership practices is a skill with which most mortals are born. And none can be taught either. For none can be captured in any form of explicit knowledge. Rather, Polanyi's (1966, 4) characterization of tacit knowledge—"we can know more than we can tell"—certainly applies to leadership. The tacit knowledge needed to engage effectively in any of these leadership practices can be acquired only through experience—with, perhaps, the guidance of some thoughtful advisors, coaches, sages, and confidants. The tacit leadership aspect of PerformanceStat is making sure that the explicit components are functioning so as to improve performance.

Putting These Leadership Practices into Practice

Unfortunately, when you've seen one PerformanceStat, you've seen only one PerformanceStat. Every one is different. Even every CompStat is different. For every effective one, the leadership team will employ these leadership practices differently. After all, every organization has different performance deficits; consequently, the details of the strategy that the members of its leadership team employ to improve performance will be, necessarily, different. Still, they are somehow employing each of these practices. But they are adapting them not just to achieve their specific purposes but also to mesh with their organizational culture and political circumstances. And, in the process, they will hold both their organization and themselves accountable.

Accountability for What Performance?

No one is opposed to accountability for performance. Still, the accountability holders and the accountability holdees each conceptualize it differently, define it differently, and think differently about how it should work. Unfortunately, for the accountability holdees—for the public executives who (whether they like it or not) will be held accountable for performance—most of the accountability holders think that accountability for performance is operationally indistinguishable from accountability for finances and fairness.

Unfortunately—and fortunately—the burden of rethinking accountability for performance thus falls to the accountability holdees. This is unfortunate because, if these executives fail to redefine what it means for them to be accountable for performance, others will do it for them. At the same time, this is fortunate because, if public executives accept and adopt the performance-target ethic, they will be able to define the nature of the performance for which they will be accountable.

Employing a PerformanceStat leadership strategy is not the only way to do this, but it is one way. By articulating a clear public purpose, establishing specific performance targets, and then mobilizing their organization to achieve those targets, the leadership team of a public agency is, indeed, establishing the basis for which it will be accountable for performance.

This of course makes the leadership team and its organization vulnerable. For if they fail to achieve their performance targets, the accountability holders will yell and scream. Employing traditional accountability-holding behavior, they will demand that heads must roll.

But by failing to articulate its public purpose and establish its performance targets, the leadership team is also making itself vulnerable. For this permits the accountability holders to choose the purposes, measures, and targets that they think are appropriate. Inevitably, they will choose purposes, measures, and targets that the organization is failing to achieve.

Accountability for performance requires a clear definition of the expectations for performance. The only question is who will create these expectations. Will the members of the leadership teams of a public agency or government jurisdiction implicitly delegate this responsibility to others? Or will they establish their own, very explicit expectations? A PerformanceStat leadership strategy is one way to do this.

NOTES

1. If a public agency is producing results that are below (or above) its usual level of performance, what should we expect in the future? Answer: The agency will "regress" or move towards its normal mean. Regardless of what its managers or employees do, if a public agency has been performing very badly, we would expect it to improve. Conversely, if an organization has been doing particularly well, we would expect its performance to slip. (Hint to would-be public managers: Don't take a job managing a well-performing agency; for even if you are brilliant, regression towards the mean may undermine your efforts. Instead, do take a job managing a poorly performing agency; as long as you avoid big mistakes that make things worse, regression towards the mean can help your reputation.)
2. It would be tempting to pass a law or promulgate a rule requiring all agencies to set performance targets. And if we do so, all agencies will comply. They will, however, see this requirement as just another regulatory hoop-jumping exercise. Yes, they will jump through it. But they will not take the hoop seriously.
3. These data are constructed from the FBI's Uniform Crime Reporting Statistics, using the "UCR Data Tool" at<http://www.ucrdatatool.gov/> (February 5, 2012). Also note: After a clash with New York Mayor Guiliani, Bratton resigned as NYPD's commissioner in the spring of 1996, having served not three full years but only two years and three months. In 2014, New York's Mayor-Elect Bill de Blasio reappointed Bratton to be NYPD's commissioner.

REFERENCES

Behn, R. D. 2001. *Rethinking Democratic Accountability*. Washington, DC: Brookings Institution Press.

Behn, R. D. 2006a. "The Varieties of CitiStat." *Public Administration Review*, 66: 332–40.

Behn, R. D. 2006b. "On Why Public Managers Need to Focus on Their Performance Deficit." *Bob Behn's Performance Management Report*, 4(1 September).

Behn, R. D. 2007. *What All Mayors Would Like to Know About Baltimore's CitiStat Performance Strategy*. Washington, DC: IBM Center for the Business of Government.

Behn, R. D. 2008a. "On Why Every Evaluation Begins with the Question: 'Compared with What?'" *Bob Behn's Performance Leadership Report*, 6(1 September) <http://www.ksg.harvard.edu/The BehnReport/September2006.pdf>.

Behn, R. D. 2008b. "On Why Citizens Need to Establish the Performance-Target Ethic." *Bob Behn's Performance Leadership Report*, 6 (3 November).

Behn, R. D. 2008c. "Designing PerformanceStat: Or What Are the Key Strategic Choices that a Jurisdiction or Agency Must Make When Adapting the CompStat/CitiStat Class of Performance Strategies?" *Public Performance and Management Review*, 32: 206–35.

Behn, R. D. 2014. *The PerformanceStat Potential: A Leadership Strategy for Producing Results*. Washington, DC: Brooking Institution Press.

Bratton, W. and Knobler, P. 1998. *Turnaround: How America's Top Cop Reversed the Crime Epidemic*. New York: Random House.

Buntin, J. 2007. "Solid Brass. Public Official of the Year William J. Bratton." *Governing*, 21: 30.

Chilvers, M. and Weatherburn, D. 2004. "The New South Wales 'Compstat' Process: Its Impact on Crime." *The Australian and New Zealand Journal of Criminology*, 37: 22-48.

Dabney, D. 2010. "Observations Regarding Key Operational Realities in a Compstat Model of Policing." *Justice Quarterly*, 27: 28–51.

Duncan, W. J. 1989. *Great Ideas in Management: Lessons from the Founders and Foundations of Managerial Practice*. San Francisco: Jossey-Bass.

Economy League of Greater Philadelphia. July 20, 2007. *Best Practices: Baltimore's CitiStat*. Retrieved from <http://economyleague.org/node/183>.

Government Accountability Office. 2011. *Government Auditing Standards*. Washington, DC: U.S. Government Printing Office.

Hackman, J. R. 1986. The Psychology of Self-Management in Organizations, pp. 89–136 in *Psychology and Work: Productivity, Change, and Employment*, eds. M. S. Pallack and R. O. Perloff. Washington, DC: American Psychological Association.

Jannette, J. 2006. *COMPSTAT for Corrections*. Irvine, CA: Center for Evidence-Based Corrections, University of California.

Latham, G. P., Borgogni, L., and Petitta, L. 2008. "Goal Setting and Performance Management in the Public Sector." *International Public Management Journal*, 11: 385–403.

Latham, G. P. and Pinder, C. C. 2005. "Work Motivation Theory and Research at the Dawn of the Twenty-First Century." *Annual Review of Psychology*, 56: 485–516.

Locke, E. A. and Latham, G. P. 1984. *Goal Setting: A Motivational Technique That Works*. Englewood Cliffs, NJ: Prentice Hall.

Locke, E. A. and Latham, G. P. 2004. "What Should We Do About Motivation Theory?" *The Academy of Management Review*, 29: 388–403.

Mazerolle, L. G., Rombouts, S., and McBroom, J. 2007. "The Impact of COMPSTAT on Reported Crime in Queensland." *Policing*, 30: 237–56.

Meyer, B. 2006. CitiStat Begins Tracking of Operations. *The Buffalo News*, June 17.

Moore, M. H. 1995. *Creating Public Value: Strategic Management in Government*. Cambridge, MA: Harvard University Press.

Perez, T. and Rushing, R. 2007. *The CitiStat Model: How Data-Driven Government Can Increase Efficiency and Effectiveness*. Washington, DC: Center for American Progress.

Poister, T. H. 2004. Performance Monitoring, pp. 98–125 in *Handbook of Practical Performance Evaluation* (second edition), eds. J. S. Wholey, H. P. Hatry, and K. E. Newcomer. San Francisco: Jossey-Bass.

Polanyi, M. 1966. *The Tacit Dimension*. Chicago: The University of Chicago Press.

Power, M. 1994. *The Audit Explosion*. London: Demos.

Power, M. 2005. The Theory of the Audit Explosion, pp. 326–44 in *The Oxford Handbook of Public Management*, eds. E. Ferlie, L. E. Lynn Jr. and C. Pollitt. Oxford: Oxford University Press.

Spreitzer, G. M. and Sonenshein, S. 2004. "Toward the Construct Definition of Positive Deviance." *American Behavioral Scientist*, 47: 828–47.

Weisburd, D., Mastrofski, S., Greenspan, R., and Willis, J. 2004. *The Growth of Compstat in American Policing*. Washington, DC: Police Foundation.

Williams, K. D., Harkins, S., and Latané, B. 1981. "Identifiability as a Deterrent to Social Loafing: Two Cheering Experiments." *Journal of Personality and Social Psychology*, 40: 303–11.

Williams, K. D., Nida, S. A., Baca, L. D., and Latané, B. 1989. "Social Loafing and Swimming: Effects of Identifiability on Individual and Relay Performance of Intercollegiate Swimmers." *Basic and Applied Social Psychology*, 10: 73–81.

CHAPTER 29

INDEPENDENT REGULATORS

COLIN SCOTT

INDEPENDENT REGULATORS AS ACCOUNTABILITY FORUMS

THIS chapter addresses the contribution of independent regulators to public account-ability. Independent regulators comprise mechanisms established at one remove from elected politicians and government departments for overseeing the activities of busi-ness, governmental, and third sectors (cf. Selznick 1985) through setting rules or norms and engaging in practices of monitoring and enforcement (Black 2002). The rise of the regulatory state has been one of the key policy trends of the late twentieth and early twenty-first centuries, involving the proliferation of agencies operating at arm's length from government and a tendency towards formalization of relationships (Majone 1994; Braithwaite 1999; Moran 2003; Dubash and Morgan 2012). Whilst the implications of this phenomenon for public policymaking and implementation have been extensively explored, the question of the contribution of independent regulators to the accountabil-ity of government generally has been little addressed.

Independent regulators offer both potential weaknesses and strengths as account-ability mechanisms. A key strength of independent regulators lies in the dispersal of power which their existence entails. Even where elected politicians and their depart-ments retain policy responsibilities in particular domains, the existence of an indepen-dent regulator creates an alternative source of knowledge and authority through which both government and regulated organizations may be held to account. A potentially negative aspect of this dispersal of power and authority is the capacity for actors to shift blame on to others for failings, facilitating an avoidance of accountability (Hood 2011, 149–50, 160–170). A further distinct problem is that actors with overlapping knowledge and power may be caught in an "accountability conspiracy" in which it is against the interests of key actors to blow the whistle on others because failures of one are seen as failures of others (Dowding 1995, 70).

Overall the existence of independent regulators contributes to the transparency of governmental activities with a tendency to diminish the concentration of power with ministers and their departments. In certain sectors, such the network industries, the establishment of independent regulators has become a core principle of good governance. A normative imperative to establish independent regulatory capacity arguably underpins the significant increase in numbers of independent regulatory agencies across the industrialized countries since the 1970s, extending beyond economic regulation to other key sectors and also to cross-sectoral economic and social policy domains such as competition, occupational health and consumer protection, and the regulation of government by supreme audit institutions, ombudsman schemes, and other types of oversight body. The emergence of independent regulators at supra-national level and in private or non-state governance arrangements adds further complexity to a picture of diffused governance which is, increasingly, not wholly within the control of national governments. This chapter evaluates the accountability case for these trends and its effects on governance more generally.

THE PROLIFERATION OF INDEPENDENT REGULATORS

Independent regulation emerged in the eighteenth and nineteenth centuries within European and North American government systems as a response to the demands of urbanization and industrialization and a recognition of the limited capacity for executive action of central government administrations (Chadwick 1829; Neocleous 1998; Raeff 1983; Rhodes 1981). The US independent regulatory agencies, which are perhaps the best established and best known, appear to owe their origins to the quasi-judicial tribunal form which had developed in the UK in bodies such as the Railways and Canals Commission (Dimock 1933). The Interstate Commerce Commission, established in 1887, was the first example at federal level. In their original conception as quasi-judicial bodies, the accountability contribution of these independent regulators was similar to that of courts, involving robust independence and systems of appeal against administrative decisions (Sharfman 1931). Something of this character remains in the US independent agencies which are characterized by relatively high degrees both of delegation and independence, subject to judicial oversight of both an internal and an external kind. Within many European systems independent regulation was established rather more clearly as an executive rather than a judicial function. Within the UK and other non-US common law systems a degree of ambiguity on this issue characterizes regulatory governance institutions. Arguably the strongest independence is attributed to regulators of public sector bodies, such as supreme audit institutions and ombudsman offices, which require a high degree of autonomy to discharge constitutional or quasi-constitutional functions (Hood et al. 1999). In respect of business regulators the nature and extent of independence is variable.

The proliferation of independent regulators as instruments of government has been remarkable throughout the member countries of the Organization for Economic Co-operation and Development (OECD) and beyond since the 1970s and surely justifies the claim of "the rise of the regulatory state" (Majone 1994). Recent research collecting time series data across 15 sectors in 48 countries (including all OECD member states), shows that the 1990s were the peak period for the creation of regulatory agencies at national level and that by 2007 regulatory agencies were present in nearly three quarters of the 720 case study sectors (Jordana, Levi-Faur, and Marín 2011, 1344). Various explanations have been advanced for the rise of independent regulatory agencies across the developed countries and also at supranational level and amongst private actors. This research sees the proliferation of agencies as a product of a variety of forms of policy transfer rather than as an isolated response to a pressing policy problem. The pattern of growth can only be properly explained as an international policy trend (Jordana, Levi-Faur, and Marín 2011). Indeed, a significant strand of research suggests that the spread of independent regulators has been driven as much by a desire for legitimacy through adoption of internationally accepted institutional models, as by a concern for enhanced regulatory policy and practice (Gilardi 2008). A further distinct set of arguments suggests that independent regulation has been extended in scope to demonstrate both the commitment to addressing major policy failures such as infected blood products in France and BSE in the UK and more significantly a commitment to the protection of capital (Roberts 2010, 99–100).

The rise of agencies is not restricted to the level of the nation state. Within the European Union (EU) some limited regulatory capacity has been assigned to independent EU-level agencies, for example in the fields of food safety and pharmaceuticals (Geradin, Munoz, and Petit 2005). Just as significant at the European level are the networks of national regulators, for example in energy and communications. These regulatory networks enhance the capacity of national regulators through sharing of strategic and operational knowledge. Additionally they bolster the legitimacy of national regulators to act independently of their national governments in pursuit of the integrity of the regulatory regime over political concerns (Eberlein and Grande 2005; Levi-Faur 2011). On one view the establishment of European regulatory networks is an acknowledgement of the problem that national regulatory agencies operating regimes substantially determined at the level of the EU are agents to two principals: national governments and the European Union institutions, notably the Commission (Coen and Thatcher 2008, 54–5). The networks enhance the capacity of national regulators to hold governments to account for deviations from European policy objectives.

Though the growth of independent regulators of business has received most attention in the literature, a more direct contribution of independent regulators to public accountability lies with those organizations whose remit is to scrutinize governmental activities, offering a form of horizontal accountability for state actors (Hughes, Mears, and Winch 1997). The gradual enhancement to the powers and role of supreme audit institutions and ombudsman schemes (addressed in Posner's chapter in this volume) can be seen as the application of the independent regulation model to government and an acknowledgement of the limits on the capacity of parliaments to hold government effectively to account (MacCarthaigh 2012). Indeed, such constitutional offices are frequently characterized by greater independence from elected government, sometimes achieved through a relationship with legislators, in order to provide reassurance as to their capacity to act independently of governmental agendas (Hood et al. 2004; Hood et al. 1999). The range of independent regulators with responsibilities for overseeing government as their exclusive or partial role include, at national level, human rights bodies, freedom of information and data protection regulators, and a wide range of inspection bodies. Key supranational organizations also oversee governments. In the European Union these organizations include the European Commission itself (overseeing both compliance with the treaty obligations generally and implementation of particular legislative and expenditure activities in particular (Majone 1996)), the anti-fraud unit, OLAF, and the European Court of Auditors (the principal focus of the European Ombudsman being the EU institutions themselves) (Hood et al. 1999).

Internationally, beyond the EU, the United Nations Human Rights Committee oversees national compliance with human rights obligations (Egan 2011), the World Trade Organization offers a form of regulatory oversight for compliance by governments with trade rules (Cass 2005), and a variety of other bodies also oversee compliance with international norms in areas such as environmental policy and labor rights (Abbott and Snidal 2009). At least as significant in the international context has been the growth of private regulatory organizations, particularly engaged in the setting of rules and standards (Brunsson and Jacobsson 2000), and increasingly engaged in a wider range of regulatory functions across many policy domains (Büthe and Mattli 2011; Scott, Cafaggi and Senden 2011). These private regulators sometimes compete with governments, for example in the setting of environmental standards, and sometimes hold governments to account more directly, for example through setting and monitoring for compliance with human rights standards.

Independent Regulators and the Enhancement of Accountable Governance

Whether explained as providing solutions to particular policy problems or as an example of policy transfer of various kinds, the establishment of independent regulators has grown beyond these origins to assume a place amongst the canons of good governance. For example, the OECD Recommendations on Regulatory Policy and Governance suggest that governments consider the establishment of independent regulatory agencies where this is required for public confidence or to provide assurance of competitive neutrality (for example between state-owned and privately-owned undertakings) (OECD 2012, paragraph 7.3). Examples of agencies established at one remove from government to promote public confidence include human rights bodies. *The Paris Principles relating to the Status of National Institutions* [for protecting human rights] emphasize a number of organizational requirements which can guarantee the independence of human rights regulators from government, since it is chiefly government itself which is regulated (United Nations Human Rights Commissioner 1993). In the case of human rights, oversight may involve review both of the legislative and administrative actions of government. The network industries provide the core example for agencies established at one remove from government to promote competitive neutrality. In the EU it is a core doctrine of EU policies in communications and energy sectors that member states should have independent regulators to oversee such matters as competition and universal service provision (Coen and Héritier 2005). The underlying policy reason for this is that it reduces the capacity of ministers to give priority to industrial policy or fiscal needs by favoring publicly owned operators or privately owned "national champions," thus imperiling competition in the single European market (Thatcher and Stone Sweet 2002).

More generally the relative insulation from politics, which is a defining characteristic of independent regulation, is rationalized as enabling the state to credibly commit to a degree of continuity in the application of regulatory policies driven by the functional needs of the sector or policy domain rather than wider political considerations (Thatcher 2002). The extent of the imperative to establish such independent regulatory organizations in some sectors is dependent on understandings of the wider political environment. Research for the OECD suggests that independent regulation is particularly important in political systems which are subject to pendulum swing politics, where industrial policies may change radically over quite short periods (Levy and Spiller 1996). Similar conclusions have been reached in a European context also (Gilardi 2008, 7).Whilst these arguments apply in particular to network industries, where businesses fearing political changes might be reluctant to invest in costly infrastructure, application of the arguments in respect of social regulation might emphasize the significance of independent regulation for achieving social stability, for example in the context of industrial relations. In the case of oversight of human rights, public expenditure, and other aspects of governmental activity, arguments for independent regulation are based on the direct interest of government in the matters overseen.

Independent agencies are frequently described as non-majoritarian institutions because their leaders are typically appointed rather than elected. Evidence from the United States suggests that elected commissioners in state public utility commissions are liable to favor consumer over industry interests (for example by favoring low prices over building up capacity for long term investment) (Besley 2002). Perhaps because of the risk of an excessive consumer orientation, most governments favor appointed leaders. The appointment of regulators is typically made by elected politicians in recognition of the limits of democratic decision-making.

From the perspective of good governance, the establishment of independent regulators is liable not only to insulate certain decision-making from political interference, but also to increase its transparency, because key relationships are put on a more formal footing and decisions and decision-makers become more visible (Scott 2000). The quality and intensity of the transparency may depend on the forms of decision-making. Regulators established for their expertise, for example, may choose to engage in participatory and even deliberative processes with key stakeholders. Other things being equal requirements to report on broad performance are likely to challenge both regulators and government more than the adoption of narrow compliance indicators (Heald 2006, 39). With such an approach we are evaluating the performance of an entire regime rather than any single actor within it, and consequently not calling any one state actor to account but rather the combination of state and non-state actors responsible for contributing to broad outcomes (Black 2008; May 2007). Such an approach may make it more difficult for elected politicians to deploy agency strategies to escape accountability for weaknesses in systems designed and legislated by them (Hood 2011, 149–50, 160–170; May 2007, 12).The contribution of more transparent regulation to the accountability of government will be variable, typically higher where the regulator regulates government itself, and thus reports directly on its finances, its maladministration, compliance with human rights obligations, and so on, and more tangential where regulation is of businesses. In this latter case the most significant enhancement to transparency of government is likely to arise from putting government–industry relationships on a more formalized footing, with less discretion to act over both publicly-owned and private companies by ministerial fiat and a greater tendency to write obligations down (Prosser 1997). In some cases an agency may, through enhanced transparency, be considerably more accountable for its public actions than the ministerial department from which its functions were carved (Prosser 2010, 317) and may thus enhance governmental accountability overall. Examples include not only the well-investigated network industries, but also food and pharmaceutical policies.

Variety in Regulatory Powers and Design

The capacity of independent regulators to act as mechanisms of accountability is dependent on highly varied arrangements in respect of: first, extent of delegation and second, the structure of their relations to other actors. The extent and nature of delegation is highly variable. Willis (1958) described Canadian (and by extension US) independent regulators which had rule-making, monitoring, and enforcement powers delegated to them as "governments in miniature." The appropriateness of combining these powers in single agencies has long been questioned in the United States (Black 2008, 141; Landis 1938). Growth in regulatory agencies in the United Kingdom from the 1980s and elsewhere in Europe has tended to involve only limited delegation of rule-making powers (if any) and reserved formal application of sanctions to the courts, often involving regulators in convoluted and practically unusable processes of enforcement. At the level of the European Union, the European Commission has for many years exercised direct enforcement powers, acting as a kind of independent regulator directly over anti-competitive conduct by businesses and other undertakings within the EU (Majone 1996). A shift amongst national governments in the EU to similarly assign direct enforcement powers (notably the power to issue substantial fines) may be traced in part to changes in competition law enforcement under which duties and powers were to be shared between the European Commission and national competition authorities (Wilks 2005). There has, however, been a wider trend to assigning direct enforcement powers (without the need for an application to a court) to independent regulators in the UK and elsewhere within the EU (Baldwin 2004).

At the level of the EU generally, independent agencies have tended towards having rather more limited powers. The European Food Safety Authority (EFSA), established in 2002, has, for example, no powers to make or enforce rules, but is largely restricted to information gathering and advisory functions. This is not to suggest that soft power is unimportant. In the case of EFSA its power largely derives from its building a reputation for scientific expertise and independence from interests including political pressures (Randall 2006, 414). Distinctly EU governance arrangements for regulation have been very much affected by the growth of networking arrangements as mechanisms of steering activity both of governments and regulators. Indeed, Maggetti (2012, 175) identifies participation in regulatory networks as a key factor in bolstering capacity for regulators vis-à-vis regulatees, enhancing their "emancipation from the regulatees."

Concerning the relations of independent regulators to others, the nature and extent of agency independence is important both to understanding the limitations placed on democratic governance and, relatedly, the extent to which agencies have their decisions on regulatory matters insulated from politics. In this context we are thinking chiefly of independence relative to ministers (though it is also possible to think about independence relative to regulatees when concerned with understanding the extent of regulatory capture). Gilardi's (2008, 7) major study of regulatory agencies in Europe found a tendency towards greater formal independence for agencies in the utilities sectors, where insulation from the vagaries of political change was most significant for fostering credible commitment to the stability of regulatory policy as a means of encouraging investment. Whilst it is possible to make an assessment of the extent of formal independence for any particular regime by looking at such matters as the division of responsibilities between agencies and ministers and powers of ministers to make interventions, such as directions (Gilardi 2008), it is arguable that an assessment of the de facto independence is more significant in any particular case (Maggetti 2012). It has frequently been observed, for example, that even agencies with relatively limited formal powers can take on considerable de facto power (and thus independence) through establishing authority and reputation in their sphere of activity (Carpenter 2010; Hall, Scott, and Hood 2000; Maggetti 2012, 35). Maggetti (2012, 39), noting the wide range of different concepts of autonomy deployed in research on agencies, offers a simple, two part definition of de facto independence premised on

(1) *the self-determination of agencies' preferences*, and (2) *the agencies' autonomy throughout the use of regulatory competencies*, that is, during the activity of regulation [italics in original].

To assess the extent of de facto independence Maggetti looked at a range of factors in selected national agencies in European states, including the extent to which agency staff had or would work in the central public administration, frequency of contacts between agencies and ministries, budgetary autonomy, organizational autonomy, board composition, vulnerability of board members to replacement at will of politicians, and extent of involvement of government actors in agency rule-making. Maggetti (2012, 74–5) concluded that the extent of de facto independence of agencies from ministers and their departments was highly variable, with variations both by policy domain and by country. De facto independence was most commonly high where there many veto players (and thus a form of extended accountability to others (Scott 2000)) and where the agency was long established, de facto independence growing over time. Examining processes of law-making, Maggetti's (2012, 139–40) research found that the line between implementation of regulatory policy, the traditional role of independent regulators in Europe, and the making of policy in legislation, traditionally the role of government and legislature, had become blurred, with regulatory agencies taking on a key role in the early and formal stages of policy making in key sectors studied. From this analysis we might equate the observation of de facto independence of regulatory agencies with a capacity to hold others, in particular government ministers and departments, to account, not only in respect of the operational matters which are traditionally the concern of independent regulators, but also in respect of policy and legislative processes with which they are seen increasingly to be involved.

Courts and tribunals may also be seen as a form of independent regulator, albeit with a different underlying logic, thus creating a form of competition with agencies over independent authority. Courts traditionally have seen their role as underpinning the integrity of the legal system and commitments to formal procedural requirements which comprise the rule of law (Teubner 1998). In contrast the logic of regulators is likely to have a functional orientation tied, for example, to the substantive objectives set down in their statutory mandates such as ensuring the efficient operation of the market, promoting safety, protecting the environment, and so on (Parker et al. 2004). Formal procedural concerns are likely to be secondary. It is perhaps not coincidental that in the United States, where there is the longest developed experience of independent regulatory agencies, the courts are seen to have moved somewhat from more formal to more substantive modes of reasoning in addressing issues for decision, with more developed ways for collecting policy evidence, and for evaluating competing claims to efficiency of outcomes (Atiyah and Summers 1991; Horwitz 1992). It is possible to hypothesize that the courts' frequent engagement with substantive regulatory issues in the United States has created a form of accountability which has shifted their reasoning towards a more substantive model. Thus whilst the tendency towards adversarial legalism in much of American life (Kagan 2003), including regulatory affairs (Kagan 2000), is widely noted, it is a form of legalism involving a more substantive and less procedural form of law than would be true for many other jurisdictions.

EFFECTS OF INDEPENDENT REGULATORS AS ACCOUNTABILITY MECHANISMS

Evidence as to the effects of independent regulators on public accountability generally is limited, in part because few research projects have directly addressed the role of independent regulators as accountability forums. The establishment of an independent regulator and the delegation of powers to it, frequently transfers powers that might otherwise be exercised by a minister, but such transfers are frequently not total, so ministers retain responsibilities and typically have staffs within their departments which shadow regulation in the sector so they may be advised as to when and how to exercise the powers. Such mechanisms are designed to protect against the capture of regulators by regulatees. However, they also act as a form of accountability for ministers, since a regime structured in this way establishes an independent source of public authority and judgment. Where, for example, a minister uses her power in a manner contrary to the regulator's view of the best interests of the sector, or the public interest, there is the capacity to complain privately or to go public with the misgivings, for example in evidence to committees of legislative bodies or in litigation. The establishment of independent regulators is thus a mechanism for increasing transparency of regulation generally, but also of ministerial exercise of power more particularly. Other things being equal, a minister with powers in a sector or a policy domain with an independent regulator is likely to be more accountable because the regulator's opinion of the minister's actions is likely to be well-informed and underpinned by the authority of public independence.

The precise form such ministerial accountability takes depends on whether powers shared with the regulator are exercised in serial or parallel fashion. A requirement of serial exercise of powers (for example ministers make the rules and agencies implement them) gives both ministers and agency powers of veto over the other. Where powers are held serially, Gilardi (2008, 136) suggests that independent regulators "reinforce stability, because they constitute additional veto points." From a government perspective ministers cannot move without the agency and vice versa. Where powers are held in parallel, either formally or in substance, either party may act without the other to engage or implement change. Gilardi (2008, 136) suggests that the relative autonomy of independent regulators, both formally, as he demonstrates, and de facto, as Maggetti discusses (see above), may commonly establish parallel capacity. Clearly, as regards ministers this is a different form of accountability since independent regulators can, to a degree, act where a minister does not, possibly using powers in a way that was not envisaged. Gilardi

(2008, 136) refers to the example of the Swiss telecoms regulator achieving a more rapid liberalization of the sector than ministers sought. Similarly, the UK telecoms regulator used powers to modify licenses to turn itself into a competition authority for the sector (Hall, Scott and Hood 2000). This potential for parallel authority being exercised, even though perhaps rarely, creates a form of day-to-day mutual accountability between regulators and ministers.

In the case of regulators of government it is common to find that powers assigned to them are very restricted, frequently limited to monitoring and reporting. The tendency towards assigning limited powers is an acknowledgement both that formal enforcement over public actors is challenging (Lodge and Wegrich 2012, 123–5; Wilson and Rachal 1977) and also that in many instances the process of correcting deviant behavior is assigned to political rather than bureaucratic processes. To be effective in holding public actors to account much regulation of the public sector requires political support and acceptance.

Accountability of Regulators: Quis Custodet Ipsos Custodes?

Discussion of the contribution of independent regulators to public accountability would not be complete without acknowledging that the establishment of independent regulators can be seen as creating a challenge to democratic governance generally and public accountability in particularly (Maggetti 2010; Maggetti 2012, 141, 187; Thiel et al. 2012, 433; Vibert 2007). Within the political science and economics literature the accountability issues are frequently presented as generic problems of agency—notably risks of "bureaucratic drift," a concern that agencies will, over time, develop and prioritize their own agendas at the expense of their legislative mandate (Horn 1995) or be subject to capture by those they are supposed to regulate (Bernstein 1951; Makkai and Braithwaite 1992; Stigler 1971). Indeed, in his study of European agencies Gilardi (2008, 4) shows that practices of delegation to independent regulators do not conform to standard expectations about delegation precisely because the agencies' preferences do not appear to conform sufficiently to those of the principals, the governments which created them and delegated to them, and because the extent of ex post control appears weak. Whilst in the US, administrative procedure requirements have underpinned an extensive involvement for the courts in oversight of agencies, the intensity of the relationship between judges and regulators varies greatly across different states, and courts have sometimes shown deference to the expertise of the organizations concerned. Audit and grievance-handling mechanisms have been relatively slow to bring independent regulators effectively within their remit (Humpherson 2010). Furthermore regulatory issues frequently lack the salience required to attract sustained social or media scrutiny. Variation in the extent of delegation has implications both for the efficiency and accountability of regulatory regimes. The fragmented character of much regulatory capacity, with responsibility for rules, monitoring, and enforcement lying with different parts of government, reduces the power and thus an aspect of the problems associated with delegation to regulatory agencies. Such fragmentation not only reduces the accountability demands of any one component of a regulatory regime but also, distinctly, creates a form of interdependence which may to a degree substitute for formal accountability (Scott 2000).

Partly as a response to concerns that regulation might be captured by industry actors, neo-liberal governments of the early 1980s initiated policies to deregulate key sectors, telecommunications, trucking, and aviation in the United States, and network industries in the United Kingdom (Armstrong 2000; Majone 1990). These policies were accompanied by a wider challenge to "red tape" in general strategies to challenge the political urge to introduce new regulation to address issues of high political salience (Froud, Boden, and Ogus 1998). Over time the emphasis of these policies has shifted away from de regulation to better regulation (Weatherill 2007) and regulatory impact assessment (Jacobs 2007). Policies of better regulation, adopted throughout the OECD countries do, in principle, extend to both legislative activities and their implementation within regulatory regimes and create a form of accountability for both for activities of government in initiating regulation and implementation by agencies. Arrangements for oversight of regulation are highly diverse. The OECD principles are supportive both of political leadership for better regulation policies and the establishment of independent capacity to oversee their execution (OECD 2012, 22–3).

Research Agenda

The contribution of independent regulators to the accountability of government overall has rarely been directly considered. Empirical research on regulatory regimes offers some hints as to how we might begin to conceptualize this potential.

A significant strand of politics research on regulation has emphasized the non-majoritarian character of independent regulators. On one view this deviation from democratic governance principles is tolerated because of the advantages it presents in terms both of expertise and capacity for credible commitment. Consideration of the accountability-of-government question offers another rationale for independent regulators which can be presented as part of a strengthening of democratic governance rather than as an exception to it. They can thus be conceived as an aspect of "monitory democracy," one of numerous mechanisms with the potential to give greater visibility to state activities (Keane 2009). The strongest version of this argument is made with the case of regulators of government, who require independence from government to provide assurance over such matters as public expenditure, human rights, and maladministration. In the case of supreme audit institutions and grievance handlers the independent regulators often report to committees of the legislature, thus tying them directly to democratic governance arrangements. The position of other forms of independent regulator could be bolstered through similar arrangements, going beyond the idea of hearings around appointments, common in some jurisdictions, to include more systematic engagement over the holding of government to account, even in respect of regulation of business.

Independent regulators characterized as private and/or supranational in character, present a different kind of challenge for further research. The idea of tying their capacity for holding governments to account to democratic institutions is more challenging and more mixed in prospect (Curtin and Senden 2011). In the case of the European Union, there has been a trend towards greater involvement of parliamentary committees in reviewing the activities of EU-level regulators, both in business domains (e.g. food and energy) and regulation of government (for example audit). Such engagement offers parliamentarians a more systematic basis for evaluation both of the European institutions and, in some policy domains, member state governments. The European institutions are always likely to be the main focus of European parliamentarians.

In the cases both of other international governmental organizations and of private regulators, it is less obvious who or what might constitute the appropriate demos to bolster and take advantage of the capacity of independent regulators to create forms of accountability. More fundamentally there might be doubts as to how strong a source of alternative accountability such organizations might be. With inter-governmental organizations they have missions organized typically around setting standards for securing objectives of the international community concerned for example with trade and human rights. Their practices provide an alternative source of thinking around such matters as human rights obligations. But the practical capacity of such organizations is rather limited, depending on the activities of states to hold each other to account, through complaints and litigation in the case of trade (Cass 2005), and through processes of periodic review in the case of human rights (Gaer 2007). We might say of such regimes that it is the international community which supplies both the standards and the limited accountability capacity associated with them.

Private regulators emerge for a wide variety of reasons. Some are trade associations which have gone beyond lobbying government (a practice which itself creates a form of accountability for government policymaking) to establish their own capacity for setting and/or enforcing norms. Where the activities are targeted directly at government, as with organizations such as Amnesty International and Transparency International (TI), we can see rather clear patterns of accountability, for example in the publication of the corruption index by TI which ranks states by reference to perceptions of corruption. Such practices exemplify "private regulation of the public sector" (Scott 2002).With other kinds of organization, for example technical standards bodies, and environmental NGOs, the links to government may be limited. For both sorts of organization the question arises as to where lies the source of their legitimacy to act. For standards bodies and environmental regulators we may argue that the regulatees choose to adopt their regime (though for some it may be imposed through contracts). Few governments choose to be overseen by Amnesty or TI. If the legitimacy of such organizations is weak this is liable to reduce their capacity to act as accountability forums.

Overall, understanding of the role of independent regulators in establishing public accountability is not yet well understood. Much of the activity arises out of informal rather than formal power with the consequence it is difficult to identify precisely, and may be highly variable in effects depending on particular contexts. For some the absence of strong hierarchical power might cause them to dismiss the role of independent regulators, or equate it to that of the media who similarly lack formal mandates to hold government to account. An alternative vision is to suggest that, as with governance generally, accountability increasingly occurs through participation in networked arrangements within which few actors, whether national or supranational, public or private, exercise true autonomy, but rather must be constantly accounting for their actions to others within the network (Goodin 2003; Scott 2000). On this view a solution to weaknesses in accountability in any particular domain might consist of bolstering the numbers and capacities of actors within the network who can remedy these problems (Dunsire 1996; Morgan 2006).

REFERENCES

Abbott, K. and Snidal, D. 2009. The Governance Triangle: Regulatory Standards Institutions and the Shadow of the State, pp. 44–88 in *The Politics of Global Regulation*, eds. W. Mattli and N. Woods. Princeton: Princeton University Press.

Armstrong, K. 2000. *Regulation, Deregulation, Reregulation*. London: Kogan Page.

Atiyah, P. S. and Summers, R. S. 1991. *Form and Substance in Anglo-American Law: A Comparative Study in Legal Reasoning, Legal Theory, and Legal Institutions*. Oxford: Oxford University Press.

Baldwin, R. 2004. "The New Punitive Regulation." *Modern Law Review*, 67: 351–83.

Bernstein, M. H. 1951. *Regulating Business by Independent Commission*. Princeton: Princeton University Press.

Besley, T. 2002. "Elected Versus Appointed Regulators: Theory and Evidence." *Journal of the European Economic Association*, 1: 1176–1206.

Black, J. 2002. "Critical Reflections on Regulation." *Australian Journal of Legal Philosophy*, 27: 1–35.

Black, J. 2008. "Constructing and Contesting Legitimacy and Accountability in Polycentric Regulatory Regimes." *Regulation and Governance*, 2: 137–64.

Braithwaite, J. 1999. "Accountability and Governance Under the New Regulatory State." *Australian Journal of Public Administration*, 58: 90–97.

Brunsson, N. and Jacobsson, B. 2000. The Contemporary Expansion of Standardization, pp. 1–17 in *A World of Standards*, eds. N. Brunsson, B. Jacobsson, and Associates. Oxford: Oxford University Press.

Büthe, T. and Mattli, W. 2011. *The New Global Rulers: The Privatization of Regulation in the World Economy*. Princeton, NJ: Princeton University Press.

Carpenter, D. 2010. *Reputation and Power: Organizational Image and Pharmaceutical Regulation at the FDA*. Princeton: Princeton University Press.

Cass, D. 2005. *The Constitutionalization of the World Trade Organization: Legitimacy, Democracy, and Community in the International Trading System*. Oxford: Oxford University Press.

Chadwick, E. 1829. "Preventive Police." *London Review*, 1: 252–308.

Coen, D. and Héritier, A. 2005. *Refining Regulatory Regimes: Utilities in Europe.* Cheltenham: Edward Elgar.

Coen, D. and Thatcher, M. 2008. "Network Governance and Multilevel Delegation: European Networks of Regulatory Agencies." *Journal of Public Policy*, 8: 49–71.

Curtin, D. and Senden, L. 2011. "Public Accountability of Transnational Private Regulation: Chimera or Reality?" *Journal of Law and Society*, 38: 163–88.

Dimock, M. E. 1933. *British Public Utilities and National Development.* London: Allen and Unwin.

Dowding, K. 1995. *The Civil Service.* London: Routledge.

Dubash, N. K. and Morgan, B. 2012. "Understanding the Rise of the Regulatory State of the South." *Regulation and Governance*, 6: 261–81.

Dunsire, A. 1996. "Tipping the Balance: Autopoiesis and Governance." *Administration and Society*, 28: 299–334.

Eberlein, B. and Grande, E. 2005. "Beyond Delegation: Transnational Regulatory Regimes and the EU Regulatory State." *Journal of European Public Policy*, 12: 89–112.

Egan, S. 2011. *The UN Human Rights Treaty System: Law and Procedure.* Dublin: Bloomsbury.

Froud, J., Boden, R., and Ogus, A. 1998. *Controlling the Regulators.* London: Macmillan.

Gaer, F. D. 2007. "A Voice Not an Echo: Universal Periodic Review and the UN Treaty Body System." *Human Rights Law Review*, 7: 109–39.

Geradin, D., Munoz, R., and Petit, N., eds. 2005. *Regulation Through Agencies: A New Paradigm for EC Governance.* Cheltenham: Edward Elgar.

Gilardi, F. 2008. *Delegation in the Regulatory State.* Cheltenham: Edward Elgar.

Goodin, R. E. 2003. "Democratic Accountability: The Distinctiveness of the Third Sector." *European Archives of Sociology*, XLIV: 359–96.

Hall, C., Scott, C., and Hood, C. 2000. *Telecommunications Regulation: Culture, Chaos and Interdependence Inside the Regulatory Process.* London: Routledge.

Heald, D. 2006. Varieties of Transparency, pp. 25–43 in *Transparency: The Key to Better Governance?* eds. C. Hood and D. Heald. Oxford: Oxford University Press.

Hood, C. 2011. *The Blame Game: Spin, Bureaucracy and Self-Preservation in Government.* Princeton: Princeton University Press.

Hood, C., James, O., Peters, G., and Scott, C. 2004. *Controlling Modern Government: Variety, Commonality and Change.* Cheltenham: Edward Elgar.

Hood, C., Scott, C., James, O., Jones, G. and Travers, T. 1999. *Regulation Inside Government: Waste-Watchers, Quality Police, and Sleaze-Busters.* Oxford: Oxford University Press.

Horn, M. 1995. *The Political Economy of Public Administration.* Cambridge: Cambridge University Press.

Horwitz, M. J. 1992. *The Transformation of American Law 1870-1960.* Oxford: Oxford University Press.

Hughes, G., Mears, R., and Winch, C. 1997. "An Inspector Calls? Regulation and Accountability in Three Public Services." *Policy and Politics*, 25: 299–314.

Humpherson, E. 2010. Auditing Regulatory Reform, pp. 267–82 in *The Regulatory State: Constitutional Implications*, eds. D. Oliver, T. Prosser, and R. Rawlings. Oxford: Oxford University Press.

Jacobs, S. H. 2007. Current in Trends in the Process and Methods of Regulatory Impact Assessment: Mainstreaming RIA into Policy Processes, pp. 17–35 in *Regulatory Impact Assessment: Towards Better Regulation?* eds. C. Kirkpatrick and D. Parker. Cheltenham: Edward Elgar.

Jordana, J., Levi-Faur, D., and Marín, X. F. 2011. "The Global Diffusion of Regulatory Agencies: Channels of Transfer and Stages of Diffusion." *Comparative Political Studies*, 44: 1343–69.

Kagan, R. A. 2000. "Introduction: Comparing National Styles of Regulation in Japan and the United States." *Law and Policy*, 22: 225–44.

Kagan, R. A. 2003. *Adversarial Legalism: The American Way of Law*. Cambridge, Mass.: Harvard University Press.

Keane, J. 2009. *The Life and Death of Democracy*. London: Simon and Schuster.

Landis, J. 1938. *The Administrative Process*. New Haven: Yale University Press.

Levi-Faur, D. 2011. "Regulatory Networks and Regulatory Agencification: Towards a Single European Regulatory Space." *Journal of European Public Policy*, 18: 810–29.

Levy, B. and Spiller, P., eds. 1996. *Regulation, Institutions and Commitment*. Cambridge: Cambridge University Press.

Lodge, M. and Wegrich, K. 2012. *Managing Regulation: Regulatory Analysis, Politics and Policy*. Palgrave Macmillan: Basingstoke.

MacCarthaigh, M. 2012. Governance and Accountability: The Limits of New Institutional Remedies, pp. 24–42 in *Irish Governance in Crisis*, ed. N. Hardiman. Manchester: Manchester University Press.

Maggetti, M. 2010. "Legitimacy and Accountability of Independent Regulatory Agencies: A Critical Review." *Living Reviews in Democracy*, 2: 1–9.

Maggetti, M. 2012. *Regulation in Practice: The De Facto Independence of Regulatory Agencies*. Colchester: ECPR.

Majone, G., ed. 1990. *Deregulation or Reregulation? Regulatory Reform in Europe and the United States*. London: Pinter.

Majone, G. 1994. "The Rise of the Regulatory State in Europe." *West European Politics*, 17: 77–101.

Majone, G., ed. 1996. *Regulating Europe*. London: Routledge.

Makkai, T. and Braithwaite, J. 1992. "In and Out of the Revolving Door: Making Sense of Regulatory Capture." *Journal of Public Policy*, 12: 61–78.

May, P. 2007. "Regulatory Regimes and Accountability." *Regulation and Governance*, 1: 8–26.

Moran, M. 2003. *The British Regulatory State: High Modernism and Hyper-Innovation*. Oxford: Oxford University Press.

Morgan, B. 2006. Technocratic v. Convivial Accountability, pp. 243–70 in *Public Accountability. Design, Dilemmas and Experiences*, ed. M. Dowdle. Cambridge: Cambridge University Press.

Neocleous, M. 1998. "Policing and Pin-making: Adam Smith, Police and the State of Prosperity." *Policing and Society: An International Journal of Research and Policy*, 8: 425–49.

OECD. 2012. *Recommendation of the Council on Regulatory Policy and Governance*. Paris: OECD Publishing.

Parker, C., Scott, C., Lacey, N., and Braithwaite, J. 2004. Introduction, pp. 1–12 in *Regulating Law*, eds. C. Parker, C. Scott, N. Lacey, and J. Braithwaite. Oxford: Oxford University Press.

Prosser, T. 1997. *Law and the Regulators*. Oxford: Oxford University Press.

Prosser, T. 2010. Conclusion. Ten Lessons, pp. 306–18 in *The Regulatory State: Constitutional Implications*, eds. D. Oliver, T. Prosser, and R. Rawlings. Oxford: Oxford University Press.

Raeff, M. 1983. *The Well-Ordered Police State: Social and Institutional Changes Through Law in the Germanies and Russia 1600–1800*. New Haven: Yale University Press.

Randall, E. 2006. "Not That Soft or Informal: A Response to Eberlein and Grande's Account of Regulatory Governance in the EU with Special Reference to the European Food Safety Authority (EFSA)." *Journal of European Public Policy*, 13: 402–19.

Rhodes, G. 1981. *Inspectorates in British Government*. London: Allen and Unwin.

Roberts, A. 2010. *The Logic of Discipline: Global Capitalism and the Architecture of Government*. Oxford: Oxford University Press.

Scott, C. 2000. "Accountability in the Regulatory State." *Journal of Law and Society*, 27: 38–60.

Scott, C. 2002. "Private Regulation of the Public Sector: A Neglected Facet of Contemporary Governance." *Journal of Law & Society*, 29: 56–76.

Scott, C., Cafaggi, F., and Senden, L. 2011. "The Conceptual and Constitutional Challenge of Transnational Private Regulation." *Journal of Law & Society*, 38:1–19.

Selznick, P. 1985. Focusing Organizational Research on Regulation, pp. 363–68 in *Regulatory Policy and the Social Sciences*, ed. R. Noll. Berkeley: University of California Press.

Sharfman, I. L. 1931. *The Interstate Commerce Commission: A Study in Administrative Law and Procedure*. New York: Commonwealth Fund.

Stigler, G. J. 1971. "The Theory of Economic Regulation." *Bell Journal of Economics*, 2: 3–21.

Teubner, G. 1998. Juridification: Concepts, Aspects, Limits, Solutions, pp. 389–440 in *Socio-Legal Reader on Regulation*, eds. R. Baldwin, C. Scott, and C. Hood. Oxford: Oxford University Press; originally published 1987.

Thatcher, M. 2002. "Delegation to Independent Regulatory Agencies: Pressures, Functions and Contextual Mediation." *West European Politics*, 25: 125–47.

Thatcher, M. and Stone Sweet, A. 2002. "Theory and Practice of Delegation to Non-Majoritarian Institutions." *West European Politics*, 25: 1–22.

Thiel, S. van, Verhoest, K., Bouckaert, G., and Laegreid, P. 2012. Lessons and Recommendations for the Practice of Agencification, pp. 413–39 in *Government Agencies: Practices and Lessons from 30 Countries*, eds. K. Verhoest, S. van Thiel, G. Bouckaert, and P. Laegreid. Basingstoke: Palgrave Macmillan.

United Nations Human Rights Commissioner. 1993. *Principles relating to the Status of National Institutions (The Paris Principles)*. New York: United Nations.

Vibert, F. 2007. *The Rise of the Unelected: Democracy and the New Separation of Powers*. Cambridge: Cambridge University Press.

Weatherill, S. 2007. The Challenge of Better Regulation, pp. 1–18 in *Better Regulation*, ed. S. Weatherill. Oxford: Hart Publishing.

Wilks, S. 2005. "Agency Escape: Decentralization or Dominance of the European Commission in the Modernization of Competition Policy?" *Governance*, 18: 431–52.

Willis, J. 1958. "Administrative Decision and the Law: The Views of a Lawyer." *Canadian Journal of Economics and Politics*, 24: 502–11.

Wilson, J. Q. and Rachal, P. 1977. "Can Government Regulate Itself?" *Public Interest*, 46: 3–14.

CHAPTER 30

....

AUDIT INSTITUTIONS

....

PAUL L. POSNER AND ASIF SHAHAN

AUDIT INSTITUTIONS AND COMPLEXITY

....

AUDIT institutions can be critical to the ability of government and elected officials to gain the confidence and trust of the many publics who look to government to answer numerous needs and demands. These institutions have become even more important as the programs and commitments of government have become more complex and specialized, making it more difficult for media, citizen groups, and elected officials to oversee government without the input of sophisticated audit and other accountability professionals.

This chapter will focus on the evolving roles played by audit institutions in responding to the accountability challenges facing public officials. These agencies are part of a broader set of accountability institutions and actors both within and outside of government that seeks to ensure that government meets the expectations placed on it for three major goals: to ensure that governmental programs and officials comply with applicable laws and values; to provide that government accurately accounts for spending public funds; to guarantee that programs achieve their goals in the most effective and efficient manner. These three types of accountability—legal, financial, and performance—have become the keystones for managers and auditors alike.

TYPES OF AUDIT

....

Governmental audits are conducted to provide an independent assessment of the extent to which public agencies meet acceptable standards of legal, financial, and performance

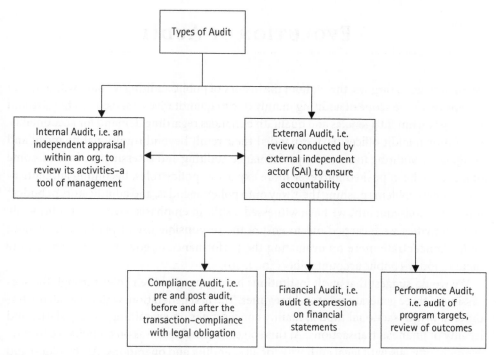

FIGURE **30.1** Various types of audit

accountability in implementing public programs. Audits can simply provide information to policymakers about public policy implementation, but most often they make recommendations to either executive or legislative officials to take corrective actions. Furthermore, audit also performs a preventive role, i.e., audit activities also provide a guideline that aims to prevent future breaches in accountability.

Most governments today provide concurrently for several types of audit. Figure 30.1 shows the basic typology of audits.

As Figure 30.1 shows, there are two primary types of audit: internal and external. Internal audit has been defined as an independent appraisal activity that has been established inside an organization by the head of the department to examine, evaluate, and report on its accounting, financial, and other operations. Even though this particular type of audit is helpful for internal control, it is not viewed as an independent assessment that external auditors can perform. On the other hand, external audit is a form of external review conducted by an organization that is independent of the audited entities. In general, the Supreme Audit Institutions (SAIs) are given, due to their statutory authority, the responsibility of this external review and these institutions report on the financial transactions, financial statements, operations, and programmatic activities carried out by government organizations or their agents, including contractors or other private or nonprofit third parties. For this chapter, we have concentrated on the external audit.

EVOLUTION OF AUDIT

As Suzuki (2004) argues, throughout the history of public auditing we have witnessed an expansion of the scope of auditing mainly due to quantitative expansion in the size and role of government agencies and qualitative changes regarding demand for accountability. National audit offices have expanded their remit beyond traditional financial and compliance auditing to focus on performance auditing and assessments. Indeed, some offices have been pushed into ever more expansive policy roles, becoming authenticators of new problems pushing their way onto policy agendas, and adjudicators of budget forecasts. Consequently, we have witnessed a shift in emphasis—whereas traditionally audit activities were carried out to ensure the responsible use of public money, now, audits concentrate more on evaluating the performance of government agencies, the focus of today's public accountability (2004, 40).

We would suggest that audit institutions have expanded their roles through the succession of three generations of audit regimes. The first generation, which we call the traditional or transactional model, mainly concentrates on examining the regularity and legality of financial transactions. At this stage, the emphasis was on compliance by government officials with legal authority for all spending and operations. As the oldest and most basic form of auditing, the traditional audit was introduced to address the concern regarding financial corruption. In their early development, these offices performed this function through the ex ante review and approval of financial transactions entered into by government agencies in their early evolution. As the complexity of government transactions and operations grew exponentially, these offices shed their ex ante roles in exchange for their more contemporary and familiar ex post role reviewing financial accounts and controls.

The early experience of US Government Accountability Office (GAO) is illustrative. Prompted partly by the growing role and scope of government, the Progressive era ushered in new governance reforms, including a new focus on financial management and professionalization of bureaucracy. The Budget and Accounting Act of 1921 established new accountability institutions by creating a central budget office for the executive branch and a national audit office for the Congress: the GAO. This legislative audit agency was responsible for reviewing and approving the transactions of the thousands of federal disbursing offices around the government and of the supporting documents and vouchers that accompanied them (Mosher 1984). At the same time, the GAO rendered opinions on the matters of law as the agency enjoyed the power to provide final interpretation in laws related with appropriations. Similarly, in the United Kingdom, when the Exchequer and Audit Department Act of 1866 established the office of Comptroller and Auditor General (C and AG), the SAI mainly checked every transaction performed by the government and evaluated whether these transactions complied with the financial rules.

The second generation audit regime, which we will call the systems based or financial audit, came about when continuing the ex ante review and approval function became almost impossible as, over time, the functions of government exploded. In order to deal with this situation, the SAIs agreed to devolve financial management and transaction approvals to the agencies' financial managers and internal auditors. Instead of examining every transaction, the SAIs focused on assuring the reliability of internal control systems within an organization which have been set up to control the processing of individual transactions (White and Hollingsworth 1999, 28). Consequently, the SAIs tested the internal control system by sampling specific transactions to reach conclusions about the validity and reliability of all transactions.

In the case of the USA, the second generation audit model was introduced and exercised during the period 1945–1966. World War II overwhelmed the GAO with paperwork and the agency faced a backlog of 35 million unaudited vouchers in 1945. In response to this, the agency shifted its focus from voucher audit and approvals to comprehensive auditing of the economy and efficiency of agencies' management and operations. The basic responsibility for control and internal auditing was devolved to the operating agencies while the GAO assumed the role of prescribing principles and standards to govern all federal accounting and auditing. In the case of the UK similar changes were brought through enacting the Exchequer and Audit Departments Act of 1921.

The third generation audit regime was ushered in during the late 1960s, what we will call the performance audit regime. The relative priorities of national audit offices shifted from the nearly exclusive focus on financial controls and compliance to the performance of agencies' programs. As the scope and expectations placed on government grew, policymakers and publics alike began to clamor for assessments of the efficiency and effectiveness of government programs. Schick (1966) has noted that the shift from financial controls to performance and program reviews and evaluations constituted a formative change in the across the board focus of public management. In the US the shift toward performance auditing was led by the GAO. The GAO conducted the first program evaluation in 1967 and this encouraged the agency to develop the program results audit in the 1970s.

The shift in focus toward performance of government was also reflected in the reforms in the administrative and financial system based on the New Public Management theory of the late 1980s. These reforms were first introduced in the UK, New Zealand, and Australia and later expanded to Sweden, Finland, the Netherlands, and France. The NPM movement has significantly redefined the accountability movement (Power 2005, 328) from a focus on processes and control over inputs to an emphasis on efficiency and effectiveness in attaining program goals and objectives. Consequently, Pollitt et al. (1999, 55–7) points out that this redefinition of public management swept over national audit offices, encouraging them to adopt the performance audit. Thus, the advent of performance auditing reinforced the thrust of the New Public Management movement by refocusing the reviews of audit offices away from detailed agency management processes and controls toward the ultimate outcomes and goals underlying agency programs and operations.

As we have indicated earlier, the performance audit is now practiced by most of the western developed democracies and the developing countries are also being encouraged to adopt this practice. However, while analyzing the evolution of audit regimes, we should bear in mind that the significance of performance audit does not necessarily mean that the other types of audit, such as compliance and financial, have become irrelevant. In fact, most of the SAIs perform a combination of these three types of audit and the evolution mainly shows a shift in emphasis.

The modern evolution of the audit process has generated significant controversy. Many scholars have raised concern about the "audit explosion" and indicated that the new forms of auditing, which include performance audit, enable auditors to play a political and policy role beyond their purview and undermine the authority of elected representatives in designing new policies and programs (Power 2005; Dubnick 2002; Funkhouser 2011).

As articulated by Michael Power, the audit explosion posits that traditional managers and service professionals have seen their roles eclipsed by auditors, inspectors, and evaluators who have reinvented the audit to become an instrument of performance assessment under the National Performance Review (NPR) banner. The audit function outgrew its traditional role as a strategy of verification and attestation to become an anvil on which to hammer out an agenda of performance and productivity reforms with significant policy and political content.

The growing prominence of auditing as a central performance management reform process has developed both from the pull of governmental officials and reformers seeking to rationalize and transform the traditional instrumentalities of the state as well as the push of the audit community intent on expanding their influence and prominence. While Power suggests that the audit explosion was mainly UK based, in fact it has taken root in the United States in recent years. For instance, under President Obama's stimulus program, additional funding and prominence was conferred on auditors to serve as the critical players to review the management and performance of the nearly $800 billion in federal funds provided to jump start the economy. While facing extraordinary burdens to spend this new money expeditiously and effectively, managers received no comparable funding increases or higher institutional recognition or authority (Posner 2010).

The audit explosion has had pervasive effects on management and leadership in public agencies by encouraging organizations to adopt a risk management approach to anticipate the reviews of audit and inspector agencies. The implications of audits on management is less in the burden or response to individual reviews and more in the anticipatory actions management takes to define its own internal processes and controls in ways to reduce their risk of being accused of fraud, abuse, and waste, as defined by auditors. This "control of controls" is what Power conceives of as the most profound regulatory impact of the audit explosion on public management.

The focus of managers on controlling risks through internal controls corresponds with the shift in audit focus from reviewing discrete financial transactions and programs to the assessment of management systems and controls. Since the early 90s, the Risk-Based Audit (RBA) has been introduced by auditors to better target and rationalize their own scarce resources on the highest priority areas considered to be most vulnerable to risk. Instead of focusing on compliance with rules or measuring the performance of organizations, these audits target the resources of audit institutions on those controls and processes that carry the greatest risks of undermining organizational goals and integrity. Risk is measured by assessing the environment within which the organization performs, the competence of its personnel, results of previous audits, size of assets, materiality, and other vulnerability factors (World Bank 2005). Once risk is identified, the risk factors are then converted from qualitative data into a quantitative risk score derived by scoring and weighting the risk factors. Based on this risk score, the scarce audit resources are deployed to high risk areas.

TYPES OF SAI

In order to explore the effectiveness of the SAIs in making the government accountable, it is necessary to understand how different governance systems create different types of SAIs. Existing literature divides the SAIs into four groups (International Management Consultants Limited 2003; Lekorwe 2008). These are:

a. The Napoleonic Court of Accounts
b. The Collegiate Body
c. The SAIs as government department
d. The Legislative Audit Office

The typology provided above allows a helpful classification of SAIs which reflects not only the differences between the structures of various SAIs but also their functional variations.

Court of Accounts

The Napoleonic Court of Accounts is modeled on the French system which was first established in 1807 to ensure the compliance of government agencies with financial rules. This particular type of SAI enjoys judicial authority and remains independent from both the legislature and the executive. The French *Cour des comptes* has always remained a "court of justice" and its jurisdictional activity includes "judging the accounts of the *comptables publics*" (Morin 2011). However, since 1958, the role of the French Court of Accounts has been changing and as per the constitution, it is now obligated to provide assistance to the parliament and government about non-judicial matters. Even though the court still performs jurisdictional functions, the share of such activity is now considered to be less than 10 percent (Morin 2010; 2011). Today, the French SAI's activities can be categorized into three groups: verification of proper use of the credits, funds, and securities managed by the State's departments; verification of management activities by evaluating financial statements submitted by the accountants; and cooperation with parliament in verifying the performance of the budget. Even though the role of the SAI has shifted from legal compliance to financial and performance audit, the organization structure and status enjoyed by the judges of the courts have not changed. All the judges of the Court of the Accounts are appointed by the Council of Ministers and these judges are appointed for life. At the same time, the court also enjoys significant independence in appointing its employees and controlling the budget.

The Court of Accounts model of SAI is followed in a number of other European countries including Belgium and Greece. The Belgian Court of Accounts, like its French counterpart, also performs financial, legal compliance and performance audits and also enjoys judicial authority. Similarly to the French SAI, the Belgian Court of Accounts has financial independence and can recruit and dismiss its staff. However, there are some structural differences between the two. Unlike the French one, the Belgian Court of Audit is divided into two chambers, one French Speaking and one Dutch speaking, and each chamber has one Presidency and four councilors and a secretary general. The members of the chambers are appointed by the House of Representatives for a term of six years and they can be reappointed (Belgian Court of Audit 2013a; 2013b). The Court of Accounts Model is also exercised in many Francophone Sub-Saharan African countries including Mali, Benin, Senegal, etc. (Wynne 2010).

Collegiate Body

There are some SAIs, which even though called Courts, do not enjoy any judicial authority. In fact, these SAIs cannot judge or impose sanctions on those responsible for public expenditure. In almost all cases, the courts perform a combination of compliance, financial, and performance audit. The Algemene Rekenkamer of the Netherlands and Bundesrechnungshof of Germany are examples of these particular type of SAIs. For instance, in the case of the Netherlands, the Court consists of three members and it functions are based on the principles of collegial governance, i.e., all the decisions taken by the Court are a reflection of the opinions of all the members and not just of the President or majority of the Board members. The members of the court are appointed for life. A similar constitution and legal protection are provided to the Federal Court of Germany. Like the Court of Audit in the Netherlands, the Presidents and Vice-Presidents are selected by the legislature through a secret ballot, but these officials are appointed for terms of 12 years.

In the cases of the collegiate bodies, the legal framework ensures the independent functioning of the SAIs. For instance, in the Netherlands, the Court of Audit enjoys the status of a "High Council of State," i.e., it is independent of the government and is on equal footing with the Senate, the House of Representatives, and the National Ombudsman. It mainly concentrates on investigating whether central government revenue and expenditure are received and spent correctly and whether central government policy is implemented as intended. However, while analyzing the outcome of a law or policy, the Court takes every effort to provide a neutral assessment and never expresses political opinion. Just like the Court of Accounts described earlier, the Court of Audit is free to decide its audit activities and even though it receives requests from the parliament to carry out specific types of audit, the elected bodies or the government cannot determine their audit coverage or limit their independence. The federal court of Germany also enjoys the same degree of independence.

Government Department

The SAI as government department is probably the rarest type of audit institution. In this case, the independence of these audit offices is a concern, as the institution is under the rubric of the executive that is the subject of most audits. The National Audit Office of China can be cited as a model of this type of SAI. The modern auditing system of China was developed as a response to the financial irregularities of the 70s and early 80s and in 1982 during the 5th Plenary Session of the 5th National People's Congress, a resolution was passed to set up the National Audit Office of the People's Republic of China (CNAO) (Gong 2009). The legal status and functions of the CNAO have been established through the constitution and Audit Law of the People's Republic of China. The CNAO works directly under the leadership of the Premier of the State Council. The Auditor General is nominated by the premier and approved by the State Council and he himself is a member of the council (Gong 2009; Ding 2000; Pei 2006). Its scope is broad and involves the audit of revenues and expenditures of public finance of departments of the State Council and local governments at various levels, as well as the operations of state banking institutions and state enterprises and undertakings (CNAO 2013). A similar type of SAI is found in Vietnam (KTC 2012).

Legislative Audit Office

The final model is known as the Legislative Audit Office model and is found mainly in the commonwealth countries (e.g. UK, Australia, India, Bangladesh, Sub-Saharan Anglophone African countries, etc.) and in Presidential systems like the United States. In this particular system, a Comptroller and Auditor General (C and AG)/Auditor General (AG) heads the Office. The C and AG remains free from the executive organ and reports directly to the parliament or congress. In general, the role and functions of the Westminster SAIs are defined by the constitution or statutory authorities. Contrary to the Court of Accounts, the Westminster SAI serves no judicial function; rather it emphasizes compliance, financial, and performance auditing. The audit reports are submitted to the entire parliament or to specific committees, such as the Public Accounts Committee of the parliament, or substantive committees of congresses which use audits to inform their oversight function.

While the taxonomy of audit offices is useful in identifying the variation in internal structure of different SAIs and understanding the connection of the SAIs with different branches of the government, we need to go further to understand the actual roles played by SAIs in promoting accountability. For this we need to examine not only the structure of the audit office itself but also the broader political and administrative system in which it is nested.

Conditions Underpinning the Independence of SAIs

In order to understand how the SAIs are performing in terms of ensuring accountability, it is necessary to consider the extent of independence enjoyed by these institutions. In fact, without being independent, it is not possible for the SAIs to hold the government accountable. The International Organization of Supreme Audit Institutions (INTOSAI), the umbrella organization of the international government audit community, acknowledged this as early as 1977 and the Lima declaration adopted by the organization stated that the "Supreme Audit Institutions can accomplish their tasks objectively and effectively only if they are independent of the audited entity and are protected against outside influence" (Fiedler 2004, 108). This focus on independence was further highlighted in the 2007 Mexico Declaration of SAI independence. The basic principles of the independence of SAI include:

a. Independence from different branches of the government, i.e. the SAIs should remain free from the influence of both the legislature and the executive. As the main goal of the SAIs is to audit the activities of the executive organ, it should perform this while remaining outside of the executive which will protect itself from undue influence. Independence of the SAI from the legislature is a complex issue as the SAIs of most countries work with or on behalf of the legislature. However, an independent SAI should be able to prioritize and conduct its audits based on its own professional standards and judgments, informed by legislative guidance and input.

b. Organizational independence, i.e. the Auditors General or heads of the SAIs should have tenure security and they should not perform at the pleasure of the government. It has been argued that if the appointment and removal procedure of the head and members of the SAIs are not clearly stipulated in the constitution and legal framework, the SAI may not be able to perform independently. Furthermore, an independent SAI should enjoy the authority to employ and dismiss its own employees (INTOSAI 2004).

c. Functional independence: The concept of functional independence comprises two dimensions—an SAI should have the ability to decide its audit activities and guidelines and due importance should be placed on the reports submitted by the SAI to the appropriate bodies. If the SAI does not enjoy discretion in discharging its audit activities, it will eventually depend on the other organs of the state and may become a political tool. If, on the other hand, SAIs' reports and recommendations are not considered to be important, they will not be able to hold the government agencies accountable.

d. Financial independence: The SAIs should have adequate independence in determining the size of their budgets and in allocating it appropriately.

Three of these models (court, collegiate and audit office) can be considered as more "independent" than the remaining one (government department). However, within these first three models, there are variations regarding the degree of independence enjoyed by the SAI. All of these three types of SAI are legally and constitutionally separated from the other branches of the government and even though these three are almost completely free from executive influences, their relationship with the legislature varies. In most cases, the collegiate SAIs enjoy a significant degree of discretion in deciding on their audit activities. In fact, the Court of Audit of Netherlands has made it clear in its website: "We are an independent institution. That means that we decide what we audit. We often receive requests to carry out audits from members of parliament, ministers and state secretaries who need an independent expert opinion on a particular matter. But they cannot order us to do so because the Court of Audit is independent" (The Netherlands Court of Audit 2013). Once they moved towards performing performance audit, however, their discretion has decreased and now they often take audit activities as per the request of the parliament.

The experience of the Court of Accounts of France is interesting from this perspective. When the first attempt of adherence to the request of the parliament was taken in 1958, the court reacted sharply and declined to perform accordingly. The court emphasized that its main goal was to perform jurisdictional activities and it planned to continue with that. Today, however, the Court undertakes many performance audits at the request of the parliament (Morin 2011).

The legislative audit offices maintain complex relationships with parliaments and congresses. In some cases, especially for the National Audit Office of the UK, Australia, or New Zealand, even though they listen to the requests of the parliament, they enjoy independence in deciding on their audit activities. In the case of GAO of USA, 92 percent of their audit reports are done having been requested by members of Congress. While Congress appears to steer most of the work of its audit agency, in fact much of the Congressional requests are generated collaboratively through the exchange of ideas between Congressional offices and GAO experts. When setting their research agenda, the agency must delicately steer between responding to these legitimate information needs while sustaining their independence in developing findings and reports. The GAO issues broad terms of engagement which set the boundaries of this relationship. In essence, the Congressional offices can determine GAO's agenda for audits, but the audit staff has autonomy in determining both how to scope and design the audits and what the ultimate report will conclude and recommend. GAO's broader engagement with media, universities, and other actors promotes its credibility and support and limits the potential for interference. However, the involvement of accountability professions in reviewing program results and effectiveness carries obvious political risks for audit institutions—many have charters that limit their coverage of these issues and constrain them from making recommendations on policy and program design issues (Schwartz 2000).

While the formal organizational models are important, informal organizational factors, such as capacity limitations and the underlying political environment and tradition, also shape the actual roles played by SAIs in many nations. Thus, while legal and constitutional provisions ensure the independence of the SAIs in the developing countries, in practice a number of these countries suffer from executive manipulation or inertia. For instance, even though the Courts of Accounts of Benin, Somalia, and Mali are designed according to the French model, in practice they suffer from a number of problems. For instance, up to 2002, the Court of Accounts of Mali was severely understaffed and a study conducted in 2002 concluded that the court would need 60 more Magistrates to perform its duties effectively. The Court of Accounts of Somalia suffers from the same problem. Another key problem for Mali is the inertia of the parliament members in discussing the reports submitted to them: "in 2006, it was concluded that the Parliament of Mali does not effectively control budget execution and accounting since the report of the Court of Accounts are not discussed in the parliament" (Wyne 2010). Even though the SAI of Bangladesh is modeled after the Westminster audit system, it lacks financial independence and does not have the power to initiate its own audit activities. With a powerful executive, the Bangladesh Ministry of Finance controls the SAI budget and the Parliamentary Accounts Committee seldom takes the recommendations of the audit agency into consideration.

Limits on the independence and efficacy of audit agencies in developing and transitional countries stem from experiences of colonialism or long periods of authoritarian rule. In most of these nations, the authoritarian, or colonial, rulers never placed a high priority on developing an independent accountability framework to prevent or disclose financial irregularities. In these countries, SAIs were set up either due to external pressure exerted by the development organizations or by the post-colonial rulers following the framework of colonizers. Therefore, it is no accident that Bangladesh and Anglo Sub-Saharan countries, which were part of the British Empire, developed Audit Office SAIs and the Francophone Sub-Saharan countries, which were French colonies, followed the court system. At the same time, in most of the transitional countries, democratic practices are still not well-established and the executives play a dominant role in the political and policy process. The interaction between dominant executive and dormant legislature often undermines the actual autonomy and effectiveness of audit institutions (Institute of Governance Studies 2009). In a political environment dominated by the executive branch, executives have a clear set of expectations for the SAIs and of boundaries that limit their independence and autonomy. While retaining the formal institutional trappings of audit institutions in the developed world, in many of these nations audit institutions function similarly to audit offices under the government department model.

An Alternative Typology

To more fully capture the range of actual influence achieved by SAIs, we have developed an alternative typology, which looks beyond the organizational structure and captures the variation in the degree of independence enjoyed by SAIs. In order to do that we have found it useful to draw on Romzek and Dubnick's (1987) model of accountability. According to Romzek and Dubnick, accountability means the processes through which the bureaucracy attempts to manage expectations that have been generated by actors operating within and outside the organizations. In their analysis they have proposed four systems of accountability based on variations in two critical factors: whether "the ability to define and control expectations is held" by inside or outside actors; and "the degree of control that the entity enjoys" in defining the expectations. According to them, the four systems of accountability are:

- Political accountability, where the bureaucrats are expected to be responsive to the policy and program goals as determined by the political representatives.
- Professional accountability, i.e. the placement of control over agency activities in the hands of expert employees to get the job done. The professional norms and standards eventually determine the expectations as managed internally by the employees.
- Legal accountability, where the expectations are determined by outside actors in a position to impose legal sanctions.
- Hierarchical accountability, where the expectations are managed through focusing attention on the priorities of those at the top of the organization.

Relying on Romzek and Dubnick's framework, we have made an effort to develop an alternative typology of SAIs which takes under consideration the variation in independence of the SAIs. We have defined independece of SAIs as the process through which the institutions make efforts to manage the expectations imposed on them by the external political environment. The variation in the performance of SAIs will rely on two factors: the influence of the external environment in controlling the function of the SAI, i.e., whether it is high or low; and the level of professional autonomy of the SAIs staffs, i.e., high or low. The interaction between these two will eventually result in four distinct types of SAI: Professional, Political, Legal, and Hierarchical. Figure 30.2 illustrates that.

Political SAIs

Political audit institutions function in a unique environment. In case of these SAIs, the political actors can exercise a certain degree of political influence over the SAIs; they have control over the budget of the institutions and they can also determine the function

Degree of external influence / Degree of professional autonomy	High	Low
High	Political (GAO)	Professional (NAO, Collegiate bodies)
Low	Hierarchical (government department)	Legal (Court of Accounts)

FIGURE **30.2** An alternative typology of audit institutions

of these SAIs. They therefore enjoy a certain degree of advantage in implementing their sets of expectations. In the case of political SAIs, however, the audit staffs are generally highly skilled and enjoy a degree of discretion in performing their designated role of auditing. Therefore, for both the actors, political and SAI, it is difficult for either set of actors to dominate. They can be expected to reach a compromise solution where the political actors determine the roles, responsibilities, and the basic set of expectations and the SAI actors depend on their professional norms in carrying out their duties, so that their professional standards are never compromised. Ironically, in order to be of value to political officials in advanced democratic systems, audit agencies must sustain their professional autonomy and credibility. The GAO of USA is an example of that. In this case, the budget of the institution is set by the Congress and the GAO actually undertakes performance audits in response to specific congressional requests. However, while performing these audits, the GAO exercises complete autonomy and their professional abilities are rarely questioned.

Professional SAIs

In the case of professional SAIs, the control of political actors over institution's activities is quite minimal. The SAIs enjoy complete independence in setting their work, and they also enjoy adequate financial and organizational independence. Audit offices exercising professional autonomy have pursued several different strategies. For some professional SAIs, performance audit has introduced a new opportunity through which they can extend their professional autonomy. Many scholars, such as Power (2005), have raised concern about this and argue that it puts unequivocal authority in the hands of the auditors. Behn (2001, 202–3) argues that performance audit eventually extends the sense of autonomy of the auditors as it makes auditors believe that "theirs is the only profession that is capable, authorized, or entitled to do it." Performance auditing allows the auditors to redefine performance and the government agencies remain accountable only when they comply with the performance indicators set by the SAIs. Naming these auditors as members of an epistemic community, Christensen et al. (2010, 4) also acknowledge their influence in shaping the agenda of NPM reform. But other audit offices in this quadrant recognize limits on their roles stemming from the need to safeguard their vaunted professional autonomy from the political controversy and potential interference that may very well accompany more ambitious policy roles. Thus in these cases, for these national audit offices the price of autonomy is limited influence over policymaking.

Hierarchical SAIs

These SAIs mainly function in developing and authoritarian countries. In their cases, the political influence of the actors over the activities of the SAI is extremely high and these SAIs lack necessary skills to defy the influence of political actors or to extend their mandates. As such, they mainly adhere to the demands placed on them by the political actors and they either fail to ensure accountability or their roles are largely ignored. The SAIs of China, Bangladesh, Benin, and Mali are all examples of this type of SAI.

Legal SAIs

The Courts of Accounts are mainly considered as legal SAIs. As the example of the French Court of Accounts indicates, these SAIs enjoy a considerable degree of independence. They remain outside the other organs of the state and they can command control over their budgetary and financial issues. As a result, the political actors cannot influence the role of the SAIs in implementing their expectation sets. However, in the case of these SAIs, the auditors do not make any effort to extend their influence. Rather they adhere to a narrow legalistic framework in defining their roles, performing audits as established in their constitution or legal framework.

THE IMPACT OF AUDIT AGENCIES ON POLICY-MAKING AND IMPLEMENTATION

As the foregoing suggests, audit institutions have emerged as powerful actors with great potential for framing performance and accountability expectations for both executives and legislatures, as well as for the broader publics they serve. As noted before, the actual impact of these institutions on policy agendas, decisions, and implementation regimes is a critical dimension in assessing the relationships between audit institutions and accountability.

There are many factors that determine whether and how these institutions shape public policy and management agendas. As we have suggested, some of these pertain to the structure and capacity of audit institutions themselves. However, broader public values, political systems, administrative norms and routines, and nongovernmental accountability networks all play important roles in determining the agenda and actual impacts of public policies.

Understanding how accountability mechanisms affect decisions in democratic organizations is thus essential as their role and importance in public management grows. Alongside expectations for positive accountability outcomes, observers identify potential for several negative, unintended, consequences, including inhibition of innovation and risk taking, tunnel vision (teaching to the test), focus on short-term objectives, focus on more easily quantifiable measures, and diversion of resources from core work (Power 1997; Behn 2001; Dubnick 2005). While positing differing outcomes from auditors' work, all of these observations assume that audit institutions have in fact formative influence on public managers and legislators but the actual influence of audit institutions is highly uncertain and an issue that calls for considerably more research.

When considering the impact of audit institutions on public policy, it is useful to consider the roles of audit institutions in relationship to a wider range of accountability institutions that have emerged in recent decades in advanced nations. In many developed nations the supply chain of accountability institutions and mechanisms has thickened in recent years. Indeed, as Koppell (2005) pointed out, there are multiple accountability actors in most government settings, and agencies can suffer from what he calls "multiple accountabilities disorder" from the sheer number of conflicting values and opinions expressed through these numerous channels and actors. Internal auditors, evaluation offices, budget and financial management units, are among the institutions within government agencies that oversee internal operations and program results. Legislatures, prime ministers, cabinet offices, and ombudsmen are among the other official organs that are constituted to review government finances and performances. In addition, many policy advocates and analytic organizations outside of government work tirelessly to transmit information to policymakers either by putting new issues on the table or providing oversight and insight on existing programs or operations.

We might call these processes the accountability issue network, using Heclo's (1978) term. Actors in this network play crucial roles in framing accountability for government by defining implicit standards for performance, expectations for implementation, types of information considered to be legitimate and necessary, and actions to be taken in response to perceived problems. In many nations, consensus often exists across these actors in defining accountability expectations and norms.

Audit agencies often play a lead role in articulating accountability systems and norms that have presumptive influence over other accountability actors. When compared to other accountability actors, audit institutions often benefit from high levels of credibility and legitimacy. With few exceptions audit institutions have no independent "power" to force any government ministers to do anything they don't want to do. Rather their influence stems from their expertise and legitimacy—ministers and civil servants alike, as well as legislators, cannot ignore with impunity the recommendations and findings of auditors.

One useful way to assess the relative influence of audit institutions within the network of accountability mechanisms is the framework developed by political scientists McCubbins and Schwartz (1984). They differentiate between police-patrol and fire-alarm oversight. Under police-patrol oversight, government officials actively use information to highlight problems and change programs. By contrast, under fire-alarm oversight, government officials establish the infrastructure of information and provide open doors for others to raise alarms, which officials may act on at their own discretion.

Active police-patrol oversight is associated with the work of audit institutions. When compared to more informal accountability information provided by nongovernmental groups and analysts, formal governmental audit agencies have greater potential to have the issues they raise gain traction and agenda status. On the other hand, fire-alarm oversight has far less certain prospects. Although established by governmental leaders, information reports and other fire-alarms are a more passive tool of accountability requiring actors in or out of government to actually use it to impact policy and management decisions.

As the accountability institutions move along the continuum from fire-alarm to police-patrol, greater prospects for policy impact are coupled with greater risks to independence and autonomy. The independence of audit institutions is fortified through career nonpolitical staffs and the appointment of agency leaders with exceptionally long tenure. But even with such institutional protections, these agencies can become a magnet for criticisms when their studies affect deeply held partisan or pluralist interests.

Notwithstanding critiques of the audit explosion, in fact audit agencies in many nations are reluctant power brokers at best. For the most part, audit institutions can be expected to sidestep major policy issues and debates in order to safeguard their autonomy and independence from other policy actors (Posner and Schwartz 2008). However, in so doing, they purchase independence at the cost of insulation from and possible irrelevance to the broader policy agendas facing nations.

The foregoing suggests that accountability institutions achieve their influence in highly contestable systems, rife with competing values. Far from hegemonic influence, these systems appear to veer from accountability deficits to accountability excesses, depending on such variables as the strength of the accountability offices and the receptivity of the broader political system (Bovens 2005). The interests and power prospects of audit institutions can be expected to differ from those of other accountability actors who represent actors and institutions carrying conflicting interests and values.

Yet as Power's audit explosion hypothesis rightly predicts, audit institutions achieve their influence not in determining policy outcomes or problem agendas, but rather in governing how actors present their claims and justifications in the policy process. Given the presumptive legitimacy accorded to audit institutions in most nations by the public media, agencies defy this professional agenda at their own risk. The influence of audit institutions in government agencies can be best described as a process of internalization and socialization of the norms of epistemic communities comprised of financial managers, evaluation specialists, and other related groups. While the adoption of this agenda by government agencies may be initially inspired by fear of the reactions of external media and other actors in the accountability network, these norms often become solidified through a process of internalization and institutional isomorphism, as agencies seek to hire auditors and create audit offices that mirror many of the characteristics of supreme audit offices.

Continued debate can be expected over whether the growing role and penetration of audit offices in public administration produces salutary or deplorable outcomes for public policy and management. However, given their expanded roles and influence, public administration practitioners and scholars alike must treat auditors as central, not peripheral, actors that warrant far more research than has been done to date.

References

Behn, R. 2001. *Rethinking Democratic Accountability.* Washington: Brookings Institution Press.

Belgian Court of Audit. 2013a. *Organisation.* Retrieved from <https://www.ccrek.be/EN/Presentation/Organisation.html>.

Belgian Court of Audit. 2013b. *Tasks and Powers.* Retrieved from <https://www.ccrek.be/EN/Presentation/TasksAndPowers.html>.

Bovens, M. 2005. Public Accountability, pp. 182–208 in *The Oxford Handbook of Public Management,* eds. E. Ferlie, L. E. Lynn Jr., and C. Pollitt. Oxford: Oxford University Press.

Christensen, M., Newberry, S., and Potter, B. N. 2010. *The Role of Global Epistemic Communities in Enabling Accounting Change: Creating a "More Business-Like" Public Sector.* In 6th AHIC (Accounting History International Conference). Wellington, 18–20 August 2010.

CNAO (National Audit Office of the People's Republic of China). 2013. *Legal Status.* Retrieved from <http://www.cnao.gov.cn/main/AboutUs_ArtID_726.htm>.

Ding, X. L. 2000. "The Illicit Asset Stripping of Chinese State Firms." *The China Journal,* 43: 1–28.

Dubnick, M. 2005. "Accountability and the Promise of Performance in Search of Mechanisms." *Public Performance and Management Review,* 28: 376–417.

Dubnick, M. J. 2002. *Seeking Salvation for Accountability.* In APSA (The American Political Science Association) Annual Meeting. Boston, 29 August –1 September 2002.

Fiedler, F. 2004. The Independence of Supreme Audit Institutions, pp. 108–121 in *INTOSAI: 50 Years (1953-2003): A Special Publication of the International Organization of Supreme Audit Institutions.* Retrieved from <http://www.intosai.org/uploads/4124efestschrift.pdf>.

Funkhouser, M. 2011. Accountability, Performance and Performance Auditing: Reconciling the Views of Scholars and Auditors, pp. 209–30 in *Performance Auditing: Contributing to Accountability in Democratic Government,* eds. J. Lonsdale, P. Wilkins, and T. Ling. Northampton, MA: Edward Elgar.

Gong, T. 2009. "Audit for Accountability in China: An Incomplete Mission." *Australian Journal of Public Administration,* 68: 5–16.

Institute of Governance Studies (IGS). 2009. *Institutions of Accountability: Office of the Comptroller & Auditor General.* Dhaka: IGS. Retrieved from <http://www.igs-bracu.ac.bd/UserFiles/File/archive_file/OCAG_Background_Paper.pdf>.

International Management Consultants Limited (IMCL). 2003. *Organization of a Supreme Audit Institution.* Andover: IMCL. Retrieved from <http://info.worldbank.org/etools/docs/library/108496/sai_organization.pdf>.

INTOSAI. 2004. *Standards and Guidelines for Performance Auditing Based on INTOSAI's Auditing Standards and Practical Experience.* Retrieved from <http://www.intosai.org/issai-executive-summaries.html>.

Koppell, J. 2005. "Pathologies of Accountability: ICANN and the Challenges of Multiple Accountabilities Disorder." *Public Administration Review,* 65: 94–107.

KTC. 2012. *Overview on the Audit Practice in Vietnam.* Retrieved from <http://russellbedford.vn/index.php?option=com_content&view=article&id=38&catid=10>.

Lekorwe, M. H. 2008. Supreme Audit Institution, pp. 77–87 in *Transparency, Accountability and Corruption in Botswana,* ed. Z. Maundeni. Cape Town: Made Plain Communication.

McCubbins, M. D. and Schwartz, T. 1984. "Congressional Oversight Overlooked: Police Patrols versus Fire Alarms." *American Journal of Political Science,* 28: 165–79.

Morin, D. 2010. "Welcome to the Court." *International Review of Administrative Sciences,* 76: 25–46.

Morin, D. 2011. "Serving as Magistrate at the French Cour des Comptes: Navigating Between Tradition and Modernity." *Accounting, Auditing & Accountability Journal,* 24: 718–50.

Mosher, F. C. 1984. *A Tale of Two Agencies: A Comparative Analysis of the General Accounting Office and the Office of Management and Budget.* Baton Rouge and London: Louisiana State University Press.

Pei, M. 2006. *China's Trapped Transition: The Limits of Developmental Autocracy.* Boston, MA: Harvard University Press.

Pollitt, C., Girre, X., Lonsdale, J., Mul, R., Summa, H., and Waerness, M. 1999. *Performance or Compliance? Performance Audit and Public Management in Five Countries.* London: Oxford University Press.

Posner, P. L. and Schwartz, R. 2008. *Accountability Institutions and Information in the Policy Making Process.* Paper for Kettering Accountability Forum. Dayton, 22–23 May 2008.

Posner, P. L. 2010. The Recovery Act: An Accountability Test for Our Federal System, pp. 17–29 in *Framing a Public Management Research Agenda,* eds. J. D. Breul, K. Newcomer, J. P. Goldman, P. L. Posner, and S. L. Schooner. Washington, DC: IBM Center on Business of Government.

Power, M. 1997. *The Audit Society: Rituals of Verification.* Oxford: Oxford University Press.

Power, M. 2005. The Theory of the Audit Explosion, pp. 326–46 in *The Oxford Handbook of Public Management,* eds. E. Ferlie, L. E. Lynn Jr., and C. Pollitt. Oxford: Oxford University Press.

Romzek, B. S. and Dubnick, M. J. 1987. "Accountability in the Public Sector: Lessons from the Challenger Tragedy." *Public Administration Review,* 47: 227–38.

Schick, A. 1966. "The Road to PPB. The Stages of Budget Reform." *Public Administration Review,* 26: 243–58.

Schwartz, R. 2000. "State Audit-Panacea for the Crisis of Accountability? An Empirical Study of the Israeli Case." *International Journal of Public Administration,* 23: 405–34.

Suzuki, Y. 2004. "Basic Structure of Government Auditing by a Supreme Audit Institution." *Government Auditing Review,* 11: 39–53.

The Netherlands Court of Audit. 2013. *Organisation.* Retrieved from <http://www.courtofaudit.nl/english/Organisation>.

White, F. and Hollingsworth, K. 1999. *Audit, Accountability and Government.* Oxford: Clarendon Press.

World Bank. 2001. *Features and Functions of Supreme Audit Institutions.* Washington, DC: World Bank. PREM Notes.

World Bank. 2005. *Risk-Based Audit: Lessons from Kenya Pilot.* Washington, D.C.: World Bank. FM Notes.

Wynne, A. 2010. "Independence of Supreme Audit Institutions in Sub-Saharan Africa." *International Journal of Governmental Financial Management*, 10: 55–62.

CHAPTER 31

······························

TRANSPARENCY

······························

ALBERT MEIJER

> Secrecy, being an instrument of conspiracy, ought never to be the system
> of a regular government.
>
> —Jeremy Bentham

TRANSPARENCY AS THE NEW "RELIGION"

BENTHAM's ideas on openness—transparency as the key to the prevention of abuses of power—have had a strong influence on the development of the modern public sector. The most important transparency measures, such as opening up archives, public sessions of representative bodies, and the publication of government documents, can all be traced back to Bentham's ideas on openness. These measures have become basic requirements of democratic governance. The trend towards more open government has not yet ended; the current attention to transparency builds upon a longer existing discourse on openness in government. Since the late 1990s, after access to documentation had become mainstream, the call for the active release of government documents has only gained in strength (Hood 2006): Transparency is expanding further into new domains.

Government transparency—in the sense of Bentham's openness—takes various forms (Heald 2006; Meijer et al. 2012). The minutes of the meetings of popular representatives are published and people can attend those meetings. Laws and legal regulations are published so that all people know the law. Government documents are published or available on request through Freedom of Information Acts. All together, these measures open up arenas of governmental decision-making to accountability to formal institutions such as Parliaments and Courts of Audit, but also to horizontal accountability to civil society organizations, stakeholders, the media, and the people at large. These forms of transparency potentially alter the accountability landscape in a fundamental manner by rearranging access to official information.

The increase in transparency is a worldwide phenomenon (see Roberts (2006) for an in-depth analysis of this trend). Erkkilä (2012, xiv) speaks of a "transnational discourse" on transparency. Roberts (2006) emphasizes that the idea of freedom of information has become to be considered as a hallmark of (democratic) governance and, therefore, countries all around the world are making an effort to institutionalize government transparency. Roberts (2010, 925) highlights that established liberal democracies (such as the UK and Germany), but also new democracies (e.g. South Africa) and even non-democratic countries (such as China), have adopted freedom of information laws in the past fifteen years. Worldwide, freedom of government information is on the rise.

While new technologies facilitate transparency (Margetts 2006; Meijer 2009), the surge in "active transparency" can be attributed to the desire of political leaders to enhance the accountability of governments. This was most clearly formulated by the American President Barack Obama (2009): "Government should be transparent. Transparency promotes accountability and provides information for citizens about what their Government is doing." Similar statements can be found in the policy intentions of governments all around the world. Even in authoritarian states such as China, where it is regarded as a tool to fight corruption, transparency is considered to be crucial in forging a connection between citizens and government (Roberts 2006, 8; Tan 2012). Transparency is often even regarded as a self-evident good in society (Etzioni 2010, 389), and Hood (2006, 3) provocatively argues that "more-transparent-than-thou" has become the secular equivalent of "holier-than-thou" in debates about modern governance. Indeed, one could argue that the all-seeing eye of God has been replaced by public eyes: both the eye of God and the public eyes convey the idea that we are being watched and, therefore, we should behave.

Political rhetoric assumes a strong relation between transparency and accountability (Fox 2007). The clearest proponent of this argument is, again, President Obama (2009): "A democracy requires accountability, and accountability requires transparency." For academics, this relation is less trivial. A more substantial understanding of the relation between transparency and accountability requires that we deconstruct these concepts and analyze the various relations between them. The expectations of the contribution of transparency to accountability are exceedingly high but our academic understanding of this relation is limited. This chapter aims to open up the "black box" of the relation between transparency and accountability. The expanding body of literature on government transparency is examined and used to shed light on the changing role of transparency in accountability. The chapter will examine the nature and effectiveness of the new transparency, its influence on accountability arrangements, and, finally, the remaining gaps in our knowledge of the relation between transparency and accountability.

HISTORICAL ROOTS

Transparency is both an old and a new concept. It is new in the sense that it now primarily refers to publishing government information on websites but it is old in the sense that the basic idea that watching others influences their behavior has been around for a long time. Hood (2006, 8) recalls that French revolutionaries embraced the idea of a transparent society "as one in which there was no space for the sort of social darkness in which they assumed injustice or unhappiness would breed" and mentions Rousseau as a key proponent of transparency. Rousseau equated opaqueness with evil and considered transparency as the way back to the lost state of nature. One could even understand this as a return to paradise when Adam and Eve were also fully "transparent."

The idea that people behave correctly when they are being watched can be traced back to Bentham's "panopticon." A panopticon is a prison in which all inmates are constantly visible to the guards in the central tower. Their visibility is expected to result in norm compliance. Although Bentham developed this idea for prisoners, the general argument that transparency results in better behavior can also be applied to civil servants and politicians. Bentham regarded transparency as a cornerstone of government since it would prevent "conspiracy." In a similar vein, Rousseau argued that civil servants should operate in full view of the public and that this would be a mechanism to avoid destabilizing intrigues (Hood 2006, 7).

Not all philosophers in the 18th century argued in favor of transparency. The French philosopher Jean Bodin defended the secrecy of the imperial policy—the Arcana Imperii—and stressed that the King's ability to maintain the integrity of the state would be undermined by transparency (Roberts 2006, 10). Even though the advocates of transparency "won" this intellectual conflict—through the French revolution—the arguments for—Rousseau's natural state—and against—Bodin's integrity of the state— openness continue to shape the debate about transparency (Roberts 2006).

The history of transparent government starts in the nineteenth century, with European countries and the US enacting legislation for openness of decisions, treaties, and access to meetings. Roberts (2006, 10, 11) summarizes:

> By the end of the nineteenth century, the Western democracies had achieved what we might call a level of basic transparency: the rule of law was established, the process of lawmaking (including the business of taxing and spending) was open to public view, and the right to speak freely about governmental affairs was protected.

Sweden was the first to adopt access to information legislation in its 1766 transition from absolutist to liberal bourgeois rule (Erkkilä 2012, 6). It was not until 1951, however, that Finland became the second country to enact transparency legislation. Freedom of information (FOI) legislation gained popularity after the Johnson Administration adopted this type of legislation in the US in 1966 and the example was followed by a spread of FOI legislation from the 1970s onwards. Erkkilä (2012, 5) shows how several West European countries (Denmark, Norway, Netherlands, France, Luxembourg) and also New Zealand adopted information access laws in the 1970s while Austria, Australia, and Canada followed suit in the 1980s. FOI legislation became really popular after the fall of the Berlin Wall: 19 European countries between 1992 and 2005. FOI has now become a standard element of Western-style democracy and this type of legislation is now being adopted in a wide variety of countries all around the world (Roberts, 2006).

While freedom of information is predominantly about access to information *on request*, a new generation of legislation has more recently been introduced that focuses on the *active* publication of government information. President Obama issued the Open Government Directive in 2009 and this directive requires agencies to take several steps to embed a culture of transparency into the way they operate (McDermott 2010). This directive emphasizes that information should be published in a timely fashion, in accessible formats, and with adequate use of new technologies. Government agencies should also provide opportunities for citizens to give feedback on, and assess the quality of, published information. The Open Government Directive is, for now, the last stage of a development in transparency legislation from passive access to a limited number of documents through lengthy legal procedures, to proactive access to large quantities of information in accessible formats. At present, most government agencies in democratic societies have complex structures and technologies for making their information available to citizens (Welch and Wong 2001).

Transparency as an Institutional Information Relation

When used in political debates, the term "transparency" is often not defined and kept ambiguous. Scholtes (2012, 341) highlights that the ambiguity of the concept makes it attractive to politicians, since transparency can be used to underpin a broad variety of political arguments. She shows how transparency can be connected to democratic value, administrative control, public accountability, the promotion of market forces, and an attitude of openness. Transparency can be regarded as an "ideograph" (McGee 1980), something nobody can be opposed to but that is conceptually empty and can be filled in different strategic ways.

The academic debate about transparency is hardly less confusing than the political debate, as many academics do not (precisely) define transparency. General definitions highlight that something is happening behind "veils" and once these "veils" are removed, everything is out in the open and can be scrutinized (Davis 1998, 121; Den Boer 1998, 105). Patrick Birkinshaw (2006, 189) puts it as follows: "Transparency is the conduct of public affairs in the open or otherwise subject to public scrutiny." Julia Black (1997, 476) completes the definition by stating what it is not: "[Transparency] is contrasted with opaque policy measures, where it is hard to discover who takes the decisions, what they are, and who gains and who loses." Although there is wide agreement on this general idea, more precise conceptualizations vary considerably. Economists regard transparency as a precondition for optimal markets, political scientists conceptualize it as a precondition for political participation, and legal scholars stress that transparency is a precondition for administrative legality. Debates between scientists from these disciplines therefore often result in misunderstandings and confusion (Meijer et al. 2012).[1]

In an effort to reduce this confusion, three basic perspectives on transparency can be distinguished: transparency as a virtue, a relation, and a system. Transparency is defined as a *virtue* of an actor when someone is considered to be transparent when s/he is open about his or her behavior, intentions, considerations, etc. Similar to certain definitions of accountability, transparency is then used as a normative concept, as a set of standards for the evaluation of the behavior of public actors (cf. Bovens 2010, 946). This type of definition can be found among legal professionals. The former European Ombudsman, Jacob Söderman (1998) defined the term transparency as follows: "the process through which public authorities make decisions should be understandable and open; the decisions themselves should be reasoned; as far as possible, the information on which the decisions are based should be available to the public." According to Lord Nolan (1995, 14) transparency is said to require that "holders of public office should be as open as possible about all decisions and actions they take." These definitions emphasize that an actor should be open but they do not mention to whom the actor should be transparent.

A second perspective defines transparency as an institutional *relation* between an actor and a forum. Cornelia Moser (2001, 3), for example, defines being transparent as "to open up the working procedures not immediately visible to those not directly involved, in order to demonstrate the good working of an institution." Oliver (2004, 2) indicates that transparency can be described through three elements: an observer; something available to be observed; and a means or method for observation. This type of definition builds upon principal–agent theory: a principal requires information about the agent to check whether the agent sticks to the "contract" (Prat 2006, 92). This type of definition comes close to Bovens's (2010) definition of accountability as a mechanism. Transparency is seen as an institutional relation or arrangement in which an actor is rendered transparent to another actor (cf. Bovens 2010, 946).

Thirdly, this institutional information relation is not isolated but exists within a *system* of these relations. Democratic decision-making in local councils, for example, is made transparent in similar fashions all across the Netherlands. These councils all have relations with their citizens and the same sets of (formal and informal) rules apply to transparency in all cities. This means that one can describe and analyze transparency not only at the level of specific relations but also at the level of sets of relations in a system. At this level, the analysis focuses on the rules that guide the behavior of actors in the system. The criteria of Transparency International (www.transparency.org) refer to transparency as a system and they qualify governments on the basis of a transparency index. In debates about good governance, transparency also refers to the system level.

In this chapter, the definition of transparency as an institutional relation provides a basis for my analysis, since it connects best to the way accountability is defined in this handbook. Our research team at Utrecht University has developed the following definition of transparency (see also Grimmelikhuijsen 2012; Meijer et al. 2012; Meijer 2013): *Transparency is defined as the availability of information about an actor allowing other actors to monitor the workings or performance of this actor.* The definition consists of an institutional relation in which an information exchange takes place which relates to the workings or performance of an actor. Transparency can be realized passively (through freedom of information requests), pro-actively (through websites or documents), and through forced access (leaking and whistleblowing); and all of these forms are argued to contribute to public accountability.[2]

Transparency and Accountability: Direct, Indirect, and Inverse Relations

Although transparency can contribute to a broad range of substantial values such as democracy, responsiveness, and legitimacy, its instrumental value is often connected to accountability: The availability of relevant information is one of the prerequisites for the information phase of any accountability process (Bovens 1998; Meijer 2003; Bovens 2007). Heald (2012, 33) argues that transparency provides rulers with a vehicle to account to citizens for their stewardship. This basic argument is identical to policy-makers' and stakeholders' arguments for transparency: Transparency facilitates accountability. This argument is nuanced here by proposing three routes between transparency and accountability: direct, indirect, and inverse.

Direct Route: Facilitating Horizontal Accountability

The direct route from transparency to accountability highlights that new horizontal forms of accountability are facilitated by growing transparency. Accountability has broadened in recent years as citizens and other stakeholders are offered ever more opportunities to scrutinize an actor's exploits, to debate results, and to pass judgment. Accountability to citizens and stakeholders has been labeled "direct" accountability, "stakeholder" accountability, or, most often, "horizontal" accountability. Horizontal accountability does not replace the traditional vertical accountability of organizations to the minister and parliament but serves as an addition (Schillemans 2008; Schillemans 2011). Michels and Meijer (2008) argue that horizontal accountability forms a logical response to the accountability gap that results from the horizontalization of government. Horizontal accountability is characterized by the absence of formal formats for information provision and debating, and, most importantly, the absence of formal sanctions (Meijer 2007). Increased transparency has been argued to make a significant contribution to facilitating this type of accountability by providing citizens, stakeholders, and media with better access to information (Meijer 2007).

Indirect Route: Strengthening Vertical Accountability

In addition to facilitating horizontal accountability, transparency can also strengthen vertical accountability by providing signals that something could be wrong. The "fire alarm" metaphor, often cited in the accountability literature (May 2007), is applicable here. A fire alarm only rings when there is a fire, doing away with the need to constantly check if everything is OK, like a "policeman on patrol." An accountability arrangement can be used in similar fashion: The accountability forum is warned by a third party as soon as something untoward is observed in the conduct of a public official or a public organization (McCubbins and Schwartz 1984). Citizens or pressure groups calling a public organization to account have no formal power over this organization but they can send a signal to vertical accountability forums (Fox 2007). To create a "fire alarm", access to raw data is crucial; unpolished information is more likely to contain clues to anything untoward than information which is carefully prepared for publication. Access to information enables citizens and other stakeholders to contribute by acting as a fire alarm for formal accountability forums. Increased transparency gives them the opportunity to scrutinize the functioning of the public sector and send signals to the established forums. The theoretical reasoning behind the idea of such strengthened accountability is that once enough people scrutinize governmental action, wrongdoing will always come to light. Or, as they say online, "Given enough eyeballs, all bugs are shallow."

Inverse Relation: Transparency Reduces the Need for Accountability

While the direct and indirect relations suggest a positive relation between transparency and accountability, some authors highlight that transparency may also diminish the need for formal accountability mechanisms. Erkkilä (2012, 9 a.f.) argues that the New Public Management emphasis on performance measurement and transparency merge in the (reductionist) idea of accountability as providing public information about government performance. Accountability is reduced to information provision and "public eyes" are expected to stimulate correct behavior (Meijer 2007). The idea of a debate between actor and accountability forum about performance disappears since "the numbers tell the full story" and sanctions do not need to be imposed since transparency is, by itself, considered to be a sanction since it can be seen as a form of public shaming (or faming). In this line of argument, transparency is an instrument to ensure that actors conform to public standards that reduces the need for another instrument, accountability, to achieve this objective.

The relationships between transparency and accountability are thus classified as potentially facilitating horizontal accountability and strengthening vertical accountability, but also potentially reducing the need for accountability. While many authors assume or test positive relations between transparency and accountability, Hood (2010) highlights that a friendly relation cannot be assumed. Using evocative terms, Hood categorizes the relations between these two components as "Siamese twins," "matching parts," and an "awkward couple." The idea of Siamese twins is that accountability and transparency cannot be meaningfully distinguished, the idea of matching parts is that they complement each other, and the idea of an awkward couple is that there may be a tension between the two. These arguments indicate that there is no ex ante reason to assume that transparency and accountability are "friends": we need to evaluate their relation on the basis of empirical research. We will now zoom in on the relationships between transparency and accountability and pose the question whether such theoretical links can be observed in practice. Does transparency indeed facilitate horizontal accountability and strengthen vertical accountability? Does it reduce the need for accountability?

Lessons from Empirical Research into Transparency and Accountability

The academic literature shows that there is not as much impact of transparency on accountability as one might expect, and that the impacts are not as straightforward as is often assumed (Fox 2007, 664). Based on international research and some of our research projects at Utrecht University, we will see what lessons are to be learned on how the relationship between transparency and accountability pans out in practice.

Lesson 1: Citizen Accountability Through Transparency is Often an Illusion

Governmental rhetoric portrays transparency as a way of being accountable to citizens. In the absence of other accountability arrangements, citizen accountability may indeed play a role. Freedom of Information Acts (FOIA) have resulted in effective forms of accountability in weak states. Roberts (2006, 4) shows how FOIA has helped Thai parents to call schools to account about their favoring, even corrupt, treatment of the children of wealthy parents. However, evidence for citizen accountability in states with more developed accountability arrangements is limited. Even in high profile cases such as transparency on school performance (Meijer 2007), air quality (Grimmelikhuijsen 2007), and government corruption (Lindstedt and Naurin 2010), only very few citizens use the information to call public organizations to account. One could even ask whether this should be expected since in the internet age transparency often results in an information overload. Roberts (2010) and Etzioni (2010) highlight that government data requires substantial handling and interpretation before most citizens can use it, something which can hardly be expected from them. To put it somewhat crudely, citizens simply have better things to do than to process large amounts of government data. Put another way, citizens have created specialist organizations for public accountability, such as Parliament, the municipal council, the Court of Audit, the Ombudsman, and also the media (cf. Hibbing and Theiss-Morse 2002).

Lesson 2: Media Accountability Through Transparency is a Reality

Empirical research shows that increased transparency first and foremost facilitates media transparency (Meijer 2007; O'Neill 2002; Lindstedt and Naurin 2010). The Watergate Investigation by reporters of the Washington Post is the key example of how transparency resulted in media accountability (Bernstein and Woodward 1974). This investigation is by no means an isolated incident; the academic literature presents many examples of media accountability that is facilitated by (proactive, passive, and forced) transparency. Data-journalism is an important new form of news production: journalists analyze data sets and write news stories on the basis of the data. Deuze (2002) already concluded that journalists spend more and more time online to find their stories, including scrutinizing public reports. Processing public information can result in various sorts of accountability processes. Meijer (2007) shows how a Dutch newspaper used passive transparency to obtain access to information about school performance and how this was used to call schools to account. Lindstedt and Naurin (2010) describe how mass media play a key role in using the transparency of government expenditure for accountability. And Roberts (2006, 5) highlights how access to information legislation was used by a Japanese newspaper to expose the influence of corporate businesses on cabinet affairs.

Lesson 3: Stakeholder Accountability Through Transparency is also a Reality

In addition to citizens and media, stakeholders, such as interest groups, form an important potential forum for horizontal accountability. Although quantitative research into this type of use has not been conducted, there is much anecdotal evidence for this relation. Both proactive and passive transparency have stimulated horizontal accountability. Grimmelikhuijsen (2007) analyzes how the Dutch chapter of the NGO Friends of the Earth uses air quality data to call municipalities to account on their air quality policy. Roberts (2006, 1–6) mentions a large number of instances in which NGOs use information to expose government corruption and to push for more integrity in government in countries such as India. He also recounts how a Ugandan environmental NGO used transparency to call their government to account for a controversial agreement about a hydroelectric dam. These NGOs have both the capacity and the desire to use transparency for accountability, and qualitative research underlines that changes in the "information playing field" stimulate stakeholder accountability.

Lesson 4: Transparency Enables Fire Alarms for Vertical Accountability

The increased transparency in the public sector via the internet has created a rise in the numbers of "fire alarms." Individual citizens play a key role as whistleblowers but this occurs on the basis of confidential information and is not facilitated through transparency. Although systematic research is lacking, a review of the transparency literature indicates that few fire alarms come from individual citizens processing public information. Again, people need an incentive to scrutinize government and, generally, most people have better things to do. Some exceptions have been documented. In the Dutch City of Utrecht, two citizens found out that the municipality of Utrecht only published online so-called model calculations on air quality not the actual recorded measurements. In reaction to these efforts, local representatives called the responsible alderman to account about this issue. While citizen fire alarms are rare, media fire alarms abound (May 2007; Schillemans 2012). Media accountability through transparency can also have a strengthening effect on political accountability when journalists can function as the fire alarm. Again, the Watergate Investigation is the prime example because it shows how media accountability resulted in political accountability (Bernstein and Woodward 1974), as did many of the other "gates" later on (e.g. Irangate, Monicagate).[3]

Lesson 5: Proactive Transparency has Limited Value for Accountability

When transparency is not enforced, governmental bodies are able to exercise a degree of discretion and make a strategic choice on which information to disclose. The academic literature provides many more examples of successful horizontal accountability processes and fire alarms for vertical accountability processes facilitated by forced or passive transparency than by pro-active transparency (Roberts 2006). This shows in the difference in the amount of information released pro-actively, but also in the selection and in the way the information is presented. Grimmelikhuijsen (2007) shows how two-thirds of municipalities only show positive information about the local air quality on their websites and Pasquier and Villeneuve (2007) argue that organizational barriers often result in distorted or incomplete transparency. Tan (2012) shows how actual transparency in China is limited because of fragmented bureaucracy and Brandsma et al. (2008) show how the European Commission does not stand up to its own transparency practices because of the difficulties of organizing transparency. Hood (2007, 200) highlights how presentational strategies are used to avoid or limit blame by spin, timing, stage-management, or argument, and Fox (2007) shows that even mandatory disclosure often does not result in accessible and reliable reporting. On the basis of a quantitative analysis, Lindstedt and Naurin (2010) show that agent-controlled transparency is far less effective in stimulating accountability than non-agent-controlled transparency. All these findings underpin the conclusion that the value of proactive transparency for accountability is limited.

Lesson 6: Third Party Transparency Reduces the Need for Accountability

While agent-controlled transparency seems to be of limited value, third party transparency may actually stimulate organizations to be more sensitive to external demands. The crucial difference here is that actors cannot decide for themselves what information will be made available to citizens and, as a consequence, information may also include underperformance, mismanagement, or other forms of falling short of public standards. Meijer (2007) shows how public schools started to pay more attention to public standards when the School Inspection Service published its reports online. The research showed that, even though there was little interest from citizens, media, and stakeholders, transparency still had an effect on the actions and decisions of school management. Fox (2007) argues that the imagined counterforce can lead to actual effects when a more transparent organization starts behaving according to public standards mobilized by the "power of shame." Not (media, stakeholder, citizen) accountability itself but mere transparency as such stimulates organizations to consider external expectations.

Lesson 7: Transparency is Limited to Certain Domains of Government Activity

Grand narratives about government transparency suggest that there is an overall increase of government transparency in all policy sectors. Roberts (2006, 18) highlights however that there are certain "enclaves" within governments in which transparency has made little headway. He specifically refers to the security sector: "In many countries, disclosure laws have been carefully tailored to ensure that the security sector survives as an enclave of secrecy." He concludes that—partly due to the 9/11 attacks—the proposition that transparency could be used as a tool for controlling human rights within the security domain was not carried forward (see also: Blanton 2003). Specified systems of classification are developed to prevent the disclosure of sensitive information in these domains of government activity. At the same time, active transparency became increasingly focused on strengthening control over quasi-markets: Governments withdrew and started using indirect instruments of disclosure to control public sector organizations (Meijer and Homburg 2009).

Lesson 8: Transparency and Accountability Reinforce One Another

A last lesson to be drawn concerns the specific relationship between transparency and accountability. While the literature often assumes that transparency only facilitates accountability, there are clues that they reinforce one another. Grimmelikhuijsen (2007) shows that the availability of air quality data facilitates new forms of accountability, and the result of this accountability process often is that there needs to be more transparency. Meijer (2007) shows how attention to school performance rose after more transparency had been created and the resulting push for more accountability also resulted in more school transparency. Accountability processes often provide information about the limits of transparency and, therefore, result in a push for more transparency.

These eight empirical lessons offer scant hope for strengthening direct democracy. Or, to put it bluntly once again—citizens usually have better things to do than to go through all sorts of transparent government data. And yet there are reasons to see the contribution of transparency to public accountability in a more positive light. For one, it is not the number of citizens that counts. As we have seen, all it takes are one or two vigilant members of the public to strengthen accountability. In addition, transparency is frequently used by stakeholders and media to call government agencies and politicians to account. Furthermore, there are interactions between horizontal and vertical accountability to Parliament. Members of Parliament use the available information from public organizations, as well as information from intermediaries such as interest groups and the media. Also the mere idea of information being disclosed in a systematic fashion can create an open culture (Hood 2006). And lastly, transparency may reduce the need for accountability when the power of shame mobilizes organizations to behave according to public standards (Fox 2007).

The review of studies into the relation between transparency and accountability shows that, under certain conditions and in certain situations, transparency may contribute to accountability. Therefore, Fox (2007) argues that we should not ask *whether* transparency facilitates accountability but *under which conditions* it does so. The lessons teach us that transparency facilitates accountability when it actually presents a significant increase in the available information, when there are actors capable of processing the information, and when exposure has a direct or indirect impact on the government or public agency. This raises the question whether these impacts are something to be desired. Does transparency-facilitated accountability produce benefits for society? This question has triggered an intense academic debate.

PANACEA, POISON, OR PHARMACON?

Proponents argue that—in spite of the limitations that we see when it is applied in practice—transparency disciplines institutions and their office-holders by making information about their performance more public, deters corruption and poor performance, and secures a basis for better and more trustworthy performance (O'Neill 2006, 76; Worthy 2010). Proponents argue that transparency can stimulate public officials to improve their performance or prevent them from being corrupt (Lindstedt and Naurin 2010). Proponents—many policymakers but also gurus such as David Brin (1998) and Richard Oliver (2004)—do not close their eyes to potential perverse effects, but stipulate that governments can avoid these by implementing transparency adequately. In the end, lifting the veil will be beneficial to all of us. Karl Popper's Open Society (1945) is the guiding idea for proponents of transparency: Openness will, in the end, make for stronger accountability since government flaws will be exposed and criticized.

The proponents argue that internet transparency gives people better information and thus contributes to the rationalization of society. The rationalization of society results in more democratic and more affluent societies. The exposure of the Watergate scandal prevented further abuses of presidential power through public accountability, disclosure of information about ENRON forms the basis for restructuring the financial sector, and transparency of effects of smoking on health conditions facilitated a public debate on regulatory measures. They will argue that WikiLeaks will help to ensure that governmental diplomacy serves the interests of the people and not those of a small but powerful elite. Opponents of transparency are not opposed to democracy but doubt whether transparency will make these contributions to society. They argue that internet transparency will result in a loss of societal trust (O'Neill 2002). Building friendly relations between countries may become difficult in the aftermath of WikiLeaks.

Opponents see perverse effects as an inseparable attribute of internet transparency. Roberts (2006), for example, highlights the threat to personal privacy through *personalized accountability*. He indicates that the growth of data in electronic form may enable private organizations to use such capabilities to assemble extensive knowledge about individuals from (widely distributed) public records. The recent publication of the performance of individual teachers in public schools by the Los Angeles Times seems to provide evidence for this argument (www.projects.latimes. com/value-added). The newspaper publishes estimates of the effectiveness of teachers by looking at the standardized test scores of students. Whereas previous forms of transparency in education focused on the school, the LA Times now renders transparent the performance of individual teachers. Bannister and Connolly (2011) identify a range of phenomena that may make transparency inimical to good governance, such as the (opportunity) cost of realizing transparency, the avoidance strategies that may evolve in response to it, and the potential misinterpretations of transparency by the public.

Other opponents argue that transparency may lead to a collective action trap and opaqueness may, in certain situations, contribute to the common good. Onora O'Neill (2002, 68) argues that transparency will erode trust: "...trust seemingly has receded as transparency has advanced" (see also Greiling in this volume). O'Neill argues that a flood of unsorted information may lead to more uncertainty and will confuse accountability. This is not an issue to be solved easily because misinformation is directly connected to transparency. O'Neill (2002, 73) emphasizes that those who know that everything they say or write is to be made public may "massage the truth." The fact that it is often not clear who has asserted, compiled, or endorsed the "supposed information" makes this even worse. O'Neill argues that transparency gets us lost in a forest of misinformation and this will eventually produce less trust. She argues that the explosion of transparency may produce a "culture of suspicion" (see also Fung and Weil 2010). Roberts (2006, 237) partly agrees with her and emphasizes that the rhetoric of anti-secrecy advocates may produce detachment of citizens and a cynical attitude towards government.

Opponents such as O'Neill are not opposed to transparency and openness but regard trust as the more important goal. If openness produces less trust, secrecy may be better: "...secrecy and lack of transparency may not be the enemies of trust" (O'Neill 2002, 70). This places O'Neill's work in the broader context of building trust in societies and, more specifically, building more trust in the public sector. Whereas Popper guides the ideas of the proponents, the work of Robert Putnam (2000) and Francis Fukuyama (1996) guides the ideas of those critical of increasing transparency. Internet transparency can interfere with a sense of community and belonging and, therefore, one should be careful in strengthening it. This debate is quite similar to the classic Friedrich–Finer debate about accountability in the US in the 1940s where Finer emphasized the need for exposure while Friedrich argued against the undue concentration on external scrutiny (Mulgan 2000). One can imagine that Finer would be on the side of the proponents of transparency and Friedrich on the side of its opponents.

Much of the debate revolves around the relation between transparency and government legitimacy or trust. Supporters of transparency, such as Brin (1998) and Oliver (2004), see it as beneficial to all. After all, only those who have something to hide have reason to object to transparency. At the other end, Bovens (2003) warns against the dark side of transparency and its potential to drag government through the mud time and time again. Empirical research shows that when it comes to facilitating horizontal accountability through transparency, supplying people with policy information on air quality can have a positive effect on trust in the municipal government (Grimmelikhuijsen 2007; Tolbert and Mossberger 2006). Therefore, transparency can contribute to the government's legitimacy but the tone of the disclosed information is an important factor here. In case of strengthened vertical accountability as a fire alarm, as when whistle-blowers report foul play, transparency is more likely to have a detrimental effect on governmental legitimacy.

One could say that the proponents see transparency as a panacea—or multivitamin (Scholtes 2012, 335)—for all kinds of ills, while opponents see it as a poison that kills many good things in society. Intense as the debate may be, slowly there seems to be emerging a consensus that transparency may have both its upsides and its downsides. Etzioni (2010) is not opposed to transparency but argues that it is overvalued and Heald (2003) explicitly conceptualizes transparency as a trade-off between the "value of sunlight" and the "danger of over-exposure." The normative debate becomes more meaningful when it focuses on the forms and levels of transparency. Dror (1999) conceptualizes transparency as a *pharmacon*: It heals in correct doses and kills when the doses are too high. This conceptualization is helpful in taking the debate from a war in the trenches to a constructive underpinning of emerging practices.

In sum, this chapter has shown that transparency is certainly not a miracle instrument for accountability. The assumption that citizens find government so interesting and important that they want to scrutinize its records simply does not hold true. At the same time, transparency does open up the playing field of accountability by giving more prominent roles to the media and stakeholders. This may result in a reduction of public trust but also may also help to curb corruption and agency drift. The challenge for democratic societies is to develop levels and forms of transparency that strengthen checks and balances and stimulate engagement but do not result in cynicism and a turning away from public affairs. Further research is needed to understand different responses to this challenge and identify conditions that stimulate favorable outcomes.

Acknowledgments

The author would like to thank Maarten Hillebrandt, Stephan Grimmelikhuijsen, Danielle Fictorie, and the editors for their comments on draft versions of this chapter.

Notes

1. While most definitions focus on what transparency is, a more complete understanding can be obtained by exploring what it is not. Some authors contrast transparency with secrecy (Pozen 2010). In this line of argument, a lack of transparency is the result of intentional actions to limit transparency. Roberts (2006) indicates that the US Government is intentionally limiting transparency on the basis of the argument of national security. Pozen adds that this secrecy may take a shallow form (i.e., known unknowns) but also a deep form (i.e., unknown unknowns). The latter form of secrecy refers, for example, to documents that have not been registered. But a lack of transparency does not only result from intentional actions; it may also result from a lack of capacity or simply the fact that a need for transparency has not been recognized. The impact of the internet on these different forms of opaqueness may expected to be different; the internet will basically change the capacity to produce transparency and, therefore, primarily influence non-intentional opaqueness.
2. Leaking is often ignored but plays an important role in transparency (Piotrowski 2007; Bok 1982). Roberts (2006, 73) convincingly argues that leaking became a crucial source of transparency during the Bush Administration.
3. One can question whether media always act as fire alarms for vertical accountability forums or whether they construct their own accountability processes and force political actors to react. See Schillemans (2012) for a broader reflection on the role of the media in these accountability processes.

References

Bannister, F. and Connolly, R. 2011. "The Trouble with Transparency: A Critical Review of Openness in e-Government." *Policy & Internet*, 3(1), art. 8.

Bernstein, C. and Woodward, B. 1974. *All the President's Men*. New York: Simon and Schuster.

Birkinshaw, P. J. 2006. "Freedom of Information and Openness. Fundamental Human Rights." *Administrative Law Review*, 58: 177–218.

Black, J. 1997. *Transparent Policy Measures*. Oxford Dictionary of Economics. Oxford: Oxford University Press.

Blanton, T. S. 2003. National Security and Open Government in the United States: Beyond the Balancing Test pp. 31–71 in *National Security and Open Government: Striking the Right Balance*, eds. A. Roberts and H. Darbishire. Syracuse, NY: Campbell Public Affairs Institute.

Boer, M. den. 1998. Steamy Windows: Transparency and Openness in Justice and Home Affairs, pp. 91–105 in *Openness and Transparency in the European Union*, eds. V. Deckmyn and I. Thomson. Maastricht: European Institute of Public Administration.

Bok, S. 1982. *Secrets. On the Ethics of Concealment and Revelation*. New York: Pantheon Books.

Bovens, M. A. P. 1998. *The Quest for Responsibility: Accountability and Citizenship in Complex Organisations*. Cambridge: Cambridge University Press.

Bovens, M. A. P. 2003. *De Digitale Republiek. Democratie en Rechtsstaat in de Informatiemaatschappij*. Amsterdam: Amsterdam University Press.

Bovens, M. A. P. 2007. "Analysing and Assessing Accountability: A Conceptual Framework." *European Law Journal*, 13: 447–68.

Bovens, M. A. P. 2010. "Two Concepts of Accountability: Accountability as a Virtue and as a Mechanism." *West European Politics*, 33: 946–67.

Brandsma, G. J., Curtin, D. and Meijer, A. 2008. "How Transparent are EU 'Comitology' Committees in Practice?" *European Law Journal*, 14: 819–38.

Brin, G. D. 1998. *The Transparent Society: Will Privacy Force Us to Choose Between Privacy and Freedom?* Reading MA: Perseus.

Davis, J. 1998. Access to and Transmission of Information: Position of the Media, pp. 121–26 in *Openness and Transparency in the European Union*, eds. V. Deckmyn and I. Thomson. Maastricht: European Institute of Public Administration.

Deuze, M. 2002. *Journalists in The Netherlands*. Amsterdam: Het Spinhuis.

Dror, Y. 1999. Transparency and Openness of Quality Democracy, pp. 25–43 in *Openness and Transparency in Governance: Challenges and Opportunities*, ed. M. Kelly. Maastricht: NISPAcee Forum.

Erkkilä, T. 2012. *Government Transparency: Impacts and Unintended Consequences*. New York: Palgrave Macmillan.

Etzioni, A. 2010. "Is Transparency the Best Disinfectant?" *The Journal of Political Philosophy*, 18: 389–404.

Fox, J. 2007. "The Uncertain Relationship Between Transparency and Accountability." *Development in Practice*, 17: 663–71.

Fukuyama, F. 1996. *Trust: The Social Virtues and the Creation of Prosperity*. New York: The Free Press.

Fung, A. and Weil, D. 2010. Open Government and Open Society, pp. 105–13 in *Open Government: Collaboration, Transparency and Participation in Practice*, eds. D. Lathrop, and L. Ruma. Beijing: O'Reilly.

Grimmelikhuijsen, S. G. 2007. *Transparency of Government and Political Trust.* Paper presented at the International Conference on Experimental Methods in Political Science. Brussels, December 14, 2007.

Grimmelikhuijsen, S. G. 2012. *Transparency and Trust: An Experimental Study of Online Disclosure and Trust in Government.* PhD Thesis. Utrecht University.

Heald, D. A. 2003. "Fiscal Transparency: Concepts, Measurement and UK Practice." *Public Administration*, 81: 723–59.

Heald, D. 2006. Varieties of Transparency, pp. 25–43 in *Transparency: The Key to Better Governance?* eds. C. Hood and D. Heald. Oxford: Oxford University Press.

Heald, D. 2012. "Why is Transparency About Public Expenditure so Elusive?" *International Review of Administrative Sciences*, 78: 30–49.

Hibbing, J. and Theiss-Morse, E. 2002. *Stealth Democracy: Americans' Belief About How Government Should Work.* New York: Cambridge University Press.

Hood, C. 2006. Transparency in Historical perspective, pp. 4–23 in *Transparency: The Key to Better Governance?* eds. C. Hood and D. Heald. Oxford: Oxford University Press.

Hood, C. 2007. "What Happens When Transparency Meets Blame-Avoidance?" *Public Management Review*, 9: 191–210.

Hood, C. 2010. "Accountability and Transparency: Siamese Twins, Matching Parts, Awkward Couple." *West European Politics*, 33: 989–1009.

Lindstedt, C. and Naurin, D. 2010. "Transparency is Not Enough: Making Transparency Effective in Reducing Corruption." *International Political Science Review*, 31: 301–22.

Margetts, H. 2006. Transparency and Digital Government, pp. 197–207 in *Transparency: The Key to Better Governance?* eds. C. Hood and D. Heald. Oxford: Oxford University Press.

May, P. J. 2007. "Regulatory Regimes and Accountability." *Regulation & Governance*, 1: 8–26.

McCubbins, M. D. and Schwarz, T. 1984. "Congressional Oversight Overlooked: Police Patrols Versus Fire Alarms." *American Journal of Political Science*, 2: 165–79.

McDermott, P. 2010. "Building Open Government." *Government Information Quarterly*, 27, 401–13.

McGee, M. C. 1980. "The 'Ideograph': A Link Between Rhetoric and Ideology." *Quarterly Journal of Speech*, 66: 1–16.

Meijer, A. J. 2003. "Transparent Government: Parliamentary and Legal Accountability in an Information Age." *Information Polity*, 8: 67–78.

Meijer, A. J. 2007. "Publishing Public Performance Results on the Internet: Do Stakeholders use the Internet to Hold Dutch Public Service Organizations to Account?" *Government Information Quarterly*, 24: 165–85.

Meijer, A. 2009. "Understanding Modern Transparency." *International Review of the Administrative Sciences*, 75: 255–69.

Meijer, A. J. and Homburg, V. 2009. "Disclosure and Compliance: The 'Pillory' as an Innovative Regulatory Instrument." *Information Polity*, 14: 263–78.

Meijer, A. J., Curtin, D. and Hillebrandt, M. 2012. "Open Government: Connecting Vision and Voice." *International Review of Administrative Sciences*, 78: 10–29.

Meijer, A. J. 2013. "Understanding the Complex Dynamics of Transparency." *Public Administration Review*, doi: 10.1111/puar.12032

Michels, A. and Meijer, A. J. 2008. "Safeguarding Public Accountability in Horizontal Government." *Public Management Review*, 10: 165–73.

Moser, C. 2001. *How Open is "Open as Possible"? Three Different Approaches to Transparency and Openness in Regulating Access to EU Documents.* HIS Political Science Series, No. 80. Vienna: Institute for Advanced Studies.

Mulgan, R. 2000. "'Accountability': An Ever-Expanding Concept?" *Public Administration*, 78: 555–73.

Nolan, L. 1995. *First Report of the Committee on Standards in Public Life*. Cm 2850-I. London: HMSO.

Obama, B. 2009. *Transparency and Open Government: Memorandum for the Heads of Executive Departments and Agencies*. Retrieved from <http://www.whitehouse.gov/the_press_office/TransparencyandOpenGovernment>.

Oliver, R. W. 2004. *What is Transparency?* New York: McGraw-Hill.

O'Neill, O. 2002. *A Question of Trust*. Cambridge: Cambridge University Press.

O'Neill, O. 2006. Transparency and the Ethics of Communication, pp. 75–90 in *Transparency: The Key to Better Governance?* eds. C. Hood and D. Heald. New York: Oxford University Press.

Pasquier, M. and Villeneuve, J. P. 2007. "Organizational Barriers to Transparency: A Typology and Analysis of Organizational Behaviour Tending to Prevent or Restrict Access to Information." *International Review of Administrative Sciences*, 73: 147–62.

Piotrowski, S. J. 2007. *Governmental Transparency in the Path of Administrative Reform*. Albany, NY: State University of New York Press.

Popper, K. 1945. *The Open Society and Its Enemies*. Volumes 1 and 2. London: Routledge.

Pozen, D. E. 2010. "Deep Secrecy". *Stanford Law Review*, 62: 257–340.

Prat, A. 2006. The More Closely We Are Watched, the Better We Behave?, pp. 91–103 in *Transparency: The Key to Better Governance?* eds. C. Hood and D. Heald. Oxford: Oxford University Press.

Putnam, R. D. 2000. *Bowling Alone: The Collapse and Revival of American Community*. New York: Simon and Schuster.

Roberts, A. 2006. *Blacked Out: Government Secrecy in the Information Age*. Cambridge: Cambridge University Press.

Roberts, A. 2010. "A Great and Revolutionary Law? The First Four Years of India's Right to Information Act." *Public Administration Review*, 70: 925–33.

Schillemans, T. 2008. "Accountability in the Shadow of Hierarchy: The Horizontal Accountability of Agencies." *Public Organization Review*, 8: 175–94.

Schillemans, T. 2011. "Remedies for the Accountability Deficit of Agencies Does Horizontal Accountability Work? Evaluating Potential Remedies for the Accountability Deficit of Agencies." *Administration & Society*, 43: 387–416.

Schillemans, T. 2012. *Mediatization of Public Services: How Organizations Adapt to News Media*. Frankfurt-am-Main (Germany): Peter Lang.

Scholtes, E. 2012. *Transparantie, Icoon van een Dolende Overheid*. PhD Thesis. Tilburg University.

Söderman, J. 1998. *The Citizen, the Administration and Community Law*. General Report for the 1998 Fide Congress. Stockholm, 3–6 June.

Tan, Y. 2012. "Transparency Without Democracy: The Unexpected Effects of China's Environmental Disclosure Policy." *Governance*, doi: 10.1111/gove.12018

Tolbert, C. and Mossberger, K. 2006. "The Effects of E-Government on Trust and Confidence in Government." *Public Administration Review*, 66: 354–69.

Welch, E. W. and Wong, W. 2001. "Global Information Technology Pressure and Government Accountability: The Mediating Effect of Domestic Context on Web Site Openness." *Journal of Public Administration Research & Theory*, 11: 509–38.

Worthy, B. 2010. "More Open but Not More Trusted? The Effect of the Freedom of Information Act 2000 on the United Kingdom Central Government." *Governance*, 23: 561–82.

CHAPTER 32

WATCHDOG JOURNALISM

PIPPA NORRIS

THE FOURTH ESTATE

THE notion of watchdog journalism as a mechanism for strengthening accountability in democratic governance has long been advocated by liberal theorists. The watchdog ideal reflects the long-established liberal conception of the news media as the fourth estate, an independent guardian located in civil society and counterbalancing the power of executive, legislative, and judiciary branches in government. Muckraking reporting has deep historical roots in the Anglo-American journalistic tradition; its origins can be traced back to early radical political pamphlets, cartoons, and posters in Britain and America, as well as to the development of the modern newspaper during the seventeenth century. The crusading role of investigative journalism expanded with the growth of mass circulation newspapers in nineteenth century America, tackling a range of social ills. A long series of newspaper investigations into corruption contributed to the reforming zeal displayed during the progressive era. The contemporary wave, seizing the popular imagination, followed release of the Pentagon Papers and the dramatic events of Watergate, unleashing forces capable of toppling an American president (Serrin and Serrin 2002; Shapiro 2003). Investigative journalism continues to be actively promoted in Anglo-American cultures through journalism education and training, and to be glorified in popular accounts, reflecting deep-rooted liberal values (Berry 2008; Burgh 2008).

Classical liberalism, ever skeptical about the trustworthiness of government and powerful leaders, advocates that journalists should be watchdogs of the public interest. Through fulfilling this role, independent media are believed to strengthen the accountability of powerful decision-makers. The core notion of "watchdog" journalism can be understood to encompass both a direct *primary* role, when investigating the behavior of the powerful and instigating reports about alleged malfeasance, as well as a more diffuse and weaker *secondary* role, when disseminating general information about public affairs which was previously hidden from public attention, such as reporting hearings from public inquiries or court prosecutions.[1] When fulfilling these twin functions, watchdog journalists question the accuracy of information, interrogate officials, and investigate whether actual conduct reflects high standards of public life. Through this process, the news media is thought to help safeguard the public interest, spotlighting cases of misinformation, incompetence, scandal, corruption, and criminality in both the public and private sectors (Donsbach 1995; Schultz 1998; Cammaerts and Carpentier 2007; Norris 2010). In democratic states, government officials are expected to explain the reasons underlying their behavior with this information conveyed via reporters to the general public. In the classic cliché, hard-hitting independent reporters ask tough questions of the powerful. If the public remains dissatisfied with the answers, officials face sanctions. Accountability, in this sense, means that leaders need to answer for their actions, decisions, or policies, where the media serves as interlocutor, with their peers or the public ultimately functioning as judge and jury. As the Nieman Foundation (2010) expressed the general argument: "The premise of watchdog journalism is that the press is a surrogate for the public, asking probing, penetrating, questions at every level from the town council to the state house to the White House, as well as in corporate and professional offices, in union halls, on university campuses and in religious organizations that seek to influence governmental actions. The goal of watchdog journalism is to see that people in power provide information the public should have."

As well the primary role of instigating stories about the abuse of power, secondary news coverage can also strengthen other accountability mechanisms. We can distinguish analytically between the potential direct and indirect effects of watchdog journalism upon public opinion.

Political information provided by the independent media helps citizens to evaluate the performance of their elected leaders, both individually and collectively. In multi-party liberal democracies, informed citizens have opportunities to "throw the rascals out" at regular intervals, ensuring the *electoral* accountability of legislative representatives and, indirectly, the bureaucratic accountability of public servants.

In the private sector, as well, documentaries and news reports—exposing events such as the Enron scandal or the risks to consumers arising from the fast food or tobacco industries—can potentially strengthen corporate governance and the *managerial* accountability of CEOs to stockholders and consumers. The media can give whistleblowers a voice, spearhead the downfall of powerful executives, and expose widespread corporate corruption.

The news media can also reinforce *legal* accountability, through catalyzing or reporting official hearings, whether by the legislature, courts of audits, ombudsmen, inspectorates and regulatory agencies; investigative reports conducted by civil society organizations; or formal inquiries by the police, courts, prosecutors, and judiciary.

Public disclosure and transparency, though not sufficient by itself to stamp out corruption (Lindstedt and Naurin 2010), is assumed to bring government and corporate misconduct to the attention of the public and the courts, and deter others from similar behavior. Liberal theories claim therefore that news coverage can inform the public and official bodies, catalyze electoral, managerial, or legal sanctions against transgressors, and thus provide incentives for better performance. For all these reasons, watchdog journalism is widely believed to be intrinsically valuable for accountability.

THE WATCHDOG ROLE IN PRACTICE

Despite the popularity of these idealized claims, especially in Anglo-American culture, do these values translate into actions? This raises a series of questions, which are progressively more difficult to answer with any degree of certainty. In particular, is there good evidence that:

(i) reporters around the world accept the normative role of watchdog journalism;
(ii) the news media actually serve as active or reactive watchdogs of the public interest in practice, through their coverage of public affairs; and that, by so doing,
(iii) the news media serve as effective mechanisms of accountability, triggering public outrage and effective actions by policy-makers, thereby fulfilling lofty democratic principles?

Several critiques are common, replete with canine metaphors, throughout the literature (Donsbach 1995). In practice, reporters can prove to be timid lapdogs, the poodle breed, if restricted by autocratic state controls and repression, or even actively engaged in promoting state propaganda. Or they may prove subservient by pandering to the interests of powerful political and corporate elites, becoming guard-dogs (Donohue, Tichenor, and Olien 1995). A common criticism of American news media is that reporters chase "soft" news, typically about glamorous celebrities, sensationalist crime, and infotainment (Patterson 1993), thereby becoming inattentive to serious investigative reporting about public affairs. Alternatively, journalists may have become attack-dogs, the Rottweilers of public affairs. Videomalaise theories, originating with Lang and Lang (1966) and Michael Robinson (1976), suggest that bellicose talk show commentary, exposé reports, and hostile interviewing of public officials has undermined trust in government institutions and fuelled public discontent with democracy (Norris 2000). Or it is also possible that the old-fashioned notion of watchdog journalism as the primary instigator of stories revealing scandals has simply become as redundant for democratic governance today as the ticker-tape machine, the equivalent of an urban sheepdog, with the reporter's primary function becoming irrelevant in the digital world of instant blogs, WikiLeaks websites, Facebook pages, YouTube phone videos, and Twitter feeds. Of course these scenarios need not necessarily be regarded as alternatives, since complex tendencies may be operating simultaneously in different parts of the world and in multi-platform, diverse, and fragmented communication industries.

Do the News Media Accept the Normative Role of Watchdog Journalism?

What empirical evidence allows us to throw light on these rival interpretations? One common approach to monitor perceptions about the importance of diverse journalistic roles and functions has been to conduct surveys of news professionals and the public. The results largely confirm that the ideal of watchdog journalism is widely endorsed by journalists in the United States, although this is only one of multiple roles (Johnstone, Slawski, and Bowman 1976; Weaver and Wilhoit 1986; Weaver 2007; Beam, Weaver, and Brownlee 2009). Several distinct role conceptions of journalists have been identified by successive studies, including those of disseminating information, interpreting complex problems, mobilizing audience members, and being "adversaries" of business and government officials. Nevertheless these empirical measures often map poorly to the underlying concept of watchdog journalism. To publish stories revealing malfeasance in public life, and to report official hearings from regulatory bodies and court prosecutions, does not necessarily imply the adoption of an adversarial stance per se. The American Society of News Editors (ASNE) surveyed a representative sample of American newspaper staff to monitor the perceived functions of newspapers.[2] Overall the importance of "investigating claims and statements made by the government and political candidates" was endorsed as "extremely" or "very" important by eight out of ten journalists. The role of "investigating claims and statements made by businesses and other institutions" was also endorsed by seven out of ten journalists. Nevertheless this measure also poorly captures the more complex notion of watchdog journalism. The ASNE survey also found, not surprisingly, that other journalistic roles, including interpreting events and providing information, were regarded as equally important.

American public opinion polls also suggest that the watchdog role of the media receives fairly widespread popular approval. The Pew Research Center for the People and the Press Poll has monitored American public attitudes towards the news media on an annual basis since 1985, including attitudes towards the statement: "By criticizing political leaders, news organizations...keep leaders from doing things which should not be done." The 2011 Pew survey found that the majority (58 percent) of Americans supported this notion. Moreover attitudes have remained fairly stable in annual surveys. The 2011 Pew survey report concluded that the press is widely criticized today in America, but nevertheless the public expresses more trust in news organizations than in government and business institutions.

In other journalistic cultures, however, evidence suggests that the role and practice of watchdog reporting is often less widely endorsed by reporters, even in many established democracies within continental Europe (Köcher 1986; Deuze 2002). For example, comparative surveys by Deuze (2002) found that the proportion of journalists agreeing that it was "extremely" or "very" important to investigate claims made by government was widespread in Anglo-American news cultures (endorsed by 88 percent of journalists surveyed in Britain, 81 percent in Australia, and 67 percent in the United States) but it was not widely supported in Continental Europe (endorsed by just 25 percent of journalists surveyed in the Netherlands and only 12 percent in Germany). Chalaby (2004) suggests that investigative journalism in France has been a relatively recent development, starting only in the 1980s. Support for the normative value of watchdog journalism, and reporting practices, varies substantially among low-income societies in many global regions (Norris 2010). Waisbord (1996) argues that in Latin America, investigative reporting used to be marginal and clandestine under the dictators but it developed during the 1980s, accompanying broader processes of democratization, so that it is now mainstream in newsrooms. The broadest comparison is based on a recent survey of journalists conducted by the World of Journalism project covering 18 diverse nations by Hanitzsch et al. (2011).[3] The study demonstrates varied cross-national support for the idea that journalists should "act as watchdogs of government." Overall among all journalists in the countries under comparison, this item proved the 3rd highest ranked of all the institutional roles listed in the survey, ranked below the roles of "providing citizens with information" and being "an absolutely detached observer." Endorsement for watchdog journalism was particularly high in contemporary liberal democracies, including the United States, Brazil, Australia, and Germany. But this item was far less widely endorsed by reporters in countries with more autocratic regimes, including China and Russia, as well as, perhaps more surprisingly, in places such as Israel, Mexico, Romania, and Chile. There was also little consensus in the 18 countries under comparison about whether journalists should also act as watchdogs of business elites. On balance, the evidence suggests that many news professionals in liberal Anglo-American democracies, skeptical of powerful elites, probably regard the primary or secondary watchdog role as central to their mission. In other cultures, however, this claim is more strongly contested.

Do the News Media Serve As Watchdogs in Practice?

Even where the principles of watchdog journalism are accepted, however, it remains unclear whether journalists actually follow these ideal roles in the news room, even in Anglo-American cultures, and thus how much reporting falls into the watchdog category. Values may shape behavior, but journalists often face serious economic, technological, and political constraints in fulfilling these ideals.

In many affluent post-industrial societies with widespread access to digital technologies, especially the United States, one increasingly severe challenge to watchdog journalism arises from the contemporary economic pressures facing newspapers, magazines, and broadcasting channels, threatening the traditional business model (Picard 1989; 2002; 2010; Barnhurst 2011; Pew 2011). The American print media are struggling to maintain profitability and adapt to an environment of dwindling advertising revenues (especially classified ads), falling subscriptions, rising paper and distribution costs, the need to offer multi-platform delivery mechanisms, and the proliferation of alternative online news sources. Local, regional, and metropolitan newspapers in the United States have been particularly badly hit, experiencing thousands of layoffs in newsrooms, buy-outs, bankruptcies, and some major closures. The rapid growth of digital communica-tions is a threat to the commercial viability of traditional for-profit news outlets. This new financial environment constrains all aspects of newspaper production in the United States. It may have the most serious repercussions for catalytic investigative report-ing, however, since this commonly requires editors and publishers to invest weeks and months of staff resources before eventual publication. It should be noted, however, that the erosion of newspaper sales is not a global phenomenon (WAN 2011), as circulation figures continue to rise in emerging economies and democratic societies, such as India, South Africa, and Brazil. Newspapers are expanding in places with widespread freedom of expression, a growing middle class, rising levels of literacy and education, and lim-ited access to digital news media (at least in its web-based extended form). In addition, in many societies, public television and specialist news channels following the British Broadcasting Corporation (BBC) model, continue to invest in the production of inves-tigative journalism in documentary and commentary programs. Even here, however, the overall audience share for public television has shrunk since the 1980s, following the proliferation of commercial cable, satellite, and online channels, and public televi-sion also faces growing constraints on public funding (especially Public Broadcasting Service (PBS) in the United States).

The technological proliferation of social media, such as Twitter, blogs, and WikiLeaks, challenges traditional forms of watchdog journalism. Social media have rapidly become an invaluable information resource for reporters, as well as an important outlet for professional journalists and for citizens who blog online. The traditional news media have been adapting to new interactive formats, including delivering news through multi-platform channels for mobile devices, and posting readers' comments to accom-pany stories, integrating live video feeds and images of events derived from participants, and incorporating live blogging into online commentary of breaking events. Due to rapid shifts in communication and information technologies, the role of journalists has been evolving into an aggregator of multiple sources, bringing order to the chaos, filter-ing information, and structuring narrative understanding.

By contrast, in many autocracies lacking freedom of expression, watchdog report-ers critical of the current regime continue to suffer from political restrictions arising from state pressure, censorship, and outright violence and intimidation. Organizations such as Human Rights Watch, Reporters Without Borders, and Freedom House reg-ularly document these limits to freedom of the independent media in countries such as Syria and Zimbabwe. Nevertheless, investigative reporting can still play a role, within certain constraints, providing autocratic regimes with feedback mechanisms and forms of local accountability. In China, for example, investigative journalism has expanded in some newspapers, providing a professional ideology for journalists. This provides information which helps the state to root out local corruption or malfeasance in public office, although criticism of the central state authorities and the party leader-ship remains extremely limited (Bandurski and Hala 2010). In China, pressures from both the Communist party and from advertisers limit the opportunities for watchdog journalism. As a result, Tong and Sparks (2009) report that the contemporary picture remains mixed. Some Chinese television channels and newspapers have largely abandoned investigative journalism while others retain the practice but with a strategy of caution.

The Impact of Watchdog Journalism

In practice, does watchdog journalism actually strengthen accountability? As Protess et al. (1991) emphasized, popular folklore glorifying the image of investigative journalism tends to mythologize vigilant reporters, the impact of this coverage upon an informed citizenry, and the responsiveness of politicians to public outrage. In practice this chain of accountability can break down at several fragile points. Reporters have many conflicting priorities, they work within constraints, and they may only pay lip-service to the watchdog role. Even where well-documented and credible exposures of wrong-doing are published, the general public and policymakers may well react with yawning indifference. Moreover muckraking can result in sanctions being applied to specific individuals found guilty of misconduct, a few heads may roll in public without necessarily mobilizing support for broader policy reforms designed to tackle the underlying causes. The potential impact of watchdog coverage upon elites and the public, like other media effects, can be understood as *agenda setting* (raising concern about the importance of certain issues), *framing* (shaping understanding of issues and perceptions of events within familiar narrative conventions), and *priming* (attributing responsibility and assigning praise or blame for certain outcomes). There is little consensus about whether watchdog journalism generates any of these multiple effects and several approaches can be used to explore the evidence.

Experimental research design is the "gold standard" for establishing causal effects, but until recently this technique has not been commonly employed to determine the impact of reporting practices. Nevertheless in several low-income democracies, natural and field experiments indicate that more information about the political process and the performance of representatives improves electoral accountability, so that those found guilty of improper conduct are removed from office (Pande 2011). A study of Italian legislators by Chang, Golden, and Hill (2010) also found that voters did not punish alleged miscreants with loss of office unless judicial findings were first aired in the press. On the other hand there are many counter-examples which suggest that media coverage by itself is insufficient to produce electoral accountability; Prime Minister Silvio Berlusconi was repeatedly returned to office in Italy despite an extensive record of criminal allegations, including mafia collusion, false accounting, tax fraud, child prostitution, corruption, and bribery of police officers and judges.

Some of the most rigorous and systematic evidence for testing the impact of watchdog journalism on corruption is derived from cross-national and time-series comparisons using econometric techniques. A series of studies using these methods have tested whether press freedom (measured at national level function) acts to promote the quality of governance, particularly the extent of corruption. Using this approach, in a widely-cited article Brunetti and Weder (2003) tested the impact of press freedom on corruption. They concluded that an increase by one standard deviation in a country's level of press freedom generally reduces the perceived level of corruption in that country by 0.4 to 0.9 points, on a six-point scale. This result was found to prove robust using different model specifications, country samples, and measures. The reasons, the authors suggest, are that the press provides a platform for the private sector to voice complaints. In addition, with a free press, journalists have incentives to investigate misconduct by officials. A series of other aggregate-level cross-national econometric studies, incorporating standard controls, generally point to similar conclusions (Stapenhurst 2000; Chowddhury 2004; Freille, Haque, and Kneller 2007; Keefer 2007; Charron 2009). For example, Lederman, Loayza, and Soares (2005) analyzed the effects of democracy, parliamentary systems, and freedom of the press on corruption, and their results confirm that press freedom inhibits corruption. In addition, media access has also been found to be important. Bandyopadhyay (2006) reported that the degree of media and ICT penetration is associated with less corruption, with the strongest effect where newspaper circulation was deepest. The diffusion of the internet has also been tested for its effects on perceptions of corruption. Lio, Liu, and Ou (2011) analyzed a panel of 70 countries from 1998 to 2005 and observed that internet adoption had a significant but weak effect by reducing (perceived) levels of corruption. Nevertheless other scholars caution that transparency by itself is insufficient to produce accountability; Lindstedt and Naurin (2010) note that unless there are ways for citizens to act on information, through channels such as electoral and legal accountability, then transparency alone will be insufficient to reduce corruption.

To update and explore the evidence, we can compare how freedom of the press (monitored by Freedom House) relates to perceived control of corruption (measured by the World Bank Institute Kaufmann-Kraay indices) for different types of regimes. The Freedom House measure of freedom of the press is one of the most widely used cross-national indicators and it is strongly correlated with alternative indices, such as the Index generated by Reporters Without Borders. The Freedom House scale is designed to measure how far the free flow of news is influenced by the legal, political, and economic environments. The *legal environment* subdivision encompasses "both examination of the laws and regulations that could influence media content as well as the government's inclination to use these laws and legal institutions in order to restrict the media's ability to operate." In this category Freedom House assesses several issues such as legal and constitutional guarantees of press freedom, penalties for libel and defamation as well as penal codes, the independence of the judiciary, and other factors. The *political environment* evaluates "the degree of political control over the content of news media." This includes the editorial independence of the media, intimidation and threats to journalists, access to informational sources, and also repressive actions such as arrests, imprisonment, physical violence, and assassinations. Finally, under the *economic environment* category, the characteristics examined are related to "economic considerations that can influence the media's activities." Within this category, Freedom House evaluates the existence of competitive pressures leading to biased press reports and investigations, the extent of sponsoring, subsidies, and advertisement, and their effect on press coverage and content, the impact of bribery by self-interested actors on what is published, and the structure and concentration of media ownership.

Both the "legal" and "economic" categories vary from 0 (complete freedom) to 30 (lack of freedom) while the "political" sub-index ranges from 0 to 40. A country's overall press freedom score is simply the sum of the scores in each of the sub-categories. The assessment of press freedom by Freedom House distinguishes between the broadcast and print media, and the resulting ratings are expressed as a 100-point scale for each country under comparison. The index is based on expert ratings derived from overseas correspondents, staff and consultant travel, international visitors, the findings of human rights and press freedom organizations, specialists in geographic and geopolitical areas, the reports of governments and multilateral bodies, and a variety of domestic and international news media.[4] It is strongly correlated with Reporters Without Borders annual Index of Press Freedom. For an intuitively clearer interpretation, the Freedom House index is reversed, so that a higher score represents greater press freedom.

The Kaufmann-Kraay indices have been developed to monitor multiple dimensions of the quality of governance (Kaufmann, Kraay, and Mastruzzi 2008). This includes control of corruption in the public sector, defined as "perceptions of the extent to which public power is exercised for private gain, including both petty and grand forms of corruption, as well as 'capture' of the state by elites and private interests." Their methodology identifies many individual sources of data on governance perceptions that are then assigned to six broad categories. The control of corruption index combines sources such as data provided by Transparency International, the World Economic Forum Global Competitiveness Survey, and the Political Risk Services International Country Risk Guide. An unobserved components model is used to construct aggregate indicators from these individual measures. These aggregate indicators are weighted averages of the underlying data, with weights reflecting the precision of the individual data sources.

Figure 32.1 illustrates the simple correlation summarizing the link between the 2010 Freedom House's annual index of press freedom and the perceived levels of the control of corruption, as measured in 2010 by Kaufmann-Kraay, without applying any controls. The results show that the curvilinear regression line provides the best fit for the data, generating a strong and significant relationship (R^2 =.578***). Perceived control of corruption sharply accelerates for those democracies which are above average for press freedom. Societies such as Iceland, Canada, Chile, and South Africa rank highly on both indices; in these places, a plurality of media outlets and a flourishing independent media sector generate the transparency which encourages clean government. The figure also highlights certain important outliers to the general pattern, such as Singapore. The least democratic states display high levels of perceived corruption. In this regard, the pattern is similar to the curvilinear relationship commonly observed between levels of liberal democracy and many other indices of the quality of governance (Norris 2012).

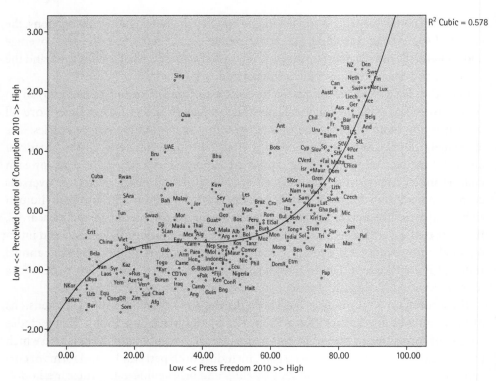

FIGURE 32.1 Press freedom and perceived control of corruption, 2010

Note: Press Freedom–Freedom House 2010; Perceived control of corruption 2010, Kaufmann-Kraay World Bank Institute indicators.

Case Study Evidence

Nevertheless while the aggregate correlation between the free press and control of corruption appears quite robust, little is understood about how this relationship works in practice and thus what needs reforming to strengthen effective democratic governance (Vaidya 2005; Oscarsson 2008). It is commonly assumed that the *availability* of information underlies the relationship, where more information is expected to generate more efficient political markets. Scandal headlines sell newspapers. In multiparty democracies, a more informed public, aware of the short-comings of corrupt elected officials, can decide to throw the rascal out (Pande 2011). Informed agencies can also use legal redress. But the available measures of media freedom at national level remain extremely general and abstract. In practice, even in the case of long-established democracies such as the United States, where electoral accountability mechanisms should be effective, there are many cases of high-ranking officials who have been charged and even convicted of corruption in cases attracting widespread headline publicity, yet who are subsequently reelected to office.[5] Berlusconi is only the tip of the iceberg. Moreover it remains difficult to determine causality using econometric techniques, even with instrumental variables, well-specified models, broad country and time-series coverage, and non-missing data. We need to dig deeper to know, in particular cases, what aspects of media systems, what forms of journalism, what types of media outlets, genres, and formats, and what societal conditions, legal contexts, and political environments, help to establish the link between watchdog journalism and its ultimate effects.

South Africa

Case studies help to illuminate these processes and that of South Africa exemplifies the underlying factors in the relationship between a plural media system and government transparency. Following the transitional democratic elections in April 1994, the media landscape was transformed through substantial reforms including the liberalization and deregulation of state control of broadcasting, the diversification of the print sector, constitutional and legal guarantees of freedom of access to state-held information, and growing use of the internet (Jacobs 2002; Tomaselli 2000; Hyden, Leslie, and Ogundimu 2002; Harber 2004). Deregulation, in particular, led to a proliferation of radio stations. Listeners in Johannesburg can tune into more than forty radio services. The South African Broadcasting Corporation (SABC) operates three national TV networks and two pay-TV channels, while commercial national broadcasters offer free and pay-TV channels, offering the usual mix of news and current affairs, sports and entertainment, movies, reality shows, and soaps, combining locally-produced and imported programming. The constitution provides for freedom of the press, and this is generally respected. In 2010, for example, out of 178 nations worldwide, Reporters sans Frontières (2010) ranked South Africa 38th from the top in press freedom, higher than France (44th) and Italy (49th), and roughly similar to Uruguay and Spain. Laws, regulation, and political control of media content are considered moderate in South Africa. Human Rights Watch (2008) praises the progress that South Africa has made in freedom of expression, despite remaining critical of the country's human rights record on other issues. Newspapers and magazines publish reports critical of the government and the state-owned SABC is far more independent now than during the apartheid era. As a result, although there remain tensions in the complex relationship between journalists and the African National Congress (ANC), during the last decade the news media has emerged as an increasingly autonomous actor, less closely aligned with the interests of the government or political parties. In the index of perceptions of corruption by Transparency International (2011), South Africa also ranks 54th out of 178 nations worldwide, similar to Malaysia and Kuwait.

Syria

By contrast, countries such as Zimbabwe, Uzbekistan, Syria, and Belarus rank poorly in Figure 32.1 in both press freedom and perceived levels of corruption. Even before the crackdown caused by the Arab uprisings, the Syrian case under President Bashar al-Assad illustrates state restriction of freedom of expression. The Syrian government owns and controls much of the media, including the daily newspapers *Al-Thawra* ("The Revolution"), *Tishrin*, and the English-language *Syria Times*, while the Baath party publishes *Al-Baath*. A brief flowering of press freedom occurred after Bashar al-Assad became president in 2000. The normally staid government newspapers cautiously started to discuss reform and democracy. For the first time in nearly 40 years, private publications were licensed. The new titles included political party papers *Sawt al-Shaab* and *Al-Wahdawi*, and a satirical journal. But within a year, under pressure from the old guard, the president cautioned against over-zealous reform, a subsequent press law imposed a new range of restrictions, and publications could be suspended for violating content rules. Criticism of President Bashar al-Assad and his family has long been banned and the domestic and foreign press is censored over material that is deemed to be threatening or embarrassing. Journalists practice self-censorship and foreign reporters rarely get accreditation. Reporters Without Borders (2007) documents common abuses, even prior to the recent crackdown caused by the Syrian war: "Journalists and political activists risk arrest at any time for any reason and are up against a whimsical and vengeful state apparatus that continually adds to the list of things banned or forbidden to be mentioned. Several journalists were arrested in 2006 for interviewing exiled regime opponents, taking part in conferences abroad or for criticizing government policies. They were subjected to lengthy legal proceedings before the Damascus military court that, under a 1963 law, tries anyone considered to have undermined state security." Critical journalists outside the country write for the Lebanese or pan-Arab press, such as the Beirut daily *Al-Nahar*, and the influential London daily *Al-Hayat*, as well as contributing to Al-Jazeera and other regional satellite channels (Campagna 2001). Syrian TV, operated by the Ministry of Information, operates two terrestrial and one satellite channel. Prior to the uprisings, it cautiously began carrying political programs and debates featuring formerly taboo issues, as well as occasionally airing interviews with opposition figures. Since the uprisings, the regime has stepped up censorship and persecution of independent journalists, depicting international criticism of its repression as a "foreign conspiracy." Syria also licensed some privately-owned radio stations in 2004 but these were restricted from airing any news or political content. With an estimated 1.5 million internet users in Syria, social media have emerged as a vehicle for dissent, a process of critical importance for connecting information among dissenters engaged in the Arab Revolt. In the view of Reporters Without Borders, however, Syria is one of the worst offenders against internet freedom, as the state censors opposition bloggers and independent news websites. Human Rights Watch (2007) notes that the government of Syria regularly restricts the flow of information on the internet and arrests individuals who post comments that the government deems too critical. Overall Syria ranked 173rd out of 178 countries in the RWB 2010 Worldwide Press Freedom index. Similarly, in terms of press freedom, Freedom House (2010) ranks the country 179th out of 195 states worldwide. In terms of perceptions of corruption, according to Transparency international, Syria currently (2010) ranks 127th out of 178 nations, around the same level as Uganda and Belarus.

Media and Corruption

These observations are also supported by a growing number of detailed case studies which illustrate the ways that the news media perform their watchdog role in the fight against corruption. Hence a study of Madagascar's educational system by Francken, Minten, and Swinnen (2005) found that the effect of anti-corruption campaigns varied by the type of media; in particular, in areas of high illiteracy, radio and television—especially local broadcasts—are more effective at curbing corruption than newspapers and poster campaigns. Ferraz and Finan (2008) studied Brazil, where the government published the findings of audits of expenditures of federal funds in selected municipalities. The authors report that in regions where local radio stations covered the findings of the audit, non-corrupt incumbents experienced a vote bonus. Finally, there is the well-known World Bank example; Reinikka and Svensson (2005) reported that in 1995, only one fifth of the money allocated to schools in Uganda actually made it to the schools. The government of Uganda initiated a media campaign to enable schools and parents to monitor the handling of school grants by local governments. By 2001, 80 percent of the allocated funds were indeed spent on the schools. The government's newspaper campaign was the major factor in the change.

Overall, therefore, case studies cannot be regarded as definitive, due to potential selection bias limiting their generalizability. Nevertheless case-studies combined with the more systematic econometric evidence suggest a systematic link between the roles of the press as watchdogs over the powerful and the transparency and accountability of government. At the same time, there are also clearly certain important exceptions to this rule, such as Singapore, which is widely regarded as low on corruption despite restrictions on press freedom, as well as cases such as Papua New Guinea, Mali, and the Philippines which continue to be afflicted with corruption despite a relatively flourishing and pluralistic independent media sector.

Many conditions limit watchdog journalism, including those arising from lack of freedom of expression to criticize autocratic and repressive states, commercial pressures from private owners and advertisers, and also a more deferential culture of journalism which does not recognize watchdog journalism as an important, or even appropriate, role for the news media. Contrasts in role expectations are found even among journalists living within similar European post-industrial societies (Köcher 1986). In fragile states and among those engaged in peace-building, such as in Iraq, Sudan, and Ethiopia, reporters can see other short-term priorities as more important, with investigative journalism regarded as a destabilizing force for countries seeking to restore public confidence in governing authorities. It is true that "attack-dog" journalism, where partisan commentators launch fierce and bitter personal assaults on political rivals, can reinforce mistrust within divided multi-ethnic communities. Nevertheless even in these difficult conditions, in the long-run, public trust and confidence in the process of reconstruction is most likely to be established and reinforced where independent investigative journalists can highlight cases of misappropriations of public funds, human rights abuses, and examples of corruption. Watchdog journalism helps to raise standards in public life, ensuring that development funds are used for the purpose for which they were intended, deterring future misdeeds, and ensuring conditions of openness and transparency which attract further investment, and aid and which ultimately strengthen confidence in government.

CONCLUSIONS

The defining feature of watchdog journalism is to ask hard or probing questions of the powerful, to maximize transparency, and to serve the public interest. In its stronger version, journalists are the key actors demanding that leaders provide reasons for their actions, uncovering the abuse of power, and thereby triggering public outrage and legal actions. In the weaker, more routine version, journalists are secondary actors bringing other accountability bodies to public attention. Investigative reporting has a special role when highlighting failures in government and business, especially those arising from cases of bribery, corruption, and malfeasance; from abuse of power; or from incompetent management of public service delivery. More routine news coverage can also strengthen open governance.

The evidence reviewed here suggests that the watchdog role for journalism is most pervasive in Anglo-American democracies, where a long liberal tradition has encouraged skepticism towards the potential abuse of state power. In other countries, the more critical role for the independent news media seems to have developed with processes of democratization, although even in China, watchdog journalism (within limits) plays a role. Much American literature glorifies the role of the vigilant reporter, speaking truth to power, righting social injustices, informing citizens, and serving the public interest. Dramatic exaggeration and selective bias colors some popular accounts. Nevertheless, in practice, a growing body of evidence derived from experimental research, econometric cross-national analysis, and from specific cases, tends to confirm the effects of the press on the quality of governance, especially control of corruption. In the right circumstances the independent media does contribute towards accountability, especially where coverage of abuse of power by the press generates widespread concern among the public, and where other electoral, legal, and managerial accountability mechanisms provide effective sanctions.

NOTES

1. Arnold's (2004) research on the media and political accountability focuses on this secondary role of the news media. He analyzed the extent to which local American newspapers reported on the activities of local representatives in Congress in order to establish whether citizens were sufficiently informed about their representatives and, thus, were in a position to hold them accountable for their actions or lack thereof.

2. See <http://www.mrc.org/node/29212>.
3. For more details, see <http://www.worldsofjournalism.org/>.
4. For more methodological details and results, see <http://www.freedomhouse.org/report/freedom-press/freedom-press-2010>.
5. One such case is Alaska's Senator Ted Stevens, returned in the November 2008 elections despite being indicted on seven charges by a federal grand jury.

REFERENCES

Arnold, R. D. 2004. *Congress, the Press, and Political Accountability*. Princeton and Oxford: Princeton University Press

Bandurski, D. and Hala, M., eds. 2010. *Investigative Journalism in China*. Washington: University of Washington Press.

Bandyopadhyay, S. 2006. *Knowledge-Driven Economic Development*. Economics Series Working Papers, No. 267. University of Oxford, Department of Economics.

Barnhurst, K. 2011. "The New 'Media Affect' and the Crisis of Representation for Political Communication." *The International Journal of Press/Politics*, 16: 573–93.

Beam, R. A., Weaver, D. H., and Brownlee, B.J. 2009. "Changes in Professionalism of US Journalists in the Turbulent Twenty-First Century." *Journalism & Mass Communication Quarterly*, 86: 277–98.

Berry, S. J. 2008. *Watchdog Journalism: The Art of Investigative Reporting*. Oxford, NY: Oxford University Press.

Brunetti, A. and Weder, B. 2003. "A Free Press is Bad News for Corruption." *Journal of Public Economics*, 87:1801–24.

Burgh, H. D., ed. 2008. *Investigative Journalism*. London: Routledge.

Cammaerts, B. and Carpentier, N., eds. 2007. *Reclaiming the Media: Communication Rights and Democratic Media Roles*. London: Intellect Inc.

Campagna, J. 2001. *Syria Briefing Sept. 2001: Stop Signs*. Committee to Protect Journalists. Retrieved from <http://www.cpj.org/Briefings/2001/Syria_sept01/Syria_sept01.html>.

Chalaby, J. K. 2004. "Scandal and the Rise of Investigative Reporting in France." *The American Behavioral Scientist*, 47: 1194–1207.

Chang, E. C. C., Golden, M. A. and Hill, S. J. 2010. "Legislative Malfeasance and Political Accountability." *World Politics*, 62: 177–220.

Charron, N. 2009. "The Impact of Socio-Political Integration and Press Freedom on Corruption." *Journal of Development Studies*, 45: 1–22.

Chowddhury, S. K. 2004. "The Effect of Democracy and Press Freedom on Corruption: An Empirical Test." *Economics Letters*, 85:93–101.

Deuze, M. 2002. "National News Cultures: A Comparison of Dutch, German, British, Australian, and US journalists." *Journalism and Mass Communication Quarterly*, 79: 134–49.

Donohue, G. A., Tichenor, P. J., and Olien, C. N. 1995. "A Guard Dog Perspective on the Role of Media." *Journal of Communication*, 45: 115–32.

Donsbach, W. 1995. "Lapdogs, Watchdogs and Junkyard Dogs." *Media Studies Journal*, 9: 17–30.

Ferraz, C. and Finan, F. 2008. "Exposing Corrupt Politicians: The Effects of Brazil's Publicly Released Audits on Electoral Outcomes." *The Quarterly Journal of Economics*, 123:703–45.

Freedom House. 2010. *Global Press Freedom 2010*. Retrieved from <http://www.freedomhouse.org>.

Freille, S. M., Haque, E., and Kneller, R. 2007. "A Contribution to the Empirics of Press Freedom and Corruption." *European Journal of Political Economy*, 23:838–62.

Hanitzsch, T., Hanusch, F., Mellado, C., Anikina, M., Berganza, R., Cangoz, I., Coman, M., Hamada, B., Hernández, M. E., Karadjov, C. D., Moreira, S. V., Mwesige, P. G., Plaisance, P. L., Reich, Z., Seethaler, J., Skewes, E. A., Noor, D. V., and Yuen, E. K. W. 2011. "Mapping Journalism Cultures Across Nations: A Comparative Study of 18 Countries." *Journalism Studies*, 12: 273–93.

Harber, A. 2004. "Reflections on Journalism in the Transition to Democracy." *Ethics & International Affairs*, 18: 79–87.

Human Rights Watch. 2007. *Syria: Stop Arrests for Online Comments: Two Internet Activists Held Incommunicado, May Be "Disappeared."* Retrieved from <http://hrw.org/english/docs/2007/10/08/syria17024.htm>.

Human Rights Watch. 2008. *Universal Periodic Review of South Africa: Human Rights Watch's Submission to the Human Rights Council.* Retrieved from <http://hrw.org/english/docs/2008/04/11/global18513.htm>.

Hyden, G., Leslie, M. and Ogundimu, F. F., eds. 2002. *Media and Democracy in Africa.* Uppsala: Nordiska Afrikainstitutet.

Jacobs, S. 2002. "How Good Is the South African Media for Democracy? Mapping the South African Public Sphere After Apartheid." *African and Asian Studies*, 1:279–302.

Johnstone, J. W. L., Slawski, E. J., and Bowman, W. W. 1976. *The News People.* Urbana, IL: University of Illinois Press.

Kaufmann, D., Kraay, A., and Mastruzzi, M. 2008. *Governance Matters VII: Aggregate and Individual Governance Indicators, 1996–2007.* World Bank Policy Research Working Paper, No. 4654. World Bank.

Keefer, P. 2007. "Clientelism, Credibility, and the Policy Choices of Young Democracies." *American Journal of Political Science*, 51:433–48.

Köcher, R. 1986. "Bloodhounds or Missionaries: Role Definitions of German and British Journalists." *European Journal of Communication*, 1:43–64.

Lang, K. and Lang, G. 1966. The Mass Media and Voting, pp. 455–72 in *Reader in Public Opinion and Communication*, eds. B. Berelson and M. Janowitz. New York: Free Press.

Lederman, D., Loayza, N.V., and Soares. R. R. 2005. "Accountability and Corruption. Political Institutions Matter." *Economics & Politics*, 17:1–35.

Lindstedt, C. and Naurin, D. 2010. "Transparency is Not Enough: Making Transparency Effective in Reducing Corruption." *International Political Science Review*, 31:301–22.

Lio, M. C., Liu, M. C., and Ou, Y. P. 2011. "Can the Internet Reduce Corruption? A Cross-Country Study Based on Dynamic Panel Data Models." *Government Information Quarterly*, 28:47–53.

Francken, N., Minten, B., and Swinnen, J. F. M. 2005. *The Impact of Media and Monitoring on Corruption in Decentralized Public Programs: Evidence from Madagascar.* LICOS Discussion Paper, No. 155/2005. Katholieke Universiteit Leuven.

Nieman Foundation. 2010. *The Nieman Watchdog Journalism Project.* Harvard University. Retrieved from <http://www.niemanwatchdog.org/index.cfm?fuseaction=about.Mission_Statement>.

Norris, P., ed. 2010. *Public Sentinel.* Washington, DC: The World Bank.

Norris, P. 2000. *A Virtuous Circle.* New York: Cambridge University Press.

Norris, P. 2012. *Making Democratic Governance Work: The Impact of Regimes on Prosperity, Welfare and Peace.* New York: Cambridge University Press.

Oscarsson, H. 2008. *Media and Quality of Government: A Research Overview.* Quality of Governance Working Paper Series, No. 12.Gothenberg: University of Gothenburg.

Pande, R. 2011. "Can Informed Voters Enforce Better Governance? Experiments in Low-Income Democracies." *Annual Review of Economics*, 3: 215–37.

Patterson, T. E. 1993. *Out of Order*. NY: Knopf.

Pew. 2011a. *The State of the News Media 2011*. Washington, DC: The Pew Research Center's Project for Excellence in Journalism.

Pew. 2011b. *Press Widely Criticized, But Trusted More than Other Information Sources: Views of the News Media: 1985–2011*. Washington, DC: The Pew Research Center's Project for Excellence in Journalism.

Picard, R. G. 1989. *Media Economics: Concepts and Issues*. Newbury Park, Calif.: Sage Publications.

Picard, R. G. 2010. *Value Creation and the Future of News Organizations: Why and How Journalism Must Change to Remain Relevant in the Twenty-First Century*. Lisbon: Media XXI.

Picard, R. G., ed. 2002. *Media Firms: Structures, Operations, and Performance*. Mahwah, N.J.: Lawrence Erlbaum Associates.

Protess, D. L., Cook, F. L., Doppelt, J. C., Ettema, J. S., Gordon, M. T., Leff, D. R., and Miller, P. 1991. *The Journalism of Outrage: Investigative Reporting and Agenda-Building in America*. NY: Guilford Press.

Reinikka, R. and Svensson, J. 2005. "Fighting Corruption to Improve Schooling: Evidence from a Newspaper Campaign in Uganda." *Journal of the European Economic Association*, 3:259–67.

Reporters Without Borders. 2007. *Syria—Annual Report 2007*. Retrieved from <http://ar.rsf.org>.

Reporters Without Borders. 2010. *Worldwide Press Freedom Index 2010*. Retrieved from <http://en.rsf.org/press-freedom-index-2010,1034.html>.

Robinson, M. 1976. "Public Affairs Television and the Growth of Political Malaise: The Case of the Selling of the President." *American Political Science Review*, 70: 409–32.

Schultz, J. 1998. *Reviving the Fourth Estate: Democracy, Accountability, and the Media*. Cambridge: Cambridge University Press.

Serrin, J. and Serrin, W., eds. 2002. *Muckraking! The Journalism That Changed America*. NY: New Press.

Shapiro, B., ed. 2003. *Shaking the Foundations: 200 Years of Investigative Journalism in America*. NY: Nation Books.

Stapenhurst, R. 2000. *The Media's Role in Curbing Corruption*. World Bank Institute Working Papers.

Tomaselli, K. 2000. South African Media 1994–7: Globalizing via Political Economy, pp. 279–92 in *De-Westernizing Media Studies*, eds. J. Curran and M. Park. London: Routledge.

Tong, J. R. and Sparks, C. 2009. "Investigative Journalism in China Today". *Journalism Studies*, 10:337–52.

Vaidya, S. 2005. "Corruption in the Media Gaze." *European Journal of Political Economy*, 21: 667–87.

Waisbord, S. R. 1996. "Investigative Journalism and Political Accountability in South American Democracies." *Critical Studies in Mass Communication*, 13:343–63.

Weaver, D.H. 2007. *The American Journalist in the 21st Century*. Mahwah, N.J.: L. Erlbaum Associates.

Weaver, D.H. and Wilhoit, C. G. 1986. *The American Journalist*. Bloomington: University of Indiana Press.

WAN (World Association of Newspapers). 2011. *World Press Trends 2011*. Paris: WAN.

PART VI

DEBATING ACCOUNTABILITY

CHAPTER 33

....

ACCOUNTABILITY DEFICITS

....

RICHARD MULGAN

DEFICITS AS ABSENCE OF POLITICAL CONTROL

....

THE notion of an "accountability deficit" has played an important role in accountability studies, stimulating both conceptual analysis and empirical investigation. The first half of this chapter discusses the main themes in the accountability deficit literature, noting that an accountability deficit has been most commonly linked with the absence of political control by democratically elected political representatives. Such deficits have been identified in two governmental areas: the international sphere which lacks any clear, overriding political authority that can undertake the obligations of accountability; and certain aspects of domestic government where executive leaders have decoupled themselves from responsibility and accountability through mechanisms such as outsourcing and the establishment of executive agencies. More broadly, a similar accountability deficit has been found in decentered networks, understood as non-hierarchical relationships lacking a single source of authority, which are found in both the international and domestic arenas (as well as crossing the boundaries between the two). Though each of these different proposed sites for an accountability deficit share a common feature—the absence of political control—they merit separate discussion.

The second half of the chapter builds on this discussion, further clarifying the notion of an accountability deficit in the light of a more multi-faceted understanding of accountability. It also explores the varying normative assumptions behind alleged accountability deficits. The general concept of a deficit usually has both empirical and normative aspects, implying, firstly, an observable lack or deficiency of some substance or quality and, in addition, an attitude of regret or disapproval towards such a lack or deficiency. Even in economics, the notion of a virtuous fiscal deficit, as advocated by Keynesians, can easily be made to sound paradoxical and morally suspect. When applied to accountability, certainly, a deficit almost always carries an implication of normative disapproval. Yet the normative values used to support claims of accountability deficits have generally remained unexamined. On analysis, these values turn out to be contestable, as does the notion of an accountability deficit itself. Whether the notion itself will maintain its current prominence in the light of the necessary analytical complications, both definitional and normative, remains open to speculation.

The Accountability Deficit in International Politics

In the international sphere, the concept of an accountability deficit came to prominence on the coat-tails of the more widely cited "democracy deficit" that was said to occur in international politics generally and, more particularly, in the European Union (EU). According to mainstream democratic theory, the key mechanism in modern democracy is the periodic free election through which citizens in a territorially defined political community choose their legislative representatives and executive leaders. Beyond the boundaries of the nation state, however, there is no citizen body or demos, and therefore no possibility of elections or popularly elected leaders and legislators, resulting in a major "democracy deficit" (Lord 1998; Dahl 1999; Scharpf 1999; Held 2004).

The claim of an international democracy deficit has not gone without challenge. In part, the question turns on the model of democracy being employed as a benchmark. If democracy is identified not with the election of representatives but with more open-ended features which can be conceptually separated from electoral processes, such as deliberative dialogue or political responsiveness, these features can then be discovered in the international sphere, thus refuting, or at least blunting, the charge of a democratic deficit (Moravcsik 2004). In this context, the European Union is best treated as a special case because it has some institutional elements of a democratic political community, including an elected parliament and an authoritative court. It cannot stand as a typical instance of international political association, or its institutions as typical international institutions. Even in the broader field of international relations, the lack of representative institutions is not universally deplored (Slaughter 2004). For the most part, however, the existence of a major democratic deficit in international politics is generally conceded, particularly if elections and political control by elected representatives are taken to be essential elements of democracy.

From the early 1990s (Schmitter and Karl 1991), analysts of democracy increasingly began to incorporate accountability as another essential element in democracy, particularly when democracy was viewed through the prism of principal–agent theory in which principals (voters) choose agents (representatives) who are then accountable to them (Przeworski, Stokes, and Manin 1999). Accountability and democracy became an almost insuperable twosome in political science. If international politics, through its lack of a voting demos, suffered a major deficit of democracy it must also suffer a corresponding deficit of accountability. Without a principal–agent relationship between international actors and the people affected by their decisions, those actors were clearly unaccountable. The "accountability deficit" thus entered the vocabulary of international relations (Held and Koenig-Archibugi 2004; Grant and Keohane 2005), including the study of the European Union (Harlow 2002; Benz, Harlow and Papadopoulos 2007; Bovens, Curtin, and 't Hart 2010, Ch. 1).

This seductive connection, however, overlooked the fact that democracy and accountability, though conceptually linked and even overlapping, are far from identical in meaning, at least according to generally accepted definitions. As international relations scholars discovered when turning to analyze the supposed accountability deficit of international organizations such as the United Nations, accountability through elected agents is not the only possible mechanism for exercising accountability. In the international sphere, the absence of an electoral process for holding leaders to account certainly removes one important means of accountability, as does lack of an effective international authority to enforce international law. But these limitations are far from excluding all possibilities of making international organizations accountable. Public administration has long recognized that the political relationship between voters and elected leaders is only one aspect of government accountability and is supplemented by a wide range of additional mechanisms, legal, administrative, professional and so on (Romzek and Dubnick 1987; Day and Klein 1987). From this sub-disciplinary perspective, the operation of some of these accountability mechanisms internationally without the backing of democratic political control would appear quite predictable. For instance, the bureaucracy of the United Nations is subject to several accountability mechanisms which can operate independently of political control, such as fiscal transparency, bureaucratic control, and independent audit. It was the failure of these mechanisms, rather than the absence of electoral accountability, that led, for instance, to the corrupt administration of the Iraq Oil-for-Food scheme (Mulgan 2009).

Those analyzing world politics and international relations have naturally been attracted to a more expansive view of accountability. In their much-cited article on accountability in world politics, Grant and Keohane (2005) list seven mechanisms of accountability that can occur beyond the nation state: hierarchical, supervisory, fiscal, legal, market, peer, and public reputational. For the most part, the list is unexceptional and accords with earlier typologies produced by public administration scholars analyzing the complexity of accountability relationships within nation states. Closer acquaintance with this literature, however, would have revealed that the inclusion of markets and reputational effects as accountability mechanisms is open to question. It depends on whether one's preferred definition of accountability allows voluntary responsiveness without voice or without the possibility of two-way dialogue to count as accountability. In international relations, however, because of the absence of some core mechanisms of domestic accountability which depend on a democratic state, it has been tempting to cast the definitional net as widely as possible. Any institution or process that serves the general purpose of aligning powerful institutions with popular preferences can thus be counted as an instance of accountability.

In similar, if still more radical, vein, Goodhart (2011) seeks to circumvent the supposed accountability deficit at the international level by arguing for a wholly alternative model of global democratic accountability. Instead of placing elections and representation at the centre of accountability, his model is constructed in terms of accountability for certain democratic norms, such as freedom and equality, which can more readily be achieved in global government. However, the conceptual innovation appears to come at the cost of abandoning any prospect of a universal understanding of accountability which could apply to any sphere of government, domestic or international. Again, this extreme consequence is less necessary if the analysis of accountability moves beyond the more blinkered approach of mainstream democratic theory and embraces the more multi-faceted approaches developed in public administration.

Two general conclusions emerge from this brief discussion of a supposed accountability deficit in the international sphere. First, the concept of an accountability deficit needs to be kept conceptually distinct from any supposed democracy deficit because of the different connotations of the two terms. Accountability through democratic processes, though essential to the presence or absence of democracy, is only one possible channel of public accountability. Secondly, analysis of how accountability operates in the absence of democratic political control may encourage more expansive conceptions of accountability in order to compensate for the absence of such control. While such expansiveness may accord with standard views of accountability, especially those found in public administration, it does run the risk of extending too far into uncharted waters. If the concept of an accountability deficit is to be meaningful it should be built on a universally applicable concept of accountability (Koenig-Archibugi 2010).

THE ACCOUNTABILITY DEFICIT IN DECOUPLED GOVERNMENT

Another major site of claims about accountability gaps or deficits is located within nation states where the control of elected leaders via a hierarchical chain of command has been breached or weakened in some way. Such breaches have been identified, for example, in relation to executive agencies, such as the UK Next Steps agencies. Executive agencies are established at arm's length from ministerial control and receive funding and responsibility for implementing particular government policies with the intention of making the agencies and their chief executives accountable for administrative decisions taken in the course of such implementation.

In Westminster systems, and other similar parliamentary systems, delegation of responsibility and accountability in this way can be seen as breaking traditional conventions of ministerial responsibility (Barberis 1998). The normal expectation is for ministers, as elected leaders answerable to Parliament, to be accountable for all actions taken within their departments, including not just major policy matters but also detailed administrative decisions. Ministers may not be held personally responsible for such decisions but they are expected to answer for them in parliament and the media, giving reasons for the decisions and, if necessary, imposing remedies. However, when agencies become formally decoupled from their ministers, ministers can legitimately refuse to answer for administrative decisions, instead handing accountability over to the agency and its chief executive.

This separation is said to create a serious accountability deficit or gap because political accountability through ministers is seen as a particularly powerful avenue of public accountability (Rhodes 1997, 54, 101–03; Flinders 2002; Mulgan 2003, 177–8; Schillemans 2008; 2011). In modern democracies, the 24-hour media cycle is dominated by political conflict between ministers and their opposition counterparts. Public questioning of ministers, particularly over controversial issues, therefore provides the most direct and effective mechanism for holding governments to account. If ministers can pass the buck, shifting blame on to public service managers, the public is deprived of the fierce level of scrutiny driven by ministers' political opponents and fanned by media publicity.

A similar accountability gap can occur when governments outsource the provision of public services to external contractors, by mechanisms such as public–private partnerships (Mulgan 1997; Hodge and Coghill 2007; Willems and Dooren 2011). Again, the formal separation of purchasers and providers, which limits the responsibility of governments and ministers to providing funds and setting general objectives, leaves accountability for detailed service provision in the hands of arm's length providers. Particularly when contractors are private sector companies not subject to the same degree of transparency and scrutiny as government departments, the level of political accountability is much less than when programs are administered by departmental public servants under direct ministerial control.

In practice, the de facto deficit in political accountability has not always been as serious as the critics claimed and the theory demanded, particularly in the case of executive agencies. The line between policy and implementation is often difficult to draw, with the result that political leaders have often not been able to distance themselves entirely from detailed decisions where these decisions have been affected by actions taken by the central government, such as policy priorities or levels of funding. More important, public opinion has proved intolerant of politicians who attempt to pass the blame on to subordinates. In Westminster jurisdictions, opportunistic opposition politicians and the media keep alive expectations that ministers will exercise traditional conventions of ministerial responsibility and answer for all government actions.

In the United Kingdom, after several high-profile cases of buck-passing between ministers and agency chief executives, with each trying to pin the blame for failure on to the other, ministers resumed their traditional role of answering publicly for all government decisions, while still allowing agency executives to share some of the direct public scrutiny (Gains and Stoker 2009, 448–9). Even in the case of privatized services, such as railways, where ministers and their departments are clearly not to blame for service failures, ministers can still feel the heat of public anger and can be under pressure to front up to media scrutiny. Even so, in spite of the undoubted resilience of long-standing expectations of political accountability and marked variation in administrative and constitutional traditions, the institutional separation of purchasers and providers inspired by managerialist reforms has certainly led to a significant reduction in the level of government activity carried out by public servants under direct political control and therefore to a reduction in political accountability through ministers (Pollitt and Bouckaert 2011, Ch.4). Increasingly, governments rely on a range of more or less arm's length organizations, such as agencies, statutory authorities, administrative boards, and private sector contractors. In each case where responsibility is formally devolved, the heads of the organizations concerned are regularly called to answer independently for their administration in a way that bypasses accountability of ministers or other political leaders. In this sense, the existence of a de jure accountability deficit in terms of political accountability is undeniable, though the de facto extent of such a deficit may be contestable.

THE ACCOUNTABILITY DEFICIT IN NETWORKED GOVERNANCE

Decoupled government arrangements and purchaser–provider separation can be subsumed into networked governance, which is an increasing (or, at least, increasingly noticed) feature of democratic government. Networks are usually defined in terms of horizontal, non-hierarchical relationships and include intra-governmental as well as inter-governmental and multi-level government relationships, thus covering both the domestic and international spheres. Networks make up the main elements of "governance," understood as a non-hierarchical style of governing commonly contrasted with bureaucratic hierarchies and with markets. Networked governance has the advantage of respecting equality of status (in contrast to hierarchy) and recognizing shared values (in contrast to markets). It may also provide a more realistic model for the wide range of government activity that involves public managers exercising initiative and responsibility in their own right, as advocated by the supporters of "public value" (Moore 1995). However, networks have also been criticized for causing accountability deficits because of a lack of direct political control (Michels and Meijer 2008; Papadopoulos 2006; Rhodes 2006).

In all networks, responsibility is shared, ruling out any single point of accountability and giving rise to intensified problems of "many hands" (Bovens 1998, 229). If no one person or body is formally in charge, nobody can be called to account for the network's collective outcomes or made to impose remedies in the wake of acknowledged failure. In the face of controversy, networks encourage buck-passing or blame-shifting and are therefore less open to public scrutiny from political oppositions and the media. The apparent susceptibility of governance to a serious accountability deficit has posed a major challenge to its many champions (Stoker 2006).

As with the international sphere, the issue of an alleged accountability deficit in networked governance has been defused in two ways, first, by stressing the operation of alternative avenues of accountability and, secondly, by extending the understanding of accountability itself. Thus one response has been to downplay the importance of political accountability and hierarchical control and to give particular emphasis to other accountability mechanisms which can apply particularly to networks. For instance, networks may be subject to horizontal mechanisms of accountability, such as media scrutiny (Michels and Meijer 2008; Papadopoulos 2006; Schillemans 2011). Indeed, the pluralistic nature of many networks, in which different members pursue different, if overlapping, agendas, often allows for more open disclosure of information than is found in more closed, hierarchical structures (Mulgan 2003, 211–14). Networks also provide scope for mutual accountability between professional peers as they discuss and scrutinize each other's actions. Where networks involve devolution of responsibility to street-level service providers, they can increase opportunities for bottom-up accountability directly to local communities (Hupe and Hill 2007; Hendriks 2009).

In addition, it may be claimed that networks have less need for traditional mechanisms of accountability, including hierarchical accountability. Networks are typically built on trust and cooperation, sharing some of the features of the not-for-profit sector which relies more on shared values and mutual dialogue than external scrutiny in order to keep its members acting responsibly (Goodin 2003). The relative lack of political accountability may therefore be less problematic than in other types of institutional structure, particularly when not-for-profit NGOs form part of key governance networks.

Alternatively, and more radically, the concept of accountability itself can be redefined (Weber 1999) to include, for instance, government responsiveness to the needs or preferences of citizens and communities without any obligation to answer publicly through the normal processes of accountability (Considine 2002). Accountability in governance has also been identified with public justifications made in terms of public reason and the public interest, again circumventing the need for political control (Weale 2011).

SPECIFYING ACCOUNTABILITY DEFICITS

Most recent discussions of an accountability deficit have exhibited two general features. First, the focus of the deficit has been the extent of political accountability of government institutions through political leaders, as understood, for example, in related notions of democratic representation, principal–agent delegation, or ministerial responsibility. Second, consideration of a deficit in such political accountability has paved the way for broader analyses of the concept of accountability, widening its scope to include other mechanisms of accountability in an attempt to mitigate the extent of the deficit and even redefining the core meaning of accountability with the purpose of defining the deficit out of existence. But if the concept of an accountability deficit is to play any valuable role in future accountability studies, analysis needs to move beyond such approaches.

In the first place, consideration of possible accountability deficits needs to be based on a stable, agreed definition of accountability which will yield verifiable assessments of the extent of accountability in particular institutional settings. If discussion of deficits always leads into further analysis of the meaning of accountability and to the construction of new approaches that will most suit the analyst's chosen context, little progress will be made. As is now generally recognized, the wide variation in preoccupations and values among those analyzing accountability means that no single definition of accountability will be universally acceptable. Any discussion of a deficit can begin to make sense only within an agreed understanding of accountability and should not be used primarily as a means of constructing such an understanding. Otherwise, the landscape of deficit studies will resemble a housing development replete with new foundations but without any completed buildings.

In this respect, the recent study of accountability and a possible accountability deficit in the European Union, edited by Bovens, Curtin, and 't Hart (2010), provides a welcome exception to the general pattern of deficit studies. The authors begin with an agreed understanding of accountability (essentially similar to the "social mechanism" version described by Bovens, Schillemans, and Goodin in this volume) and then use this to frame their empirical investigation from various perspectives of the extent of accountability in various EU institutions.

Secondly, assuming an expansive view of public accountability as constituting a complex network or web of different accountability mechanisms, the concept of an accountability deficit must be widened to allow for all the different possible dimensions where accountability may be found to be lacking. The concentration on gaps in political accountability, found in most of the deficit literature, provides a distorted view of possible accountability deficits. Each of the commonly distinguished types of accountability such as legal/judicial, administrative/managerial, peer professional, media, etc., can also be subject to significant gaps or deficits. For example, judicial accountability through the courts, while offering powerful redress for individuals who question their personal treatment by governments, is heavily skewed in favor of those with sufficient resources to embark on legal proceedings. This litigation bias therefore produces an accountability deficit for less well-off citizens.

Similar gaps or deficits can be located in other types of accountability. Indeed, political accountability through elected representatives, which has been held up as the key type of accountability, an absence of which gives rise to an accountability deficit, is itself prone to serious deficiencies. Ministerial responsibility, though rightly championed as a corner-stone of accountability in parliamentary democracies, has also proved inadequate in guaranteeing the accountability of both ministers and departmental public servants. In Westminster systems, the great wave of accountability reform beginning in the 1960s and 1970s, which led to the introduction of ombudsmen, extended scrutiny by parliamentary committees, performance audits by government auditors, and freedom of information legislation, was driven by an acknowledgment that traditional ministerial responsibility shielded governments, particularly public servants, from public scrutiny.

From this perspective, traditional ministerial responsibility suffered from an accountability deficit in its failure to expose public servants to direct public investigation. Conversely, the reforms may be said to have gone some way to remedying the deficit, opening government departments up to more mechanisms of horizontal accountability while still preserving the right of ministers to take vertical responsibility and impose remedies. Even so, some inadequacies and gaps can still be discerned in the operation of ministerial responsibility, as in all mechanisms of principal–agent accountability through political representatives.

The proliferation of possible accountability deficits means that any alleged deficit must be clearly specified and contextualized. Talk of a single, unqualified accountability deficit assumes a single variable which is somehow in the red (as a budget deficit implies a negative financial result in the government's total revenue and expenditure). Public accountability, however, is not a simple quantum in this way. It consists of countless relationships, between different accountees and account-holders over different issues, not reducible to a single measure or variable. For any accountability deficit, as for any accountability relationship, we must always specify answers to the standard questions: who, to whom, for what, and in what way.

For example, the accountability deficit commonly alleged in relation to international organizations or arm's length service providers needs to be specified as a deficit in political accountability, especially the accountability of public officials to elected politicians through representative institutions and a chain of hierarchical command under political leadership. Once the deficit is clearly specified, as a gap in a particular avenue of accountability, the way is open for acknowledging the operation of other accountability mechanisms and processes which may compensate, to some extent, for the identified deficit in political accountability.

Thirdly, if the significance of any specified accountability deficit is to be meaningfully assessed, it should be against a realistic yardstick of how that type of accountability could be expected to operate if the deficit in question were absent. For example, in the case of the alleged deficit in political accountability in relation to international organizations or government contractors, such a deficit should be assessed against a realistic view of how political accountability actually operates in the standard case of representative government where public officials are under the direct control of elected leaders and accountable to elected legislatures.

Such an analysis is likely to reveal that representative government has its own obvious defects in political accountability (Bovens, Curtin, and 't Hart 2010, 187). Political accountability is very haphazard in its effectiveness and depends heavily on political context. Where political oppositions are hot on the trail of ministerial incompetence, urged on by a sensation-seeking media, accountability will often be swift and decisive. On the other hand, where government activities are protected by a cozy consensus between political parties combined with lack of media interest, political accountability is often deficient and needs to be supplemented by other channels, such as audit and regulation. A reasonable yardstick for political accountability would therefore include a level of public debate and vertical rectification, without requiring complete performance under these headings. From this perspective, arm's length organizations may have a greater deficit in political accountability than government departments under direct political control because they lack the latter's exposure to political direction in response to high-profile public concern. But the difference is one of degree.

In legal accountability before the courts, if an accountability deficit arises because of unequal access to professional legal advice and assistance, we should also acknowledge that providing equal access would not remove all deficiencies in legal accountability, such as the cumbersome and time-consuming nature of legal proceedings. A yardstick for legal accountability would therefore require reasonable levels of access and promptness without demanding unrealistically high standards. Accountability deficits, in other words, are to be seen as typically relative and comparative, indicating a particular deficiency in comparison to some other, somewhat less unaccountable institution, on the assumption that all accountability systems are deficient in some respects.

WHAT MAKES AN ACCOUNTABILITY DEFICIT WRONG?

Finally, apart from being clearly specified and context-dependent, judgments of accountability deficits need to be made against an explicit normative view of why the deficit is regrettable and why it should, if possible, be mitigated or removed altogether. Though the concept of an accountability deficit can be understood in an ethically neutral sense to apply to empirically observable phenomena (the comparative absence of certain specifiable relationships and processes), in practice the term is not usually adopted unless with the intention of signifying some form of normative disapproval of that absence. What values, then, are at stake in identifying an accountability absence as a "deficit"?

Accountability studies in modern western societies usually assume a frame of democratic values. On this view, as articulated in the principal–agent perspective on democracy, the underlying purpose of public accountability is to encourage governments, as agents, to act in accordance with the preferences of citizens, their principals. Any absence of an aspect of accountability which, if present, would improve the responsiveness of governments to their citizens would therefore appear to be regrettable and classifiable as a deficit. Such thinking clearly supports the usual complaints of accountability deficits, particularly when they are linked so closely with the concept of a democratic deficit and when they focus on barriers to the exercise of political accountability by elected representatives responsive to the views of voters.

But the normative setting of accountability systems, like the actual structure of these systems themselves, is much more complex than envisaged in any simple principal–agent model. In the first place, the purposes of accountability mechanisms are not always to be located in any straightforward translation of citizen opinion into government actions. Some well-established accountability mechanisms, such as judicial review or compliance audit, historically predate the full development of representative democracy and are more concerned with questioning the legality of government actions rather than their popularity. Here, the ultimate goal is the maintenance of liberal constitutional government and the rule of law, with checks and balances and general constraints on government power, rather than government responsive to public opinion. Other mechanisms of transparent government, such as freedom of information legislation and media inquiry, can also be seen as primarily aimed at open and lawful government rather than democratic responsiveness.

Given the chameleon-like meaning of "democracy," the connotation of democratic values is contestable, as is the distinction between democratic government and constitutional government. "Democratic" often stands for all principles valued in modern societies, including civil liberties and human rights. Thus, for example, in Keane's (2009) influential concept of "monitory" democracy, liberal constitutional values become subsumed under democracy as another model. Bovens, Schillemans, and 't Hart (2008), on the other hand, clearly distinguish between a "democratic perspective," which privileges popular control and political accountability, and a "constitutional perspective" which emphasizes the prevention of corruption and abuses of power (Bovens, Curtin, and 't Hart 2010, 50–2).

Regardless of terminology, however, the substantial point is that the political goals of accountability are multiple and, potentially, in conflict. For instance, when dealing with unpopular minorities such as refugees, elected politicians are under popular pressure to adopt draconian policies. Any failure to follow public opinion could be seen as an accountability deficit in terms of democratic responsiveness. On the other hand, governments that respond to public opinion by reducing refugees' rights of access to the courts could be accused of opening up another, more serious, accountability deficit in terms of judicial review. The actual existence of an accountability gap may be empirically determinable. But whether it is treated as a regrettable gap or deficit becomes a matter of normative judgment.

Moreover, a gap in accountability can be viewed positively as well as negatively. In the above example, the supporters of refugees applaud a gap in political accountability as needed to protect refugees' rights. Conversely, the populist democrats would welcome a reduction in the legal accountability rights of refugees as a necessary corollary of the majority's rights to determine policy. Accountability is a type of process of which one can have too much as well as too little. The topic of accountability overload is the subject of Halachmi's chapter in this volume. But we need to recognize the conceptual link between the two notions, particularly when adopting a normatively neutral understanding of accountability itself. Accountability is a process susceptible to both deficit and overload, depending on one's point of view.

Another area in which conflict of values has led to disputes over accountability deficits is in the role of political control over administrative actions. As already noted, complaints of accountability deficits have been common where the provision of public services has been decoupled from detailed political direction, for instance through executive agencies and other purchaser–provider separations. The main rationale for such decoupling came from managerialist thinking which sought to improve efficiency and effectiveness by giving public managers clear mandates or objectives and then allowing them the autonomy to make their own decisions about how best to achieve these objectives. Though the rationale was mainly expressed in the instrumental values of efficiency and effectiveness it also contained an accountability agenda which can be expressed in terms of accountability deficits (and overloads) (Mulgan 2003, 154–6).

For managerialists, traditional bureaucratic government suffered from serious weaknesses in accountability. One was a misguided emphasis in terms of the subject matter of accountability (*for what* governments were accountable): accountability was too concerned with process but insufficiently focused on results. Public managers should be freed from some of the more constraining procedural red tape while being made more accountable for achieving given objectives. Secondly, public managers were too beholden upwards to their political masters, particularly for day-to-day administrative decisions where political interference tended to compromise good decision-making. The solution was to decouple managers from political control (other than for the general functions of providing resources and setting objectives) while subjecting their performance to more transparent monitoring by regulators and auditors. This managerial perspective can also be described as a "learning perspective" which emphasizes the role of accountability mechanisms in providing feedback to public managers and helping them to improve their performance (Bovens, Curtin, and 't Hart 2010, 52).

Where democratic champions of political control saw decoupling as leading to serious accountability deficits, for managerialists it was a welcome reduction in what amounted to a surfeit of political accountability and a means of reducing a more significant accountability deficit, the failure to hold public managers properly accountable for achieving specified results. Thus, from a managerial or "good governance" perspective, accountability is to be valued in terms of contributing to government that is efficient and effective in meeting agreed administrative objectives. Conversely, accountability deficits are to be identified as deficiencies in accountability which detract from those values.

The concept of an accountability deficit is, to some extent at least, in the eye of the beholder. It depends on the political values adopted, including the preferred model of democracy as well the approach taken to other principles of government, such as constitutionalism, the rule of law, and good governance. The best recent analyses of accountability deficits, such as Bovens, Curtin, and 't Hart on the European Union (2010) and Schillemans on executive agencies (2011), sensibly embrace a form of normative pluralism. They not only carefully specify the different empirical dimensions of accountability but also assess them for possible deficits in terms of a range of different value perspectives.

CONCLUSION

The concept of an accountability deficit has clearly played an important part in the analysis of accountability, particularly in underlining the variety of accountability mechanisms other than political accountability through elected representatives and also in stimulating the search for alternative understandings of accountability. As a consequence of more finely-grained understandings, talk of *an* unqualified accountability deficit appears too categorical and in need of contextual specification. Accountability can certainly be deficient but only in terms of a specific accountability relationship (who? to whom? for what? how?) as well as in contrast with some related accountability situation and from some value perspective.

REFERENCES

Barberis, P. 1998. "The New Public Management and a New Accountability." *Public Administration*, 76: 451–70.
Benz, A., Harlow, C., and Papadopoulos, Y. 2007. "Introduction." *European Law Journal*, 13: 441–46.
Bovens, M. 1998. *The Quest for Responsibility: Accountability and Citizenship in Complex Organisations.* Cambridge: Cambridge University Press.
Bovens, M., Curtin, D., and 't Hart, P. 2010. *The Real World of EU Accountability.* Oxford: Oxford University Press.
Bovens, M., Schillemans, T., and 't Hart, P. 2008. "Does Public Accountability Work? An Assessment Tool." *Public Administration*, 86: 225–42.
Considine, M. 2002. "The End of the Line? Accountable Governance in the Age of Networks, Partnerships and Joined-Up Services." *Governance*, 15: 21–40.
Dahl, R. 1999. Can International Organizations Be Democratic? A Skeptic's View, pp. 19–36 in *Democracy's Edges*, eds. I. Shapiro and C. Hacker-Cordon. Cambridge: Cambridge University Press.
Day, P. and Klein, R. 1987. *Accountabilities: Five Public Services.* London: Tavistock.
Flinders, M. 2002. *The Politics of Accountability in the Modern State.* Aldershot: Ashgate.
Gains, F. and Stoker, G. 2009. "Delivering 'Public Value': Implications for Accountability and Legitimacy." *Parliamentary Affairs*, 62: 438–55.
Goodhart, M. 2011. "Democratic Accountability in Global Politics: Norms, not Agents." *Journal of Politics*, 73: 45–60.
Goodin, R. E. 2003. "Democratic Accountability: The Distinctiveness of the Third Sector." *Archives Européenes de Sociologie*, 44: 359–96.
Grant, R. W. and Keohane, R. O. 2005. "Accountability and Abuses of Power in World Politics." *American Political Science Review*, 99: 29–43.
Harlow, C. 2002. *Accountability in the European Union.* Oxford: Oxford University Press.
Held, D. and Koenig-Archibugi, M. 2004. "Introduction." *Government and Opposition*, 39: 125–31.

Held, D. 2004. "Democratic Accountability and Political Effectiveness from a Cosmopolitan Perspective." *Government and Opposition*, 39: 364–91.

Hendriks, C. M. 2009. "The Democratic Soup: Mixed Meanings of Political Representation in Governance Networks." *Governance*, 22: 689–715.

Hodge, G. and Coghill, K. 2007. "Accountability in the Privatized State." *Governance*, 20: 675–702.

Hupe, P. and Hill, M. 2007. "Street Level Bureaucracy and Public Accountability." *Public Administration*, 85: 279–99.

Keane, J. 2009. *The Life and Death of Democracy*. New York: Simon and Schuster.

Koenig-Archibugi, M. 2010. "Accountability in Transnational Relations: How Distinctive Is It?" *West European Politics*, 33: 1142–64.

Lord, C. 1998. *Democracy in the European Union*. Sheffield: Sheffield Academic Press.

Michels, A. and Meijer, A. 2008. "Safeguarding Public Accountability in Horizontal Government." *Public Management Review*, 10: 165–73.

Moore, M. 1995. *Creating Public Value: Strategic Management in Government*. Cambridge, Mass.: Harvard University Press.

Moravcsik, A. 2004. "Is There a 'Democratic Deficit' in World Politics? A Framework for Analysis." *Government and Opposition*, 39: 337–63.

Mulgan, R. 1997. "Contracting Out and Accountability." *Australian Journal of Public Administration*, 56: 106–16.

Mulgan, R. 2003. *Holding Power to Account: Accountability in Modern Democracies*. Basingstoke: Palgrave Macmillan.

Mulgan, R. 2009. AWB and Oil for Food: Some Issues of Accountability, pp. 334–52 in *Sanctions, Accountability and Governance in a Globalised World*, eds. J. Farrall and K. Rubinstein. Cambridge: Cambridge University Press.

Papadopoulos, Y. 2006. "Problems of Democratic Accountability in Network and Multilevel Governance." *European Law Journal*, 13: 505–22.

Pollitt, C. and Bouckaert, G. 2011. *Public Sector Reform*. Third edition. Oxford: Oxford University Press.

Przeworski, A., Stokes, S. C., and Manin, B. eds. 1999. *Democracy, Accountability and Representation*. Cambridge: Cambridge University Press.

Rhodes, R. A. W. 1997. *Understanding Governance: Public Networks, Governance, Reflexivity and Accountability*. Buckingham: Open University Press.

Rhodes, R. A. W. 2006. Policy Network Analysis, pp. 425–47 in *The Oxford Handbook of Public Policy*, eds. M. Moran, M. Rein, and R. E. Goodin. Oxford: Oxford University Press.

Romzek, B. S. and Dubnick, M. J. 1987. "Accountability in the Public Sector: Lessons from the Challenger Tragedy." *Public Administration Review*, 47: 227–38.

Scharpf, F. W. 1999. *Governing in Europe: Effective and Democratic?* Oxford: Oxford University Press.

Schillemans, T. 2008. "Accountability in the Shadow of Hierarchy: The Horizontal Accountability of Agencies." *Public Organization Review*, 8: 175–94.

Schillemans, T. 2011. "Does Horizontal Accountability Work? Evaluating Potential Remedies for the Accountability Deficit of Agencies." *Administration and Society*, 43: 387–416.

Schmitter, P. C. and Karl, T. L. 1991. "What Democracy Is … and Is Not." *Journal of Democracy*, 2: 75–88.

Slaughter, A. M. 2004. *A New World Order*. Princeton: Princeton University Press.

Stoker, G. 2006. "Public Value Management: A New Narrative for Networked Governance?" *American Review of Public Administration*, 36: 41–57.

Weale, A. 2011. "New Modes of Governance, Political Accountability and Public Reason." *Government and Opposition*, 46: 58–80.

Weber, E. P. 1999. "The Question of Accountability in Historical Perspective." *Administration and Society*, 31: 451–94.

Willems, T. and Dooren, W. van 2011. "Lost in Diffusion? How Collaborative Arrangements Lead to an Accountability Paradox." *International Review of Administrative Sciences*, 77: 505–30.

CHAPTER 34

....

ACCOUNTABILITY OVERLOADS

....

ARIE HALACHMI

ACCOUNTABILITY AND ORGANIZATIONAL PATHOLOGIES

....

POLITICIANS, public employees, journalists, and taxpayers support the need for more public accountability. This notion is shared by the commons at face value without consideration of the possible dysfunctional implications of "accountability." Slowing down governmental response to a need, the added cost, possible interference with the implementation of other governmental functions, or any other aspect of what is commonly labeled as "red tape" are examples of such dysfunctions. Nobody questions the need for accountability to assure the proper functioning of organizations in general, and public ones in particular. Few, though, consider the prospect that too much emphasis on accountability may result in unintentional, but systematic, undermining of efficiency and effectiveness.

The thesis of this chapter is that the overload of accountability demands undermines productivity, responsiveness, and service quality. Arrangements for assuring accountability may cause the onset of organizational pathologies. Such a development can manifest itself in several ways but may not be easily detected or corrected.

An organizational pathology is likely to develop whenever demonstrated accountability becomes the paramount consideration in evaluating organizational performance—making efficiency and effectiveness secondary in importance.

THE ACCOUNTABILITY OVERLOAD

....

Overload evolves when arrangements to assure accountability in various respects, political, legal, professional, social, bureaucratic, or environmental, become dysfunctional—when good intentions end up undermining the effectiveness and efficiency of the organization or a particular program; when it reduces responsiveness and flexibility or discourages innovations. The paradox is that the accountability fervor meant to assure performance can have direct and indirect consequences that undermine it. The direct dysfunctions manifest themselves in various ways— such as delays or red tape from the perspective of service recipients; dwelling too long on short term success; excessive use of resources when compared with private organizations; slowness in or lack of responsiveness; interference with the execution of other programs; siphoning of critical resources from operations to underwrite the overhead cost of accountability; and the discouragement of innovation and improvisation to address rapidly changing circumstances. Extreme cases of accountability overload may dissuade innovations in other organizations that consider alternatives for addressing a public need. Such deterrence may have adverse effects on the polity's welfare. The disturbing consequences of excessive accountability arrangements have already caught the attention of several writers. Power (1997) coined the term "the audit society" in his treatise on this subject, while Bovens, Schillemans, and 't Hart (2008) and others underscore the undesired attributes of accountability overload. However, the gaming and pathologies that result from such attributes is still not a salient item on the public agenda.

Bovens, Schillemans, and 't Hart (2008, 225) suggest that:

> The ideas and impulses for increased control and accountability mechanisms have come partly from outside the realm of national government. Idea brokers in the "new public management" mould, such as the OECD, have been instrumental in spreading the gospel about benchmarking, monitoring, accreditation, and planning and control cycles.

Box 34.1 Dysfunctional Pathologies of Accountability Overloads

The literature on public accountability has identified, described and discussed a large number of dysfunctional pathologies. Most of these are discussed or mentioned in this chapter. As a guide to future systematic research on accountability overloads, this text box presents the most important pathologies and some references to key publications.

- Large opportunity and transaction costs (Halachmi 1976)
- The audit society, a society devoting too much attention to the "rituals of verification" (Power 1997)
- Discouraging innovation: fixed accountability standards may thwart and discourage innovation (De Bruijn 2002)
- Awakenings syndrome: dwelling on short-term success, while disregarding future goals (Halachmi 2005b)
- Gaming: actors exploiting the indicators and mechanisms for accountability (Pollitt 2003)
- Blame games: the accountability process results in fault-finding only, not in remedial action (Behn 2001; Hood 2002)
- Multiple accountability: the demands for accountability from different relevant stakeholders invoke confusing expectations (Romzek and Dubnick 1998; Schillemans and Bovens 2011)
- Multiple Accountabilities Disorder: conflicting demands for accountability may paralyze agents (Koppell 2005)

There might be other factors, though, that may contribute, if not induce, excessive accountability. These factors have to do with the political economy of the public sector environment and the dynamics of organizational behavior.

Signed into law by President George W. Bush on January 8, 2002, the No Child Left Behind Act (NCLB) was the principal federal law affecting education from kindergarten through high school in the US. The law was a response to growing demands for greater accountability about the use of tax revenues by the government in general, and the performance of public schools in particular. It provided a rigorous framework for measuring the achievement of students while allowing meaningful performance comparisons across the board between schools and teachers. But important parts of the law were suspended on September 22, 2011 by President Obama. The President's action was a response to two major developments. There had been stories in the media about widespread cheating by several school districts such as Atlanta (Turner 2011) and Houston (Radcliffe 2010) in an effort to manufacture the needed data for compliance with the law. Teachers' unions had opposed the law from its inception on grounds such as the cost (Hoxby 2002), or the holding of teachers responsible for students' progress when they have no control over the ability or willingness of students to do the work (Banchero 2012). These reservations are consistent with the Levitt, Janta, and Wegrich (2008) review of the literature about teachers' accountability.

Criticizing Congress for months of inaction in updating No Child Left Behind, President Obama lifted the law's most onerous provisions, including its 2014 deadline for bringing all students to proficiency in reading and math. States that promised to follow his Administration's school improvement agenda and develop their own schemes for evaluating teachers' performance, were granted exceptions from the law (Dillon 2011). Teachers' organizations asked for this change since they have more influence at the state than at the national level. Most importantly, allowing states to develop their own measurements of school performance eliminated the threat of accountability by comparisons.

On the face of it, President Obama was addressing the difficulties of school districts and states to comply with the law. It is as likely, however, that he was reacting to demands from an important interest group for his re-election campaign and his other policy initiatives (e.g., health care). His actions illustrate one of the issues in the political economy of public accountability, namely, the need to appease interest groups with conflicting demands. By changing or shifting the venue of the educational accountability debate, Obama was trying to appear as one supporting the political symbol of (teachers') accountability while avoiding the political cost of being involved in an unpopular process to assure it.

This case illustrates two things: The context or the environment of government programs can affect an overload or a deficit of accountability. Organizational pathologies can emerge where there is a gap between an unrestricted quest for absolute accountability and limited feasibility of attaining it, beyond a basic threshold that is acceptable to those held accountable. This issue has to do with organizational behavior. With this case in mind, one may ask whether accountability overload evolves due to concerns that in certain respects accountees can dodge accountability. Layers of accountability can be added to assure the reporting of the truth, the whole truth, and nothing but the truth, and for the political symbolism of such reporting being assured. Undesired consequences, such as unintended overload, are rarely considered because first, adding safeguards to guarantee accountability do not have an opportunity cost for their proponents, and second, there is nothing to flag an overload evolvement. Thus, one may ask two questions. What is there to induce economic rationality into this regulatory process? And what is the role of the accountees in facilitating or undermining the feasibility of the accountability process? This last question has not been explored by researchers in spite of its possible implications for the theory and practice of management in general, and organizational behavior in particular. The importance of this question becomes evident while considering the use, abuse, and possible pathologies of performance measurement, a common approach to assure accountability.

A widely used cliché suggests that what is being measured by the organization is being attended to because it leads to accountability. As noted by Williamson (2006), "*what gets measured gets done*" has been attributed to Peter Drucker, Tom Peters, Edwards Deming, Lord Kelvin, and others. But what are overlooked by many writers on performance measurement are some of the undesired side effects of this approach for assuring accountability (see Van de Walle and Cornelissen in this volume). Put another way, the quest for accountability and transparency in general, and the use of performance measurement in particular, assure that things are done *right* but not necessarily that the *right things* are done. One of the reasons for this is the short-term perspective used to establish accountability. The possible dysfunction, abuse, and pathologies of performance measurements have been addressed elsewhere (Halachmi 2002) and are beyond the scope of this chapter. A move from performance measurement to a broader conceptual framework of performance management (Halachmi 2005a) is, however, a possible way of reducing accountability overload. The reason is the better perspective that results from the longer time horizon of performance measurement.

Another under-researched issue is the prospect that managers are trying to address issues of "informal accountability" by adding formal ones. This important topic is addressed in Romzek et al. (2012).

THE NEED FOR DYNAMIC ACCOUNTABILITY

The need to demonstrate accountability based on short-term information results in a single periodic report of organizational performance. The short perspective of such a report can be very misleading. It condones, if not encourages, sub-optimization. To look great for the moment at the expense of long-term achievements is an example of such sub-optimization. Another and more serious example is the case where a sub-unit pushes its own performance in a way that jeopardizes the systemic ability to excel. Using a strong hand to collect more tax may lead to popular resentment of government and resistance to or lack of cooperation with anything attempted by its other agencies. Practices that overlook the long-term consequences of pursuing certain objectives or doing things in a particular way, are influenced by the need to show results on short-term report cards. Though such an approach is suitable for elected officials whose frame of reference is the electoral cycle, from a systemic, i.e., the polity, point of view it is dysfunctional. This approach is not in the best interest of society. The preferred approach for serving the societal interest is *dynamic accountability*.

The following analogy illustrates the differences between the two approaches. The short-term performance report is a snapshot that freezes a situation and allows some evaluation. Dynamic accountability, however, is more like time lapse photography that catches the evolution of the administrative process and program implementation. Such a view captures not only what is being done but also reactions and counter-reactions within and from outside an agency. This facilitates a better understanding of what took place. Dynamic accountability facilitates organizational learning, which, in turn, fosters true accountability.

Dynamic accountability is also a promising antidote to the organizational pathology called "awakening syndrome." This pathology got its name from the movie *Awakenings*, based on a true story (Halachmi 2005b). Awakening syndrome is the tendency to dwell too much on momentary success before assuring that the long-term consequences of the "cure" are not worse than receiving no cure. The temporary "high" experienced by members of the organization when a short-term performance report indicates greater than expected achievements may numb and undermine learning and caution. This, in turn, may contribute to risky, but unjustified, behavior by members of the organization leading to underperformance in the long term. The consequences of such behavior trigger the addition of more accountability arrangements to prevent its re-occurring and the prospect of accountability overload.

From a conceptual point of view, a possible difference between short-term accountability and long-term, or dynamic, accountability is similar to the difference between the concepts of "general will" and "general welfare" (Amadae 2003). General will is the cumulative popular vote, e.g., against a higher tax. General welfare is the ultimate interest of the polity, unachievable without hiking the tax. In America, this imminent conflict between the short-term and the long-term interests of the polity was resolved by making members of the House stand for re-election every two years while members of the Senate are elected every six years. In organizations, various annual reports allow for short-term accountability. However, public agencies lack feasible means for assuring long-run accountability. The simplistic assumption that more short-term accountability arrangements assure or facilitate long-term accountability contributes to the overload but not to the needed dynamic accountability.

The Costs of Assuring Accountability

With the evolution of the age of government austerity (Lodge and Hood 2012; Ferlie, Lynne, and Pollitt 2004; Schwartz 2012), the cost of assuring accountability becomes a salient economic and a political liability that cannot be ignored. The explosion of the audit culture, which Power (1997) labeled as the "audit society," is not without cost (Power 2000; Hoxby 2002). Reflecting on the merit of this development, Power (2003, 1) asks, "Can we no longer think of accountability without elaborately detailed policing mechanisms?" Until the recent economic crisis the opportunity cost of excess auditing was ignored by elected officials for reasons outlined earlier. Legislatures are now increasingly becoming aware of the opportunity cost of government transparency. They start to see how unlimited reporting requirements and numerous oversight reviews are syphoning resources from operations to cover the cost of the accountability overhead. In the evolving culture of government austerity, it is easier to understand what drives elected officials to reconsider past demands for reporting and reviews. Awareness of the fact that new resources cannot be easily mobilized became a motivation to reduce the cost of overhead expenses, in general, and those involving accountability, as symbolic rituals, in particular. The example that follows illustrates this trend.

Republicans and Democrats have largely praised oversight provisions in President Obama's $840 billion 2009 economic stimulus bill, despite a deep and highly partisan divide over the economic value of the bill itself. But when the cost of enforcing these provisions to assure accountability became more tangible, the US Congress took action to reduce it by lowering the threshold under which recipients of Federal grants and loans under this program must file reports. Reacting to this development, the US Energy Department Inspector General (IG), Gregory Friedman, is on record claiming, "Less burdensome reporting likely will come with higher levels of waste, fraud and abuse." According to a published report, the IG asserted:

> If the body politic is prepared to accept [a new] threshold and understands the risk associated with that threshold... that's OK," Friedman said. "But if, at the end of the day, we're going to adopt such a mechanism and then have people criticize the fact that there wasn't adequate reporting or oversight below the threshold, we will have ended up moving the ball backward rather than forward. (Marks 2011)

When the costs involved were too high, an effort was made to place the financial reporting burden on the recipients of stimulus money rather than on agencies. This, in turn, resulted in a barrage of complaints about the reporting requirements, perceived to be overly burdensome and burying the small staffs of some recipients in paperwork (Marks 2011). Reducing the overhead cost of administering the Stimulus Program on the administration side did not reduce the overall overhead cost.

Transparency and Accountability Overload

"Transparency Demands Cost Governments Money" (Rich 2011) was the headline of a media report regarding the elimination of the State of California's Transparency website on November 3, 2011. Governor Jerry Brown, according to Rich, did it because maintaining the site became "too expensive." At face value, the possible functional relationship between transparency and accountability seems to be very clear. However, close examination suggests otherwise. The truth is that more emphasis on transparency can be dysfunctional rather than a force that leads to more accountability. Greater transparency can induce behavior that makes blind following of the letter of the law and the desire to do things *right* prevail over the need to consider the spirit of the law and do the *right thing* from a rational, fairness, or equity point of view. As such, transparency can harm and do injustice to those who are least capable of mobilizing intervention by higher-ups to assure reasonable behavior of bureaucrats and justice. In addition, transparency provides government employees with an unintended shield from accountability. It allows ineffective administrators to use the transparency of the process to excuse or spin their poor performance metrics.

The relationship between transparency and accountability is complex (see Meijer's chapter in this handbook). It should be noted though, that the advent of e-government, as a common and desired mode for conducting government business increases accountability (Moon 2002; Yigitcanlar 2003; Tolbert and Mossberger 2006).

CAN ANYTHING BE DONE TO REDUCE THE PATHOLOGY THAT RESULTS FROM ACCOUNTABILITY OVERLOAD?

In the private sector, there are ways to estimate the cost of oversight and other control mechanisms. These calculations can be used to assure that the price of gaining a higher level of accountability does not exceed the expected benefits. Diagram 34.1 illustrates this prospect where curve M (mistakes) shows how the calculated cost of errors

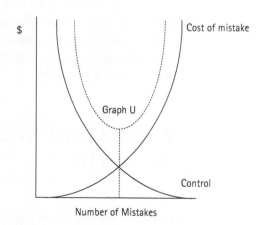

FIGURE 34.1 Financial and operational "costs" of accountability

is escalating when oversight is low. The diagram also shows graph C (cost of control), demonstrating how the cost of oversight is growing as greater effort is made to prevent mistakes. A point on the U-shaped curve represents the sum of the corresponding values on each of the two graphs in the diagram. The lowest point of the U-shaped curve corresponds to the intersection of curve M (cost of mistakes) and curve C (the cost of control, i.e., assuring no greater mistakes). We can calculate these values to reflect actual fluctuations of the corresponding prices for each over time. Balancing the demands for a reasonable level of accountability and an acceptable price for assuring it, is achieved at the point where graph M and graph C intersect. As illustrated by graph U, which shows the combined cost of graph M and graph C for every combination of errors and control costs, at this intersection point the combined cost is the lowest. Any move to the right or the left of this point results in a higher economic price.

However, as elaborated in an earlier publication, such an economic approach for checking that the price of accountability (or administrative control) does not exceed the expected economic benefits of assuring it, does not exist in the public sector (Halachmi 1976). In the private sector, managers are not expected to spend a dollar to find out where the missing quarter (25 cents) is. The expectation in the public sector, however, is they have to find the missing money regardless of cost because of the principle. As the saying goes, "if you cannot account for the missing quarter what else might you be missing or be unaware of?" Such expectations by auditors, the media, and the public create a pressure that leads to over-accountability. In addition, in the public sector the cost of a mistake has a political price that often exceeds the economic cost of the blunder. On the other hand, to insist on a greater level of oversight, regardless of its opportunity cost, can generate political benefits because of the symbolic value that such actions have for naive observers who form the majority of prospective voters.

Hoxby (2002) asserts that the cost of accountability in the public sector cannot readily be estimated because the cost of the overhead for it is allocated and reported in different ways by states and local authorities. Hoxby suggests that in the case of education, some of the accountability cost can be estimated by looking at the reported revenues of the companies that develop the student assessment tests. Such data provide limited information. Still missing from the bottom line is the cost of administering and reporting test results by teachers and other employees of the educational system. Testing company revenues also do not capture the costs of compliance with the sanctions and oversight regulations that are required in poorly performing schools.

Hospitals use market mechanisms to weed out poorly performing doctors by publishing data about success, complications, and mortality rates. But when it comes to the case of teachers, such attempts have been met with resistance. For example, the initiative of the Governor of Louisiana to move in this direction resulted in massive demonstrations outside the State Legislature (MSNBC 2012). The Governor wanted to use market forces to bring about greater teacher and school accountability. His reasoning was that publishing data about school performance and giving parents vouchers they could use in public, charter, or private schools of their choice would weed out poor performers. A similar reaction by teachers' unions to proposals involving the publication of testing scores has been reported in other places in America (Banchero 2012).

The reality, it seems, is that the public, the media, and many elected officials still cannot differentiate between the expected monetary (economic) value (EMV) of adding additional levels of scrutiny and oversight and the respective utilities that result from added accountability as a political symbol.

For the unsophisticated, it is simply better when new layers of reviews and audits are added. Power (1997) notes, however, that there is little data to support the notion that the presence of internal audit, an Inspector General, or an Ombudsman contribute to greater effectiveness, efficiency, or accountability. From an economic point of view, the added overhead cost resulting from establishing such staff units must be justified by a clear demonstration that the cost is less than the costs resulting from the aggregated cost of actual wrongdoing, poor judgment, and abuse of power by public employees. The following example might help underscore the importance of this issue.

In 2011, the media reported a scandal involving the Inspector General of the US Department of Health and Human Services (HHS). The fiasco involved the handling of alleged misconduct at the Center for Devices and Radiological Health (CDRH). Specifically, the HHS Inspector General overlooked serious wrongdoing within CDRH when it rejected whistleblower complaints about the center allowing unsafe medical devices onto the market. According to Dickinson (2011), Project on Government Oversight (POGO), an "[i]ndependent activist watchdog group," mailed a written request to HHS secretary Kathleen Sebeluis to "open a new investigation of CDRH misconduct." POGOs letter noted the inadequacy of the IG's 2009 investigation stating that it "ignored noncriminal misconduct and retaliation." Additionally, POGO pointed out that deaths from the use of unsafe medical devices allowed on the market could have easily been avoided.

"The broad, underlying problem is managerial misconduct," POGO alleged. "When CDRH managers fail to heed the advice of their own medical and scientific experts within CDRH, they often overrule these experts by circumventing the FDA's regulations."

This report illustrates the fact that the cost of the Office of the Inspector General for HHS could not be justified by the resulting greater accountability of employees at CDRH. Accountability in this case resulted from scrutiny by a civil society advocacy group, POGO, whose activities did not cost taxpayers any money. The initial complaint to the Office of the IG about low standards at CDRH (POGO 2010) was ignored and only a subsequent intervention by Congress fostered corrective action. One of the Pork Reports (Coburn 2011) identifies at least $4,837,900 in wasteful Washington spending overlooked by auditors raising a similar question about the justification of the cost to underwrite auditing operations.

The example given suggests that the mere creation of administrative units within an agency to enhance accountability is not enough to assure it. Ad hoc environmental and contextual forces may be more potent in turning such arrangements into cost centers. Such arrangements may have political value as political symbols assuring the public of orderly conduct by officials. However, there is nothing in their mere existence to suggest that they can generate tangible benefits, i.e., greater efficiency, effectiveness, responsiveness, transparency, or answerability.

Similarly, the value of intra-organizational schemes for enhancing accountability may be limited to their questionable worth as political symbols. A case in point is the Congressional investigation in connection with a misconceived scheme by the Justice Department known as "Fast and Furious" (Savage 2011). The aim of the operation was to identify drug dealers in Mexico by allowing criminals from that country to purchase guns from American stores without asking too many questions. The investigation was prompted by the murder of an American Border Patrol Agent with one of those weapons (Frieden 2011). Some of the documentation requested by the investigating committee was refused by the Attorney General (AG). Some of the provided documents turned out to be misleading. The hearing revealed lack of accountability within the Justice Department and resulted first in calls for the AG's resignation or impeachment (Politico 2011; Boyle 2011). The lack of cooperation by the AG reached a climax when the US House of Representatives held the AG in contempt (ABC News 2012) and filed suit to force him to turn in the requested documents, that is, to be held accountable. This unprecedented act had no consequences for the AG or for the Obama Administration. Media coverage of that development, if any, was focused more on the precedent created by that vote than on the merit of the issue at hand (Chastain 2012). Note that this case raises a question about the role of legislators in assuring accountability and any other inter-organizational arrangements. This case suggests that holding an official to account may depend on the willingness of that individual to be held accountable. It may also explain the tendency to add accountability safeguards in anticipation of such unwillingness to cooperate and, thus, the creation of an accountability overload. These issues at HHS and the Justice Department suggest at least two things. First, an administrative and political culture that emphasizes accountability is more important than having such arrangements actually in place. Second, relative transparency and external oversight by civil society-based organizations can spotlight accountability issues and foster corrective actions more effectively and more efficiently than administrative units. In other words, in addition to other benefits, a transition from governing to governance may enhance accountability in the most economical way.

CONCLUDING REMARKS

State governments where there was a high risk for corruption was the subject of a March 2012 report by the Associated Press. The study generated a lot of media attention. In the midst of a heated political debate in connection with the election season in the USA, the study is setting the stage for contending candidates to pledge new efforts to address this issue, which is loaded with political symbolism. The use of market mechanisms, such as a better and more frequent report of data, along with greater involvement of civil society advocacy groups in audit and review processes are possible economic ways to address the concerns raised by the study. The growing use of e-government helps to increase transparency and reduce the opportunities for wrongdoing. However, such efforts are not tangible enough for candidates who seek office. Promises to add new layers of internal and external reviews by Inspector Generals, Ombudsmen, performance reporting, and other things are more tangible and have greater political value. The opportunity cost and the possible reductions in productivity resulting from prolonged administrative processes are not, however, a consideration on the campaign trail. Yet, the efforts to assure accountability without generating additional expenses is still important.

Reports indicate (Wade 2012) the University of Connecticut returned $890,000 to the government after suspecting that one of its employees was publishing falsified research results. The university did not wait for the 600,000 pages of the government report of the alleged fraudulent research before taking action to protect its reputation. This case illustrates the possibility that systemic forces might be triggered to assure accountability when organizational survival is threatened. In this case, the concerns of university administrators and professors about their own professional reputation and the good name of the university were enough to trigger corrective action from within even before outside bodies with oversight powers called the university to account. There is a prospect that similar forces might exist in other organizations as the labor force becomes more educated and as information technology generates greater transparency. As employees and outsiders get more timely and comprehensive pictures of organizational processes and their results, more questions are likely to be asked of employees and their supervisors. These may force, or at least foster, greater accountability but may also increase the odds for creating an overload. At the same time, a growing realization by managers and elected officials of the opportunity cost of imposing various schemes to assure accountability may signal the dawn of a new age. In this new age, the notion of accountability, as being in some respect responsible for something or being held to account by someone, is not discarded. Rather, an evolving political culture, administrative ethos, and professionalism may replace the need for periodic reporting, auditing, and other modes of oversight. Under these circumstances, the accountability overload that results from attempts to assure accountability at a price that greatly exceeds the economic value of preventing possible transgressions by public employees or elected officials may be reduced. As government austerity (Lodge and Hood 2012) becomes the rule, the design and introduction of new schemes for assuring accountability for their symbolic value are likely to become less and less attractive to the tax weary public and its elected officials.

The culture of accountability that would evolve with the advent of this new age would support a review of accountability schemes put in place in the past with the utmost disregard of their economic value or opportunity cost. This, in turn, would free resources to sustain, if not improve, operations and reduce overhead and other organizational pathologies like the ones that have been discussed in this chapter.

REFERENCES

ABC News. 2012, June 27. *House Holds Eric Holder in Contempt.* Retrieved from <http://abc-news.go.com/blogs/politics/2012/06/house-prepares-for-holder-contempt-vote/>.

Amadae, S. M. 2003. *Rationalizing Capitalist Democracy.* Chicago: University of Chicago Press.

Associated Press. 2012, March 18. *State Governments at High Risk for Corruption.* Retrieved from <http://www.foxnews.com/politics/2012/03/19/study-state-governments-at-high-risk-for-corruption/>.

Banchero, S. 2012, February 25. *Teacher Ratings Aired in New York.* Retrieved from <http://online.wsj.com/article/SB10001424052970203918304577243591163104860.html?mod=djem_jiewr_JM_domainid#articleTabs%3Darticle>.

Behn, R. D. 2001. *Rethinking Democratic Accountability.* Washington, D.C.: Brookings Institution Press.

Bovens, M., Schillemans, T., and 't Hart, P. 2008. "Does Public Accountability Work? An Assessment Tool." *Public Administration,* 86: 225–42.

Boyle, M. 2011, April 12. *Ariz. Congressman: Pressure to Resign is Getting to Eric Holder.* Retrieved from <http://dailycaller.com/2011/12/04/ariz-congressman-pressure-to-resign-is-getting-to-eric-holder/#ixzz1jER2JSrI>.

Chastain, M. 2012, August 14. *Contempt Lawsuit Against Holder: NBC Ignores, ABC and CBS do Bare Minimum.* Retrieved from <http://www.breitbart.com/Big-Journalism/2012/08/13/NBC-Ignores-ABC-and-CBS-Do-Bare-Minimum-Over-Contempt-Lawsuit-Against-Holder>.

Coburn, T. 2011, August 1. *The Pork Report: How Washington Politicians, Bureaucrats, and Lobbyists are Spending Your Tax Dollars.* Retrieved from <http://www.coburn.senate.gov/public/index.cfm/washingtonwaste?ContentRecord_id=3b228ac9-acf9-4873-89d0-5e7d9c5d1866>.

De Bruijn, H. 2002. "Performance Measurement in the Public Sector: Strategies to Cope With the Risks of Performance Measurement." *International Journal of Public Sector Management,* 15: 578–94.

Dickinson, J. 2011, January 25. *FDA Taking 25 Steps to Improve 510(k) Process: Critics Say that Delaying Some of the Changes is a Concession Made for Industry; FDA Disagrees.* Retrieved from <http://www.mddionline.com/article/fda-25-steps>.

Dillon, S. 2011, September 22. *Obama to Waive Parts of No Child Left Behind.* Retrieved from <http://www.nytimes.com/2011/09/23/education/23educ.html>.

Ferlie, E., Lynne, L., and Pollitt, C. 2004. *The Oxford Handbook of Public Management.* Oxford: Oxford University Press.

Frieden, T. 2011, December 2. *Justice Department Sends Congress 1,400 Pages on "Fast and Furious."* Justice Department. Retrieved from <http://articles.cnn.com/2011-12-02/politics/politics_fast-and-furious-documents_1_operation-fast-and-furious-atf-justice-department?_s=PM:POLITICS>.

Halachmi, A. 1976. "Using Simulations for Better Policy Analysis." *Indian Journal of Public Administration,* 12: 48–64.

Halachmi, A. 2002. "Performance Measurement, Accountability, and Improved Performance." *Public Performance & Management Review,* 25: 370–4.

Halachmi, A. 2005a. "Performance Measurement is Only One Way of Managing Performance." *International Journal of Productivity and Performance Management,* 54: 502–16.

Halachmi, A. 2005b. "Performance Measurement: Test the Water Before You Dive In." *International Review of Administrative Sciences*, 71: 255–66.

Hood, C. 2002. "The Risk Game and the Blame Game." *Government and Opposition*, 37: 15–37.

Hoxby, C. M. 2002. *The Cost of Accountability*. NBER Working Paper, No. 8855. National Bureau of Economic Research.

Koppell, J. G. 2005. "Pathologies of Accountability: ICANN and the Challenge of 'Multiple Accountabilities Disorder.'" *Public Administration Review*, 65: 94–109.

Levitt, R., Janta, B. and Wegrich, K. 2008. *Accountability of Teachers: Literature Review*. Santa Monica, CA: Rand Cooperation.

Lodge, M. and Hood, C. 2012. "Into an Age of Multiple Austerities? Public Management and Public Service Bargains Across OECD Countries." *Governance*, 25: 79–101.

Marks, J. 2011, November 30. *It's Waste vs. Cost in the Transparency Debate*. Government Executive. Retrieved from <http://www.nextgov.com/technology-news/2011/11/its-waste-vs-cost-in-the-transparency-debate/50207/>.

Moon, M. J. 2002. "The Evolution of E-Government Among Municipalities: Rhetoric or Reality?" *Public Administration Review*, 62: 424–33.

MSNBC. 2012, March 13. *Teacher Protest Closes Schools in Louisiana*. Retrieved from <http://usnews.msnbc.msn.com/_news/2012/03/14/10685511-teacher-protest-closes-schools-in-louisiana>.

POGO. 2010, September 28. *POGO's Letter to Deputy HHS IG on FDA's CDRH's Low Standard of Medical Devices Approval*. Retrieved from <http://www.pogo.org/our-work/letters/2010/ph-fda-20100928-1.html>.

Politico. 2011, February 12. *Top Officials Sent False Fast and Furious Denials, Documents Reveal*. Retrieved from <http://www.politico.com/news/stories/1211/69680.html#ixzz1jEPbhdjE>.

Pollitt, C. 2003. *The Essential Public Manager*. London: Open University Press / McGraw-Hill.

Power, M. 1997. *The Audit Society: Rituals of Verification*. Oxford: Oxford University Press.

Power, M. 2000. "The Audit Society: Second Thoughts." *International Journal of Auditing*, 4: 111–19.

Power, M. 2003. *The Audit Explosion*. London: Demos. Retrieved from <http://www.demos.co.uk/files/theauditexplosion.pdf>.

Radcliffe, J. 2010, March 5. *HISD Test Cheating Inquiry Stalls District's Accreditation: HISD Cheating Inquiry Stalls Accreditation: Status is Now "Pending" as TEA Probes Reports of Test Irregularities*. Houston Chronicle. Retrieved from <http://www.chron.com/news/houston-texas/article/HISD-test-cheating-inquiry-stalls-district-s-1712030.php>.

Rich, S. 2011, November 3. *Transparency Demands Cost Governments Money: California Gov. Jerry Brown*. Government Technology. Retrieved from <http://www.govtech.com/e-government/Calif-Transparency-Website-Shuttered.html>.

Romzek, B. S. and Dubnick, M. J. 1998. Accountability, pp. 6–11 in *International Encyclopedia of Public Policy and Administration, Vol. 1: A-C*, ed. J. M. Shafritz. Boulder: Westview Press.

Romzek, B. S., LeRoux, K., and Blackmar, J. M. 2012. "Preliminary Theory of Informal Accountability Among Network Organizational Actors." *Public Administration Review*, 72: 442–53

Savage, C. 2011. *Holder, Grilled on Gun Inquiry, Says He Won't Resign*. The New York Times. Retrieved from <http://www.nytimes.com/2011/12/09/us/politics/holder-clashes-with-republicans-on-fast-and-furious.html>.

Schillemans, T. and Bovens, M. 2011. The Challenge of Multiple Accountability: Does Redundancy Lead to Overload?, pp. 3–21 in *Accountable Governance: Problems and Promises*, eds. M. J. Dubnick and H. G. Frederickson. Armonk: M.E. Sharpe.

Schwartz, N. D. 2012, January 2. *Austerity Reigns in Europe as Crisis Deepens*. The New York Times. Retrieved from <http://www.heraldtribune.com/article/20120102/ARTICLE/120109955>.

Tolbert, C. J. and Mossberger, K. 2006. "The Effects of E-Government on Trust and Confidence in Government." *Public Administration Review*, 66: 354–69.

Turner, D. 2011, July 17. *Atlanta Schools Cheated Through Fear: Officials Forced Teachers to Comply, Probe Reveals*. Associated Press. Retrieved from <http://www.theblaze.com/stories/2011/07/16/178-teachers-principals-named-atlanta-schools-created-culture-of-cheating-fear/>.

Wade, N. 2012, January 11. *University Suspects Fraud by a Researcher Who Studied Red Wine*. The New York Times. Retrieved from <http://www.nytimes.com/2012/01/12/science/fraud-charges-for-dipak-k-das-a-university-of-connecticut-researcher.html>.

Williamson, R. M. 2006. *What Gets Measured Gets Done: Are You Measuring What Really Matters?* Retrieved from <http://www.swspitcrew.com/articles/What%20Gets%20Measured%201106.pdf>.

Yigitcanlar, T. 2003. *Bridging the Gap Between Citizens and Local Authorities via E-Government*. In *Symposium on E-Government: Opportunities and Challenges*. Muscat, Sultanate of Oman, May 10–12, 2003.

CHAPTER 35

ACCOUNTABILITY AND TIME

JERRY L. MASHAW

ADDING THE "WHEN" QUESTION

OUR standard "grammar of governance" (Mashaw 2006) distinguishes accountability regimes according to six features. *Who* is accountable? To *whom* are they accountable? For *what* is accountability demanded? Assessed by *what standards*? Determined through *which processes*? And, attended by *what effects*? To those six questions, we should add another: *When* are the relevant actors be called to account?

Looking at current arrangements we know that there is a vast menu of options. In electoral politics some systems use fixed durations in office. Others allow elections to be called at the option of some office-holder—think parliamentary snap elections—or at the option of some segment of the electorate. As we have had reason to experience several times recently in the United States, many states, perhaps most of them, permit office-holders to be subject to recall if a sufficient number of voters request a recall election (Streb 2011). Fixed durations can vary across offices in order to trade off concerns about maintaining representatives' closeness to voters, current policy preferences against citizens' equally important background preferences for some stability in governing coalitions and therefore government policies.

The timing of accountability is often at the discretion of the overseer, the "to whom" person or institution in a particular accountability regime. Legislatures may investigate the performance of administrators whenever they feel the need (or perhaps merely the desire) to do so. Legal accountability is fundamentally at the option of plaintiff or prosecutor initiative in adversary systems, or judicial initiative in more inquisitorial arrangements. As a parent I can oversee my children's school performance episodically at report card time, or I can check whether they are doing their homework and understanding their lessons on a nightly basis. Some accountability systems are in continuous operation like quality assurance systems in both the public and private sectors. Others are highly episodic as when accountability to the people, or to someone else, is based on the happenstance of journalistic investigation.

We need not pursue further examples of current practice to see that time is a crucial design parameter that serves multiple purposes. One of these purposes is precisely to protect against accountability overload and the disruption of ongoing decision processes. Legislatures cannot function if their members must constantly stand for election. Administrative agencies cannot do their job if they can be called into court to justify their decisions before they are made final, or sometimes before they are applied. More fundamentally, the timing of occasions for accountability is crucial for the preservation of liberty and autonomy. Were we continuously accountable to others, individual moral agency would be eliminated.

This is not to say that getting the time dimension right is easy. Accountability reinforces effectiveness and efficiency but can undermine both of those things as well. The tradeoffs are many. But this is only to say that designing institutions is an uncertain business. From this perspective time is just a dimension of designing accountable and effective governments or firms—or families, for that matter.

Time can enter into the design of accountability regimes in other ways as well. Writers have been concerned that time, in the sense of "history," may be ignored in accountability analyses. Failure to consider the history of accountability successes and failures when attempting to design or reform institutions is surely a mistake (Brandstrom, Bynander, and Hart 2004). Time also figures into the analysis of accountability regimes when considering the effects of path dependency on organizational designs and when considering how to make accountability regimes durable over time (Pollitt 2008).

My concern in this chapter, however, is with a different dimension of the time problem, one that causes particular problems for institutional design. How can or should contemporary accountability regimes deal with time lags, that is, long separations between decisions and their effects? This question emerges in two different forms. In the first, current effects are seemingly attributable to historical actions or policies whose authors have long passed from the scene. A prominent example is the longstanding debate over reparations for the lingering effects of chattel slavery in the United States. Slaves and slave owners, along with the policymakers who instituted and preserved this institution and others who bore its benefits and burdens have long since past from the scene. Is it possible to craft acceptable current policies of repair when the benefits and burdens of reparations as a remedial accountability device would necessarily affect persons in the present?

A second lag problem concerns decisions made (or not made) and actions taken (or not taken) today that are anticipated to affect events or situations that will occur sufficiently far in the future that the responsible actors or deciders will not then be available to be called to account. Policy decisions by governments sometimes turn out badly, but only after the decision-makers have moved on. For contemporary Americans the Iraq War and the deregulation of the banking sector spring immediately to mind. Governments may make improvident expenditures and commitments that result much later in unsustainable national indebtedness. The current malaise of the Eurozone is an example fresh to the European mind. And the failure to recognize the dangers of CO_2 emissions over the past century, and current procrastination in doing anything decisive about it, may well have catastrophic consequences in the next century—or perhaps this one. Long lag times between decisions or actions and effects are a real problem, both for decision-making itself and for making decision-makers accountable for their actions. Are these problems for which institutional designers lack solutions?

Distinguishing Policy Mistakes from Accountability Failures

In gauging just how serious lag times are in the design of accountability systems, we should not confuse policy mistakes with accountability failures. There are available mechanisms that can make current actors accountable for risky decisions. That decisions turn out badly does not, without more, signal an accountability failure. Let us take the financial collapse of 2008 in the US as an example.

Much ink has been spilled concerning the "real causes" of the 2008 financial meltdown (Gorton 2010; Rajan 2010; Shiller 2008). Banking regulation had become too lax, thus allowing banks to take risks that could have dire systemic consequences. The US Federal Reserve System's approach to monetary policy was too expansionist in the face of a housing bubble. Rating agencies gave overly optimistic ratings to complex debt instruments. The government's promotion of home ownership through the quasi-private entities that manage the secondary mortgage market caused lenders to ignore risks that they should have considered. And so on.

To be sure, as a contrite administrator testifying before Congress once remarked, mistakes were made. And some of those mistakes were made well over a decade before the financial collapse to which they contributed. Nevertheless, it is far from obvious that the lag time between decisions and effects raises an issue of accountability that should trouble us. The political decisions concerning regulatory reform in the banking sector were made within the usual accountability restraints applicable to legislation. And, at the time, there were many reasons for thinking that those reforms reduced financial risks in the banking sector by permitting banks to diversify their investment portfolios. Similarly, ratcheting down the requirements concerning mortgage risks necessary to access the secondary mortgage market carried out a pro-home ownership policy approved by the political branches of the national government. Collateralizing these loans was subject to the usual constraints of marketability. If those collateralized debt obligations were believed to be too risky, they could not be sold in the private market. But sold they were, at substantial gains for Fanny Mae and Freddy Mac, the relevant secondary market makers. The purchasers of many collateralized debt obligations certainly ended up holding paper that was a lot riskier than they believed it to be, but the riskiness of those ventures had been certified in the usual way by the accounting firms to which the federal government has made various purchasers accountable. There may be an accountability system flaw in this process, the conflict of interest created by having rating agencies paid by the issuers of the paper that they are rating. But that flaw had nothing to do with time lags.

Not to put too fine a point on it, all decisions made under conditions of uncertainty about the future—which means virtually all decisions—have risks. But there are front-end mechanisms to make current actors accountable for their current risky decisions. In the financial crisis scenario, elected officials were electorally responsible for decisions concerning deregulation of the banking sector. Market actors were responsible in the usual way, through fear of loss or bankruptcy, for decisions to hold certain forms of debt obligations. There has been much complaint that those who caused the crisis have not been held accountable because some of them were bailed out by the government and few have been criminally prosecuted. But we should recognize that the bailouts short-circuited the market processes and, economic losses, including bankruptcy, that would have, in the normal course, made the banks (and some non-bank institutions) accountable for their risky decisions. A political decision was made that standard market accountability should be forestalled in order to protect the financial system as a whole. And while many citizens of the countries affected are understandably angry at the bankers whose practices caused this mess, few bankers have been prosecuted because few if any engaged in any criminal activity. Virtually no one anticipated the combination of events that turned a bubble in the housing market—a market that is, after all, a small portion of the total economy—into a global meltdown of the financial system. To be sure, real estate and other bubbles have caused crashes before but, in the words of the title of a book published soon after the crash, everyone thought "this time is different" (Reinhart and Rogoff 2010).

Mistakes were made, but within the standard political and market accountability regimes. Delayed effects posed no special accountability problems. Moreover, where there are relatively well-known tendencies for policymakers to fail to anticipate the future, or to over-weight the present, we often find accountability mechanisms that require sober second looks at what the relevant actors are doing. The tendency of legislatures to spend now in the hope of paying later—on someone else's watch—often results in both substantive and procedural constraints on incurring public debt. Virtually all states in the United States, for example, have balanced budget requirements in their constitutions (National Conference of State Legislatures 2010). These do not always work as planned, but they do limit future trouble by making legislatures legally accountable now for public budget decisions. At the local level, again in the United States, one finds common requirements that localities submit proposals for the issuance of municipal bonds to local referenda. Hence, in many circumstances localities cannot acquire debt without the immediate approval of the taxpayers whose taxes will retire it. Where risks are unavoidable, but their incidence uncertain, we may demand that individuals or firms post bonds or carry insurance so that any future harm from their current activities can be compensated, at least monetarily.

We should remember that the absence of explicit governmental accountability regimes for protection against future harms does not necessarily indicate that no alternative accountability regimes are in place. Indeed, markets and social accountability regimes may be particularly good at both limiting future "bads" and incentivizing the production of future "goods." Lenders avoid bad credit risks; people with a reputation for poor judgment are not given decision-making authority in firms, families, or other organizations. On the other hand good track records tend to be rewarded with money, power, and social esteem. There is a substantial literature on how these normative systems substitute for and sometimes displace law and legal accountability (Ellickson 1991; McAdams 1995).

To put the points that I have just been making in another way, in many situations time, the lag between decisions or actions and their ultimate effects, is not really the problem. The problem is uncertainty. We have a limited capacity to forecast the future, even if the future is tomorrow. Extended time periods simply exacerbate uncertainties because a host of other contextual factors shift over time in ways that could not have been anticipated. And, while we have mechanisms to hold actors or decision-makers accountable by requiring sober second looks at risky decisions, we do not want to overdo front-end accountability mechanisms to protect against the risks of all decisions and actions having future consequences. Preventing all risky actions or judgments by burdensome front-end accountability mechanisms—even if it were possible—would hardly be desirable. Risks also have rewards.

Moreover, other values are at stake. Lots of parents seem to be pretty bad at providing their offspring with the environment and guidance that promote future success in life. And social constraints on "bad parenting" may be quite weak, particularly where cultural and economic factors tend to reinforce unsuccessful parenting approaches. The human costs of bad parenting are high. But, as a policy matter we tend to want to hold parents accountable legally only for extremes of abuse or neglect. Routine accountability to government "parenting coaches" might conceivably improve the lot of a substantial number of children. But liberty and family privacy count for something.

We also know that something like 7 out of 10 new businesses will fail, and yet the prospects for failure, at least as a statistical matter, do not seem to deter over-optimistic entrepreneurs from trying to make a go of yet another pizza parlor or high tech startup. This involves a lot of wasted resources. But we hardly want to try to license every pursuit (although I sometimes think we are getting close) in order to make sure that entrepreneurs know what they are doing, have the requisite skills to make their businesses a success, and have the financial wherewithal to make it through an almost inevitable slow start. Such a licensing scheme is a sure-fire recipe for economic stagnation. Knowing that, we leave accountability for business success largely to the market, even though a market accountability system that produces only 30 percent successes and 70 percent failures seems to do a reasonably bad job of informing entrepreneurial judgment.

To summarize, time, with its attendant uncertainties, is a problem. Long lag times between decisions or actions and consequences exacerbate risk and uncertainty. But we should not take that to mean that there are no ex ante constraints or accountability mechanisms that make actors consider the future. Mistakes are not necessarily accountability failures and much success is due to luck, not to the fact that actors knew that they could be held accountable for the risks their actions or decisions posed for the future. Neither failures nor good outcomes in the future are necessarily the result of accountability system successes or failures in the present. Second, society has other values besides ensuring that people are accountable. Liberty, privacy, and economic welfare may demand loose accountability controls. We should be prepared to find an accountability deficit only when a different accountability regime would produce better results without too high a tradeoff in relation to other social values.

So where is the deep problem of accountability and time—if there is one? If there are such problems it seems to me that they tend to combine long lag times with major uncertainties about how to answer one or more of my original six questions about the construction of an accountability regime. To test this intuition let's consider a couple of rather hard cases—reparations for past injustices and the problem of intergenerational equity. As we shall see, accountability of the present to the past raises rather different and les tractable issues than accountability in the present for potential future effects.

Reparations for Enslavement

Accountability for the historical injustice of slavery through reparations paid to the descendants of slaves has been debated in the United States and elsewhere for many decades. Arguments for reparations have been made by some Caribbean countries as well and African countries which were the countries of origin for the slave trade have asked for reparations to them for loss of population (Brennan and Packer 2012; Howard-Hassmann 2008). In 1865 who should be accountable to whom and with what effects seemed relatively straightforward to General William Tecumseh Sherman. Having military authority over a portion of the occupied South, Sherman used the property of former slave owners to settle nearly 40,000 slaves on 400,000 acres of tillable land. Around the same time, Congress created the Freedman's Bureau and authorized it to rent and eventually sell land to freedmen. But when Andrew Johnson assumed the presidency after Lincoln's assassination, he reversed Sherman's order and similar actions by the Freedman's Bureau, thereby undermining two Acts of Congress. Congress failed to address the issue of reparations for the rest of Reconstruction (Foner 1988).

The passage of time seems to have made all these questions increasingly complicated. For General Sherman, who should be accountable was relatively straightforward: the slave holders who had benefitted directly from slave labor. But the slave holders are now gone and their descendants, including some ex-slaves, long since dispersed. Other candidates abound. The United States government is one. The US House of Representatives did pass a resolution apologizing for slavery and subsequent discriminatory laws on July 30, 2008, but proposals for reparations have never made any substantial headway. There is also much controversy about where the obligation should lie. Should it be only the responsibility of former slave- holding states or of the whole country? Slavery existed for a time in the North as well as the South and northern merchants were heavily involved in the slave trade itself.

The plot thickens. Prior to the formation of the United States of America, slavery was permitted because of the legal regimes enforced by the colonial powers, Spain, France, and the United Kingdom. Merchants in all those countries, as well as others, were heavily involved in the slave trade. Moreover, the slave traders received their cargoes from Africans as well as Europeans. And, to complicate matters further, none of the European or African countries implicated in this slave trade have retained the forms of government that existed in the late eighteenth century.

Private companies are also a potential target. Publicity campaigns have elicited apologies for involvement in the slave trade from companies like Aetna Insurance, J.P. Morgan Chase, and Wachovia. But suits for reparations against private companies have foundered. In 2006 Judge Richard Posner, in an opinion for the United States Court of Appeals for the Seventh Circuit, outlined the high legal hurdles that such a lawsuit would have to clear:

> If one or more of the defendants violated the state law by transporting slaves in 1850, and the plaintiffs can establish standing to sue, prove the violation despite its antiquity, establish that the law was intended to provide a remedy... to lawfully enslaved persons or their descendants, identify their ancestors, quantify the damages incurred, and persuade the Court to toll the statute of limitations, there would no further obstacle to the grant of relief. (Posner 2006, 759).

To state these criteria is essentially to deny the possibility of a successful lawsuit.

The ease with which General Sherman issued his reparations order compared with the difficulties of legal accountability, and the long unsuccessful pursuit of reparations from legislatures, highlight the importance of the process through which accountability is to be established. The legislative process seems to be the only available approach. And even that would seem under-inclusive if foreign governments and enterprises should bear some responsibilities. No international court has jurisdiction over all or even most of the relevant potential defendants.

But these complications concerning processes and potential collective defendants pale beside the more fundamental questions raised by the passage of time. Holding the United States responsible means holding current taxpayers responsible. And, while it may be true that the wealth of the United States has been enhanced by the exploitation of black slave labor (Horton and Horton 2005), not all Americans have shared equally in that wealth. Taxpayers would share the burden of reparations in proportion to their tax liabilities, not in proportion to their benefits from slavery in the past. Indeed, the descendants of white abolitionists and soldiers in the Union Army seem odd persons to hold accountable for the effects of an institution that their ancestors sacrificed themselves to abolish. The "to whom" question is similarly complicated. General reparations whether in money or in time would be over-inclusive. Large proportions of the current African-American population are not the descendants of slaves, and in some cases it would seem quite unjust, as in the case of the descendants of free blacks who owned slaves themselves. Yet a more targeted approach is confounded by the obvious difficulties—perhaps "impossibility" is closer to the mark—of tracing ancestry.

Finally, time complicates the question of under what standard one should judge past conduct. Slavery was, after all, not illegal in the United States prior to the 13th Amendment to the US Constitution, which was ratified in 1865. And, the Jim Crow laws passed in the South following Reconstruction, which for many years disadvantaged freed slaves and their descendants, were not repealed or declared unconstitutional until much later. The standard for reparations would have to be a moral one, not one based in violation of law. And, while many believed slavery immoral even when legal, many did not. A consensus on the immorality of slavery can perhaps only be established at the time that the legal institutions were changed. But, if the moral fault begins when slavery was abolished, then the claim for reparations must be based on failures to compensate and repair in the subsequent period. Which means that the claim for reparations would be based in some sense on the failure to make reparations. This is not a morally incoherent position, but over time it raises the same conundrum concerning who is accountable to whom as slavery itself.

In the reparations case it seems clear that passage of time raises a host of questions, questions so fundamental that they implicate the broader issue of whether accountability in this form can be justified at all. Yet, I hasten to add that the legal, moral, and practical difficulties with establishing a reparations regime as the accountability mechanisms for the historical injustice of chattel slavery does not mean that all forms of accountability are absent.

Notice that various federal, state, and private institutions have apologized for their historic role in United States slavery. Who is accountable is being determined by political, social, and market forces that cause various institutions at various times to accept responsibility for the past. The processes through which these acceptances are made are the usual processes of public and corporate governance. To whom these accountable parties are apologizing is also determined by a process of self-selection. The groups that have formed to demand reparations, in-kind benefits, and the acceptance of responsibility, are the agents for a much broader class of persons who self-identify as the persons to whom these apologies have been directed.

Moreover, one can easily argue that a number of public and private policies to end discrimination and to engage in affirmative action to assist those disadvantaged by the history of slavery result from a similar political and social accountability regime. And because these institutional actions are tied to conventional public and private governance structures, the "voluntary" actions to apologize and to seek to compensate for disadvantage represent a broader acceptance of responsibility by the constituencies that control these institutional actors through yet another set of accountability arrangements.

To be sure this is an accountability system or regime that is loose-jointed, disaggregated, and indirect. Time has made answering the basic questions about how a reparations accountability regime should be structured much more difficult. But, asking those questions reveals that if one shifts the answer to the question of "with what effects?" to include apologies, non-discrimination requirements, and affirmative action, some forms of accountability re-emerge.

Where reparations are concerned, an important opportunity was lost when President Johnson revoked General Sherman's military order and Congress was unable to act. Time has made seizing that opportunity ever more problematic. Time has not eliminated all accountability for slavery's historic injustice, but it has radically reshaped its focus.

Intergenerational Equity and Accountability

Accountability for the future poses a somewhat different set of issues. At a superficial level we know that the question of how a later generation could hold a former one accountable for the mix of consumption and savings that it chose is unanswerable. When we employ "generation" in this way we mean to reference populations that do not share political or economic power, or perhaps inhabit the earth, at the same time. If a later generation finds that its prospects have been diminished by a prior generation's resource use (consumption) that prior generation is beyond reach. If the *who* is accountable to *whom* questions concern a former generation's accountability to a later, the game seems to be up. Time gets in the way.

On the other hand we have already seen that certain ex ante techniques of accountability can enforce norms of conduct that limit future risks to acceptable levels. Perhaps if we could agree on an acceptable norm concerning intergenerational equity, then we could translate the problem of accountability into a question of how to structure an accountability regime for the present generation that tends to implement that norm by appropriate processes, standards, incentives, and sanctions. The present generation would be accountable to itself for making good on its normative commitments. And every subsequent generation could do the same, even if it agreed on different norms of intergenerational equity.

It is obvious from ordinary public conversation that people do care about these matters and have beliefs about the current generation's obligation to its successors. There is at least some inchoate theory of intergenerational equity in commonplace complaints that current generations are beggaring future generations by overspending, or exhausting the Earth's resources and polluting its atmosphere so that future generations have lesser life chances—or perhaps no life at all. Indeed, in recent years environmental equity has been a major focus for debates about intergenerational equity (Gundling 1990; Westra 2006).

Moreover, it is widely recognized that this problem is a deep-seated one. Our all-too-human tendency to privilege the present over the future is one of the most robust findings of the behavioral social sciences (Kahneman 2011). And here the findings are about whether people tend to discount their own futures excessively, much less the futures of some as yet unborn generations. This tendency surely suggests that we need some social norm to counter this so-called cognitive bias and some accountability mechanisms to reinforce those normative commitments.

Under the scheme I am imagining it is up to each generation to decide what those normative commitments might be. Our concern is with what sort of accountability regime might make present generations accountable for acting on their normative commitments. But we need to specify some norm in order to see where the difficulties in constructing such a regime might lie.

To be sure, at a philosophical level, intergenerational equity is a difficult problem. For present purposes I am going to assume that we cannot do much better than some variant of the old Lockiean proviso concerning property (Locke 1988; Nozick 1974). We are morally entitled to make use of property (here think the resources of the Earth) to the extent that as much and as good is left for others. Translated into intergenerational terms, the present generation is entitled to use the resources of the Earth to carry out its life plans just to the extent that resources remain available to the next or following generations to carry out theirs.

Rawls's (1971) famous maximin principle would seem to lead down a similar path. If one agrees with Rawls's approach, a hypothetical contract across generations would specify that resources could be used by a present generation so long as that use of resources maximized the position of the least advantaged in that society—and also the least advantaged persons in subsequent generations as well.

Utilitarianism might lead to a different approach: Current generations might be obliged to forego resource use that would increase that generation's happiness provided that the next generation's happiness would be increased by an amount that exceeded the current generation's loss. But it is not clear why one generation's happiness should be more important than another's. Nor is it clear why one generation's capacity for happiness should exceed another's. Hence, utilitarian commitments could lead to similar results as the Lockean or Rawlsian approach. And non-individualistic normative systems that tend to collapse generations into a "people" or "mankind" across time recognize these obligations to the future almost as a matter of course (Bickham 1981).

But we can leave these theory questions aside. The issue is how to translate any of these general norms into rules of conduct that would actually implement the norm. So, assume for present purposes that we adopt the Lockean proviso. How are we to make the current generation accountable for living up to this normative commitment? Can political, market, and/or social accountability mechanisms be put in place that will likely be effective? Perhaps, but the difficulties are immense because time exacerbates uncertainties.

Consider just two of the unknowns concerning the future—the rate of technological change and population growth (Solow 1974). We might assume that natural resources are finite, but that does not mean that we know either what the finite quantity is today or what natural resources will be important for the production of human well-being in the future. Technological change can easily alter both. A decade ago, for example, we tended to think that our access to carbon-based energy was reliably quantifiable in terms of known reserves, and was diminishing fairly rapidly given then current rates of use. New processes of extraction have altered this picture dramatically. Further technological innovations, such as deep sea bed mining, may alter the picture yet again. A decade ago we seemed to be violating the principle of leaving as much and as good for following generations. But given unanticipated technological advances, with further yet unknown advances perhaps in the offing, conserving carbon-based energy resources may be entirely unnecessary to carry out our obligation to leave as much and as good resources for future generations.

And, of course, "resources" is a vague term whose operational meaning may change with time as well. "Carbon-based energy resources" may seem well-specified, but the real question for human well-being is access to energy that is usable in producing goods and services. Given future technological advances, carbon-based energy may turn out to be a passing energy phase, like the almost exclusive reliance on the power of animals, wind, and water by earlier generations. Nuclear energy is having something of a renaissance and the whole energy equation would be transformed by an ability to harness fusion power. Who is to say that geo-thermal energy is not the wave of the future or indeed that wind and water might not make a comeback. What technology is going to be available is not a difficult question if we are talking about the day after tomorrow. If we're talking about the generation after the next, time introduces radical uncertainty. In order to assure that the least advantaged in each generation might have the same advantage as those in the preceding or following ones, technological advance might demand rapid consumption of current resources even if they are thought finite at the moment. Otherwise the current generation will be short-changed.

The rate of population increase or decrease may also confound our expectations. If populations are static, the present generation needs to pass on resources equivalent to those that it inherited—assuming it can determine what that means. In the face of a growing population, equally advantaging future generations would mean providing them with greater resources than were available to the present one. And, of course, just the opposite would be true if populations shrink. We may believe that overall population growth is a virtual certainty, but the long history of the Earth provides no assurance that that is the case. To make the current generation accountable for implementing its normative commitments to the next we need a standard that can be operationalized in the face of unbridgeable gaps in our knowledge about the state of the world in the future.

Uncertainty is not the only issue plaguing intergenerational accountability. Up to now I've treated the question of who the current generation is as essentially non-problematic. But a "generation" is just an abstraction—a way of describing those who are in control or alive on the planet, or some part of it, at a particular time. That abstraction cannot be held accountable even though we might have described it as having obligations or normative commitments.

So who is the "who," that is, the persons or institutions to be held to account for carrying out one generation's responsibilities to future ones? To be responsible for, and therefore properly to be held accountable for, the implementation of a norm, persons or institutions must have a capacity to act or refrain from acting in ways that would tend to produce that result (Copp 1991). But we are speaking globally here about the responsibility of current inhabitants of the planet to future ones. And there is no world government that can be made responsible, and hence accountable, for implementation.

If we think of the accountability problem as one entailing extant governmental structures we must redefine generations to be generations of Americans or Nigerians or Chinese. But, if so, those governments can be made accountable for acting on the desires or normative commitments of their populations concerning intergenerational equity in the same ways that they are made accountable for other policy choices. The problem of time and uncertainty in intergenerational equity poses daunting problems of prediction, but if those could be solved, existing and well-understood accountability regimes seem as serviceable here as elsewhere.

The problem, of course, is that national governments, acting alone, do not have the capacity to fully implement citizens' normative commitments. The world is too interconnected. Resources are found here that are consumed or used there and the utilization of resources by those not within a particular national government's control makes it impossible for any government to reliably enact and implement an intergenerational equity program. What future populations of Americans, Nigerians, or Chinese have by way of resources to carry out their life plans is too dependent upon the actions of others for their national governments to be sensibly charged with the responsibility of carrying out their citizens' desires concerning intergenerational equity. In order to make the "who" problem tractable, we really need to redefine the "what." We have to think of national governments not as responsible for intergenerational equity in the sense of fully implementing their citizens' desires in that regard, but instead as responsible for attending to the issue and attempting to manage the problem as best they can in the face of both daunting uncertainties and limited control over the relevant actors who ultimately determine outcomes.

This is hardly the place to attempt to catalogue the various means available to the national government for implementing a commitment to intergenerational equity. But it is worth noting that many such efforts are already underway. States participate in international organizations that have recognized and promoted intergenerational justice, particularly with regard to environmental resources. The interests of future generations are recognized in statutes and constitutions. Some countries have instituted particular offices, ombudsmen, or parliamentary commissions, which have specific auditing and consultative functions designed to bring to bear the interests of future generations in both parliamentary and administrative decision-making. Some courts have recognized the standing of existing parties to represent the interests of future generations and numerous environmental agencies have respect for the interests of future generations as a part of their statutory mandates. In short, there is an array of techniques for instantiating concern for intergenerational equity in state legislative, judicial, and administrative processes and in their participation in international affairs (Gopel 2011; Science and Environmental Health Network 2008).

The problem of time is not a problem that defeats current accountability for attending to intergenerational equity. Governments are already accountable in myriad ways for implementing the preferences of their populaces. There may be accountability deficits in the rough and ready way in which all citizen preferences are factored into the responsibilities of a particular government. But, if those preferences include a concern for equity across generations, then governments are already responsible and accountable for intergenerational equity through standard political processes. If governments are not attending to this issue, or attending to it as effectively as they might, the deficit may lie in the preferences or normative commitments of the citizenry. We can make ourselves accountable to future generations by making our governments accountable to us for attending to that issue in as effective ways as they or we can devise. The problem of accountability over time is soluble even here, at least to a degree, but we have to want to solve it.

Conclusion

Time is both an ubiquitous feature of accountability regimes and a troublesome problem in their construction. Long lag times between actions and effects can problematize virtually all the who, whom, what, and how standards, and effect issues that help us characterize and analyze accountability regimes. Inquiry into time's hard questions, like reparations for historic harms and responsibility for intergenerational equity, also illuminates the fundamentally normative nature of accountability discourse. Designing accountable political, social, or economic institutions is much more than a technocratic enterprise.

This chapter has focused on time as duration, on lags between decisions and effects and lags between actions and accountability demands. From this perspective time is a confounding contextual factor in designing accountability regimes and in assessing the normative appropriateness of demanding accountability at all. Time as periodicity, the setting of appropriate temporal occasions for accountability demands, was mentioned only in passing. But this aspect of accountability and time obviously requires much greater exploration before an even minimally adequate account can be given. And struggles over the need for and desirability of various accountability regimes may in some sense be disputes about the appropriate time horizon within which actions or decisions should be judged. Economically oriented actors may be functioning in what Ruggie (1998) has termed "incremental time," characterized by relatively predictable discrete actions and events, whereas environmental activists may be thinking in terms of "conjunctural" or even "epochal" time, where uncertainty reigns. Accountability and time are both deep subjects. The agenda for further reflection is large.

REFERENCES

Bickham, S. 1981. "Future Generations and Contemporary Ethical Theory." *The Journal of Value Inquiry*, 15: 169–77.

Brandstrom, A., Bynander, F., and 't Hart, P. 2004. "Governing by Looking Back: Historical Analogies in Crisis Management." *Public Administration*, 82: 191–210.

Brennan, F. and Packer, J., eds. 2012. *Colonialism, Slavery, Reparations and Trade: Remedying the Past?* New York: Routledge.

Copp, D. 1991. "Responsibility for Collective Inaction." *Journal of Social Philosophy*, 22: 71–80.

Ellickson, R. C. 1991. *Order Without Law: How Neighbors Settle Disputes*. Cambridge: Harvard University Press.

Foner, E. 1988. *Reconstruction: America's Unfinished Revolution, 1863-1877*. New York: Harper and Row.

Gopel, M. 2011, January 6. "Guarding our Future: How to Protect Future Generations." *Solutions*, Volume 1, Issue 6. <http://www.thesolutionsjournal.com/node/821>.

Gorton, G. 2010. *Slapped by the Invisible Hand: The Panic of 2007*. Oxford: Oxford University Press.

Gundling, L. 1990. "Our Responsibility to Future Generations." *American Journal of International Law*, 84: 207–12.

Horton, J. and Horton, L. 2005. *Slavery in the Making of America*. New York: Oxford University Press.

Howard-Hassmann, R. E. 2008. *Reparations to Africa*. Philadelphia: University of Pennsylvania Press.

Kahneman, D. 2011. *Thinking Fast and Slow*. New York: Farrar Strauss and Giroux.

Locke, J. 1988. *Second Treatise of Government*. Cambridge: Cambridge University Press.

Mashaw, J. L. 2006. Accountability in Institutional Design: Some Thoughts on the Grammar of Governance, pp. 115–56 in *Public Accountability, Designs, Dilemmas and Experiences*, ed. M. W. Dowdle. Cambridge: Cambridge University Press.

McAdams, R. H. 1995. "Cooperation and Conflict: The Economics of Group Status Production and Race Discrimination." *Harvard Law Review*, 108: 1003–84.

National Conference of State Legislatures. 2010. *State Balanced Budget Provisions*. Retrieved from <http://www.ncsl.org/documents/fiscal/StateBalancedBudgetProvisions2010.pdf.>.

Nozick, R. 1974. *Anarchy, State and Utopia*. New York: Basic Books.

Pollitt, C. 2008. *Time, Policy, Management: Governing With the Past*. Oxford: Oxford University Press.

Posner, R. A. 2006. *In re African-American Slave Descendants' Litigation*. 471 F.3d 754 (7th Cir. 2006).

Rajan, R. G. 2010. *Fault Lines: How Hidden Fractures Still Threaten the World Economy*. Princeton: Princeton University Press.

Rawls, J. 1971. *A Theory of Justice*. Cambridge: Harvard University Press.

Reinhart, C. M. and Rogoff, K. S. 2010. *This Time is Different: Eight Centuries of Financial Folly*. Princeton: Princeton University Press.

Ruggie, J. G. 1998. *Constructing the World Polity: Essays on International Institutionalization*. New York: Routledge.

Science and Environmental Health Network. 2008. *Models for Protecting the Environment for Future Generations*. Retrieved from <sehn.org>.

Shiller, R. J. 2008. *The Subprime Solution: How Today's Global Financial Crisis Happened and What to Do About It*. Princeton: Princeton University Press.

Solow, R. M. 1974. "Intergenerational Equity and Exhaustible Resources." *Review of Economic Studies*, 41: 29–45.

Streb, M. J. 2011. *Rethinking American Electoral Democracy*. New York: Routledge.

Westra, L. 2006. *Environmental Justice and the Rights of Unborn and Future Generations*. London: Earthscan.

CHAPTER 36

....

ACCOUNTING FOR CRISES

....

SANNEKE KUIPERS AND PAUL 'T HART

CRISIS MANAGEMENT: COPING WITH THE INTOLERABLE

....

NOT so long ago crises and disasters were likely to enter collective memory as an unfortunate incident or "Act of God." Such unfortunate incidents challenged or defeated available administrative and political repertoires of prevention and response (Boin et al. 2009, 85). Academic research primarily focused on operational response and mass behavior during crises, and on post-crisis recovery, collective traumas, and solidarity impulses (Barton 1969; Drabek 2009; Perry and Quarantelli 2005).

Times have changed. Even natural disasters immediately evoke an intense debate on responsibility and guilt (Boin et al. 2009; Quarantelli 1998; Steinberg 2000; Perry and Quarantelli 2005). Today, nearly any significant disturbance of life as usual is liable to being labeled—and indeed being felt to be—a "crisis" in the process of public and political meaning-making that such non-routine events provoke. Crises are commonly defined as situations that are being experienced as seriously threatening to core values or structures, requiring urgent action, yet also highly uncertain as to their origins and consequences (Boin et al. 2005). When labeled as such, "crises" dramatize the vulnerability of key tenets of the existing socio-political order (e.g. the belief in the power and capability of the state to protect citizens from collective harm or in the fundamental integrity of public office-holders and institutional practices) and individuals and institutions that are supposed to epitomize and defend this order. They are, in societies that pride themselves as being stable, well-ordered, peaceful, and safe, viscerally intolerable.

As crises abate, endure, or reoccur, this perceived intolerability adds to or even supersedes the collective stress that the "on the ground" events themselves have triggered. Something unacceptable has happened, therefore somebody, some organization, or entity must be held responsible. Societies need a purification ritual to "bounce back" and "move on" from crises. Without an authoritative pinpointing of "whodunnit" and, more often than not, some form of public reckoning and "lesson-drawing," it is very difficult for communities to achieve a stable post-crisis equilibrium.

Notwithstanding this legitimate desire for public scrutiny and societal re-equilibration, post-crisis accountability processes are also always intensely political. From a normative, rational perspective, truth-finding dialogues, justifications, and learning efforts would be expected. By contrast, during and after crisis situations a much more political high-stakes game tends to ensue among office-holders, agencies, and other interested parties involved. Through media and internet coverage, crises focus public attention on all parties involved in their development: victims, responders, planners, regulators, corporations, politicians, investigators. All of these wish to influence how events get publicly depicted and understood. Moreover, as Boin et al. (2009, 95) observe, "media are not just the backdrop against which crisis actors operate, they constitute a prime arena in which incumbents and critics, status-quo players and change-advocates have to perform to obtain or preserve political clout. Crisis actors need to convince news-makers to pay attention to their particular crisis frame, and, if possible, support it." Consequently, crises are accompanied by "accountability management". Incumbent officials and agencies explain their actions prior to, during, and after the occurrence of a major societal disturbance, whilst their opponents seek to expose their alleged failures. Through accountability, crises can make, break, or transform political and public service careers, agency mandates and reputations, and policy paradigms.

In this chapter, we review the terrain of crisis-induced accountability processes. We follow Bovens' (2010) conceptualization of accountability as involving the interplay between forums, actors, and consequences. Throughout we ask what makes crisis-induced accountability processes and outcomes special. Do they differ in kind or just in degree from those occurring in more "business as usual" circumstances? We argue here that they do differ, in the sense that they are invariably intensely political and strategic. As a result the rational drive to "learn" from the events has to contend with the politics of blame, political survival, and political exploitation. If we wish to understand the conduct of politicians and civil servants in accountability processes during and after crises, we must embrace this perspective. We start by examining where post-crisis accountability is enacted (forums), we then examine the strategies accountees (actors) may adopt in response to crisis-induced demands for accountability, followed by an overview of what is known about the outcomes (consequences) of crisis accountability processes. We end by offering some avenues for further research in this area.

How Crises are Scrutinized: Forums

The intense attention and raw emotions that crises generate tend to spur equally intense activities of various accountability forums. First and foremost, of course, the *mass media and the internet* are abuzz with reporting, speculation, and judgments of the performance of relevant actors and stakeholders in the case at hand. In some cases, this public scrutiny of the causes and management of crises, while intense at its peak, abates quickly. This is most likely if the crisis is seen as having been responded to adequately. Such is the case if authorities' first accounts of what happened are deemed credible and official, authoritative forms of inquiry have been announced early. If nothing "fishy" and no "smoking gun" have emerged in the public reporting and interpretation, the media are likely to move on to the next big story and cease devoting scarce resources to further penetrate a crisis that has become yesterday's news. The web, anarchic as it is, may see continued discussion and speculation, where worst-case scenarios and conspiracy interpretations may thrive among relatively small sub-communities.

Rational search behavior (most effective use of limited resources) and commercial rewards for the bigger news stories direct media to produce punctuated equilibria in their reporting (Baumgartner and Jones 2002). Media immediately latch on to what emerges as a "bigger story" that can be unearthed as a result of the initial reporting on the crisis. If, for example, journalists report an industrial accident and speak to workers, unions, and Occupational Health and Safety (OH and S) experts criticizing the company's safety policies and management practices, they will keep pushing the envelope. This may lead them on to the role of government licensing and oversight practices, with ample scope for finding faults that lead them to matters of policy and politics. This then brings a new set of angles and reporters into the picture, as the crisis story expands and morphs into a bigger tale of negligence, mismanagement, and competing values and interests. A second reason why media will continue to intensely monitor and report a particular crisis is if the on-the-ground manifestations of it don't go away quickly, and particularly if this appears to be related to problems in the initial response to the crisis. Hurricane Katrina and the BP oil spills in the Gulf of Mexico are cases in point. In both cases, the responses to the initial disaster were unsatisfactory and in fact clearly aggravated the damage and suffering caused, presenting the media with both continued public salience and a clear path of inquiry. The result was merciless hyper-scrutiny that damned the reputations of organizations and leaders and upped the ante of all the official hearings and inquiries that were set in motion partly as a result of the painful displays of incompetence amplified by continued media coverage.

Above and beyond media and internet coverage, crisis scrutiny may take place in a range of more formal accountability forums, often in parallel and occasionally even overtly competing streams of investigation, debate, and evaluation. First, *regulatory bodies tasked with oversight and incident investigation* are often authorized and sometimes even compelled to investigate major incidents within their domain of competence. Think of environmental protection agencies, transport safety bodies, school inspectorates, medical licensing authorities, OH and S regulators, and so on. Though their final reports end up in the public domain, these agencies tend to operate within a *technical, professional paradigm of accountability*, work behind closed doors, and focus on drawing and disseminating lessons for the future. However, in the context of a major crisis, pressures can build on these agencies to work faster and hit harder if only to dispel any notions that they themselves are tainted by regulatory capture, or to prove the relevance of their specific line of inquiry amidst what might well be a clamor of investigative voices and accountability conversations.

Second, judicial authorities representing the rule of law may see fit to, or again be required to, launch their own investigations: coroners, police, public prosecutors, and—sooner or later—courts. Though they each have their own particular angles and pre-occupations, broadly speaking all these investigations operate on a *forensic paradigm of accountability*, where the main aim is not just to establish causality, but to ascertain responsibility and indeed culpability. In the context of high-consequence events such as crises, this lends these investigations a particularly grave and potentially intensely adversarial bent, threatening not just on-site operators but managers, executives, and corporate coffers. The legal shadow that crises cast may, as a result, be long (the 1984 Union Carbide explosion at Bhopal, India has been in the Indian and US courts for over two decades) and extremely costly.

Third, governments confronted with a major crisis occurring on their watch will anticipate or respond to public pressures for accountability by launching a major and public ad hoc independent investigation of their own. This could take the form of a blue ribbon panel, an academic authority, a current or former judge, or—in Westminster-style political systems—a Royal Commission. Authorities that commission such inquiries walk a fine line in designing their briefs. In order to properly fulfill its symbolic, cathartic function, the investigation needs to be bestowed with public authority. This presupposes that people of impeccable, non-partisan credentials are selected to head it, that they be given a wide brief, unlimited access to information and actors, ample resources to conduct their business, and freedom to organize their work as they see fit. But by granting all of that, governments may also be setting up a body that can prove to be a major thorn in their own side, which will end up finding fault not just "out there" and "down the line," but tracing responsibilities back to "in here" and "up at the top", or proposing policy changes that are politically controversial and finan-cially unpalatable. So, in practice, the relationships between governments and official investigations are full of ambiguity and latent tensions that need to be carefully man-aged in order for both to come out the other end unscathed (Weller 1994; Prasser 2006; Dekker 2007; Boin et al. 2008).

Finally, inquiries of a more explicitly political nature are often initiated in the wake of crisis, with legislatures (and particularly opposition forces within them) keen to show their involvement and robustness in holding executive power to account. Also, victim organizations may set up their own inquiries, often explicitly designed in overt opposi-tion to the existing array of official, but insufficiently probing, inquiries.

In many instances, these four streams of inquiry and accountability intersect. In fact, major incidents often trigger a whole gamut of inquiries whose briefs and purposes par-tially overlap and partially conflict—presenting a formidable management challenge to governments and other actors whose performance is being put under the public micro-scope. The next section examines how they cope with this challenge.

Managing Crisis-Induced Accountability: Actors and their Strategies

The bulk of the literature on accountability for crises focuses on the behavior of agents who anticipate or respond to questions about their performance prior to and during the crisis response phase raised by these different types of accountability forums. Or, to put it more bluntly, on how parties actually play the "blame game" (Hood 2011). Different but overlapping lines of inquiry generate roughly similar sets of findings. Two patterns emerge in the academic literature on how actors account for their contribution to a particular situation (the crisis at hand) in response to the accountability forums presented in the section above. In general the perceived need to tackle the issue of blame (and thus liability) for real or perceived contributions to the occurrence or escalation of a crisis seems a primary driver for political actors. As a result, the chief accountability strategies they employ involve (1) the (re)allocation of blame and (2) the exhibition of empathy and responsiveness. We examine each briefly.

Blame Allocation

If events are perceived as intolerable, and as a blameworthy violation of substantive values such as justice, democracy, liberty, or national security, a blame firestorm may erupt (Brändström and Kuipers 2003). Factors that increase the level of perceived "guilt" are (1) the unequivocality of the social norms violated; (2) the alleged intentionality and awareness of the actors involved; (3) the rarity of the blameworthy incident; (4) the presence of images and simplified causal scripts; and (5) the brutality of the harm perpetrated and public identification with the victims involved (Hearit 2006). When a story about negative political performance catches on, attempts at blame avoidance have run their course and give way to blame management strategies which accountable actors employ to avoid being pinpointed as culpable and/or responsible for the problems that have been identified (McGraw 1991). They do so because negative events affect their reputation more than positive ones (Weaver 1986).

Blame assignment and avoidance in the accountability process involves framing the course of events—both by incumbents and their opponents—to influence the dominant perception of what happened and who did it. This is the "art" of strategic rhetoric. Actors whose behavior comes under critical scrutiny can attempt to escape the searchlights of the accountability debate by referring to a set of recurrent defensive scripts such as accusing the accusers, disqualifying critics, blaming the messenger, extenuating their own behavior, shifting the burden of proof onto critics, or blaming others. Actors employ these and other tactics sequentially (Bovens et al. 1999). In order to avoid blame, actors start with crisis or problem denial, then adopt other responses such as admitting the crisis but blaming others; or admitting partial responsibility but denying substantial involvement, until their strategy becomes untenable and actors are forced to admit both problem and culpability (cf. Boin et al. 2009).

To be sure, some actors seem better at dodging the blame bullet than others, even in the most adverse circumstances. Personality and persona come into play, in ways that are difficult to pinpoint analytically. Some politicians elicit forgiveness. "Teflon Tony" Blair managed to dissociate himself from whatever mire or difficulties he himself or his ministers became involved in—until the Iraq war proved to be one crisis too many. Vladimir Putin's popularity defied a range of embarrassing crisis management fiascoes such as the Kursk disaster (2000), the Dubrovska theatre siege (2002), and the Beslan school hostage crisis (2004).

Given the fact that most humans lack a Teflon skin, what do implicated leaders do to duck responsibility? Brändström and Kuipers (2003) distinguish two dimensions along which government elites reframe a crisis to escape blame: one, by depicting the failures committed as technical, operational matters for which blame remains limited to lower-level operators than themselves; and two, by depicting any critical failures or weaknesses as incidental (as opposed to symptomatic or structural).

This model helps to diagnose actor strategies in accountability debates, and even helps account for accountability outcomes. Brändström et al. (2008) explain why similar government failure to respond timely and adequately to the 2004 Tsunami disaster had different political consequences in Sweden, Norway, and Finland. Stark (2011) demonstrates that crisis escalation by opponents in the English and Scottish school exam crises is sequential (as Hood et al. (2009) suggested earlier) and proceeds along the dimensions discerned by Brändström and Kuipers. Initially, technical policy failures were framed as a threat to larger values (trust in each education system), then associated to higher level errors by politically responsible actors (Estelle Morris in Britain, and Samuel Galbraith in Scotland), and finally portrayed as symptoms of endemic governmental failure (substantiated by the Tomlinson inquiry and the Deloitte and Touche investigation, respectively).

An even more consummate strategy involves deflecting blame towards institutionalized scapegoats. This presupposes that prior to the crisis, blame management has been considered in the design of the formal delegation structures. Responsibility for unpopular or risky endeavors can be limited through delegation by design, a tradition that goes back to Machiavelli's *The Prince*. Scapegoats can also deliberately take the fall for their bosses and patrons. Ellis's (1994) "presidential lightning rods" are a case in point. Proto-culprits, such as the wingman or the spin doctor, designed into the very fabric of the power structure, provide office-holders with an extra option to survive scandal and demonstrate resolute "crisis management" (cf. Jones 2000). Government agencies even deliberately delegate risk to autonomous or privatized agencies, with varying success (see Hood, this volume). But usually, in response to crisis, this ship has sailed and the delegation strategy is no longer available. We therefore continue here to discuss other presentational strategies in the accountability process, such as exhibition of empathy and manipulation of process and procedures.

Exhibition of Empathy and Responsiveness

Besides denying the problem, defending oneself, and passing the buck, accountability considerations can actually also result in actors embracing responsibility for what happened prior to and during a crisis. Government elites are not necessarily all self-interested, nor even cynical yet resourceful survivors. Another strand of research points out that immediate and public display of empathy is an important response category in the accountability process. Responses to crisies can also be seen as ritualized opportunities for the public display of compassion, solidarity, and reassurance. Prominent officials visiting the disaster site, the organization of state funerals or collective mourning remembrance ceremonies, protest marches, setting up an evacuation shelter (whether necessary of not), or the lowering of flags to half-mast are all significant forms of crisis-related ritual ('t Hart 1993).

Failure to grasp the symbolic dimension of crisis management can be an important factor influencing later accountability "trials." The Swedish Minister of Foreign Affairs paid a high political price for her visit to the theatre on the evening of the Asian tsunami disaster on December 26, 2004: Her emotional dissociation from the fate of the 30,000 Swedes on holiday in the affected region ignited a blaze of criticism. The same happened to Victorian police commissioner Christine Nixon during the inquiry that followed a massive and deadly bushfire on the outskirts of greater Melbourne: The inquiry commissioners, the tabloid press, and the larger public never forgave her that she and her husband had gone out for a pub meal with friends while communities were burning, even though she had no command responsibilities that evening.

One step down the ladder of symbolic displays of empathy is contrition: the art of apology (Hearit 2006; cf. Benoit 1995; Nobles 2008). Research suggests that acts of self-mortification by besieged elites can be usefully understood and evaluated in terms of their: truthfulness—an apology needs to be accompanied by full disclosure of relevant information; sincerity—an apology needs to come across as an authentic attempt to reconcile rather than a desire to escape further scrutiny; timing—apologies lose force when they come late (i.e. well after an actor has first tried to ignore or deny responsibility); voluntarism—contrition in the absence of duress has more impact than apology that is perceived to be forced; comprehensiveness—the degree to which it encompasses all victims and affected parties; and dramaturgy—the extent to which it is performed in an appropriate, dignified public context (Hearit 2006, 64–9).

In addition, actors invoke procedural rationality and due process to appease indignant stakeholders. Clarke (2000, 8), for example, notes that "crises, disasters and scandals result in public disquiet and in loss of confidence in the body of politics. Confidence can be effectively restored only by thoroughly investigating and establishing the truth and exposing the facts to public scrutiny." The initiation of a commission of inquiry creates a new venue for all stakeholders to influence accountability outcomes. Boin et al.'s (2009) analysis of 15 cases suggests that officeholders and their opponents do so by affecting the way the inquiry process itself is managed. Incumbents try to keep an inquiry assignment out of the adversarial, politicized legislative domain, and attempt to assign the inquiry task to blue ribbon commissions or senior lawyers.

Incumbent actors assume that the establishment of an inquiry can help to avoid political sanctions, and at least temporarily shed the tabloids (Sulitzeanu-Kenan 2010). Elliot and McGuinness (2001) posit that the appointment of an inquiry allows office-holders to get out of the limelight in what has often become a glare of media attention and public criticism. While the inquiry commission is at work, political actors can legitimately refrain from addressing the issue and from answering uncomfortable questions. According to Parker and Dekker (2008) incumbent officeholders better avoid inquiries into crises happening on their watch. Both the admission of the problem that is conveyed with the inquiry appointment, and the risk of receiving a critical report, increase incumbents' wariness.

That said, manipulating accountability procedures, processes, and story lines remain tempting tactical ploys for officeholders to—somehow—"manage" the intolerable. In the next section we will discuss to what extent their accountability strategies are successful, and what conditions the variety of outcomes of blame avoidance, apology, and inquiry ploys.

Post-Crisis Accountability Impacts

The investment of resources, time, and energy that generally goes into strategies to avoid blame after crisis, suggests that actors widely believe in the effectiveness of those strategies to influence outcomes of the accountability process. Hood (2011) warns that this belief is not borne out by empirical research, which suggests that the causal relation between political behavior (presentational strategies to influence the accountability process) and outcome (blame attribution) remains opaque. Crisis-induced "blame games," as he calls them, take place in a fuzzy context: Office-holders always have a prior reputation, other pressing issues may gain salience, symbolic incidents may unleash a media frenzy. Seeking to find method to the apparent madness, Boin et al. (2009, 100) studies fifteen cases of post-crisis public discussion and inquiry, and conclude that incumbent officials are more likely to survive if one or more of the following conditions apply:

(1) they have a good stock of pre-crisis political capital with key media actors;
(2) they cogently, proactively, and consistently communicate their own, self-disculpating crisis frames;
(3) they manage to have an "expert commission" as the main locus of official inquiry into the crisis, as opposed to being judged by a more political layman commission;
(4) they are new in office and able to turn themselves into critics of the status quo ante, committing to reform;
(5) there is a predominant view that the crisis had exogenous as opposed to endogenous "within system" causes

Time and place shape the way blame plays out, when actors at different levels attempt to re-allocate culpability to others by framing the crisis to their advantage. And whether as a result of this tactical maneuvering or of broader contextual influences, audiences sometimes attribute blame to executive leaders and elites, and at other times are satisfied that the roots of failure lay with ground operators or simply bad luck.

Effects of Apologies

The effect of apology has been studied empirically in the corporate literature on public relations. Studies on crisis management by apology draw on the "Stealing Thunder" tradition in corporate communication literature. This field offers many invaluable insights for private and public organizations alike. If an organization breaks the news about its own crisis (stealing thunder), this enhances rather than diminishes its stature with clients and markets (Arpan and Roskos-Ewoldsen 2005). Besides, self-disclosure allows the organization to avoid explicitly taking or rejecting responsibility by means of a crisis response strategy (Claeys and Cauberghe 2012).

Coombs (2007) offers a framework to assess reputational threat as a result of crisis, and argues that if the threat is mild, timely disclosure of information provides a sufficient remedy. Claeys and Cauberghe (2012, 88) add to this by concluding that self-disclosure strategies particularly help to avoid reputational damage. If the reputational threat is severe, or if the actor or organization's initial lines of defense did not "steal thunder," more comprehensive and painful image repair strategies are required, such as an apology.

Repercussions of Inquiries

Research explicitly focused on the consequences of exploitation of procedures and processes, concludes that appointing inquiries may serve to buy time, but in the end only postpones condemnation by legislative committees and audit bodies, as media attention continues to focus on the inquiry (Hood et al. 2009, 716). This finding is in line with Sulitzeanu-Kenan's (2007) research on attenuation in media salience of 40 British events: The appointment of a political inquiry does not make the media go away, often the contrary.

Earlier empirical research by the same author is even more discouraging for incumbents: The proactive appointment of an inquiry does not reduce the likelihood of blame being attributed to the appointing officeholder (Sulitzeanu-Kenan 2006). In addition, a negativity bias plays up regarding the inquiry's conclusions: Denunciations of government by public inquiries are considered more credible by observers than praise (Sulitzeanu-Kenan 2006). In sum, empirical research offers little hope to incumbent authorities that holding an inquiry is an effective way to avoid some form of public stigma (Hood 2002; Hood et al. 2009; Parker and Dekker 2008; Schwartz and Sulitzeanu-Kenan 2004; Sulitzeanu-Kenan 2006, 2007, 2010).

These findings are partly explained by underlying citizen predispositions. It has been argued that voters, for example, have the tendency to pay more attention to negative than to positive information, and politicians often receive less credit for successes than blame for failures (Hood and Lodge 2006; James and John 2007; cf. Weaver 1986), even in the event of an uncontrollable catastrophe. In fact, Arceneaux and Stein (2006) argue that particularly in case of natural disasters, citizens are inclined to attribute responsibility to government, because it alone can do something to prevent the extremity of a natural catastrophe, and because people expect governments to have an infinite capacity for safeguarding their citizens from all kinds of harm and adversity (Yates 1998).

Being blamed does not necessarily mean paying the ultimate price (dismissal, electoral defeat, agency and policy termination), of course. Post-crisis scrutiny often does produce a certain amount of damage to leaders' public standing and political strength (Boin et al. 2009), though there is no clear generic evidence of causality between crisis management performance and hard political outcomes such as results in the first post-crisis elections, since many other factors are usually at play. It happens only in rare cases, such as when Spanish Prime Minister Aznar's conservative party paid a heavy price for his misguided claim that Basque terrorists were behind the 2004 Madrid train bombings, which took place just days before a scheduled election (Olmeda 2008). The implosion of President George W. Bush's public standing following the federal government's ill-handling of the emergency response after hurricane Katrina is another case in point (Preston 2008).

That said, most political and organizational elites "survive" the accountability process. Dowding and Kang's (1998) longitudinal study of ministerial resignations in the United Kingdom indicates that only one third of the serious calls for resignation leads to direct ministerial resignation. Everywhere, in fact, the bulk of the leaders whose role and performance were scrutinized in the wake of crisis keep their jobs (Boin et al. 2008, 291). But for how long? In a later study on the same UK ministerial resignation data, Berlinksi and colleagues (2010, 563) show that though resignation calls may not lead to direct resignation, they do certainly damage a politician: "only 30 percent of the ministers who have faced one or more resignation calls see out their term."

Still, in the large majority of cases executive reputations appear to recover as time elapses. In some cases, some of their associates may pay the price for their survival: Firing or moving on other, lesser, figures as "lightning rods" for the top tiers of executives is not an uncommon strategy (Ellis 1994).

Policy Consequences

If crisis-induced accountability is to contribute to "learning," we would expect reform in precisely those areas where the accountability conversation has revealed deficiencies in risk management and crisis preparedness. Post-crisis inquiry reports are subjective reconstructions of an incident, and the story is built at least partially around the preferred lessons and desired recommendations for action (Boudes and Laroche 2009). Disruptions of societal routines open up political space ("opportunity windows") for actors inside and outside government to redefine issues and, propose policy innovations and organizational reforms (Boin et al. 2009).

Yet, even in the wake of the most dramatic crisis episodes, incremental rather than radical change appears to be the norm (Boin et al. 2009, 100). Evaluations after crisis often report technical problems for which incremental fixes are possible. The deeper causes are often more complex, ambiguous, and less easy to repair. Investigative reports increasingly point at underlying causes, such as organizational culture, regulatory regime, or human interaction (Reason 2008, 131), but they rarely lead to removing or neutralizing the system-level risk factors (Heyse et al. 2006).

In most cases, governments choose to adopt secondary (e.g. technical, instrumental adjustments in regulation and implementation practices) changes (Boin et al. 2009). In hazardous systems, incidents generally result in the increasing tightening of safety measures (Busenberg 1999). However, Schwartz and Sulitzeanu-Kenan (2004) do not even find evidence for such limited policy change after crises. They conclude that disasters of sufficient dread do reach the governmental agenda, but lead only to symbolic action if there is no coherent advocacy coalition to push for reform (Schwartz and Sulitzeanu-Kenan (2004), 98).

The presence and efficacy of advocacy coalitions could account for the variety we find for policy change after "focusing events" in different policy domains. Birkland (2007) concludes from his comparison of policy change after crises in the homeland security, earthquake response, and aviation security domains that at least one major advocacy coalition is required to press for actual change to occur. Because active advocates made sure that ideas for improvement were already on the shelf when shortcomings of the system were dramatically revealed on 9/11, rapid adoption of new policies in aviation security was possible (Birkland 2007, 176–7). When such a coherent coalition is absent, policy change often fails to materialize (Nohrstedt and Weible 2010).

The general absence of drastic policy changes after crises, and the importance of framing in the accountability process, indicate that at the end of the day all the scrutiny that takes place might well be more relevant "for the management of crises as mediums of political communication rather than agents of reform or lesson learning" (Stark 2010, 9), though other research suggests that much substantive learning does take place after crises, far removed from the public limelight of inquiry politics in the domain of professional bureaucracies (Van Duin 1992) and resilience-oriented organizational cultures (Weick and Sutcliffe 2007).

From Crisis to Breakdown to Re-Equilibration

The study of crisis-induced accountability is a small but developing endeavor. It fundamentally examines how polities cleanse themselves in the wake of disruptive and disconcerting episodes. Our review of the existing literature concerning the design of accountability procedures, the use of strategies and tactics by actors, and the impact of crisis-induced accountability processes leaves us with inconclusive answers to pivotal questions concerning "what works when, and for whom." What we can safely conclude is that accountability after crises is a complex, uncertain, ambivalent, and often intensely political affair. The impulse to blame co-exists with the desire of incumbents to survive in office; the wish to learn conflicts with the need for societal and political catharsis; and the opportunity to forge a radical break with the now traumatic past jars with institutional reflexes to "normalize" the situation (Nohrstedt 2011). Crisis inquiries are designed and conducted in a context of intense public interest and, often, vigorous public debate. Depending on that context, inquiries can be seen as more or less authoritative; they can be well or poorly equipped and empowered; they can be more or less independent from the agents whose behavior they are supposed to assess.

At the end of the day, crisis-induced accountability episodes can be usefully described, compared, contrasted, and even evaluated, in terms of their role in the eventual re-equilibration process. Inspired by examples like Parker and Dekker's (2008) investigation of the 9/11 commission in the US, we suggest that more rigorous comparative study is needed of the ways in which crisis inquiries contribute to the diagnostic work of "truth-telling"; the therapeutic work of publicly acknowledging the plight of those experiencing risk, harm, and trauma; the inquisitorial work of establishing responsibilities; and the reconstructive work of lesson-drawing and adapting to the new realities as constituted by the narratives emerging from investigative efforts and the accountability conversations they elicit.

References

Arceneaux, K. and Stein, R. M. 2006. "Who is Held Responsible When Disaster Strikes?" *Journal of Urban Affairs*, 28: 43–53.

Arpan, L. M. and Roskos-Ewoldsen, D. R. 2005. "Stealing Thunder: Analysis of the Effects of Proactive Disclosure of Crisis Information." *Public Relations Review*, 31: 425–33.

Barton, A. H. 1969. *Communities in Disaster: A Sociological Analysis of Collective Stress Situations*. New York, NY: Doubleday.

Baumgartner, F. R. and Jones, B. D. 2002. *Policy Dynamics*. Chicago, Ill: University of Chicago Press.

Benoit, W. L. 1995. *Accounts, Excuses and Apologies: A Theory of Image Restoration*. Albany, NY: State University of New York Press.

Berlinski, S., Dewan, T. and Dowding, K. 2010. "The Impact of Individual and Collective Performance on Ministerial Tenure." *Journal of Politics*, 72: 559–71.

Birkland, T. A. 2007. *Lessons of Disaster: Policy Change After Catastrophic Events*. Washington, DC: Georgetown University Press.

Boin, A., 't Hart, P., and McConnell, A. 2009. "Crisis Exploitation: Political and Policy Impacts of Framing Contests." *Journal of European Public Policy*, 16: 81–106.

Boin, A., 't Hart, P., Stern, E., and Sundelius, B. 2005. *The Politics of Crisis Management: Public Leadership under Pressure*. Cambridge: Cambridge University Press.

Boin, A., McConnell, A., and 't Hart, P. 2008. *Governing After Crisis: The Politics of Investigation, Accountability and Learning*. Cambridge: Cambridge University Press.

Boudes, T. and Laroche, H. 2009. "Taking off the Heat: Narrative Sensemaking in Post-crisis Inquiry Reports." *Organization Studies*, 30: 377–96.

Bovens, M. 2010. "Two Concepts of Accountability: Accountability as a Virtue and as a Mechanism." *West European Politics*, 33: 946–67.

Bovens, M., 't Hart, P., Dekker, S., and Verheuvel, G. 1999. The Politics of Blame Avoidance: Defensive Tactics in a Dutch Crime-Fighting Fiasco, pp. 123–47 in *When Things Go Wrong:Organizational Failures and Breakdowns*, ed. H. K. Anheier. London: Sage.

Brändström, A. and Kuipers, S. 2003. "From 'Normal Incidents' to Political Crises: Understanding the Selective Politicization of Policy Failures." *Government and Opposition*, 38: 279–305.

Brändström, A., Kuipers, S. and Daléus, P. 2008. The Politics of Blame Management in Scandinavia After the Tsunami Disaster, pp. 114–47 in *Governing After Crisis:The Politics of Investigation, Accountability and Learning*, eds. A. Boin, P. 't Hart, and A. McConnell. Cambridge: Cambridge University Press.

Busenberg, G. 1999. "The Evolution of Vigilance: Disasters, Sentinels and Policy Change." *Environmental Politics*, 8: 90–109.

Claeys, A. S. and Cauberghe, V. 2012. "Crisis Response and Crisis Timing Strategies, Two Sides of the Same Coin." *Public Relations Review*, 38: 83–8.

Clarke, Rt. Hon Lord Justice 2000. *Thames Safety Inquiry: Final report*. London: HMSO, Cm 4558.

Coombs, W. T. 2007. "Protecting Organization Reputation During a Crisis." *Corporate Reputation Review*, 10: 163–76.

Dekker, S. 2007. *Just Culture: Balancing Safety and Accountability*. Aldershot: Ashgate.

Dowding, K. and Kang, W. T. 1998. "Ministerial Resignations 1945–1997." *Public Administration*, 76: 411–29.

Drabek, T. E. 2009. *The Human Side of Disaster*. Boca Raton: CRC Press.

Duin, M. van. 1992. *Van Rampen Leren*. Den Haag: Haagse Drukkerij en Uitgeversmaatschappij.

Elliot, D. and McGuinness, M. 2001. "Public Inquiry: Panacea or Placebo?" *Journal of Contingencies and Crisis Management*, 10: 14–25.

Ellis, R. 1994. *Presidential Lightning Rods: The Politics of Blame Avoidance*. Lawrence, KS: University Press of Kansas.

Hart, P. 't 1993. "Symbols, Rituals and Power: The Lost Dimensions of Crisis Management." *Journal of Contingencies and Crisis Management*, 1: 36–50.

Hearit, K. M. 2006. *Crisis Management by Apology: Corporate Response to Allegations of Wrongdoing*. Mahwah, NJ: Lawrence Erlbaum Associates.

Heyse, L., Resodihardjo, S., Lantink, T., and Lettinga, B. 2006. *Reform in Europe: Breaking the Barriers in Government*. Aldershot: Ashgate.

Hood, C. 2002. "The Risk Game and the Blame Game." *Government and Opposition*, 37: 15–37.

Hood, C. 2011. *The Blame Game: Spin, Bureaucracy, and Self-Preservation in Government*. Princeton, NJ: Princeton University Press.

Hood, C. and Lodge, M. 2006. *The Politics of Public Service Bargains: Reward, Competency, Loyalty—and Blame*. Oxford: Oxford University Press.

Hood, C., Jennings, W., Dixon, R., Hogwood, B., and Beeston, C. 2009. "Testing Times: Exploring Staged Responses and the Impact of Blame Management Strategies in Two Examination Fiasco Cases." *European Journal of Political Research*, 48: 695–722.

James, O. and John, P. 2007. "Public Management Performance Information and Electoral Support for Incumbent English Local Governments." *Journal of Public Administration Research and Theory*, 17: 567–80.

Jones, D. 2000. *Sultans of Spin: The Media and the New Labour Government*. London: Orion Books.

McGraw, K. M. 1991. "Managing Blame: An Experimental Test of the Effects of Political Accounts." *American Political Science Review*, 85: 1133–57.

Nobles, M. 2008. *The Politics of Official Apologies*. Cambridge: Cambridge University Press.

Nohrstedt, D. 2011. Uncertainty, Accountability, and the Conduct of Post-Crisis Inquiries, pp. 199–216 in *Ethics and Crisis Management*, ed. L. Svedin. Charlotte: Information Age Publishing.

Nohrstedt, D. and Weible, C. M. 2010. "The Logic of Policy Change After Crisis: Proximity and Subsystem Interaction." *Risk, Hazards & Crisis in Public Policy*, 1: 1–32.

Olmeda, J. A. 2008. A Reversal of Fortune: Blame Games and Framing Contests After the 3/11 Terrorist Attacks in Madrid, pp. 62–84 in *Governing After Crisis: The Politics of Investigation, Accountability and Learning*, eds. A. Boin, P. 't Hart, and A. McConnell. Cambridge: Cambridge University Press.

Parker, C. and Dekker, S. 2008. September 11 and Post-crisis Investigation, pp. 255–84 in *Governing After Crisis: The Politics of Investigation, Accountability and Learning*, eds. A. Boin, P. 't Hart, and A. McConnell. Cambridge: Cambridge University Press.

Perry, R. W. and Quarantelli, E. L. 2005. *What is a Disaster? New Answers to Old Questions*. Philadelphia, PA: XLibris Press.

Prasser, S. 2006. *Royal Commissions and Public Policy in Australia*. Chatswood: Butterworths.

Preston, T. 2008. Weathering the Politics of Responsibility and Blame: The Bush Administration and its Response to Hurricane Katrina, pp. 33–61 in *Governing After Crisis: The Politics of Investigation, Accountability and Learning*, eds. A. Boin, P. 't Hart, and A. McConnell. Cambridge: Cambridge University Press.

Quarantelli, E. L. 1998. *What is a Disaster? Perspectives on the Question*. New York: Routledge.

Reason, J. 2008. *The Human Contribution*. Farnham: Ashgate.

Schwartz, R. and Sulitzeanu-Kenan, R. 2004. "Managerial Values and Accountability Pressures: Challenges of Crisis and Disaster." *Journal of Public Administration Research and Theory*, 14: 79–102.

Stark, A. 2010. "Legislatures, Legitimacy and Crises." *Journal of Contingencies and Crisis Management*, 18: 2–13.

Stark, A. 2011. "The Tradition of Ministerial Responsibility and its Role in the Bureaucratic Management of Crises." *Public Administration*, 89: 1148–63.

Steinberg, T. 2000. *Acts of God: The Unnatural History of Natural Disaster in America*. New York: Oxford University Press.

Sulitzeanu-Kenan, R. 2006. "If They Get it Right: An Experimental Test of the Effects of the Appointment and Reports of UK Inquiry Committees." *Public Administration*, 84: 623–53.

Sulitzeanu-Kenan, R. 2007. "Scything the Grass: Agenda Setting Consequences of Appointing Public Inquiries in the UK." *Policy & Politics*, 35: 629–50.

Sulitzeanu-Kenan, R. 2010. "Reflection in the Shadow of Blame: When Do Politicians Appoint Commissions of Inquiry?" *British Journal of Political Science*, 40: 613–34.

Weaver, K. 1986. "The Politics of Blame Avoidance." *Journal of Public Policy*, 6: 371–98.

Weick, K. E. and Sutcliffe, K. M. 2007. *Managing the Unexpected: Resilient Performance in an Age of Uncertainty*. San Francisco, CA: Wiley and Sons.

Weller, P. 1994. *Royal Commissions and the Making of Public Policy in Australia*. Melbourne: Macmillan.

Yates, S. 1998. "Attributions About the Causes and Consequences of Cataclysmic Events." *Journal of Personal & Interpersonal Loss*, 3: 7–24.

CHAPTER 37

ACCOUNTABILITY AND BLAME-AVOIDANCE

CHRISTOPHER HOOD

BLAME-AVOIDANCE: ACCOUNTABILITY'S EVIL TWIN?

ACCOUNTABILITY is an abstract noun that notoriously has many shades of meaning, partly because of all the various adjectives that human ingenuity can attach to it (Romzek and Dubnik 1998; Behn 2001; Koppell 2005, 2011). But one of those meanings, and perhaps the commonest one in practice, denotes ways of pinning down blame in the sense of identifying responsibility for what is seen as avoidable harm or loss by some individual or group. After all, just as "leadership" is most frequently mentioned in conjunction with the words "lack of," calls for "accountability" in practice usually come in the aftermath of accidents, disasters, and policy failures. More formally, Pollitt (2003, 89) has defined the essence of accountability as some sort of communicative interaction among "accountors" and "accountees" in which the former evaluate and judge the latters' behavior in some way.

By contrast, blame-avoidance is a compound noun whose range of meanings has not been elaborated by scholars to the same extent as that for accountability. That is perhaps because in its current form at least it has not been in the language of political science for so long. The term itself only dates from the 1980s, although the underlying concept is of course much older than that (Weaver 1986, 1988; Hood 2002, 2011, 15). It ordinarily denotes ways of trying to minimize, evade, or transfer culpability for harm or loss perceived to have been avoidable, and in Weaver's usage to a common tendency on the part of politicians to prefer blame-avoidance over credit-claiming where the two come into conflict. Confusingly, the words accountability and blame-avoidance can both denote an *outcome* (responsibility successfully identified, or blame successfully avoided) and an *activity* or *process* (boxes ticked, procedures followed, excuses given, attempts made to pass the buck, etc.). But outcome and activity are by no means the same thing.

At first sight those two terms look like mirror-image concepts in several ways other than the one already mentioned. Accountability is a word that has mostly positive resonance, meaning that as well as its various analytic meanings it has strong normative connotations as a feature of "good governance" (Bovens 2005; Koppell 2011, 55). It is true that an increasing number of writers on the topic seek to distinguish between "good" and "bad" accountability or argue accountability can be taken too far. Examples include Anechiarico and Jacobs' (1996) claim that proliferating anti-corruption laws and procedures at some point start to undermine effective government; Dubnick's (2005) claim that more accountability does not necessarily produce better government; Mansbridge's (2010) attack on sanctions-based accountability as potentially subversive of democratic pluralism; Koppell's (2005, 3) argument that multiple contradictory accountabilities lead to bureaucratic dysfunctions. Related observations about the potentially negative effects of bureaucratized accountability systems include criticisms of "management to audit" (Power 1997) and of performance indicator regimes that are so complex and frequently changed that they are impenetrable to all but a small group of insiders (Pollitt 2011). But even though Mansbridge (2010) boldly uses the title "Against Accountability" for her analysis, none of these writers goes so far as to dismiss accountability altogether—only what they consider to be the *wrong kind* of accountability. Blame-avoidance, on the other hand, is a term for something often generally considered negative or disreputable, which would not happen in some imagined ideal world of upright behavior, honest admission of mistakes, and just sanctions imposed on those office-holders whose conduct or judgment is found to be lacking (Hood 2011, 163ff). Up to now, "wrong kind of" arguments have seldom been made about blame-avoidance, though I have argued (Hood 2011) that there are "good" as well as "bad" variants of blame-avoidance behavior.

Accountability often further denotes an *intended* effect that institutional arrangements are designed or presumed to bring about (and reformers claim will be enhanced by changes they propose), while blame-avoidance often denotes unintended or unwanted ways in which individuals or groups somehow manage to slip through a net to escape the censure or sanctions that accountability systems are designed to trigger. At first sight the two concepts thus seem to be in many ways symmetrical, even though the two epistemic worlds of accountability and blame-avoidance only partially intersect in political science and often use rather different terminology. Part of the reason for that "separate tables" relationship (in a well-known phrase used by Almond (1988) to denote fragmentation among political science subfields) between the two fields of study is that the epistemic world of accountability studies tends to be more closely linked to normative theory and to constitutional and public-law scholarship, whereas the epistemic world of blame-avoidance studies tends to be more closely linked to behavioral studies of politics and public policy and to draw in concepts from social psychology, particularly in relation to negativity bias and blame-attribution (Sulitzeanu-Kenan 2006).

So are accountability and blame-avoidance just opposite sides of the same coin; should we see blame-avoidance as accountability's evil twin? Even though they happen to have originated in different parts of the political science forest, could both of those ideas be more economically and less confusingly described by using a common terminology? At first sight there seems much to be said for making such a move. After all, both accountability and blame-avoidance are directional concepts, in that they involve attribution of responsibility in some sense to one or a set of actors. Both concepts also centrally involve counterfactuals, in the sense of trying to answer sometimes tricky causal questions about what might have happened in the absence of some key act of commission or omission by one or more actors. Both are concerned with contestable perceptions of harm and human agency. And both are temporally specific phenomena, in that much turns on when things happened, in what order, and who made what judgments on the basis of what information at what point in time.

However, this chapter argues that accountability and blame-avoidance are only mirror-image concepts up to a point. They are mirror images for that sense of accountability that denotes attempts to attribute responsibility for activities and outcomes and to bring about positive or negative consequences for those who have created value or loss that would not otherwise have occurred, and for that sense of blame-avoidance that denotes evasion or dilution of responsibility as an outcome of strategy or institutional architecture. But there are different ways of conceiving and defining both concepts in their respective analytic literatures, and the mirror image tends to disappear once we move to those alternatives. So this chapter aims to set out the analytic issues that arise both when accountability and blame-avoidance are mirror-image concepts and (perhaps more interestingly) when they are not.

ACCOUNTABILITY AND BLAME-AVOIDANCE AS MIRROR IMAGES

To the extent that accountability (in its pinning-down-blame sense) and blame-avoidance (in its wriggling-out-of-blame sense) are opposite sides of the same coin, we can think of the politics of responsibility as a cat-and-mouse game between accountability-seekers and blame-avoiders. Accountability-seeking/blame-avoidance games are of course central to electoral and public-opinion politics, for example when government ministers come under fire for their personal behavior or the alleged fiascos they have presided over (Hood et al. 2009). But such games also often figure in the design of institutions and even (perhaps especially) to the small print of public policy and service delivery in the byzantine world of organizational and corporate politics, for example in the architecture of risk regulation (Black 2005; Hood, Rothstein, and Baldwin 2001). In principle interaction between accountability-seekers and blame-avoiders could be modeled in a similar way to other well-known cat-and-mouse-type interactions, such as predator–prey dynamics, the evolution of viruses in response to new drug applications, or law enforcement games such as that between drivers seeking to outwit the traffic authorities and the counter-responses of those authorities.

If the logic of that line of thinking about accountability-seeking/blame-avoidance dynamics is to turn it into a formal model of interaction among rival strategizing parties, such an approach has not really been adopted either in the accountability or blame-avoidance literatures up to now (some limited formalization can be found in Sulitzeanu-Kenan and Hood 2005; Sulitzeanu-Kenan 2007; Hood et al. 2009). Part of the reason for that is that both the accountability and blame-avoidance literatures have hitherto tended to be dominated by qualitative case studies and the sort of conceptual analysis that eschews formal or game-theoretic modeling. Part of the reason is that the terrain over which the game is played—electoral politics, the organization of government, and the detailed design and operation of public policy—tends to be divided into different specialist political science bailiwicks, whose boundaries it is intellectually hazardous to cross in a world of specialized peer-reviewing. And part of the reason is the complication that (in contrast to, say, viruses and drug researchers or drivers and traffic police) the same players can be both accountability-seekers and blame-avoiders in the classic form of "blame game" in which two or more parties seek to put the blame on others, which makes neat modeling more difficult.

The point about drawing a parallel with predator–prey games and similar dynamics is that if we think about accountability and blame-avoidance as the outcome of interactions between rival strategizing parties we can in principle identify equilibria or at least limits both of accountability-seeking and blame-avoidance strategies. In a situation where for every blame-avoidance tactic, there is a corresponding accountability-sharpening response and vice versa, the two forces can ordinarily be expected to be in dynamic balance rather than for one ever to achieve outright victory over the other. Outcomes will fall somewhere between "perfect accountability" (an imaginary world in which no one ever escapes identification and culpability for actions that create avoidable harm or loss) and "perfect blame-avoidance" (an imaginary world in which "no one is responsible for anything that he does," as Jeremy Bentham (1983, 173–4) once famously complained about the institutional architecture and policy processes of early nineteenth-century British government).

An example of such dynamic balancing is the contest between increased transparency requirements in the form of Freedom of Information (FOI) laws (intended to sharpen the answerability of public bureaucracies and office-holders by removing opportunities for concealment of key information), and the corresponding counter-strategies by those exposed to FOI, for example increased use of organizational types not subject to FOI, such as private companies, less explicit record-keeping, and more centralized control over information (Roberts 2006). Another in the corporate world is the sharpening up of corporate governance requirements through elaborated governance codes and similar requirements in the 1980s and 1990s and corresponding counter-strategies by those at whom such measures were aimed, particularly in moves towards private equity institutions and the de-listing of formerly public companies.

If one possible analytic advantage from seeing accountability and blame-avoidance as mirror-image concepts is to focus on limits and equilibria more clearly than would arise if the two concepts were considered separately, another is the possibility of pinning down more clearly the social mechanisms that underpin accountability and blame-avoidance. For instance, if the literature of blame-avoidance distinguishes agency, presentational, and policy strategies as different ways of minimizing, shifting, sharing, or avoiding blame (Hood 2011), we should, on the mirror-image principle, be able to identify corresponding agency, presentational, and policy strategies for enhancing accountability.

Agency strategies denote the use of institutional architecture to shape responsibility. Much has been made in the blame-avoidance literature of the responsibility-avoiding possibilities of delegation to flak-catchers and lightning-rods (Ellis 1994). That theme, which goes back to Machiavelli (1961, 106), has been developed in rational-choice modeling, and its ultimate application takes the form of nominally private or independent militias or police forces operating as "unacknowledgeable means"(Mitchell 2004). But there are corresponding accountability-enhancing strategies that aim to counter such responses. Examples include no-delegation rules in law (as variants of Locke's (1980, 74) famous doctrine that "the Legislative can have no power to transfer their Authority of making laws, and place it in other hands") and requirements for principals to take responsibility for the actions of their agents (the vicarious liability principle, as in the doctrine of ministerial responsibility and often applied to other types of corporate responsibility).

Presentational strategies denote the framing of events and arguments to shape responsibility. Much has been made in the blame-avoidance literature of the responsibility-avoiding possibilities of spin-doctoring through devices such as careful timing, the use of diversions, and creative presentation (Kurtz 1998; Bovens et al. 1999; Crawford 2005). But there are corresponding accountability-enhancing strategies that aim to limit framing and presentational discretion, for example by imposing rules about what should be published when (for example in the time government office-holders have to prepare their responses to, or interpretations of, official statistics before they are published), thereby blocking off some of the opportunities to exercise the "dark arts" of spin-doctoring.

Policy strategies denote the use of policies and procedures to shape responsibility, and the blame-avoidance literature contains discussions of "avoidance" and "assurance" behavior, the former denoting avoidance of areas or people with a high blame risk and the latter denoting procedures that are designed to limit blame (Duke Law Journal 1971, 942; Bernzweig 1973). Those particular terms originate in the analysis of "defensive medicine," that is, the practice of medicine primarily for the purpose of minimizing the risk of malpractice claims, though other terms are often used for the same phenomena in other contexts. And here too there are corresponding accountability-enhancing strategies, for example in compelling individual rather than group decision-making through variations of the *einheitssystem*—the principle of single-person responsibility—stressed by classical authors such as Max Weber (1948) and Jeremy Bentham (1983), and enforcing record-keeping in the IT-age equivalent of the "registrar" function that Bentham saw as central to the rule of law. A modern example is the practice of recording each individual member's recommendations for interest-rate changes for some monetary policy committees advising central banks, such as that of the UK.

In all of those cases accountability enhancement and blame avoidance can be seen as involving inverse processes of engineering, using the same basic principles. But is that all there is to the relationship between accountability and blame-avoidance?

Beyond Polar Opposition Between Accountability and Blame-Avoidance: Spheres of Synergy

It has been argued above that much can be gained analytically from looking at accountability and blame-avoidance as opposite sides of the same coin or as some sort of zero-sum game in which gains to blame-avoiders mean corresponding losses to accountability-seekers and vice versa, and in which agency, presentational, and policy strategies can be used both for accountability and blame-avoidance. But as was pointed out at the outset, that opposition comes from taking only one, albeit common, meaning of accountability (as an attempt to pin down blame). If we consider other important meanings or dimensions of the A-word, that logical opposition tends to disappear, such that blame-avoidance and accountability can in principle run together in several ways, thus reinforcing rather than pulling against one another. Consider the following three examples.

One is the case where accountability is more concerned with explanation and diagnosis—the "answerability" dimension of accountability that many authors have identified (Marshall 1984)—than with establishing culpability. Indeed, the form of accountability that Mansbridge (2010) targets in her *Against Accountability* referred to earlier is precisely that which puts the emphasis on establishing culpability and applying sanctions, rather than the "answerability" form. Mansbridge sees that "sanctions model" as most applicable to "relatively corrupt" regimes, as against a less heavy-duty approach of simply relying on intrinsically motivated representatives on the basis of a shared sense of purpose. From a different part of the intellectual forest, Tim Besley's (2006) *Principled Agents* makes exactly the same point, using social sorting theory to challenge conventional principal–agent assumptions about voter–politician relationships in democracies, which rest on presuppositions of inherent conflict.

Now if failure to secure re-election is counted as a sanction, elected representatives may well be highly motivated to pursue blame-avoidance strategies. Indeed, much of Kent Weaver's (1986) analysis of the blame-avoidance approach relates precisely to the behavior of elected politicians fearful of the effects of negativity bias (that is, the tendency for negative information to produce more political activity than positive information) and retrospective voting (that is, voting that focuses on past performance of individuals and parties rather than promises for the future) on their prospects for re-election. And that in turn will tend to translate itself into incentives passed down to bureaucrats to pay more attention to avoiding blame than claiming credit. But even then, if the emphasis on blame-avoidance activity results in the production of valid reasons why no one should be to blame for any given instance of perceived harm or loss, that outcome can itself be accountability-enhancing in the sense that action or inaction has been convincingly explained and justified to the relevant "accountors."

Alternatively, even if issues of blame cannot be argued away, accountability and blame-avoidance will not be polar opposites to the extent that that "answerability" dimension can be separated from the fault-finding and sanctioning dimension of accountability. And indeed it is often argued that the only way to obtain the quality of information about past errors or malfunctions that can serve as the basis for effective learning and system redesign is precisely to remove blame and fault from the equation, so that provision of information is not hampered by injunctions, lawyers' letters, "Fifth Amendment" silences to avoid self-incrimination, and all the other forms of legal defensiveness that prevent free and timely flow of the kind of information needed for effective corrective action to be taken. That is why promises of immunity from prosecution often figure so large in efforts to secure information in criminal inquiries, and also why no-fault reporting is so commonly identified as a key feature of "safety culture" and "high-reliability organizations" in organization theory (Sagan 1993). The same sort of thinking lies behind criticisms of the "blame and shame" approach to dealing with medical failures (Bristol Royal Infirmary Report 2001) and the related idea of blaming systems rather than individuals for such failures (Braithwaite, Healy, and Dwan 2005, 18). A well-known practical application of the "no-fault model" of answerability is the various forms of voluntary and anonymous reporting systems for safety-critical mishaps such as medical errors and aviation near-misses, which in principle allow for speedy analysis and system modifications without years of convoluted or deadlocked inquiry (Webb et al. 1993; Kaplan et al. 1998). It is hardly surprising that rates of incident reporting tend to be higher under anonymous or non-punitive conditions, for instance in those US states where critical incident reporting counts as "peer review" activity that is protected from legal discovery processes (Wald and Shojania 2001, 46).

But we know relatively little about what Douglas (1992: 16), perhaps ironically, called "the conditions for these delightful no-fault cultures." Such systems often tend to break down politically when they are challenged by those who advocate the "culpability" approach to accountability, and anonymous error-reporting systems are always vulnerable to collapse under legal, political, and media pressure when particularly serious faults come to light. Indeed, the trade-off between the acquisition of timely information that can be used for swiftly improving safety or performance and the establishment of culpability at a standard that permits legal or formal sanctions to be applied is a well-known general dilemma in the design of accountability regimes. A relevant example, occurring as this paper was first drafted, was the high-profile shipwreck of a large Italian cruise liner (the *Costa Concordia*) off the coast of Tuscany in 2012, in consequence of the vessel sailing close to Isola del Giglio to greet the inhabitants and accidentally running onto a reef, resulting in 34 deaths. Commenting on the post-wreck recriminations, Admiral John Lang, former UK chief inspector of marine accidents commented that "the concept of a marine accident has been overtaken by the need to find criminal behavior" (*Daily Telegraph* 17 January 2012, letters page). What Lang was pointing out was that important information that could be used to enhance safety systems in large cruise liners (such as the design of the boats) was tending to be sidelined or ignored in the drive to place all the legal responsibility for the accident onto a single individual's alleged errors of judgment. The general point is that accountability systems designed to promote learning and adaptation on the basis of rich information flows may have to stress the "answerability" dimension of accountability at the expense of the "culpability" dimension, and to the extent that they do, blame-avoidance and accountability will not be polar opposites.

A second way in which blame-avoidance (construed in this case as activity rather than outcome) and accountability can go hand in hand is through the perhaps unintended effects of organizational efforts to avoid or shift blame by at least some key players. Here we need to return to the distinction made earlier between blame-avoidance as activity and blame-avoidance as outcome. If blame avoidance activity results in blame being shifted from less to more appropriate "blamees," that activity can be conducive to sharper and more targeted forms of accountability. An example is the delegation of responsibility by high-level office-holders in an attempt to shift blame away from themselves—perhaps the most commonly discussed "agency strategy" for blame-avoidance. In some conditions, such delegation can result in that responsibility falling onto the shoulders of individuals with more relevant expertise than the delegators, or more ability to affect the outcomes of the system concerned, and so targets accountability more efficiently. By "efficiency" is meant placing the obligation to answer and perhaps to face sanctions as well, onto those best placed to prevent avoidable loss or harm in any given system, in the same way as is implied by a long tradition of discussing where legal liability should be placed among various parties in tort or delict systems (Hood 2011, 172).

In particular, it is often argued that the traditional "ministerial responsibility" doctrine of Westminster model systems of government, which holds that the minister is expected to be answerable (and in some more extreme variants of the doctrine, culpable as well) for every action taken by his or her department, will tend to make ministers over-accountable and senior civil servants under-accountable if it is followed strictly. That convention often gives ministers concerned with blame-avoidance an incentive to hive off parts of their departments to separate agencies under independent control or to expert advisory bodies, as happened for example in the UK over food safety in the aftermath of the BSE crisis of the 1990s, over central banking some years after the British pound crashed out of the then European Exchange Rate Mechanism in 1992, and over the deportation of released foreign convicts in the aftermath of a prisoner-release scandal that claimed a senior minister's scalp in the mid-2000s. When delegation of that type occurs, designed to shift blame from ministers to agency heads, the outcome can in principle be one that redresses that traditional over- and under-accountability problem, by forcing the experts and officials who make the key decisions to be directly answerable for their actions and judgments rather than only through ministers.

The problem that commonly prevents that sort of blame-shifting by ministers from improving the efficiency of accountability in the system of executive government is that the distribution of powers is often left blurred or ambiguous in practice, meaning that blame does not stay shifted to the delegatees when a blame crisis strikes. Unless such delegation by ministers takes a relatively "hard" constitutional form, for example to other elected bodies, by systems of appointment that limit government influence on office-holders (such as no-reappointment rules) or by a clean break between the responsibilities of an agency and those of the ministry it has been carved out of, the result in practice can be very different from the theoretical possibility of more efficiently targeted accountability. When those conditions do not apply, messy delegation arrangements can easily lead either to a blame-avoidance outcome arising from an inconclusive blame game (in which delegators accuse delegatees, and delegatees in turn accuse delegators of backdoor influence) or to an outcome in which it is ministers who become under-accountable for their string-pulling behind the scenes and civil servants, managers, or experts who become over-accountable for decisions they were not wholly responsible for, producing a new accountability imbalance that is the opposite of the previous one (Barker 1998).

Another case in which the pursuit of blame-avoidance can in principle serve to enhance accountability is when a desire to avoid blame leads to "protocolization" of standards of conduct, so that beleaguered individuals can offer a "following rules or best practice guidelines" defense when they find themselves under fire for some adverse outcome. In principle such developments can heighten accountability by making standards of proper behavior clearer. The stock examples of this kind of blame-avoidance behavior are the "due diligence" approach to financial transactions, originating in a key clause of the 1933 Securities and Exchange Act in the United States, and the "assurance" approach to defensive medicine in the United States that has been already mentioned, arising from changes made by several US state Supreme Courts in the 1960s to the rules of evidence for medical malpractice. But such behavior is widely observable in many other domains as well. If the rules and guidelines that emerge from such a process are properly grounded on a model of effective behavior, such developments can make it easier to pin down responsibility for careless or willfully idiosyncratic behavior. The problem in practice with such arrangements is that that box-ticking to avoid blame and liability can often distort behavior and make it harder to challenge poor exercise of judgment. It is possible that we could draw a parallel with what has been said by some about target-setting for public services (Barber 2007, 273), that such practices may help to move aggregate performance from very low to more adequate levels, but are much less likely to facilitate excellent performance, but that possibility has not been systematically explored up to now.

In a third way, blame-avoidance activity can in principle go hand in hand with accountability in both the answerability and culpability sense, in conditions where "blame games" work as part of a social discovery process. A rough parallel can be drawn here with the idea (typically associated with Friedrich Hayek) of markets as social discovery processes about values, wants and trade-offs. Hayek (1978, 170–90) and others argued that markets will often work better as discovery systems than alternatives such as expert planning and coordination of economic processes, and Charles Lindblom (1965) controversially advanced a parallel argument about the "intelligence" of partisan mutual adjustment relative to expert determination in developing public policy. Exactly the same sort of argument can be made about the "blame games" that result from efforts to dodge blame, in the form of mutual finger-pointing among various parties who are in the frame for possible censure over some avoidable loss or harm resulting from acts of commission or omission. If alternative methods of establishing culpability, for example by expert determination or complete specification of all the relevant rules of engagement in advance, are inherently limited for the same sort of reasons as apply to central economic planning and coordination, then blame games can serve as discovery processes that can help to sharpen rather than to blunt accountability in all of its senses. But, as Schillemans and Bovens (2011, 7) point out, blame games by no means always effectively perform such a discovery function, often serving to obscure rather than to clarify responsibility. The problem for analysts of blame and accountability is then to explore what distinguishes "good" blame games from "bad" ones, and whereas, as was mentioned earlier, there is a growing literature on "good" and "bad" accountability, a parallel analysis for mutual blaming is still in its infancy.

CULTURES OF ACCOUNTABILITY AND BLAME-AVOIDANCE

This chapter has argued that while there are ways in which blame-avoidance and accountability are mirror-images—the more you have of one, the less you have of the other—there are important senses of both concepts that do not lead them to be polar opposites. If blame-avoidance is defined as activity rather than outcome, it can in principle be compatible with various forms of accountability, both in the sense of "answerability" and of "culpability," dependent on the discovery effects of blame games and the ability of blame-avoidance activity to shift responsibility definitively. So we cannot see blame-avoidance as simply accountability's evil twin. Nor could we simply abolish one or other of these two terms without impoverishing our ability to describe and analyze important aspects of institutional processes and behavior.

There are however, limits to the kind of analysis that catalogues types and mechanisms of accountability and blame-avoidance in a culture-free way. Many of the more challenging questions about both accountability and blame-avoidance—whether as mirror images or complementary phenomena—concern the way that such processes and outcomes are shaped by variations in culture and attitudes rather than treating accountability or blame-avoidance as if they were Platonic essences. Indeed, the anthropologist Mary Douglas's well-known work on cultural theory clearly brings out their variability, since she conceived cultural variation in terms of different forms of accountability and blame. As she put it (1990, 10–11):

> Cultural theory starts by assuming that a culture is a system of persons holding one another mutually accountable. A person tries to live at some level of being held accountable...which matches the level at which that person wants to hold others accountable. From this angle, culture is fraught with the political implications of mutual accountability.

It follows from such analysis that both accountability and blame will vary from one cultural setting to another. Douglas (1990, 15–16) suggested that, "In an individualist culture, the weak are going to carry the blame for what happens to them; in a hierarchy, the deviants; in a sect, aliens and...faction leaders." By that she meant that each of the four basic cultural types she identified comprised its own distinctive way of holding others to account and for directing blame about harm and risk, and that insight has yet to be fully incorporated into mainstream studies either of accountability or of blame-avoidance.

Accordingly, hierarchist cultures will be predisposed to have accountability systems that emphasize rule-following and will see accountability as something to be conducted by established authorities following proper procedures. They will assume that potential pathologies of accountability systems, as identified by Dubnick (2005) and other critics, can be tackled by finding "the right kind" of accountability or taking it up to some appropriate level that can be determined by the relevant professoriate, and will tend to blame those who do not follow the rules or expert-defined best practice guidelines. Corresponding blame-avoidance strategies will tend to emphasize the formal allocation of responsibilities in institutional organograms and to stress procedural rule-compliant defenses based on agreed "best practice."

Individualist cultures, by contrast, will be predisposed to accountability systems that put the emphasis on individual judgment and choice, and are more likely to see accountability as a process of contestation rather than something for which agreed standards can be established by any expert authority. They will favor the multiple and competing accountabilities that numerous writers on the subject have commented on (Schillemans and Bovens 2011), in which various rival accountability bureaucracies and committees slug it out for the time and attention of accountees. They will think of "accountability to the market" as more important than accountability to politicians, tribunals, or ethics committees, and blame will tend to focus on the poor judgment or inept choices of individuals. Corresponding blame-avoidance strategies will emphasize the limits of mutual obligation, for example through the use of disclaimers (those who don't know the rules or don't take the trouble to read the small print have no-one to blame but themselves for what happens to them) and through attributing harm or loss to "market forces."

Egalitarian cultures, in turn, will be predisposed to have accountability systems that put the emphasis on sideways or downwards answerability, seeing it principally as a way of making individuals answer to peer groups and making powerful private and public organizations answer to local community activists. They will tend to blame those outside the group or the community (or those who are portrayed as traitors within the group, such as leaders of minority factions) for any harm or loss. Corresponding blame-avoidance strategies will tend to collectivize responsibility by institutional partnership arrangements and group working methods (the horse may be a camel, but at least it was designed by a committee meeting in which everyone had their say), institutional arrangements of partnership and public-good justifications.

Mary Douglas did not spell out in the passages quoted above how she saw accountability and blaming working in fatalist cultures, and the same goes for most cultural theorists who follow her approach (such as Thompson, Ellis, and Wildavsky 1990). It can be argued that fatalists will tend to see accountability as a matter of chance and happenstance rather than something that can be guaranteed by any particular doctrine of governance or institutional design, and that is the logical corollary of the lack of faith fatalists have in established authority, individual judgment, or the wisdom of groups. But I have argued earlier (Hood 1998, 145–67) that there is some fatalist logic in institutional designs that emphasize random processes (for example in posting individuals around ramified field organizations, such that no-one can easily predict who they will be working with or when, or other comparable processes, such as unpredictable selection of peer-reviewers in the academic world). Corresponding blame-avoidance strategies will emphasize the workings of chance, for example in "Act of God" excuses, reliance on confusion and complexity in organizational arrangements as a source of protection, and reliance on sortition or random choice selection or allocation processes (Duxbury 1999). Examples include use of lotteries for work permits, conscription, or allocation of school places, rather than forms of rationing or allocation that rely on factors other than chance.

Such analysis of cultural variation can help to develop the mirror-image view of accountability and blame-avoidance, in that each cultural bias can be expected to have its matching forms of accountability and blame-avoidance. But it can also help us to go beyond the mirror-image view when cultural biases conflict or mingle, because what gets you off the hook of blame from one cultural starting-point may only dig you into a deeper accountability hole in another setting.

REFERENCES

Almond, G. A. 1988. "Separate Tables: Schools and Sects in Political Science." *PS: Political Science and Politics*, 21: 828–42.

Anechiarico, F. and Jacobs, J. B. 1996. *The Pursuit of Absolute Integrity: How Corruption Control Makes Government Ineffective*. Chicago: University of Chicago Press.

Barber, M. 2007. *Instruction to Deliver: Tony Blair, Public Services and the Challenge of Achieving Targets*. London: Politico's.

Barker, A. 1998. "Political Responsibility for UK Prison Security: Ministers Escape Again." *Public Administration*, 76: 1–23.

Behn, R. D. 2001. *Rethinking Democratic Accountability*. Washington, DC: Brookings Institution.

Bentham, J. 1983. *Constitutional Code*. Oxford: Clarendon.

Bernzweig, E. 1973. *Defensive Medicine Appendix: Report of the Secretary's Commission on Medical Malpractice*. DHEW Publication No. 73–89. Washington, DC: US Government Printing Office.

Besley, T. 2006. *Principled Agents: The Political Economy of Good Government*. Oxford: Oxford University Press.

Black, J. 2005. "The Emergence of Risk Based Regulation and the New Public Management in the UK." *Public Law*, 15: 512–49.

Bovens, M. 2005. Public Accountability, pp. 182–208 in *The Oxford Handbook of Public Management*, eds. E. Ferlie, L. Lynn, and C. Pollitt. Oxford: Oxford University Press.

Braithwaite, J., Healy, J., and Dwan, K. 2005. *The Governance of Health Safety and Quality*. Canberra: Commonwealth of Australia.

Bristol Royal Infirmary Report. 2001. *Learning from Bristol: The Report of the Public Inquiry into Children's Heart Surgery at the Bristol Royal Infirmary 1984–1995*. London: HMSO, Cm 5207.

Crawford, C. 2005. *Attack the Messenger: How Politicians Turn You Against the Media*. Lanham, MD: Rowman and Littlefield.

Douglas, M. 1990. "Risk as a Forensic Resource." *Daedalus:Journal of the American Academy of Arts and Sciences*, 119 (4): 1–16.

Daily Telegraph. 17 January 2012. *Letters to the editor*.

Douglas, M. 1992. *Risk and Blame: Essays in Cultural Theory*. New York: Routledge.

Dubnick, M. 2005. "Accountability and the Promise of Performance: In Search of the Mechanisms." *Public Performance and Management Review*, 28: 376–417.

Duke Law Journal. 1971. "The Medical Malpractice Threat: A Study of Defensive Medicine." *Duke Law Journal*, 5: 939–93.

Duxbury, N. 1999. *Random Justice: On Lotteries and Legal Decision-Making*. Oxford: Oxford University Press.

Ellis, R. 1994. *Presidential Lightning Rods: The Politics of Blame Avoidance*. Kansas: Kansas University Press.

Hayek, F. A. 1978. Competition as a Discovery Procedure, pp. 179–90 in *New Studies in Philosophy, Politics, Economics and the History of Ideas*, ed. F. A. Hayek. Chicago: University of Chicago Press.

Hood, C. 1998. *The Art of the State: Culture, Rhetoric and Public Management*. Oxford: Clarendon.

Hood, C. 2002. "The Risk Game and the Blame Game." *Government and Opposition*, 37: 15–37.

Hood, C. 2011. *The Blame Game: Spin, Bureaucracy and Self-Preservation in Government*. Princeton: Princeton University Press.

Hood, C., Rothstein, H., and Baldwin, R. 2001. *The Government of Risk: Understanding Risk Regulation Regimes*. Oxford: Oxford University Press.

Hood, C., Jennings, W., Dixon, R., Hogwood, B., and Beeston, C. 2009. "Testing Times: Exploring Staged Responses and the Impact of Blame Management Strategies in Two Exam Fiasco Cases." *European Journal of Political Research*, 48: 695–722.

Kaplan, H. S., Battles, J. B., Schaaf, T. W. van der, Shea, C. E., and Mercer, S. Q. 1998. "Identification and Classification of the Causes of Events in Transfusion Medicine." *Transfusion*, 38: 1071–81.

Koppell, J. G. 2005. "Pathologies of Accountability: ICANN and the Challenges of 'Multiple Accountabilities Disorder.'" *Public Administration Review*, 65: 94–109.

Koppell, J. G. 2011. Accountability for Global Governance Organizations, pp. 55–77 in *Accountable Government: Problems and Promises*, eds. M. J. Dubnick and H. G. Frederickson. New York: M.E. Sharpe.

Kurtz, H. 1998. *Spin Cycle: Inside the Clinton Propaganda Machine*. New York: Free Press.

Lindblom, C. 1965. *The Intelligence of Democracy*. New York: Free Press.

Locke, J. 1980. *Second Treatise of Civil Government*, ed. C. B. Macpherson. Indianapolis, Indiana: Hackett Publishing Company; originally published 1690.

Machiavelli, N. 1961. *The Prince*. Harmondsworth: Penguin.

Mansbridge, J. 2010. *Against Accountability*. Max Weber Lectures 2010–2011, European University Institute. Accessed February 2012 <http://www.youtube.com/watch?v=6whJpAMZPkE>.

Marshall, G. 1984. *Constitutional Conventions: The Rules and Forms of Political Accountability*. Oxford: Oxford University Press.

Mitchell, N. 2004. *Agents of Atrocity: Leaders, Followers and the Violation of Human Rights in Civil Wars*. Basingstoke: Palgrave Macmillan.

Pollitt, C. 2003. *The Essential Public Manager*. London: Open University Press.

Pollitt, C. 2011. Performance Blight and the Tyranny of Light? Accountability in Advanced Performance Measurement Regimes, pp. 81–97 in *Accountable Government: Problems and Promises*, eds. M. J. Dubnick and H. G. Frederickson. New York: M.E. Sharpe.

Power, M. 1997. *The Audit Society*. Oxford: Oxford University Press.

Roberts, A. 2006. *Blacked Out: Government Secrecy in the Information Age*. New York: Cambridge University Press.

Romzek, B. S. and Dubnik, M. J. 1998. Accountability, pp. 6–11 in *International Encyclopedia of Public Policy and Administration. Vol. 1:A-C*, ed. J. M. Shafritz. Boulder: Westview Press.

Sagan, S. 1993. *The Limits of Safety*. Princeton: Princeton University Press.

Schillemans, T. and Bovens, M. 2011. The Challenge of Multiple Accountability: Does Redundancy Lead to Overload?, pp. 3–21 in *Accountable Governance: Problems and Promises*, eds. M. J. Dubnick and H. G. Frederickson. New York: M.E. Sharpe.

Sulitzeanu-Kenan, R. 2006. "If They Get it Right: An Experimental Test of the Effects of UK Public Inquiries' Appointment and Reports." *Public Administration*, 84: 623–53.

Sulitzeanu-Kenan, R. 2007. "Scything the Grass: Agenda-Setting Consequences of Appointing Public Inquiries in the UK: A Longitudinal Analysis." *Policy and Politics*, 35: 629–50.

Sulitzeanu-Kenan, R. and Hood, C. 2005. *Blame-Avoidance with Adjectives? Motivation, Opportunity, Activity and Outcome*. In ECPR (European Consortium for Political Research) Joint Sessions. Granada, April 2005.

Thompson, M., Ellis, R., and Wildavsky, A. 1990. *Cultural Theory*. Boulder, Westview Press.

Wald, H. and Shojania, K. G. 2001. Incident Reporting, pp. 41–50 in *Making Health Care Safer: A Critical Analysis of Patient Safety Practices*, eds. K. G. Shojania, B. W. Duncan, K. M. McDonald, and R. M. Wachter. Rockville, MD: Agency for Healthcare Research and Quality.

Weaver, R. K. 1986. "The Politics of Blame-Avoidance." *Journal of Public Policy*, 6: 371–98.

Webb, R. K., Currie, M., Morgan, C. A., Williamson, J. A., Mackay, P., Russell, W. J., and Runciman, W. B. 1993. "The Australian Incident Reporting Study: An Analysis of 2000 Incident Reports." *Anaesthesia and Intensive Care*, 21: 520–8.

Weber, M. 1948. *From Max Weber: Essays in Sociology*, eds. H. H. Gerth and C. W. Mills. London: Routledge and Kegan Paul.

CHAPTER 38

....

ACCOUNTABILITY AND TRUST

....

DOROTHEA GREILING

Introduction

....

If we look at the relationship between public accountability and trust, there are authors who regard public accountability as a crucial factor for improving trust in the public sector (Kim 2005, 622; Fard and Rostamy 2007, 322; for a performance-trust model see Bouckaert and Halligan 2008, 16). Citizen trust is regarded by many researchers in Western Europe as indispensable for the functioning of governments (Bouckaert and Van de Walle 2003, 33). Trust is seen as the glue that keeps the system together or as a litmus test of how well government is performing in the view of the citizens (Bovens and Wille 2011, 47), although there is also a need of critical and questioning distrust in order to keep democracy in a good shape (Bovens and Wille 2011; Van der Meer and Dekker 2011, 95). Political trust tends to be high in the Nordic countries and lower in Central and Eastern Europe (Van der Meer 2010; Van der Meer and Dekker 2011, 95).

Applying the principal–agent theory it can be argued that public accountability with its control-focus is mistrust-driven and therefore directed at identifying shortcomings in the performance of politicians or public managers. As a result, mistrust in the public sector has increased. Back in the 1980s the mismatch between the citizens' needs and the services a government provided resulted in low citizen trust (Van de Walle 2011, 314). To improve trust, short-term explicit standards of performance, additional accountability levels, and numerous audit and inspection mechanisms were introduced. Thus a steering model was launched which is based on the assumption that self-interested public officials cannot be trusted (2011, 316). Under Public Governance models the relationship between public accountability and trust is likewise far from clear, as Public Governance became popular at a time when a growing range of "wicked" problems appeared, which traditional governmental mechanisms could not solve (Bovaird and Loeffler 2007, 371).

It would be naïve to assume that in the Public Governance approach all forms of citizen participation are automatically enablers for increasing citizen trust.

These standpoints demonstrate that the relationship between trust and public accountability is far from straightforward. As outlined below, trust can be the dependent as well as the independent variable. Before going into more details, the next section focuses on some terminological aspects of trust in general and trust in the public sector in particular.

TRUST AS AN ELUSIVE CONCEPT

If one looks at definitions of trust, a lack of conceptual clarity becomes apparent (Hosmer 1996, 380; Luhmann 2000, 123). As a highly ambiguous concept, trust created some confusion in the economic and organizational theory as well as in political discussions (Shapiro 1987, 624; Noteboom 2005, 55). In everyday use no clear distinction exists between trust, hope, and confidence (Ripperger 1998). Richter and Furubotn (2003, 64–5) stress the contribution of trust as a means of decreasing transaction costs. According to Dasgupta (1988, 49), trust is treated as an underlying fact, presented whenever it needs to be called upon, a sort of ever-ready lubricant that permits voluntary participation in production and exchange. Since the 1990s the idea of trust as a social kit for society has been one that has also been gaining importance in the discussions of social capital (Putnam 1993) in political science.

A literature review by Hosmer (1996, 381) shows that there is no common understanding of trust in *organizational theory*. The concepts of trust range from trust as an individual optimistic expectation, through trust as an interpersonal relation, trust as the basis for economic transactions, and trust as part of the social structure. For Hosmer (1996, 392) trust includes a positive guarantee that the rights and interests of the other party will be respected in the final outcome. *Personal trust* is "a psychological state which enables individuals to accept vulnerability and place their welfare in the hands of other parties, expecting positive intentions and behavior from other parties" (Yang 2006, 574). According to Kasperson et al. (1992) trust is a rational evaluation of a social situation where the trust-giver thinks that the object of his or her trust is competent, intrinsically committed, extrinsically committed (accountable because of encapsulated interests), and predictable. Trust in others is highly variable across people, across time, across countries, and across space (Rahn et al. 2009, 1647).

Many of the definitions so far mentioned deal with personal or interpersonal trust. Luhmann (2000) argues that personal trust is something which will only work in simple social structures. Trust in people is quite different from trust in institutions and political authorities (Putnam 2000, 137). In more complex structures, *system trust* is also necessary (Luhmann 2000). For Luhmann (2000, 90) system trust has much to do with confidence in the functioning of systems and that those systems repetitively generate reliable results in a trustworthy way. With respect to organizations, some authors do not speak of system trust but of *organizational trust*. Based on a literature review on trust and trustworthiness, Caldwell and Clapham (2003) have developed a typology which specifies elements of organizational trustworthiness. The authors differentiate between three organizational trustworthiness factors: ability (with the sub-dimensions of competence, financial balance, and outcome), benevolence (including interactional courtesy and a responsibility to inform), and integrity (legal compliance and procedural fairness).

Taking into account the body of literature which focuses on trust in the public sector, it becomes obvious that trust here is also an ambiguous and fuzzy concept. This starts with the object of trust; for example, trust in government, trust in democracy, trust in the cabinet, trust in politicians, trust in the public sector, trust in political parties (Bovens and Wille 2011, 48). This list could be augmented by taking the trust-givers into account, namely trust by citizens, trust by public employees, trust by supervising bodies, trust by national governments in supra-national institutions, and so on. In his literature review Grimmelikhuijsen (2012, 31) identifies four elements of trust in government: trust as a psychological state which goes along with the acceptance of vulnerability and positive expectations about the intentions of another actor. According to this author trust is not the same as legitimacy, confidence, and of course distrust. Grimmelikhuijsen (2012, 42) distinguishes three of public institution-based trust (Table 38.1).

In public management trust is seen as a facilitator for good governance and institutional trustworthiness as an enabler for increasing the citizens' cooperative behavior and compliance with governmental decisions (Kim 2005, 612). Many writers have pointed out that currently there is a lack of public trust in professional bureaucracies (Bovaird and Loeffler 2007, 376 with further references). There is an ongoing discussion whether political trust is withering or merely wavering (Bovens and Wille 2011). Bovens and Wille (2011, 54) observe that the rate and timing of fluctuations of different trust measures within a country are remarkably similar and a high level of trust in one institution tends to affect the trust in other institutions. According to these authors (2011, 58) the rising volatility of political trust can be attributed to the following short- and

Table 38.1 Levels and objectives of institution–based trust (Grimmelikhuijsen 2012, 42)

	Political Trust	Public Sector Trust
Macro	Trust in democracy	Trust in government (in general) Trust in bureaucracy
Meso	Trust in political institutions (e.g. parliament)	Trust in a government organization/administration Trust in public institutions (e.g. police, media)
Micro	Trust in politicians/in a particular politician	Trust in civil servants Trust in policemen, journalists, etc.

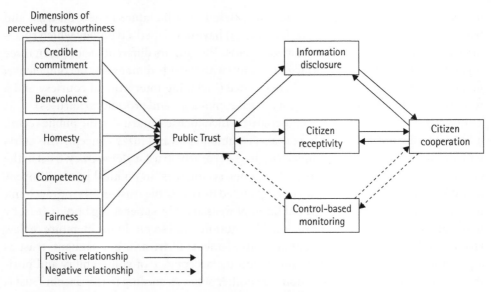

FIGURE **38.1** A conceptual model of public trust in government agencies (Kim 2005, 622)

long-term explanations: shifts in consumer confidence, shifts in the political process, and (international) crises as short-term factors, and changes in society and citizens, changes in government, and changes in the media as long-term factors.

If we look at the factors which lead to trust we find a variety of proposals. According to Kim (2005, 616) *organizational trustworthiness* in public administrations requires public-spirited employees who are competent, credible, and willing to act in the interest of the larger public. Based on a literature review, Kim developed a model of public trust and identified five dimensions of public trustworthiness (Figure 38.1).

According to Kim (2005, 622), "*credible commitment*" is the most frequently cited dimension of government trustworthiness among scholars in public administration and political science. Credible commitment goes beyond the fact that government actors honor their agreements, as it includes consistency between talk and action. Furthermore, credible commitment entails that the government actors exercise their power for the common good (2005, 624).

Benevolence means that the citizens feel that the government shows genuine care and concern for its citizens (Kim 2005, 625). *Honesty* or, to be more precise, the lack of honesty on the part of public employees, is an intensively discussed issue. When citizens feel that public servants are not acting in line with public service motivation but are concealing their activities and taking advantage for their own personal benefit, public trust will be shaken (Kim 2005, 626). *Competency*, i.e. knowledge and skills required for effective performance, is another important dimension that determines a government's trustworthiness (Kim 2005 with further references). *Fairness* has to do with the fact that public agencies treat citizens equally and do not show favoritism (2005, 627). Kim's five dimensions of trustworthiness are not only focused on the organizational or institutional dimension but also include elements of personal or inter-actor trustworthiness. This becomes apparent when Kim speaks of a "government actor" or a "public employee." Implicitly a causal positive relationship is assumed between personal and organizational trustworthiness. This is not unproblematic as high personal trustworthiness is not of great importance in organizational settings where organizational deficits prevent an efficient and effective delivery of public service.

For Grimmelikhuijsen (2012, 44–5), perceived trustworthiness of government organizations can be attributed to the following dimensions:

- Perceived competence, i.e. perceived effectiveness and skillfulness of a government organization
- Perceived benevolence consisting of the perceived intentions of the government
- Perceived honesty in the sense that government is seen as telling the truth and as acting righteously towards the citizens.

The factors which determine trust in governments are, according to Bouckaert and Van de Walle (2003, 334), not the same for every country or political culture. While in central Europe low citizen trust is associated with a crisis in democracy, in the Anglo-Saxon research community low trust is often regarded as an expression of a healthy democratic attitude. The elaborate system of checks and balances in the US political system with its focus on accountability is the result of this fear of possible abuses of power (Kim 2005). Furthermore, trust in the public sector may differ over time as the changing public attitude towards the Weberian bureaucrats shows.

As trust also has an inter-actor dimension, it is also necessary to look at the dimensions of public actors' trust in citizens. Yang (2005, 276) defines the latter as "administrators' belief that the citizens who are affected by their work (or whom they are serving) when involved in the administrative (or governing) process, will act in a fashion that is helpful (or beneficial) to administrators' performance (or goal fulfillment)." Trust in citizens is furthermore dependent on the administrators' trust in the specific citizen participation mechanism (Yang 2006, 587). According to Yang (2006) there are four main dimensions which have a positive impact on bureaucratic trust in citizens: knowledge-based trust, affective trust, trust in participation institutions, and propensity to trust. While *knowledge-based trust* has to do with citizens' knowledge and skills, affect-based trust has more to do with a set of principles the trust giver finds desirable (e.g. maintaining integrity and honesty in the decision-making process). Additionally, the trust of public administrators in the participating institutions of citizen participation influences their trust in citizens. Trust in citizen participation mechanisms is regarded by Yang (2006, 569) as a mediator between trust in citizens and the willingness to promote citizen involvement. Finally, a public administrator's trust in citizens is influenced by his or her propensity to trust, which is a personal trait. This trait has its roots in generalized expectations about the trustworthiness of others (2006, 580).

Based on a cross-country analysis of trust in parliament by the citizens, Van der Meer (2010) identified the following determinants: At the individual level, the level of education proved to be significant. If citizens are better educated they have a higher trust in their country's parliament. At the context level, corruption and survey results from former communist countries were negatively associated with trust in parliament. On the positive side, trust in parliament by the citizens is higher in a proportional electoral system. Quite unexpectedly, Van der Meer found no significance between the economic performance of a country and trust nor did he find that trust is lower if the parliament is highly fractionized. A more recent study by Van der Meer and Dekker (2011) shows that trust in parliament is higher when citizens are Protestants. Also positively associated are the following individual factors: level of education, income, age squared, degree of urbanization, being Jewish or a frequent church goer. All together these individual factors could explain about 17 percent of the variance of the country (2011, 104). Context factors had a higher explanation value.

Besides personal, inter-personal, and organizational or system trust one finds the differentiation between calculus-based, knowledge-based, and identification-based trust in the public management literature (Van de Walle 2011). *Calculus-based trust* relies on a calculus of the rewards for being trusting and trustworthy, and the effects on one's reputation of not being trusted. The fear of such effects acts as a deterrent (2011, 315). In the same line, Choudhury (2008) argues that calculus-based trust has to do with the predictability of the behavior of a person, group, organization, or public entity. Therefore, calculus-based trust is influenced by past experiences and expectations about future behavior.

Knowledge-based trust has to do with the level of information the trust giver has. Knowledge-based trust can be fostered through inserting more and better information into the system (2011, 316). Making detailed performance metrics available was seen by New Pubic Management (NPM) reformers as instrumental for creating knowledge-based trust (Van der Walle 2011 with further references).

Identification-based trust is based on shared values and goals. "Unlike calculus- and knowledge-based trust, it is not cognitive, but emotional" (2011, 316). With reference to Lewicki and Bunker (1996), Van de Walle (2011, 316) argues that identification-based and calculus-based trust are limited to a few relationships while knowledge-based trust is applicable to many relationships.

Relationships between Public Accountability and Trust

Common Factors

Public accountability and public trust have some common antecedents. Some of Caldwell's and Clapham's (2003) elements of organizational trustworthiness are also important for public accountability. The accountor's obligation to inform is an essential prerequisite for public accountability. Assuring that certain quality standards are met or demonstrating legal compliance, organizational competency or procedural fairness are prerequisites of various types of public accountability.

In line with Kim's (2005) and Grimmelikhuijsen's (2012) models (Figure 38.1) public accountability, as a social process, needs personal and inter-actor trustworthiness as preconditions for organizational or institutional trustworthiness. Demonstrating competency or showing to what extent public promises have been met, may also be an objective of public accountability. Honesty as a qualitative characteristic of public accountability reporting is embedded in the "true and fair view" principle which is relevant for reporting across the sectors. More difficult to associate with public accountability are the more subjective elements, like benevolence, individual fairness, personal integrity, or personal propensity to trust.

In Yang's (2006) model knowledge-based trust is the type of trust most easily connected with public accountability. If there is no or low trust in the participating institutions, public accountability is either a very difficult process or just a token. Affect-based trust and a propensity to trust have their basis in personal beliefs or personal traits and are, therefore, more difficult to associate with public accountability, especially if the control focus is dominant. If one recalls Bovens' (2007, 463) three perspectives of public accountability, the control model is embedded in the democratic perspective which "provides the people's representatives and the voters with the information needed for judging the propriety and effectiveness of the conduct of the government." From the constitutional perspective the prevention of corruption and abuse of power are central issues. Here the control purpose is also quite obvious. Accountability in that sense has a lot to do with the appropriateness of actions, adherence to obligations, and the threat of sanctioning. Along with the control model goes the idea that deficits, public waste, and ineffectiveness are identified and stigmatized. Like corruption, this is harmful for citizens' trust in the functioning of the public sector.

This brief review shows that public accountability has several common determinants with (organizational) trustworthiness but, where the control focus dominates, also some elements which are difficult to reconcile with trust. If one examines the possible relations between public accountability and trust, at least the following three can be identified:

- Trust as the dependent variable
- Trust as the independent variable
- Trust and public accountability as independent concepts

Trust as the Dependent Variable

In this case high or low trust is influenced by public accountability. Public accountability is regarded as one approach (among others) for creating trust in the functioning of the public sector. For Zucker (1986) the emergence of the bureaucratic form with its written rules and multiple bureaucratic accountability requirements is a basis for public trust. The liberal distrust in the government leads to intensive public accountability obligations aiming at enabling citizen trust in the government (Choudhury 2008, 602). According to this author, controls become trust-enabling if they are rule-based, impersonal, and embedded in the structures, norms, and policies of a public agency (2008, 594).

Assuming a positive relationship between trust and public accountability is in line with the Anglo-Saxon approach towards public accountability. Performance transparency created by public accountability may act as an enabler for public trust if the performance is good. Halachmi and Holzer (2010, 387) argue along the management paradigm, which regards high performance as a necessity for creating public trust. These two authors see citizen participation that allows the public to ask questions and to select the measurement methodology as a moderator for increasing the confidence in public accountability reports and the trust in the data collection process.

A second line of argument for a positive relationship is the following. As trust provision provides some risks, public accountability may act as a safety device to limit the risk for the trust-giver (Greiling 2007). Public accountability is regarded as an instrument which signals competence and organizational trustworthiness and demonstrates how compliance and procedural fairness standards are met and whether high quality standards for public service are maintained (Greiling 2013). With greater public accountability the knowledge and familiarity with the trust-receiver rises as consequently does personal and organizational closeness.

The relationship between public accountability and trust can also be a negative one. In that case more public accountability and more performance transparency is associated with a decline in public trust. This reasoning can be corroborated by looking at the negative results of a control approach towards public accountability. By applying the principal–agent theory it can be argued that public accountability with its control-focus is mistrust-driven. It is directed at identifying the shortcomings of politicians, public managers, and public agencies. The account-giver is regarded as an agent who will most likely misuse the existing discretionary freedom to gain an advantage.

If we look at the different types of accountability, such an approach towards accountability can be found in bureaucratic accountability and in managerial accountability. Bureaucratic accountability has a strong focus on procedural accountability and on detailed and highly-regulated information demands. Managerial accountability can also be motivated by detecting an inappropriate use of power or of managerial freedom given to perform public tasks. Another common denominator of these two forms of accountability is the fact that they are both forms of hierarchical accountability and are in line with a control approach.

Our *empirical knowledge* of the relationship between trust and public accountability is quite poor. The challenges start with the fact that public accountability and trust are both elusive concepts. The findings of surveys on political trust usually do not proceed from any clear account of what is meant by political trust in the first place (Bovens and Wille 2011, 49). If the dependent as well as the independent variable is fuzzy, there will be negative effects on the way of operationalizing and getting statistically significant results.

In a study by Van der Meer and Dekker (2011, 104), which is based on a European Social Survey data of 21 countries, intrinsic commitment by the trust-receiver was more important than accountability aspects. An exploratory study in Iran, conducted by Fard and Rostamy (2007, 334), indicates that public accountability, with its legal, financial, performance, political, and democratic aspects is the most important factor for the creation of public trust.

By conducting experiments Grimmelikhuijsen (2012) investigated the relationship between computer-mediated government transparency and trust along the following dimensions of transparency: decision-making transparency, policy information transparency, and policy outcome transparency. He found out that in seven out of nine trustworthiness dimensions no effects could be observed for the three transparency dimensions. Notable exceptions were a negative effect of decision-making transparency on the perceived competence and a positive effect of decision-making transparency on the perceived outcome. Therefore, the transparency skeptics seem to be more in the right. Publishing output and outcome data does not contribute in general to higher trust as the transparency optimists assume (2012, 202). With respect to direct effects, the experiments showed that there is no reward for transparency. On the contrary, transparency has negative effects on a government organization's perceived competence by providing a balanced content of policies and reporting negative policy outcomes (2012, 204). Message credibility proved to have a positive effect on the perceived trustworthiness of government actors' while knowledge only had a slightly positive effect when providing factual knowledge (Grimmelikhuijsen 2012). Therefore Grimmelikhuijsen (2012, 212) came to the conclusion that in his experiments he found hardly any positive effect of transparency on trust. These findings are surprising given the high expectations based on transparency.

Trust as the Independent Variable

Here trust is seen as a prerequisite for public accountability. It is unrealistic to assume that one can create watertight accountability mechanisms which leave the account-giver no room for making use of information asymmetries. Incomplete accountability arrangements create opportunities for the account-giving actor to present a picture which shows the agency in an overly positive way. The accountability forum cannot directly observe all actions undertaken by the account-giver and therefore has only limited knowledge of what information could be available (Schillemans 2008). If one recalls the three stages of public accountability, especially in stages one and two, the account-giving actor can use his or her information advantage for window-dressing. Typically, the accountability forum has less knowledge of organizational practices than the account-giver (Greiling and Spraul 2010). The discretionary freedom to hide information is particularly high in the information phase. It also exists in the debating phase. Although the accountability forum can ask questions, there are still great information asymmetries in favor of the account-giver. The dialogues are not usually free of tension about information access and the appropriateness of the required additional information.

In both phases of the accountability process the account-giver can also choose the strategy of overloading the accountability forum with too much irrelevant information (Greiling and Spraul 2010). Sometimes the danger of information overload is already embedded in the design of accountability obligations. March and Olsen (2004) argue if the logic of consequences is not reconciled with the logic of appropriateness, the amount of accountability information expands and information overload is more likely to occur (Greiling and Spraul 2010).

Public accountability faces at least two further challenges (Greiling and Spraul 2010). Firstly, the problem of too many hands (Bovens 2005, 198; Benz 2007, 508) entails that it is not easy to identify precisely who is responsible for which aspects of the information provision. In cases of shared responsibilities, it is difficult to disentangle the respective responsibilities which leads to a situation. Koppell (2005) labels this as multiple accountability disorders. Secondly, in public sector accountability arrangements it is not unusual for the accountability information provided by one account-giver to serve as input for the accountability obligations of the recipient accountability forum with regard to a third party. At each accountability level the incoming information has to be processed in order to meet different and sometimes conflicting accountability logics. Redundant accountability may be a safeguard for better information quality, as Schillemans (2010) advocates, but must not necessarily be a remedy against accountability overload.

Additionally to design problems, measurement challenges that lead to noisy measures also complicate the situation. Jacobides and Croson (2001, 208) argue that self-interested account-givers will develop a notoriously high ability to play "fast and loose" with the imposed accountability obligations. Problems of uncertainty and ambiguity increase the challenges further. Decades of experience with program evaluation, with its myriads of problems regarding output and outcome measurement, show that it is highly likely that often one will have to rely on proxy indicators (Greiling 2007). Performance gaming is also a well-known negative side-effect of public accountability (for various types see Radnor 2008). Irrespective of the sector, Jacobides and Croson (2001, 212) challenge the paradigm that "the more information provided the better." They argue that performance measurement may even contribute to *agency loss*. This is likely to occur in the cases of measurement imperfections, unobserved multitasking, casual ambiguity, and latent economics of continuation. In these circumstances additional performance information creates organizational dysfunctionalities.

In line with these challenges of the public accountability process it can be argued that imperfections in the design and measurement process need trust as a prerequisite to avoid a situation where there is an explosion of public accountability demands. If the reporting demands are too detailed, this may lead to situations where public officials regard public accountability as an end in itself with no public value created.

On a more positive note one may say that it is in line with Bovens's learning perspective to consider trust as a prerequisite for public accountability (Bovens 2007; Bovens, Schillemans, and 't Hart 2008). If one recalls the antecedents for (inter-)organizational learning in the public sector (for a literature review see Greiling and Halachmi 2013), it becomes obvious that trust is a crucial element. Organizational learning can only happen where public accountability goes beyond pointing an accusatory finger. A learning culture in the public sector requires a general readiness to encourage questioning and constructive criticism. This is only possible if there is a climate of trust. Yang (2009) reports a positive correlation between innovative culture and honest reporting. As Bovens, Schillemans, and 't Hart (2008, 233) suggest, organizational learning in the public sector will only happen if a sense of safety exists that minimizes the chances that defensive routines take over. On the relationship level each partner must be trustworthy. The learning perspective of public accountability requires that the account-givers see themselves as advisors and partners and not as antagonistic supervisors. All three stages of account-giving are affected. The information input of the account-giver needs to be based on honest, unbiased provision of all the relevant facts including the admission of errors. This is only possible if a certain level of trustworthiness and trust exists. From the learning perspective, the interrogating stage should be based on mutual openness and be directed towards identifying possible areas for improvement. Compared to the control model, this phase is much more reflective. Additionally, the account-giver as well as the accountability forum might actively use the dialogue for searching for actions that lead to an improvement of public services. The judgment stage ought to focus on the implementation of lessons learned. It is not sanctioning that is in the center but enabling organizational learning in order to enhance public service delivery.

Trust and Public Accountability as Independent Concepts

It can also be argued that both concepts are not related in all respects. There are elements of public trust which are difficult to reconcile with public accountability and also elements of public accountability which are difficult to connect with public trust. If one looks at the elements of interpersonal trustworthiness, it becomes obvious that some of the elements of benevolence and integrity are difficult to link to all forms of public accountability as a social mechanism. With the notable exception of accountability between the superior and a team member, some of the affective components of personal trust are not relevant in public accountability arrangements. That has to do with the fact that public accountability is more focused on knowledge-based and calculus-based trust.

As stated above, mistrust-driven public accountability arrangements that are directed at destroying the account-giver, and accountability processes where window-dressing dominates are difficult to see as trust-building devices. Not so clear-cut are arrangements where public accountability serves a symbolic function. From a neo-institutionalistic perspective it could be argued that giving account may have an instrumental effect on the account-giver as well as the accountability forum because it helps both to create legitimacy towards society.

Another argument for seeing public accountability and public trust as unrelated is that in the complex world of (post-) NPM such a linkage cannot exist. NPM with its devolution, its decentralization, and its separating of steering from rowing has resulted in coordination problems that make manageable relationships between these two broad concepts impossible. Post-NPM reform efforts to mend the negative side effects of NPM have increased the complexity further. The resulting (organizational) confusion makes it impossible to identify what is the dependent and what is the independent variable.

CONCLUSIONS AND DIRECTIONS FOR FURTHER RESEARCH

Public trust and public accountability are both elusive and multi-faceted concepts. Consequently, the relationship between the two is not a straightforward one. While we have a growing body of empirical findings about trust enablers or disablers, the empirical evidence on public accountability is smaller. Both are elusive concepts on which, on the one hand, high expectations are being placed and, on the other hand, we are witnessing a certain degree of disillusion about their instrumental value. If one takes into account the different levels of stakeholder trust and the various forms of accountability as well as cultural factors, types of political systems, and public sector reform models, the issue at hand becomes even less straightforward.

While the distrust-creating effects of public accountability under NPM are relatively well-researched, there are other reform agendas for modernizing the public sector where empirical results about the relationship between public accountability and trust are lacking. How the linkage between public accountability and trust works under public service motivation and Neo-Weberian ideas, is an open question. Yang (2009) expects that it works better. It would be also interesting to investigate under which conditions dynamic e-accountability helps to create public trust.

Looking at the current theoretical concepts referred to in the debate about public accountability and trust, the principal–agent theory and public choice play an important role in addressing the issue at hand. Within political science the idea of public trust is predominately investigated by the social capital theory, deliberative thinking, and communitarism. So far the role public accountability can play in this context has not been well researched. This also holds true for applying the stewardship theory to the issue under discussion. The unclear instrumental value of increasing public accountability as a means of increasing public trust in the public sector shows that it is far too shortsighted to investigate the relationship against one dominant theoretical approach only. Therefore, an interdisciplinary dialogue is necessary that combines economic reasoning with political science.

REFERENCES

Bouckaert, G. and Van de Walle, S. 2003. "Comparing Measures of Citizen Trust and User Satisfaction as Indicators of 'Good Governance': Difficulties in Linking Trust and Satisfaction Indicators." *International Review of Administrative Sciences*, 69: 329–43.

Bovaird, T. and Loeffler, E. 2007. The Role of Trust in Organisational Responses to Local Governance Failures, pp. 371–83 in *Stand und Perspektiven der öffentlichen Betriebswirtschaftslehre II*, eds. D. Braeunig and D. Greiling. Baden-Baden: Nomos Verlag.

Benz, A. 2007. "Accountable Multilevel Governance by the Open Method of Coordination?" *European Law Journal*, 13: 505–22.

Bovens, M. 2005. Public Accountability, pp. 182–208 in *The Oxford Handbook of Public Management*, eds. E. Ferlie, L. E. Lynn Jr., and C. Pollitt. Oxford, NY: Oxford University Press.

Bovens, M. 2007. "Analysing and Assessing Accountability: A Conceptual Framework." *European Law Journal*, 13: 447–68.

Bovens, M., Schillemans, T., and 't Hart, P. 2008. "Does Public Accountability Work? An Assessment Tool." *Public Administration*, 86: 225–42.

Bovens, M. and Wille, A. 2011. Falling or Fluctuation Trust Levels? The Case of the Netherlands, pp. 47–66 in *Political Trust: Why Context Matters*, eds. S. Zmerli and M. Hooghe. Colchester: ECPR Press.

Bouckaert, G. and Halligan, J. 2008. *Managing Performance: International Comparisons.* New York: Routledge.

Caldwell, C. and Clapham, S. E. 2003. "Organizational Trustworthiness: An International Perspective." *Journal of Business Ethics*, 47: 349–64.

Choudhury, E. 2008. "Trust in Administration: An Integrative Approach to Optimal Trust." *Administration & Society*, 40: 586–620.

Dasgupta, P. 1988. Trust as a Commodity, pp. 49–72 in *Trust:Making and Breaking Cooperative Relations*, ed. D. Gambetta. Oxford, UK: Blackwell.

Fard, H. D. and Rostamy, A. A. 2007. "Promoting Public Trust in Public Organizations: Explaining the Role of Public Accountability." *Public Organization Review*, 7: 331–44.

Greiling, D. 2007. "Trust and Performance Management in Nonprofit Organisations." *The Innovation Journal*, 12: e-journal.

Greiling, D. 2013. "Public Accountability and Citizen Participation." *Journal for Public and Nonprofit Management* (publication forthcoming).

Greiling, D. and Halachmi, A. 2013. "Accountability and Organizational Learning in the Public Sector." *Public Performance & Management Review*, 36: 380–406.

Greiling, D. and Spraul, K. 2010. "Accountability and the Challenges of Information Disclosure." *Public Administration Quarterly*, 34: 338–77.

Grimmelikhuijsen, S. G. 2012. *Transparency and Trust.* Dissertation. University of Utrecht.

Halachmi, A. and Holzer, M. 2010. "Citizen Participation and Performance Measurement: Operationalizing Democracy through Better Accountability." *Public Administration Quarterly*, 34: 378–99.

Hosmer, L. T. 1996. "Trust: The Connecting Link Between Organizational Theory and Philosophical Ethics." *The Academy of Management Review*, 20: 379–403.

Jacobides, M. G. and Croson, D. C. 2001. "Information Policy: Shaping the Value of Agency Relationships." *The Academy of Management Review*, 26: 202–23.

Kasperson, R. E., Golding, D., and Tuler, S. 1992. "Social Distrust as a Factor in Siting Hazardous Facilities and Communicating Risk." *Journal of Social Issues*, 48: 161–87.

Koppell, J. G. 2005. "Pathologies of Accountability: ICANN and the Challenge of 'Multiple Accountabilities Disorder.'" *Public Administration Review*, 65: 94–108.

Kim, S. E. 2005. "The Role of Trust in the Modern Administrative State: An Integrative Model." *Administration & Society*, 37: 611–35.

Lewicki, R. J. and Bunker, B. B. 1996. Developing and Maintaining Trust in Work Relationships, pp. 114–39 in *Trust in Organisations: Frontiers of Theory and Research*, eds. R. M. Kramer and T. R. Tyler. Thousand Oaks, CA: SAGE Publications.

Luhmann, N. 2000. *Vertrauen: Ein Mechanismus zur Reduktion Sozialer Komplexität.* Fourth edition. Stuttgart: Lucius and Lucius.

March, J. G. and Olsen, J. P. 2004. *The Logic of Appropriateness.* Arena Working Paper, WP. 04/09. Oslo.

Noteboom, B. 2005. Forms, Sources and Limits of Trust, pp. 35–58 in *Normative und institutionelle Grundfragen der Ökonomik:Reputation und Vertrauen*, eds. M. Held, G. Kubon-Gilke, and R. Sturm. Marburg: Metropolis Verlag.

Putnam, R. D. 1993. *Making Democracy Work: Civic Traditions in Modern Italy.* Princeton, NJ: Princeton University Press.

Putnam, R. D. 2000. *Bowling Alone.* New York: Simon & Schuster Paperbacks.

Radnor, Z. 2008. "Muddled, Massaging, Manoeuvring or Manipulated? A Typology of Organisational Gaming." *International Journal of Productivity and Performance Management*, 57: 313–28.

Rahn, W. M., Yoon, K. S., Garet, M., Lipson, S., and Loflin, K. 2009. "Geographies of Trust." *American Behavioral Scientist*, 52: 1646–63.

Richter, R. and Furubotn, E. G. 2003. *Neue Institutionenökonomik: Eine Einführung und kritische Würdigung.* Third edition. Tübingen: UTB.

Ripperger, T. 1998. *Ökonomik des Vertrauens.* Tübingen: Mohr-Siebeck.

Schillemans, T. 2008. "Accountability in the Shadow of Hierarchy: The Horizontal Accountability of Agencies." *Public Organizations Review*, 8: 175–94.

Schillemans, T. 2010. "Redundant Accountability: The Joint Impact of Horizontal and Vertical Accountability on Autonoumous Agencies." *Public Administration Quarterly*, 34: 300–37.

Shapiro, S. P. 1987. "The Social Control of Interpersonal Trust." *American Journal of Sociology*, 93: 623–58.

Van der Meer, T. 2010. "In What We Trust? A Multi-Level Study into Trust in Parliament as an Evaluation of State Characteristics." *International Review of Managerial Sciences*, 76: 517–36.

Van der Meer, T. and Dekker, P. 2011. Trustworthy States, Trusting Citizens? A Multilevel Study Into Objectives and Subjective Dimensions of Political Trust, pp. 95–116 in *Political Trust: Why Context Matters*, eds. S. Zmerli and M. Hooghe. Colchester: ECPR Press.

Van de Walle, S. 2011. New Public Management: Restoring the Public Trust through Creating Distrust?, pp. 309–20 in *The Ashgate Research Companion to New Public Management*, eds. T. Christensen and P. Lægreid. Farnham and Burlington: Ashgate.

Yang, K. 2005. "Public Administrators' Trust in Citizens: A Missing Link in Citizen Involvement Efforts." *Public Administration Review*, 65: 273–85.

Yang, K. 2006. "Trust and Citizen Involvement Decisions: Trust in Citizens, Trust in Institutions, and Propensity to Trust." *Administration & Society*, 38: 573–95.

Yang, K. 2009. "Examining Perceived Honest Performance Reporting by Public Organizations: Bureaucratic Politics and Organizational Practice." *Journal of Public Administration Research and Theory*, 19: 81–105.

Zucker, L. G. 1986. "Production of Trust: Institutional Sources of Economic Structure 1840-1920." *Research in Organizational Behavior*, 8: 53–111.

CHAPTER 39

ACCOUNTABILITY, LEGITIMACY, AND THE COURT OF PUBLIC OPINION

MARK H. MOORE

SOCIAL ACCOUNTABILITY, ACCOUNTABILITY AGENTS, AND THE COURT OF PUBLIC OPINION

LIBERAL societies, and the individuals who constitute them, have long been concerned about the effective control of powerful institutions that arise within them. Their principal pre-occupation has been with controlling the actions of government. Indeed, democratic societies are often defined by a set of social structures and processes that empower individual citizens vis-à-vis government by granting constitutional rights that protect citizens from arbitrary governmental action and allow them to control what the government chooses to do and how it seeks to accomplish its goals (Cunningham 2002).

But liberal societies have also often been concerned with the actions of large private organizations that grow up in their midst. Over the last century and a half, concerns have focused on the increasing power of private corporations to shape the conditions under which individuals live, and to influence democratic political processes (Dunlop 1980; Reich 2007). To protect themselves from concentrated economic power, individuals have often looked to government, but government action has been neither necessary nor sufficient to control corporate conduct (Bardach and Kagan 1982; Braithwaite and Drahos 2000). Instead, over the last decade or so, while government has been reluctant to curb the power of private corporations, the public has sought and found ways to call corporations to account *without the mediation of government* (Vogel 2006; Peters et al. 2009; Gray, Owens and Adams 1996). Using the same political and social mobilization techniques that citizens have long used to call government to account, a social and political movement has emerged to demand—and sometimes get—corporate compliance with standards of social accountability that are not necessarily enshrined in law. This has revealed the force of demands for social accountability that spring up in society, and are pressed in the "court of public opinion" even when such demands are neither backed by current law, nor a prelude to the passage of laws.

Think of the court of public opinion as an interested public composed of many different kinds of social actors who seek to impose external accountability on large, powerful organizations. These include individuals, the press, civic associations, political advocacy groups, and even political parties whose words and deeds target not only governments, but also private organizations including private corporations (Cohen and Rogers 1995). These actors can be defined as "accountability agents" who make public claims against other social actors. Accountability agents not only pay attention to the conduct and performance of powerful governmental and private institutions, but also make evaluative judgments about whether they are sufficiently respectful of the rights of individuals, or appropriately accountable for the effects of their actions, and more generally whether the enterprise seems legitimate or not. Having made such judgments, accountability agents give voice to their claims and rouse others to support them.

Often, such agents are self-appointed and self-authorized. They may or may not have a legal basis to press their claim, but feel they have a compelling moral claim that can get traction in the court of public opinion—at least in part because they assume that the public believes accountability is good per se. Only when accountability agents call powerful public and private organizations to account can anyone expect those institutions to act in the public's interest rather than their own. These assumptions embolden accountability agents to press their claims.

Ironically, the social entities that think of themselves as accountability agents are often not all that different in type or form from their targets. Very often, an accountability agent that makes a claim against another social entity quickly becomes the target of demands for accountability from the organization it has confronted: "Who are you to call me to account?" What makes a social entity an accountability agent, then, is not that it is a particular kind of social entity. Government agencies can call private social actors to account as well as be called to account. Private commercial organizations can call those with whom they have contracted to account, but they can also be called to account by their contractors, the government, and what one private executive has called "three kooks with a fax machine" speaking as the voice of the public. What makes a social entity an accountability agent is simply that it seeks to influence the conduct of other social agencies by asserting a public demand for accountability (Behn 2001).

Taken all together, accountability agents constitute the external accountability structure that all social organizations face. And it is within this structure that a court of public opinion arises and begins to shape the conduct of organizations in ways that are not fully captured by an abstract ideal of accountability, nor a legal concept of accountability, nor perhaps even by a pluralist concept of political accountability. This court of public opinion is a product that springs from the collision of accountability agents with both the targets of their demands for accountability and sometimes with one another as they press more or less conflicting claims on targeted organizations.

My purpose in this essay is to briefly examine this emerging form of social accountability through both legal and behavioral lenses in order to contribute to ideas about how accountability can be created and made forceful as individuals living in liberal societies seek to protect themselves from the power of large economic, social, and political institutions.

The Legal Structure of External Social Accountability

The structures and processes of external accountability begin with laws that give social actors (individuals and groups) outside the formal structure of existing organizations rights of action against the conduct and performance of those organizations.

The Law of Torts

Tort law provides some basic protection for all individuals who are adversely affected—whether through unsafe products, shoddy medical practices, or intrusive government security measures—by the actions of large institutions (Landes and Posner 1987). The authority of the state is engaged here insofar as state court findings will be definitive with respect to the settlement of disputes, but the activation of that state authority, like many things in liberal societies, is at the discretion of, and in service to, those who have been mistreated. For this reason, legal demands for accountability will, to some degree, follow the dispositions and capacities of individuals in a position to sue. On occasion, the individuals injured can combine their interests in class action suits (Hensler 2000). In these cases, the organizer of the collective group (the class) is often a lawyer seeking justice and compensation for his clients as well as financial returns and perhaps fame for himself! But the claim that is being represented in courts is simply the sum of individual rights.

Economic and Social Regulation of Organizations

Tort law is complemented by legislation that directs corporations to avoid actions that harm, or to take actions that advance, the public good (Bardach and Kagan 1982; Braithwaite and Drahos 2000; Mann and Roberts 2008). Sometimes such laws seek to advantage particular groups of individuals whose interests might be adversely affected by the conduct of both private and public institutions. Safety and health regulations in both private and public institutions protect workers' interests. Various regulatory regimes that impose burdens on economic suppliers protect consumers' interests. Due process protections require government agencies to treat their clients fairly (Mashaw 1985). Limitations on what charitable organizations are allowed and required to do protect donors' interests. And so on.

While complaints from citizens often activate the enforcement of these laws, government can also act on its own to bring complaints to bear on private organizations or other governments, spending public resources to discover violations of the law without being directed to do so by a particular individual, and calling both private and public agencies to account when offenses are found (Wilson 1989; Sparrow 1994). Thus, in some cases, the collective institutions and processes of democratic governance—rather than the choices of affected individuals—determine the overall level and focus of accountability.

Mandated Transparency

Other laws structure accountability for both for-profit and nonprofit organizations by requiring them to submit information to public agencies and to the public at large describing their aims, activities, and results as well as their officers, addresses, finances, and aspects of their performance (Fung, Graham and Weil 2007). Government activity is similarly made transparent by general duties to produce reports on expenditures and activities, and more specific duties created by the Freedom of Information Act which requires government agencies to refrain from conducting business in secrecy, and to divulge records of both their deliberations and actions (Foerstal 1999).

Laws like these are designed to increase the transparency of the deliberations and actions of powerful organizations. But they do not necessarily result in a legal action by someone with a right of action against the organization. In order for the laws creating transparency in both private and public organizations to have their desired effects, there has to be an interested party paying attention to take up the cause (Fung 2004). Rules mandating transparency make it easier for those who wish to call an organization to account to do so, but they do not in themselves represent a force demanding external accountability. The energy to demand accountability has to come from elsewhere.

THE SOCIAL PROCESS OF CREATING ACCOUNTABILITY

The laws set out above—those giving legal rights to individuals injured by private and public organizations, those instructing organizations how to behave in accord with the public interest, and those requiring organizations to render their activities more transparent to the outside world—create a formal structure of accountability around existing organizations. That formal structure includes a set of social actors who have legal standing to make a claim against a particular organization and a set of procedural and substantive claims that those actors can make on the conduct of an organization.

But the legal structure of accountability may be only the beginning of the story. The fact that these legal mechanisms of accountability depend crucially for their effect on the initiative of some agent in bringing the existing legal accountability to bear hints at the possibility for a wider, more behavioral conception of accountability. The laws merely create the potential for accountability. They do not enforce themselves. They need aggrieved individuals or groups to step forward to press their claims. Neither do these laws limit demands for accountability. Individuals without legal rights to demand accountability may nonetheless make a claim on some moral principle that has not yet been recognized in law.

To undertake a comprehensive social and empirical study on the construction of effective accountability, the examination of the formal, legal structure of accountability would be only part of the exercise. The other part would focus on the behavioral interactions of self-appointed "accountability agents" and the organizations they targeted.

Stakeholders and Affected Interests as Agents of Accountability

Scholars of institutional design, organizations, and management have terms to describe social actors who may be interested in calling organizations to account. They describe them as "stakeholders," or actors with "affected interests," or "political authorizers" of an organization (Freeman et al. 2010; Fung 2013; Moore 1995). Perhaps because such scholars are more empirically than normatively or legally oriented, they make no claim about the legal standing of the stakeholder or the affected interest with respect to a given organization. Of course, many stakeholders do have legal claims against organizations. Citizens have claims against government, investors and customers have legal claims they can make against business firms. But an important feature of the empirical reality of accountability is that there might well be stakeholders or affected interests who do not have legal standing to press their claims. Given that the law is at best an imperfect reflection of the moral concerns that might be important in deciding who could make a claim on an organization, and what that claim might be, it seems likely that not all morally relevant actors, nor all morally relevant substantive concerns would be reflected in the existing law. In fact, given that existing law often institutionalizes the interests of the powerful against those of the less powerful, it seems likely indeed that the existing law would have failed to recognize all the important affected parties and their interests. The inevitable result is that there will be many stakeholders who do not have the legal power to call organizations to account but—because they think they have a moral right, because they can find platforms to make their voice heard, because the public is not particularly discriminating about what constitutes a lawful demand for accountability, and because the stakeholders think the moral claim might resonate with the public—will make demands for accountability without explicit legal sanction. "There oughta be a law!" they proclaim, and wait to see what happens.

The set of demands for accountability that lack legal sanction constitute a sort of anarchic penumbra of extra-legal accountability demands. It is not that the demands for accountability are illegal (though some, of course, are, and we call these demands extortion and corruption!). Indeed, in a liberal society such demands are constitutionally protected by laws that protect the right of individuals to use their voice to exercise control over large collective institutions. Amplified and broadcast by news and social media, those politically powerful but legally unsanctioned demands for accountability can put pressure on organizations even without the implicit or explicit threat of legal action.

Those who lead large private and public organizations know well that many different social actors can and do call them to account for many different aspects of their performance (Moore 1995; Behn 2001). Public officials are a bit more used to this than private executives. But both would likely testify to the extraordinary external pressure that can be brought to bear on them when self-appointed accountability agents demand changes on some dimension or another. In this way, the context of external social accountability is both broader and less disciplined than the concept of legal accountability suggests.

Practical and Moral Pressures for Accountability

It is not hard to understand why some self-appointed accountability agent would be interested in asserting a demand for accountability even if the demand would not be supported in a court of law. The more interesting question is why such a claim would bother the executive officers of an organization. They can always say (as many do) that they have done everything the law requires them to do, and that they have exercised their discretion in using the assets entrusted to them in the best interests of those to whom they owe fiduciary responsibility. Indeed, to some, it might seem morally irresponsible to respond to demands that lie outside the boundaries of their established legal responsibility because doing so might undermine their commitment to the purposes of those who do have legal claims on them. Ideally, this legal structure would properly identify the important actors who should have standing to demand accountability from organizations and give appropriate priority to the particular claims they make on the organization, allowing the organization to focus on what is important and socially valued and to ignore claims that would cause it to be less responsible and less effective in its conduct than it otherwise would be. If these were all features of the established legal structure, moral weight as well as prudential weight might well align with a felt obligation to resist extra-legal demands for accountability—even if they resonate with wider public sentiment.

But the reality seems to be that the leaders of organizations *do* feel vulnerable to these demands for accountability. They feel obligated to hear and respond to demands made in the court of public opinion. Organizational leaders in both public and private organizations know that those who may not have legal standing or practical force in one social forum may find traction in others. Corporate executives know that such accountability agents may turn their efforts to trying to persuade customers, investors, and workers that they should not buy from, invest in, or work for a company that harms people or natural environments. Public executives know well that what is won by stonewalling or winning in court can be overturned when those who lost organize themselves politically. Given the practical threat that some accountability agents pose, leaders might wisely respond to the extra-legal demand as though they had some legal responsibility to meet it (Moore and Khagram 2004).

Beyond these practical considerations, organizational leaders may feel bound to respond to the moral issues raised by the demand for accountability. In fact, many of the practical concerns have to be gauged at least in part by a judgment about the weight, importance, and public appeal of the moral concerns raised by the accountability agents. If the moral claim is weak, or idiosyncratic, it will probably not have much economic, social, or political resonance. If it is strong, then morality will come down on the side of prudence and cause the leaders to act as though there were a legal claim. A moral claim asserted by an outside stakeholder may even stir the hearts and minds of executives and workers within the organization. Executives may feel morally compelled to use their office to express that moral commitment.

It is these practical and moral judgments that make the social penumbra of accountability as potentially important in regulating the conduct of organizations as the legal structure of rules. If what is important about external accountability is its real capacity to guide organizations towards the protection of individual rights and the achievement of the public good, then any institutional analyst or designer would have to look at the behavioral impact of the court of public opinion as well as the court of law.

The Risks and the Opportunities of Wide Social Accountability

Suppose that the observations made above are empirically true: that the actual social processes of creating and demanding accountability often slip their legal moorings and become far more anarchic, unpredictable, and dynamic that we usually imagine, or than the legal system can manage. How should one who is interested in using the idea of accountability as a guide to improving the conduct of large organizations view such a situation? Is the anarchy and dynamism good or bad for the cause of accountability and the hope that properly constructed accountability might not only meet normative demands linked to fiduciary responsibilities, but also to improved organizational performance in the pursuit of the public good?

From the point of view of those outside of organizations who either fear or hope to improve the conduct of an organization (i.e., potential accountability agents) the loose structure of accountability seems like a good thing. They can feel free to press their claims without particular concern about what the law says or the claims being made by other accountability agents. They can stand on their God-given right to demand accountability to them and their values.

Many others who have less specific interests but share concerns about the potential power of large organizations may also come down on the side of a relatively loose and free-flowing process of accountability. Constraints on demands for accountability that permit only certain actors to make them, or only certain substantive concerns to be the focus of accountability, signify the danger of large organizations that have the power to manipulate the law to protect their interests over other important interests and values.

From the point of view of those inside an organization, or those hoping that the organization (whether private or public) might produce something valuable for individuals and the society at large, however, wide-ranging and unpredictable demands for accountability create a potential hazard. They worry that those who lead powerful organizations will be distracted from their focus on producing something of value. They will be forced to be all things to all people and risk their effectiveness as producing organizations. From this perspective, responding to new and unpredictable demands for accountability—particularly on relatively narrow and idiosyncratic dimensions of performance—comes at a high cost reckoned in terms of responsiveness to more established claimants or more important social purposes.

Both these points of view have their merits. A loose system of accountability could increase the social performance of an organization by enabling it to become more responsive to a wider range of stakeholders and helping it understand the consequences of its current conduct (Ebrahim 2005). One can also see how a system of accountability in which the penumbra of extra-legal accountability was strong relative to the tighter legal structure could create serious difficulties for those trying to run organizations efficiently and effectively to achieve a simple, established set of valued results. How, then, to advise those who manage organizations, those who wish to call them to account, and all the rest of us who are interested in having a system of accountability that would allow us to gain the advantages that come from both a strict and a looser idea of accountability?

THE PURSUIT OF LEGITIMACY AS A COMPLEMENT TO MEETING THE DEMANDS FOR ACCOUNTABILITY

If the system of accountability that emerges in a liberal democratic society is anarchic and only imperfectly tamed by a legal structure that gives specific social actors legal rights to press specific claims, then it seems clear that we citizens cannot rely only on stricter enforcement of a legal structure of accountability to ensure the performance of our large institutions. We might be forced to rely more on efforts to establish principles of good practice in negotiating accountability among interested parties than legal structures and processes that permanently fix the structure of accountability (Moore and Brown 2001).

In doing so, of course, we might have to give up the idea of accountability as a fixed legal ideal, and think of it, instead, as an emergent process in which social collisions and processes of negotiating and mediating those collisions create a shared sense of accountability and concern for the overall performance of the organization among those demanding accountability and those subject to those demands. This may be a much messier, less rigorous, and less satisfying form of accountability, but perhaps comes closer to the way the world really works, and might move us towards a better way of meeting the demand for accountability as an important value in itself, and as a device that can improve the social performance of large organizations.

Instead of thinking about how we could legally control the conduct of those leading powerful organizations and, through them, the conduct of the organizations themselves, it might be useful to focus on what all of us who have an interest in their performance really want those leaders and their organizations to do, all things considered. We might decide we want to encourage executives to reach for a kind of social legitimacy within which legal accountability was just one important element. Social legitimacy could be founded on shared moral concerns *and* prudential interests as well as legal liability. Instead of talking about controlling these organizations with legal rules, we might want to encourage them to develop and use practices in managing relations with those who call them to account that would build a shared understanding about the important terms of their accountability and anticipate a new legal structure of accountability that could begin doing its work before it was established in legal form. The goal of enhancing the social legitimacy of organizations might be both a virtuous act for those leading organizations as well as being practically valuable to them in their roles.

Developing and propagating practices that allow the officers and leaders of powerful organizations to engage the anarchic world of accountability agents could help create a court of public opinion in which the plaintiffs are also part of the jury. In essence, instead of trying to resolve the issue of accountability by simply rank ordering the legal claims made against the organization, some kind of deliberation among those demanding accountability could be carried out in which each accountability agent would see the claims of others, and understand that they might have to adjust their claim in light of those claims of others. With no legal platform beneath them, or with an understanding that the existing legal platforms cannot resolve the issue, accountability agents might be more inclined to accommodate one another, and a better structure of accountability be created. Preferences might be altered and improved in this deliberative frame rather than hardened, and a more stable and reliable consensus might emerge (Cohen and Rogers 1995). Meeting undisciplined demands for accountability may feel like a thankless task. Finding the means to increase the social legitimacy of a collective enterprise and its actions, however, might be the kind of task that could attract the commitment of both practical and fair-minded leaders.

Holding out the idea of advancing social legitimacy might be particularly important if meeting the demands for accountability was neither necessary nor sufficient for the creation of legitimacy. It might also be an important shift in perspective if success in increasing the legitimacy of an enterprise might improve its functioning—partly by giving the enterprise more standing and credibility, and partly by allowing those outside and within the organization who support its functioning to support it more wholeheartedly. So, while the leaders of organizations can be *forced* to meet demands for accountability, they might actually *want* to find the means to increase their organization's legitimacy.

Social Accountability versus Social Legitimacy

In order for this argument to be plausible, there has to be some important difference between the idea of social accountability on one hand, and social legitimacy on the other. Many writing about the importance of creating powerful external accountability systems think that there is a very close relationship between the two concepts (Bovens 2005). To them, meeting legally sanctioned demands for accountability is the very definition of social legitimacy. Others, more behaviorally oriented, would say that meeting such demands for accountability is a necessary but not sufficient path towards the creation of social legitimacy (Moore and Brown 2001).

Two important questions about the idea of legitimacy lie in this difference. The first is whether legitimacy is understood as an idealist concept or a psychological judgment by those observing the conduct of an organization, or some combination of the two. By an idealist concept, I mean that an organization can be said to have the quality of legitimacy independent of the views of those who observe, oversee, or interact with the organization as investors, workers, or clients. If the organization measures up to some objective standards of conduct that define legitimacy, then the organization has legitimacy regardless of how individuals distributed across these different positions vis-à-vis the organization would evaluate its conduct and performance. In contrast, if legitimacy is in the eye of the beholder, the only way an organization can be said to have legitimacy is if it is deemed legitimate by individual members of a society who interact with that organization in various different roles.

A combination of the two would suggest that there were some idealist concepts of legitimacy that many particular individuals use in their evaluations, but that these idealist conceptions do not completely dominate individual conceptions of legitimacy. Instead, individuals in different roles, challenged to make judgments about the legitimacy of organizations and their operations, would adapt idealist concepts of legitimacy to fit the particular occasion. In deciding what is socially legitimate, many accountability agents might well be unduly influenced by their own interests at the expense of all others, and also perhaps by relatively idiosyncratic views of the public good. But perhaps some of the special interests and idiosyncrasy can be scoured away through a process that presses individual claimants to use general principles in justifying their claims and exposes them to the more or less reasonable demands of others. Ideally, this sort of process could help transform the clamorous demand for social accountability into a competent court of public opinion that would allow leaders to gain legitimacy for their organization.

The second question about our ideas of legitimacy is whether the concept is primarily concerned with deontological concerns about the degree to which an organization and its leaders conform to right fiduciary relationships with those to whom they owe legal and moral duties of loyalty and care; or with more utilitarian concerns about how well the organization performs in producing or acting in accord with a particular set of values that citizens want to see realized in operations. To some, the only important question about legitimacy is whether an organization has met its fiduciary responsibilities to report, explain, and be accountable. To others, organizations may acquire legitimacy through demonstrations of efficient and effective performance even if they depart somewhat from ordinary expectations of accountability. The end results may secure social legitimacy even if the organization did not conform to fiduciary demands for accountability. This would not be because the organization sacrificed some important value associated with a proper accountability structure, but because the accountability structure itself drew resources from the operations of the organization, reduced the flexibility in methods it needed to achieve its goals, and blunted the organization's initiative (Moore and Gates 1986; Moore 1993).

If the idea of legitimacy is both a legal and psychological concept, and if it refers to both the maintenance of proper fiduciary relationships and the real performance of the organization relative to the expectations and aspirations of those whose interests are affected by it, then there is much more room for the construction of a socially responsive structure of accountability that delivers legitimacy than there is if the idea of accountability is tethered to a static, legal, idealist view of legitimacy. A process of discussion and deliberation among accountability agents might produce a different and stronger social mandate for organizational performance than the legal system of accountability.

The Pursuit of Legitimacy as a Better Way to Promote Social Accountability

It is possible, of course, that creating a discussion about the social legitimacy of an organization's conduct and performance might be every bit as chaotic as the penumbra of demands for accountability itself. Each accountability agent may stand on his or her right to demand accountability and to expect the organization's conduct to conform to that idea. But if particular accountability agents can come to understand that they are one among many stakeholders, if they can be reminded that they and the other claimants have an interest in the overall performance of the organization, and if they come to see that performance both advancing and behaving in accord with several different dimensions of value that are important to them and others, then the way is open to create a kind of accountability that resembles a court of public opinion rather than a babble of self-authorized accountability agents.

If there is a wide public discussion about the legitimacy of a given organization, or a particular class of organizations, and if that discussion settles into a clear set of informal standards, then being accountable to those standards could be seen as the only way an organization can become legitimate. Yankelovich (1991) makes an important distinction between mere public opinion which is superficial, chaotic, and unanchored in social deliberation, and public judgment which is deeper, more settled, and more deeply rooted in a shared social understanding. He describes the process of coming to public judgment as one that depends crucially on individual reflection and social discussion. It seems reasonable to hope that, with some help, a public could come to a public judgment about the standards of accountability that could guide an organization. It is that process that would make the crucially important connection between the idea of legal accountability on one hand, and legitimacy for an organization on the other.

Needless to say, this does not happen often. As a practical matter, then, a gap remains between the idea of accountability and legitimacy. It is in that gap that the issue of legitimacy is fought out. The gap forms the arena within which diverse accountability agents make their claims—confident that they have both a right to do so and a reasonable chance of success. In this world, meeting the legally established demands for accountability does not necessarily produce legitimacy, though it can be helpful. The more difficult but ultimately more valuable path is to engage those who demand accountability in a more collective public discussion designed to properly weigh and integrate the competing demands in an effort to construct social legitimacy for the organization's operations. Such a discussion might well end up transforming the structure of legal accountability over the long run as society and its influential organizations come to understand the values at stake. But in the short run, the pursuit of legitimacy might move organizations towards improved social performance without having to change the legal structure of accountability.

CONCLUSION: CREATING A COMPETENT COURT OF PUBLIC OPINION

The argument, then, is that while thinking about accountability as a legal concept, and using that concept as a principal social mechanism for controlling the conduct of powerful organizations in liberal societies has a long, honorable, and important pedigree, it has always faced some conceptual and practical problems. More importantly, given its illustrious record in reducing organizational misconduct, the concept may cause us to miss the opportunity that lies in focusing attention on other ways to construct social legitimacy in a pluralist, dynamic world.

In that contentious world, legitimacy is constructed in the first instance by taking the demands of self-appointed accountability agents seriously, not because they have a legally supported right to demand accountability, but because the basis of legitimacy in a democratic society is the degree to which powerful organizations whose actions have direct impact on the public (even if their auspices are private) is the degree to which individual citizens grant them legitimacy. From this perspective, *any* complaint is worth taking seriously—at least until we all get a chance to look at and test its empirical and moral importance against the many other claims made on the performance of powerful organizations.

Legitimacy is thus constructed in the second instance through processes that test the empirical and moral importance of these claims and complaints. Is it true that the organization has inflicted unrecognized losses on individuals? Are the losses consequential in either a utilitarian welfare calculation or in a deontological inquiry into what principles of justice and fairness require? How big were the losses compared with the protection or advancement of other important social values? Were the losses necessary to achieve these larger utilitarian or justice aims? Could some compensation be made if the losses were necessary?

Such a process could build social legitimacy for powerful organizations through adaptation of two different kinds of mechanism that are at the core of democratic theory. There is the idea that legitimacy is built through consultation and the consent of the citizens. That gives powerful organizations a reason to be interested in and responsive to claims made against them even though they seem frivolous at the outset. The point of such consultation, however, is not simply to hear and evaluate competing claims from an executive position, but instead to use executive leadership and skills to turn the consultation process into a deliberative one in which those representing particular interests are called upon to hear and understand the claims of others (Fung 2004; Moore and Fung 2012). In such a process, self-interested or idiosyncratic ideas of the public good can become more considered public ideas of the common good.

Then there is a judicial system in which competing interests clash and are resolved in accord with some principle of justice or fairness or the public good. The process permits only certain kinds of arguments and evidence, is regulated by an impartial judge, and the verdict is rendered by a jury of peers. Obviously, not all of this apparatus of a real court can be constructed to adjudicate competing demands for social accountability. But the idea of an impartial magistrate and a jury of peers might help guide those seeking to create a deliberative process among accountability agents.

John Dewey (1927) argued forcefully (and at length!) about the importance of calling into existence a public that could understand and act on its own interests. There are many different occasions when democratic societies need to call a public into existence to legitimate social action taken by both public and private bodies. There are many different ways in which a public can be constructed (Fung and Wright 2003). But one of the important arenas for calling a public into existence is that arena in which accountability agents make claims on organizations. We can try to organize that process as a straightforward legal process. But it might be better to think of it as an occasion for deliberation. And in the background of that deliberation—creating the context for the deliberation—is a public acting as impartial magistrate and jury on the important question of what values ought to be reflected in the conduct and performance of powerful organizations.

REFERENCES

Bardach, E. and Kagan, R. 1982. *Social Regulation: Strategies for Reform*. Richmond, CA: Institute for Contemporary Studies.

Behn, R. D. 2001. *Rethinking Democratic Accountability*. Washington, DC: Brookings Institution Press.

Bovens, M. 2005. Public Accountability, pp. 182–208 in *The Oxford Handbook of Public Management*, eds. E. Ferlie, L. E. Lynn Jr., and C. Pollitt. Oxford: Oxford University Press.

Braithwaite, J. and Drahos, P. 2000. *The Global Regulation of Business*. Cambridge: Cambridge University Press.

Cohen, J. and Rogers, J. 1995. *Associations and Democracy*. London: Verso.

Cunningham, F. 2002. *Theories of Democracy: A Critical Introduction*. London: Routledge.

Dewey, J. 1927. *The Public and its Problems*. New York: Henry Holt.

Dunlop, J. T., ed. 1980. *Business and Public Policy*. Cambridge: Division of Research, Graduate School of Business Administration, Harvard University.

Ebrahim, A. 2005. "Accountability Myopia: Losing Sight of Organizational Learning." *Nonprofit and Voluntary Sector Quarterly*, 34: 56–87.

Foerstal, H. 1999. *The Freedom of Information Act and the Right to Know: The Origins and Applications of the Freedom of Information Act*. Westport: Greenwood Press.

Freeman, R. E., Harrison, J. S., Wicks, A. C., Parmar, B. L., and De Colle, S. 2010. *Stakeholder Theory: The State of the Art*. Cambridge: Cambridge University Press.

Fung, A. and Wright, E. O. 2003. *Deepening Democracy: Institutional Innovations in Empowered Participatory Governance*. London: Verso.

Fung, A. 2004. *The Political Economy of Transparency: What Makes Disclosure Politics Effective?* Cambridge, MA: Ash Institute for Democratic Governance and Innovation, John F. Kennedy School of Government, Harvard University.

Fung, A. 2013. The Principle of Affected Interests and Inclusion in Democratic Governance, pp. 215–235 in *Representation: Elections and Beyond*, eds. J. Nagel and R. Smith. Philadelphia: University of Pennsylvania Press.

Fung, A., Graham, M., and Weil, D. 2007. *Full Disclosure: The Perils and Promise of Transparency*. Cambridge, UK: Cambridge University Press.

Gray, R. H., Owen, D. and Adams, C. 1996. *Accounting and Accountability: Changes and Challenges in Corporate Social Responsibility*. Upper Saddle River, NJ: Prentice Hall.

Hensler, D. 2000. *Class Action Dilemmas: Pursuing Public Goals for Private Gain*. Santa Monica, CA: RAND Institute for Civil Justice.

Landes, W. M. and Posner, R. A. 1987. *The Economic Structure of Tort Law*. Cambridge, MA: Harvard University Press.

Mann, R. A. and Roberts, B. S. 2008. *Business Law and the Regulation of Business*. Ninth Edition. Mason, OH: West Legal Studies in Business.

Mashaw, J. L. 1985. *Due Process in the Administrative State*. Conn.: Yale University Press.

Moore, M. H. and Brown, L. D. 2001. "Accountability, Strategy, and International Non-Governmental Organizations." *Nonprofit and Voluntary Sector Quarterly*, 30: 569–87.

Moore, M. H. and Fung, A. 2012. Calling Publics into Existence: The Political Arts of Public Management, pp. 180–210 in *Ports in a Storm: Public Management in a Turbulent World*, eds. J. C. Donahue and M. H. Moore. Washington, D.C.: Brookings Institution Press.

Moore, M. H. and Gates, M. J. 1986. *Inspectors-General: Junkyard Dogs or Man's Best Friend?* New York: Russell Sage Foundation.

Moore, M. H. and Khagram, S. 2004. *On Creating Public Value: What Business Might Learn from Government about Strategic Management*. Corporate Social Responsibility Initiative Working Paper, No. 3. Cambridge, MA: John F. Kennedy School of Government, Harvard University.

Moore, M. H. 1993. *Accounting for Change: Reconciling the Demands for Accountability and Innovation in the Public Sector*. Washington, DC: Council for Excellence in Government.

Moore, M. H. 1995. *Creating Public Value*. Cambridge, MA: Harvard University Press.

Peters, A., Koechlin, L., Förster, T., and Zinkernagel, G. F. 2009. *Non-State Actors as Standard Setters*. Cambridge, UK: Cambridge University Press.

Reich, R. B. 2007. *Supercapitalism: The Transformation of Business, Democracy, and Everyday Life*. New York: Vintage Books.

Sparrow, M. 1994. *Imposing Duties: Government's Changing Approach to Compliance*. Westport, CT: Praeger.

Vogel, D. 2006. *The Market for Virtue: The Potential and Limitations of Corporate Social Responsibility*. Washington, DC: The Brookings Institution.

Wilson, J. Q. 1989. *Bureaucracy: What Government Agencies Do and Why They Do It*. New York: Basic Books.

Yankelovich, D. 1991. *Coming to Public Judgment: Making Democracy Work in a Complex World*. Syracuse, NY: Syracuse University Press.

PART VII

REFLECTIONS ON THE FUTURE OF ACCOUNTABILITY STUDIES

CHAPTER 40

....

THE ONTOLOGICAL CHALLENGE

....

MELVIN J. DUBNICK

THE CASE FOR ACCOUNTABILITY STUDIES

In an earlier chapter in this volume, I put forward the case for viewing accountability as a cultural keyword. In highlighting its importance as a rhetorical device in the hands of politicians and valued policy tool in those of reformers, that presentation implied that accountability might be nothing more than a cultural artifact of modern society, more significant as an iconic driver of our collective aspirations than as an effective aspect of dealing with the problems of governance. Implied as well was a strong critique of the basic assumptions (i.e., the promises inherent in the different reformist discourses) used to justify the development and use of accountability mechanisms as a means to measure and modify the performance of government.

The theme of this short commentary might seem to run counter to the focus and tone of that earlier analysis, for here I will make the case for the development of a field of "accountability studies" designed to extend and deepen our understanding of its actual role in governance. To put the case in the strongest possible terms, I contend that *it is not possible to comprehend the role of governance in human relationships (past and present) without a basic understanding and appreciation of accountability*. In that sense, the future of governance studies depends on the development of an organized field dedicated to the study of accountability.

OPTION-I AND OPTION-R

The main challenge for the field of accountability studies is to deal with a formidable ontological dilemma, for there are two clear paths the field might follow. Each path involves a defining ontological viewpoint about the social phenomena that comes under the purview of studying accountability. The first option, which I will refer to as Option-I, perceives accountability institutionally, as part of that assemblage of structures and mechanisms that comprise governance. The second (referenced below as Option-R) assumes a relational view of accountability, positing that account-giving behavior is a basic form of human interaction capable of (and often) existing independently of governance arrangements or any other institutional context. These alternative ontologies offer radically different answers to the key question of any research endeavor: What is it we are studying?

A case can be made against this two-options model of the field, for on the surface the two views are not mutually exclusive. The obvious overlap is found in the fact that all institutionalized forms of accountability are comprised of structures and processes (i.e., accountability mechanisms) designed to establish and foster account-giving relationships and associated behavior that serve the purposes of organization (see Aucoin and Heintzman 2000). The problem is that once institutionalized, the account-giving relationship is more often than not transformed into something quite different, e.g., a bureaucratic procedure requiring regular reports or audits, the establishment of a standard for assessing performance, etc.[1] Once a relationship becomes structured, formalized, and/or mechanized, the social dynamic that underpins account-giving relations and behaviors is altered. From the perspective of Option-R, accountability mechanisms are at least one order removed from the behaviors involved in accountability-based interactions, and can best be understood as surrogates for account-giving relationships.[2]

The governance-related literature currently associated with accountability addresses the distinction between the two ontological options whenever confronting the need to define the concept. In some instances the dilemma is resolved by equating accountability with the surrogate mechanisms themselves. Thus, the degree of agency "transparency" (i.e., openness and disclosure) is often cited as a direct measure of accountability (Hale 2008),[3] just as audits and associated reporting and compliance requirements are equated with accountability (Guthrie 1993; Power 1999). In other studies there is a passing acknowledgement of the relational nature of accountability (typically as a principal–agent relationship; see Przeworski et al. 1999), followed by the adoption of an Option-I definition ("for present purposes") that focuses the study's attention on the mechanisms rather than on the relationships underlying them.

In contrast, there exists a considerable body of work outside the realm of governance-related scholarship based on the Option-R ontology. For example, the giving and demanding of accounts has been addressed by sociologists and social psychologists who have generated many studies focusing on excuse-making, the attribution of blame, and reactions to demands to explain one's actions or decisions (e.g., Scott and Lyman 1968; Tetlock et al. 2007). The study of speech acts, initiated by analytic philosophers and applied linguists, is also relevant (Searle 1969; Smith 2008; Buttny 1993), as is the work of cognitive psychologists who explore the creation of self-identity in individual efforts to relate to others (Bandura 2001). Much of the work on the role that ethnomethodology (Garfinkel 1967) and folk psychology (Dennett 1987; Churchland

1989) play in everyday life relates to account-giving behaviors, and there have been efforts among computer scientists to integrate those notions of accountable relationships into their work (see Eriksén 2002). As significant is the contemporary focus among moral philosophers on "what we owe each other" (Scanlon 1998) and the moral identity formed by "giving an account of oneself" to others (Butler 2005).

In addition, within the field of public administration itself there are relevant Option-R case studies that can be brought to the accountability studies endeavor. Among the classics in the field, Herbert Kaufman's study of the US Forest Service (1967) can be reconsidered as an examination of the range of methods used to hold widely dispersed members of the US Forest Service accountable to the priorities of the agency. The work of Maynard-Moody and Musheno (2003) and others who study the everyday lives and dilemmas of public servants can similarly be put to use in a strong research program focused on account-giving relationships and behavior.

And there is clear evidence that such a research program is already underway. Hupe and Hill (2007) have already conducted a re-analysis of Michael Lipsky's 1980 examination of street-level bureaucracies based on the relational nature of public accountability. Lily L. Tsai (2007) has published an in-depth study of the role that "informal accountability" has played in the delivery of public services in rural China, and in the US Barbara Romzek and colleagues have undertaken research to uncover the role that informal accountability relationships play in the complex world of service delivery networks (Romzek, LaRoux, and Blackmar 2012). These and similar studies are indicative of a trend driven in large part by an awareness that there is more to accountability and its role in governance than has been explored under the previously dominant Option-I perspective.

While something of a convergence of the two ontological options seems to be emerging from these studies of informal governance mechanisms, perhaps the most significant developments may be in the efforts of Mark Bovens (2005) and Mark Philp (2009) in constructing a conceptual-theoretical bridge between the two ontologies. Going beyond mere acknowledgment of the relational nature of accountability, each demonstrates that applying what is known about account-giving relations and behavior enhances our understanding of governance and provides insights into why efforts to improve the operations and performance of governments have proven so frustrating and puzzling.

A RADICAL SHIFT TOWARD OPTION-R

While the Bovens/Philps efforts to bridge the ontological options advances the case (and rationale) for the field of accountability studies, my own approach would involve a more radical shift toward the Option-R position. Central to my argument is the contention that account-giving relationships and associated behaviors form the foundations of governance. Put otherwise, account-giving relations comprise the constitutive elements of any arrangement of the structures and process that produce and sustain governance.

This commentary is obviously not the appropriate venue for elaborating the logic and rationale for advocating such a radical ontological shift, but the implications for the study of accountable governance can be considerable. Empirically, Option-R uses account-giving relationships as the basic unit of analysis rather than institutional arrangements and mechanisms.[4] Methodologically, it gives priority to ethnography over design—i.e., critical, descriptive, and explanatory studies over evaluative and prescriptive efforts. Theoretically, it loosens the strong ties of accountability studies to the logic of neo-institutional and positive theory (see Scott 2008; Suddaby 2010) and reasserts its long-established links to moral philosophy (Smith 1759) and the re-emergence of relational social theory (e.g., Archer 2007).

Since the current thread of research on accountability was initiated more than twenty-five years ago (Day and Klein 1987; Romzek and Dubnick 1987), there have been times when one felt the need to make an open plea for greater attention to the complex nature of this critical subject (e.g., Dubnick 2002). Over the past decade (at least) those pleas have been answered. The question now is how we move the field of accountability studies forward.

NOTES

1. See Levin (1974, 364), where a survey of the literature generates four "relatively distinct concepts of accountability: (a) as performance reporting; (b) as a technical process; (c) as a political process; (d) as an institutional process."
2. The same holds true for trust relations; see Harré (1999).
3. Transparency is often perceived as the equivalence of accountability in the policy area as well; see Krotoszynski (2011).
4. A shift equivalent in nature and purpose to Simon's (1947) call for establishing decision-making and decision premises as the basic unit of analysis for the administrative sciences.

REFERENCES

Archer, M. S. 2007. *Making Our Way Through the World: Human Reflexivity and Social Mobility*. Cambridge: Cambridge University Press.

Aucoin, P. and Heintzman, R. 2000. "The Dialectics of Accountability for Performance in Public Management Reform." *International Review of Administrative Sciences*, 66: 45–55.

Bandura, A. 2001. "Social Cognitive Theory: An Agentic Perspective." *Annual Review of Psychology*, 52: 1–26.

Bovens, M. 2005. Public Accountability, pp. 183–208 in *The Oxford Handbook of Public Management*, eds. E. Ferlie, L. E. Lynn, and C. Pollitt. Oxford: Oxford University Press.

Butler, J. 2005. *Giving an Account of Oneself*. New York: Fordham University Press.

Buttny, R. 1993. *Social Accountability in Communication*. London: Sage Publications.

Churchland, P. M. 1989. "Folk Psychology and the Explanation of Human Behavior." *Philosophical Perspectives*, 3: 225–41.

Day, P. and Klein, R. 1987. *Accountabilities: Five Public Services*. London: Tavistock Publications.

Dennett, D. C. 1987. *The Intentional Stance*. Cambridge: MIT Press.

Dubnick, M. J. 2002. *Seeking Salvation for Accountability*. In APSA (The American Political Science Association) Annual Meeting. Boston, 29 August–1 September 2002.

Eriksén, S. 2002. *Designing for Accountability*, pp. 177–86 in Proceedings of the Second Nordic Conference on Human-Computer Interaction. Aarhus, October 19–23, 2002.

Garfinkel, H. 1967. *Studies in Ethnomethodology*. Cambridge, UK: Polity Press.

Guthrie, J. 1993. "Australian Public Business Enterprises: Analysis of Changing Accounting, Auditing and Accountability Regimes." *Financial Accountability & Management*, 9: 101–14.

Hale, T. N. 2008. "Transparency, Accountability, and Global Governance." *Global Governance*, 14: 73–94.

Harré, R. 1999. Trust and its Surrogates: Psychological Foundations of Political Process, pp. 249–72 in *Democracy and Trust*, ed. M. E. Warren. Cambridge, UK; New York: Cambridge University Press.

Hupe, P. and Hill, M. 2007. "Street-Level Bureaucracy and Public Accountability." *Public Administration*, 85: 279–99.

Kaufman, H. 1967. *The Forest Ranger: A Study in Administrative Behavior*. Baltimore, MD: Johns Hopkins University Press.

Krotoszynski, R. J. Jr. 2011. "Transparency, Accountability, and Competency: An Essay on the Obama Administration, Google Government, and the Difficulties of Securing Effective Governance." *University of Miami Law Review*, 65: 449–81.

Levin, H. M. 1974. "A Conceptual Framework for Accountability in Education." *The School Review*, 82: 363–91.

Lipsky, M. 1980. *Street-Level Bureaucracy: Dilemmas of the Individual in Public Services*. New York: Russell Sage Foundation.

Maynard-Moody, S. and Musheno, M. C. 2003. *Cops, Teachers, Counselors:Stories from the Front Lines of Public Service*. Ann Arbor: University of Michigan Press.

Philp, M. 2009. "Delimiting Democratic Accountability." *Political Studies*, 57: 28–53.

Power, M. 1999. *The Audit Society: Rituals of Verification*. New York: Oxford University Press.

Przeworski, A., Stokes, S. C. and Manin, B., eds. 1999. *Democracy, Accountability, and Representation*. New York: Cambridge University Press.

Romzek, B. S. and Dubnick, M. J. 1987. "Accountability in the Public Sector: Lessons From the Challenger Tragedy." *Public Administration Review*, 47: 227–38.

Romzek, B. S., LeRoux, K., and Blackmar, J. M. 2012. "A Preliminary Theory of Informal Accountability Among Network Organizational Actors." *Public Administration Review*, 72: 442–53.

Scanlon, T. 1998. *What We Owe to Each Other*. Cambridge, Mass.: Belknap Press of Harvard University Press.

Scott, M. B. and Lyman, S. M. 1968. "Accounts". *American Sociological Review*, 33: 46–62.

Scott, W. 2008. "Approaching Adulthood: The Maturing of Institutional Theory." *Theory and Society*, 37: 427–42.

Searle, J. R. 1969. *Speech Acts: An Essay in the Philosophy of Language*. London: Cambridge U.P.

Simon, H. A. 1947. *Administrative Behavior*. New York: Macmillan Co.

Smith, A. 1759. *The Theory of Moral Sentiments*. London: A. Millar.

Smith, N. 2008. *I Was Wrong: The Meanings of Apologies*. Cambridge: Cambridge University Press.

Suddaby, R. 2010. "Challenges for Institutional Theory." *Journal of Management Inquiry*, 19: 14–20.

Tetlock, P. E., Visser, P. S., Singh, R., Polifroni, M., Scott, A., Elson, S. B., Mazzocco, P., and Rescober, P. 2007. "People as Intuitive Prosecutors: The Impact of Social-Control Goals on Attributions of Responsibility." *Journal of Experimental Social Psychology*, 43: 195–209.

Tsai, L. L. 2007. "Solidary Groups, Informal Accountability, and Local Public Goods Provision in Rural China." *American Political Science Review*, 101: 355–72.

CHAPTER 41

....

THE NEED FOR A SYSTEMIC APPROACH

....

FRANK VIBERT

THIS reflection focuses on the accountability of unelected (non-majoritarian) bodies. Because such bodies are deliberately set at arm's length from politics and lie outside direct control by electorates they are seen to raise special problems in the ways in which they can be held to account (Braithwaite 1999; Thatcher and Stone Sweet 2002; Vibert 2007). In thinking about the ways in which the unelected exercise their authority, there seem to me to be three important areas that need much further exploration in future accountability studies. Most studies in accountability focus, as the majority of chapters in this handbook demonstrate, on rationalist assumptions of human behavior, static analyses, and isolated mechanisms or institutions. In order to extend our knowledge, it is imperative that future studies of accountability take up each of these three challenges.

THE BEHAVIORAL

....

A starting point for the development of accountability studies in my view would involve the incorporation of richer views of human behavior (see Patil, Vieider, and Tetlock; and Koch and Wüstemann in this volume). The prevailing model is essentially "rationalist" and connects most easily to a "deliberative" or "participatory" view of democracy. It relies on information, question and answer, and presupposes that the actor and the forum and the public speak the same language, understand each other, and are open to exchange and changing their minds and practices through persuasion—or will accept the closure of disputes through reasoned decision-rules such as those imposed by a court or, in the case of a participatory model, by a referendum (Trechsel 2010).

This model of interaction represents an over-simplified view of human attitudes and approaches to decision-taking. It is normatively attractive because it is nice to think of public policy and social interactions in these terms. Its empirical foundation however is weak. The model represents a highly stylized "ideal type" rather than the real world. It depicts a setting that is far removed from the way people, groups of experts, and unelected institutions actually form attitudes and approach decision-taking. Cognitive studies suggest that the real world is characterized by the use of heuristics (short-cut methods of decision-taking), emotion based rationalities (such as favoring the familiar), and self-deception (for example people looking for evidence that confirms a pre-existing belief).

Political science is adapting to take a more nuanced view of human behavior in the context of electoral politics. For example, it has been able to adapt to the constraints of the model of bounded rationality that emphasizes the use of heuristics (Simon 1960; Schattschneider 1975). It recognizes that much politics takes the form of short-cut forms of communication. Accounts of electoral behavior have also been able to take account of some forms of self-deception, such as seeking confirmatory evidence for a view, consistent with theories of cognitive dissonance (Festinger 1959). Electoral behavior thus meets a broad conception of political accountability that focuses on the need for parties and politicians to defend a record and the possibility of facing sanction through removal from elected office. However it does not sit comfortably with the standards of rationality expected of expert bodies. Non-elected regulatory bodies belong to the knowledge world, borrow their epistemic standards from those of the natural and social sciences, and holding them to account involves a higher standard subjecting the procedures employed by such bodies to a rigorous and challenging mechanism of review.

This higher standard creates a discontinuity with the kind of reasoning employed by electorates. It is therefore a challenge to those who think that unelected bodies should be held accountable in some way by the general public. The general public is unlikely to engage with expert discourse, and the short-cut reasoning used by the general public will not hold expert bodies to the standards to which they need to be held. The general concept of public accountability remains relevant in so far as the public may want to know that all bodies that exercise authority in society are in some way held to account (particularly when things go wrong) but approaches to accountability that stress the virtues of "participation" or "voice" have to be reshaped in a much more nuanced way. Possibly the focus should be on how unelected bodies themselves play a "representation" role and stand in for the public interest and how this role is to be defined (Norr-Cetina 1981).

A richer account of cognitive behavior also needs to be adopted in thinking further about the higher standards that apply to unelected bodies. The working assumption must be that both actors and forums, including judiciaries, exhibit the full range of cognitive characteristics including many of those biases that accompany the use of heuristics, emotion-based decision-taking and self-deception (Haas 2007).

What this suggests is that it is not sufficient for accountability studies simply to assert the truism that channels of accountability are multiple. What is important is to recognize that bodies with authority in society work to different standards of rationality and that different standards of rationality apply to different systems of social coordination. In particular, holding expert bodies to account involves much greater exploration of how to select and apply the relevant cognitive standards while concepts of accountability to the general public need to be reformulated from a different perspective (Vibert 2011).

ACCOUNTABILITY AND THE PROCESSES OF CHANGE

A second general area that might receive more attention in future accountability studies concerns the relationship between accountability and ideas about the processes of political change. Much analysis of accountability is conducted in static terms—actors, acts, and decisions at particular points of time. However, political systems, and systems of authority more generally, are not stable but in constant flux and it is therefore important to develop an approach to accountability that tracks changes over time.

From the perspective of analyzing change, accountability can be seen as a mechanism for monitoring interactions and linking processes of frequent small changes at the margins to larger scale accumulating changes. However, when it comes to theorizing about this linkage, theories of incrementalist change such as "muddling through" or "path dependency" do not seem to link very easily to theories of episodic and major change borrowed mainly from disciplines outside political science—such as "waves" of democracy from the sociology of the diffusion of innovation, "punctuated equilibrium" also from sociology or paleontology, and "paradigm shifts" from the theory of scientific discovery—and none seem to provide a particularly apt framework for the analysis of accountability as a mechanism for overseeing change.

Systems theory offers an alternative framework in making a distinction between systems that are self-reflective and possibly self-correcting and those that are not. From this perspective accountability can be seen as about mechanisms for triggering reflection and correction. This perspective also calls into play a constitutional perspective since constitutions assume that systems are not self-correcting.

SYSTEMS ACCOUNTABILITY

The third area concerns the need to think about the accountability of systems of authority as such and not just in the context of change. Much recent discussion of accountability has been framed in terms of the relationship between an actor wielding power (such as a rail safety regulator) and a forum (such as a tribunal of inquiry) monitoring how that power has been used. This way of framing the debate places the focus on the individual institutional arrangements that bring the relationship together, or on the "regime," where a complex of arrangements may be involved. It is a "micro" perspective from which it is assumed or asserted that more general inferences can be drawn about accountability.

By contrast, a systems approach looks at accountability in terms of how powers are exercised through a system or subsystem of social coordination.[1] A systems approach looks at the social system as the totality of different systems and subsystems of social coordination—including politics, the law, and the market.[2] From this viewpoint it is important to know how power and authority is being exercised within a particular system, to monitor whether or not the system is operating as envisaged, and to look at system inter-relationships and for adjustments to be made if the system is not working as intended.

Most current discussions of accountability have adopted a systems perspective only in a limited sense in the context of viewing accountability as a learning mechanism for public administration. The main focus has been on the health or performance of the individual organization or the arrangement. Under this approach the principal question posed is whether or not the organization operates to the required normative standards or whether the forum or regime works. The systems approach asks a different question. It asks about the health of the system or subsystem. Is the system of financial regulation working as intended within the market system, or the system of regulation working as intended within the system of government, or, considered as a separate system, for social coordination? Accountability from this perspective is not about informing ourselves about a particular institution or decision with possible "consequences" for that institution. It is about informing ourselves about the performance of the system to which the institution belongs and that information leading to "consequences" for the way that system is organized.[3] It involves an "integrity" approach rather than a "compliance" approach (Philp 2008).

There are three main reasons why a systems approach may be seen to be becoming more relevant. First, it no longer seems safe to make general inferences about a system from the behavior of a particular actor. The perils of moving from the particular to the general have been well illustrated by the 2008 international financial crisis. In that case individual financial actors took decisions about leverage that were rational for each in the light of the capital requirements regime of Basel II but that led to instability in the system as a whole and to collapse. Following the crisis, financial supervisors are putting intensive efforts into trying to achieve a better understanding of the financial sector as a complex system. A similar caution about the care needed in going from the particular to the collective is appropriate more generally.

Secondly, modern societies are increasingly turning to the segmentation and disaggregation of issues to solve policy problems and in this process the big picture may be lost. Modern societies are bound together only to a limited extent by shared norms and identities. Multicultural societies have populations that embrace multiple identities and conflicting norms. One reaction of contemporary societies is to approach the solving of problems of public policy not as a matter of general principle or shared norms (on which there would be no agreement) but as specific questions of "pragmatism" or technical detail. This tendency to deal with the specific has been encouraged by the need to mobilize knowledge and information from the social and natural sciences that is also compartmentalized into different disciplines and sub-disciplines and is itself constantly subdividing into new specialties. (Abbott 2001). It is also encouraged by the fact that many problems of public policy have an increasingly technical or scientific character. This may be a productive way for societies to go about problem-solving but it raises questions that go beyond the performance and accountability of individual institutions.

The third reason why it is important to adopt a systems approach is that mentioned above; that patterns of authority within societies are in constant flux and it is important to monitor and to be able to adjust to these changing patterns. Particular disquiet is sometimes expressed about what is happening to political systems. Political parties no longer seem to aggregate public opinion as effectively as in the past, the connections of the digital age seem to fracture opinion as much as bring it together, and the ability of political parties to "socialize" conflict seems therefore to have eroded (Schattschneider 1975). This disquiet is also stimulated by the increasing reliance on experts and expert bodies (Bevir 2010). Some of this disquiet is misplaced. At the same time there is a need to monitor what is happening to the different systems of authority and the way in which they interrelate. This again seems to require a "macro" perspective rather than a "micro" one.

These three areas of challenge—the behavioral, the dynamic, and the systemic—will not be easy to meet. Little research has been done on the cognitive behavior of expert bodies, most concepts of change in political systems have been borrowed from disciplines outside political science, and there is a basic lack of agreement among political scientists on how to analyze systems of authority (Eckstein and Gurr 1975).

Notes

1. The term "system" is defined by Anthony Giddens (1984, 24) to refer to "reproduced relations between actors or collectivities, organized as regular social practices."
2. One influential account of social systems is provided by Niklas Luhmann's theorizing about complex systems. For Luhmann "complexity" is "a measure for indeterminacy or lack of information" and can either reflect the complexity of the environment or the system (Luhmann 1995, 27–8; 1984).
3. The importance of a systems approach is also recognized by Bovens, Curtin, and t' Hart (2010, 53) in discussing accountability in the EU.

References

Abbott, A. 2001. *Chaos of Disciplines*. Chicago: University of Chicago Press.
Bevir, M. 2010. *Democratic Governance*. Princeton, N.J.: Princeton University Press.
Bovens, M., Curtin, D., and 't Hart, P. 2010. *The Real World of EU Accountability*. Oxford: Oxford University Press.

Braithwaite, John. 1999. "Accountability and Governance under the Regulatory State." *Australian Journal of Public administration*. 58 (1): 90-94.

Eckstein, Harry and Gurr, Ted R. 1975. *Patterns of Authority*. New York. John Wiley & Sons.

Festinger, L. 1959. *A Theory of Cognitive Dissonance*. London: Tavistock Publications.

Giddens, A. 1984. *The Constitution of Society*. Berkeley: University of California Press.

Haas, P. M. 2007. Epistemic Communities, pp. 792–806 in *Oxford Handbook of Environmental Law*, eds. D. Bodansky, J. Brunnee, and E. Hey. Oxford: Oxford University Press.

Luhmann, N. 1984. *Soziale Systeme: Grundriß einer allgemeinen Theorie*. Frankfurt am Mein: Surhkamp.

Luhmann, N. 1995. *Social Systems*. Stanford, CA: Stanford University Press.

Norr-Cetina, K. 1981. Introduction, pp. 1–47 in Advances in *Social Theory & Methodology*, eds. K. D. Knorr-Cetina and A. V. Cicourel. London: Routledge & Kegan Paul.

Philp, M. 2008. "Delimiting Democratic Accountability." *Political Studies*, 57: 28–53.

Schattschneider, E. E. 1975. *The Semi Sovereign People*. Orlando, FL: Harcourt Brace Jovanovich College Publishers.

Simon, H. A. 1960. *The Sciences of the Artificial*. Cambridge, Mass.: MIT Press.

Thatcher, M. and Stone Sweet, A. 2002. "Theory and Practice of Non-Majoritarian Institutions." *West European Politics*, 25: 1–22.

Trechsel, A. H. 2010. "Reflexive Accountability and Direct Democracy." *West European Politics*, 33: 1050–64.

Vibert, F. 2007. *The Rise of the Unelected*. Cambridge: Cambridge University Press.

Vibert, F. 2011. *Democracy and Dissent: The Challenge of International Rule Making*. Cheltenham, UK: Edward Elgar.

CHAPTER 42

....

THE FUTURE AND RELEVANCE OF ACCOUNTABILITY STUDIES

....

MATTHEW FLINDERS

THERE is little doubt that the concept of accountability appears to be emerging as the *über*-concept of the twenty-first century. And yet at the same time it appears that the concept is in some ways more nebulous, contested, and vague than it has ever been. When located within the contours of Sartori's (1970) classic work on conceptual political analysis it appears that accountability appears destined to provide an example of *conceptual stretching* (i.e. vague, amorphous conceptualizations that say more and-more about less and less) rather than *conceptual travelling*, in which a tight and broadly coherent framework is applied across a range of cases. And yet to adopt this position would be to deny the existence of a rich seam of material—much of it represented in this handbook—that has in recent years sought to increase the analytical utility and leverage of this concept through the development of multi-dimensional frameworks and an increasingly sophisticated awareness of *the politics* of accountability. It is, however, difficult to review the broader landscape of accountability studies and its main scholarly reference points and not conclude that in terms of "coming to terms with accountability," as Willems and Van Dooren (2012) argue, there remains an urgent need for a solid conceptual framework.[1]

And yet in reaching this conclusion the student of public accountability immediately slips into a pre-existing idiom whereby the field is littered with previous attempts at conceptual cartography in which various forms and types of accountability (judicial, public, managerial, market, etc.) are identified and compared (Flinders 2001). Although such an approach would dovetail with Sartori's emphasis on conceptual precision and conceptual deconstruction it has arguably mutated into a form of disciplinary path-dependency whereby the intellectual heritage of accountability studies has—to some extent—become fixated with narrow categorizations, limited case studies, and etymological explorations to the detriment of a more expansive and potentially fertile focus on a range of broader socio-political factors that in themselves have much to say about the changing nature of account-demanding, account-giving, and (critically) the role of the social and political sciences in the twenty-first century. It is in exactly this context that this chapter seeks to prod and provoke and chide and challenge in order to clear the ground for new beginnings. More specifically, this chapter seeks to set out three inter-related arguments about the future of accountability studies (broadly defined) and its position within an increasingly salient debate concerning the public relevance and visibility of the social and political sciences.

> Argument 1 (A1)—Teasing apart the concept of accountability can be usefully framed within the language of *supply* and *demand*. This provides a relatively simple and agreed-upon conceptual vocabulary that raises fresh questions about whether an 'accountability gap' actually exists and how it might be closed (Ashworth, Snape, and Aulakh 2007).
>
> ⇓
>
> Argument 2 (A2)—A focus on the dynamic and iterative relationship between supply and demand forces scholars to step back and reflect upon the nature of the 'accountability space' and their own role in creating or delimiting this terrain.
>
> ⇓
>
> Argument 3 (A3)—The future of 'accountability studies' as a fledgling field of inquiry in its own right will depend very much on the degree to which it can demonstrate its broader social relevance.

The glue that holds each of these arguments together is a focus on (the politics of) public expectations—but not simply about the public's expectations about levels and forms of accountability vis-à-vis politicians and public servants but more broadly about the public's expectations (as well as those of politicians and public servants who are under increasing pressure to deliver "more for less" across the public sector) of academics vis-à-vis society. The core aim of this chapter is therefore to encourage some reflection on the accountability of those academics who study public accountability by locating them *within* the analytical construct of a social "accountability space" that is, by definition, replete with its own demands, expectations, and tensions. This chapter is therefore trying to cover a lot of analytical and professional ground in a relatively small number of words. This will inevitably demand the use of a fairly broad brush on a wide canvas but to some extent this does not matter as the central ambition of the chapter is to encourage other students of accountability to explore, reject, or finesse the arguments offered, thereby achieving a more fine-grained understanding of the issues raised. With this caveat in place it is possible to examine the first argument.

A1: Accountability: Supply and Demand

In 2000 the American political scientist and Nobel Prize winner Elinor Ostrom (2000) outlined "the danger of self-evident truths" and warned that "the fact that something is so widely believed does not make it correct." The aim of this section is to very briefly locate the theme of challenging "self-evident truths" squarely within the parameters of public accountability studies by challenging a dominant assumption within the now burgeoning literature on accountability and in doing so focus attention on the politics of *supply* and *demand*. From Simon Jenkins' *Accountable to None* (1996) through to Janet McIntyre-Mills' *Systemic Governance and Accountability* (2010) with a number of key texts—like Jonathon Fox and David Brown's *The Struggle for Accountability* (1998), Mark Bovens' *The Quest for Responsibility* (1998), Dilip Mookherjee's *The Crisis in Government Accountability* (2004), David Held and Mathias Koenig-Archibugi's *Global Governance and Public Accountability* (2005), Goetz and Jenkins' *Reinventing Accountability* (2005), Gustavsson, Karlsson, and Person's *The Illusion of Accountability in the European Union* (2009) and Richard Bellamy and Antonio Palumbo's *Political Accountability* (2010)—in between, the conventional wisdom is relatively clear and can be summed-up in four analytical steps:

Step 1: The transition from *government* to *governance* has undermined traditional mechanisms of democratic accountability.

⇓

Step 2: As a result politicians have become more untrustworthy and bureaucracies less responsive.

⇓

Step 3: Any individual or organization that argues against greater accountability must have something to hide.

⇓

Step 4: New modes and mechanisms of accountability therefore need to be implemented (i.e. the "reformist paradox").

The "self-evident" truth that tends to pervade much of the literature on public accountability is therefore that a serious "accountability gap"—possibly even by some accounts an "accountability chasm"—has emerged due to a disconnection between the evolution of the state (i.e. from "government" to "governance") and the existing architecture for securing an account from those to whom public power is delegated. If the geological metaphor of "chasms" and "gaps" is taken a little further it is possible to suggest that a constitutional fault-line has always existed within the constitutional configurations of most modern polities as the theory of democratic government was rarely perfectly mirrored by reality. However, this initial fissure has for a number of reasons grown to the extent that Chan and Pattberg (2008, 108) have observed a number of factors that have widened "the pre-existing accountability gaps" to the extent that they now talk of an "accountability crisis."

The link between the scholarship of Chan and Pattberg and this chapter's emphasis on the politics of public expectations in relation to accountability is their emphasis on "issue framing" (i.e. the social construction or schema through which individuals try to make sense of an issue and construct a response). The framing of public accountability by the majority of scholars, irrespective of their discipline, has generally been couched in the language of "problems," "deficits," and "blame games" (Hood 2010). As a result the analytical conclusions and normative prescriptions of most scholars have tended to focus on *increasing supply* by designing and implementing new forms of accountability in an attempt to "close" the accountability gap. It is, however, possible to frame the issue of accountability as one of public understanding, political literacy, and social trust and, through this re-framing of the accountability "problem", generate alternative or complementary strategies for closing the gap that most people agree has emerged. Indeed, simply taking this focus on reframing into the discourse and language of an "accountability gap" immediately reminds us that closing any gap can be achieved by either *increasing supply* (i.e. through the implementation of new forms and mechanisms of accountability) or *reducing demand* (i.e. through forging a less high-blame, low-trust "attack politics" social context in which the public possesses a more sophisticated understanding of the complexities and challenges of modern governance and therefore a more realistic set of expectations regarding accountability)—or *a combination of both strategies*. The simple argument of this section is that the field of "accountability studies" has predominantly focused on *increasing supply* whereas this chapter focuses on the controversial and highly unfashionable idea of *reducing demand*.

This brings the argument to a focus on the politics of public expectations regarding public accountability. Is it heretical to suggest that in some situations the public's "accountability expectations" are simply unrealistic? Is it sacrilegious to suggest that *more* accountability might not always be a "good thing"? "There exists an almost unquestioned assumption", as Dubnick (2002) notes, "that the creation or enhancement of accountability mechanisms of any sort will result in greater democracy." But has no one else noticed that just as accountability, transparency, and freedom of information have become increasingly dominant within democratic governance that levels of public trust in politicians, political processes, and political institutions have declined? This is reflected in a vast literature on "disaffected democracies," "why we hate politics," and "the life and death of democracy" (Hay 2007; Pharr and Putnam 2000; Keane 2009). To suggest that public accountability may not always be the "magic concept" many suppose it to be is not a novel argument (Pollitt and Hupe 2011). Frank Anechiarico and James Jacobs's *The Pursuit of Absolute Integrity* (1996), Robert Behn's *Rethinking Democratic Accountability* (2001), Christopher Hood and David Heald's *Transparency. The Key to Better Governance?* (2006), and Dino Falaschetti's *Democratic Governance and Economic Performance* (2009), not to mention Jonathan Koppell's (2005) work on "multiple-accountabilities disorder," have each in their own ways demonstrated the sometimes pathological impacts of accountability on both organizations and individuals. Not everybody therefore agrees that accountability is a "good thing", that it is fundamental to liberal democracy and *that we need more of it* [emphasis added] (Pollitt 2008).

And yet the main aim of this section has not been to re-visit existing arguments about the "accountability–efficiency trade-off" (March and Olsen 1995), but to make the far simpler point that in analyzing accountability (and its social and political implications) scholars might consider dealing with the perceived "accountability gap" through a combination of both *increasing supply* and also *decreasing demand*. Decreasing demand in the sense of attempting to forge a more realistic set of public expectations in relation to public accountability that are in themselves informed by an awareness of the problems of "many hands" and "many eyes" in an increasingly complex and fragmented network-based governing environment (Thompson 1980; Bovens 2007; Flinders 2009).[2] This focus on re-framing, in turn, forces us to step back and shift our analytical lens to this chapter's second argument and the notion of "accountability space."

A2: THE ACCOUNTABILITY SPACE

In many ways the aim of this chapter is to situate the analysis of public accountability within its broader social and professional context and, as such, the aim of this section is to try and offer a link between the focus on conceptual vagueness or slipperiness that was emphasized in the opening section and the previous section's emphasis on *reducing demand* as a way of closing the "accountability gap" that many scholars have identified. In essence, the core argument of this section is simply that accountability is a messy and difficult concept due to the simple fact that democratic politics (i.e. the *public* element of public accountability) is innately and unavoidably messy. This, in turn, introduces Dubnick's (2011) recent focus on the notion of "accountability space" and the need for scholars to "give priority to research that maps that space as a first step toward understanding the nature and potential of accountable governance" (cf. Flinders 2011). But this chapter attempts to go much further by placing the academic scholar of public accountability within that "accountability space."

Viewed from this perspective academics are not passive or neutral analysts but are themselves one important strand of the social fabric that produces, supports, or questions dominant assumptions about the expected standard of public accountability. Put slightly differently, this chapter asks whether academics have in themselves created or contributed to the perceived "accountability crisis" by over-inflating the social expectations surrounding the concept. In asking this question it is possible to draw a modicum of support from Dubnick's (2011, 705) critique that "the reformist narrative [highlighted above] drives the current obsession with so called accountability solutions to a wide range of problems for which they are not suited." He goes on to note that "Nothing short of a break with that discourse and its associated assumptions will put our 'accountability' problems in proper perspective...It is not accountability that is undermining our aspirations for an effective democracy but the reformist aspiration for an effective democracy that is undermining accountability."

Putting accountability in its "proper perspective"—at least for the purposes of this section and chapter—involves locating the concept within an honest, pragmatic, and mature understanding of the inevitable nature of democratic politics. As Crick (1962) argued in his seminal *In Defence of Politics* almost exactly half a century ago, democratic politics is simply and inevitably *messy*. As a social process it cannot escape the existence of tensions, gridlocks, and incompatible demands; it can be slow and frustrating and tends to grate and grind for the simple reason that it is a worldly and compromise-based art. It is built, to return to Crick, on a "complex timidity" and "untidy elegance" but it was at the same time for him a quite beautiful and civilizing activity. And yet at the root of Crick's argument was a focus on public expectations and public understanding that resonates with the previous section's emphasis on the language of *supply* and *demand*. Put simply, Crick explained how political competition between parties and candidates created inflationary pressures that over-inflated public expectations. As such "people expect too much—and the disillusionment of unreal ideals is an occupational hazard of free politics." Stoker (2006) drew upon this line of reasoning to suggest that democratic politics was to some extent "destined to disappoint" because it involves the tough process of squeezing collective decisions out of multiple and competing interests and opinions.

Crick's "mere essay" has influenced a generation of scholars and social commentators who have in their own ways sought to challenge public apathy and disengagement by offering a more balanced account of democratic politics' achievements *alongside* its failings (Turner and Hogan 2004; Stoker 2006; Hay 2007). The link between this broad field of scholarship and the narrower sub-field of accountability studies is that the latter has arguably failed to acknowledge the fact that because democratic governance is inevitably messy then to some extent public accountability mechanisms will inevitably reflect this fact. More specifically there is often an epistemological and methodological bias at play in the sense that rational-choice theoretic approaches that presuppose that all individuals are selfish and self-serving will to some extent always reveal a degree of selfish and self-serving behavior. Hay (2009) laments the social consequences of public choice theory by suggesting that by accepting certain assumptions about self-interested motives academics have been unwittingly culpable in "fuelling the contemporary culture of political cynicism. Political science has, in short, been part of the problem; and only if this is acknowledged can it become part of the solution."

Phrased in these terms the problem of conceptual precision mutates from being an analytical or methodological challenge to being a social or political challenge. "Political", not in the sense of party politics, but political in the sense that public accountability is inevitably a mirror-image development of public governance that emanates from political processes and decision-making systems. Put slightly differently, could it be that too many accountability-focused scholars have failed to acknowledge the inevitable gap between *theory* and *practice* or between *ideals* and *reality*? To pose this question is not to deny that anyone should stop striving for certain ideals or stop thinking about society as they might like it to be in the future but is to inject a degree of realism into debates about public accountability that accepts that—like politics and life—accountability has limits. Could it be that by projecting unrealistic expectations and failing to promote the public understanding of democratic politics, scholars may have unwittingly played a small role in fuelling political disengagement and apathy? Let me reiterate that Herod is not in my heart but there is no escaping the fact that the wider literature on public accountability generally tends to approach the topic in a pessimistic, skeptical, and generally bleak manner that implicitly conveys the values of what Flinders (2012) labels "the bad faith model of politics" in which politicians are generally corrupt and not to be trusted and political processes are generally inefficient and self-serving. Willems and Dooren (2012, 2) pin this argument squarely on the tail of accountability studies when they argue that:

> The pessimistic narrative risks idealizing the past, as if holding a government to account was ever that easy and straightforward; and it also risks leading to *unrealistically high expectations and consequently to negative assessments of the present* [emphasis added].

Not only does this argument re-introduce the creation and management of public expectations vis-à-vis public accountability but it also provides a very direct link to Dubnick's (2011) work on "accountability space" in general, and the "reformist paradox" in particular, as a concluding topic for this section.

The "reformist paradox" is—according to Dubnick—little more than the simple fact that any effort to improve accountability through reforms generates consequences that in fact alter, often undermine, and generally complicate existing forms of accountability. More importantly, Dubnick's approach clearly demonstrates how public accountability involves the management of expectations in a setting where there are generally multiple, diverse, and often conflicting expectations (Romzek and Dubnick 1987). As a result, although Dubnick is not against reformist agendas per se, he is more skeptical than many other scholars of the value and worthiness of proposals for change that are based on the logic of "more accountability is better governance" (i.e. increasing supply). The future of accountability studies, for Dubnick (2011, 708), will be better served by adopting a more sophisticated ontological position that defines accountability, not as a *secondary relationship* governing the transfer of resources (money, food, time, etc.), but as a primary "ingredient in the building and maintenance of the social order within which structures (i.e. institutions, mechanisms, and processes) operate." In advocating a relationalist ontology that views the milieu of account-demanding and account-giving as the basic fabric of modern governance—as opposed to a more substantialist approach that is simply focused on institutions, mechanisms, and processes—Dubnick carves out an "alternative reality" that suddenly poses a completely new set of questions that concern not just the epistemology and methodologies deployed by social and political theorists in exploring public governance but also far broader questions concerning the professional responsibilities of academics to *the public*. It therefore provides a way of placing scholars of public accountability squarely within the "accountability space" they profess to study. It is to this topic and the third argument concerning "impact" and social relevance that this chapter now turns.

A3: The Social Relevance and "Impact" of Accountability Studies

This chapter is structured around three arguments or pillars that can be viewed as dissecting the field of accountability studies across three levels. The first section and argument focused on the micro level and suggested that the language of *supply* and *demand* offered new ways of understanding the "accountability gap." This linked in to critiques of the reformist narrative by daring to suggest that the "gap" might be closed from above (i.e. by reducing demand) rather than always focusing on lifting the lower bar (i.e. increasing supply). The second section then adopted a more mid-range perspective by outlining the simple argument that as democratic politics is inevitably messy, compromise-based, imperfect, and forged around the production of what economists would label "sub-optimal" or "least worst" decisions, then it was not surprising that accountability processes reflected these qualities. This, in turn, produced a set of questions about whether scholars had imposed unrealistic expectations on an inevitably messy world and as a result produced consistently negative and critical assessments (which then, in themselves, fuelled the reformist paradigm). This third and final section employs Dubnick's arguments in favor of a relationist ontology as a gateway into a far wider (macro-level) discussion about the position of accountability studies within the broader debate concerning the social relevance, impact, and future of the social and political sciences. This, in turn, allows us to generate fresh insights and novel ways of reflecting upon the past, present, and future of accountability studies.

It is, however, once again impossible within the boundaries of this short chapter to provide little more than the merest hint or flavor of the link between the study of public accountability and the broader debate about the future of the social and political sciences, let alone the potential value of a relationist ontology. This is—as already stated—a work in progress that is using big and bold brush strokes on a very wide canvas in the hope that subsequent scholars will assist with filling in the fine detail (or even erasing the parts they do not like). The link, however, between the second and third arguments of this chapter is provided by the way in which a relationist ontological position focuses attention not simply on the day-to-day operation of forms of accountability or "accountability webs" but also on the manner in which the entire process is embedded in a dynamic accountability space. A space that is constituted upon both visible institutions, mechanisms, and processes but possibly more importantly on *invisible* accountability relationships that define and orientate our ("yours," "mine," "his," "hers") expectations and understandings of not only the world around us but also our position within a rapidly changing world.

In short, the relationist perspective suddenly asks pertinent questions about the role of academics in shaping (either through omission or intent) the expectations that the public have of the world around them. From here it is little more than a small intellectual hop, skip, or jump into a broader and more urgent set of questions concerning the role, obligations, and responsibilities of social and political scientists in the twenty-first century. Or, more specifically, to a set of questions concerning the responsibilities of academics to the broader public—to the demos—in terms of helping them make sense of the world in which the traditional banisters (to paraphrase Hannah Arendt) like religion, close family units, stable employment, clear political structures, appear to have melted away into an increasingly ephemeral and mobile form of "liquid modernity" (Strong 2012; Bauman 2000). The question then becomes one of the role of academics in helping the public make sense of the world around them—to offer a politics with vision and new banisters.

These questions have become crystallized into a global debate about the social relevance and "impact" of the social and political sciences. At the core of this debate is a concern that in recent decades the incentives surrounding academic life have emphasized esoteric specialization and impenetrable publications over public engagement. The "tragedy of political science" as Ricci (1984) argued three decades ago is therefore that as the study of politics became more "professional" and "scientific," the weaker it became in terms of both its social relevance and accessibility and as a social force supportive of democracy and democratic values. More recently, Shapiro (2005) has written a devastating critique of the manner in which the social and political relevance of the study of politics arguably melted away in the 1980s and 1990s and was replaced with a malignant (and to some extent embarrassing) preoccupation with methodological masturbation, theoretical fetishism, sub-disciplinary balkanization, and the development of esoteric discourses. Leading figures within the social and political sciences have in their own ways voiced serious concerns that resonate with Shapiro's thesis and, in doing so, have suggested that a new "gap"– an "understanding gap"—has arisen due to a failure of the social sciences to promote the public understanding of politics (cf. Flinders 2012).

This focus on an "understanding gap" brings this chapter full circle and back to a focus on supply *and* demand (i.e. A1), an awareness of the "accountability space" and the role of academics within that social milieu (A2), and the simple conclusion that the future of accountability studies will to a great extent depend on the degree to which it can demonstrate its broader social relevance and impact (A3). Moreover it is possible to conclude by arguing that a clear relationship exists between the "accountability gap" and the "understanding gap" that in itself raises critical questions about the future and relevance of accountability studies.

At a fairly narrow or specialized level it is possible to suggest that the "accountability gap"/"understanding gap" reflect the *supply* and *demand* dichotomy that this chapter has sought to promote. The former is linked to the "reformist paradigm" and favors increasing supply; while the latter is linked to what could be termed the "understanding paradigm" which warns against unrealistic expectations and instead promotes the role of the academic in promoting public understanding and engaged citizenship. Whereas the "accountability gap" defines the issue to *be solved*, the "understanding gap" reframes the issue as one to *be understood*. And yet paradoxically this re-framing places new expectations and obligations on the role of an academic. From being an external observer and student of accountability the academic is suddenly placed, through a relational ontology, at the center of the "accountability space" with a clear social role and responsibility for contributing to the shaping of account-demanding and account-giving expectations. This shifting role and set of expectations dovetails with a changing social context in which academics are increasingly forced to account for their contribution to "public goods" (seen in the introduction of "impact" case studies as a core element of the Research Excellence Framework in the United Kingdom, and the spread of STAR METRICS[3] approaches beyond the United States).

Although some scholars may define the imposition of external indicators of value upon their profession as an unwarranted diminution of academic autonomy, for those interested in the issue of public accountability the future is arguably bright. Indeed, as many contributions to this collection demonstrate to great effect, this is a field of inquiry with a rich tradition of delivering theoretically informed, policy-relevant research that also has a clear and demonstrable public benefit. The challenge for the future, however, lies in moving away from well-worn clichés concerning accountability's "chameleon-like" qualities, "iconic" status, or "ever-expanding" boundaries and instead building new ways of thinking about the concept that focus on closing the "understanding gap" as much (if not more) than the "accountability gap."

Notes

1. The existence of a conceptual gap in terms of normative and epistemological interpretations can be seen through a comparison of the conclusions of Gustavsson, Karlsson, and Person (2009) on the one hand, and Bovens, Curtin, and t' Hart (2010) on the other.
2. For an empirical application of both challenges see Flinders (2009).
3. This is an acronym for "Science and Technology for America's Reinvestment: Measuring the Effect of Research on Innovation, Competitiveness and Science."

References

Anechiarico, F. and Jacobs, J. 1996. *The Pursuit of Absolute Integrity: How Corruption Control Makes Government Ineffective*. Chicago: University of Chicago Press.

Ashworth, R., Snape, S., and Aulakh, S. 2007. "Plugging the Accountability Gap? Evaluating the Effectiveness of Regional Scrutiny." *Environment and Planning C:Government and Policy*, 25: 194–211.

Bauman, Z. 2000. *Liquid Modernity*. Cambridge: Polity.

Behn, R. 2001. *Rethinking Democratic Accountability*. Washington, DC: The Brookings Institution.

Bellamy, R. and Palumbo, A. 2010. *Political Accountability*. London: Ashgate.

Bovens, M. 1998. *The Quest for Responsibility: Accountability and Citizenship in Complex Organisations*. Cambridge: Cambridge University Press.

Bovens, M. 2007. "Analysing and Assessing Accountability: A Conceptual Framework." *European Law Journal*, 13: 447–68.

Bovens, M., Curtin, D., and t'Hart, P. 2010. *The Real World of European Union Accountability: What Deficit?* Oxford: Oxford University Press.

Chan, S. and Pattberg, P. 2008. "Private Rule Making and the Politics of Accountability." *Global Environmental Politics*, 8: 103–21.

Crick, B. 1962. *In Defense of Politics*. London: Penguin.

Dubnick, M. 2002. *Seeking Salvation for Accountability*. In APSA (The American Political Science Association) 98th Annual Conference. Boston, 29 August–1 September 2002.

Dubnick, M. 2011. "Move Over Daniel: We Need Some 'Accountability Space'." *Administration & Society*, 43: 704–16.

Falaschetti, D. 2009. *Democratic Governance and Economic Performance: How Accountability Can Go Too Far in Politics, Law, and Business*. New York: Springer-Verlag.

Flinders, M. 2001. *The Politics of Accountability in the Modern State*. London: Ashgate.

Flinders, M. 2009. *Delegated Governance and the Modern State*. Oxford: Oxford University Press.

Flinders, M. 2011. "Daring to Be a Daniel: The Pathology of Politicized Accountability in a Monitory Democracy." *Administration & Society*, 43(5): 1–25.

Flinders, M. 2012. A Rallying Cry to the University Professors of Politics, in *The Relevance of Political Science*, eds. G. Peters, J. Pierre, and G. Stoker. Basingstoke: Macmillan.

Flinders, M. 2012. *Defending Politics*. Oxford: Oxford University Press.

Fox, J. A. and Brown, D. L. 1998. *The Struggle for Accountability: The World Bank, NGOs, and Grassroots Movements*. Cambridge, Mass.: MIT Press.

Goetz, A. M. and Jenkins, R. 2005. *Reinventing Accountability: Making Democracy Work for Human Development*. Basingstoke: Palgrave Macmillan.

Gustavsson, S., Karlsson, C., and Person, T. 2009. *The Illusion of Accountability in the European Union*. London: Routledge.

Hay, C. 2007. *Why We Hate Politics*. Cambridge: Polity Press.

Hay, C. 2009. "Tony Wright on Doing Politics Differently." *Political Quarterly*, 80: 575–88.

Held, D. and Koenig-Archibugi, M. 2005. *Global Governance and Public Accountability*. Chichester: Wiley-Blackwell.

Hood, C. 2010. *The Blame Game*. Princeton: Princeton University Press.

Hood, C. and Heald, D. 2006. *Transparency: The Key to Better Governance?* Oxford: Oxford University Press.

Jenkins, S. 1996. *Accountable to None: The Tory Nationalization of Britain*. London: Penguin Books.

Keane, J. 2009. *The Life and Death of Democracy*. London: Simon and Schuster.

Koppell, J. 2005. "Pathologies of Accountability: ICANN and the Challenge of 'Multiple Accountabilities Disorder'." *Public Administration Review*, 65: 94–108.

March, J. and Olsen, J. 1995. *Democratic Governance*. New York: Free Press.

McIntyre-Mills, J. 2010. *Systemic Governance and Accountability: Working and Re-Working the Conceptual and Spatial Boundaries*. New York: Springer.

Mookherjee, D. 2005. *The Crisis in Government Accountability: Essays on Governance Reforms and India's Economic Performance*. New Delhi: Oxford University Press.

Ostrom, E. 2000. The Danger of Self-Evident Truths. *PS: Political Science & Politics*, 33: 33–44.

Pharr, S. and Putnam, R. 2000. *Disaffected Democracies*. Princeton: Princeton University Press.

Pollitt, C. and Hupe, P. 2011. "Talking about Government: The Role of Magic Concepts." *Public Management Review*, 13: 641–58.

Pollitt, C. 2008. *The Essential Public Manager*. Maidenhead: Open University Press.

Ricci, D. 1984. *The Tragedy of Political Science*. Yale: Yale University Press.

Romzek, B. and Dubnick, M. 1987. "Accountability in the Public Sector." *Public Administration Review*, 47: 227–38.

Sartori, G. 1970. "Concept Misformation in Comparative Politics." *American Political Science Review*, 64: 1033–53.

Shapiro, I. 2005. *The Flight from Reality in the Human Sciences*. Princeton: Princeton University Press.

Stoker, G. 2006. *Why Politics Matters*. London: Palgrave.

Strong, T. 2012. *Politics Without Vision*. Chicago: University of Chicago Press.

Thompson, D. 1980. "Moral Responsibility of Public Officials: The Problem of Many Hands." *American Political Science Review*, 74: 905–16.

Turner, K. and Hogan, M. 2004. *The Worldly Art of Politics*. Sydney: Federation Press.

Willems, T. and Dooren, W. van. 2012. "Coming to Terms with Accountability." *Public Management Review*. doi: 10.1080/14719037.2012.662446

CHAPTER 43

MEANINGFUL ACCOUNTABILITY

MARK BOVENS AND THOMAS SCHILLEMANS

FROM ACCOUNTABILITY DEFICITS TO ACCOUNTABILITY DESIGN

EACH year, 28,000 American federal employees are required to file a SF 278 form that lists their financial interests.[1] They have to provide detailed information about their assets, their outside income, including dividends, royalties, and interests, their liabilities, about their employment-related pension schemes, leaves of absence, their transactions, gifts, travel reimbursements, and a variety of other interests. Much of this same information has to be provided about the financial interests of their spouses and dependent children. The form is rather complicated and accompanied by a 300-page "reviewers' guide." These forms, once filed, are available for inspection by external ethics offices. However, in practice very few SF 278 forms are actually scrutinized—from 2006 to 2008, the government only received an average of 130 annual requests (Clark and Embree 2013). Another 300.000 federal employees annually have to file a SF 450 form, which is only slightly less demanding.

Both the SF 278 and the SF 450 forms exemplify modern accountability practices. They operate on the principle of "better safe than sorry." Public officials and public organizations are under heavy scrutiny and each financial scandal or policy fiasco leads to new demands for more public accountability, resulting in more regulations, more intricate forms, and increasing demands for disclosure. For example, in the wake of a "Sixty Minutes" news item which suggested insider trading by some members of Congress, in April 2012 the American Congress enacted the STOCK Act.[2] This act mandates the creation of a public, searchable database of all the annual SF 278 forms, not just those of the members of Congress and their staff, but of all 28.000 federal employees.[3]

The American examples underscore the main trend in both the practice and the study of public accountability—an overwhelming focus on accountability *deficits*. In these examples, the apparent accountability deficit, politicians and civil servants with potentially hidden (financial) interests that might affect their behavior, was redressed by a standardized and publicly accessible form. In similar vein, public accountability research has been dominated by studies of accountability deficits. In a sample of over 200 accountability papers taken from a variety of disciplines, nearly two-thirds focused on various types of deficits—situations in which power-holders are decoupled from adequate accountability mechanisms (see Schillemans 2013). Heavily-researched alleged accountability deficits relate to the internationalization of decision-making (WTO, WU, World Bank, etc.), the privatization and agentification of public services, public management reforms in the core executive of most jurisdictions, and the emergence of networks of governance incorporating private and non-profit organizations in complex systems of collaborative service provision. This focus on deficits is easy to explain, as the gist of many contemporary governance reforms has been to challenge hierarchical lines of command (and thus accountability). When powers shift, slip away, or dissipate, accountability mechanisms should step into the breach. Accountability research, then, often traces the extent to which accountability has been compromised by reforms of governance. The implicit normative implication of this type of research is also, as Flinders vividly illustrates in his chapter in this part, that we simply need *more* accountability.

The cumulative evidence from two decades of accountability research (see Mulgan in this volume and Part 5 more generally), however, suggests that this problem of absent or deficient accountability may not be as grave as one would expect, given the strong emphasis on it in the literature and in public discourse. Notably, empirical analyses of apparent accountability deficits invariably reveal that allegedly unaccountable actors are scrutinized by a variety of, and in most cases increasingly *dense*, networks of more or less effective accountability mechanisms (Willems and Van Dooren 2011; Klingner, Nalbandian, and Romzek 2002; Bovens, Curtin, and 't Hart 2010).

The empirical evidence, however, also reveals that the increased focus on accountability has produced considerable collateral damage in terms of excessive costs, red tape, and negative effects on other important public values, such as effectiveness, efficiency, trust, and learning. Many empirical studies of accountability report some—and sometimes exclusively—negative (side-)effects of accountability (Schillemans 2013). This suggests that it would make sense, both in accountability studies and in practice, to focus more on the *quality* of accountability, on tackling and effectively redressing accountability *overloads* (see Halachmi in this volume). This approach necessitates a more careful look at the *design* of accountability mechanisms and practices and signals a shift in focus from demands for more (or less) accountability to questions about *what types* of accountability are relevant and the *conditions* and *contexts* in which they are effective.

Default Accountability: Burdensome, Predictable, and Decoupled

The default design of systems of public accountability, as illustrated by the SF 278 and SF 450 forms, is based on repetitive, predictable, and data-intensive mechanisms (see Van Rijn and Van Twist 2009; Schillemans, Van Twist, and Vanhommerig 2013). Most default accountability mechanisms are *generic* in nature. Accountable agents are obliged to account for their choices, conduct, and results across a broad range of issues through standardized and routine procedures such as annual reports, evaluation protocols, and fixed forms. Default accountability is often cyclical and predictable; agents can expect to be called upon to provide information on a regular basis, filling in existing protocols, data sheets, and registers in a lulling sequence of administrative activities. Default accountability also struggles with what Behn (2001) calls the *accountability bias*; because it is difficult to measure and assess outcomes, public accountability in effect heavily focuses on financial and procedural propriety. Default accountability, then, pushes public organizations towards compliance, to adhere to existing laws and regulations and to operate within strict financial parameters, possibly to the detriment of their willingness or even ability to realize their goals and missions.

One of the major disadvantages of default accountability is that it is not particularly *lean*; it easily threatens to overburden accountable agents with excessive administrative overloads. This propensity to excess often comes to the fore in interviews with practitioners and public managers (see Sinclair 1995; Schillemans, Bovens, and Le Cointre 2011) and has been broadly outlined in the academic literature. Some authors point to the large transaction costs of accountability (see Pollitt 2003, 95) while others emphasize the opportunity costs (Halachmi 2002, 233) that divert resources from core missions to administrative overheads. To many officials and public professionals, the production of accountability data appears to be "deadweight loss" and "unproductive time"; it is often found to be devoid of meaning. The fact that accountability forums will often only gloss over and scan the provided data, in effect only checking whether agents have "ticked off all the right boxes" without substantively reading the provided account let alone responding to it, further contributes to the lack of enthusiasm among those required to provide the necessary information.

In addition, default accountability easily suffers from a systemic turn. Its focus is redirected from the critical scrutiny of what people (in organizations) actually do, to critical, second-order, analysis of the organizational systems that *monitor* what people are *reporting* to be doing. As a result, accountability processes tend to focus on administrative realities and numerical categories that can be readily assessed and evaluated, instead of what actually happens on the ground. Accountability may be decoupled from actual, meaningful action (see Power 1999). Furthermore, systems of accountability may stimulate dysfunctional levels of goal displacement, where (necessarily imperfect) measurements take precedence over substantive goals and real experiences (Van de Walle and

Cornelisse in this volume). Goal displacement manifests itself when the police focus on safety statistics (instead of on safety itself), scientists on impact figures and H-indices (instead of on the "discovery" of new knowledge), and service providers on "perceptions of performance" (instead of on the real thing).

Moreover, overly intrusive accountability obligations and inquiries readily stand in the way of organizational learning and improvement (Hood 2010; Ebrahim 2005) and may easily compromise inter-organizational and interpersonal trust (Greiling in this handbook). Rigorous accountability mechanisms, threatening to punish every fluke or fault that is discovered, convert public organizations into defensive, formalistic, and rule-obsessed bureaucracies. Leaders, anticipating future accountability claims, may be disinclined from taking tough choices and may resort to the defense of the status quo, even when dysfunctional in the face of their goals. While this is at times a fruitful strategy, important opportunities for organizational learning, successful adaptation, and innovation may be missed. This negative effect on learning and performance is truly paradoxical. Accountability has been on the increase in the wake of widespread concerns regarding public sector performance. One of its paradoxical effects, however, is that organizational abilities and propensities to improve and learn are sometimes compromised in the process.

The American federal SF 278 form is a prime example of default accountability. It is standardized, and must be filed each year; it requires detailed information on a large variety of items with a focus on financial data; but it is hardly ever read by anyone, let alone discussed. Accountability is important in theory, but often seems burdensome and irrelevant in practice.

MEANINGFUL ACCOUNTABILITY

How can public accountability become more meaningful and less demanding? In the accountability literature and in the practice of accountability several avenues can be found (compare Mansbridge; Behn in this volume; Noordegraaf 2008). These avenues illustrate ways in which accountability practices could move from the repetitive, predictable, data-intensive, and easily ridiculed ("ticking of boxes") activity that it now too often is, into a more focused and substantively more meaningful process. These innovations aim to give accountability practices more added value, both for actors and for forums, as a means of, essentially, establishing the extent to which public duties are performed appropriately and successfully. These innovations are by no means a failsafe strategy for meaningful accountability; we are not writing these paragraphs as wannabe accountability consultants selling a set of one-size-fits-all solutions to whatever problem might come in our way. It is our intention rather to highlight a number of innovations in public sector accountability that aim to improve upon the widely acknowledged problems of excessive, debilitating, or counterproductive accountability. By highlighting these innovations, and more importantly by stressing the constitutive ideas beneath those practices, we hope to sketch an agenda for researchers and practitioners that may contribute to the identification and implementation of more meaningful accountability mechanisms and, in the process, help the analysis of the conditions under which specific mechanisms will be more, or less, desirable. We start by discussing a number of stimulating new *types* of accountability and proceed to discuss shifts in the *purpose* of accountability and the *conditions* for effective accountability.

Innovation in Types: Calibrated-To-Fit Accountability

Instead of focusing on a broad set of recurring items and general issues, accountability forums and agents could focus on a few, salient issues, which may differ from year to year. Also, account-giving need not necessarily be a cyclical phenomenon, recurring independently of context and change. Instead, it can be calibrated to fit specific circumstances and developments. In the past years, several innovations in accountability practices more or less embrace this rationale. Many regulatory agencies, for instance, have started to work on the basis of risk assessments, which allows them to allocate their resources according to perceived risks of specific violations and forms of misconduct. As a result, they hope to be able to lower the accountability demands on the many who are compliant, while simultaneously increasing accountability pressure on the few potential culprits (see Majone 2011). A very different example comes from the Netherlands, where a Parliamentary committee proposed to limit the annual debate about the government's annual report—a hefty 2.277 page document with numerous appendices—to just five, pre-decided issues, in an attempt to effectuate a focused Parliamentary debate about a manageable set of key policy issues. And in their interesting, comparative studies on regulation and control in governments, Christopher Hood and colleagues (1999; 2004) show how "contrived randomness," such as chance inspections and selection by lot, is both a fruitful and cheap tool in the box of contemporary accountability professionals. The common denominator in the above examples is that forums focus on just a limited and adaptable set of issues for which accountability is imminent, rather than going over all the same items each year.

A different set of innovations in accountability has been on the rise under the umbrella of PerformanceStat (see Behn in this handbook). In these examples, the amount of processed data is still formidable, yet the design of the accompanying accountability process aims to help, with variable degrees of success, actors and forums to assess the data more meaningfully and to translate accumulated information into meaningful strategic action. In these innovations, an agent is held accountable to his superiors, in a hearing in front of his peers and on the basis of key data.

PerformanceStat, initially developed by the New York police, focuses on one district at a time, comparing trends in the district to general trends. The decision on which district and which topics to focus is not set in stone, but can be adjusted to circumstances and developments. The recurring element in these innovations is "stat"—relevant statistical data on crime or the environment are condensed and integrated with the use of advanced systems of registration and projection. It operates on the basis of concise PowerPoint™ and data sheets, provided by the actor, showing the most important developments for a limited set of issues. This can still be very burdensome, as it requires a lot of preparation and calls for the condensation of large volumes of data in focused and pointed presentations. It capitalizes on the enormous wealth of crime-related data that is often available anyhow and on new computational techniques that allow organizations to organize and actually *use* this data. Subsequently, however, the data lend themselves to focused discussions in which the agent's activities can be assessed and both parties, crucially, may learn how to improve their future behavior.

A Focus on Conditions: When to Choose What Type of Accountability?

The search for improved forms of accountability raises an important and neglected issue for researchers and practitioners alike. Under what conditions will different types of accountability mechanisms be effective? This question moves the accountability debate from the trenches, where opponents and proponents fight each other's arguments for more or for less accountability, to more constructive and design-oriented explorations of specific mechanisms, underlying conditions, and processes.

In their chapter in this handbook, Patil, Vieider, and Tetlock discuss the relative merits of outcome versus process accountability, where the former is generally conducive of innovation whereas the latter is better geared towards control. This insight is of imminent importance to political and public accountability, as it raises the question whether real-world accountability mechanisms actually are compliant with these insights. Our own guess would be that they are generally not designed with this rationale in mind. The Patil et al. chapter builds on a very large body of research that aims to establish connections between different types of accountability and different outcomes. This literature, for instance, shows how accountability—the expectation that one has to explain and justify one's choices towards an audience—affects distributive choices (Adelberg and Batson 1978; Skitka and Tetlock 1992), accuracy of judgments (Mero and Motowidlo 1995), and the quality of judgment per se and for attribution of blame (Taylor 1995). Accountability helps, so Mero and Motowidlo (1995) show, to increase the accuracy with which jobs are performed, an insight that is helpful for all those situations in public policy where people have to make precise judgments on norms, applications, social services, etc. Conversely, however, as Adelberg and Batson (1978) famously showed, accountability may also lead to ineffective distributions of limited resources. Furthermore, accountability also changes the way people gather information; not only will they gather the information they need for their job but they will also gather the "political" information that is necessary to maintain their position (Doney and Armstrong 1996).

A further relevant insight, tying in to the examples of innovation discussed in the previous section, is that some deliberate levels of insecurity may be beneficial to accountability, as this fosters favorable cognitive responses. When agents know they are going to be held accountable, but are not too certain about the specific process, the parties involved, or the exact preferences of their accountability forums, they will engage in pre-emptive self-criticism (Lerner and Tetlock 1999) in order to arrive at more balanced decisions. Repeated experimental research approaches suggest that the most important effect of accountability comes from agents' anticipation of future accountability. When agents expect to be held accountable for actions or decisions in the future by a reputable accountability forum whose exact preferences are unknown, they will assess their actions and choices much more carefully in anticipation, digesting more information and taking more sides of an issue into account. In this way, anticipating accountability leads decision-makers to put more mental effort into decisions. And that is likely to lead to better decisions.

These, and similar findings from the micro perspective of social psychology and micro economics, lend themselves well to a transposition to the macro-level of governmental and public accountability. Chance inspections, on-site visits, or variable accountability procedures, can provide productive forms of insecurity.

A Shift in Purpose: Deliberative Instead of Defensive Accountability

Knowledge of the likely effects of specific accountability mechanisms as such can only help to inform institutional design choices when the purpose of accountability is clearly established. Default accountability generally stresses the beginning—the obligation to disclose information, as in the SF 278 form—and the end of the accountability process—the forum's ability to *punish* the actor (see Mansbridge in this volume). While undoubtedly indispensable and of great importance to accountability, information and punishment also stand at the root of many of the described ills of default accountability. Excessive reporting requirements seem like a meaningless affair to frustrated forums and actors alike; while an imposing arsenal of corrective mechanisms may, while aimed at compliance, invoke all sorts of undesirable defensive behavior by accountable actors. In more meaningful accountability, the "middle phase" of accountability in which actor and forum discuss and debate the former's behavior, is of more importance (see also Brandsma and Schillemans 2013).

The focus on deliberation in accountability is relevant because standards for what constitutes accountable behavior are not written in stone. They have to be interpreted and made to fit the concrete practices that are to be evaluated. In highly complex or rapidly changing circumstances, accountability standards are not given, but have to be construed in the process. In these compound, dynamic contexts, default accountability is often too crude, because it is not adaptive or sensitive to the context and the variety of interests and considerations that are relevant. Organizing accountability processes in more deliberative ways could help to provide more meaning. This could be done, for example, by inviting relevant stakeholders to the table to engage in a dialogue about the relevant standards and future norms for holding the actor accountable. Instead of filing a glossy annual report, a public service delivery organization could hold an annual account session to which both its political principal and its main stakeholders are invited and heard, resulting in a more tailored and sensible set of accountability expectations. More innovative forms of accountability, fostering less detailed data and simultaneously stimulating more policy reflection, would benefit from more "open norms," derived, for example, from organizational missions. These types of norm specify the direction in which an agent, an office holder, or organization is aiming and serve as the yardstick with which to measure his (or her) performance. Open norms serve as compasses, pointing out the general direction, and thus while being quite directive, leave it to the agent (and the relevant accountability forums) to establish how to proceed in the given circumstances. Open norms also serve as bottom lines against which strategic choices can be assessed.

FROM DEFICITS TO DESIGN

The discussion in this chapter could be wrongfully read as suggesting that "meaningful accountability" is just a juxtaposition to "default accountability." These are not two opposite archetypes however. Rather, meaningful accountability is an adjustment to, or a supplement for, existing forms of accountability. The account-giving is not organized as a mindlessly repetitive phenomenon, impervious to context and change, but is instead calibrated to fit specific circumstances and issues, which may differ from year to year. This type of accountability supports, rather than presupposes, sense-making processes. Rules, procedures, and protocols ought to be amenable to change. The process is based on adaptable formats and may also take the form of a (public) hearing, a briefing, or a conference. Finally, meaningful accountability is not about compliance with existing rules and regulations, but about whether the organization is effectively serving its mission and about whether, and how, improvements are necessary.

Would any of this now help to alleviate the pressure on the 28,000 American federal employees filling out their annual SF 278 forms? Probably. A combination of risk assessments, chance inspections (contrived randomness), and constructive dialogues about accountable behavior is likely to be more effective at tackling problems of conflicting interests than a standard form. This solution could be harder to communicate to concerned citizens, critical media, and faint-hearted administrators alike, but it might actually work by relieving many from the tedious obligation to fill in that form while simultaneously contributing to "accountable behavior" *and* raising the chance of actually catching those failing to discriminate between professional and personal interests.

The ultimate aim of this chapter, however, is not to shape the future of the SF 278 form of course. Rather, our discussion of different types of accountability, and some of the conditions under which they operate and the purposes they serve, ultimately relates to two, closely related, academic and practical challenges—a shift in focus in accountability research from the *deficits* of to the *design* of effective accountability. And a refinement of our academic and practical debates from "more versus less" accountability to questions of *what forms* of accountability are appropriate, under *what circumstances,* and for *what purposes.*

Acknowledgments

The authors wish to thank Corine Buers, Kathleen Clark, Paul 't Hart, and Mirko Noordegraaf for their constructive commentary on an earlier draft of this chapter.

Notes

1. The information on these forms and on the STOCK Act of 2012 is based on Clark and Embree (2013).
2. *Stop Trading On Congressional Knowledge Act* of 2012, 112 Pub. L. 105, 126 Stat. 291 (2012).
3. After massive protests, the database provisions were repealed by Congress in April 2013.

References

Adelberg, S. and Batson, C. D. 1978. "Accountability and Helping: When Need Exceeds Resources." *Journal of Personality and Social Psychology,* 36: 343–50.

Behn, R. D. 2001. *Rethinking Democratic Accountability.* Washington, D.C.: Brookings Institution Press.

Bovens, M., Curtin, D., and 't Hart, P. 2010. *The Real World of EU Accountability: What Deficit?* Oxford: Oxford University Press.

Brandsma, G. J. and Schillemans, T. 2012. "The Accountability Cube: Measuring Accountability." *Journal of Public Administration Research and Theory,* 23 (4): 953–975.

Clark, K. and Embree, C. 2013. "Faux Transparency: Ethics, Privacy and the Demise of the STOCK Act's Massive Online Disclosure of Employees' Finances." Washington University in St. Louis Legal Studies Research Paper No. 13-05-1. Available at SSRN: <http://papers.ssrn.com/sol3/papers.cfm?abstract_id=2269336>.

Doney, P. M. and Armstrong, G. M. 1996. "Effects of Accountability on Symbolic Information Search and Information Analysis by Organizational Buyers." *Journal of the Academy of Marketing Science,* 24: 57–65.

Ebrahim, A. 2005. "Accountability Myopia: Losing Sight of Organizational Learning." *Nonprofit and Voluntary Sector Quarterly,* 34: 56–87.

Halachmi, A. 2002. "Performance Measurement: A Look at some Possible Dysfunctions." *Work Study,* 51: 230–39.

Hood, C. 2010. Blame Avoidance and Accountability: Positive, Negative, or Neutral?, pp. 167–79 in *Accountable Governance: Problems and Promises,* eds. M. J. Dubnick and H. G. Frederickson. Armonk: M.E. Sharpe.

Hood, C., Scott, C., James, O., Jones, G., and Travers, T. 1999. *Regulation Inside Government: Waste-Watchers, Quality Police, and Sleazebusters.* Oxford: Oxford University Press.

Hood, C., James, O., Peters, B. G., and Scott, C. 2004. *Controlling Modern Government: Variety, Commonality and Change.* Cheltenham: Edward Elgar.

Klingner, D. E., Nalbandian, J., and Romzek, B. S. 2002. "Politics, Administration and Markets: Conflicting Expectations of Accountability." *American Review of Public Administration*, 32: 117–44.

Lerner, J. S. and Tetlock, P. E. 1999. "Accounting for the Effects of Accountability." *Psychological Bulletin*, 125: 255–75.

Majone, G. 2011. Strategic Issues in Risk Regulation, pp. 295–307 in *Handbook on the Politics of Regulation*, ed. D. Levi-Faur. Cheltenham: Edward Elgar.

Mero, N. P. and Motowidlo, S. J. 1995. "Effects of Rater Accountability on the Accuracy and the Favorability on Performance Ratings." *Journal of Applied Psychology*, 80: 517–24.

Noordegraaf, M. 2008. "Meanings of Measurement: The Real Story Behind the Rotterdam Safety Index." *Public Management Review*, 10: 221–39.

Pollitt, C. 2003. *The Essential Public Manager.* London: Open University Press / McGraw-Hill.

Power, M. 1999. *The Audit Society: Rituals of Verification.* Oxford: Oxford University Press.

Schillemans, T. 2013. *The Public Accountability Review: A Meta-Analysis of Public Accountability Research in Six Academic Disciplines.* Working Paper. Utrecht University School of Governance. <http://igitur-archive.library.uu.nl/USBO/2013-0517-200614/UUindex.html>.

Schillemans, T., Bovens, M., and Le Cointre, S. 2011. Publieke Managers en Publieke Verantwoording, pp. 211–39 in *Handboek Publiek Management*, eds. M. Noordegraaf, K. Geuijen, and A. Meijer. Den Haag: Lemma.

Schillemans, T., Van Twist, M., and Vanhommerig, I. 2013. "Innovations in Accountability: Learning Through Interactive, Dynamic and Citizen-Initiated Forms of Accountability." *Public Performance & Management Review*, 36: 407–35.

Sinclair, A. 1995. The Chameleon of Accountability: Forms and Discourses. *Accounting, Organizations and Society*, 20: 219–37.

Skitka, L. and Tetlock, P. E. 1992. "Allocating Scarce Resources: A Contingency Model of Social Justice." *Journal of Experimental Social Psychology*, 28: 491–522.

Taylor, K. A. 1995. "Testing Credit and Blame Attributions as Explanations for Choices under Ambiguity." *Organizational Behavior and Human Decision Processes*, 62: 128–37.

Van Rijn, R. and Van Twist, M. 2009. Verantwoorde Vernieuwing? Innovatie van Publieke Verantwoording, pp. 255–74 in *Handboek Publieke Verantwoording*, eds. M. A. P. Bovens and T. Schillemans. Den Haag: Lemma.

Willems, T. and Van Dooren, W. 2011. "Lost in Diffusion? How Collaborative Arrangements Lead to an Accountability Paradox." *International Review of Administrative Sciences*, 77: 505–30.

INDEX

Note: bold entries refer to figures and tables.